CAST OF CHARACTERS

CHARACTERS IN THE PAST

RIN OKUMURA

Born of a human mother and Satan, the God of Demons, Rin Okumura has powers he can barely control. After Satan kills Father Fujimoto, Rin's foster father, Rin decides to become an Exorcist so he can someday defeat Satan. Now a first-year student at True Cross Academy and an Exwire at the Exorcism Cram School, he hopes to someday become a Knight. When Yukio broke his Koma Sword, the [power] of Satan swallowed him, but [Meph]i called him back to himself. He [tra]veled to the past to learn the [circumst]ances surrounding his birth.

[MEPHIS]TO PHELES

[...] Cross Academy and [Exorci]sm Cram School. He [is Rin]'s friend, and now [Rin's] guardian. The [...] Gehenna and [a mo]del, King of Time.

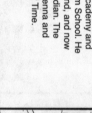

SHIRO FUJIMOTO

The man who raised Rin and Yukio. He was a clone of Azazel created in Section 13, but he made a deal with Mephisto to become an Exorcist. Later, he rose to the rank of Paladin.

YURI EGIN

Rin and Yukio's mother. She was an orphan, but after she met Shiro, Asylum took her in and she became an Exorcist. She is the only person Satan trusts and is pregnant with his child.

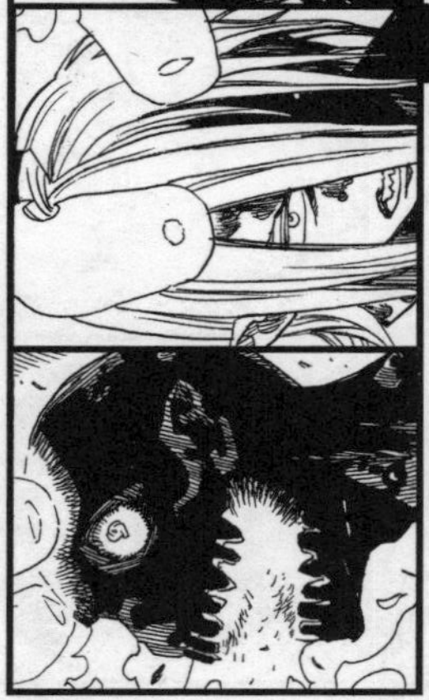

SATAN

Rin and Yukio's father. He is connected to and rules over almost all demons. He occupies Section 13 to prevent the deterioration of his body, but then the Order captures him during an escape attempt with Yuri. Later, the brain of the body he's possessing begins to deteriorate, rendering him only partially conscious. However, his obsession with Yuri causes him to return.

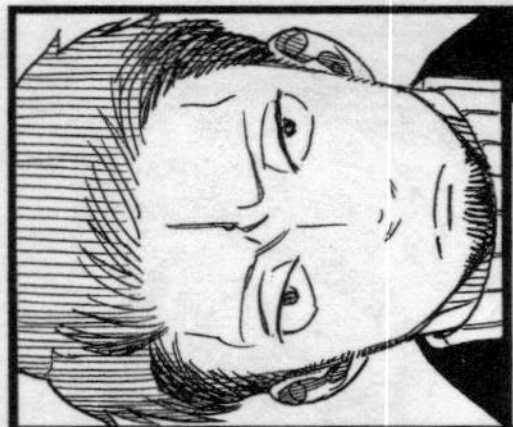

Richard "Rick" Lincoln

An Exorcist raised with Yuri at Asylum. He's a Junior Exorcist Second Class and a Tamer. He's good friends with Shiro and Yuri.

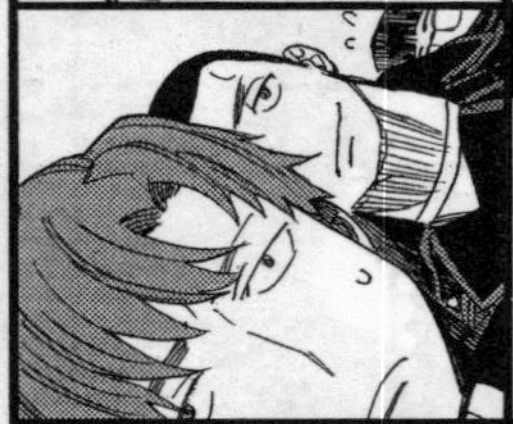

Shiro's Men

Shiro selected them personally to assist him.

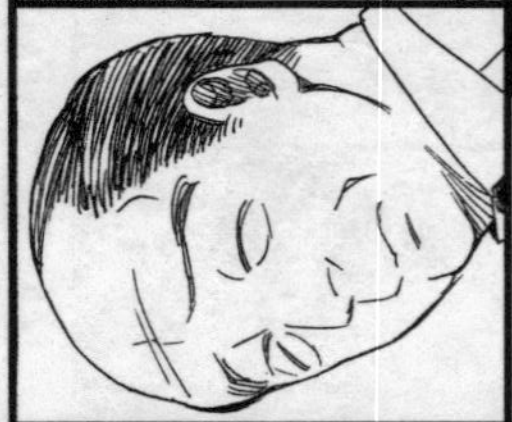

Tadashi Misumi

He was involved with researching clone technology at Section 13.

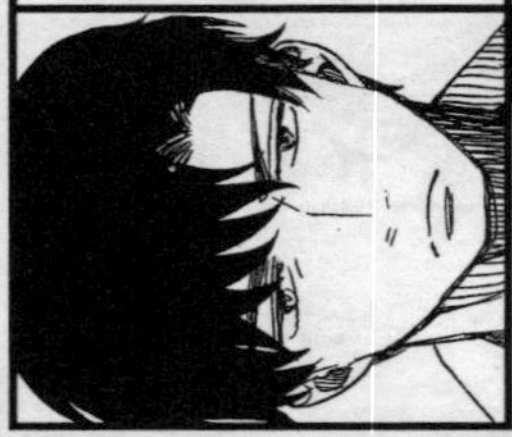

Igor Neuhaus

An expert in demon ecology at Section 13.

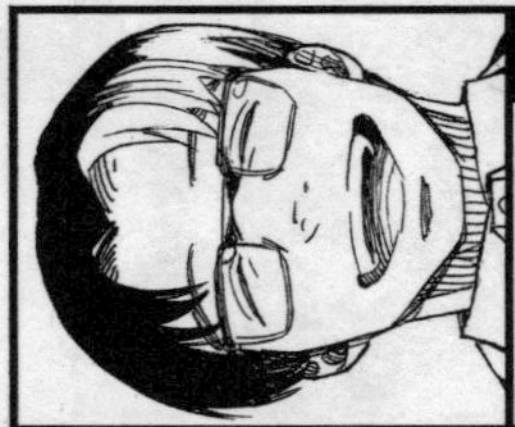

Saburota Todo

Born into the famous Todo family, known for its expertise in magic seals. He visits Section 13 in the company of his older brothers, who have undertaken a request from Mephisto.

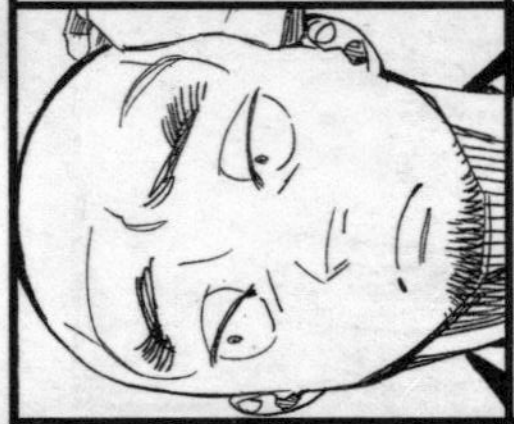

Tatsuma Suguro

Heir to the Myodha sect. He gives the Koma Sword to Shiro.

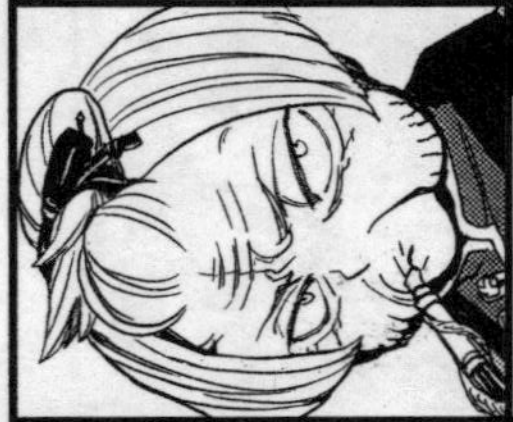

Lucy Yang

An Exorcist at the China Branch.

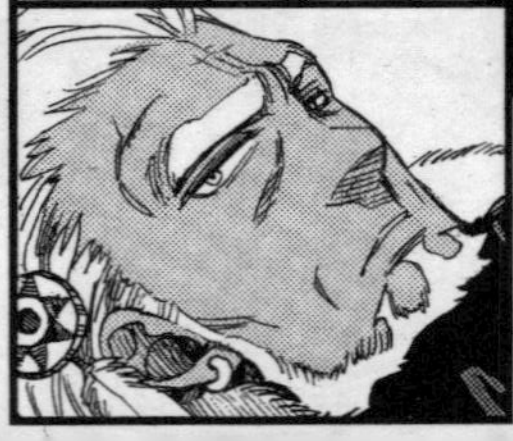

Osceola Redarm

An Exorcist at the Mexico Branch.

BLUE EXORCIST

NICOLAE EMINESCU

A researcher at Section 13. He was leading research into cloning for Satan and Lucifer. His true identity is Drac Dragulescu.

ABEL FRANKEN

The 250th Paladin.

SHEMIHAZA

A Grigori, one of the Order's highest-level advisors.

JEREMIAH UZAI

Assists Shemihaza in the Grigori Agency.

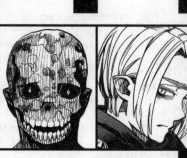

LUCIFER

Known as the King of Light, he is the highest power in Gehenna aside from Satan. The cloning and elixir research at Section 13 is for his sake. He swore fealty to Satan when Satan took corporeal form.

◉ **CHARACTERS IN THE PRESENT** ◉

YUKIO OKUMURA

Rin's brother. He's a genius who is the youngest student ever to become an instructor at the Exorcism Cram School. He has begun to question the righteousness of the Knights of the True Cross after learning that they are involved in cloning the demon kings, and he has gone to meet the Illuminati.

◉ THE STORY SO FAR ◉

BOTH HUMAN AND DEMON BLOOD RUNS THROUGH RIN OKUMURA'S VEINS. IN AN ARGUMENT WITH HIS FOSTER FATHER, FATHER FUJIMOTO, RIN LEARNS THAT SATAN IS HIS TRUE FATHER. SATAN SUDDENLY APPEARS AND TRIES TO DRAG RIN DOWN TO GEHENNA BECAUSE RIN HAS INHERITED HIS POWER. FATHER FUJIMOTO FIGHTS TO DEFEND RIN, BUT DIES IN THE PROCESS. RIN DECIDES TO BECOME AN EXORCIST SO HE CAN SOMEDAY DEFEAT SATAN AND BEGINS STUDYING AT THE EXORCISM CRAM SCHOOL UNDER THE INSTRUCTION OF HIS TWIN BROTHER YUKIO, WHO IS ALREADY AN EXORCIST.

RIN AND THE OTHERS SUCCEED IN DEFEATING THE IMPURE KING, AWAKENED BY THE FORMER EXORCIST, TODO. MEANWHILE, YUKIO FIGHTS TODO, AND AS THE BATTLE RAGES, HE SENSES THE SAME FLAME IN HIS OWN EYES AS HIS BROTHER.

LATER, MYSTERIOUS EVENTS BEGIN OCCURRING AROUND THE GLOBE ORCHESTRATED BY A SECRET SOCIETY KNOWN AS THE ILLUMINATI. FINALLY, THE JAPANESE GOVERNMENT PUBLICLY RECOGNIZES THE EXISTENCE OF DEMONS.

IN ORDER TO LEARN ABOUT SATAN INHABITING HIS LEFT EYE AND THE SECRETS SURROUNDING HIS BIRTH, YUKIO TELLS RIN GOODBYE AND GOES TO JOIN THE ILLUMINATI. RIN REALIZES HE TOO MUST KNOW ABOUT HIS BIRTH IF HE EVER WANTS TO SEE YUKIO AGAIN, SO HE TRAVELS INTO THE PAST.

AS HE OBSERVES THE LIVES OF SHIRO AND YURI, SATAN TAKES A CORPOREAL FORM. YURI KEEPS SATAN COMPANY TO PREVENT HIM FROM RAGING OUT OF CONTROL, AND HE GRADUALLY FALLS IN LOVE WITH HER.

THEY TRY TO LEAVE ASYLUM TO LIVE A QUIET LIFE, BUT THE ORDER STOPS THEM. THEN THE ORDER LEARNS THAT YURI IS PREGNANT AND SATAN IS THE FATHER. THE FIRST OF HER TWINS TO BE BORN IS RIN AND HE MANIFESTS THE BLUE FLAME AND BEGINS ATTACKING THE SURROUNDING EXORCISTS. MEANWHILE, SATAN HAS BEEN IMMOBILE DUE TO THE DETERIORATION OF HIS BODY, BUT NOW HE'S BACK!!

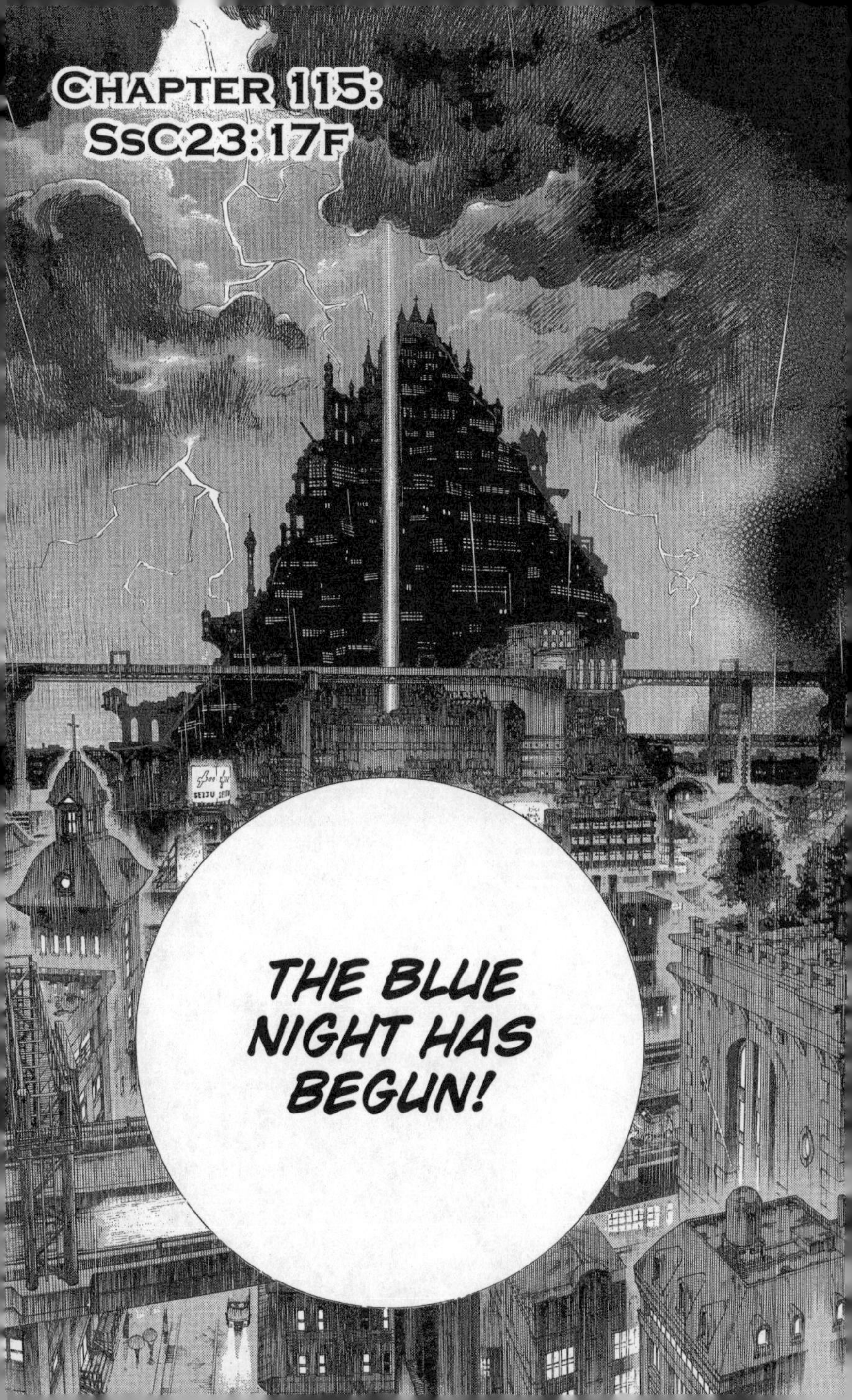
CHAPTER 115:
SsC23:17F
THE BLUE NIGHT HAS BEGUN!

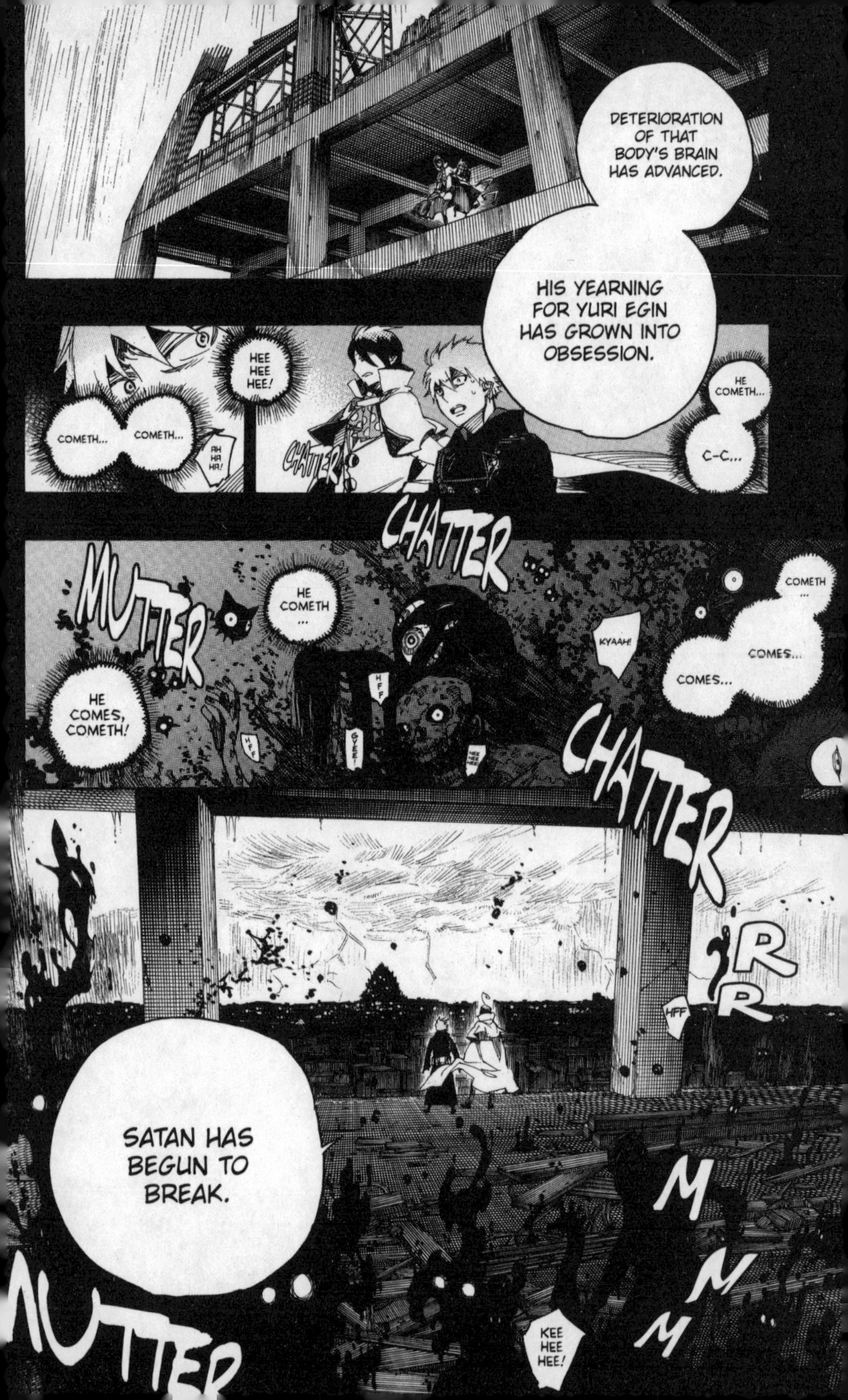
DETERIORATION OF THAT BODY'S BRAIN HAS ADVANCED.
HIS YEARNING FOR YURI EGIN HAS GROWN INTO OBSESSION.
HE COMETH...
C-C...
CHATTER
HEE HEE HEE!
COMETH...
COMETH...
AH HA HA!
CHATTER
COMETH ...
COMES...
COMES...
KYAAH!
HE COMETH ...
MUTTER
HFF
GYEE!
HEE HEE HEE!
HE COMES, COMETH!
HFF
CHATTER
RR
HFF
SATAN HAS BEGUN TO BREAK.
MMM
KEE HEE HEE!
MUTTER

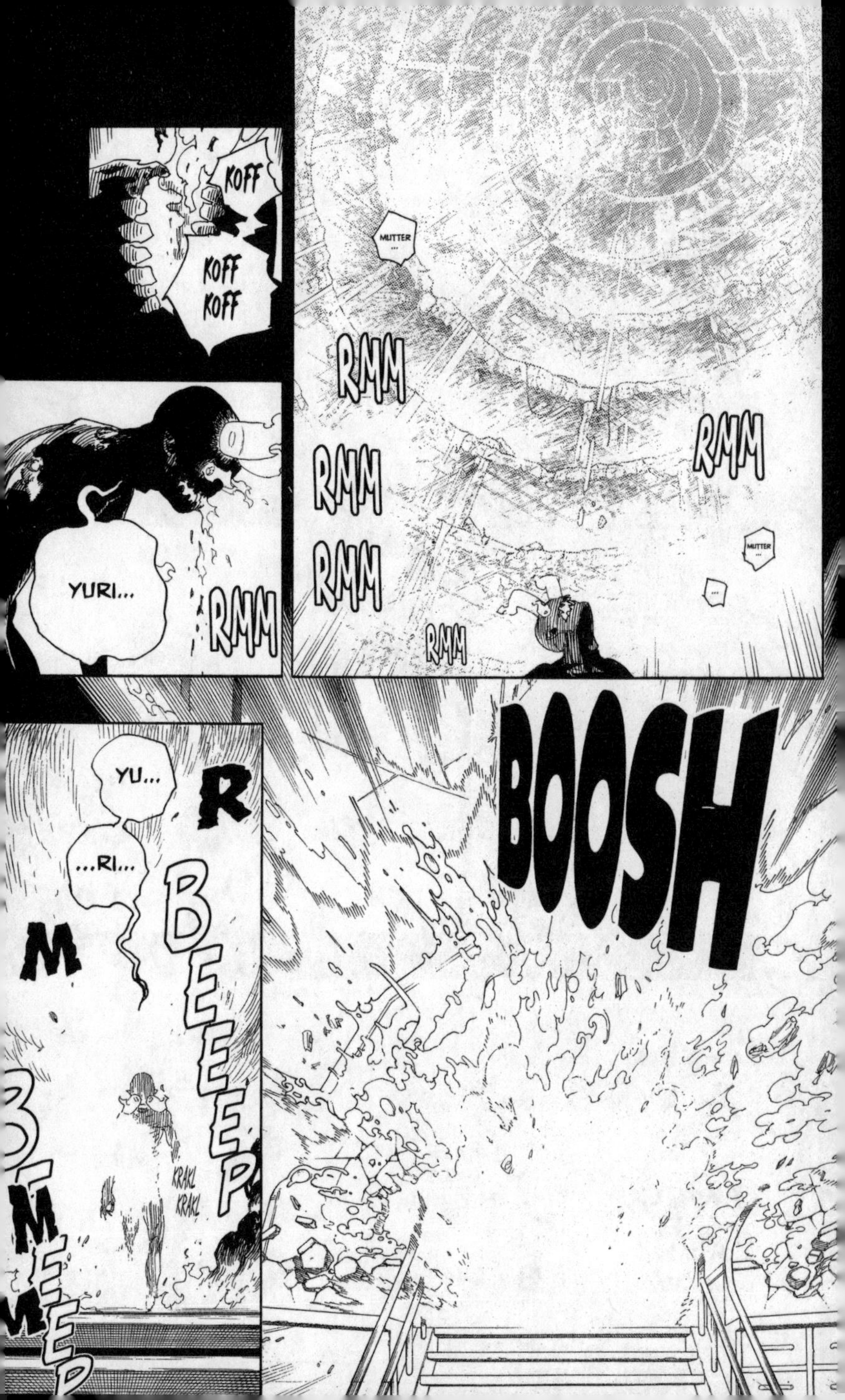

MUTTER...
RMM
RMM
RMM
RMM
MUTTER...
...
RMM
KOFF
KOFF KOFF
YURI...
RMM
BOOSH
R
BEEEEP
YU...
...RI...
M
KRAKL KRAKL

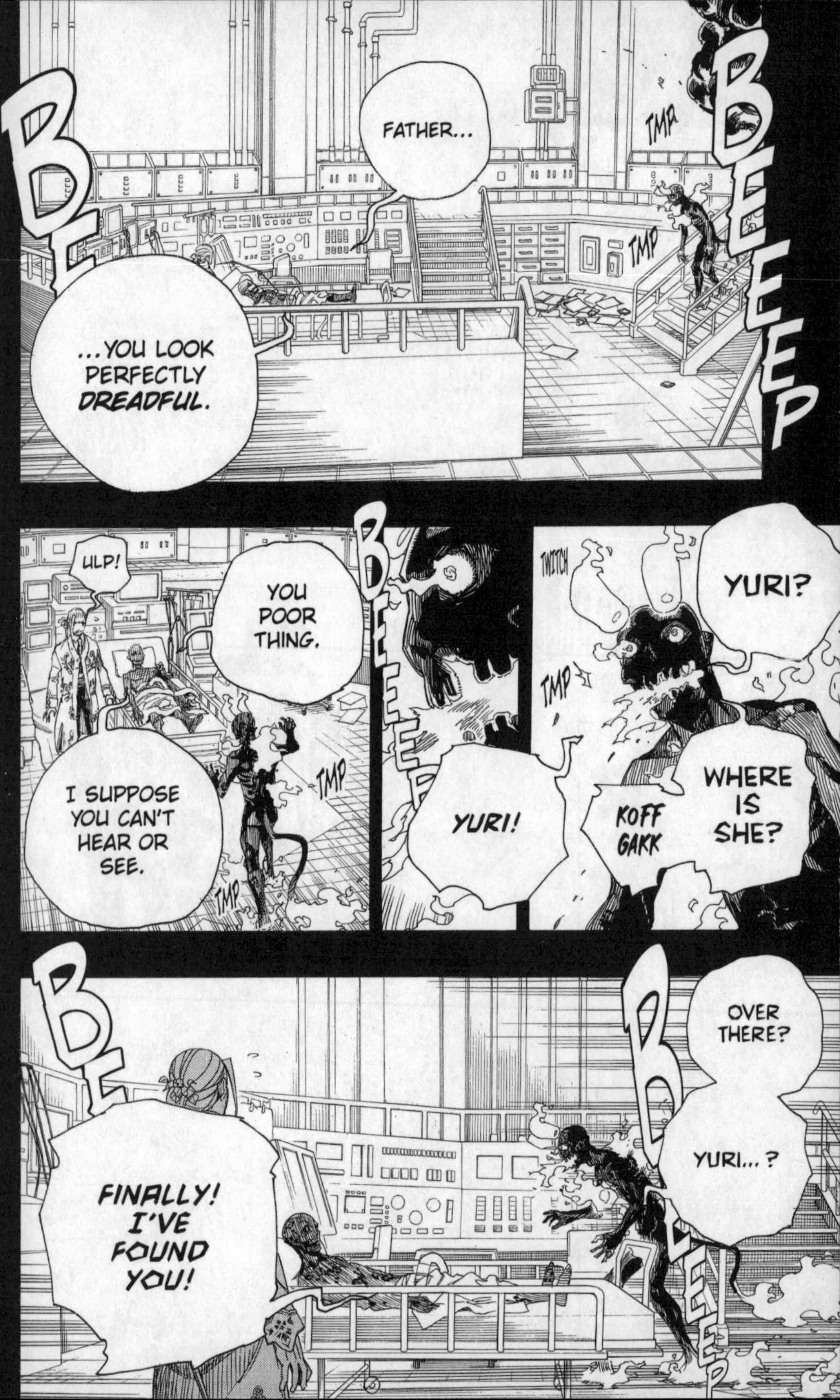
BEEEEP
TMP
FATHER...
TMP
...YOU LOOK PERFECTLY DREADFUL.
BE
YURI?
TWITCH
TMP
WHERE IS SHE?
KOFF GAKK
BEEEEP
YURI!
YOU POOR THING.
ULP!
TMP
I SUPPOSE YOU CAN'T HEAR OR SEE.
TMP
OVER THERE?
YURI...?
BBEEEP
FINALLY! I'VE FOUND YOU!
BE

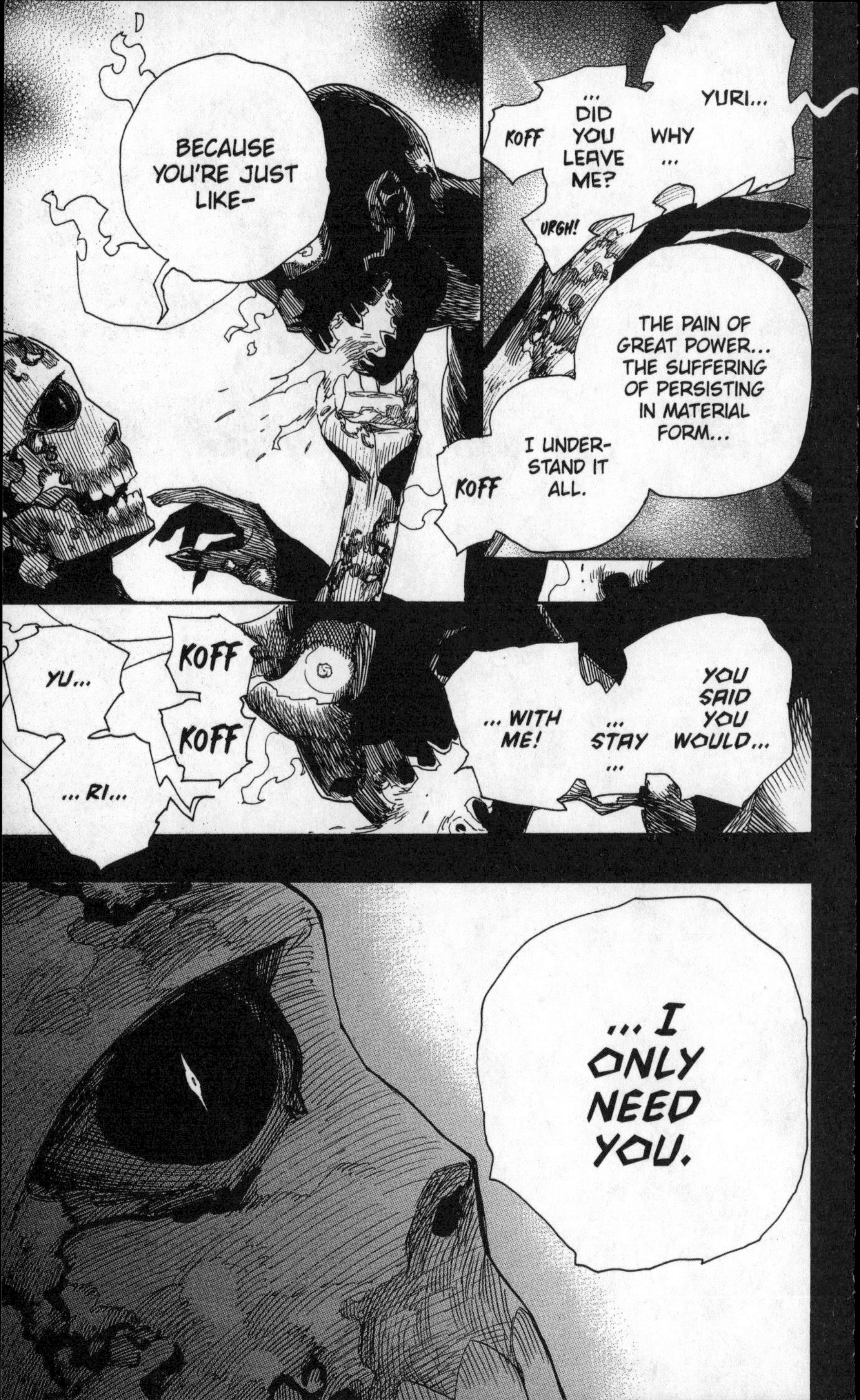
YURI... WHY... ...DID YOU LEAVE ME?
KOFF
URGH!
THE PAIN OF GREAT POWER... THE SUFFERING OF PERSISTING IN MATERIAL FORM...
I UNDERSTAND IT ALL.
KOFF
BECAUSE YOU'RE JUST LIKE-
YOU SAID YOU WOULD... ...STAY... ...WITH ME!
KOFF
KOFF
YU... ...RI...
...I ONLY NEED YOU.

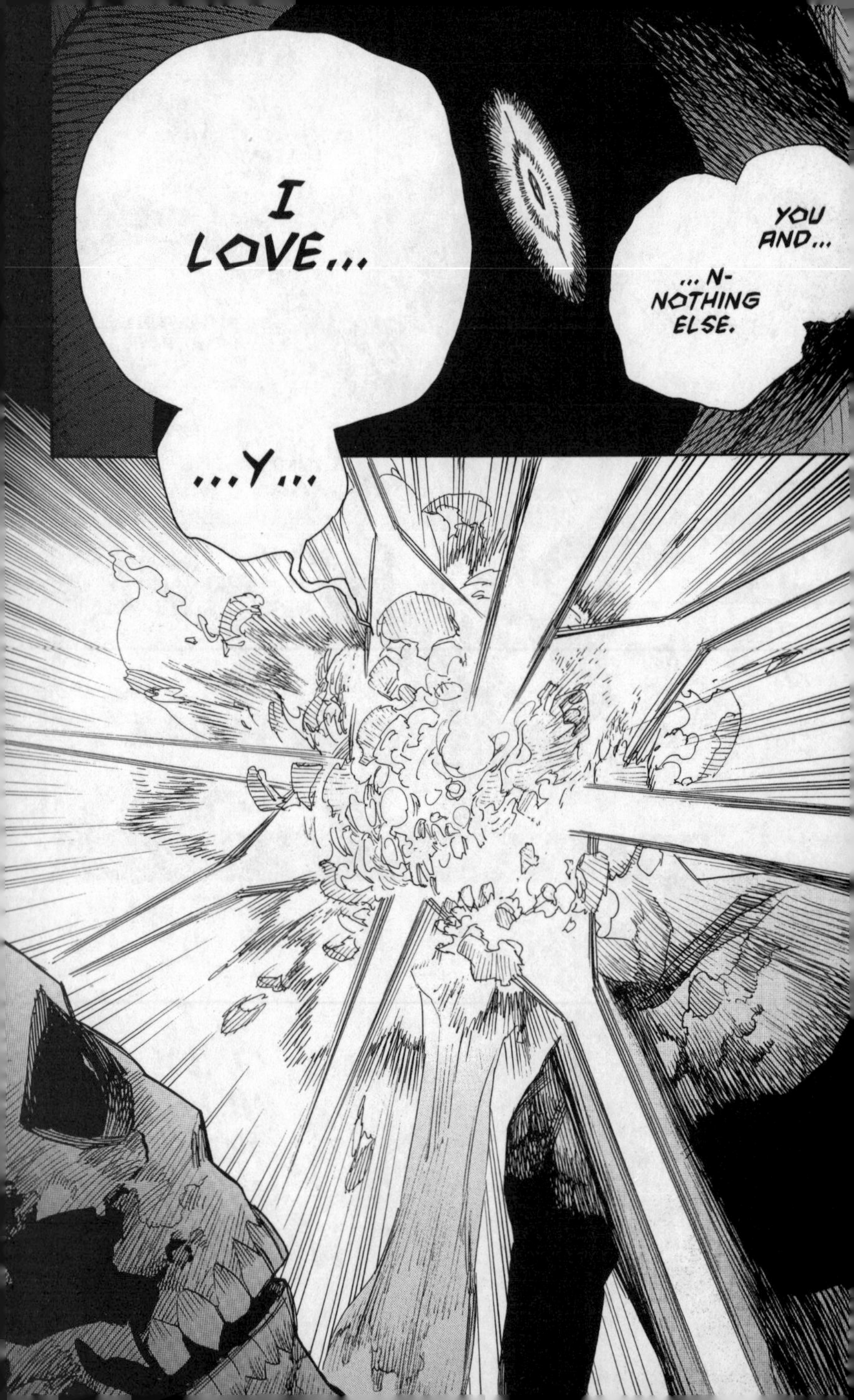
I LOVE...
...Y...
YOU AND...
...N-NOTHING ELSE.

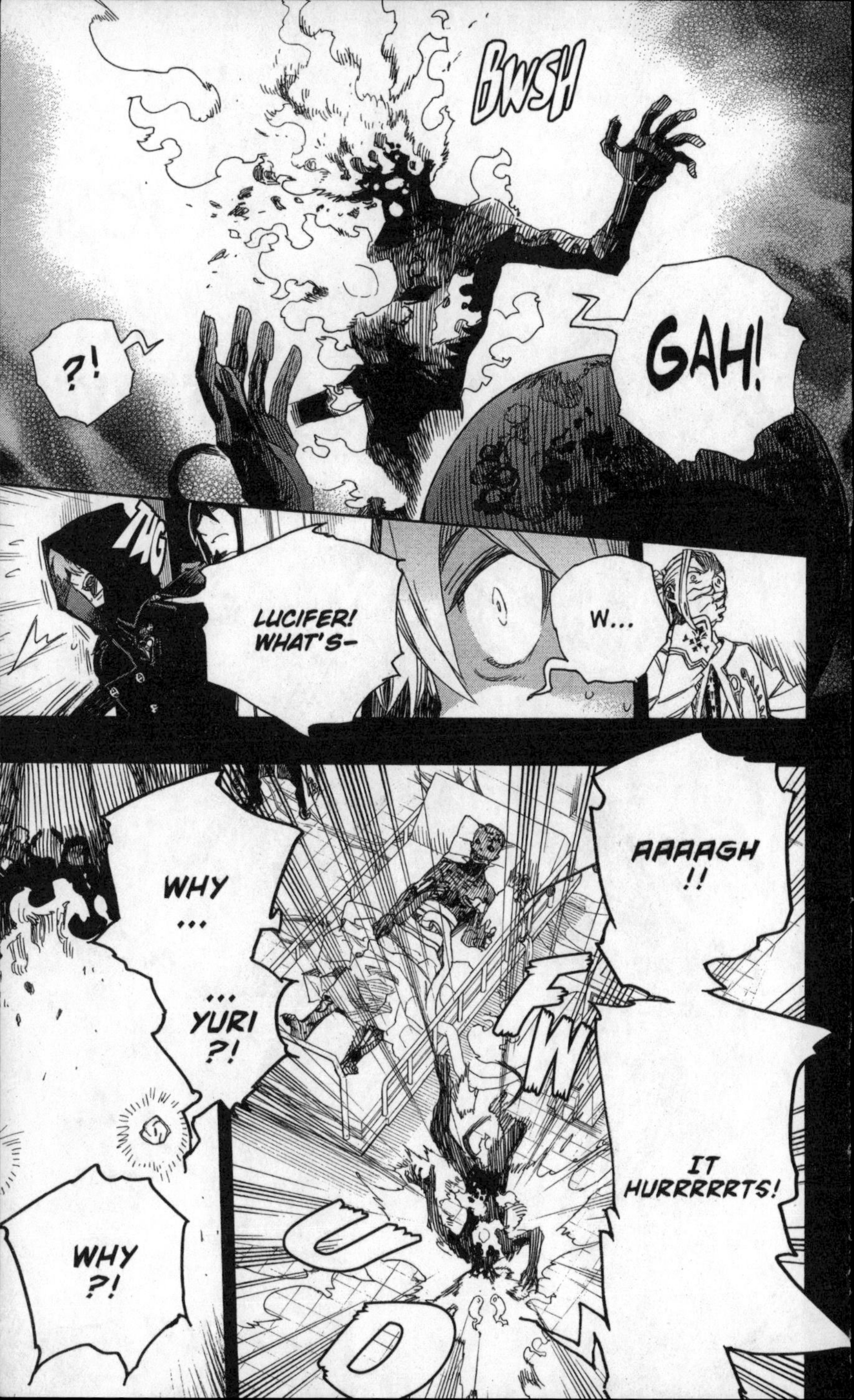

BWSH
GAH!
?!
W...
LUCIFER! WHAT'S-
THG
AAAAGH !!
IT HURRRRRTS!
FWUD
WHY ...
... YURI ?!
WHY ?!

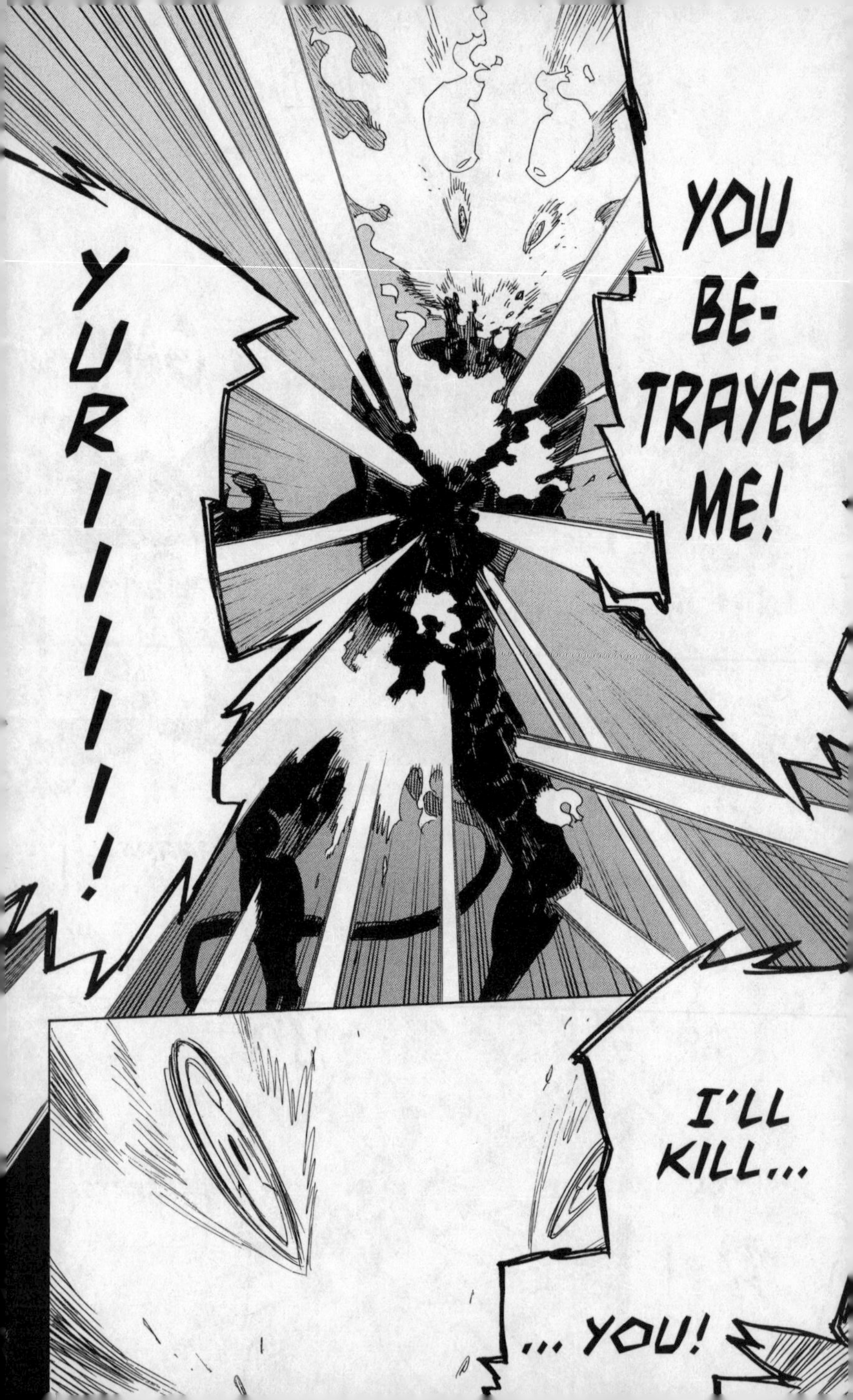
YOU BE-TRAYED ME!
YURIIIIII!
I'LL KILL...
... YOU!

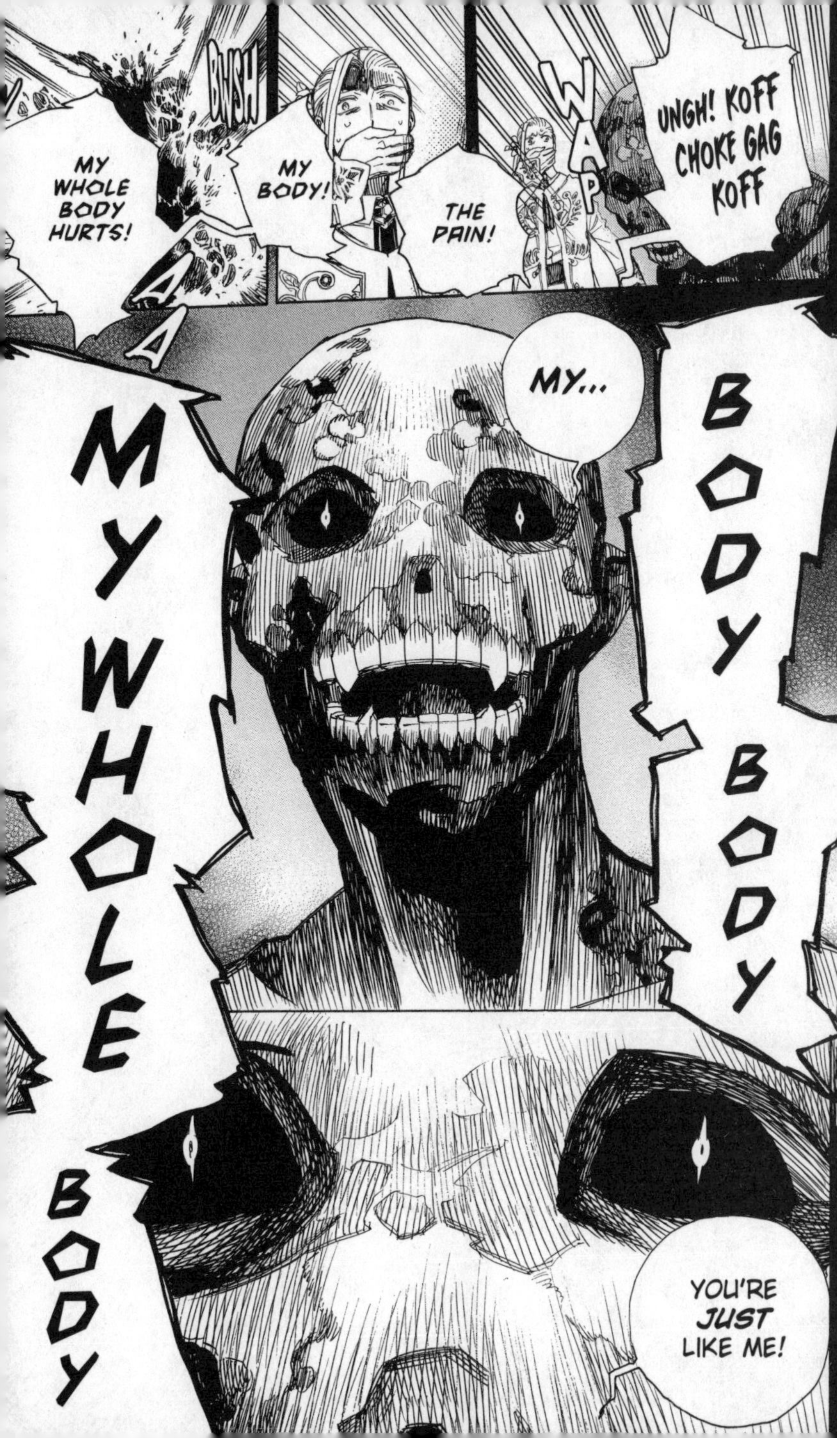
UNGH! KOFF CHOKE GAG KOFF
WAP
THE PAIN!
MY BODY!
BWSH
MY WHOLE BODY HURTS!
AA
BODY BODY BODY
MY...
MY WHOLE BODY
YOU'RE JUST LIKE ME!

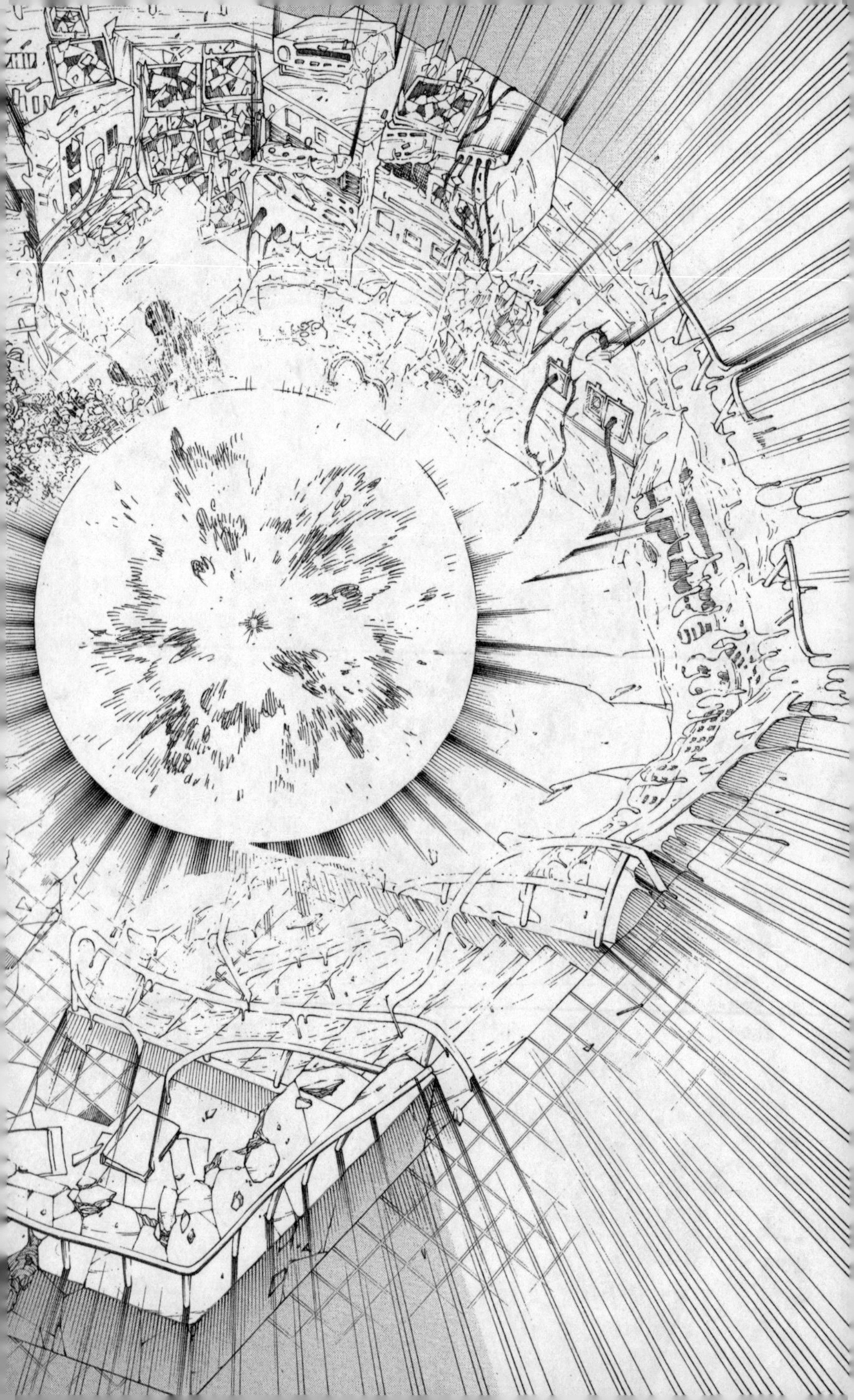

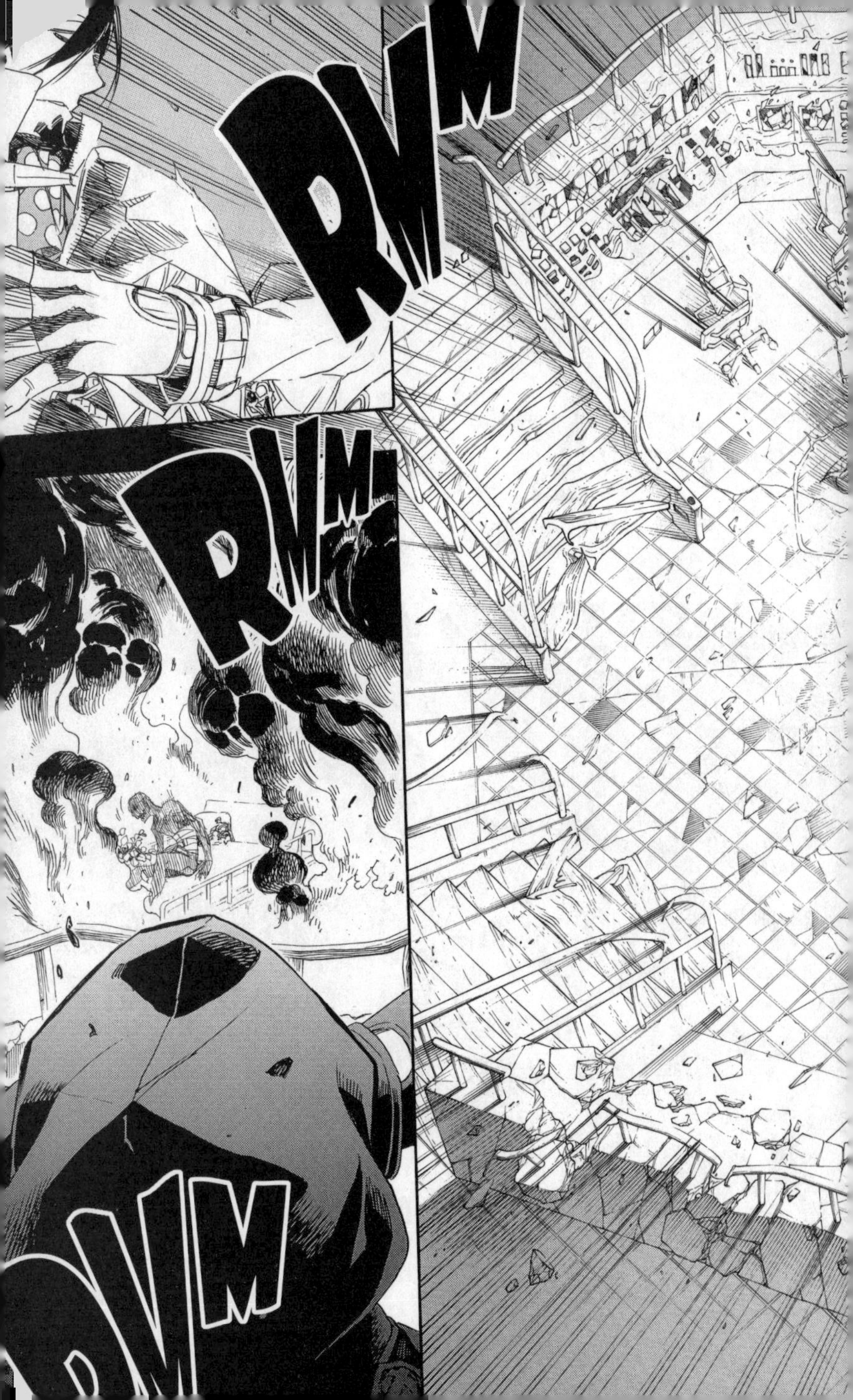
RMMM
RMMM
RMMM

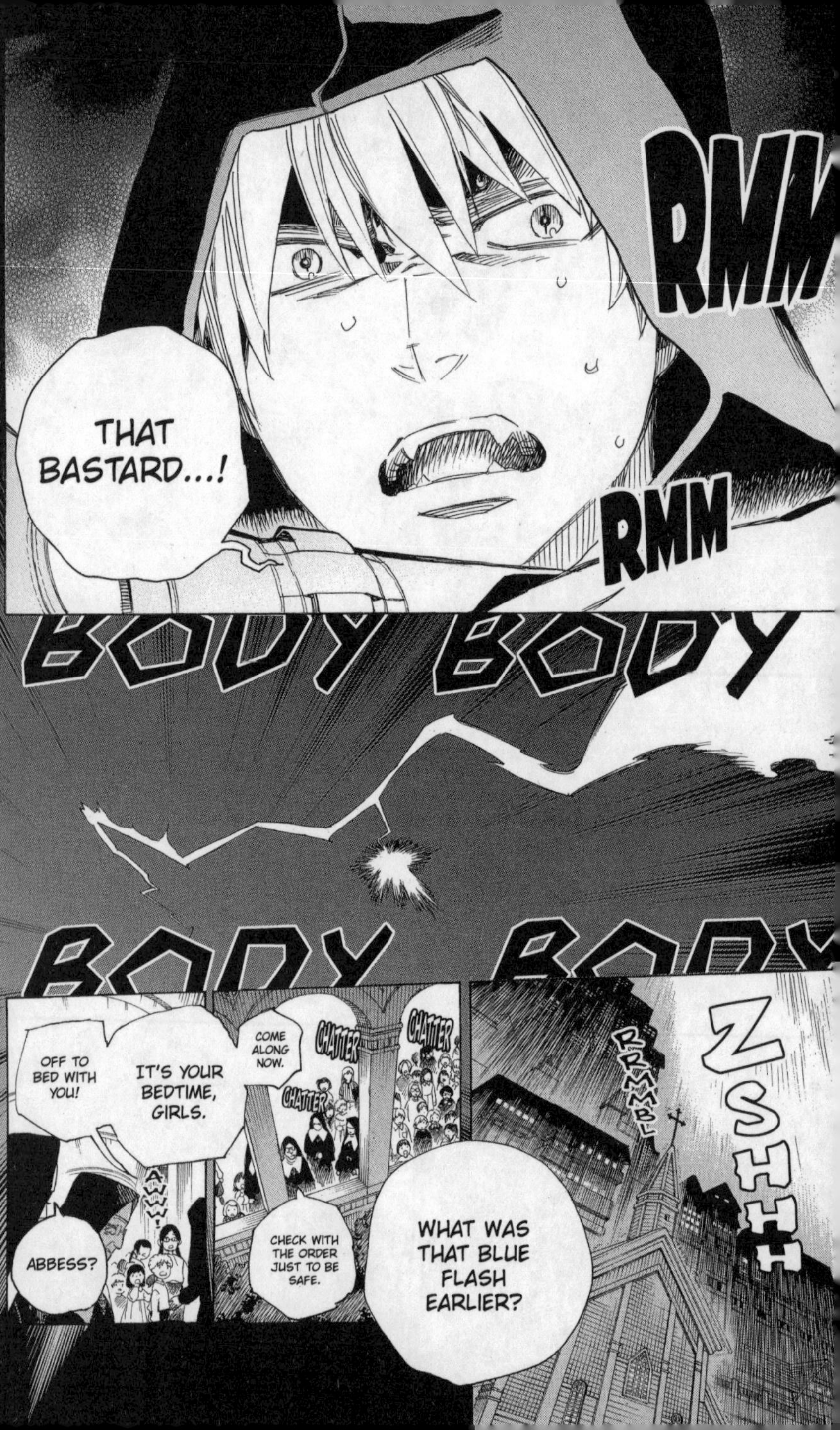
RMM
RMM
THAT BASTARD...!
BODY BODY
BODY BODY
ZSHHH
RRRMMBL
WHAT WAS THAT BLUE FLASH EARLIER?
CHATTER
CHATTER
COME ALONG NOW.
CHATTER
CHECK WITH THE ORDER JUST TO BE SAFE.
IT'S YOUR BEDTIME, GIRLS.
OFF TO BED WITH YOU!
AWWW!
ABBESS?

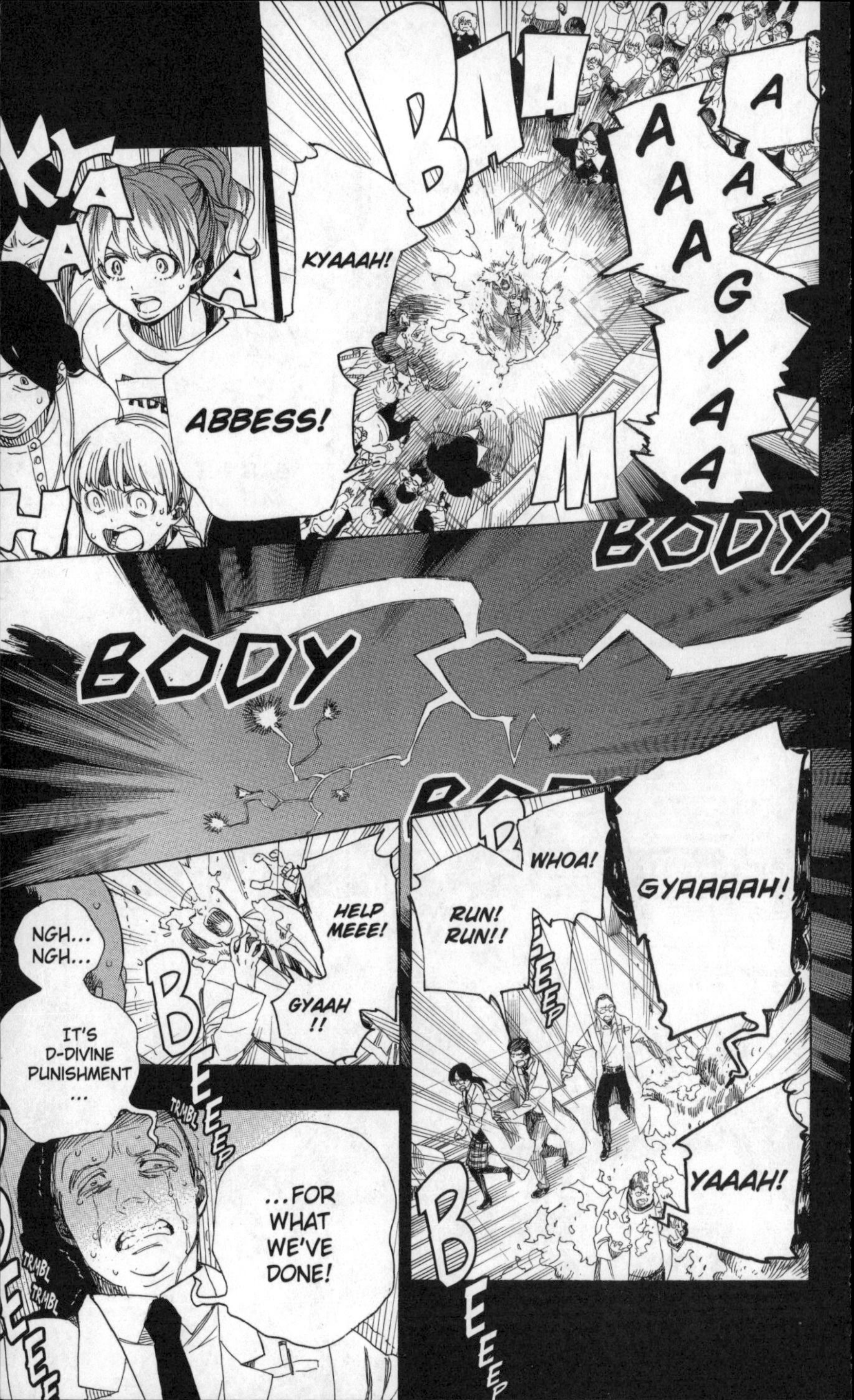
BAAAM
AAAAAGYAAA
KYAAAH
KYAAAH!
ABBESS!
BODY
BODY
GYAAAAH!
WHOA!
RUN! RUN!!
BEEEP
YAAAH!
BEEEP
HELP MEEE!
NGH... NGH...
GYAAH!!
BEEEP
IT'S D-DIVINE PUNISHMENT ...
TRMBL
...FOR WHAT WE'VE DONE!
TRMBL TRMBL
BEEEP

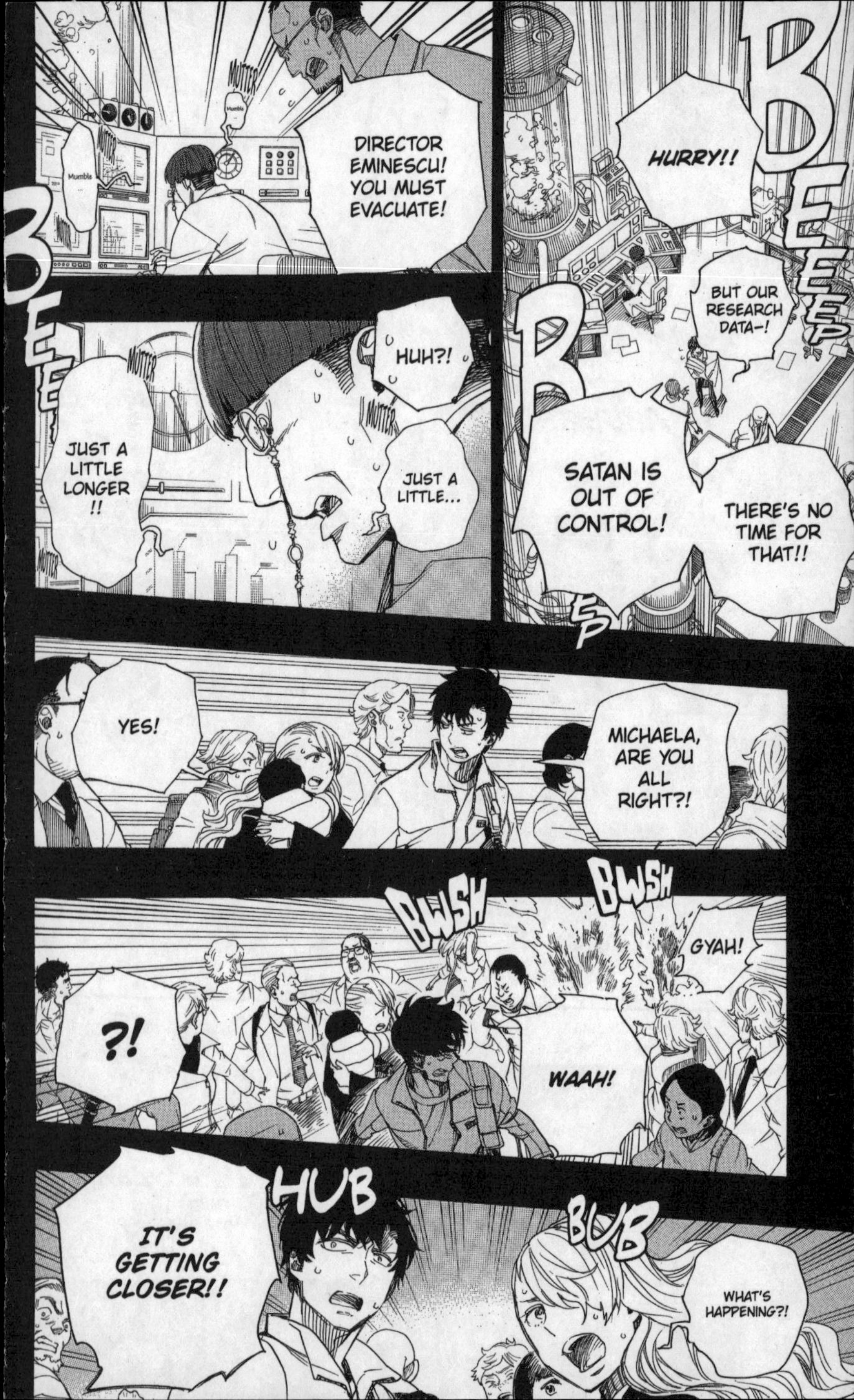
BEEEEP
HURRY!!
BUT OUR RESEARCH DATA-!
SATAN IS OUT OF CONTROL!
THERE'S NO TIME FOR THAT!!
BEEP
DIRECTOR EMINESCU! YOU MUST EVACUATE!
MUTTER
Mumble
MUTTER
Mumble
MUTTER
HUH?!
MUTTER
JUST A LITTLE...
MUTTER
JUST A LITTLE LONGER!!
MUTTER
MICHAELA, ARE YOU ALL RIGHT?!
YES!
BWSH
BWSH
GYAH!
WAAH!
?!
BUB
WHAT'S HAPPENING?!
HUB
IT'S GETTING CLOSER!!

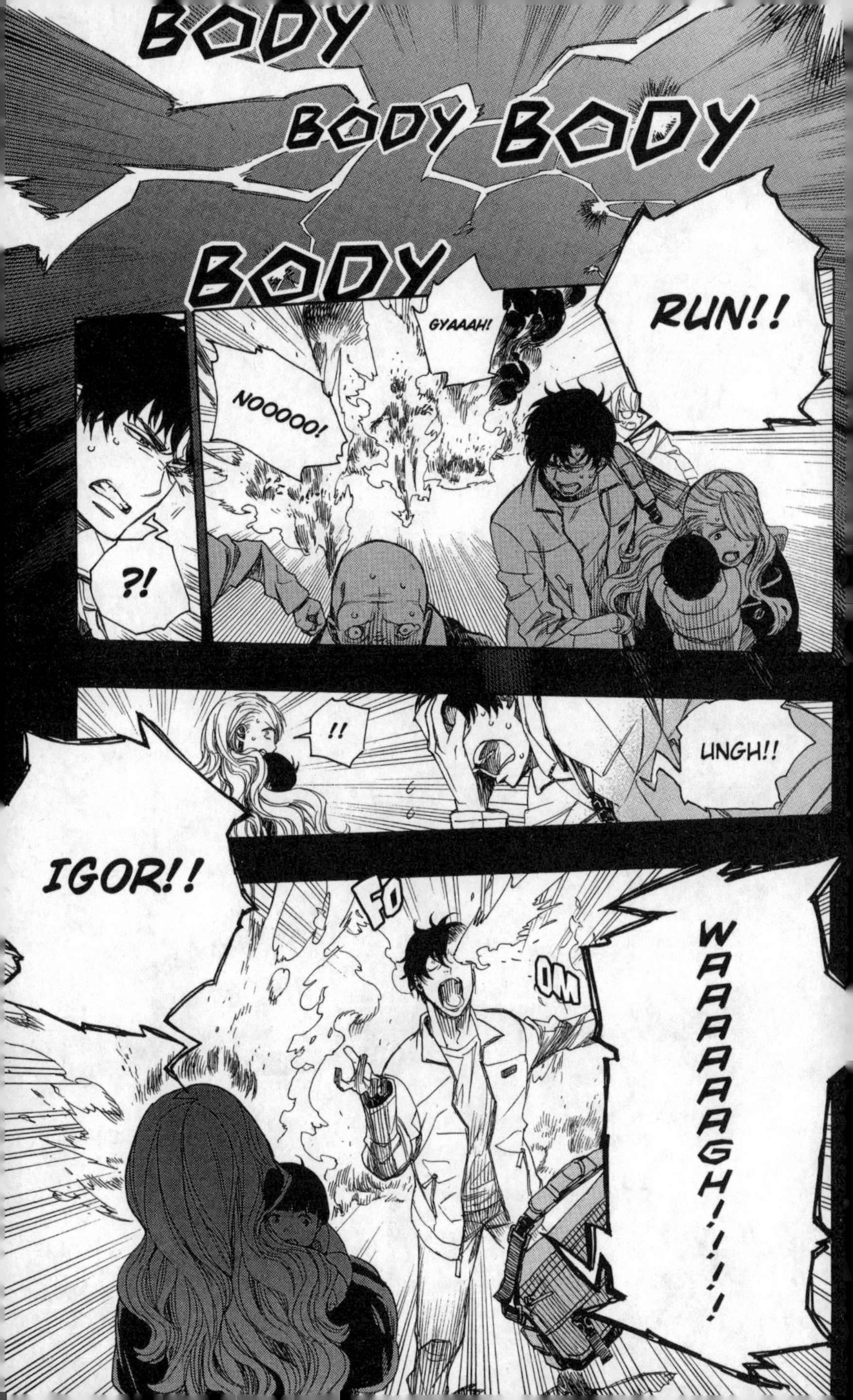
BODY
BODY
BODY
BODY
RUN!!
GYAAAH!
NOOOOO!
?!
UNGH!!
!!
IGOR!!
WAAAAAAAGH!!!!!
FOOM

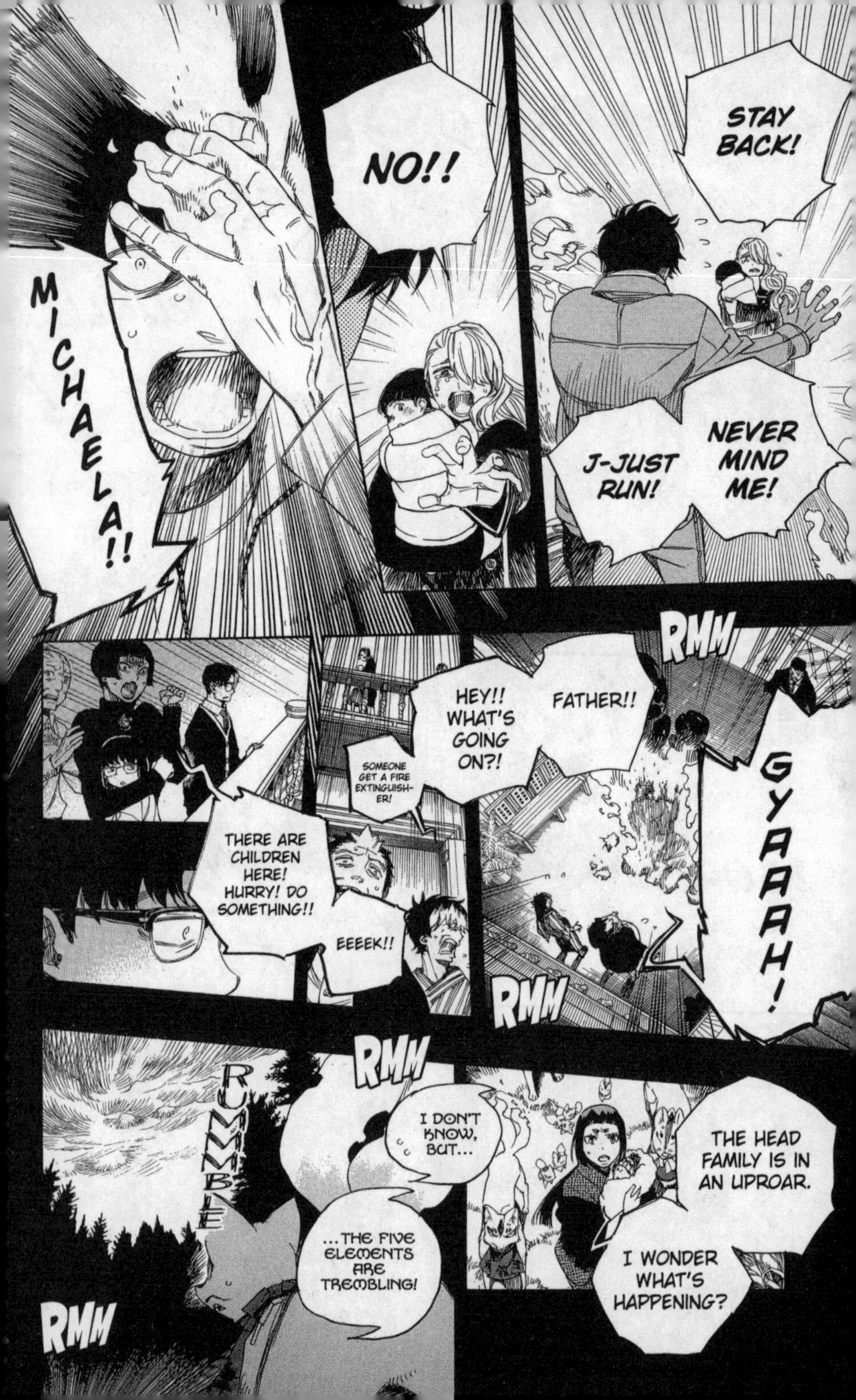
STAY BACK!
NEVER MIND ME!
J-JUST RUN!
NO!!
MICHAELA!!
RMM
FATHER!!
GYAAAH!
RMM
HEY!! WHAT'S GOING ON?!
SOMEONE GET A FIRE EXTINGUISHER!
THERE ARE CHILDREN HERE! HURRY! DO SOMETHING!!
EEEEK!!
THE HEAD FAMILY IS IN AN UPROAR.
I WONDER WHAT'S HAPPENING?
RMM
I DON'T KNOW, BUT...
...THE FIVE ELEMENTS ARE TREMBLING!
RUMMBLE
RMM

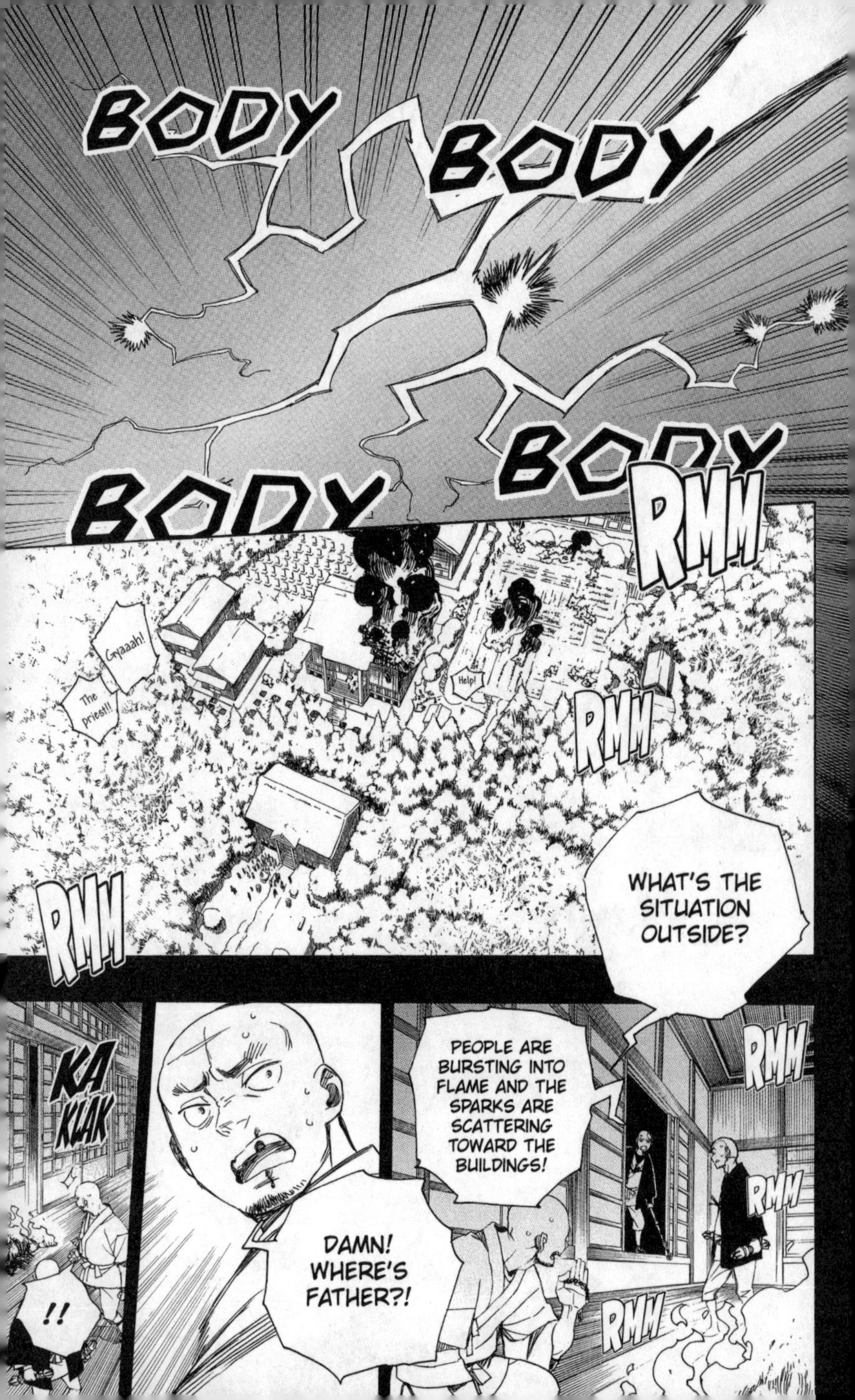

BODY
BODY
BODY
BODY
RMM
Help!
Gyaaah!
The priest!!
RMM
RMM
WHAT'S THE SITUATION OUTSIDE?
RMM
PEOPLE ARE BURSTING INTO FLAME AND THE SPARKS ARE SCATTERING TOWARD THE BUILDINGS!
RMM
RMM
DAMN! WHERE'S FATHER?!
KA KLAK
!!

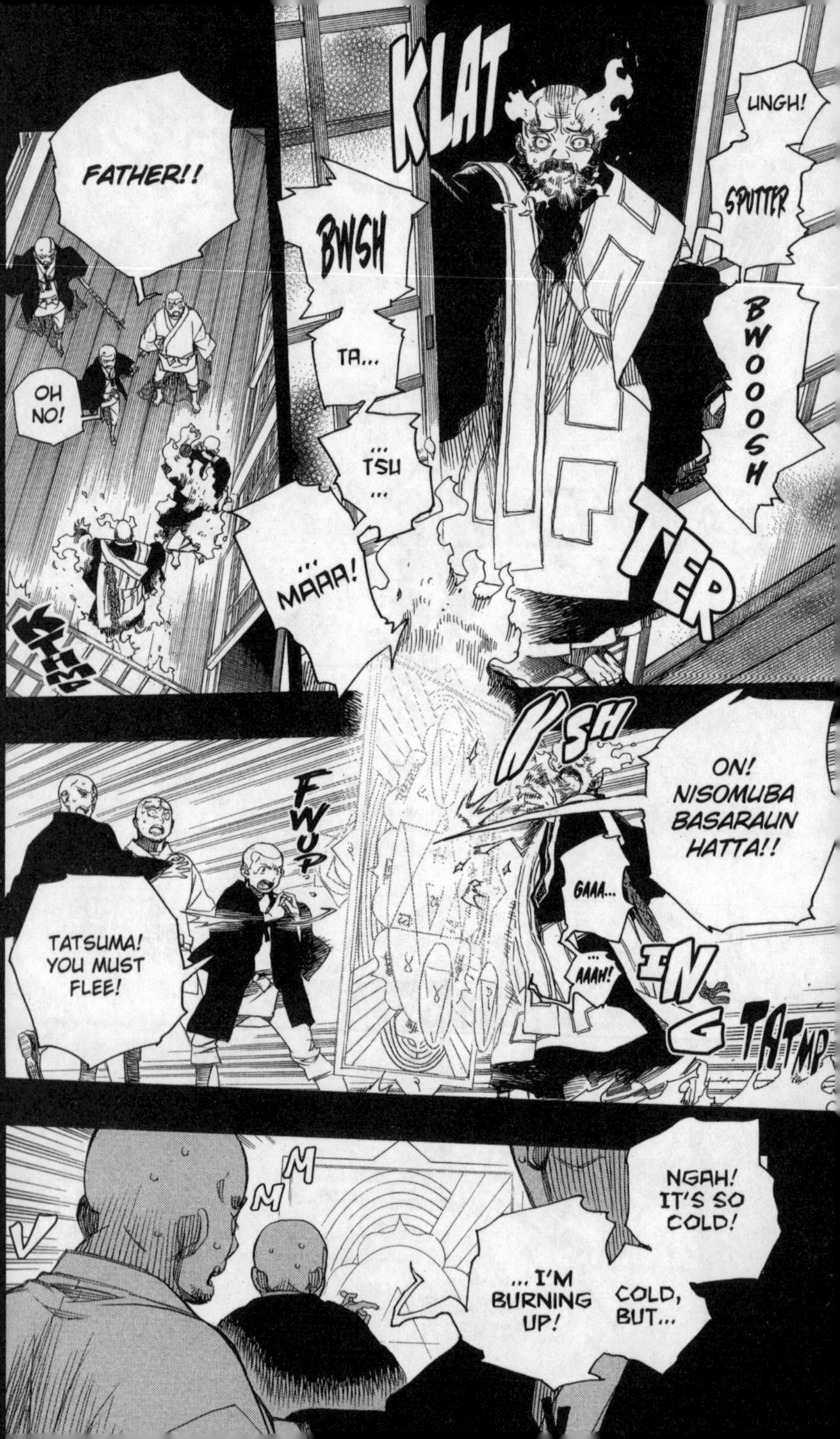
UNGH!
SPUTTER
BWOOOOSH
KLAT
TER
BWSH
TA...
... TSU ...
... MAAA!
FATHER!!
OH NO!
ON! NISOMUBA BASARAUN HATTA!!
GAAA...
... AAAH!
ING
TATMP
FWUP
TATSUMA! YOU MUST FLEE!
NGAH! IT'S SO COLD!
COLD, BUT...
... I'M BURNING UP!
M
M

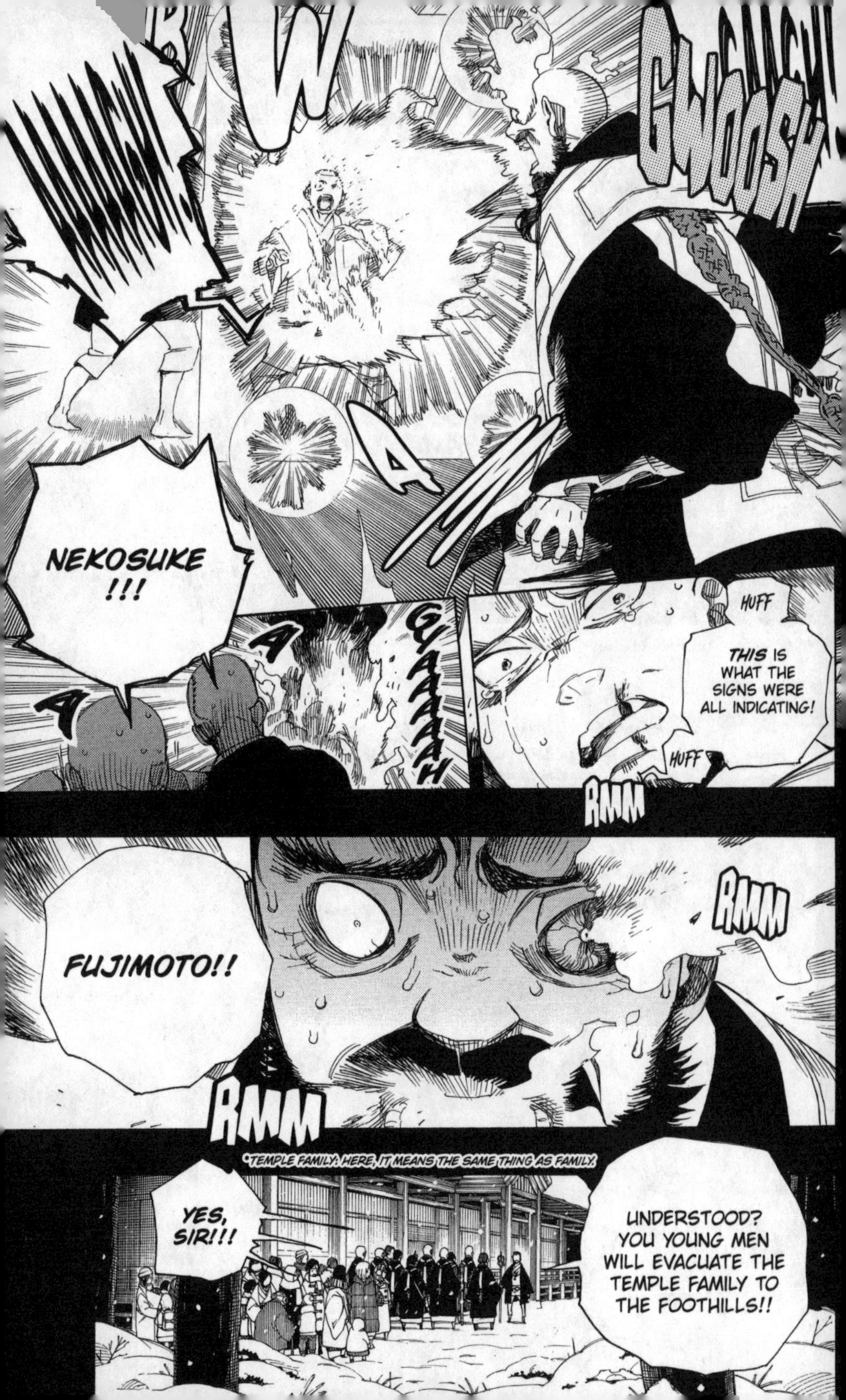
GWOOSH
WAAAGH!
A
NEKOSUKE !!!
HUFF
THIS IS WHAT THE SIGNS WERE ALL INDICATING!
HUFF
RMM
GUAAAAAH
A
A
RMM
FUJIMOTO!!
RMM
UNDERSTOOD? YOU YOUNG MEN WILL EVACUATE THE TEMPLE FAMILY TO THE FOOTHILLS!!
YES, SIR!!!

*TEMPLE FAMILY: HERE, IT MEANS THE SAME THING AS FAMILY.

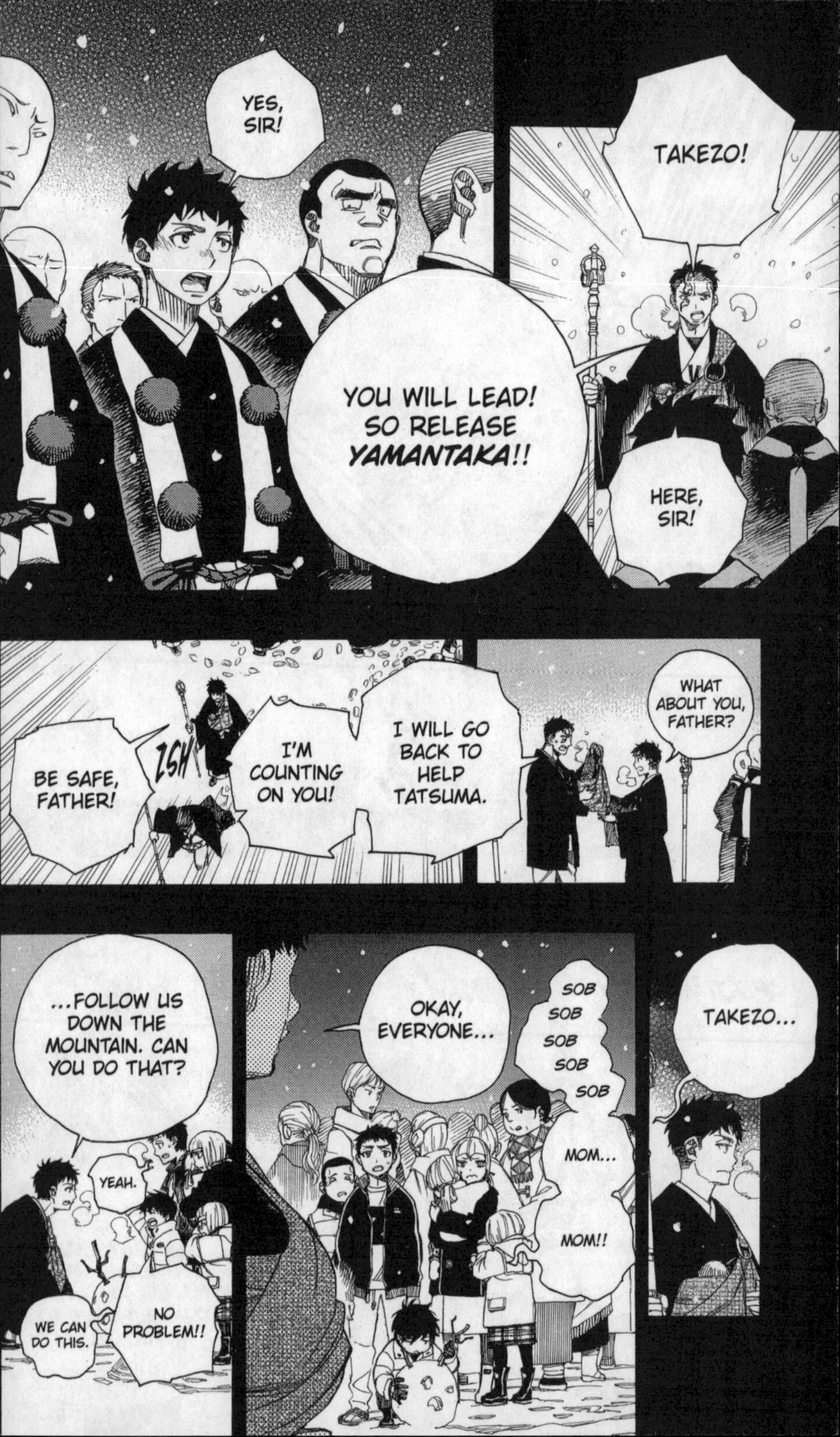
TAKEZO!
YOU WILL LEAD! SO RELEASE *YAMANTAKA*!!
HERE, SIR!
YES, SIR!
WHAT ABOUT YOU, FATHER?
I WILL GO BACK TO HELP TATSUMA.
I'M COUNTING ON YOU!
ZSH
BE SAFE, FATHER!
TAKEZO...
SOB SOB SOB SOB SOB
OKAY, EVERYONE...
MOM...
MOM!!
...FOLLOW US DOWN THE MOUNTAIN. CAN YOU DO THAT?
YEAH.
NO PROBLEM!!
WE CAN DO THIS.

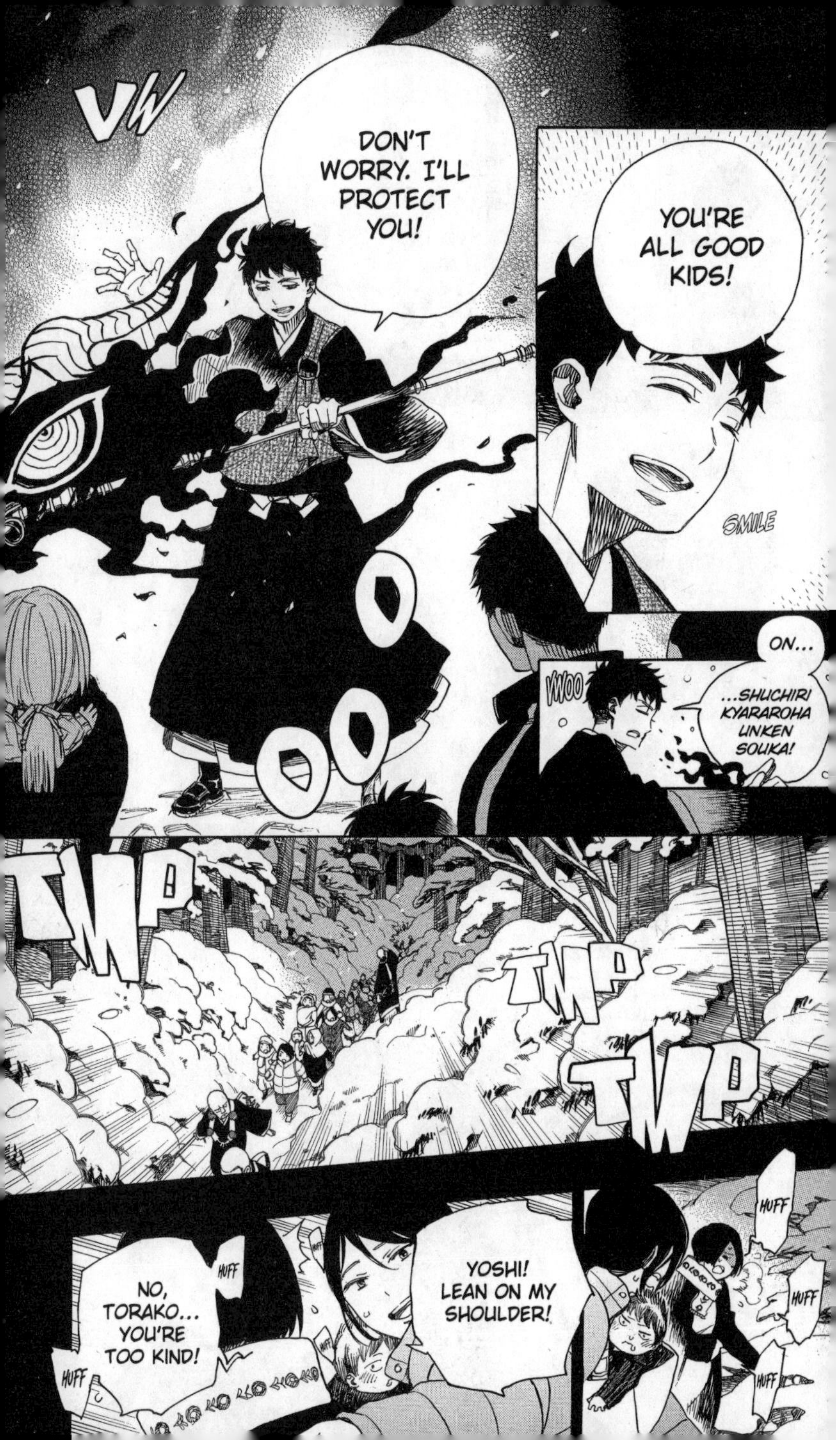
YOU'RE ALL GOOD KIDS!
SMILE
VWOO
ON...
...SHUCHIRI KYARAROHA UNKEN SOUKA!
VW
DON'T WORRY. I'LL PROTECT YOU!
TMP
TMP
TMP
HUFF
HUFF
HUFF
YOSHI! LEAN ON MY SHOULDER!
HUFF
NO, TORAKO... YOU'RE TOO KIND!
HUFF
HUFF

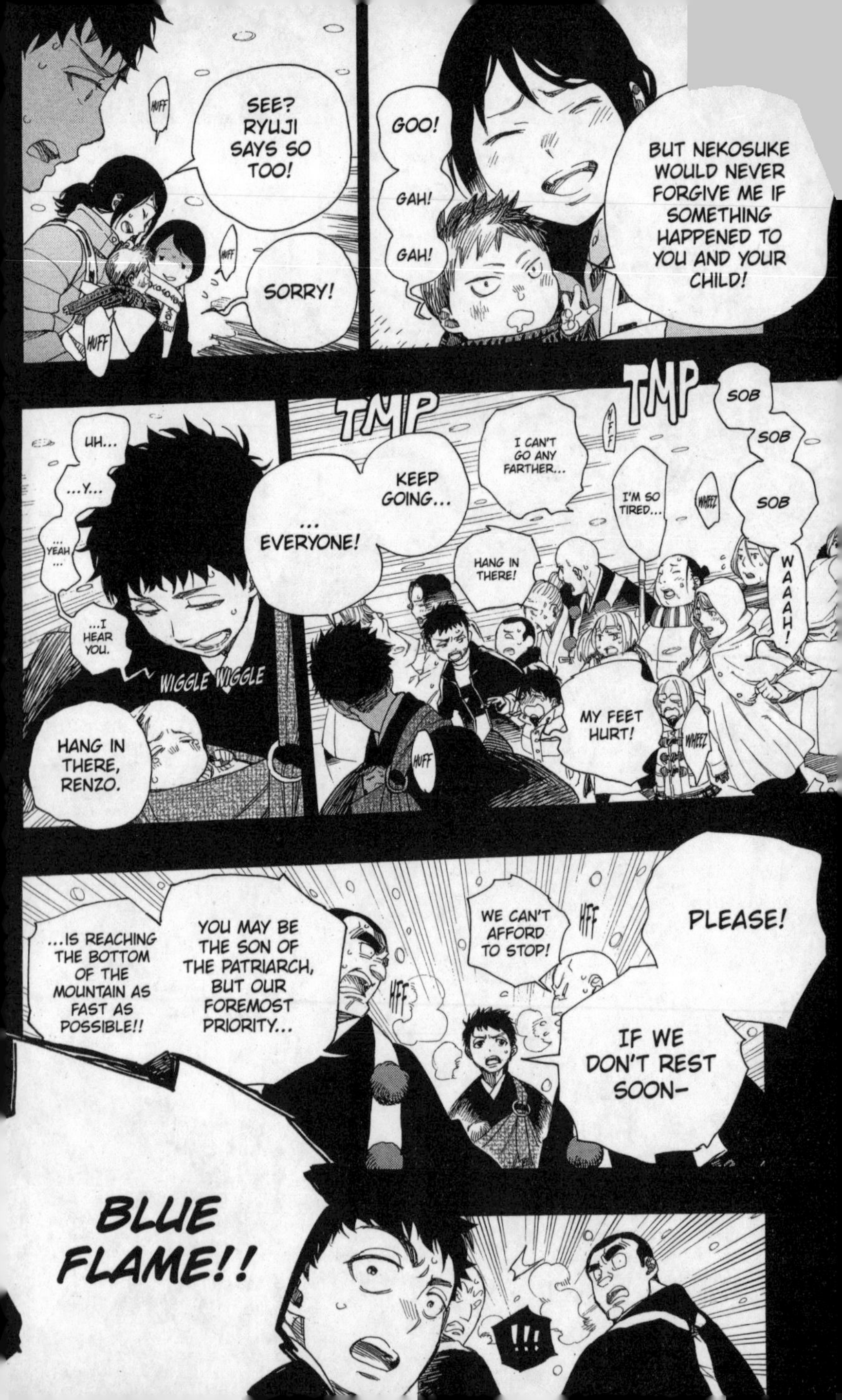
BUT NEKOSUKE WOULD NEVER FORGIVE ME IF SOMETHING HAPPENED TO YOU AND YOUR CHILD!
GOO!
GAH!
GAH!
HUFF
SEE? RYUJI SAYS SO TOO!
HUFF
SORRY!
HUFF
TMP
SOB
SOB
SOB
WAAAAH!
HFF
I CAN'T GO ANY FARTHER...
I'M SO TIRED...
WHEEZ
TMP
KEEP GOING...
...EVERYONE!
HANG IN THERE!
MY FEET HURT!
WHEEZ
HUFF
UH...
...Y...
...YEAH...
...I HEAR YOU.
WIGGLE WIGGLE
HANG IN THERE, RENZO.
PLEASE!
HFF
WE CAN'T AFFORD TO STOP!
IF WE DON'T REST SOON-
YOU MAY BE THE SON OF THE PATRIARCH, BUT OUR FOREMOST PRIORITY...
...IS REACHING THE BOTTOM OF THE MOUNTAIN AS FAST AS POSSIBLE!!
HFF
BLUE FLAME!!
!!!

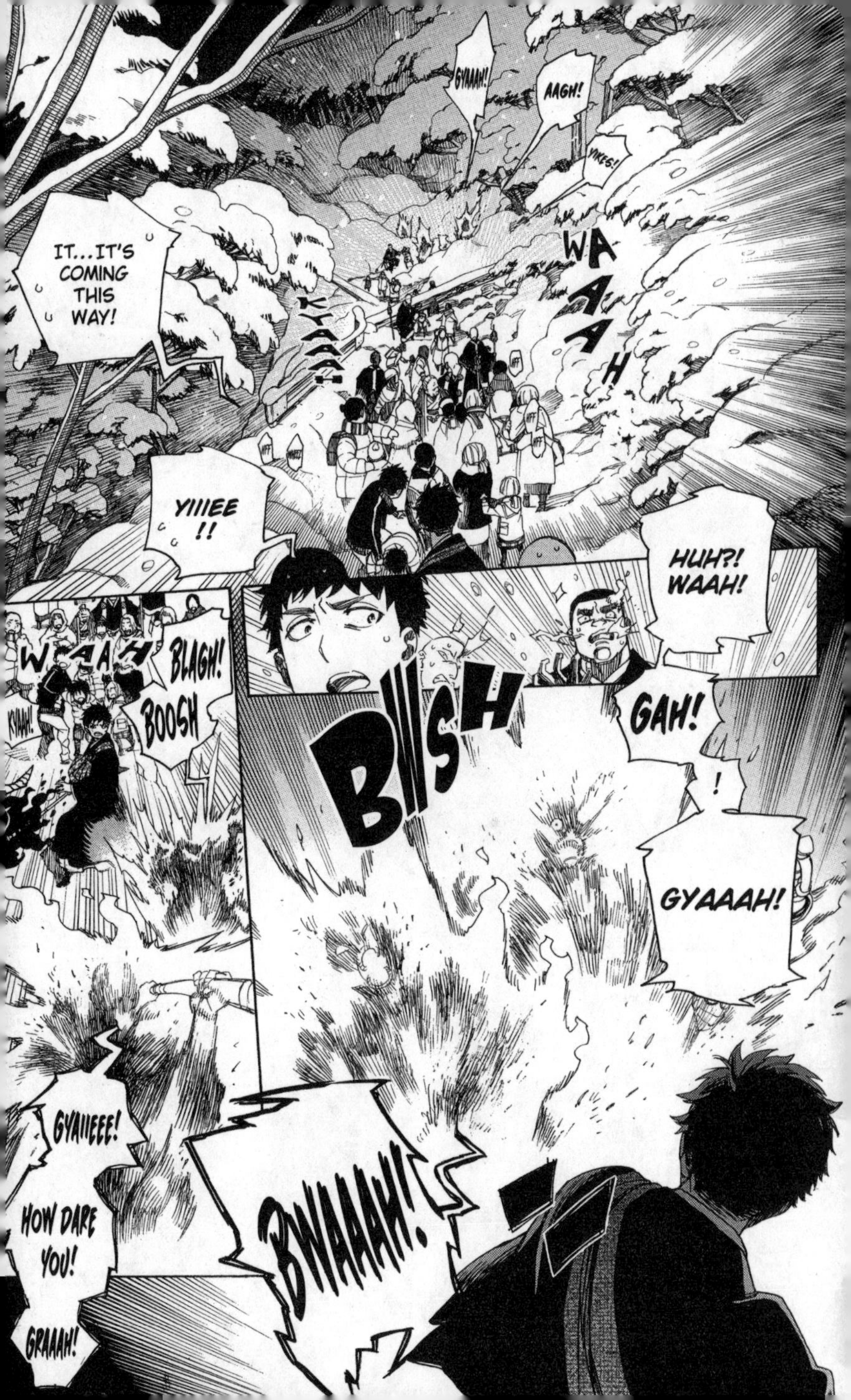
YIKES!
AAGH!
GYAAAH!
WAAAAH
KYAAAA!
IT...IT'S COMING THIS WAY!
YIIIEE!!
HUH?! WAAH!
BISH
GAH!
!
GYAAAH!
BLAGH!
WAAH
BOOSH
KYAAH!
BWAAAH!
GYAIIEEE!
HOW DARE YOU!
GRAAAH!

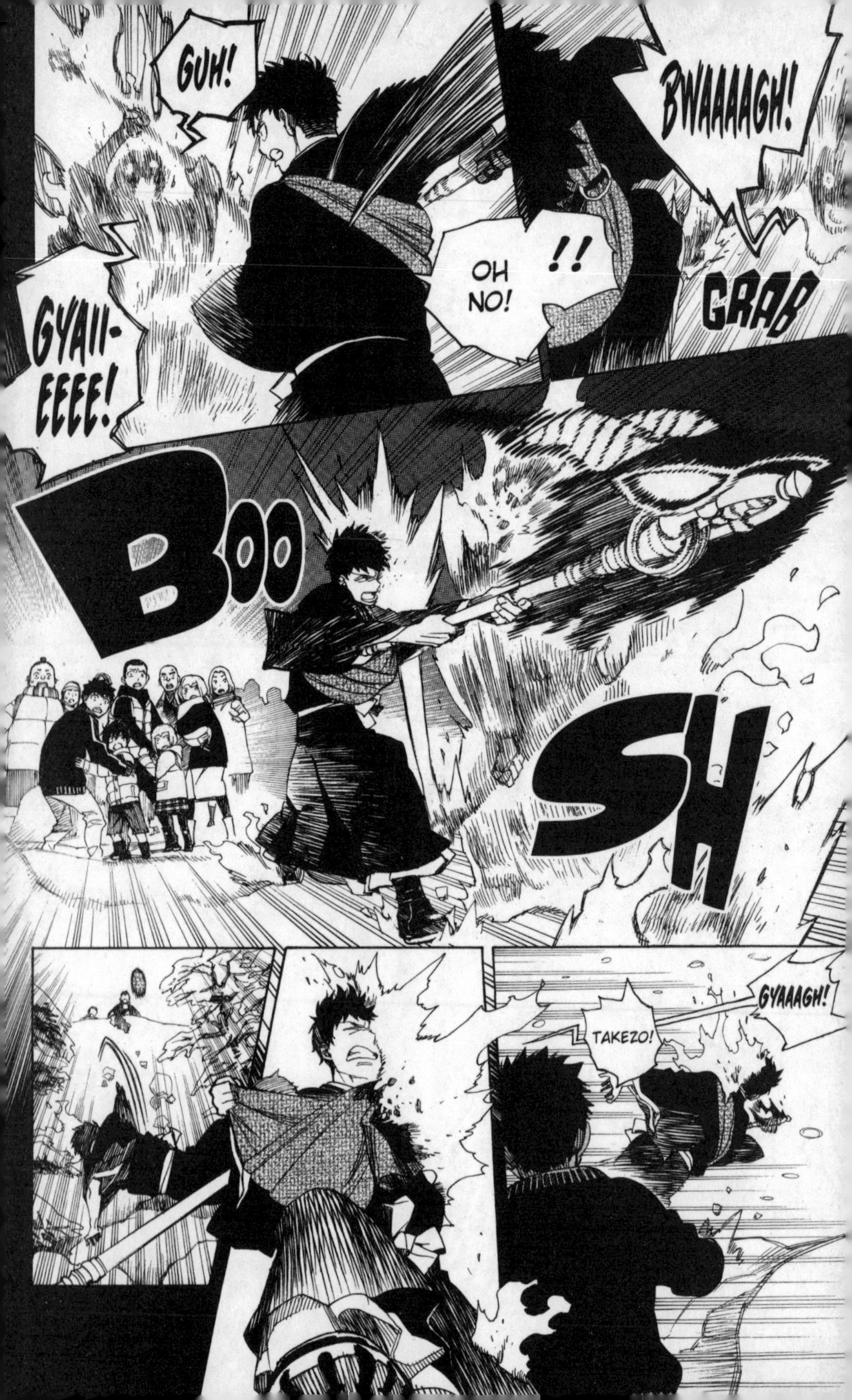
BWAAAAGH!
GUH!
!!
OH NO!
GRAB
GYAII-EEEE!
BOOSH
GYAAAGH!
TAKEZO!

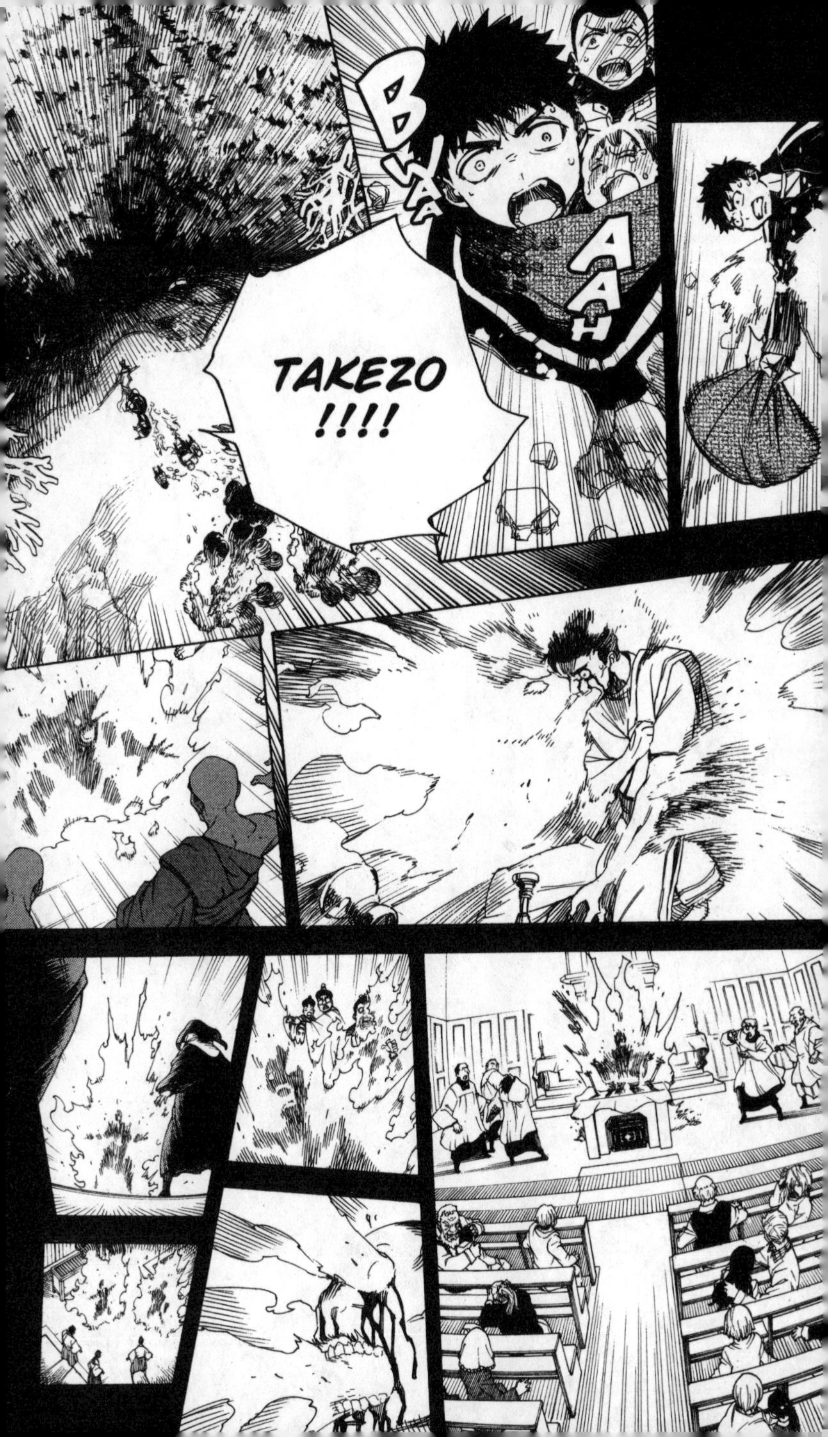
BWAA
AAAH
TAKEZO !!!!

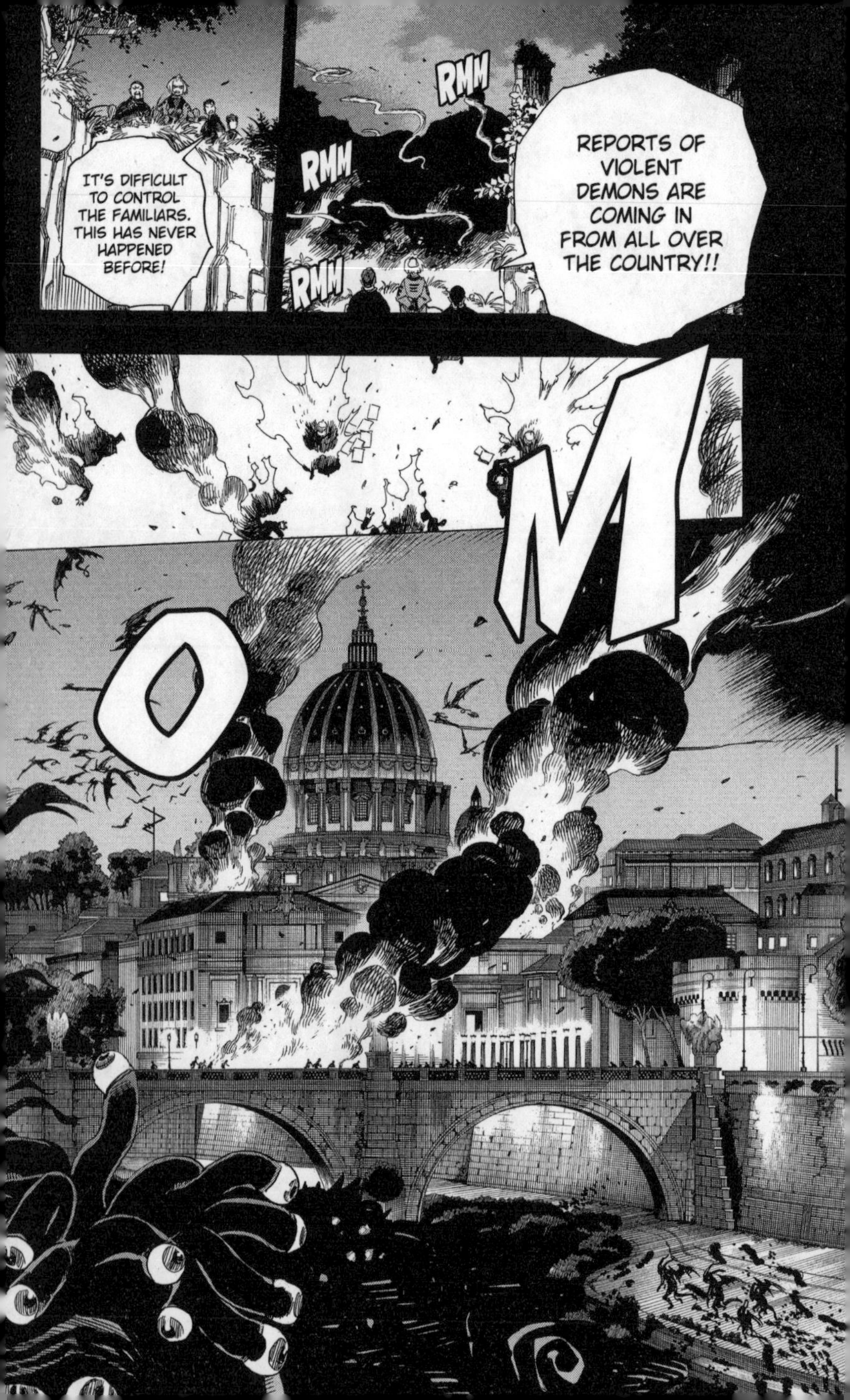
RMM
RMM
RMM
REPORTS OF VIOLENT DEMONS ARE COMING IN FROM ALL OVER THE COUNTRY!!
IT'S DIFFICULT TO CONTROL THE FAMILIARS. THIS HAS NEVER HAPPENED BEFORE!
OM

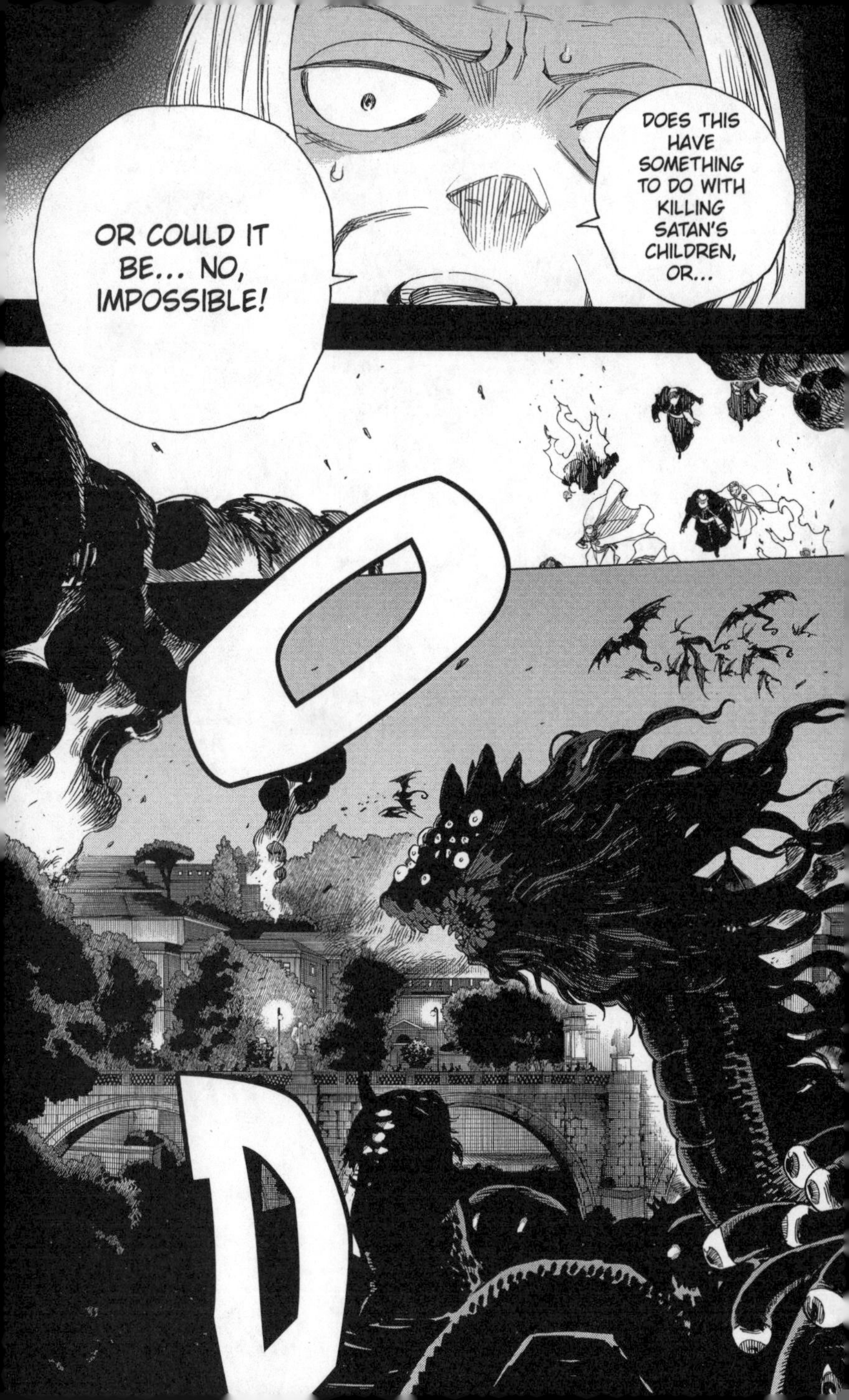
DOES THIS HAVE SOMETHING TO DO WITH KILLING SATAN'S CHILDREN, OR...
OR COULD IT BE... NO, IMPOSSIBLE!
DO

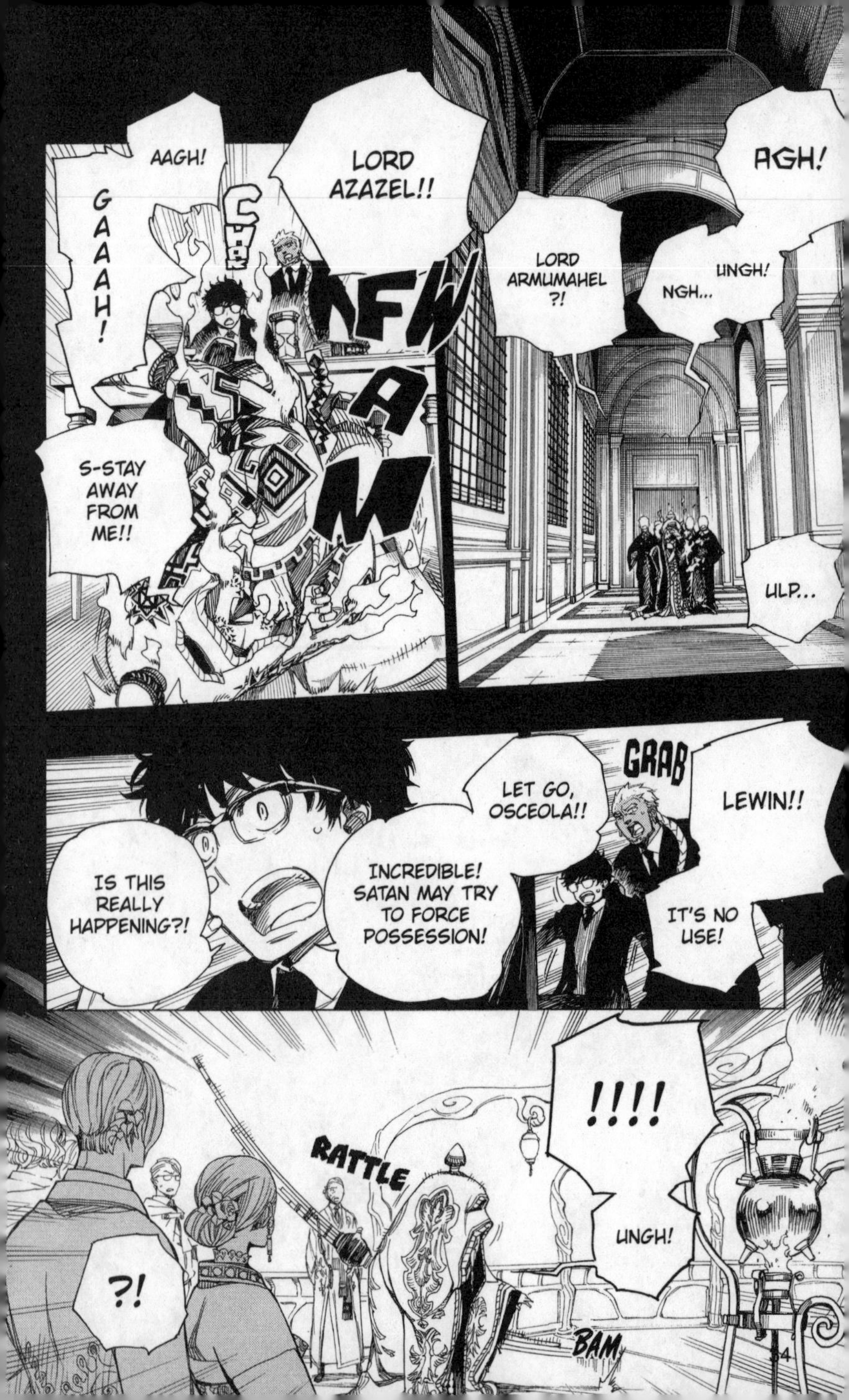
AGH!
LORD ARMUMAHEL?!
UNGH!
NGH...
ULP...
LORD AZAZEL!!
AAGH!
GAAAAH!
CHOK
FWAM
S-STAY AWAY FROM ME!!
GRAB
LEWIN!!
LET GO, OSCEOLA!!
IT'S NO USE!
INCREDIBLE! SATAN MAY TRY TO FORCE POSSESSION!
IS THIS REALLY HAPPENING?!
!!!!
UNGH!
RATTLE
BAM
?!

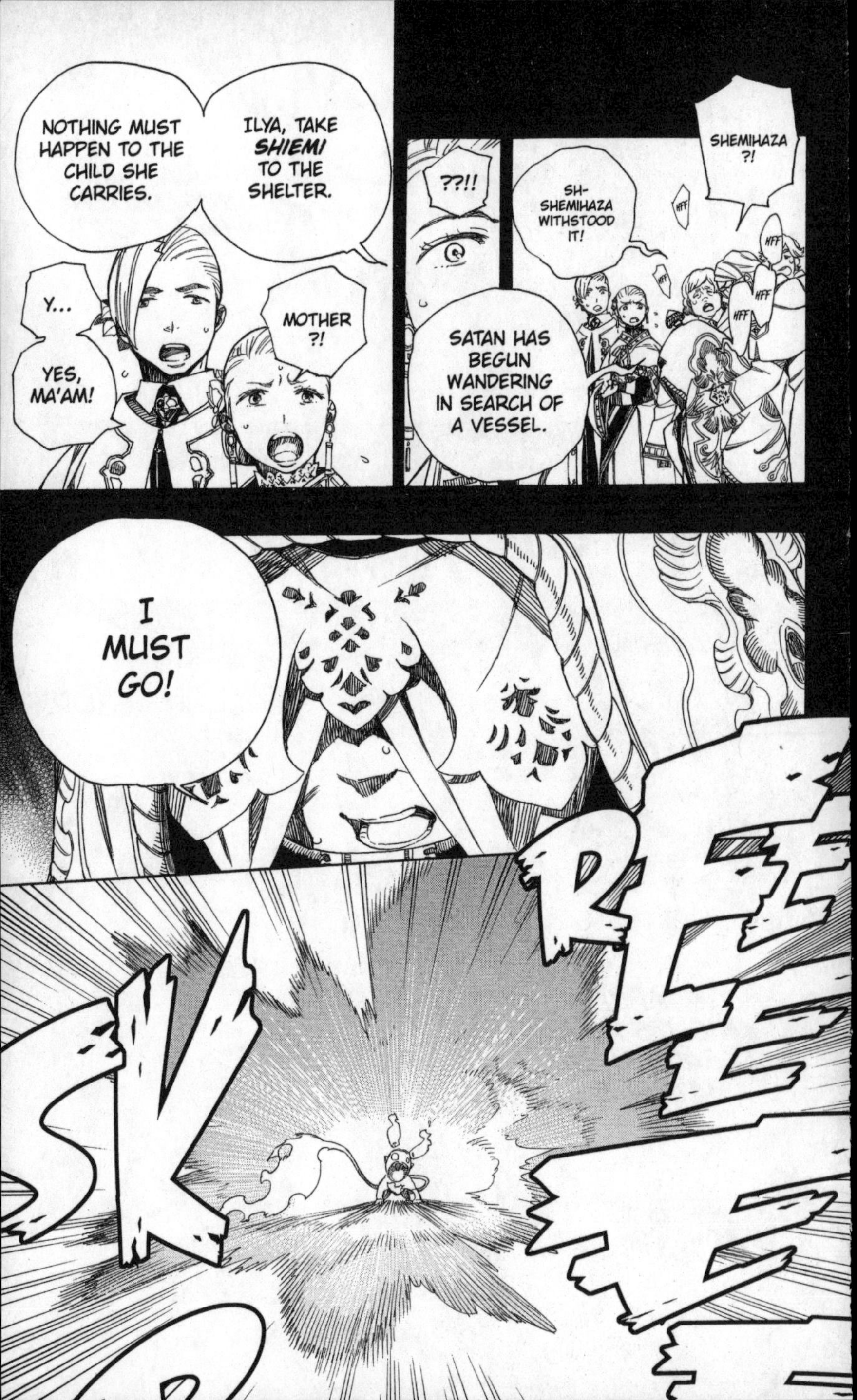
SHEMIHAZA ?!
HFF
SH-SHEMIHAZA WITHSTOOD IT!
HFF
HFF
HFF
HFF
??!!
SATAN HAS BEGUN WANDERING IN SEARCH OF A VESSEL.
ILYA, TAKE *SHIEMI* TO THE SHELTER.
NOTHING MUST HAPPEN TO THE CHILD SHE CARRIES.
MOTHER ?!
Y...
YES, MA'AM!
I MUST GO!
SK
REEE

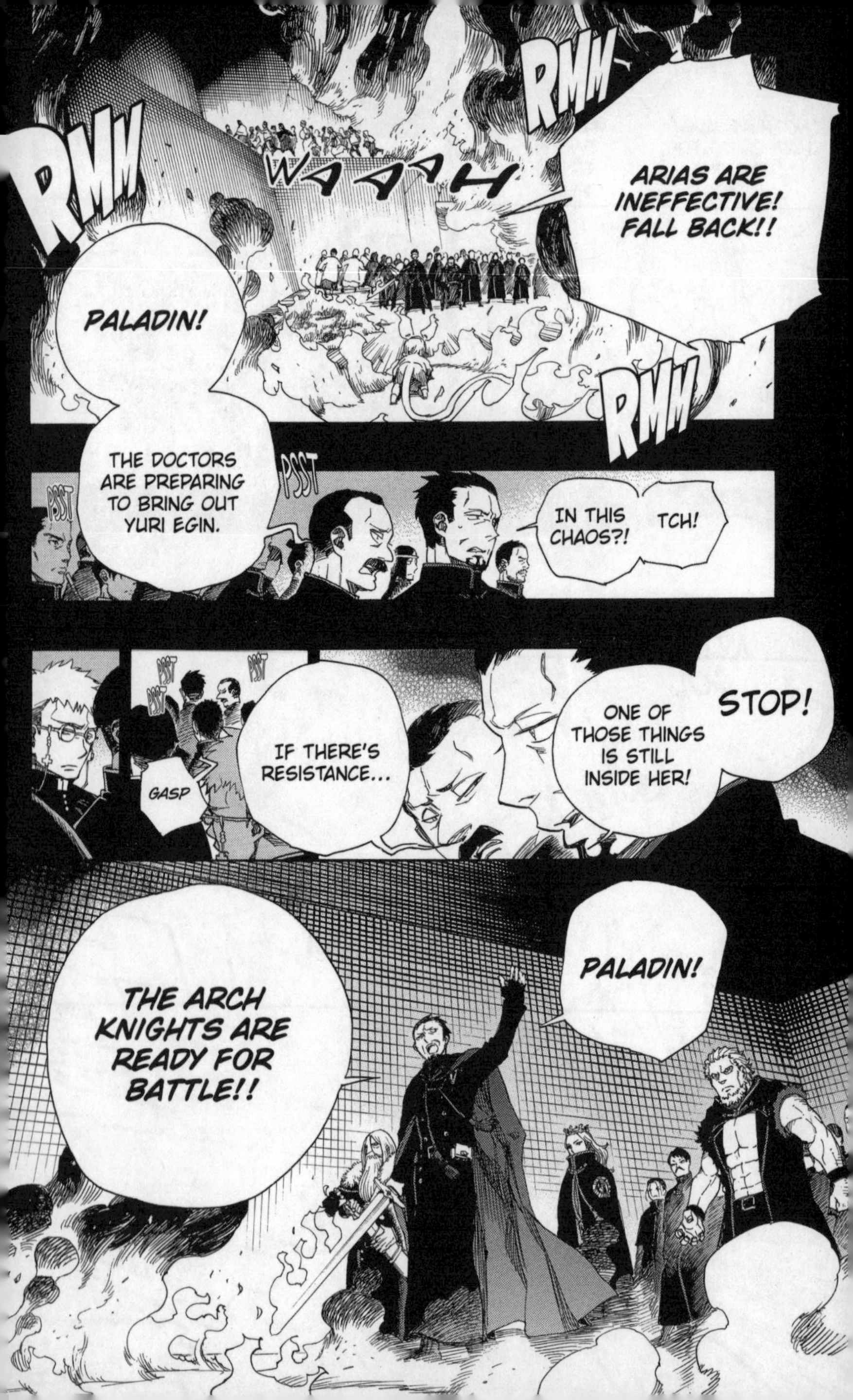
RMM
ARIAS ARE INEFFECTIVE! FALL BACK!!
WAAAH
RMM
RMM
PALADIN!
THE DOCTORS ARE PREPARING TO BRING OUT YURI EGIN.
TCH!
IN THIS CHAOS?!
PSST
PSST
STOP!
ONE OF THOSE THINGS IS STILL INSIDE HER!
IF THERE'S RESISTANCE...
PSST
PSST
PSST
GASP
PALADIN!
THE ARCH KNIGHTS ARE READY FOR BATTLE!!

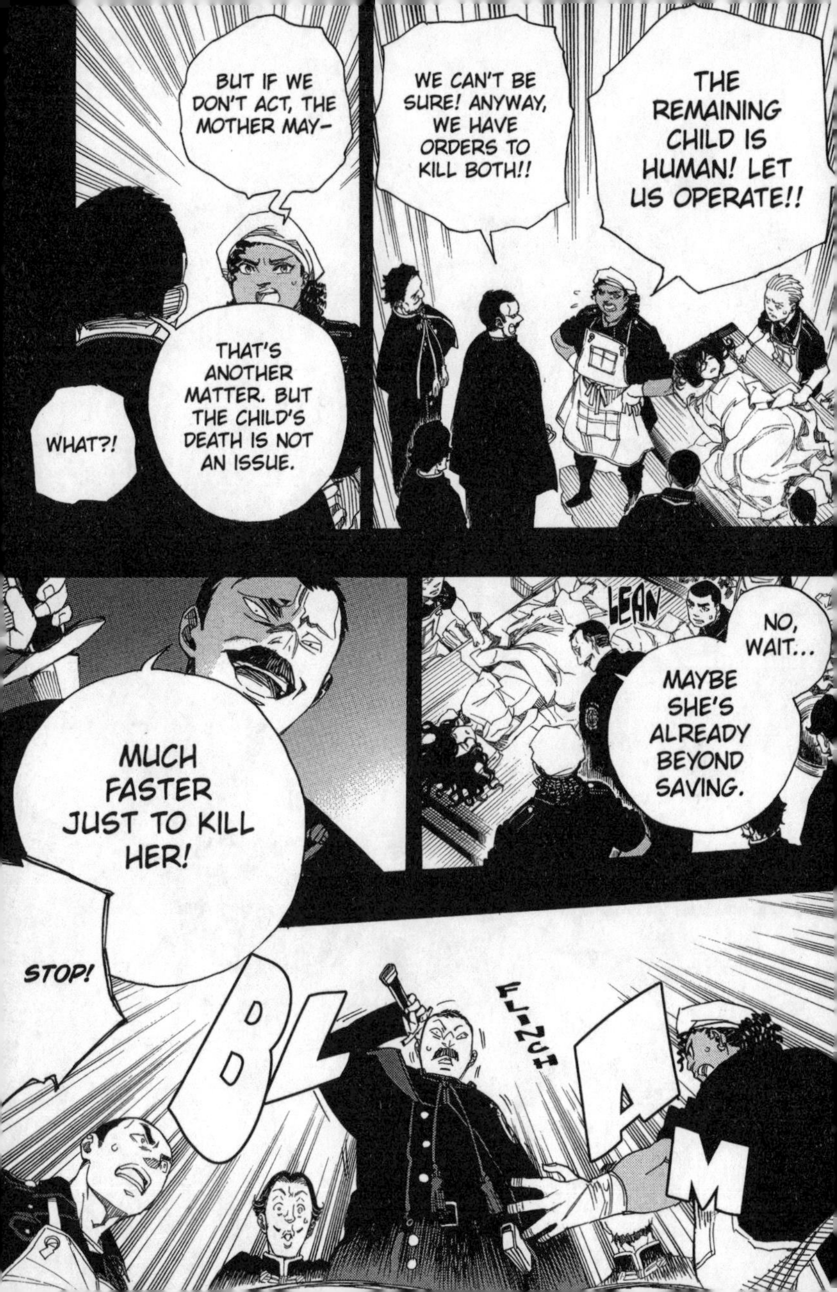
THE REMAINING CHILD IS HUMAN! LET US OPERATE!!
WE CAN'T BE SURE! ANYWAY, WE HAVE ORDERS TO KILL BOTH!!
BUT IF WE DON'T ACT, THE MOTHER MAY-
THAT'S ANOTHER MATTER. BUT THE CHILD'S DEATH IS NOT AN ISSUE.
WHAT?!
LEAN
NO, WAIT...
MAYBE SHE'S ALREADY BEYOND SAVING.
MUCH FASTER JUST TO KILL HER!
FLINCH
BLAM
STOP!

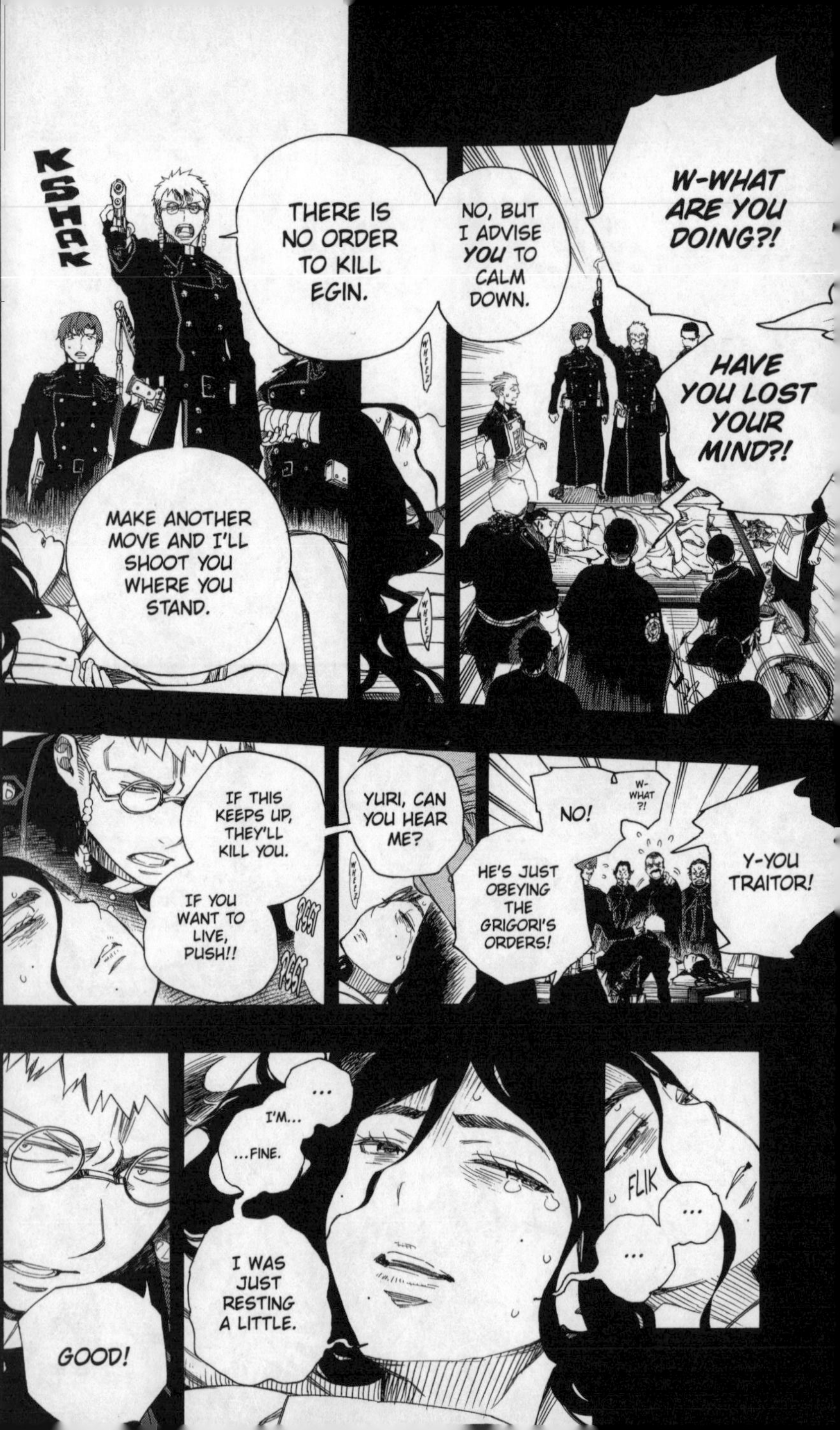
W-WHAT ARE YOU DOING?!
HAVE YOU LOST YOUR MIND?!
NO, BUT I ADVISE YOU TO CALM DOWN.
THERE IS NO ORDER TO KILL EGIN.
KSHAK
WHEEZ
MAKE ANOTHER MOVE AND I'LL SHOOT YOU WHERE YOU STAND.
WHEEZ
Y-YOU TRAITOR!
W-WHAT ?!
NO!
HE'S JUST OBEYING THE GRIGORI'S ORDERS!
YURI, CAN YOU HEAR ME?
WHEEZ
IF THIS KEEPS UP, THEY'LL KILL YOU.
IF YOU WANT TO LIVE, PUSH!!
FLIK
...
...
...
I'M...
...FINE.
I WAS JUST RESTING A LITTLE.
GOOD!

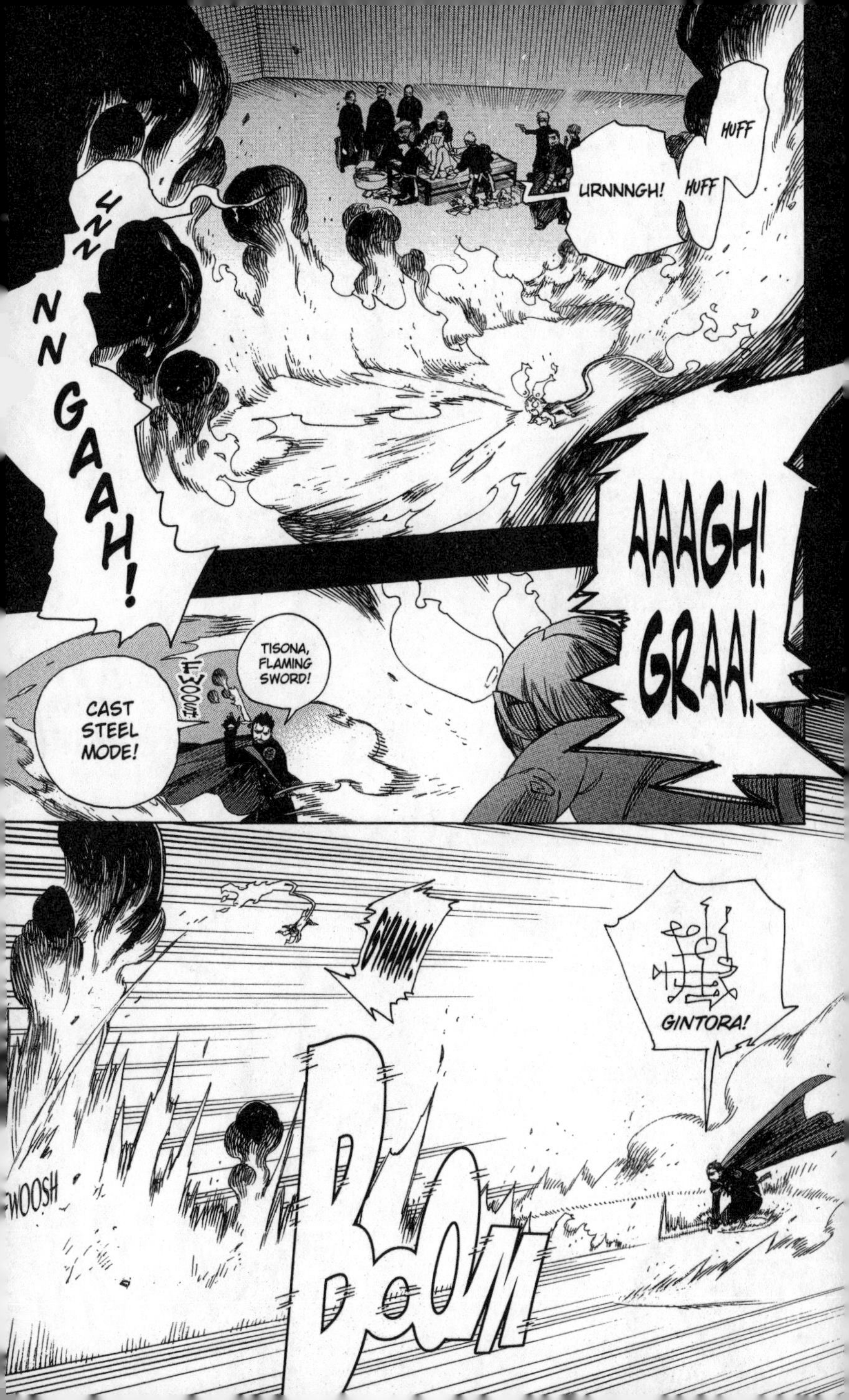
HUFF
HUFF
URNNNGH!
UNNNNGAAH!
AAAGH! GRAA!
TISONA, FLAMING SWORD!
FWOOSH
CAST STEEL MODE!
GINTORA!
GWAAH!
BOOM
WOOSH

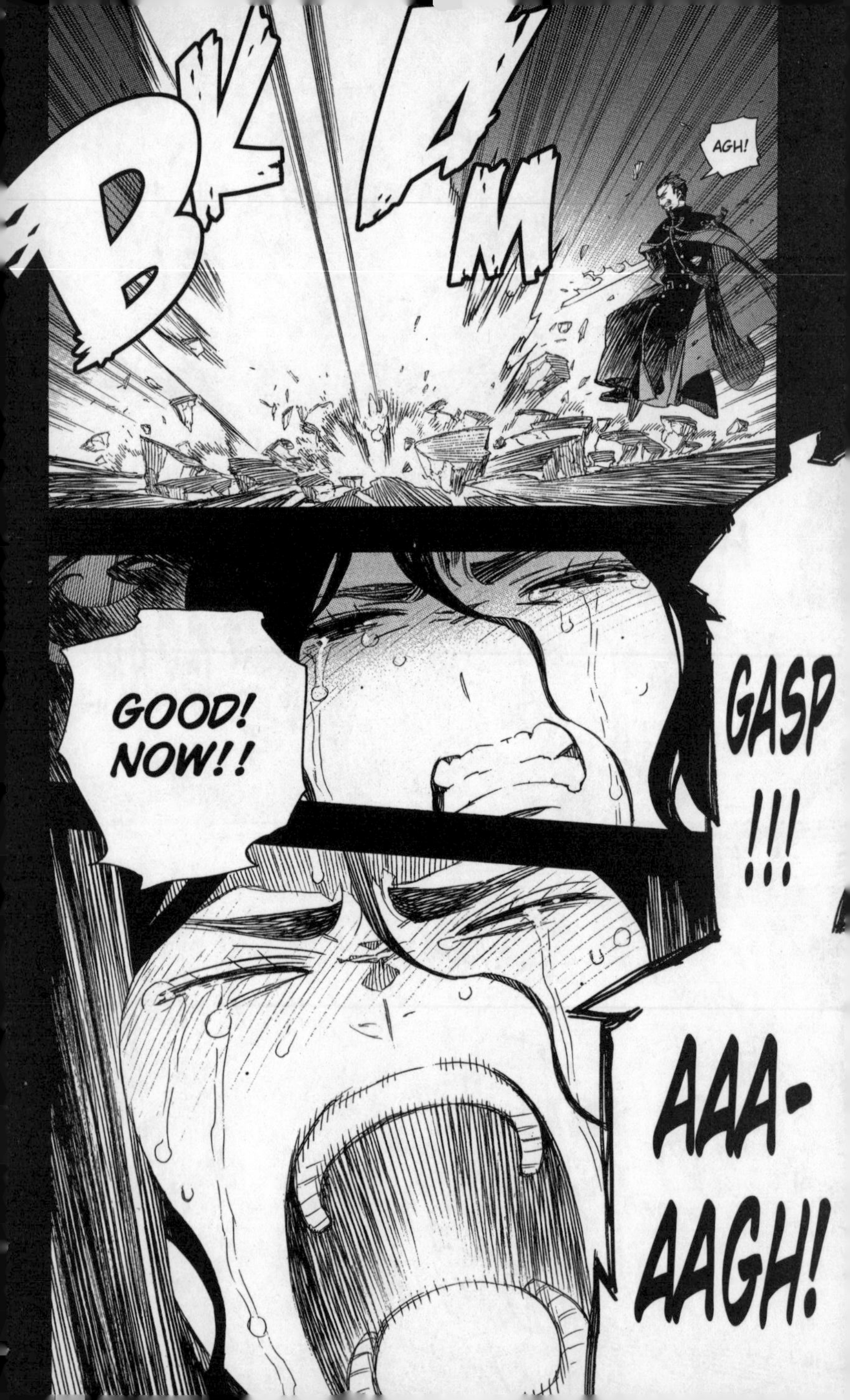
BKAM
AGH!
GASP !!!
GOOD! NOW!!
AAA-AAGH!

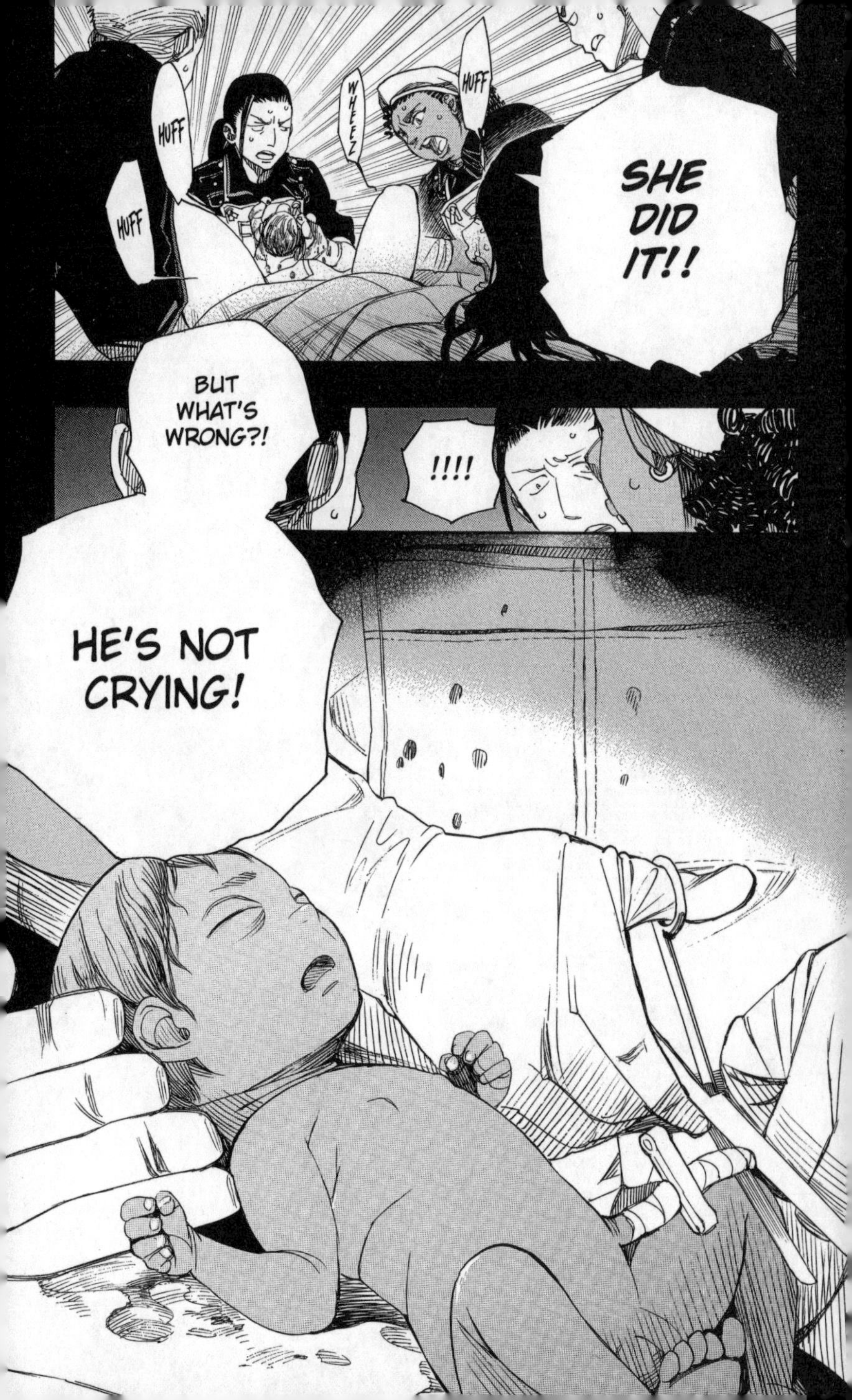
SHE DID IT!!
HUFF
WHEEZ
HUFF
HUFF
!!!!
BUT WHAT'S WRONG?!
HE'S NOT CRYING!

Blue Exorcist Chapter 115: SsC23: 17F

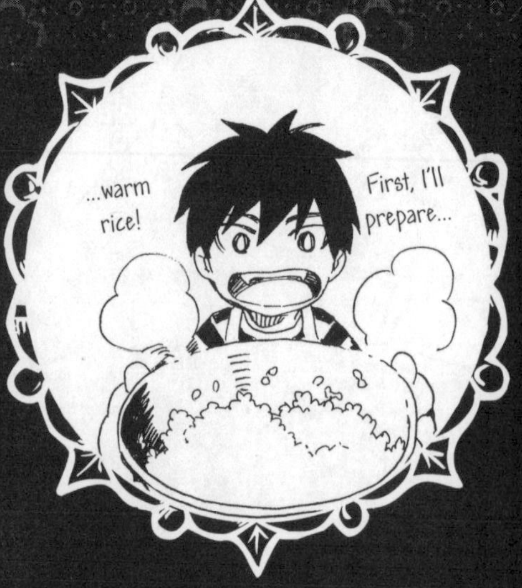
First, I'll prepare...
...warm rice!

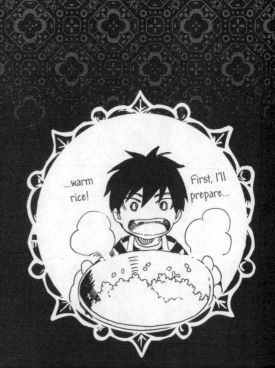

CHAPTER 116: SSC23:17G

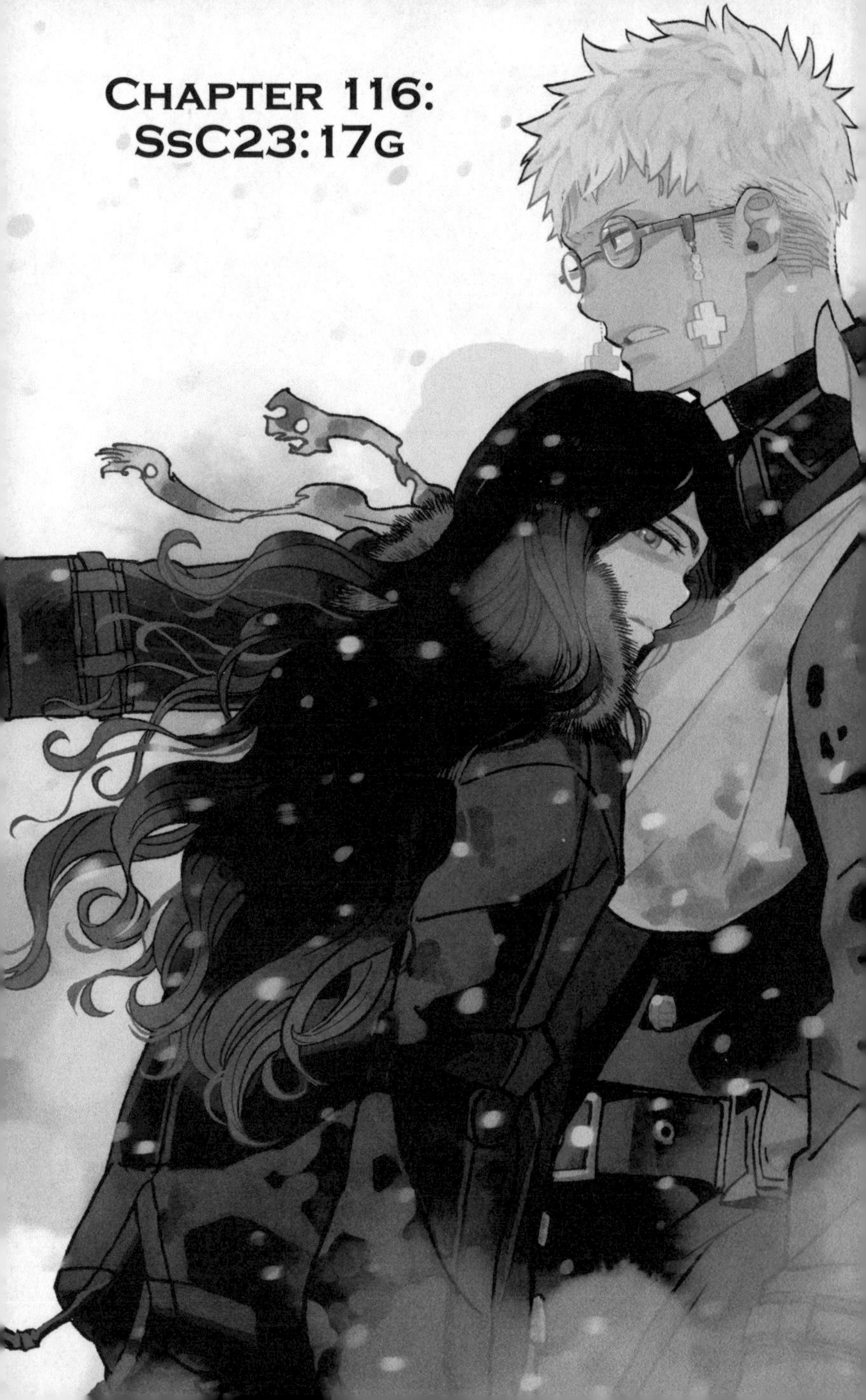

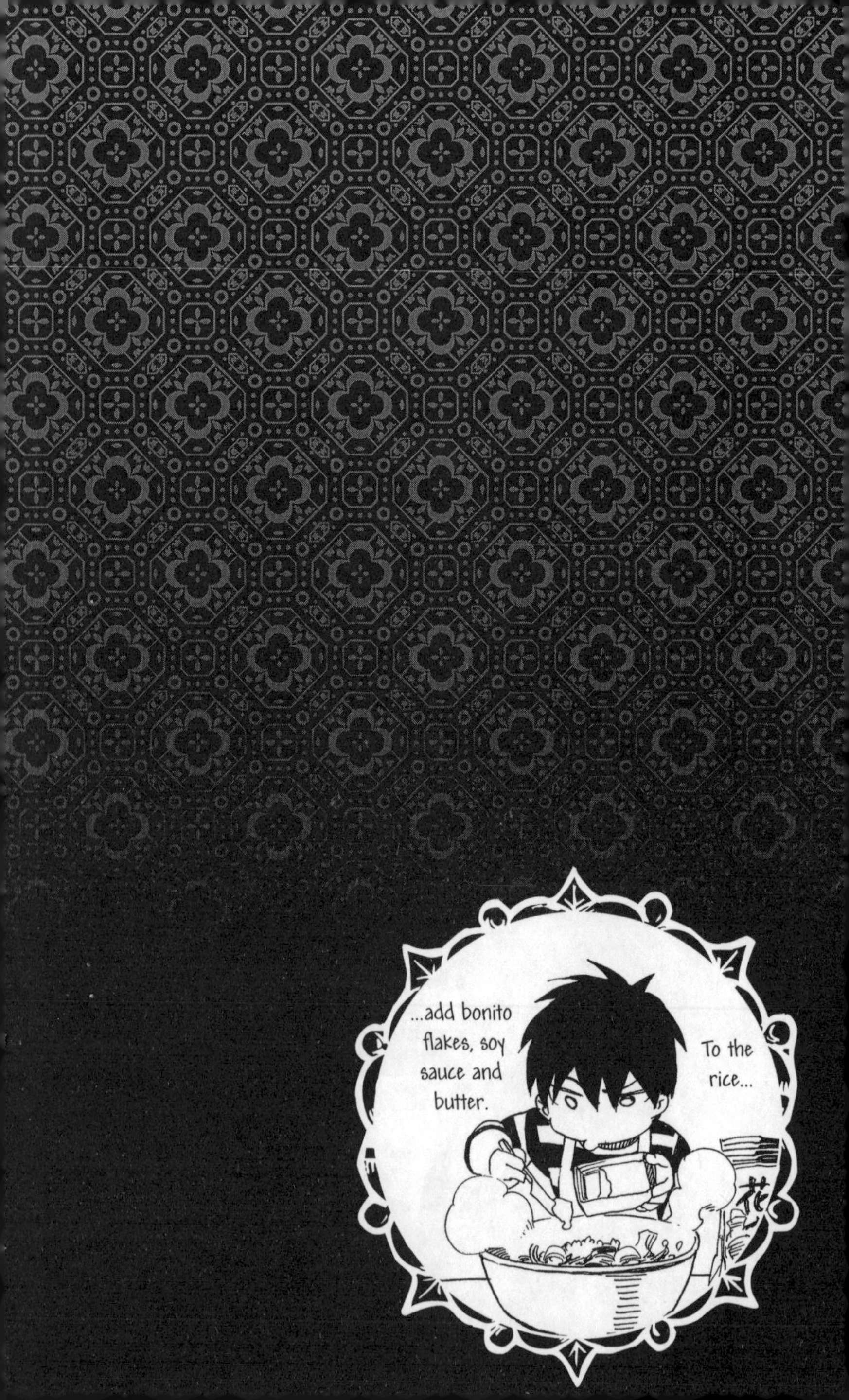
To the rice...
...add bonito flakes, soy sauce and butter.

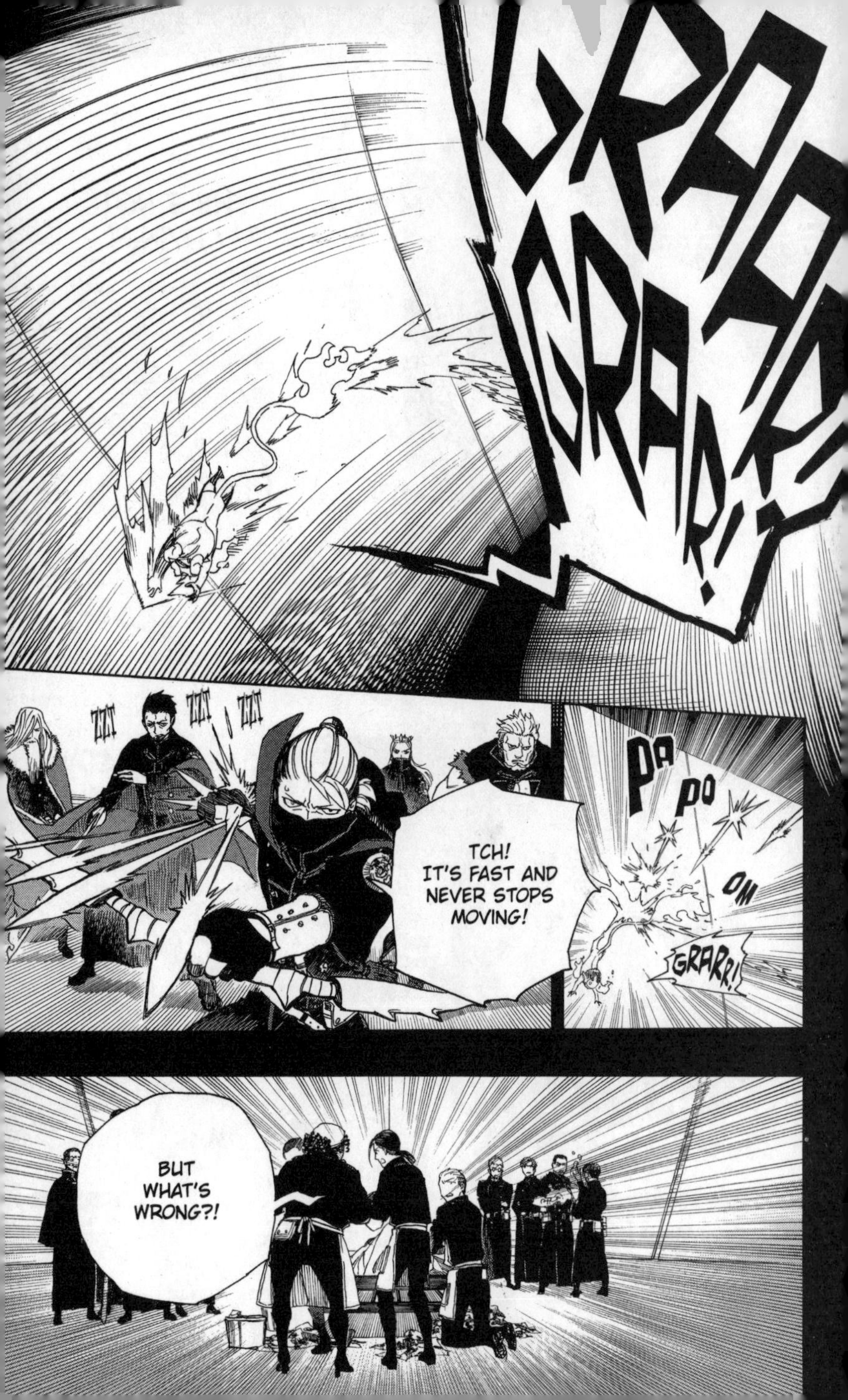
GRAO
GRAR!!
PA
PO
OM
GRARR!
ZZT
ZZT
ZZT
TCH! IT'S FAST AND NEVER STOPS MOVING!
BUT WHAT'S WRONG?!

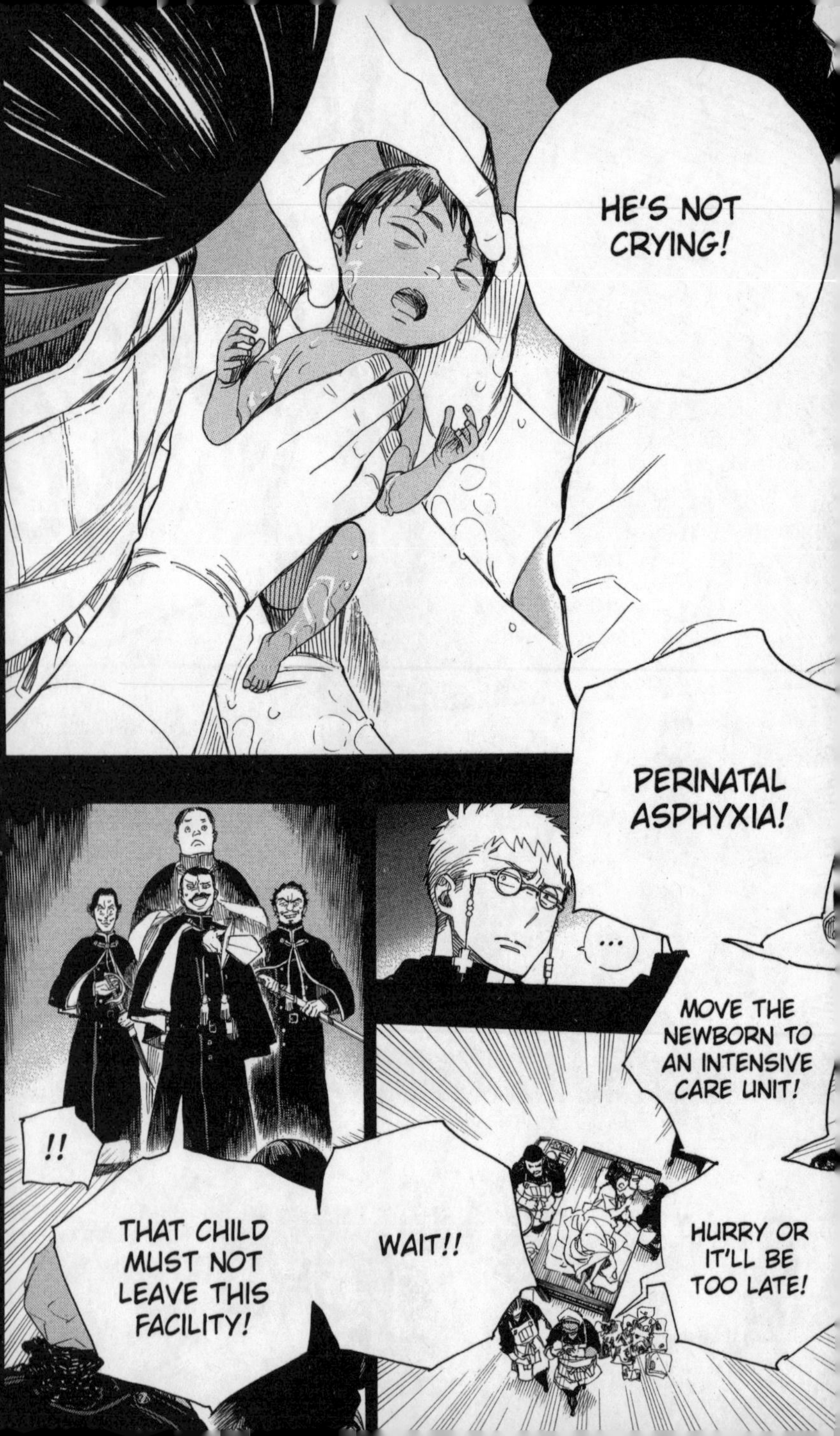
HE'S NOT CRYING!
PERINATAL ASPHYXIA!
...
MOVE THE NEWBORN TO AN INTENSIVE CARE UNIT!
HURRY OR IT'LL BE TOO LATE!
!!
WAIT!!
THAT CHILD MUST NOT LEAVE THIS FACILITY!

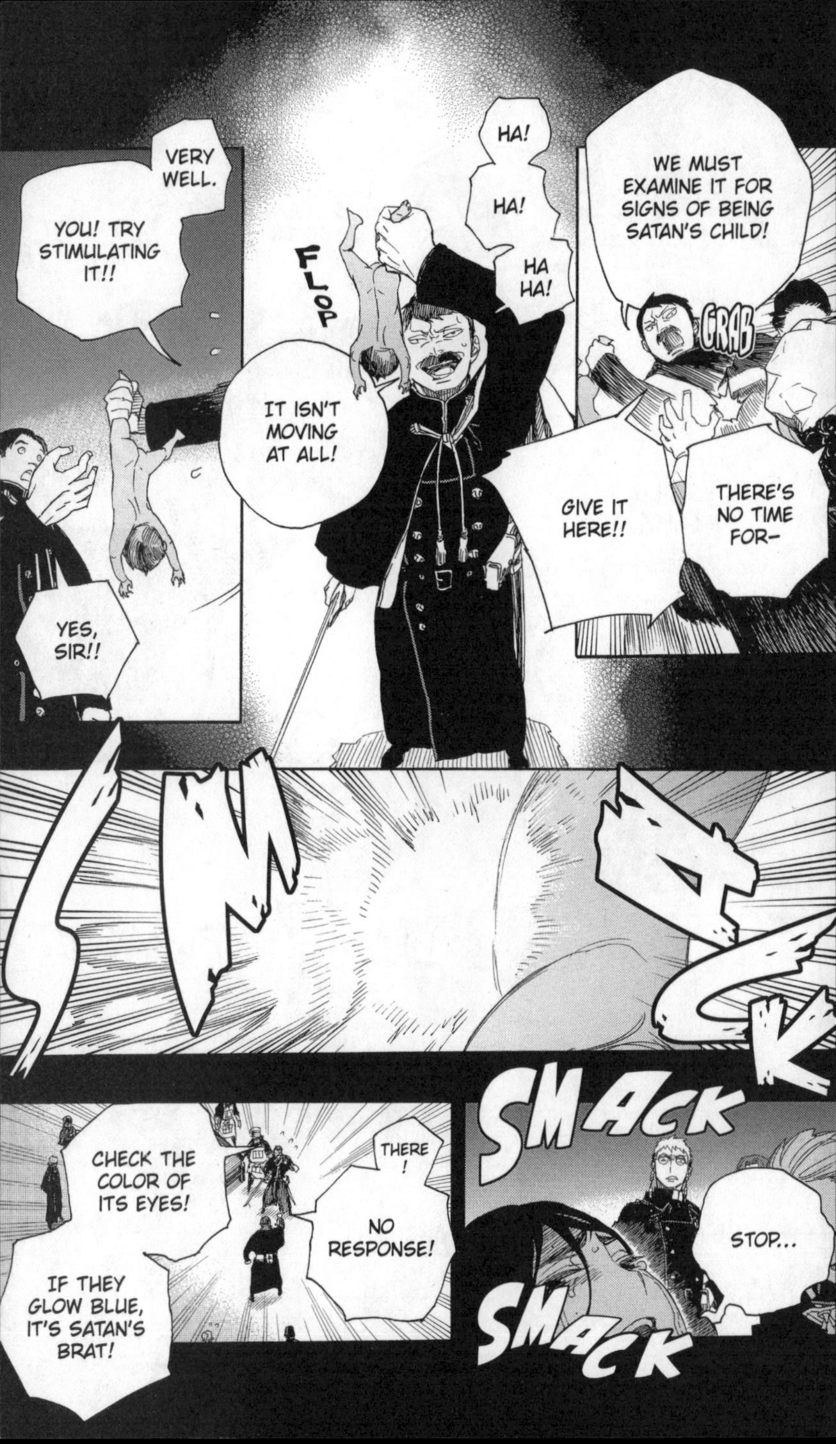
WE MUST EXAMINE IT FOR SIGNS OF BEING SATAN'S CHILD!
GRAB
THERE'S NO TIME FOR-
GIVE IT HERE!!
HA!
HA!
HA HA!
FLOP
IT ISN'T MOVING AT ALL!
VERY WELL.
YOU! TRY STIMULATING IT!!
YES, SIR!!
SMACK
SMACK
STOP...
SMACK
THERE!
NO RESPONSE!
CHECK THE COLOR OF ITS EYES!
IF THEY GLOW BLUE, IT'S SATAN'S BRAT!

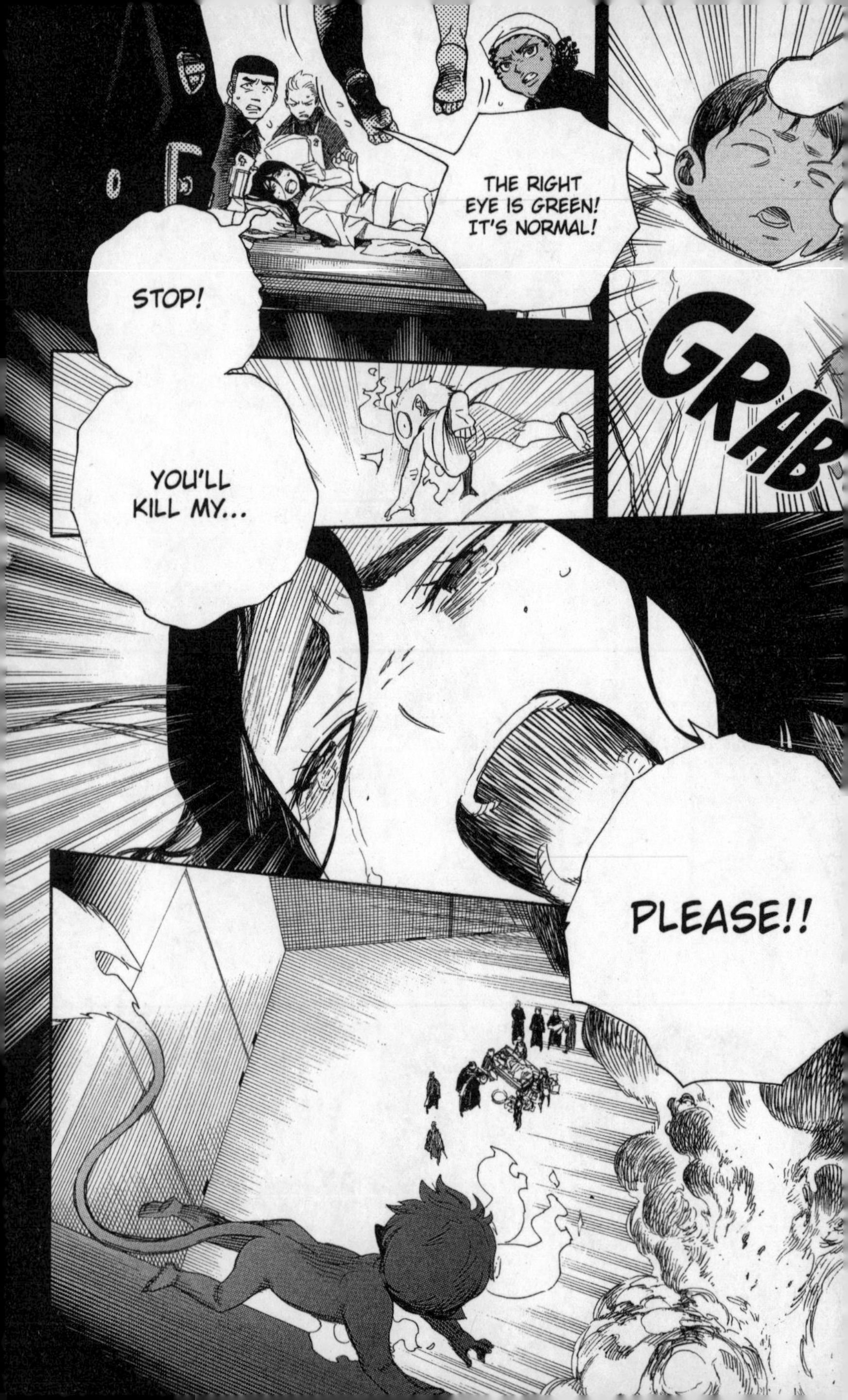
GRAB
THE RIGHT EYE IS GREEN! IT'S NORMAL!
STOP!
YOU'LL KILL MY...
PLEASE!!

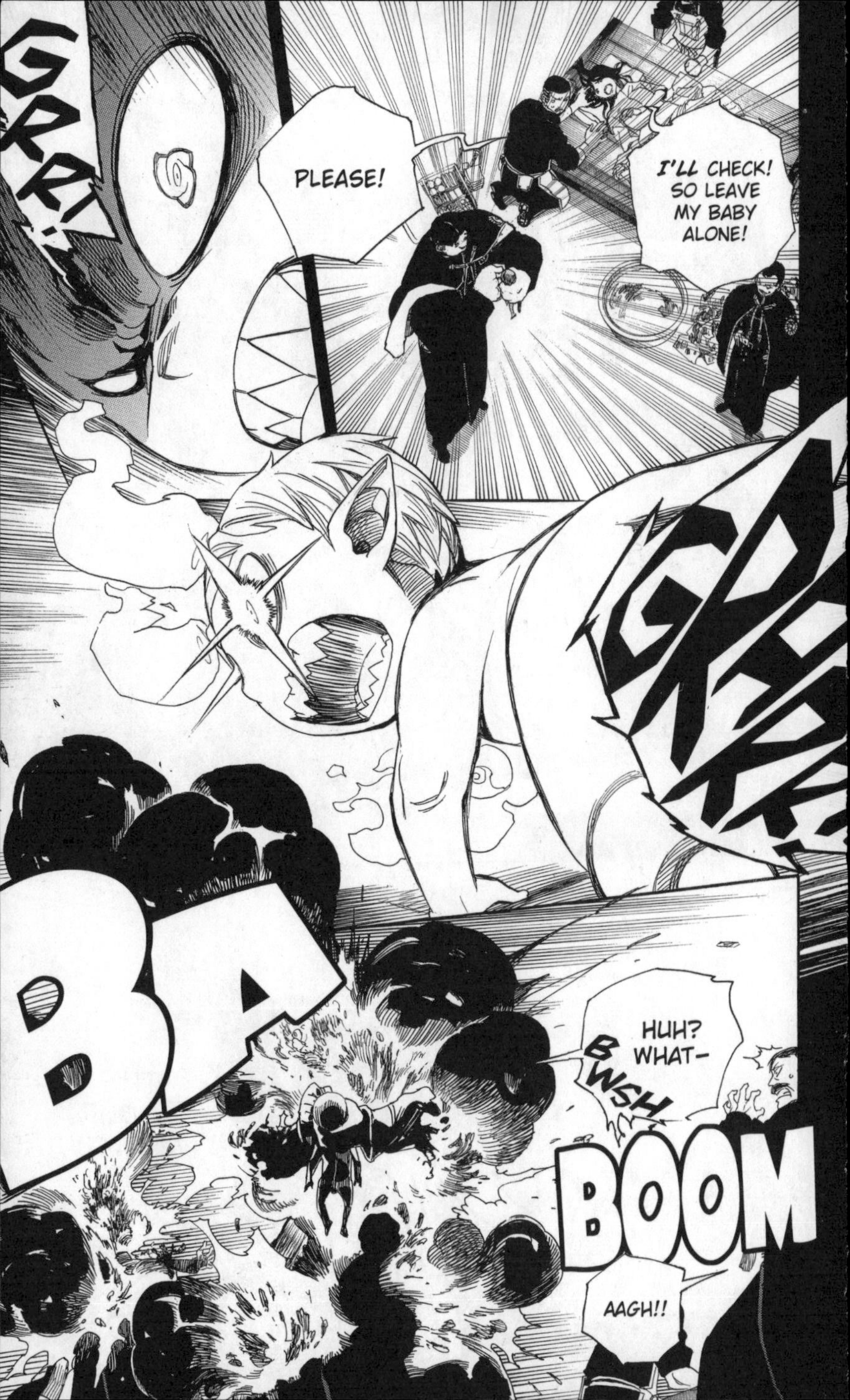
I'LL CHECK! SO LEAVE MY BABY ALONE!
PLEASE!
GRR!
HUH? WHAT-
BWSH
BOOM
AAGH!!

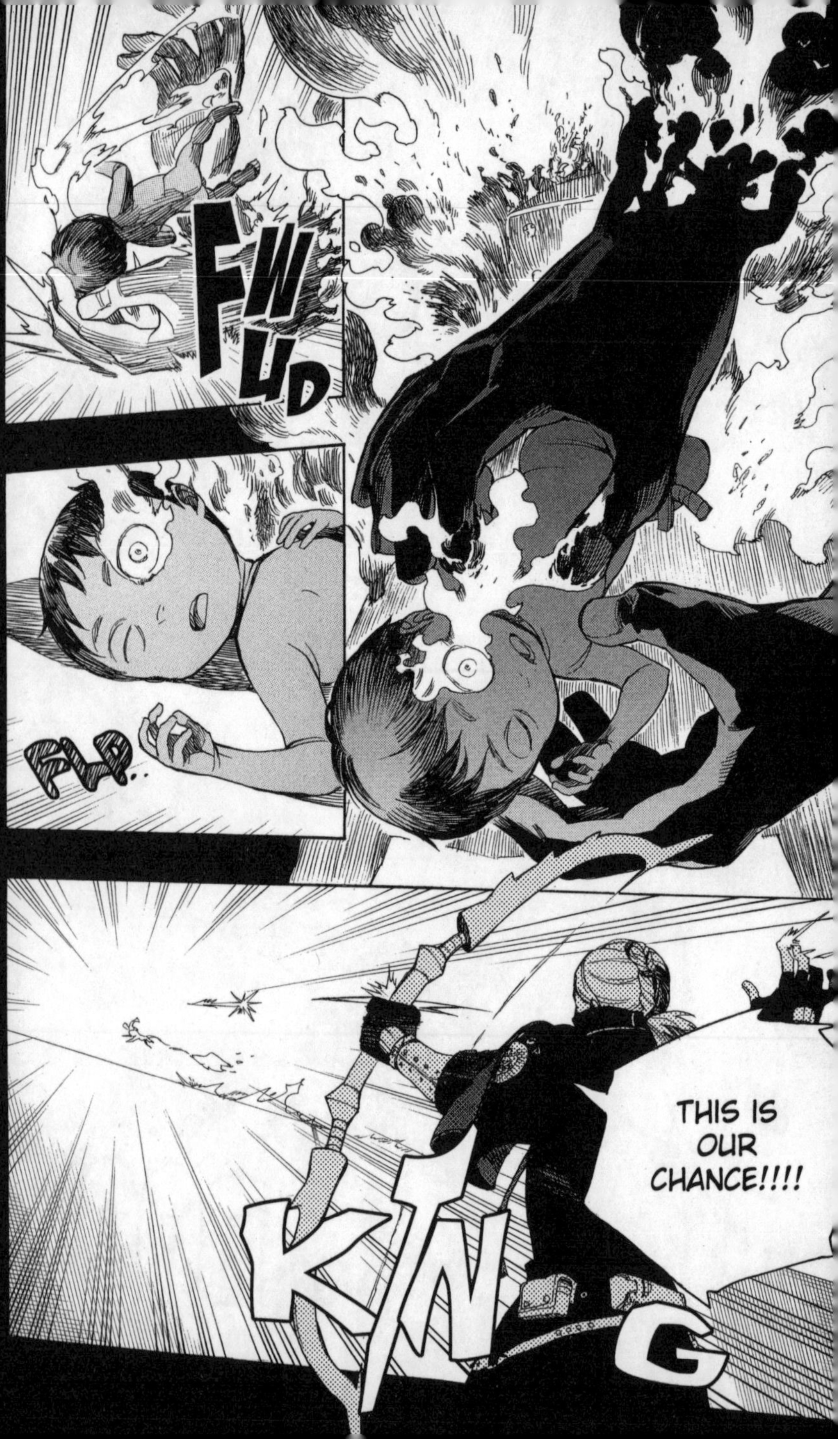
FWUD
FLP...
THIS IS OUR CHANCE!!!!
KING

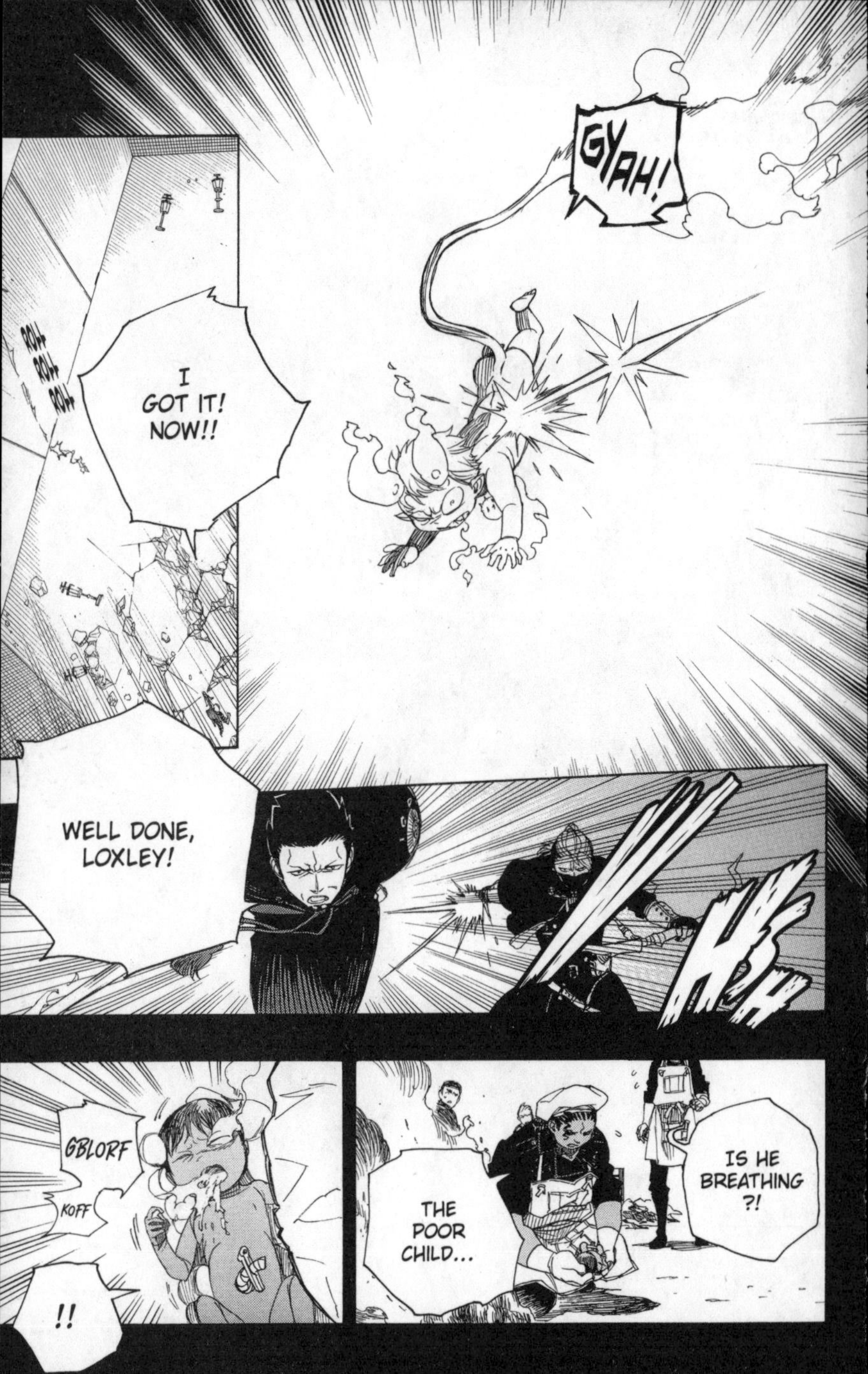
GYAH!
ROLL ROLL ROLL
I GOT IT! NOW!!
WELL DONE, LOXLEY!
IS HE BREATHING?!
THE POOR CHILD...
GBLORF
KOFF
!!

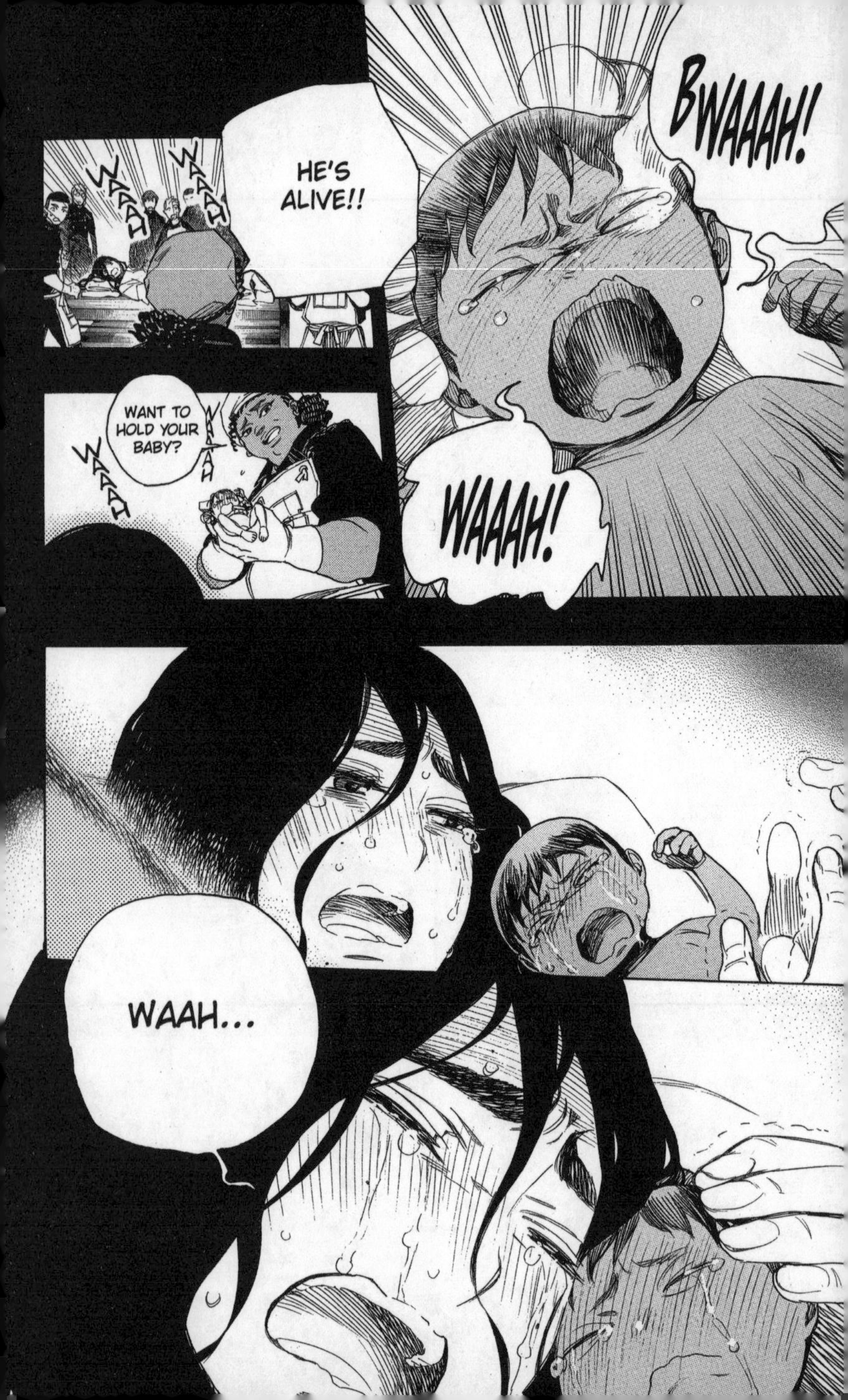

BWAAAH!
WAAAH!
HE'S ALIVE!!
WAAAH
WAAAH
WANT TO HOLD YOUR BABY?
WAAAH
WAAAH
WAAH...

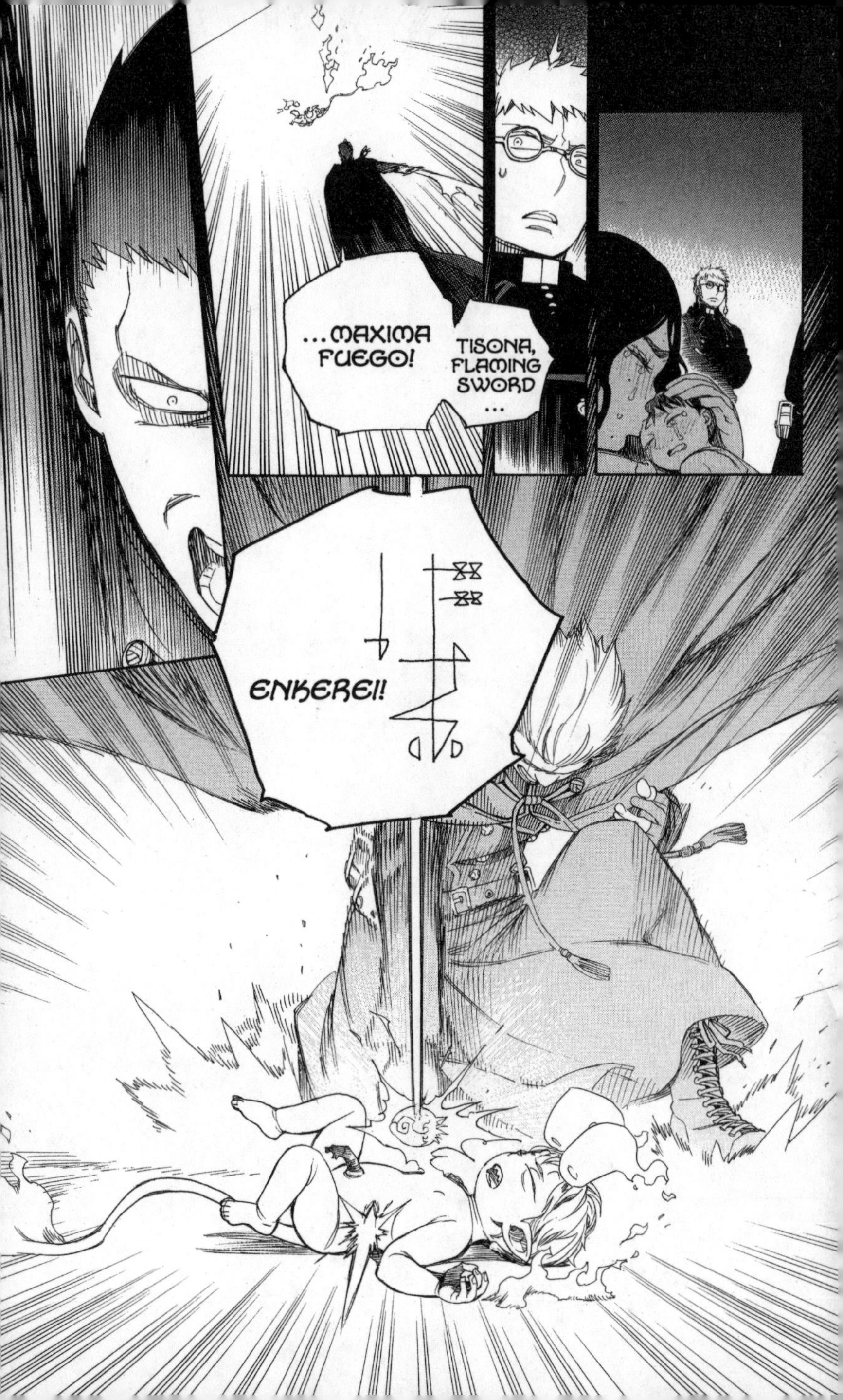
TISONA, FLAMING SWORD ...
...MAXIMA FUEGO!
ENKEREI!

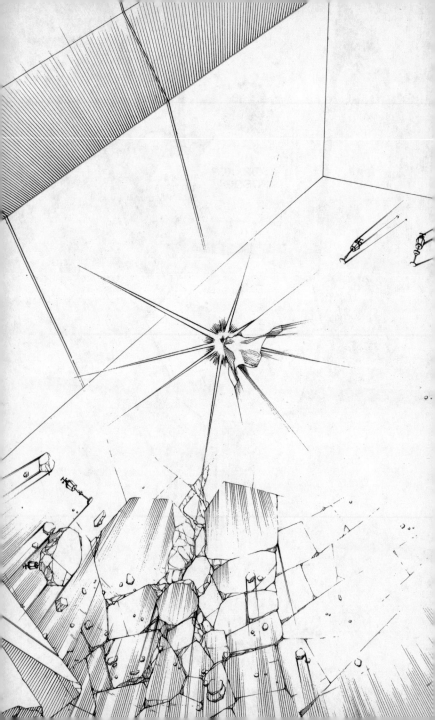

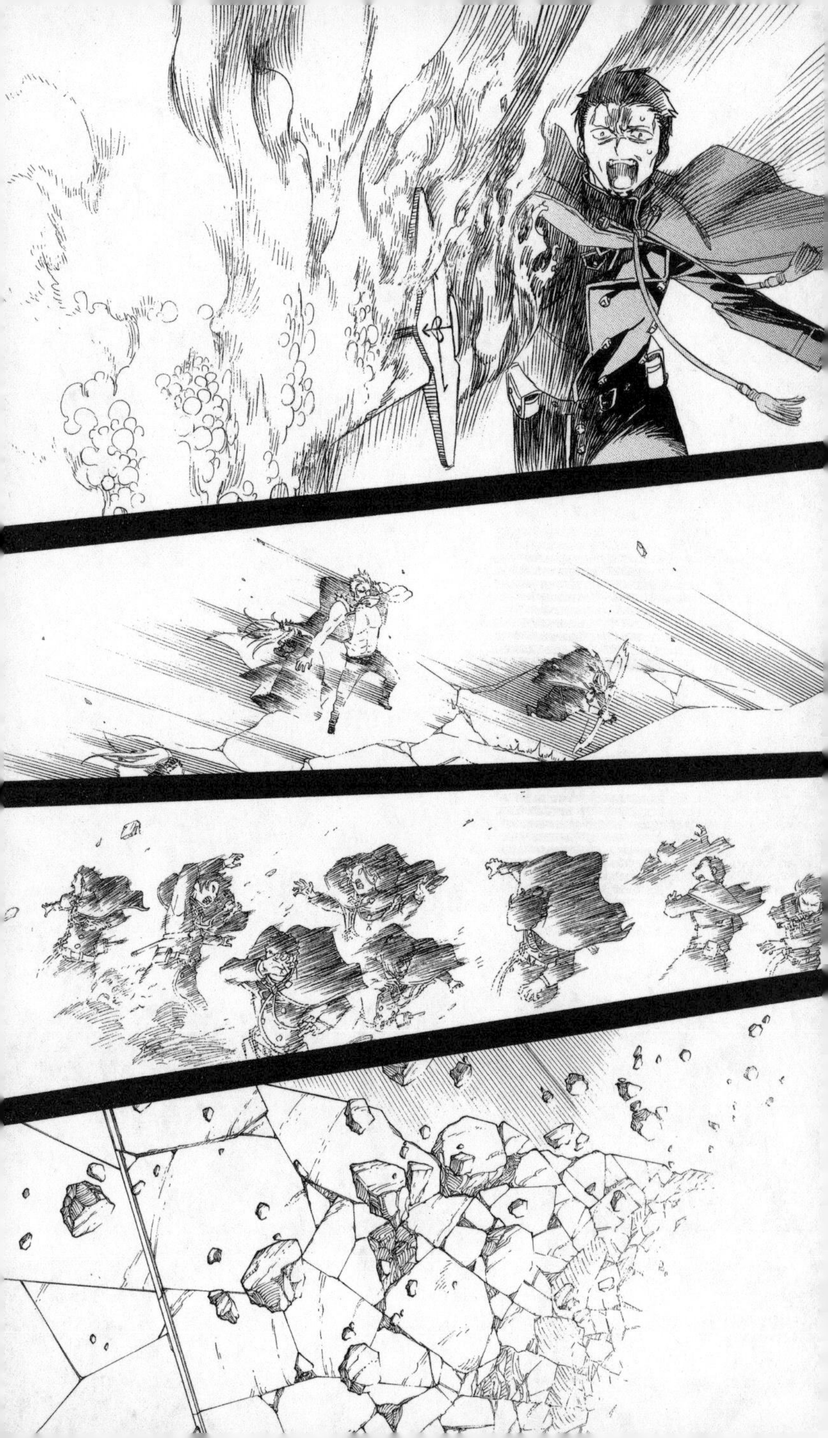

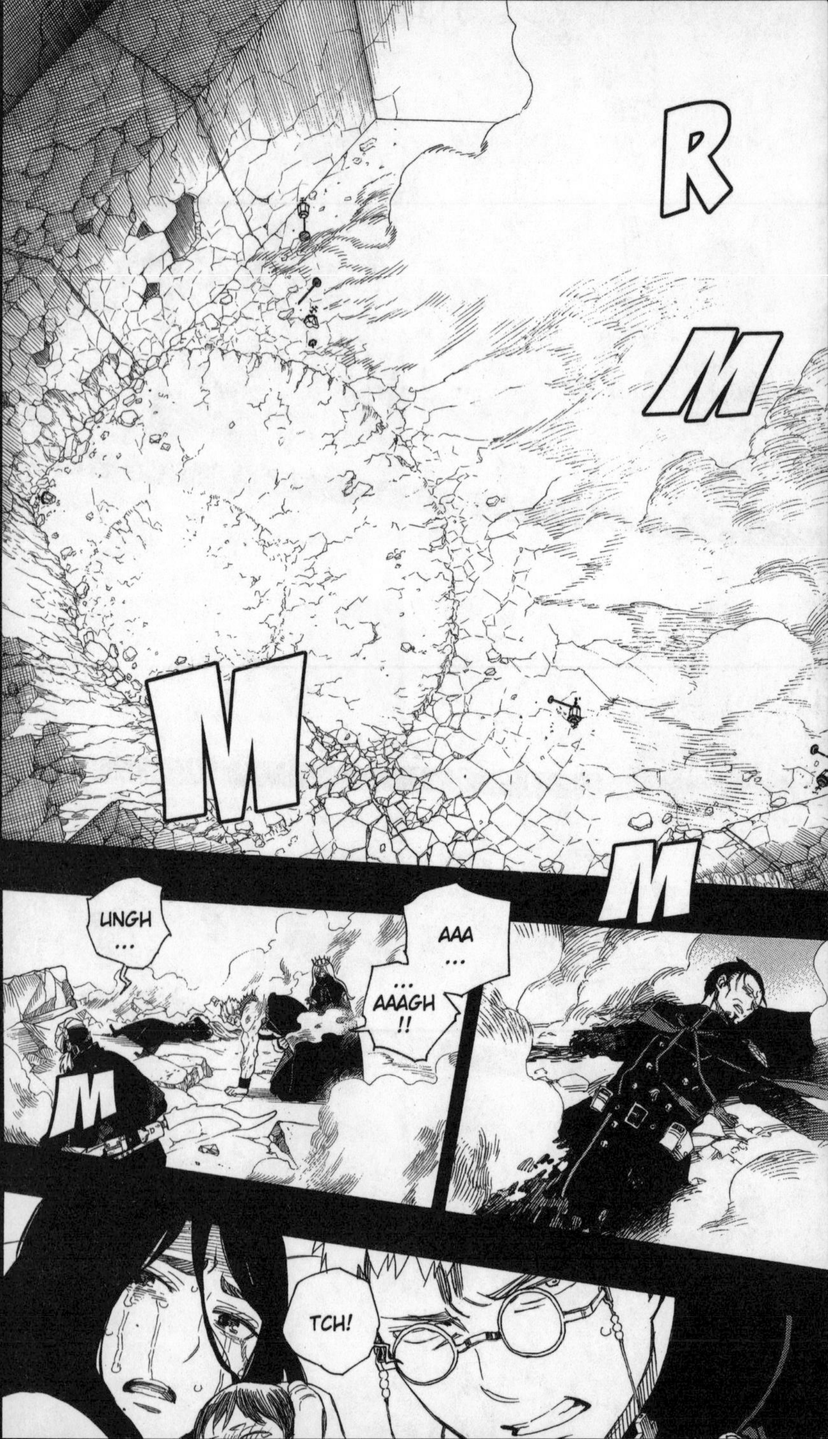
R
M
M
M
M
AAA ... ... AAAGH !!
UNGH ...
TCH!

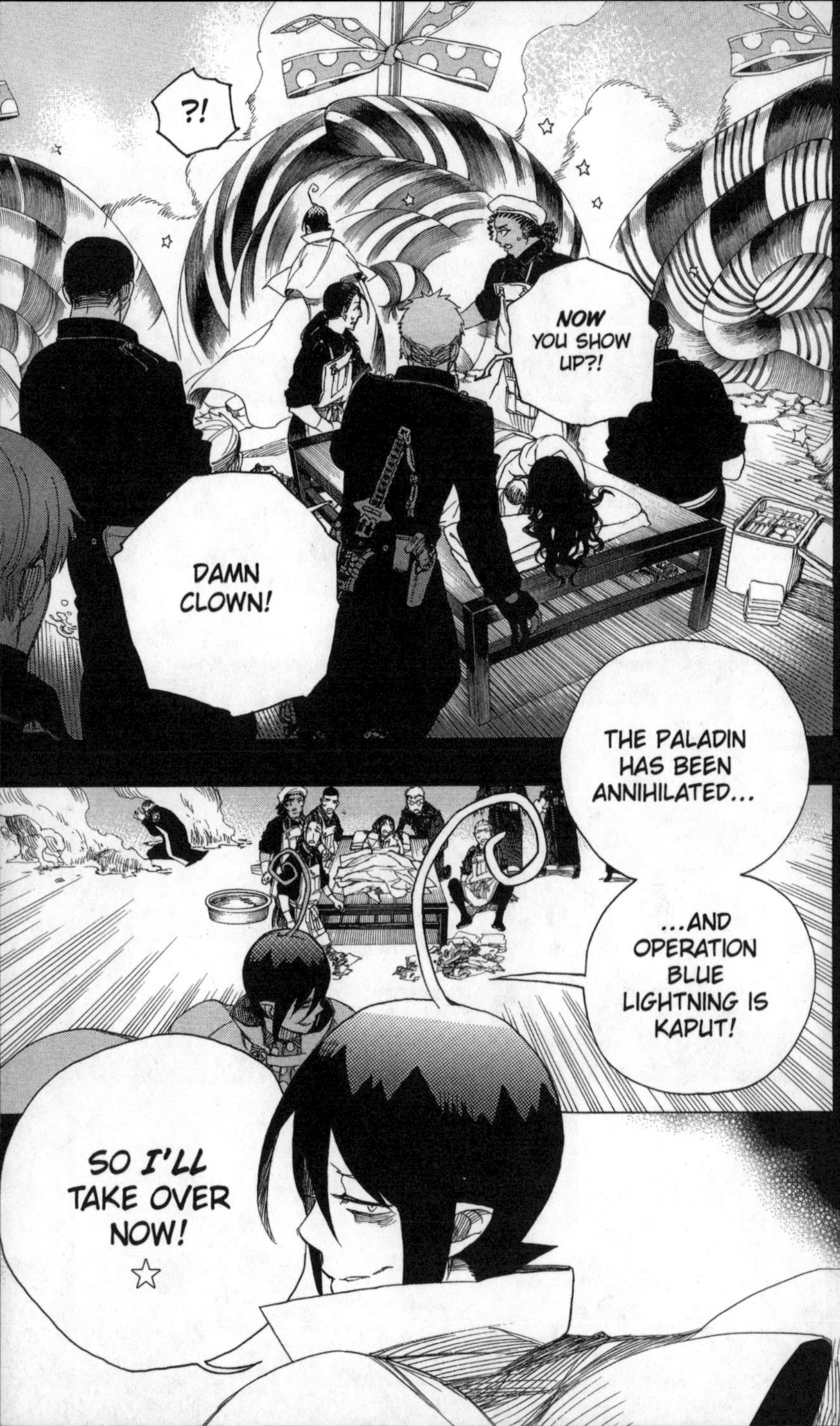
?!
NOW YOU SHOW UP?!
DAMN CLOWN!
THE PALADIN HAS BEEN ANNIHILATED...
...AND OPERATION BLUE LIGHTNING IS KAPUT!
SO I'LL TAKE OVER NOW! ☆

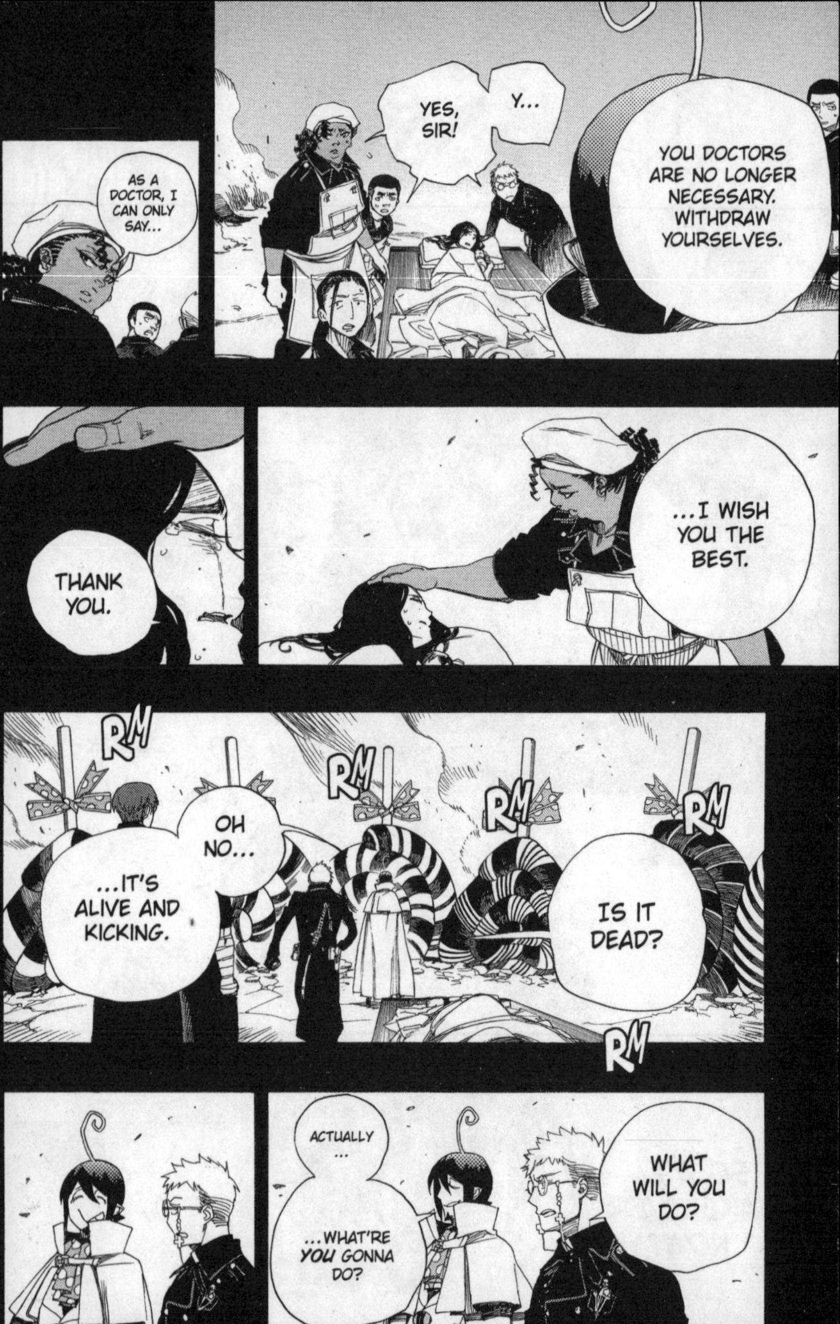
YOU DOCTORS ARE NO LONGER NECESSARY. WITHDRAW YOURSELVES.
Y...
YES, SIR!
AS A DOCTOR, I CAN ONLY SAY...
...I WISH YOU THE BEST.
THANK YOU.
RM
RM
RM
RM
IS IT DEAD?
OH NO...
...IT'S ALIVE AND KICKING.
RM
WHAT WILL YOU DO?
ACTUALLY ...
...WHAT'RE *YOU* GONNA DO?

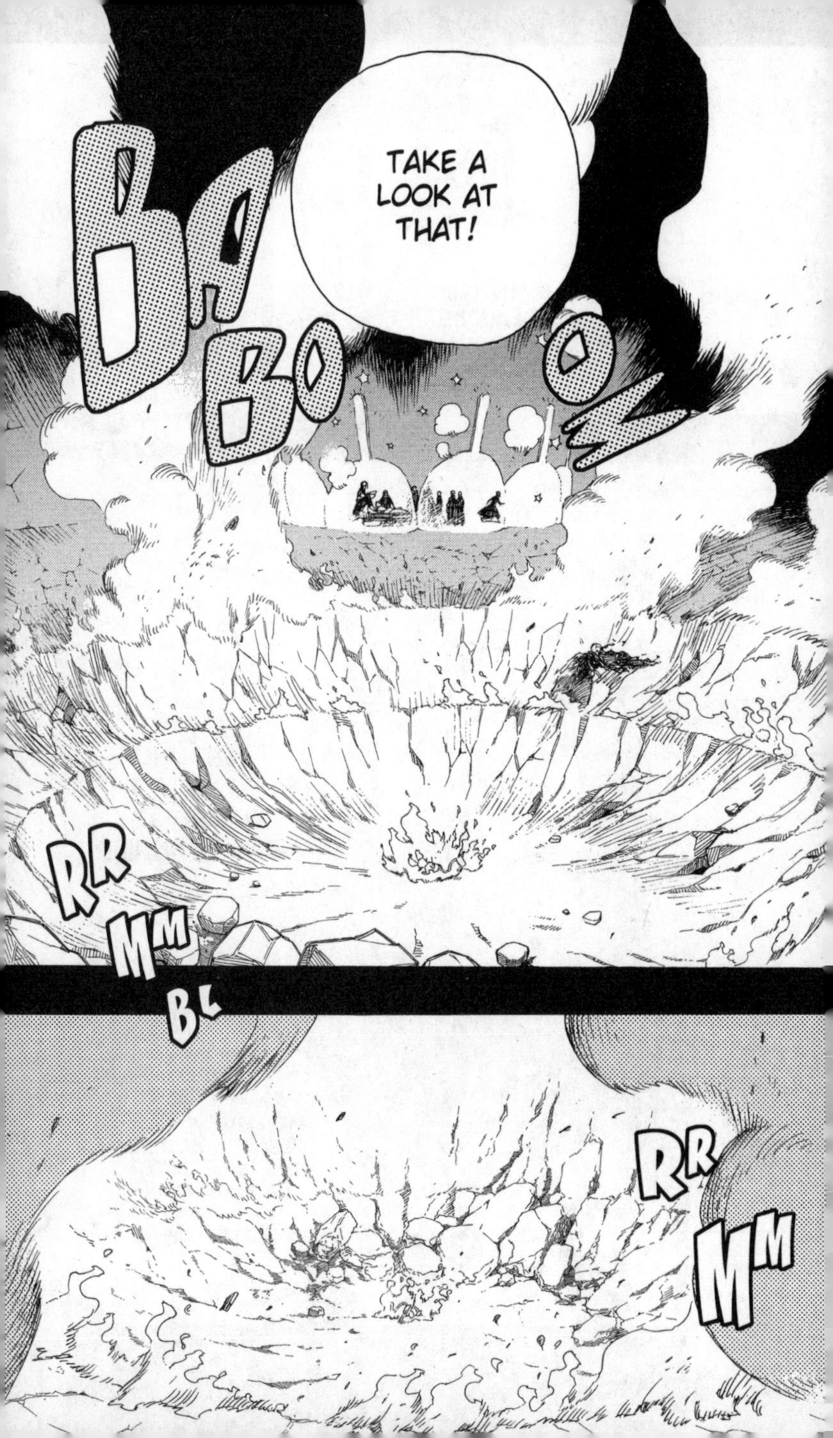
TAKE A LOOK AT THAT!
BABOOM
RRMM
BL
RRMM

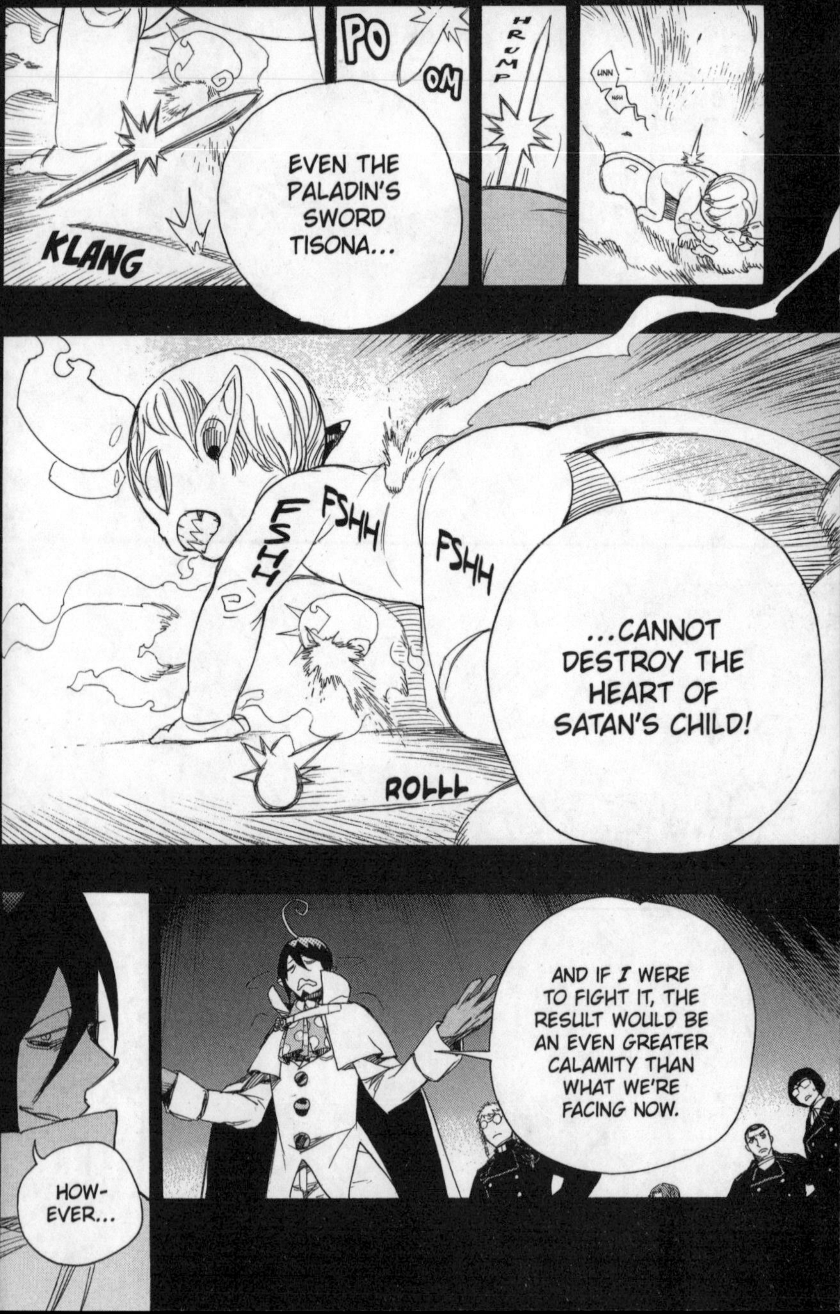
UNN
NGH
HRUMP
POOM
EVEN THE PALADIN'S SWORD TISONA...
KLANG
...CANNOT DESTROY THE HEART OF SATAN'S CHILD!
FSHH
FSHH
FSHH
ROLLL
AND IF I WERE TO FIGHT IT, THE RESULT WOULD BE AN EVEN GREATER CALAMITY THAN WHAT WE'RE FACING NOW.
HOW-EVER...

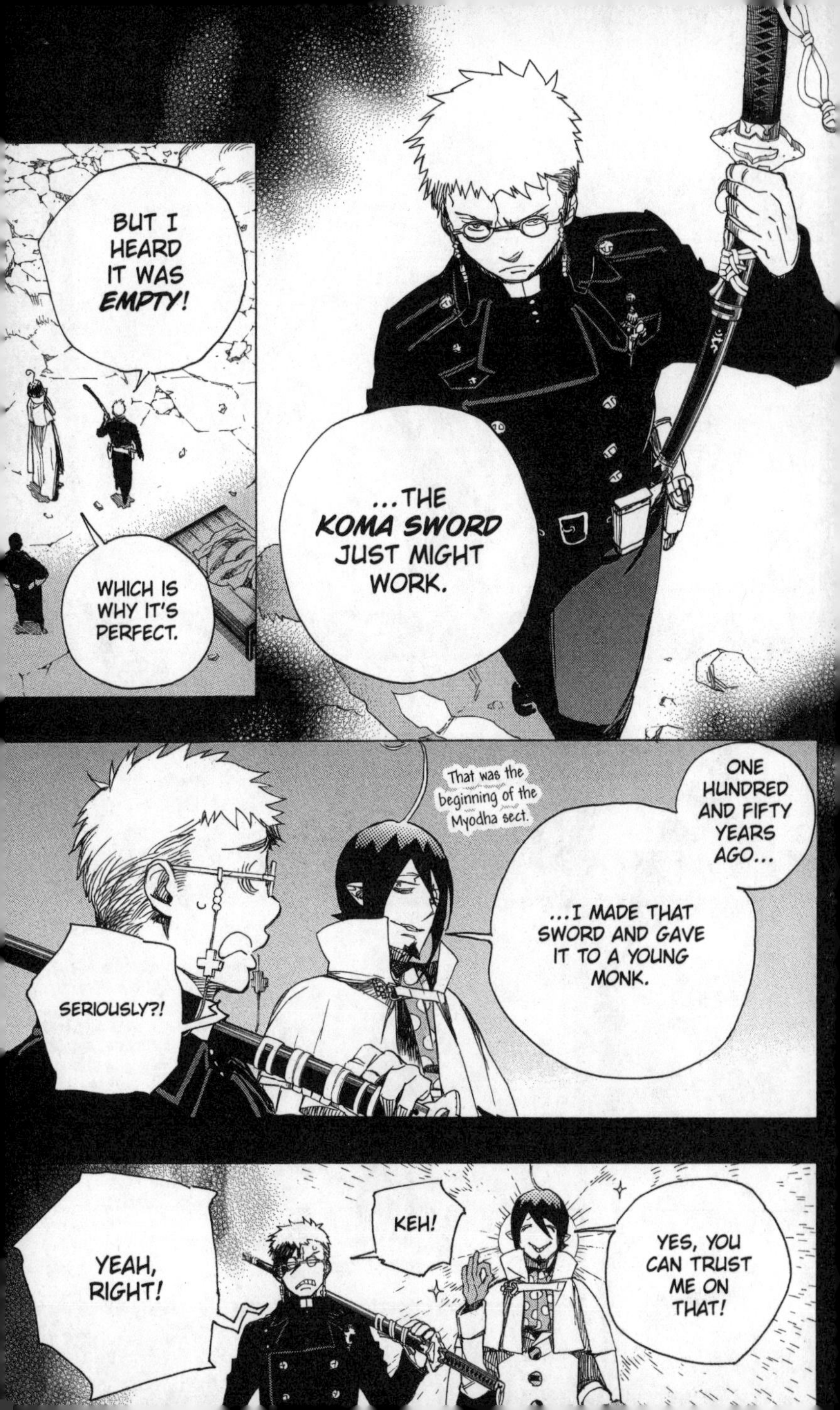

...THE KOMA SWORD JUST MIGHT WORK.
BUT I HEARD IT WAS EMPTY!
WHICH IS WHY IT'S PERFECT.
ONE HUNDRED AND FIFTY YEARS AGO...
...I MADE THAT SWORD AND GAVE IT TO A YOUNG MONK.
That was the beginning of the Myodha sect.
SERIOUSLY?!
YES, YOU CAN TRUST ME ON THAT!
KEH!
YEAH, RIGHT!

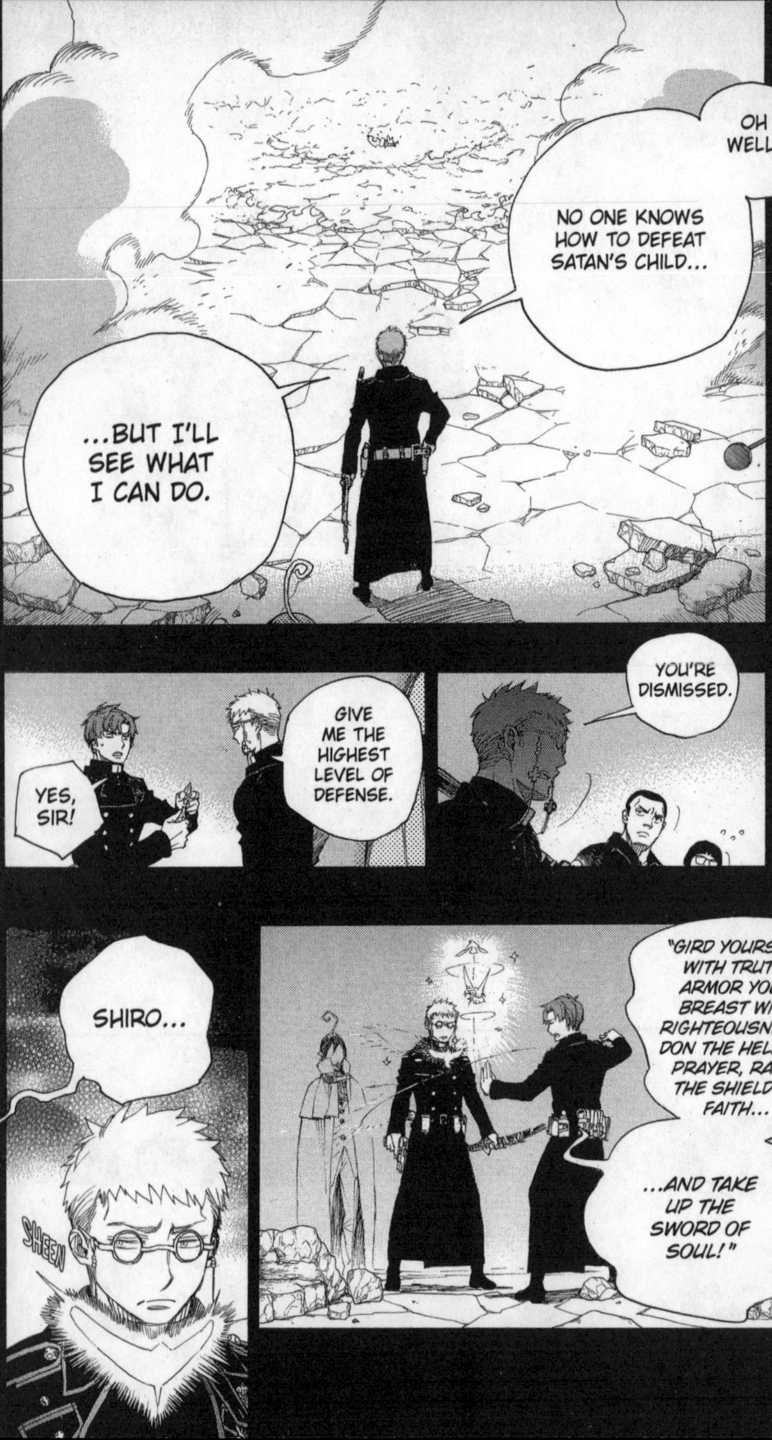
OH WELL.
NO ONE KNOWS HOW TO DEFEAT SATAN'S CHILD...
...BUT I'LL SEE WHAT I CAN DO.
YOU'RE DISMISSED.
GIVE ME THE HIGHEST LEVEL OF DEFENSE.
YES, SIR!
"GIRD YOURSELF WITH TRUTH, ARMOR YOUR BREAST WITH RIGHTEOUSNESS, DON THE HELM OF PRAYER, RAISE THE SHIELD OF FAITH...
...AND TAKE UP THE SWORD OF SOUL!"
SHIRO...
SHEEN

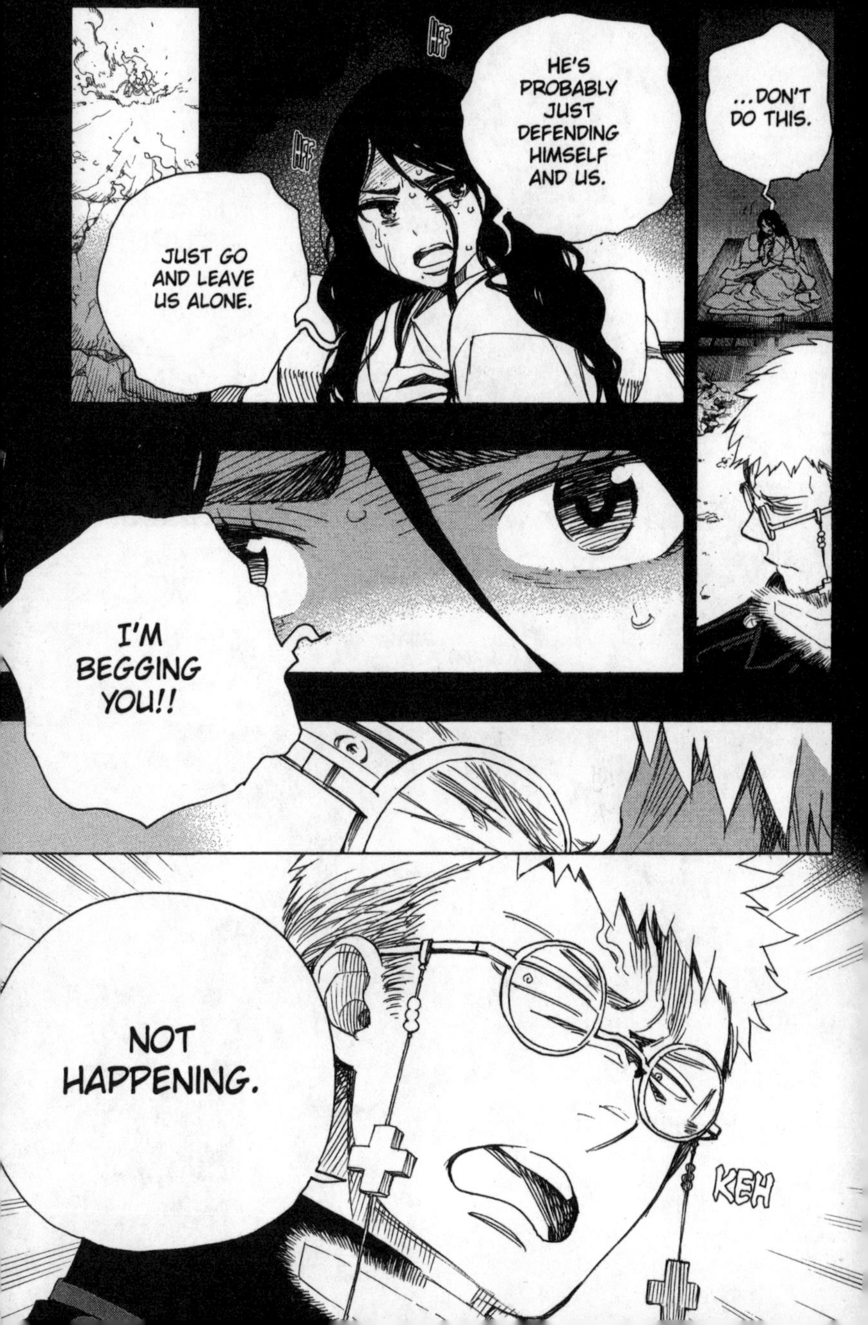
...DON'T DO THIS.
HFF
HE'S PROBABLY JUST DEFENDING HIMSELF AND US.
HFF
JUST GO AND LEAVE US ALONE.
I'M BEGGING YOU!!
NOT HAPPENING.
KEH

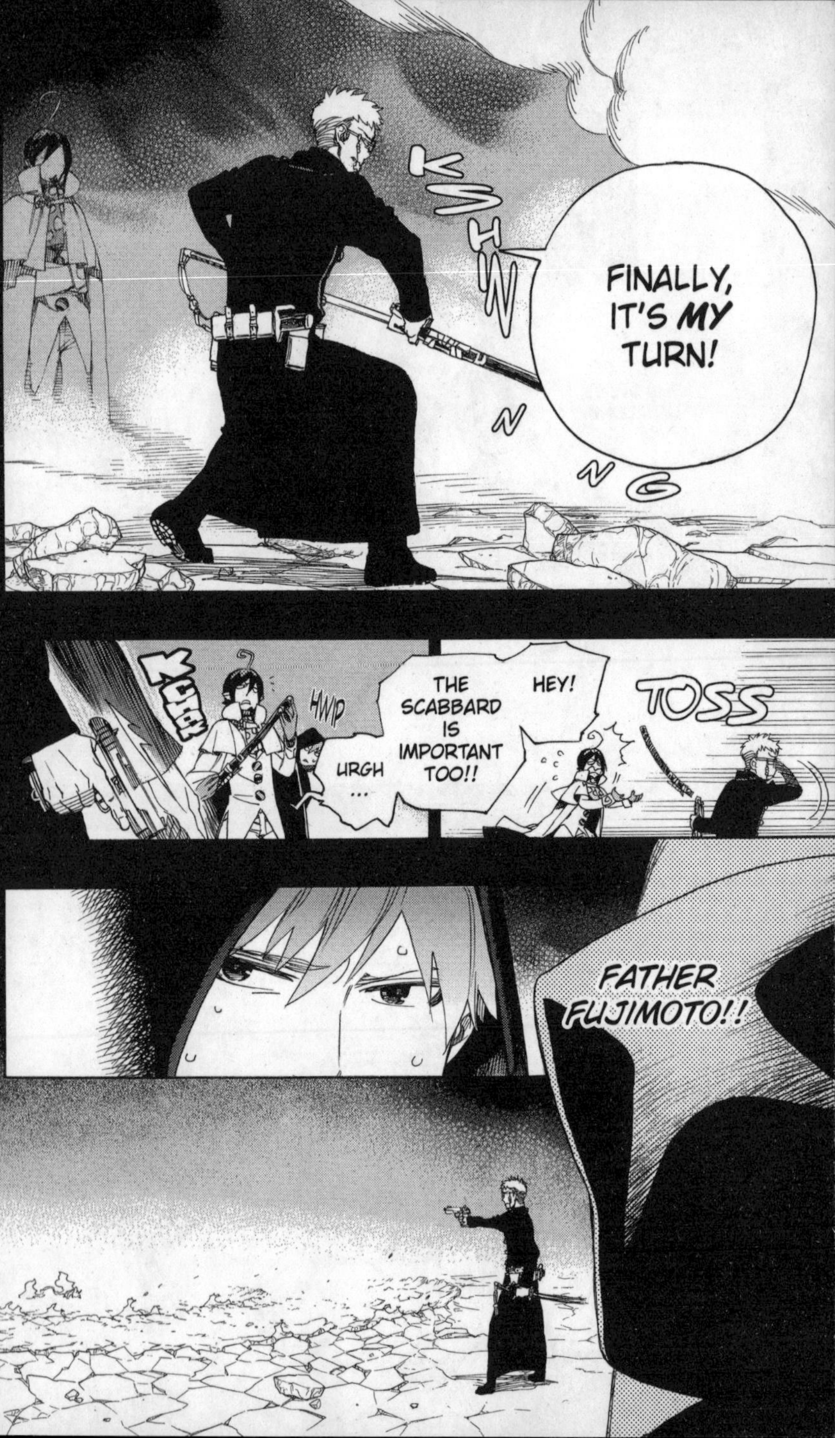
KSHIIINNNG
FINALLY, IT'S MY TURN!
TOSS
HEY!
THE SCABBARD IS IMPORTANT TOO!!
URGH ...
HWIP
KCHICK
FATHER FUJIMOTO!!

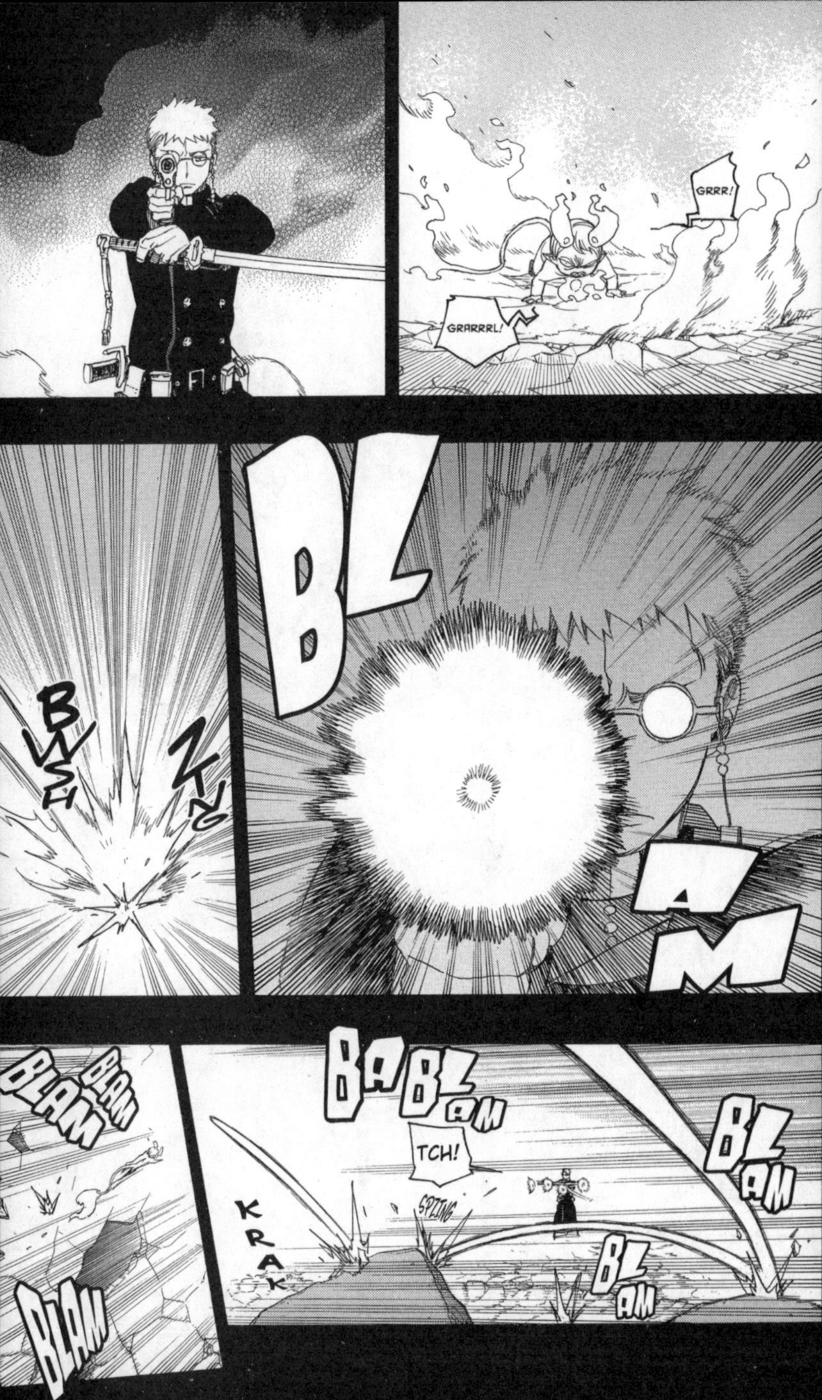
GRRR!
GRARRRL!
BLAM
ZKNG
BWSH
BLAM
BABLAM
TCH!
SPZING
BLAM
KRAK
BLAM
BLAM
BLAM

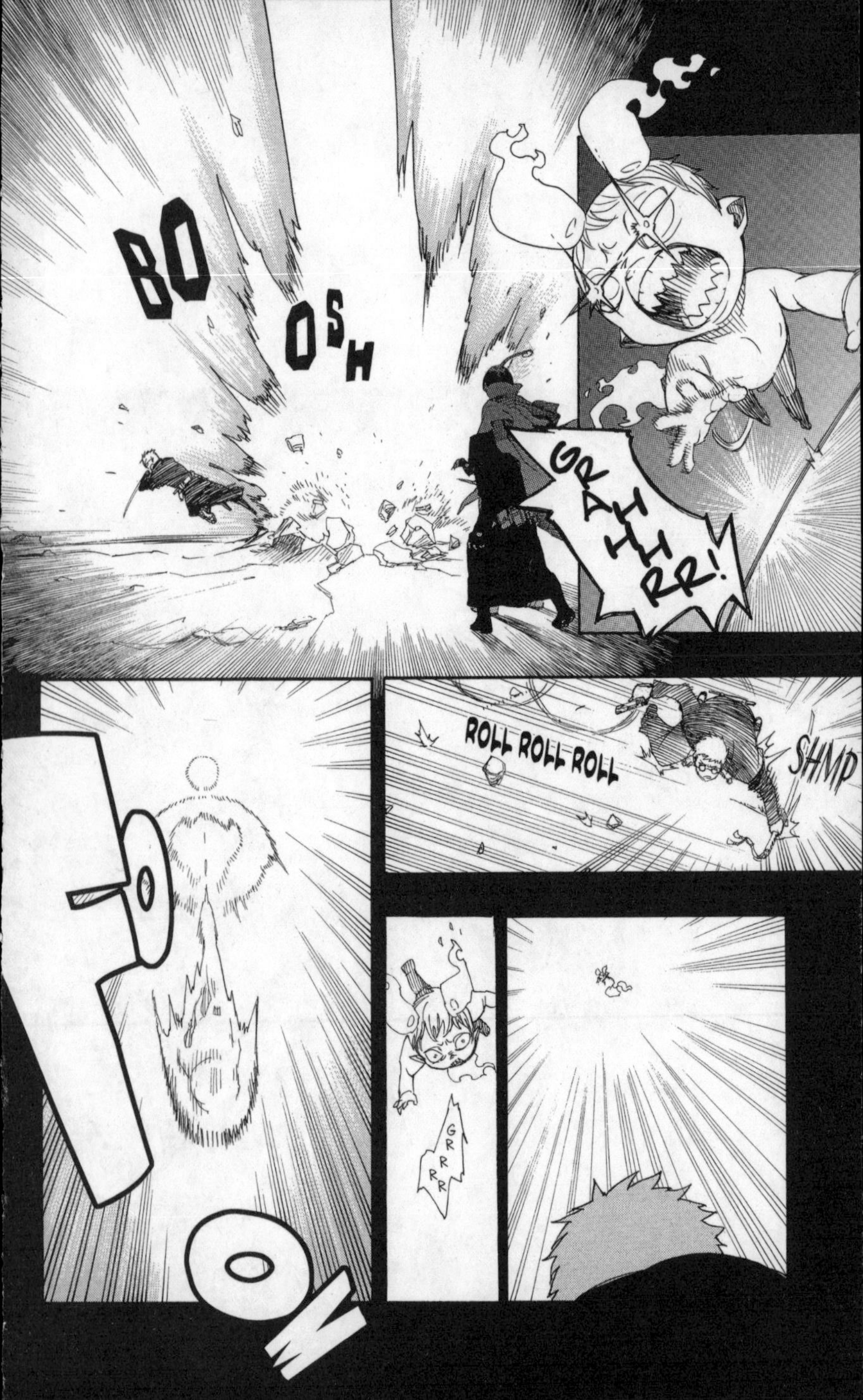
GRAHHHRR!
BOOSH
SHMP
ROLL ROLL ROLL
GRRRR

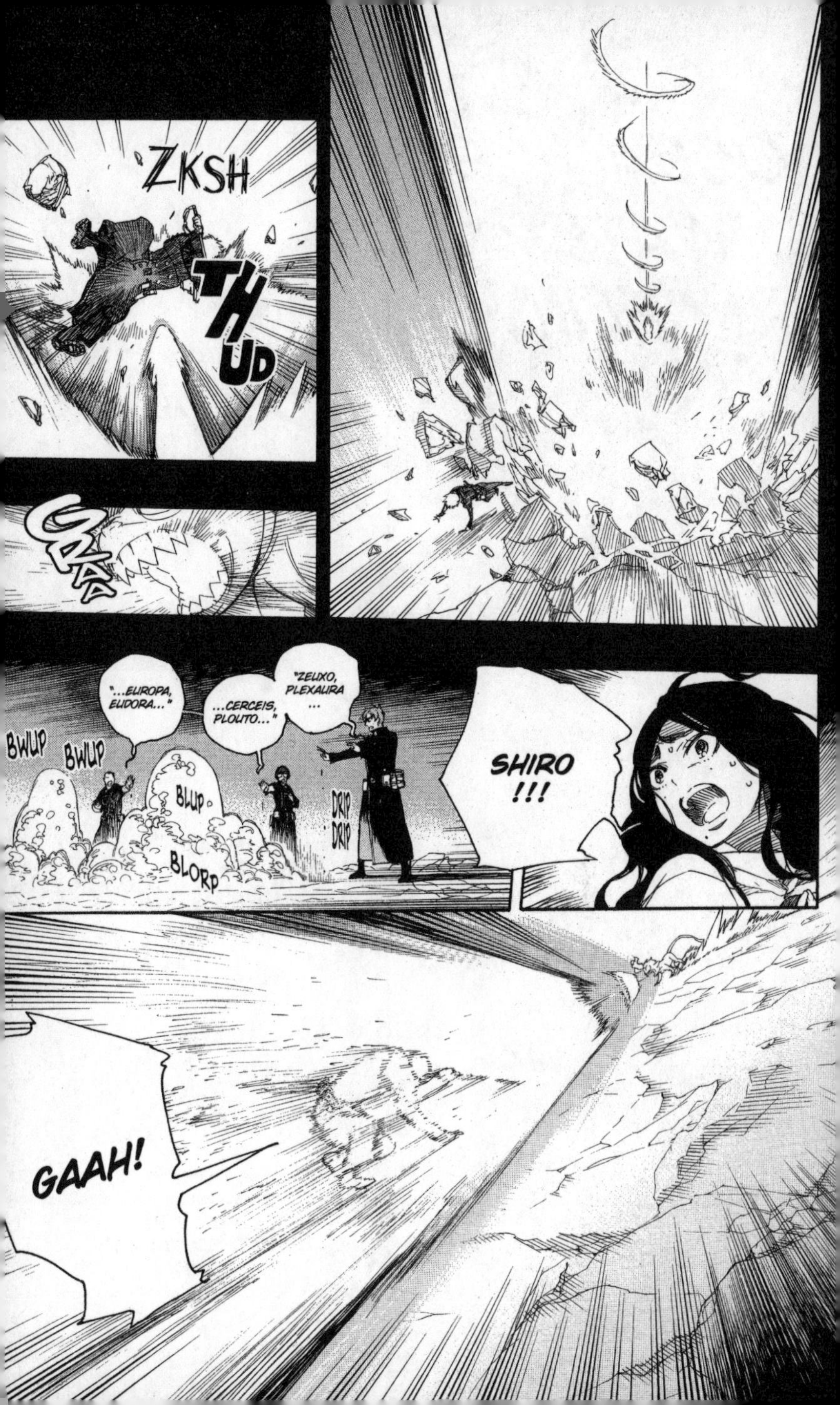

ZKSH
THUD
GRAA
SHIRO!!!
"ZEUXO, PLEXAURA ...
...CERCEIS, PLOUTO..."
"...EUROPA, EUDORA..."
DRIP DRIP
BLUP
BLORP
BWUP
BWUP
GAAH!

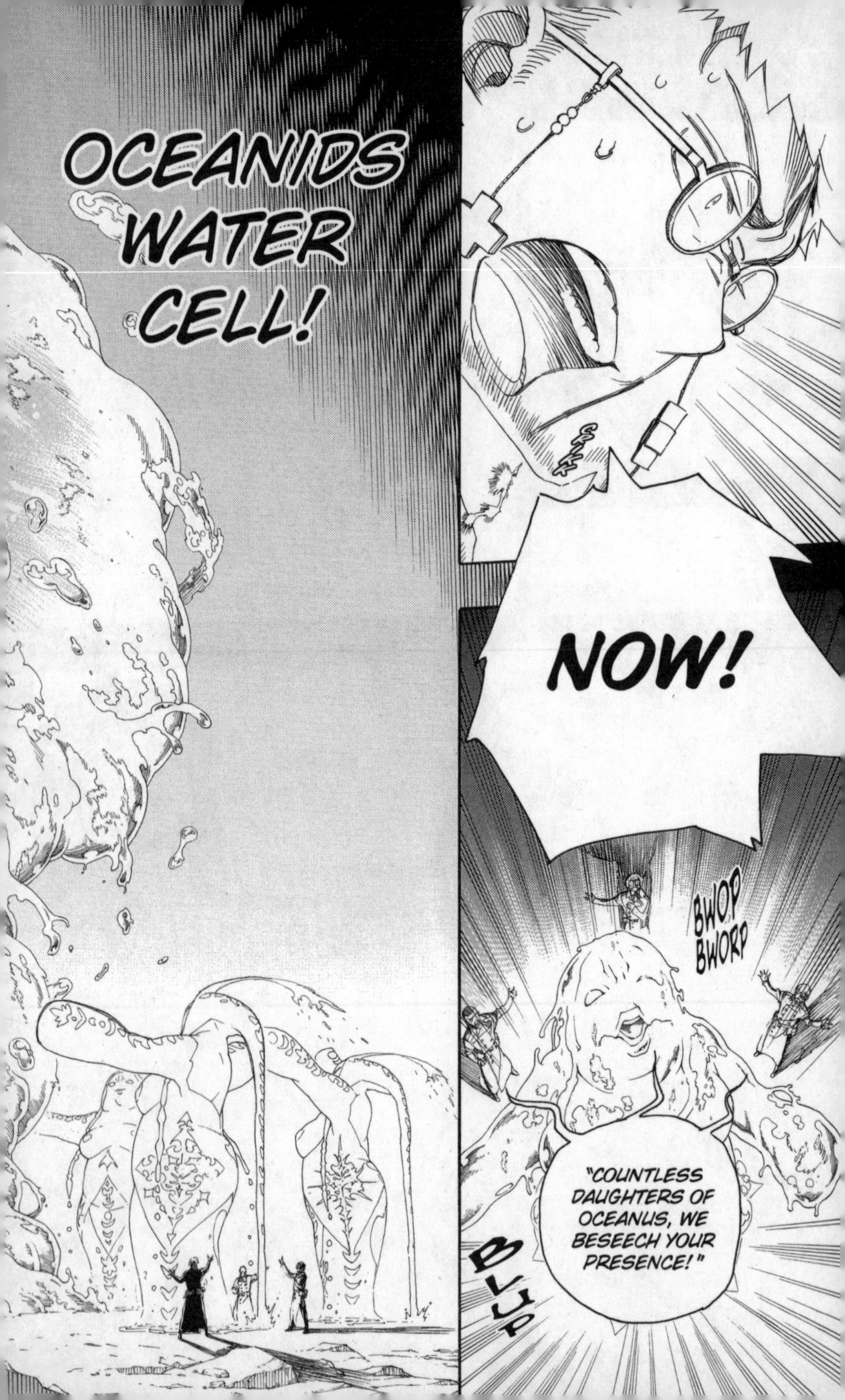
NOW!
BWOP BWORP
"COUNTLESS DAUGHTERS OF OCEANUS, WE BESEECH YOUR PRESENCE!"
BLUP
OCEANIDS WATER CELL!

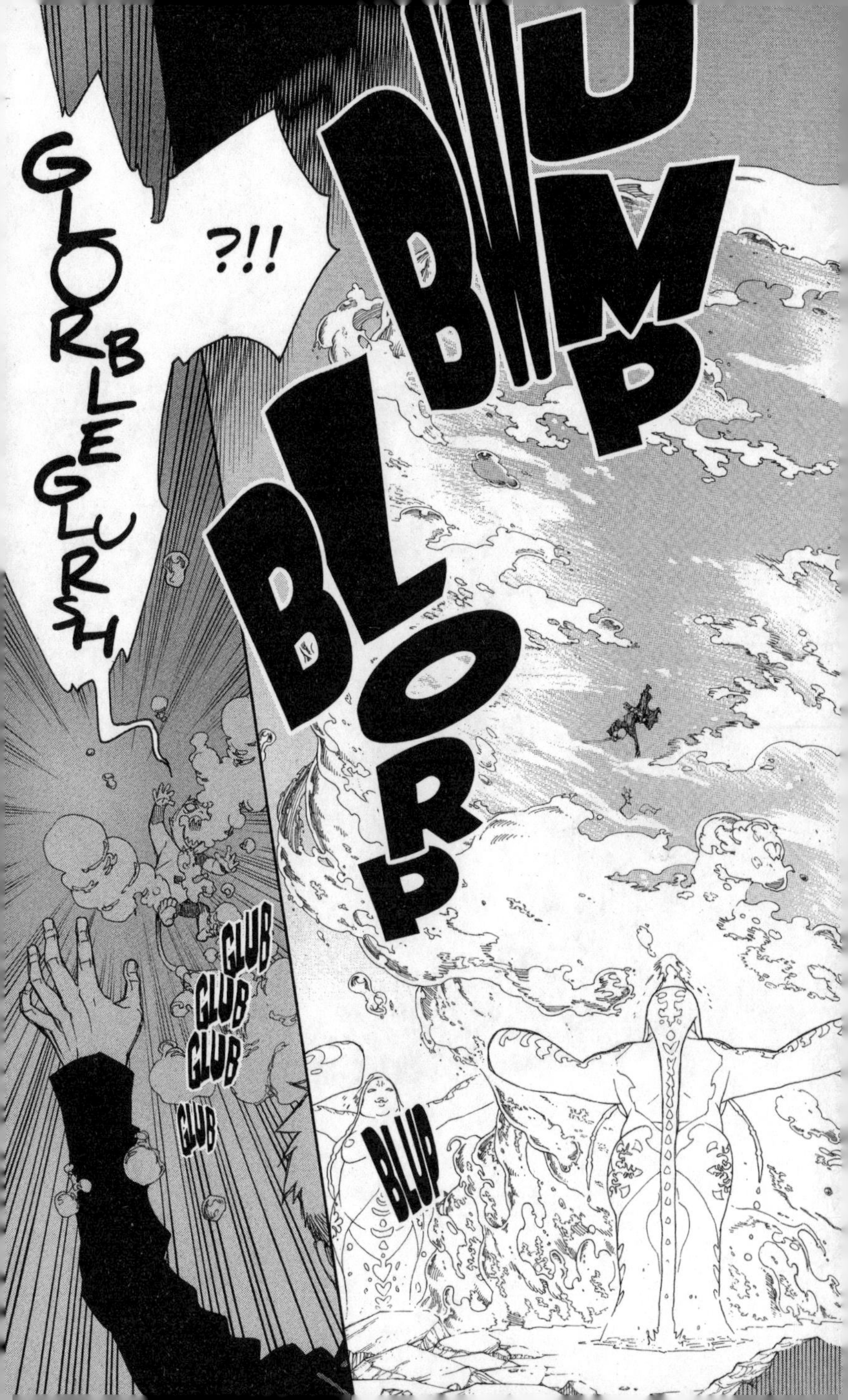
DWUMP
BLORP
BLUP
?!!
GLORBLEGLURSH
GLUB
GLUB
GLUB
GLUB

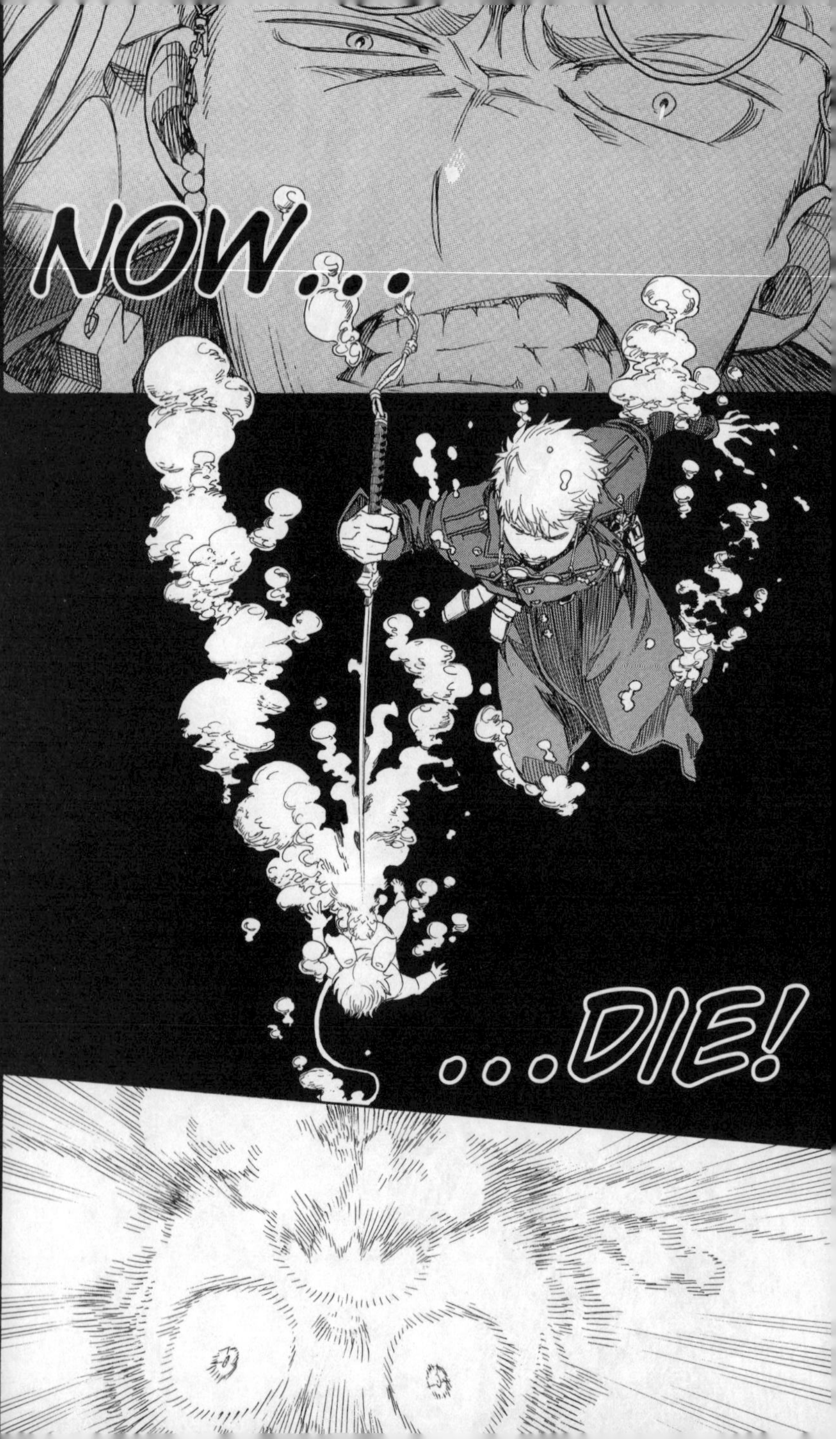
NOW...
...DIE!

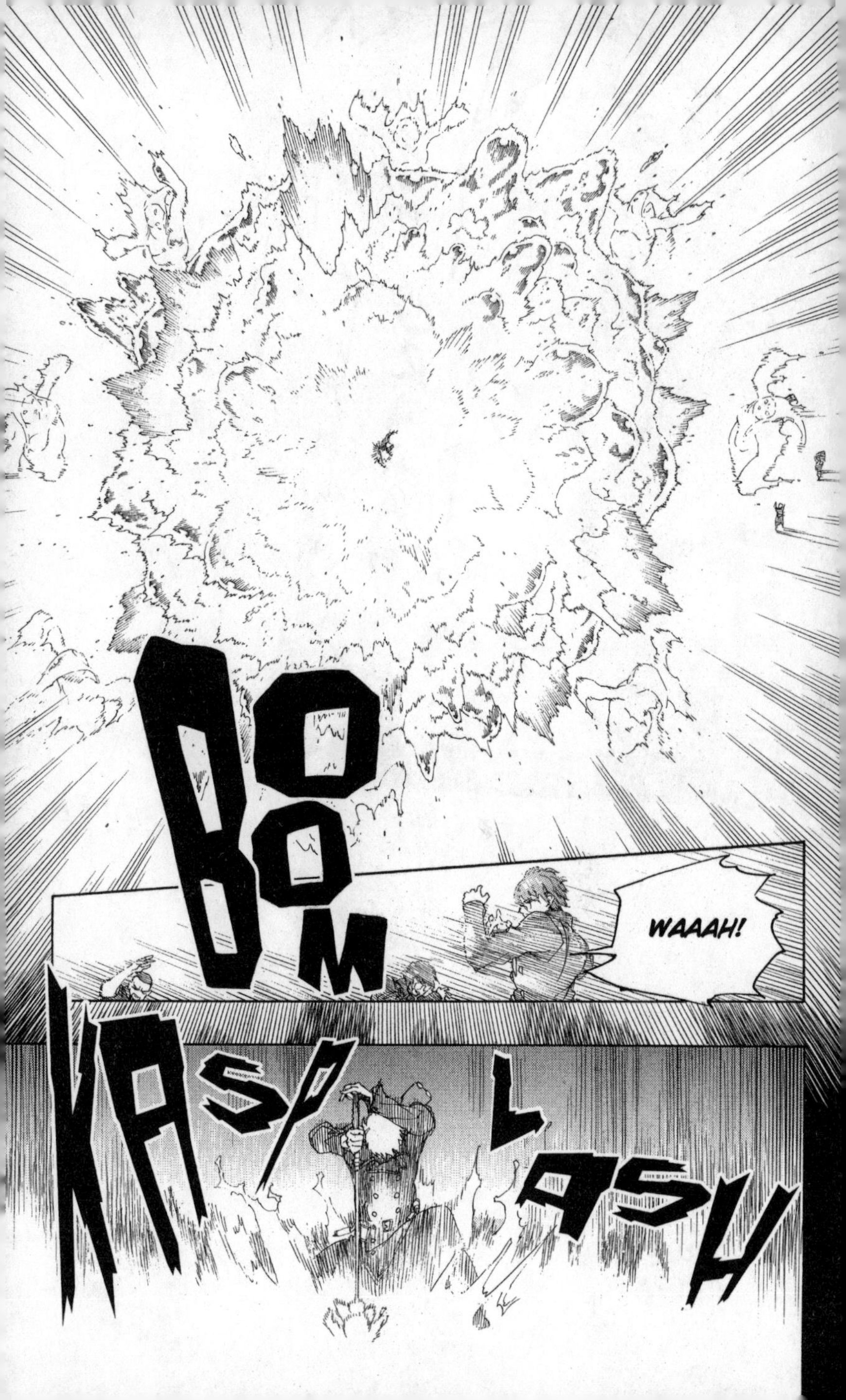
BOOM
WAAAH!
KASPLASH

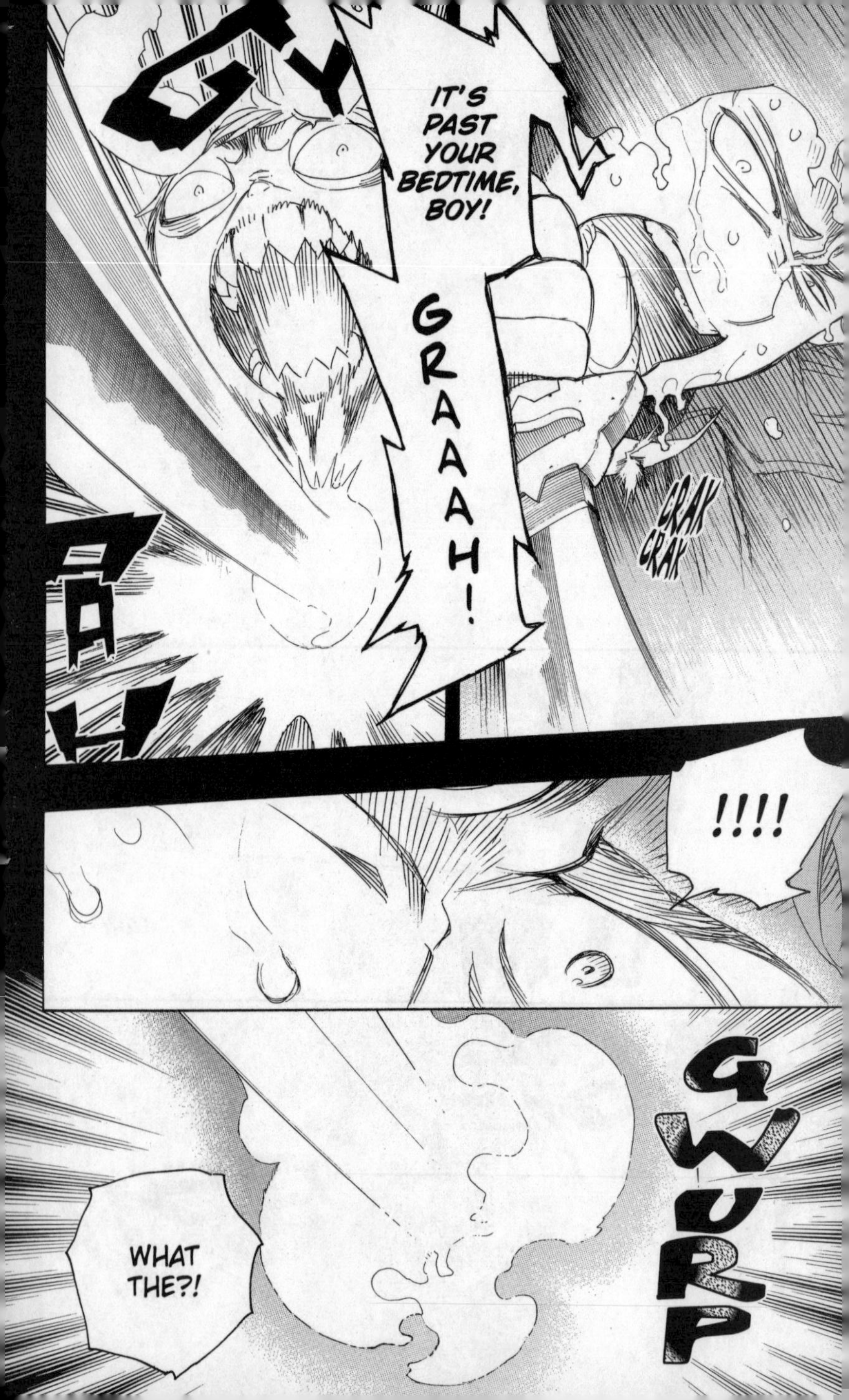
IT'S PAST YOUR BEDTIME, BOY!
GRAAAH!
CRAK CRAK
!!!!
GWURP
WHAT THE?!

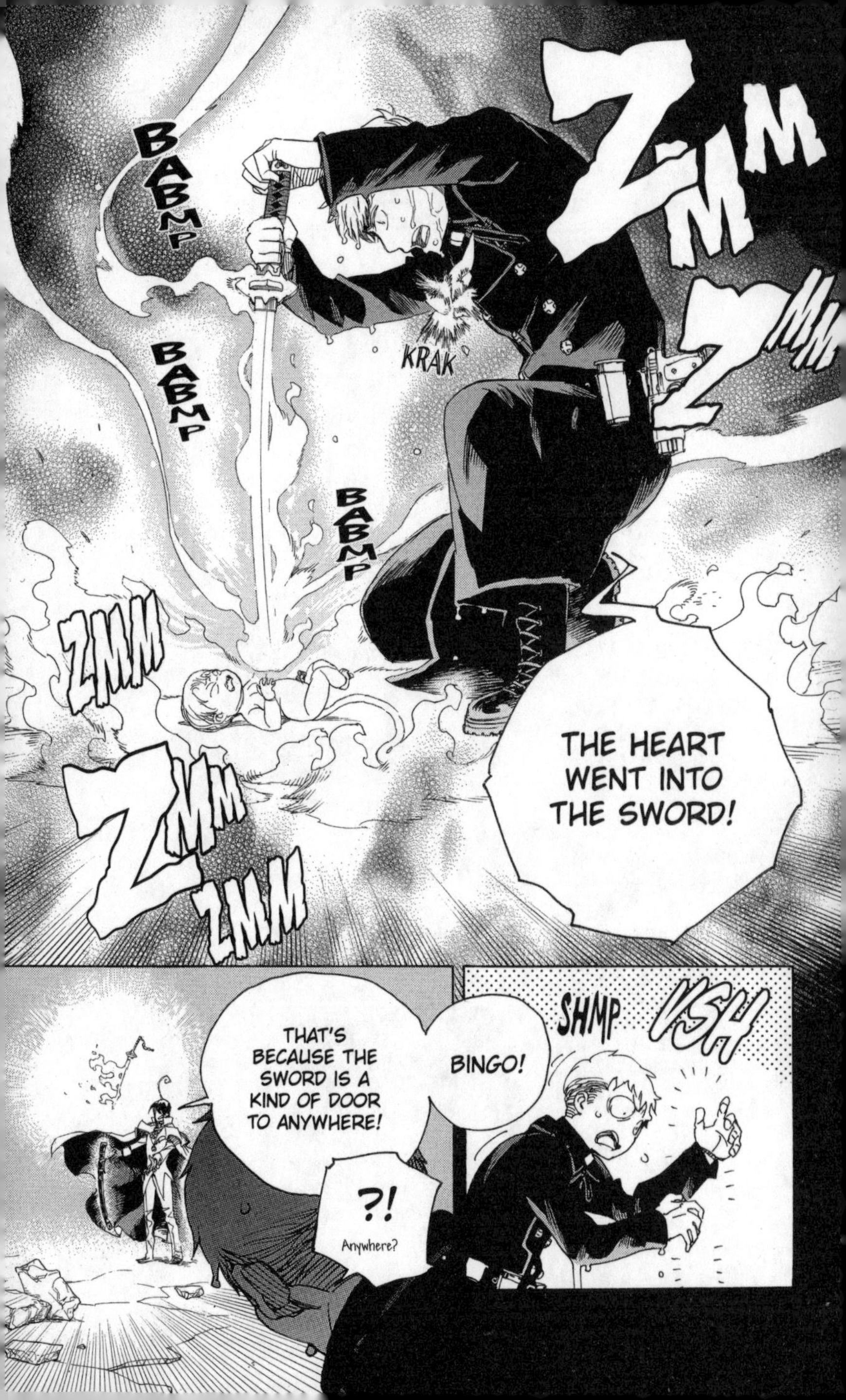
ZMMM
ZMMM
BABMP
BABMP
KRAK
BABMP
ZMM
ZMM
ZMM
THE HEART WENT INTO THE SWORD!
VSH
SHMP
BINGO!
THAT'S BECAUSE THE SWORD IS A KIND OF DOOR TO ANYWHERE!
?!
Anywhere?

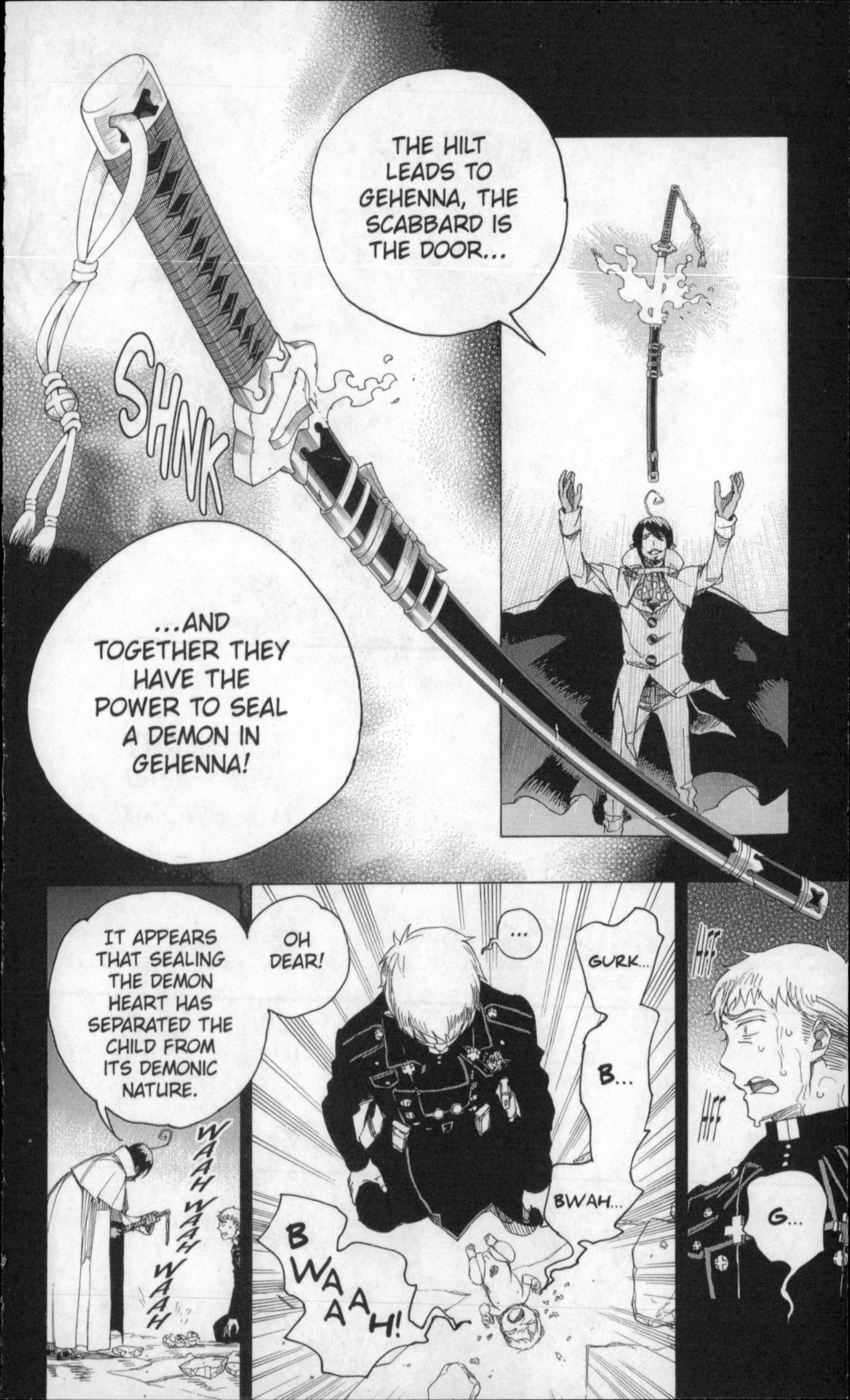
THE HILT LEADS TO GEHENNA, THE SCABBARD IS THE DOOR...
SHNK
...AND TOGETHER THEY HAVE THE POWER TO SEAL A DEMON IN GEHENNA!
HFF
HFF
G...
...
GURK...
B...
BWAH...
BWAAAAH!
OH DEAR!
IT APPEARS THAT SEALING THE DEMON HEART HAS SEPARATED THE CHILD FROM ITS DEMONIC NATURE.
WAAH WAAH WAAH

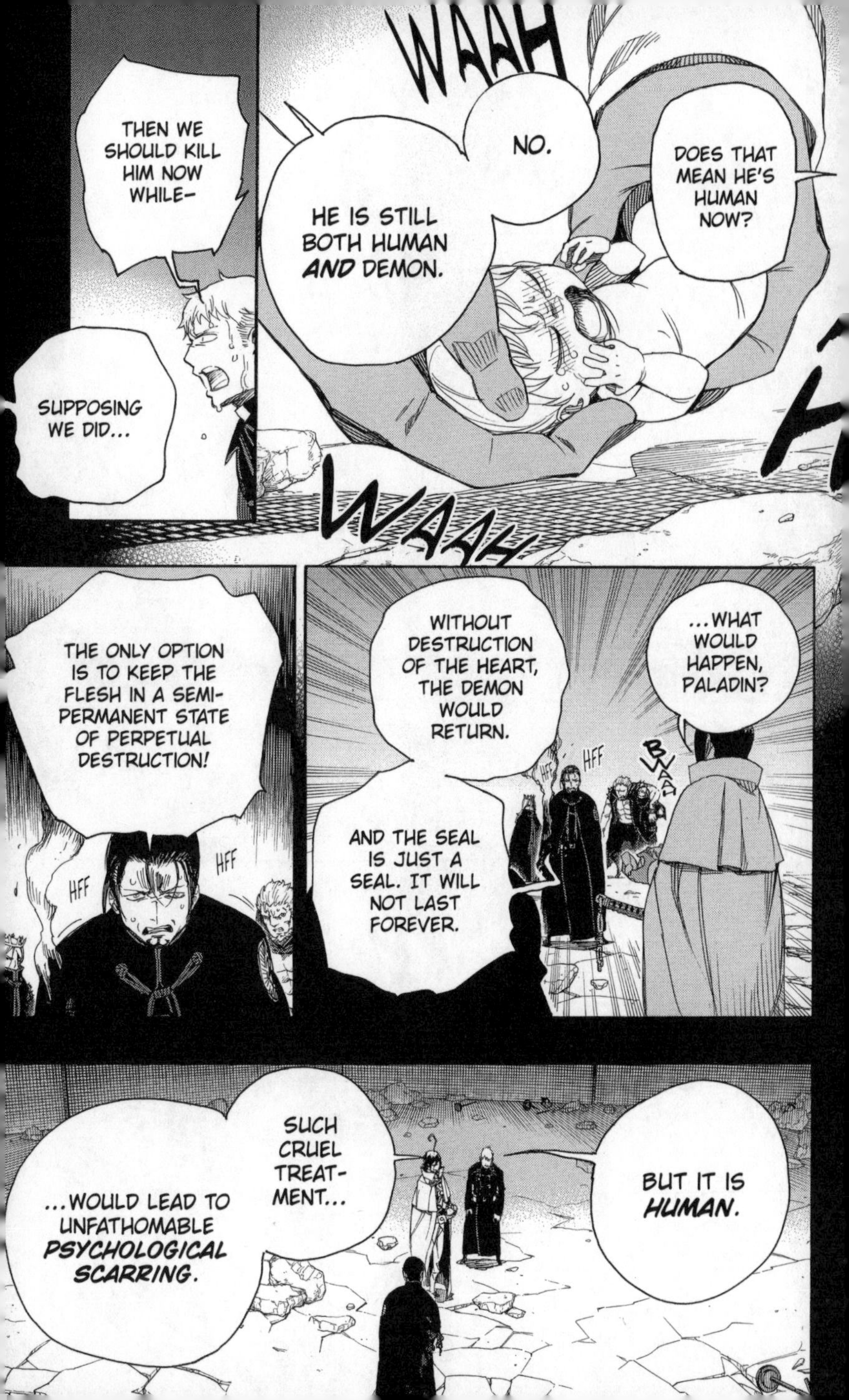
WAAH
DOES THAT MEAN HE'S HUMAN NOW?
NO.
HE IS STILL BOTH HUMAN AND DEMON.
WAAH
THEN WE SHOULD KILL HIM NOW WHILE-
SUPPOSING WE DID...
...WHAT WOULD HAPPEN, PALADIN?
WITHOUT DESTRUCTION OF THE HEART, THE DEMON WOULD RETURN.
BWAAH
HFF
HFF
AND THE SEAL IS JUST A SEAL. IT WILL NOT LAST FOREVER.
THE ONLY OPTION IS TO KEEP THE FLESH IN A SEMI-PERMANENT STATE OF PERPETUAL DESTRUCTION!
HFF
HFF
BUT IT IS HUMAN.
SUCH CRUEL TREAT-MENT...
...WOULD LEAD TO UNFATHOMABLE PSYCHOLOGICAL SCARRING.

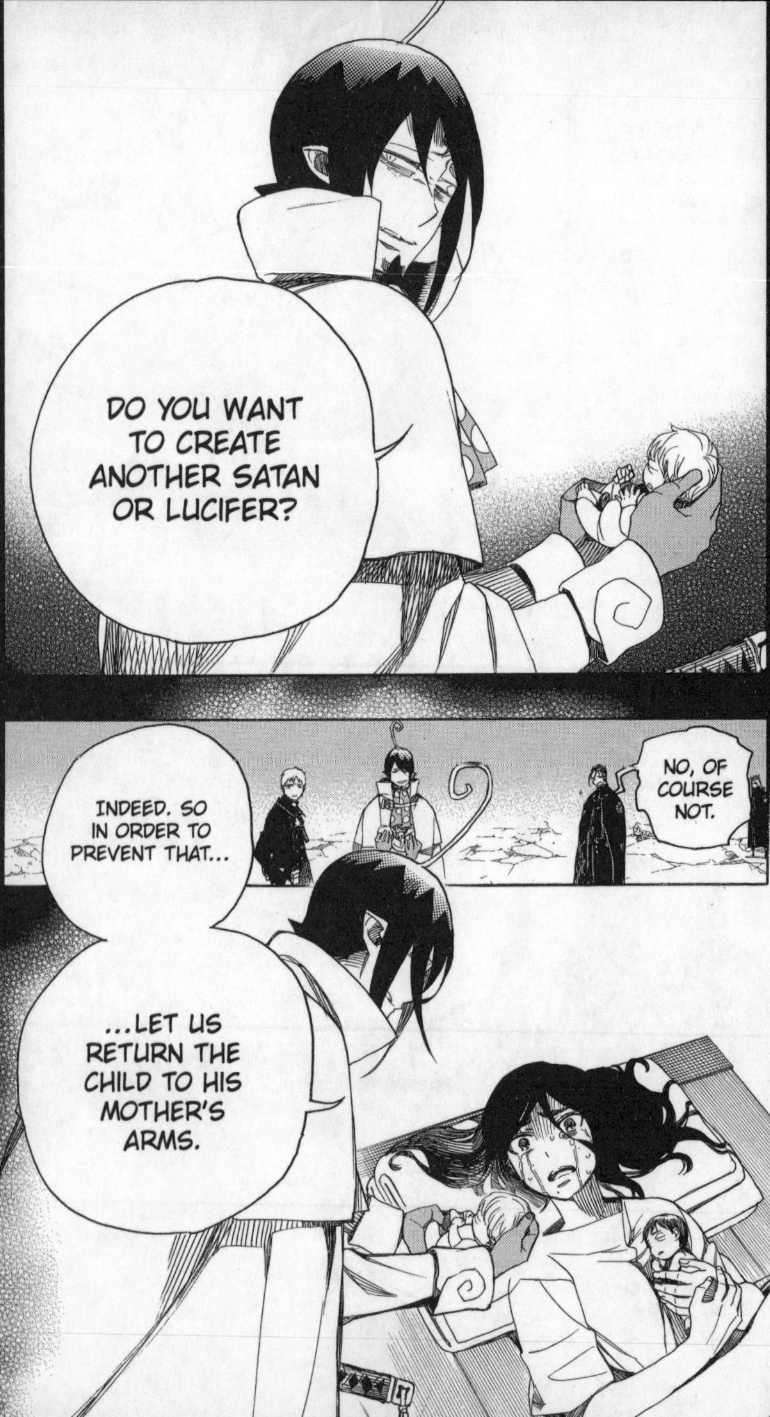
DO YOU WANT TO CREATE ANOTHER SATAN OR LUCIFER?
NO, OF COURSE NOT.
INDEED. SO IN ORDER TO PREVENT THAT...
...LET US RETURN THE CHILD TO HIS MOTHER'S ARMS.

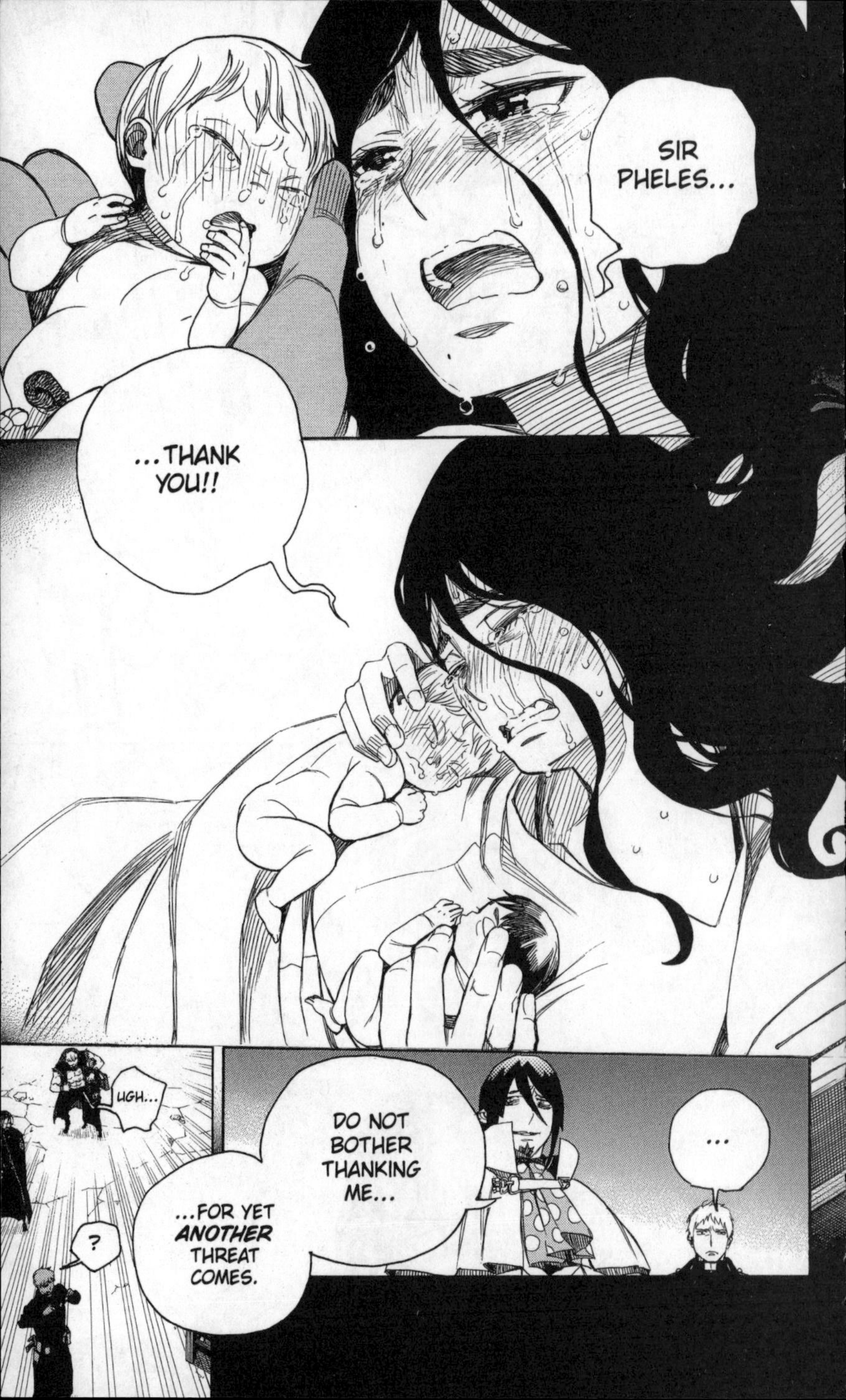
SIR PHELES...
...THANK YOU!!
...
DO NOT BOTHER THANKING ME...
...FOR YET *ANOTHER* THREAT COMES.
UGH...
?

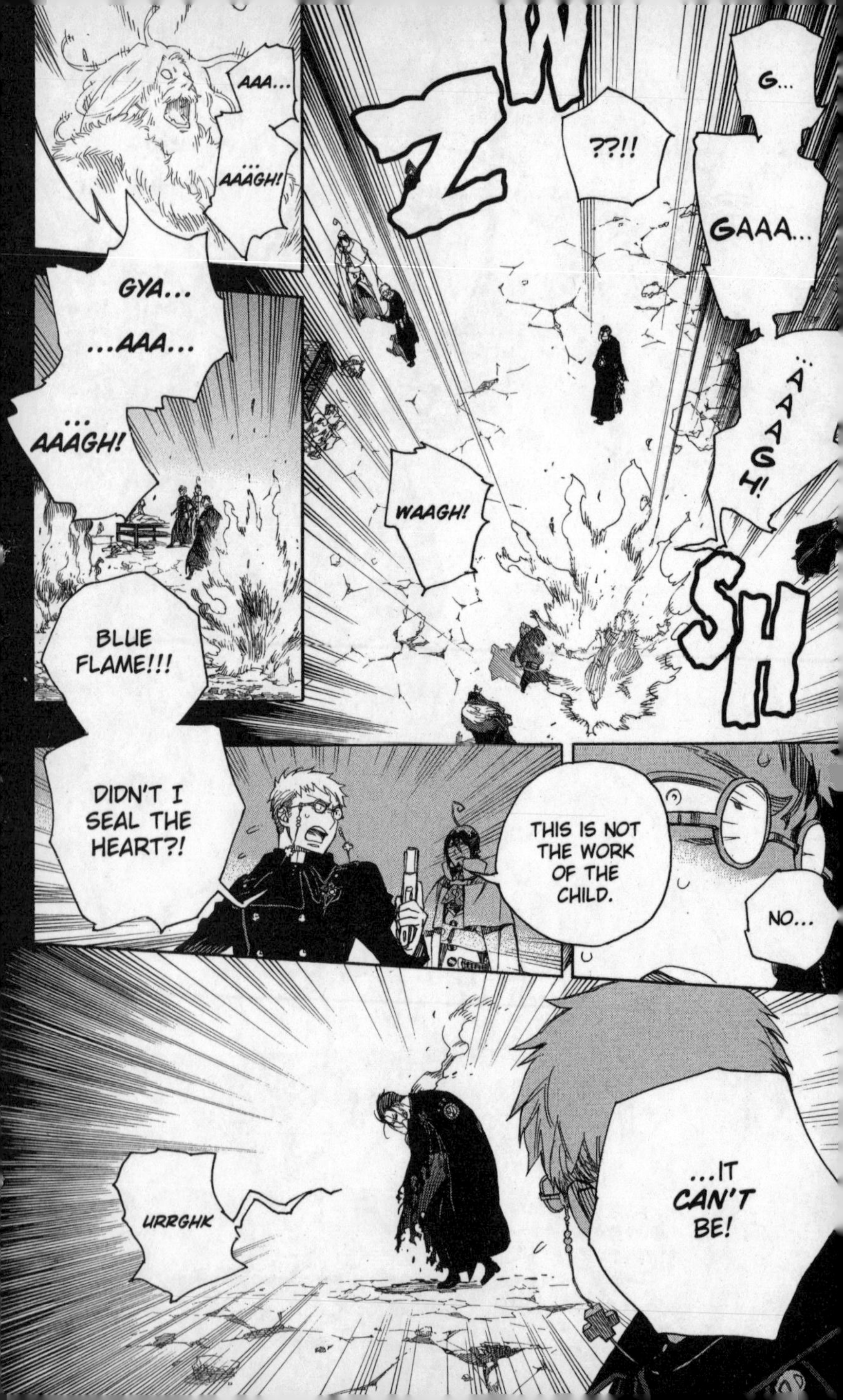
G...
ZW
??!!
GAAA...
...AAAAGH!
SH
WAAGH!
AAA...
...AAAGH!
GYA...
...AAA...
...AAAGH!
BLUE FLAME!!!
DIDN'T I SEAL THE HEART?!
THIS IS NOT THE WORK OF THE CHILD.
NO...
...IT CAN'T BE!
URRGHK

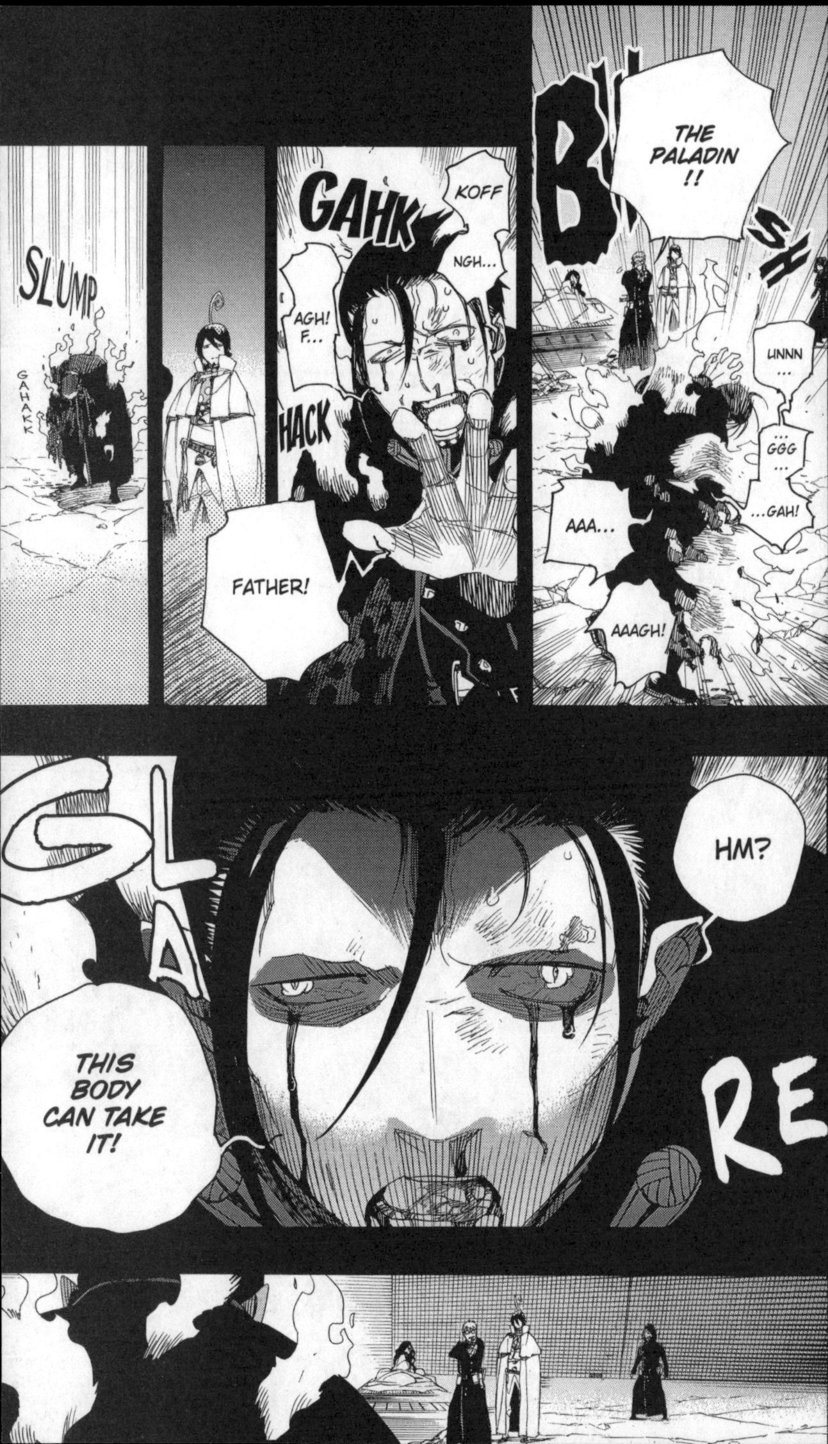
THE PALADIN !!
SH
UNNN...
...GGG...
...GAH!
AAA...
AAAGH!
GAHK
KOFF
NGH...
AGH! F...
HACK
FATHER!
SLUMP
GAHAKK
HM?
RE
GL
A
THIS BODY CAN TAKE IT!

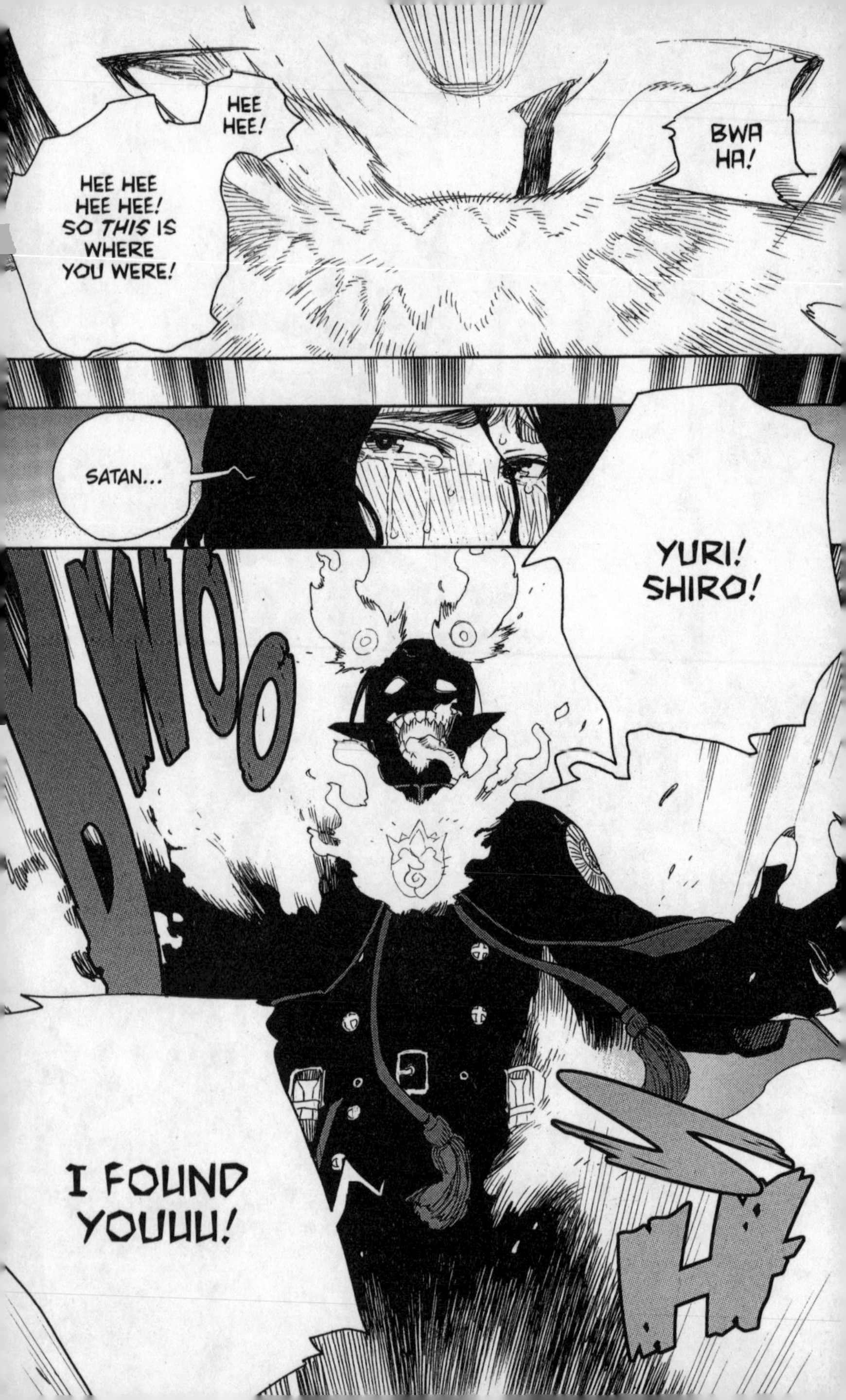
BWA HA!
HEE HEE!
HEE HEE HEE HEE! SO *THIS* IS WHERE YOU WERE!
SATAN...
YURI! SHIRO!
I FOUND YOUUU!

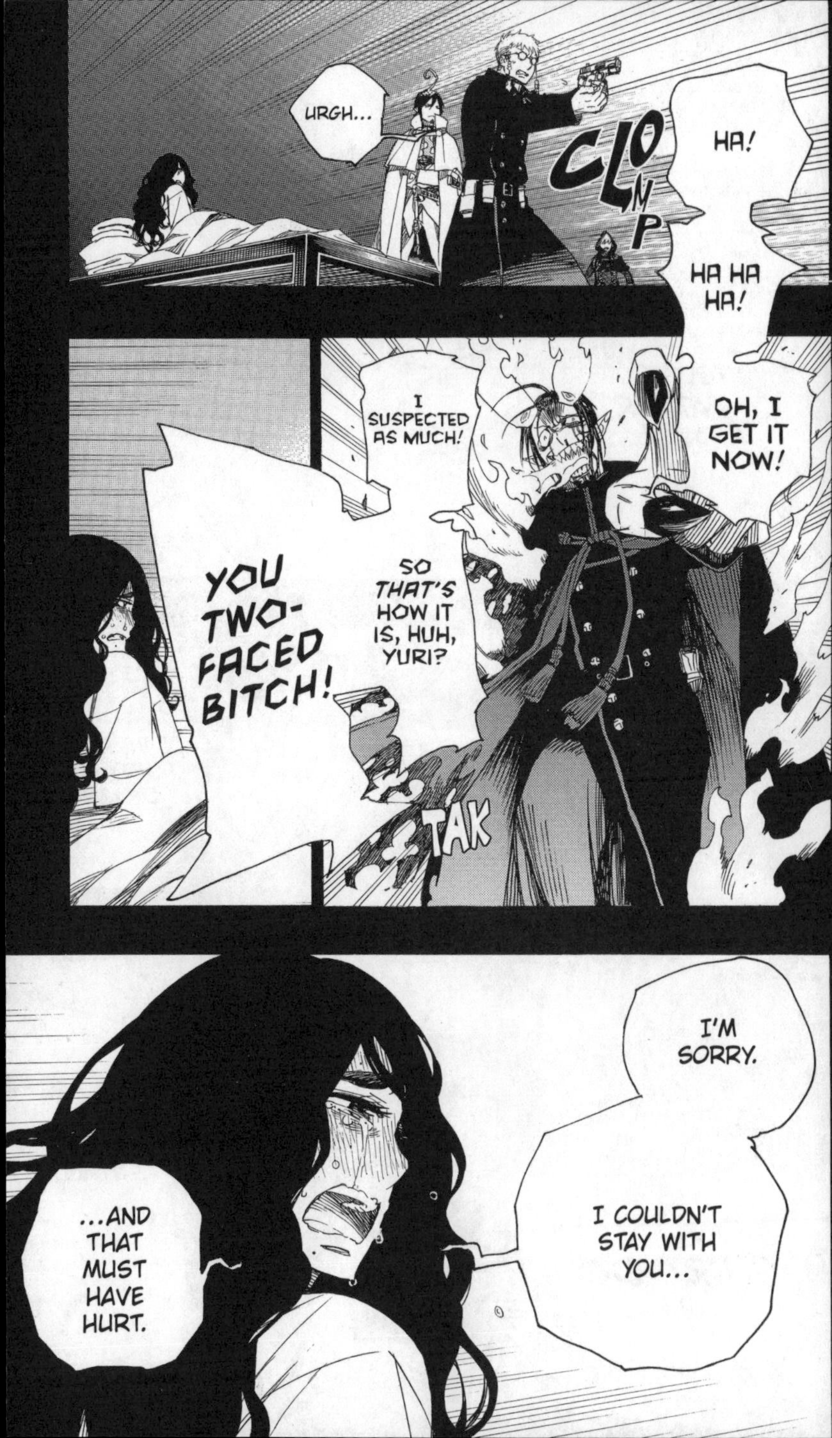
HA!
HA HA HA!
CLOMP
URGH...
OH, I GET IT NOW!
I SUSPECTED AS MUCH!
SO THAT'S HOW IT IS, HUH, YURI?
YOU TWO-FACED BITCH!
TAK
I'M SORRY.
I COULDN'T STAY WITH YOU...
...AND THAT MUST HAVE HURT.

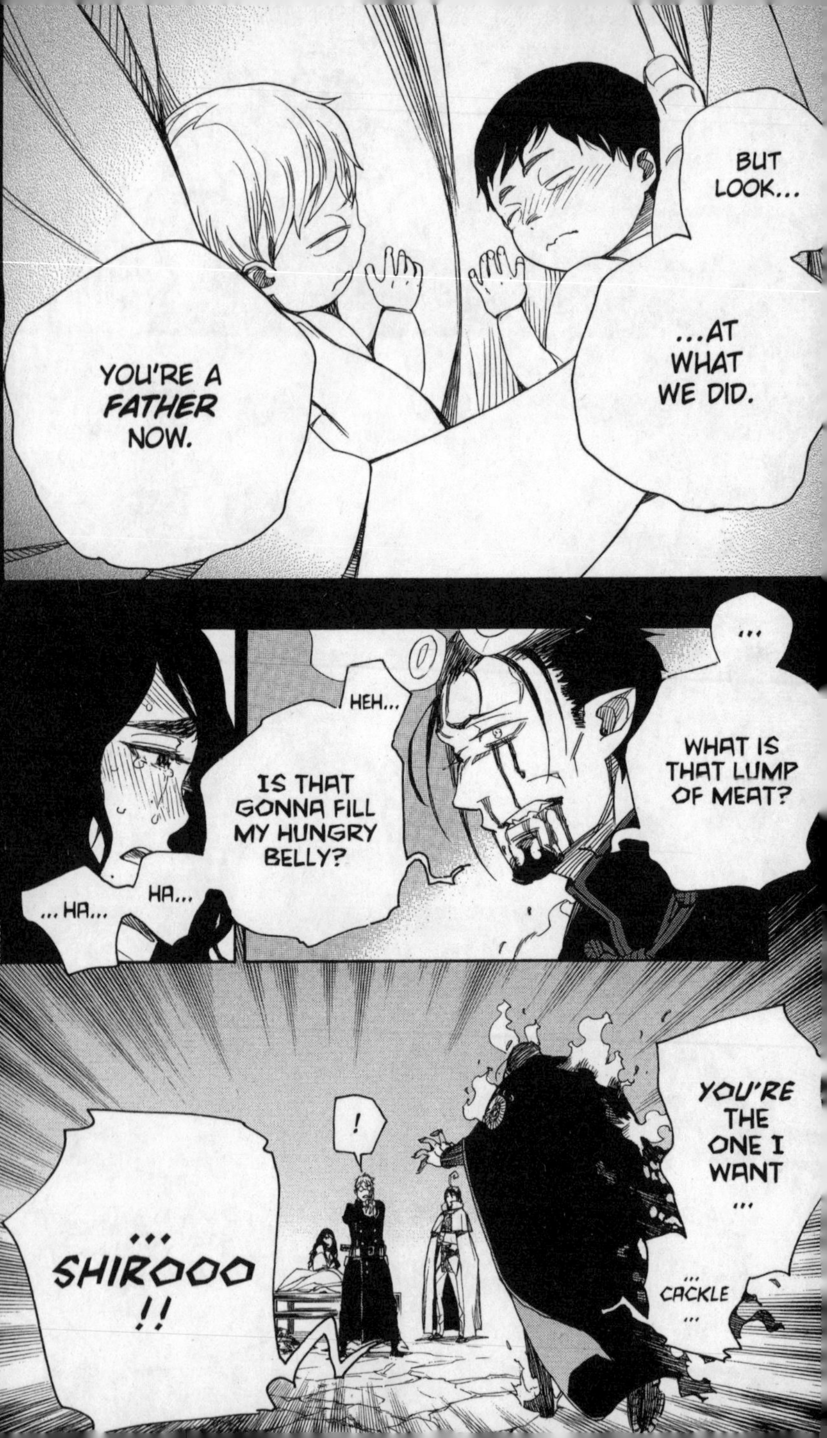
BUT LOOK...
...AT WHAT WE DID.
YOU'RE A *FATHER* NOW.
...
WHAT IS THAT LUMP OF MEAT?
HEH...
IS THAT GONNA FILL MY HUNGRY BELLY?
HA...
...HA...
YOU'RE THE ONE I WANT ...
... CACKLE ...
!
... SHIROOO !!

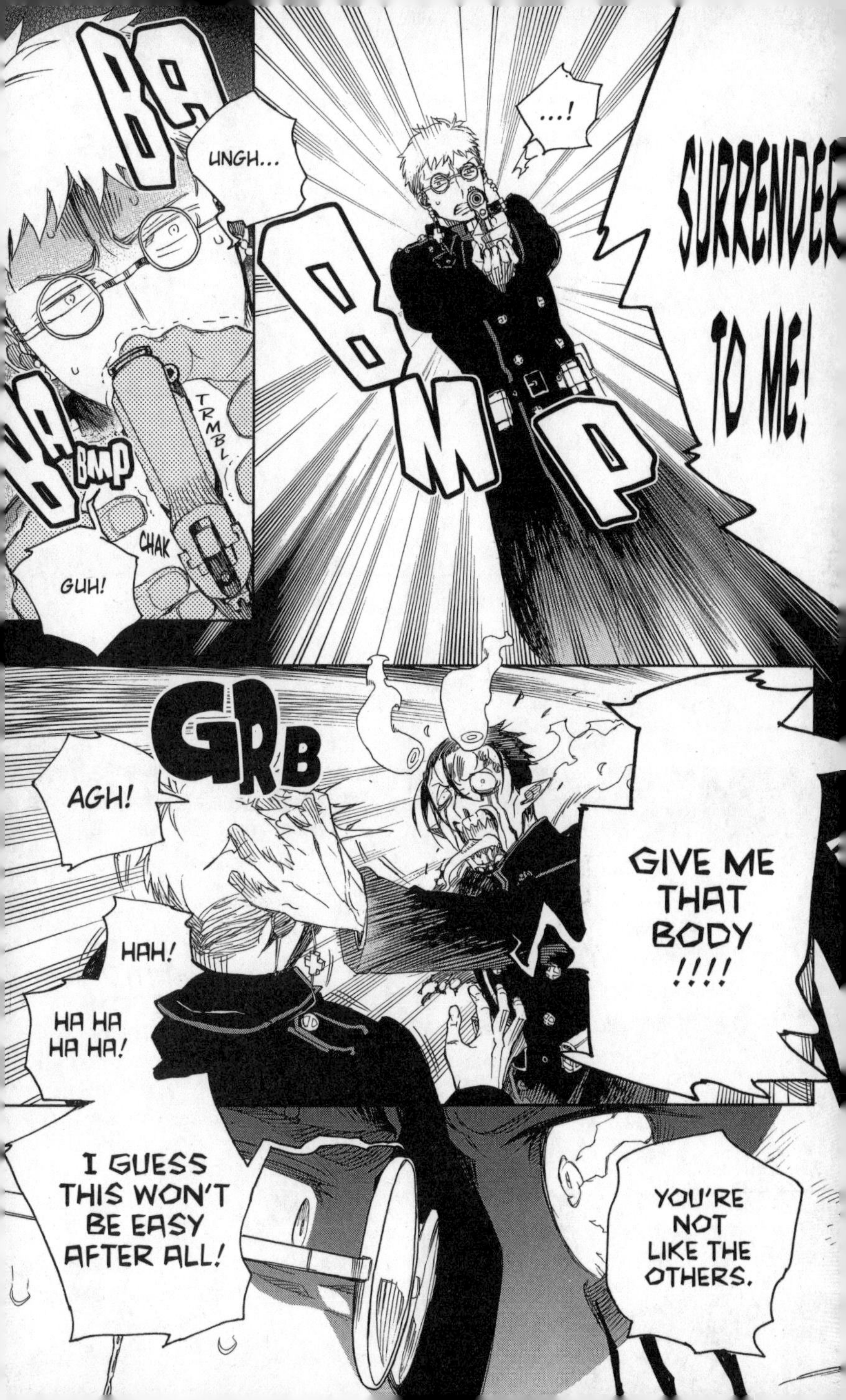

...!
SURRENDER TO ME!
BMP
BA
UNGH...
TRMBL
BA
BMP
CHAK
GUH!
GIVE ME THAT BODY !!!!
GRB
AGH!
HAH!
HA HA HA HA!
YOU'RE NOT LIKE THE OTHERS.
I GUESS THIS WON'T BE EASY AFTER ALL!

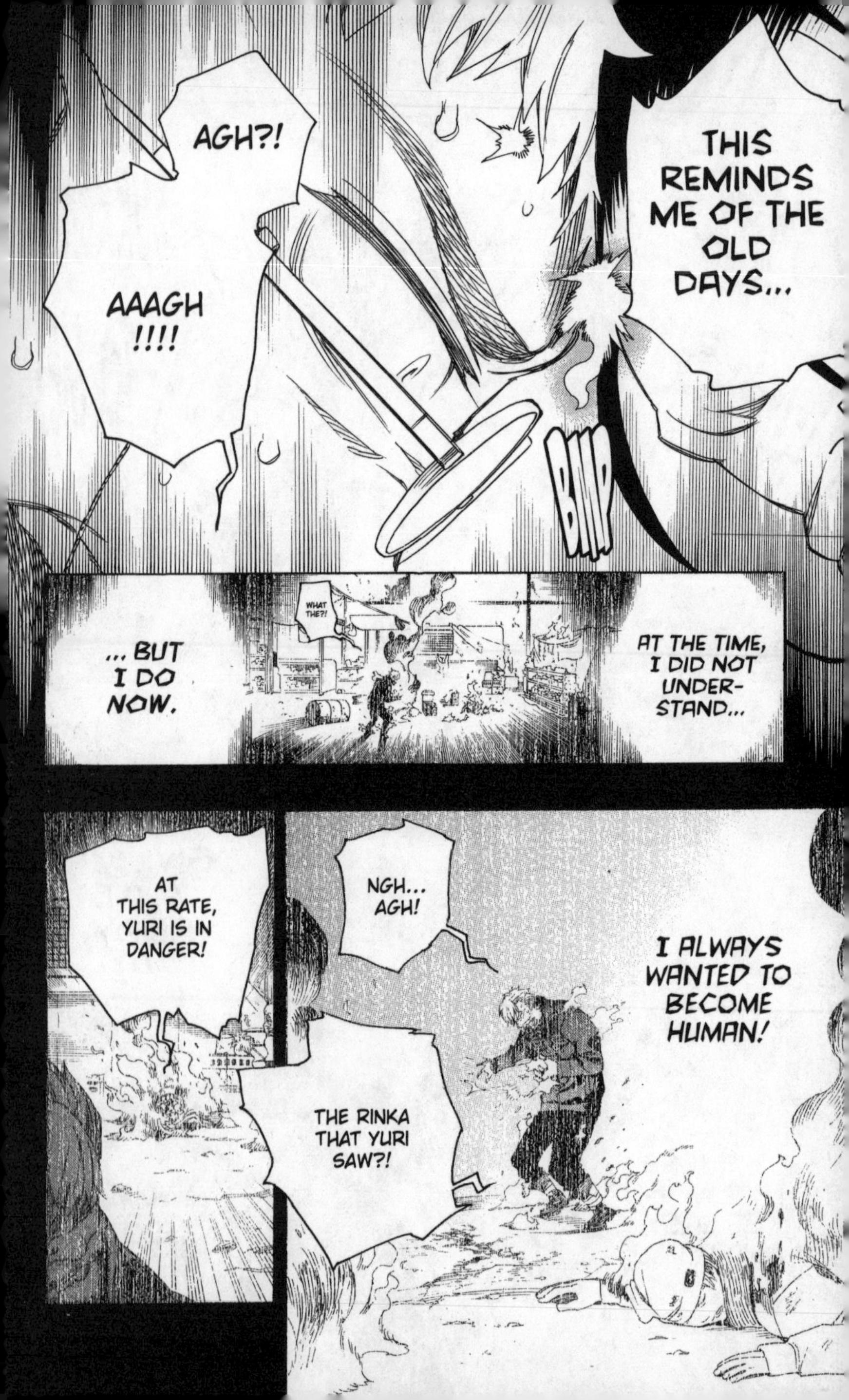
THIS REMINDS ME OF THE OLD DAYS...
AGH?!
AAAGH !!!!
BMP
AT THE TIME, I DID NOT UNDER-STAND...
WHAT THE?!
... BUT I DO NOW.
I ALWAYS WANTED TO BECOME HUMAN!
NGH... AGH!
THE RINKA THAT YURI SAW?!
AT THIS RATE, YURI IS IN DANGER!

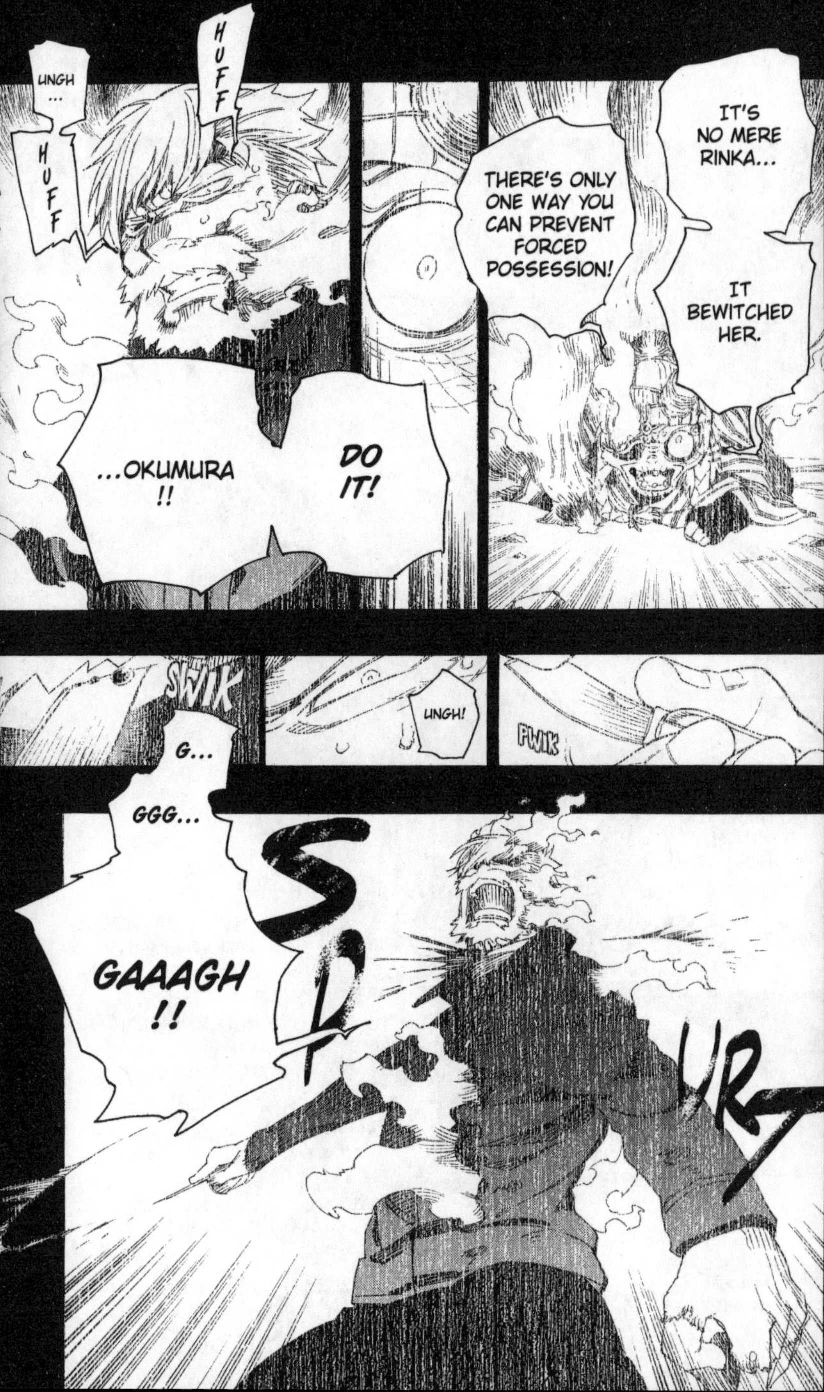

IT'S NO MERE RINKA...
IT BEWITCHED HER.
THERE'S ONLY ONE WAY YOU CAN PREVENT FORCED POSSESSION!
HUFF HUFF
UNGH...
HUFF HUFF
...OKUMURA!! DO IT!
PWIK
UNGH!
SWIK
G...
GGG...
GAAAGH!!
SPURT

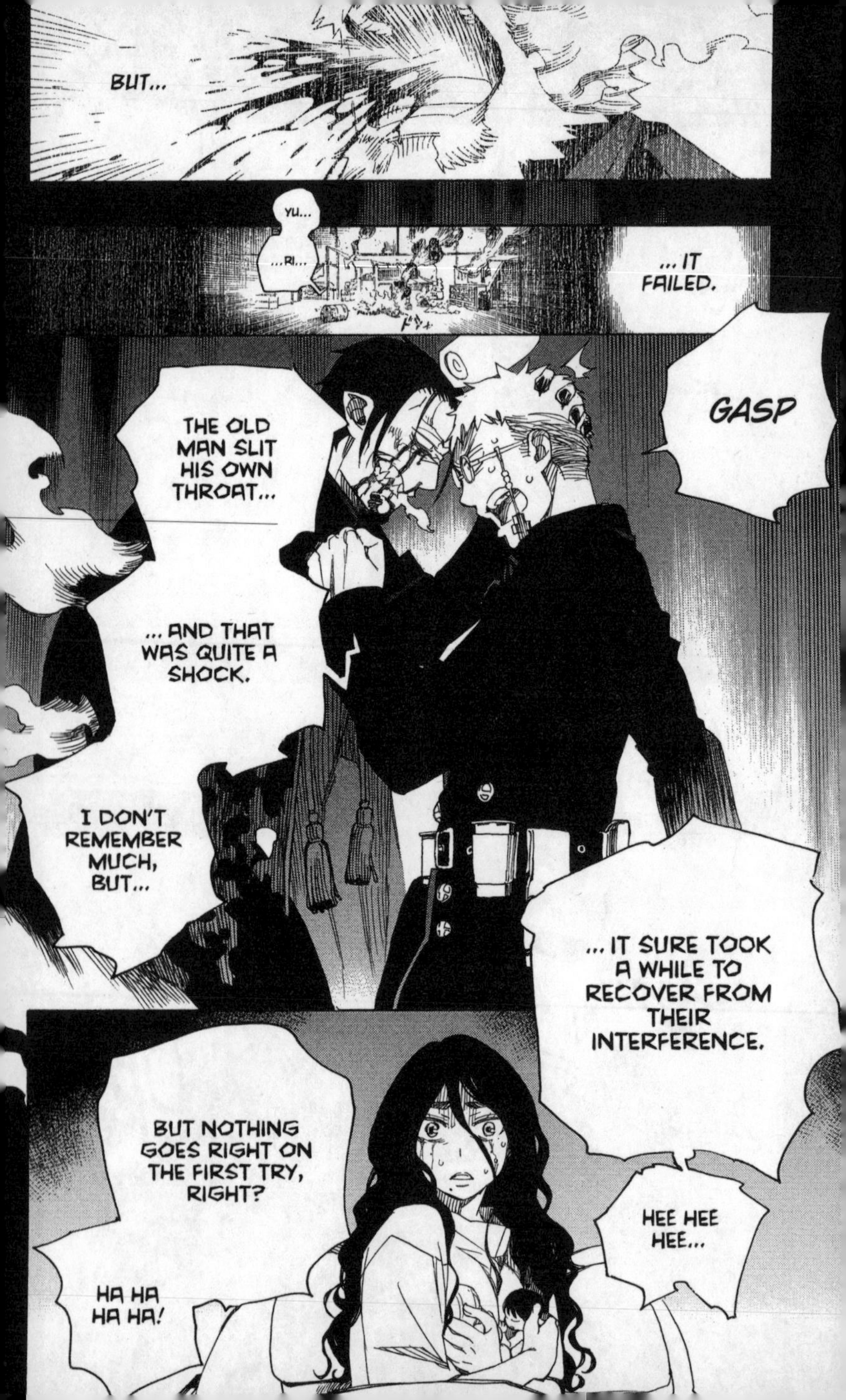
BUT...
...IT FAILED.
YU...
...RI...
GASP
THE OLD MAN SLIT HIS OWN THROAT...
...AND THAT WAS QUITE A SHOCK.
I DON'T REMEMBER MUCH, BUT...
...IT SURE TOOK A WHILE TO RECOVER FROM THEIR INTERFERENCE.
HEE HEE HEE...
BUT NOTHING GOES RIGHT ON THE FIRST TRY, RIGHT?
HA HA HA HA!

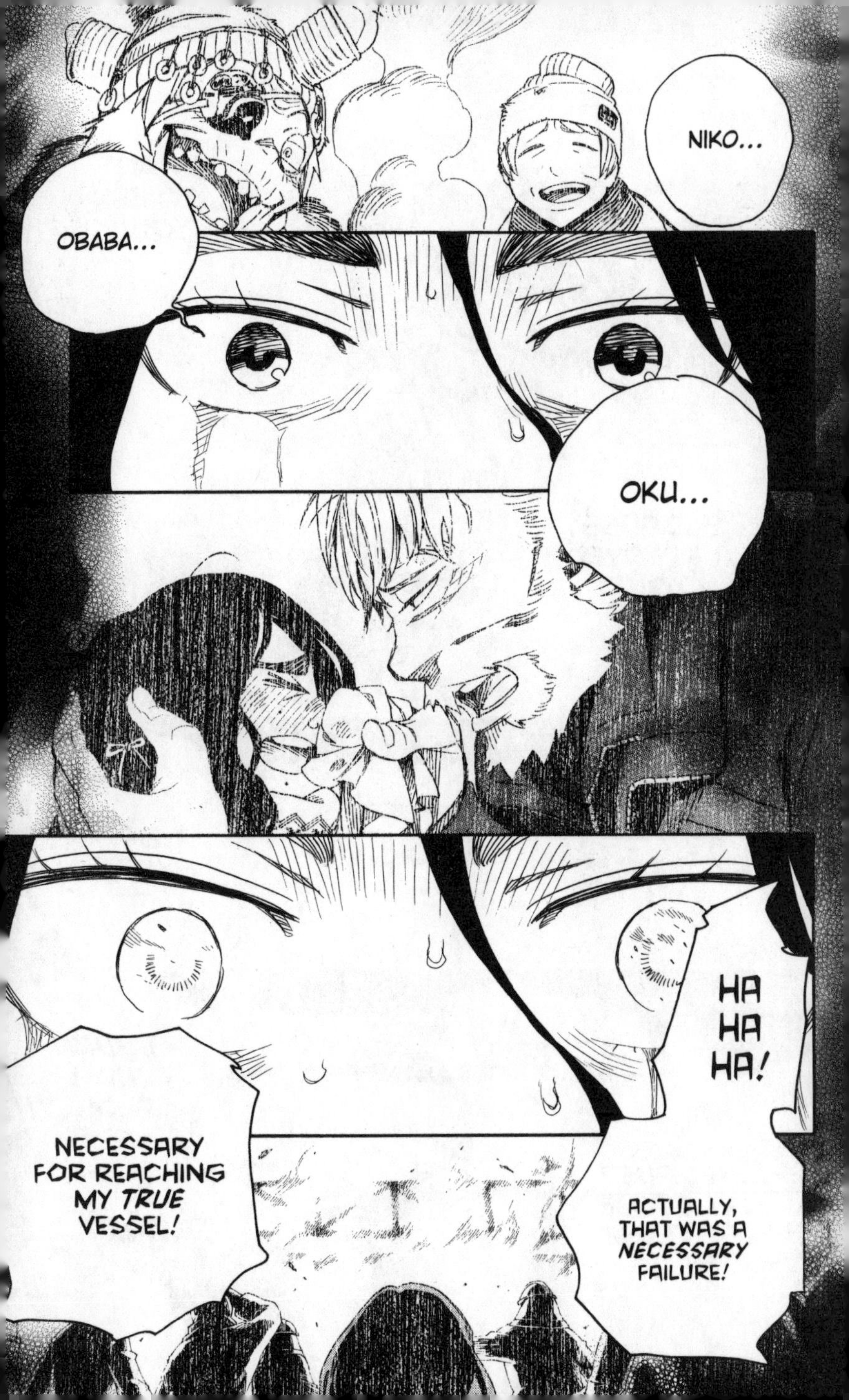
NIKO...
OBABA...
OKU...
HA HA HA!
ACTUALLY, THAT WAS A *NECESSARY* FAILURE!
NECESSARY FOR REACHING MY *TRUE* VESSEL!

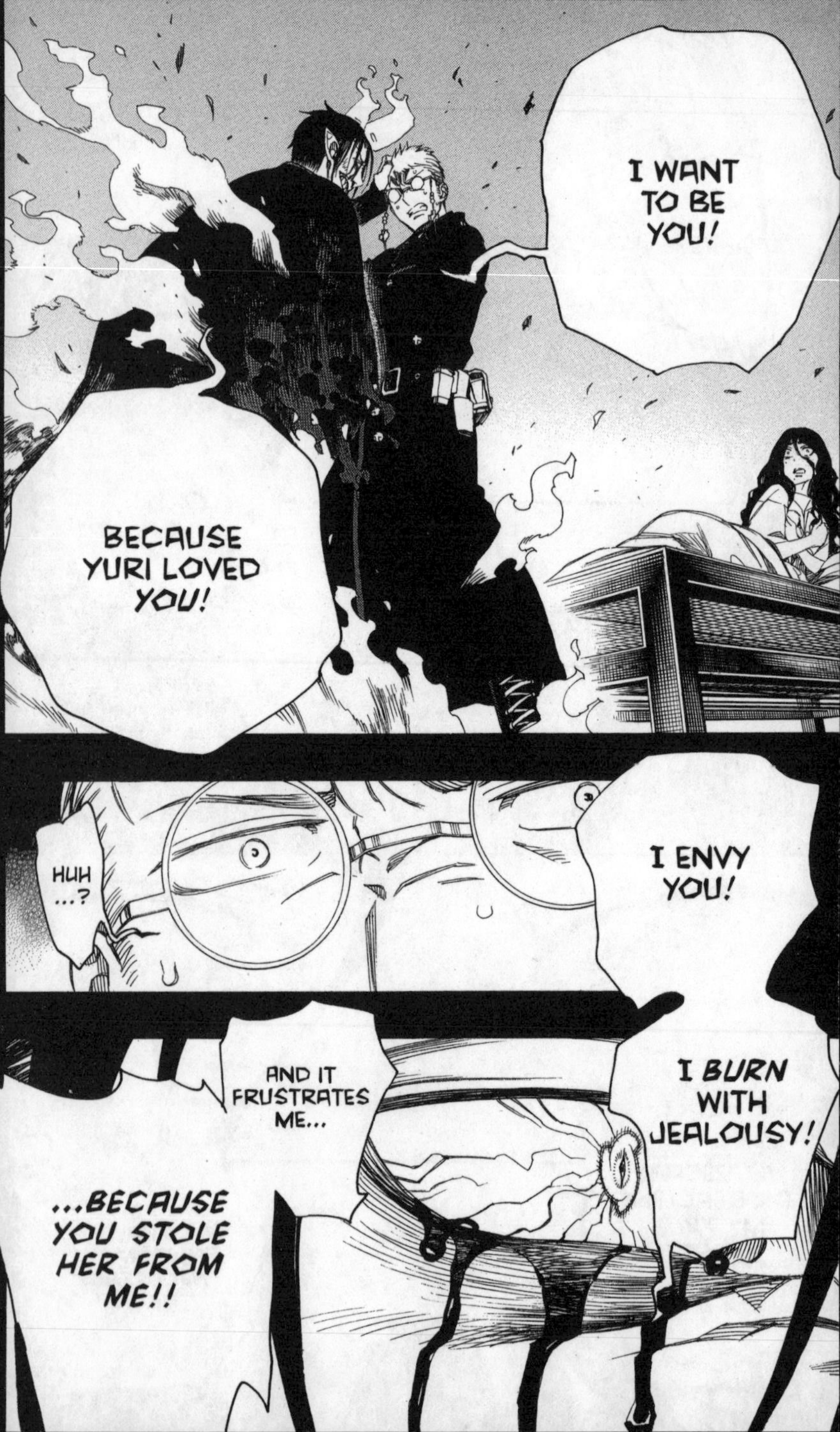
I WANT TO BE YOU!
BECAUSE YURI LOVED YOU!
I ENVY YOU!
HUH ...?
I BURN WITH JEALOUSY!
AND IT FRUSTRATES ME...
...BECAUSE YOU STOLE HER FROM ME!!

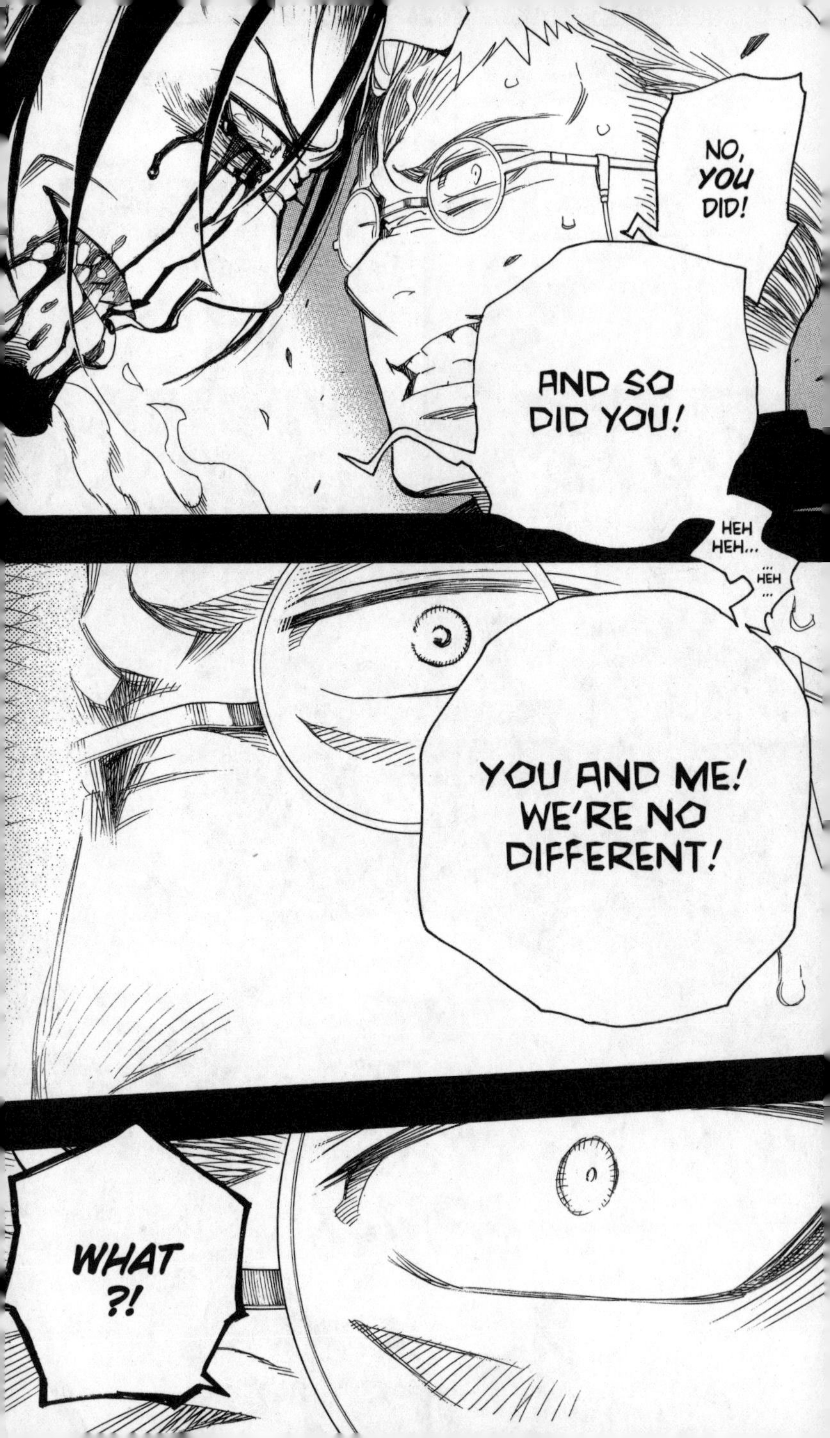
NO, YOU DID!
AND SO DID YOU!
HEH HEH...
...HEH...
YOU AND ME! WE'RE NO DIFFERENT!
WHAT?!

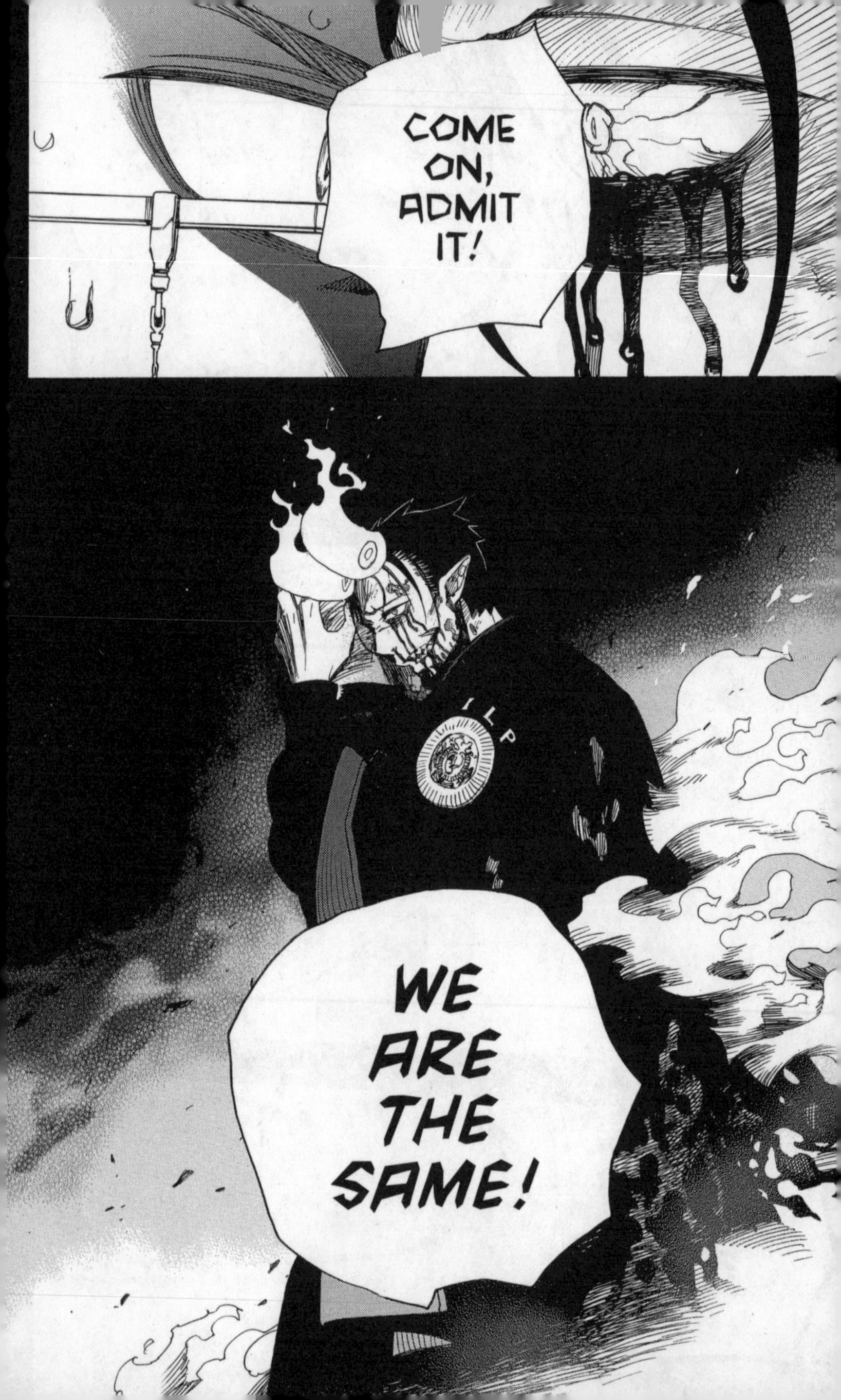
COME ON, ADMIT IT!
WE ARE THE SAME!

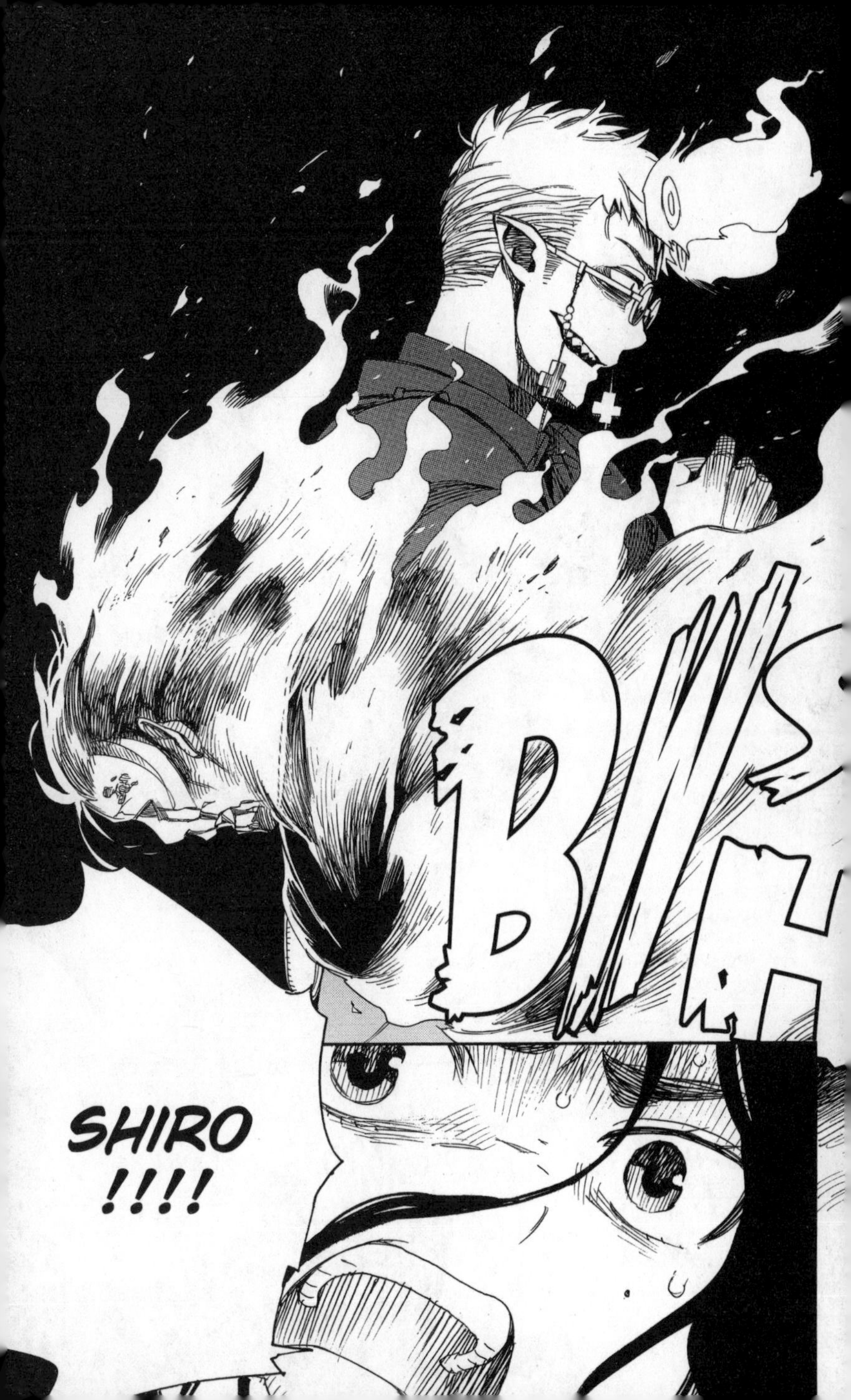
BWAH
SHIRO !!!!

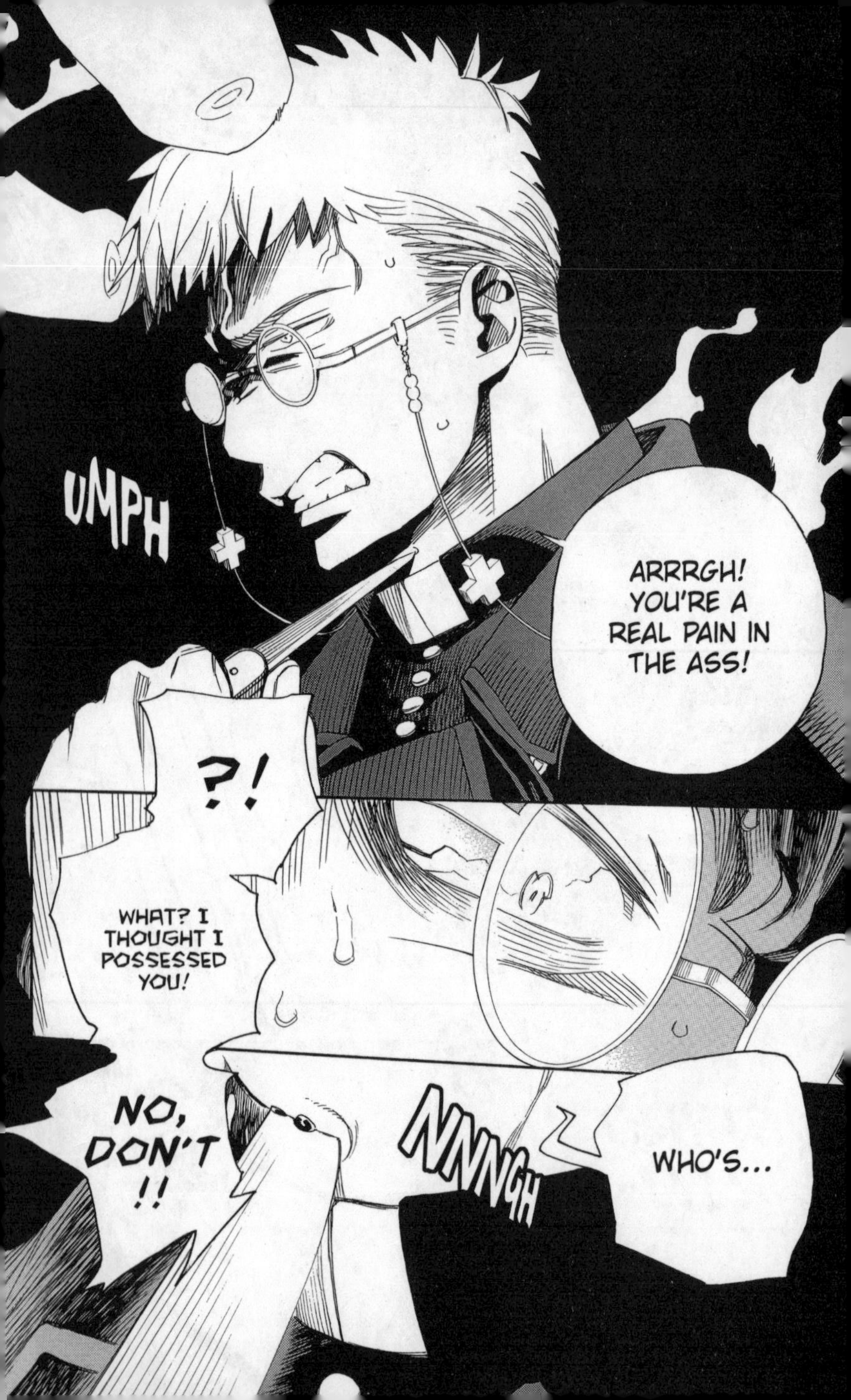
ARRRGH! YOU'RE A REAL PAIN IN THE ASS!
UMPH
?!
WHAT? I THOUGHT I POSSESSED YOU!
WHO'S...
NNNGH
NO, DON'T!!

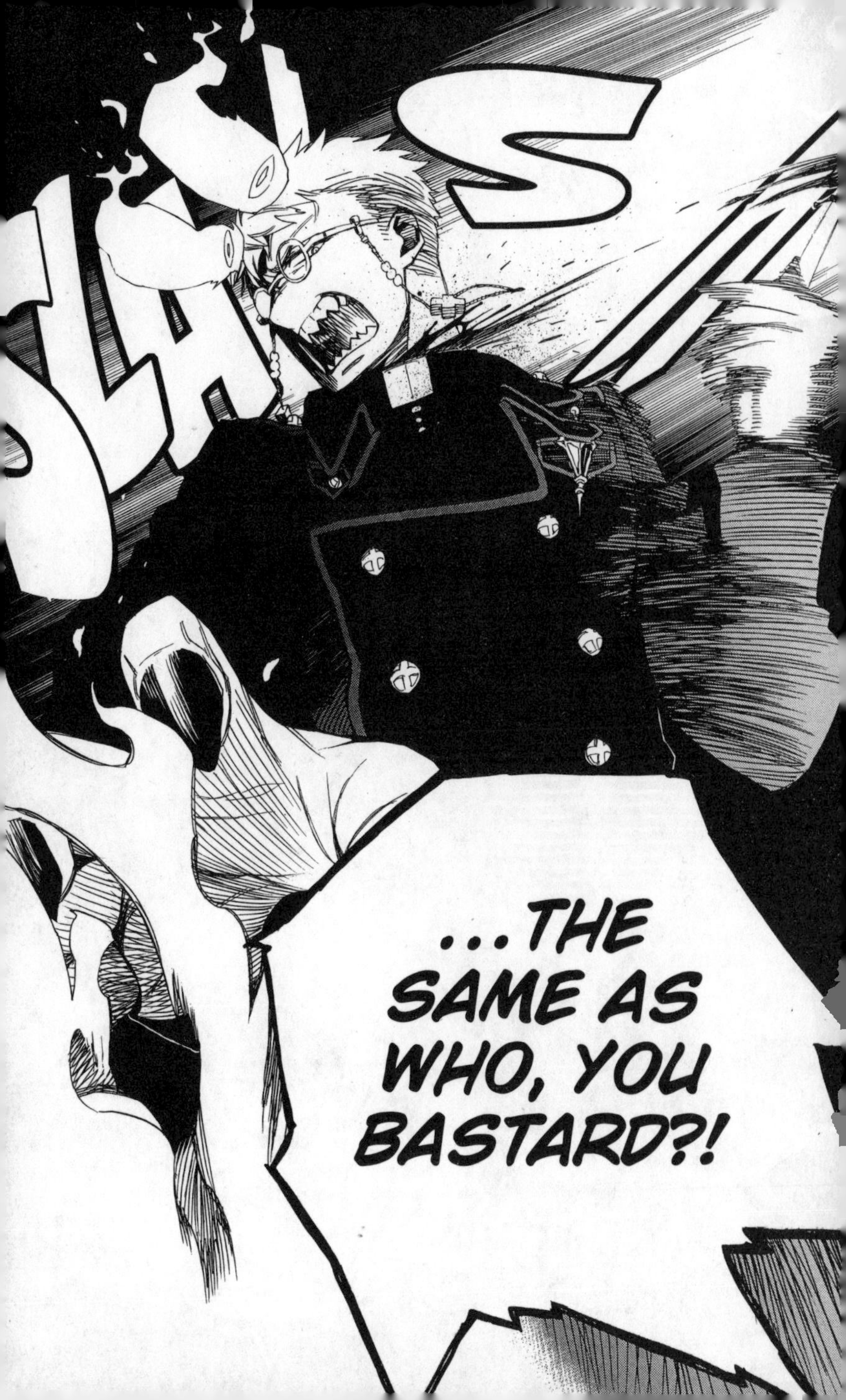
...THE SAME AS WHO, YOU BASTARD?!

BLUE EXORCIST CHAPTER 116: SSC23: 17GZ

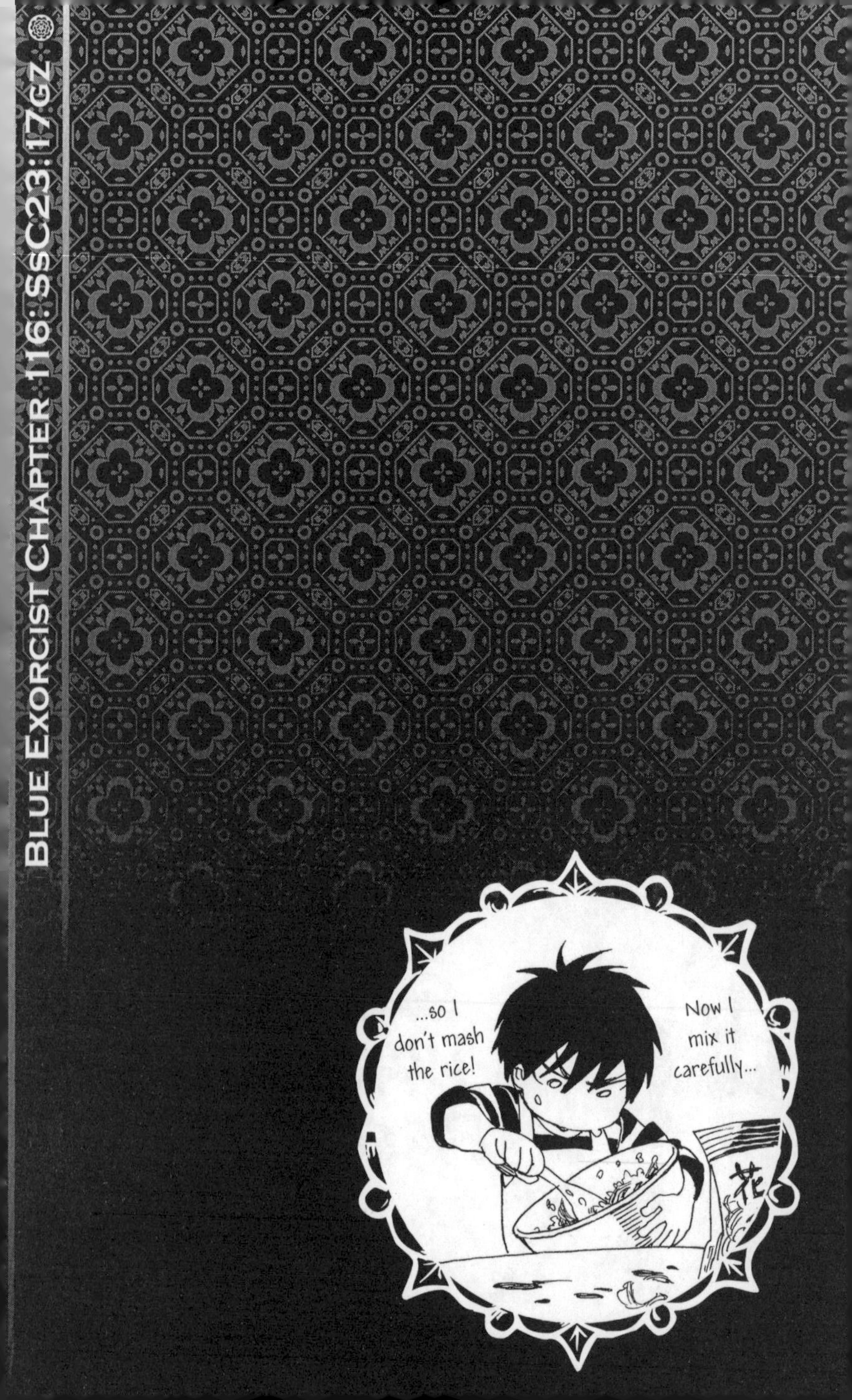
Now I mix it carefully...
...so I don't mash the rice!

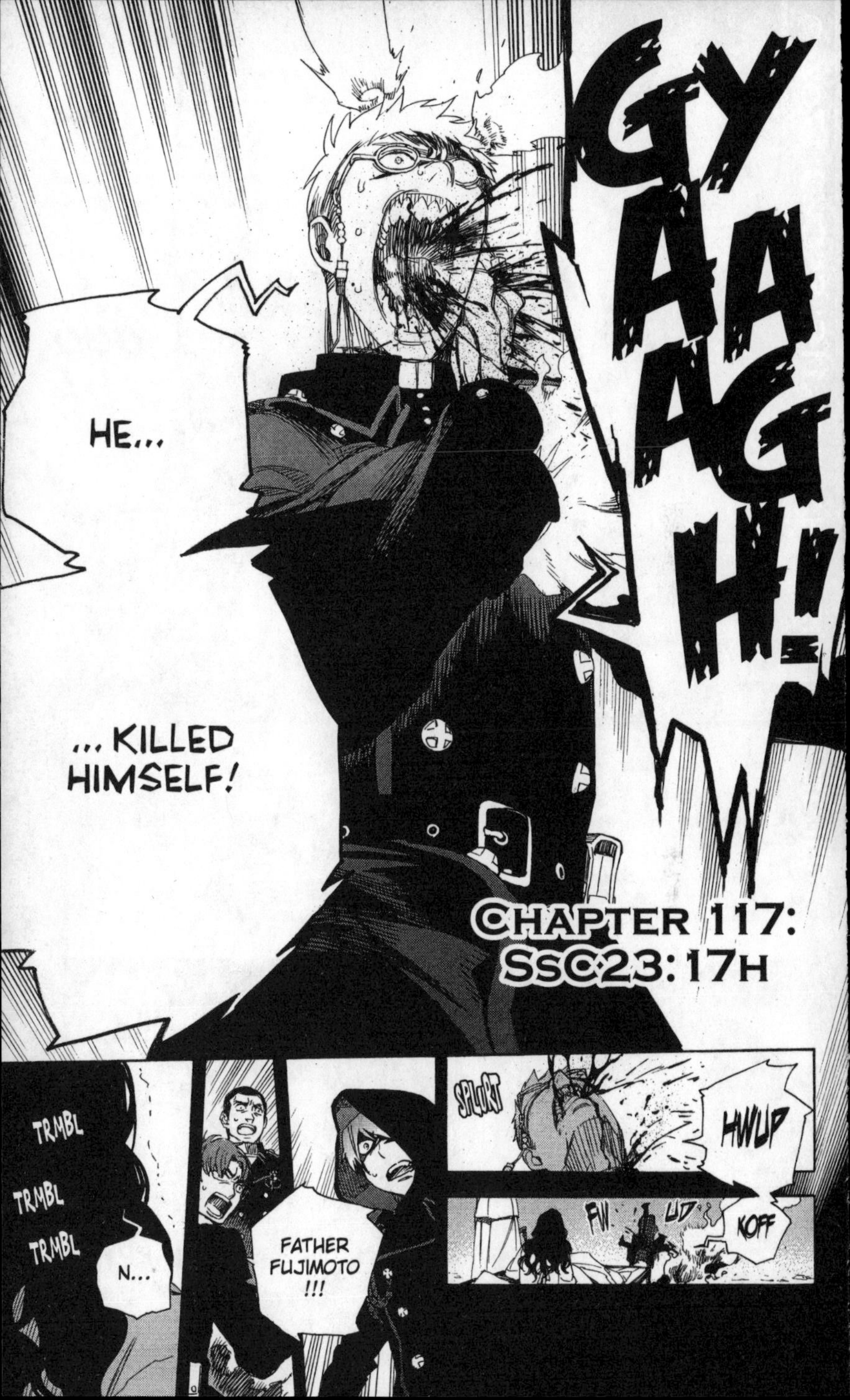
GYAAAGH!!
HE...
...KILLED HIMSELF!
CHAPTER 117: SsC23:17H
SPLURT
HWUP
FWUD
KOFF
FATHER FUJIMOTO!!!
TRMBL
TRMBL
TRMBL
N...

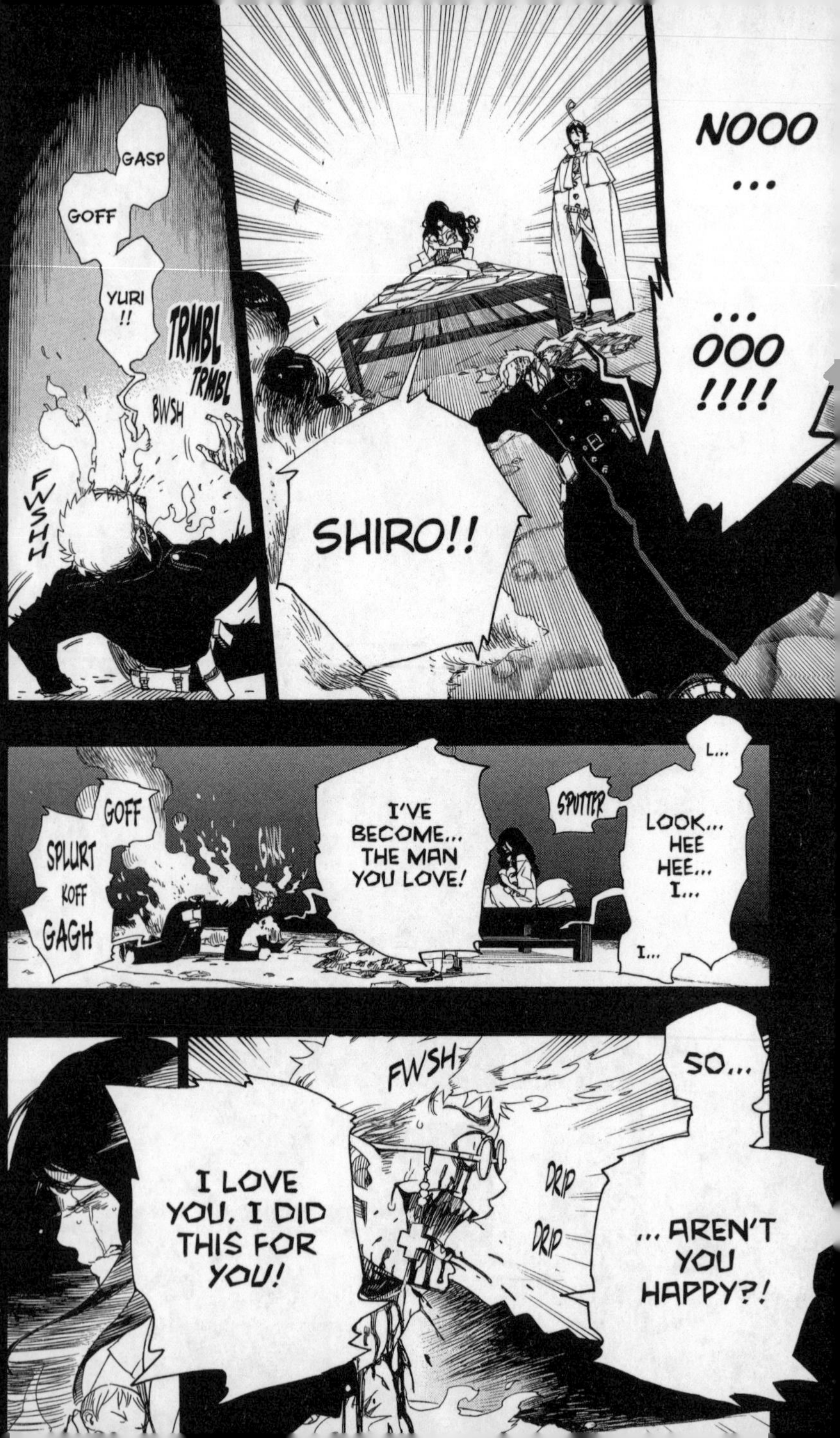
NOOO
...
...
ÖOO
!!!!
SHIRO!!
GASP
GOFF
YURI
!!
TRMBL
TRMBL
BWSH
FWSHH
L...
LOOK... HEE HEE... I...
I...
SPUTTER
I'VE BECOME... THE MAN YOU LOVE!
GOFF
SPLURT
KOFF
GAGH
SO...
... AREN'T YOU HAPPY?!
DRIP
DRIP
FWSH
I LOVE YOU. I DID THIS FOR YOU!

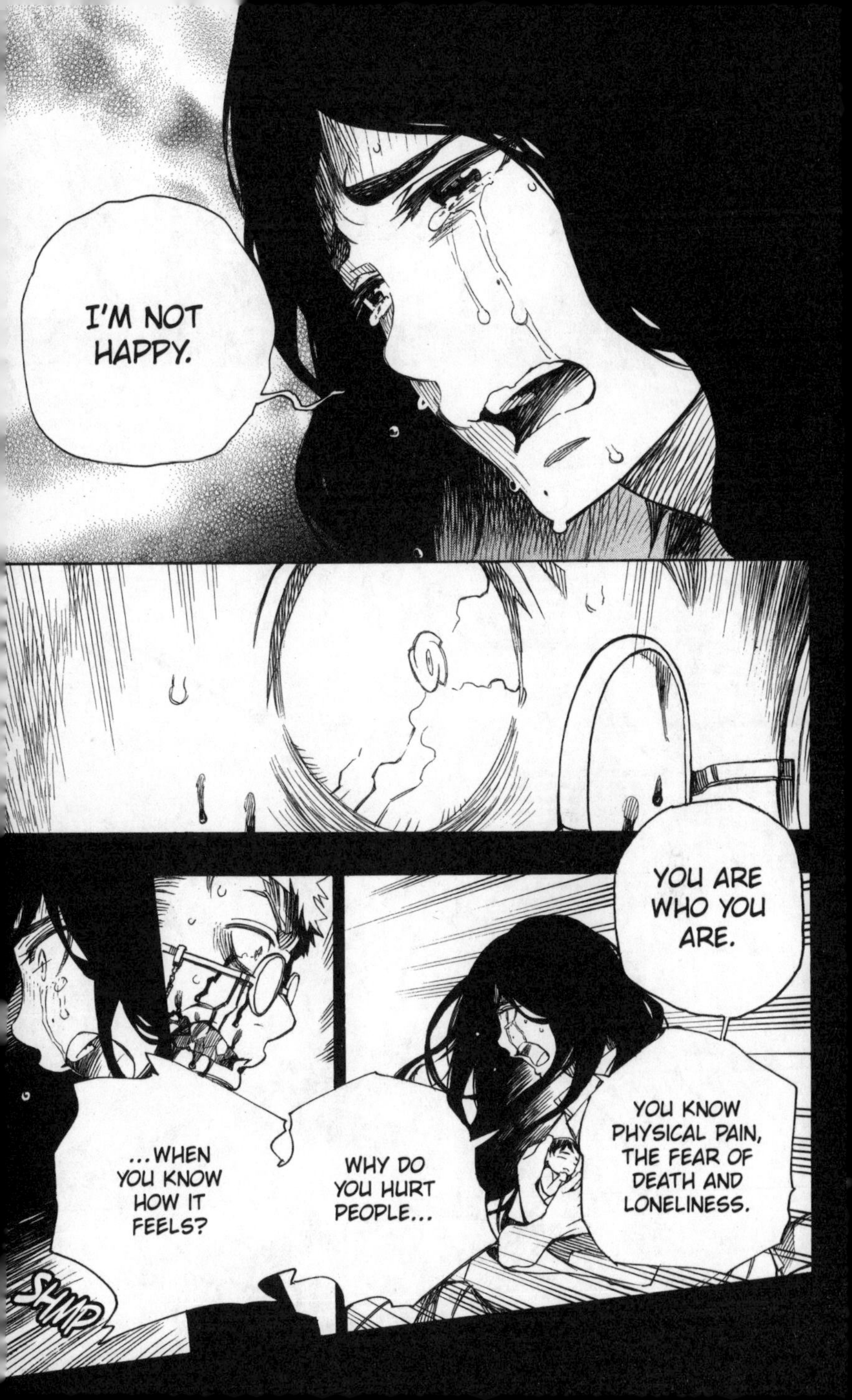
I'M NOT HAPPY.
YOU ARE WHO YOU ARE.
YOU KNOW PHYSICAL PAIN, THE FEAR OF DEATH AND LONELINESS.
WHY DO YOU HURT PEOPLE...
...WHEN YOU KNOW HOW IT FEELS?

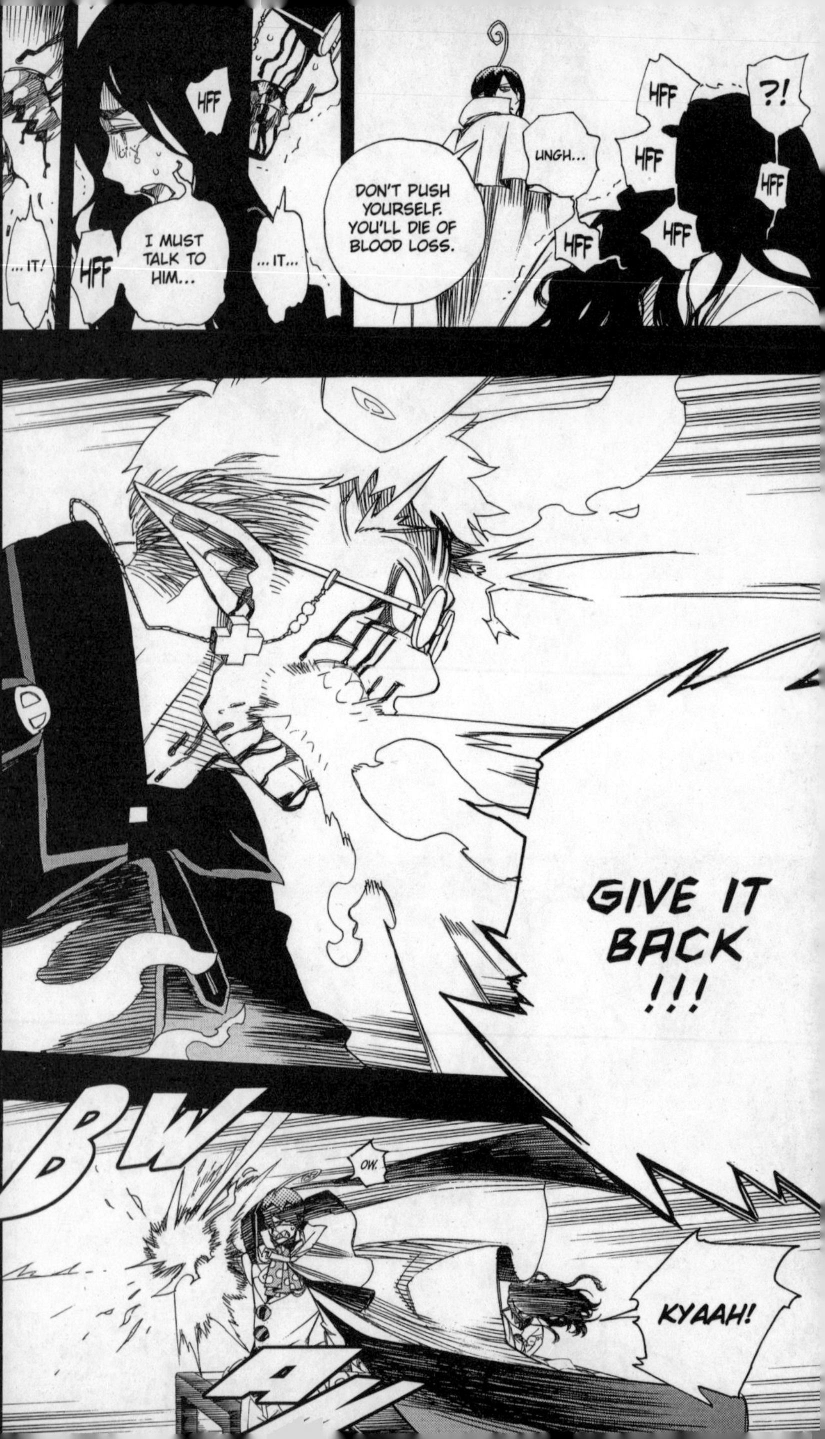
?!
HFF
HFF
HFF
HFF
UNGH...
HFF
DON'T PUSH YOURSELF. YOU'LL DIE OF BLOOD LOSS.
...IT...
HFF
I MUST TALK TO HIM...
HFF
...IT!
GIVE IT BACK !!!
KYAAH!
OW.
BWA

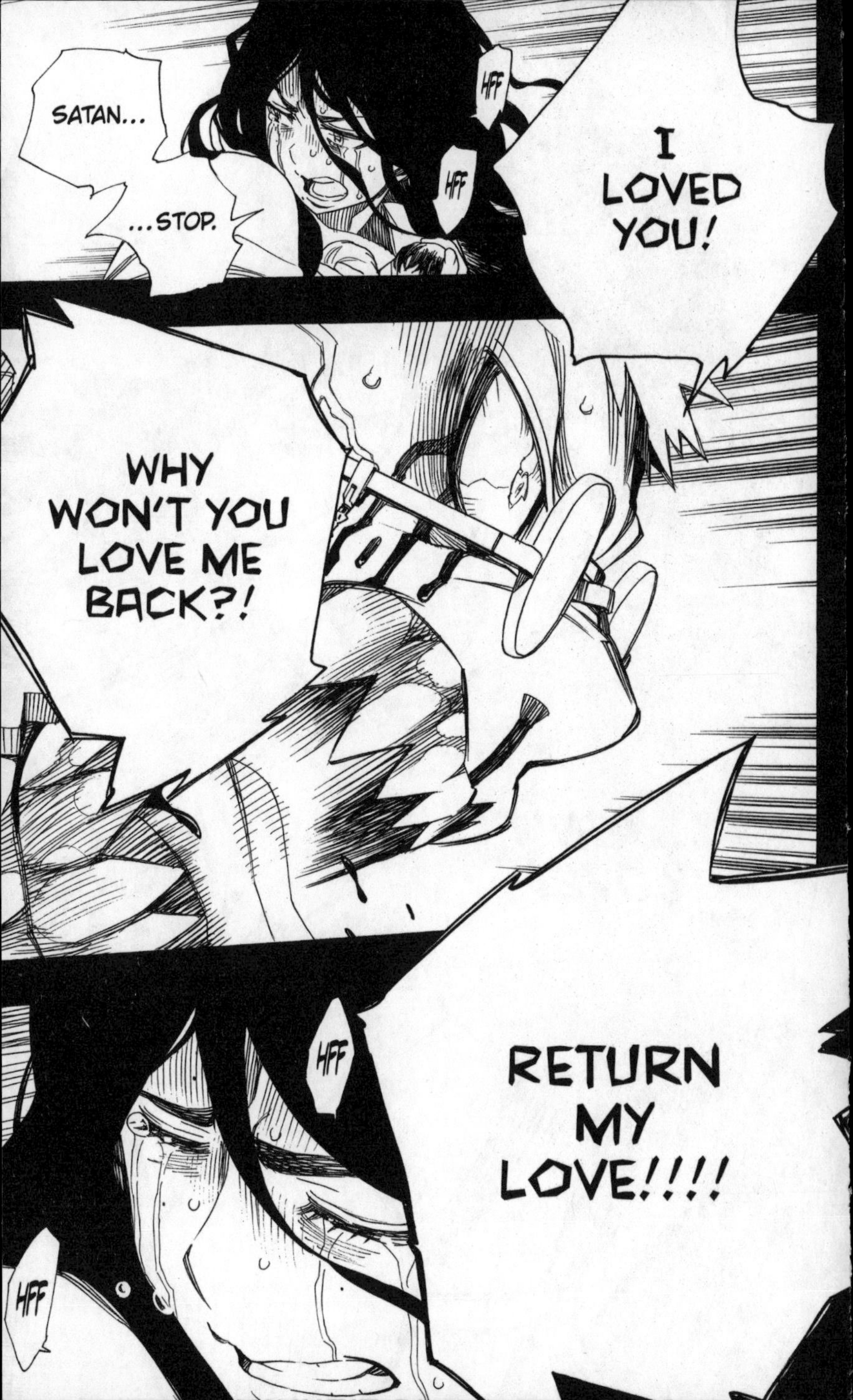
HFF
HFF
SATAN...
...STOP.
I LOVED YOU!
WHY WON'T YOU LOVE ME BACK?!
RETURN MY LOVE!!!!
HFF
HFF

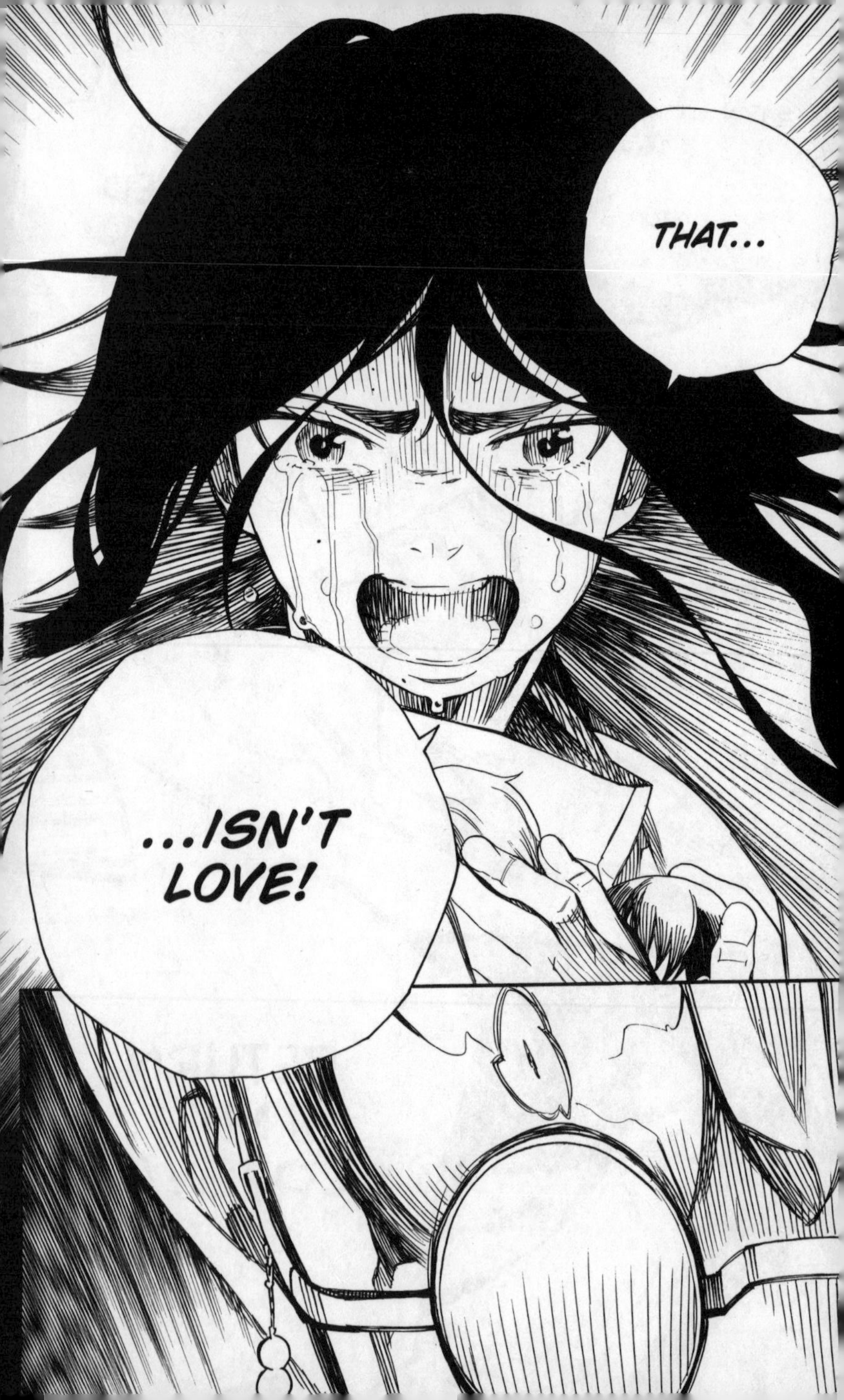
THAT...
...ISN'T LOVE!

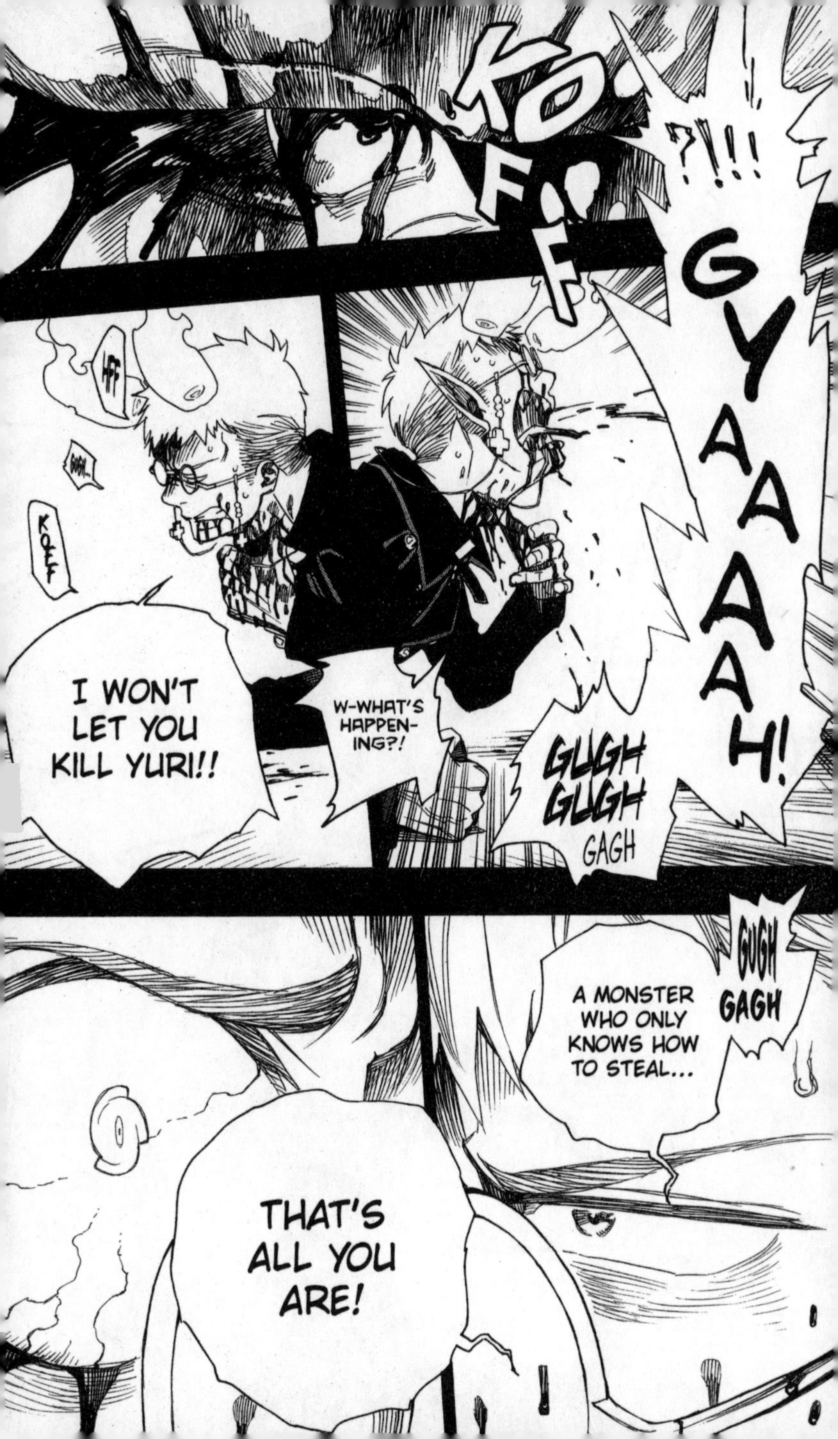
?!!!
GYAAAAH!
KOFF
W-WHAT'S HAPPEN-ING?!
GUGH GUGH GAGH
HFF
GUGH...
KOFF
I WON'T LET YOU KILL YURI!!
GUGH GAGH
A MONSTER WHO ONLY KNOWS HOW TO STEAL...
THAT'S ALL YOU ARE!

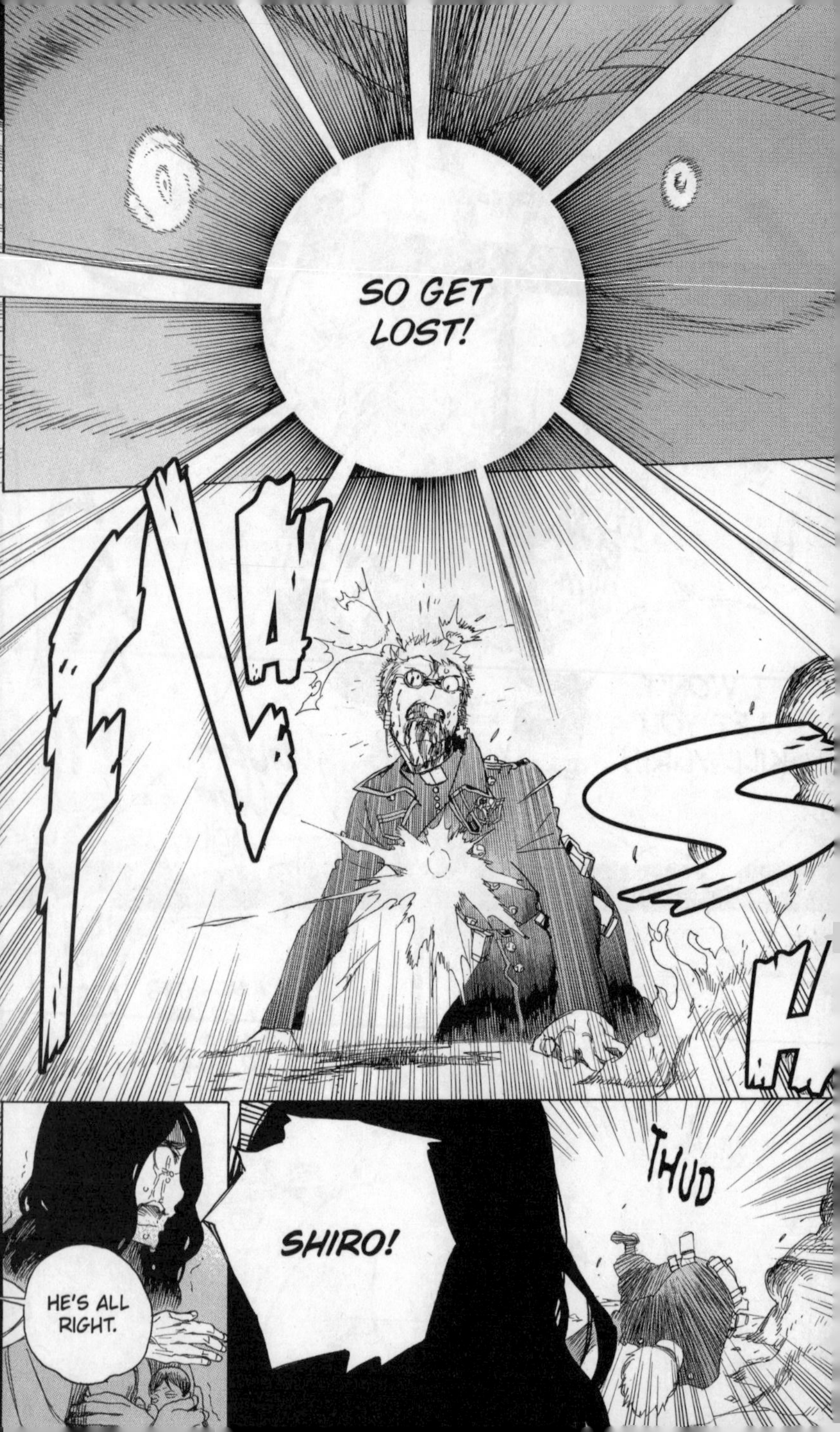
SO GET LOST!
THUD
SHIRO!
HE'S ALL RIGHT.

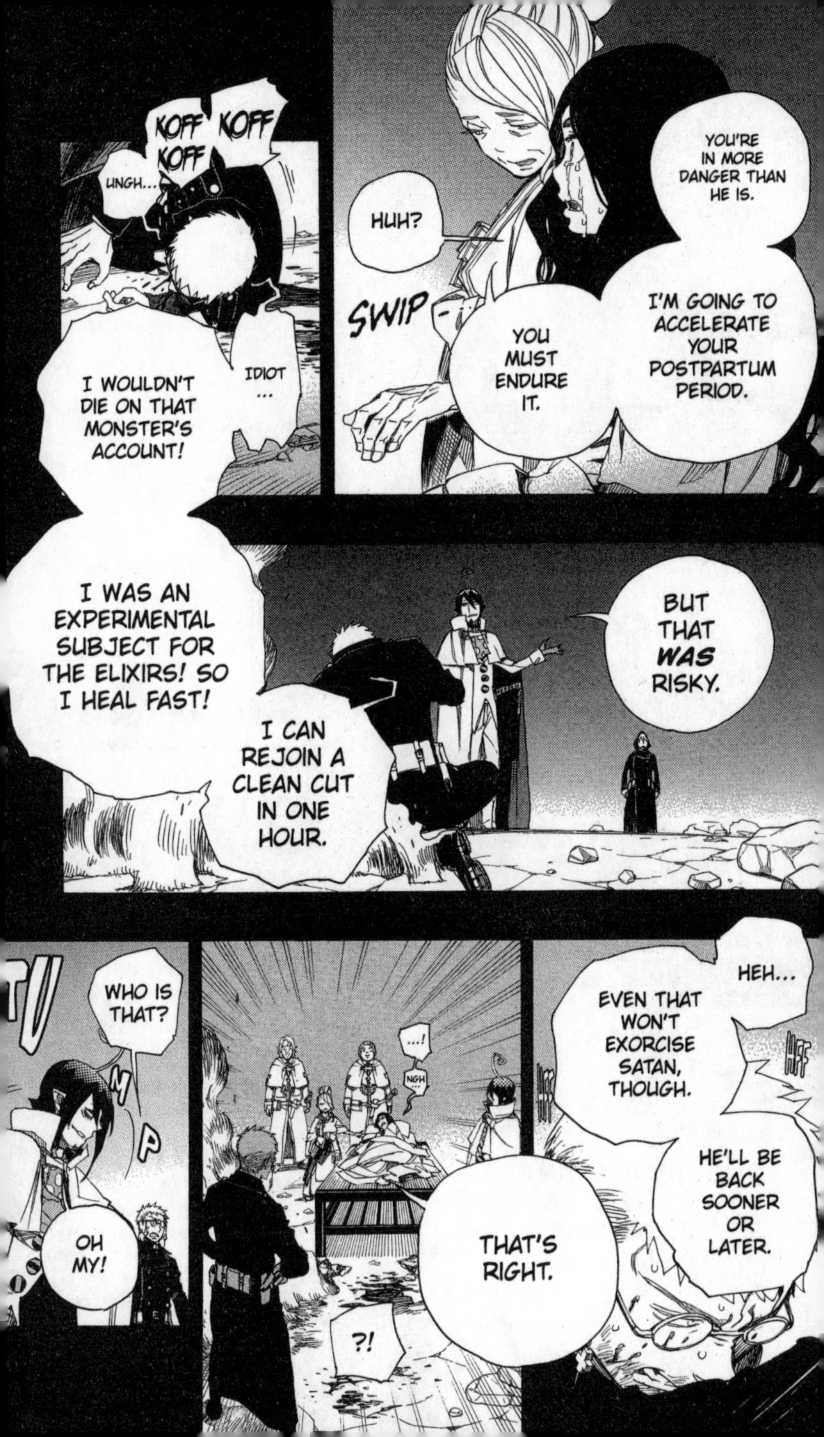
YOU'RE IN MORE DANGER THAN HE IS.
HUH?
SWIP
I'M GOING TO ACCELERATE YOUR POSTPARTUM PERIOD.
YOU MUST ENDURE IT.
KOFF KOFF
KOFF
UNGH...
IDIOT...
I WOULDN'T DIE ON THAT MONSTER'S ACCOUNT!
BUT THAT *WAS* RISKY.
I WAS AN EXPERIMENTAL SUBJECT FOR THE ELIXIRS! SO I HEAL FAST!
I CAN REJOIN A CLEAN CUT IN ONE HOUR.
HEH...
EVEN THAT WON'T EXORCISE SATAN, THOUGH.
HFF
HE'LL BE BACK SOONER OR LATER.
THAT'S RIGHT.
...!
NGH...
?!
TUMP
WHO IS THAT?
OH MY!

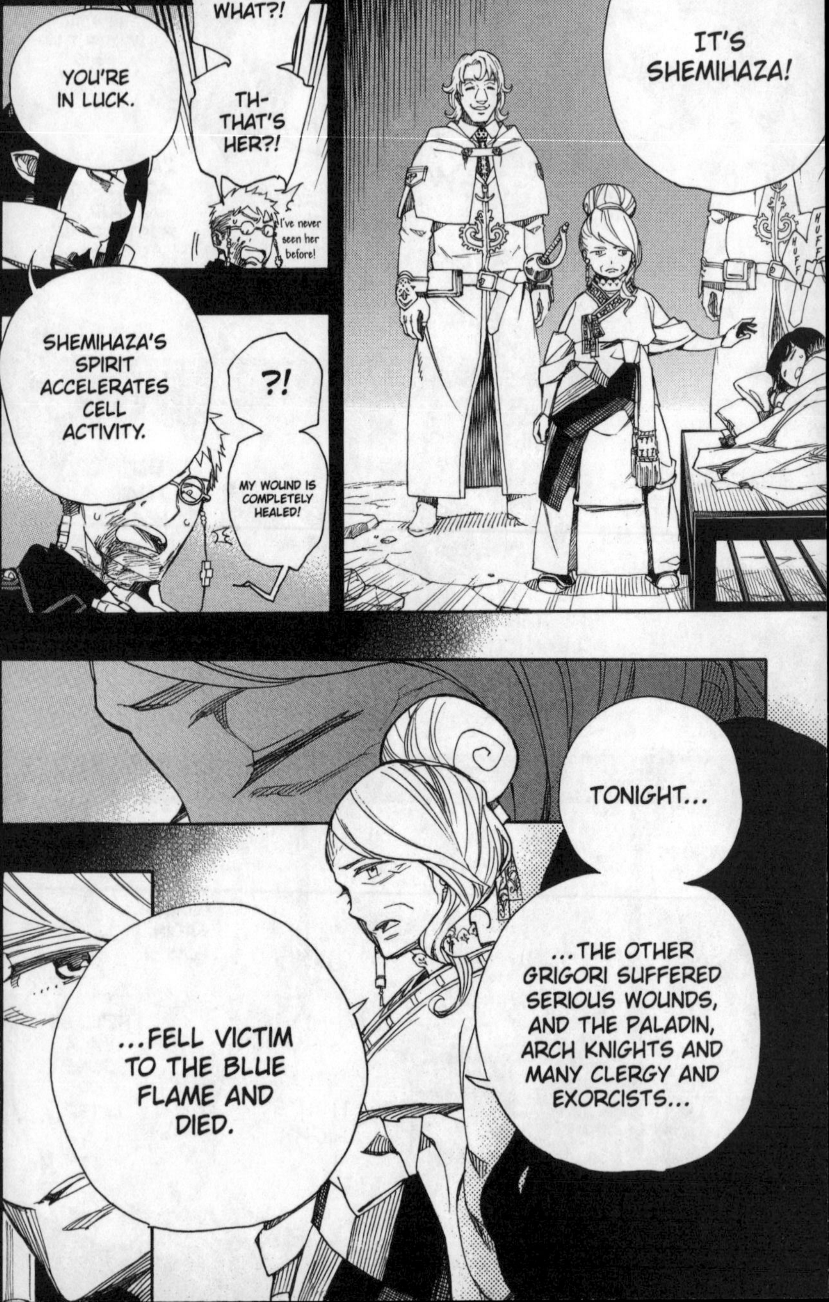
IT'S SHEMIHAZA!
WHAT?!
TH-THAT'S HER?!
I've never seen her before!
YOU'RE IN LUCK.
?!
MY WOUND IS COMPLETELY HEALED!
SHEMIHAZA'S SPIRIT ACCELERATES CELL ACTIVITY.
HUFF HUFF
TONIGHT...
...THE OTHER GRIGORI SUFFERED SERIOUS WOUNDS, AND THE PALADIN, ARCH KNIGHTS AND MANY CLERGY AND EXORCISTS...
...FELL VICTIM TO THE BLUE FLAME AND DIED.

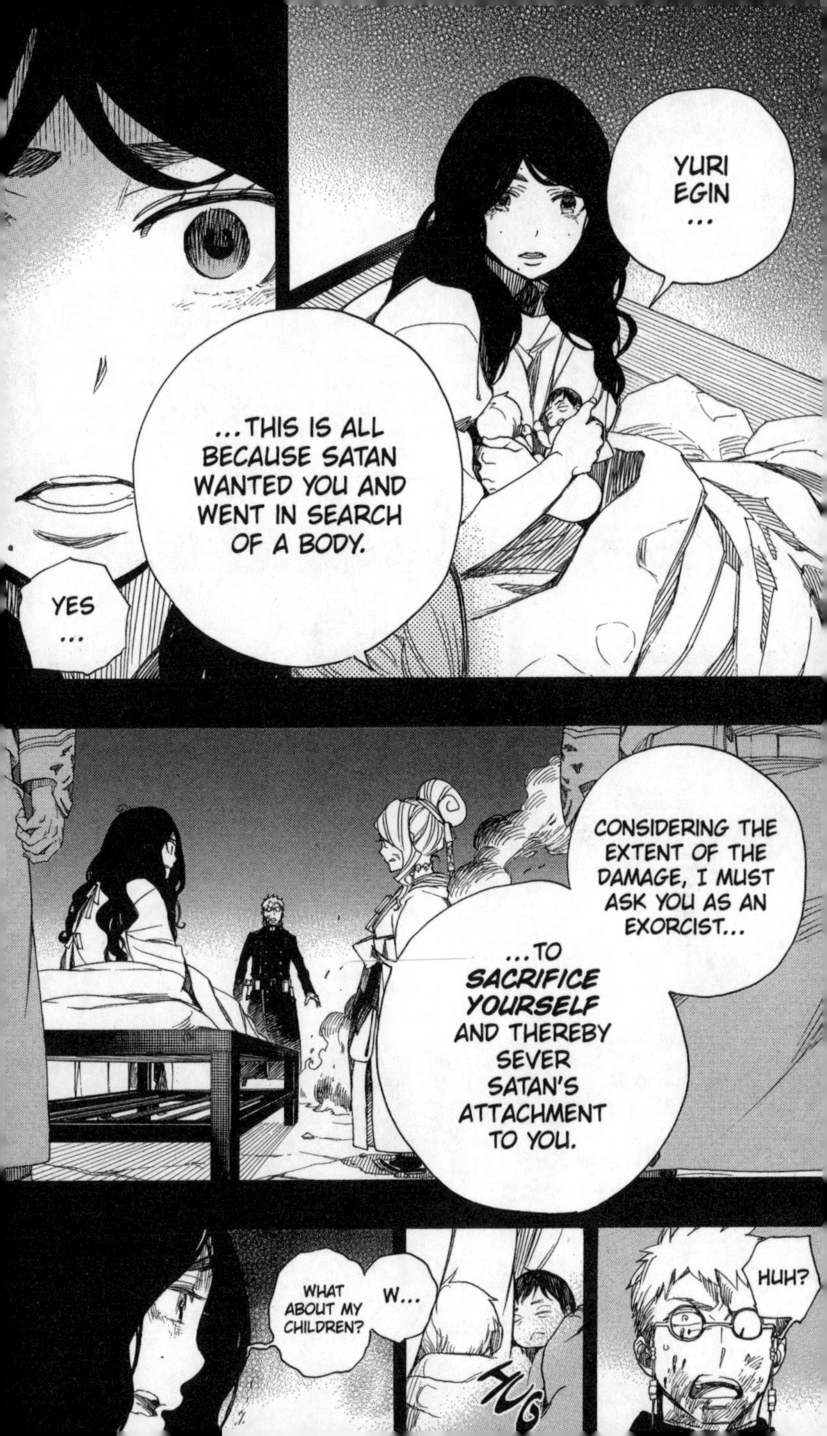
YURI EGIN ...
...THIS IS ALL BECAUSE SATAN WANTED YOU AND WENT IN SEARCH OF A BODY.
YES ...
CONSIDERING THE EXTENT OF THE DAMAGE, I MUST ASK YOU AS AN EXORCIST...
...TO ***SACRIFICE YOURSELF*** AND THEREBY SEVER SATAN'S ATTACHMENT TO YOU.
HUH?
HUG
W...
WHAT ABOUT MY CHILDREN?

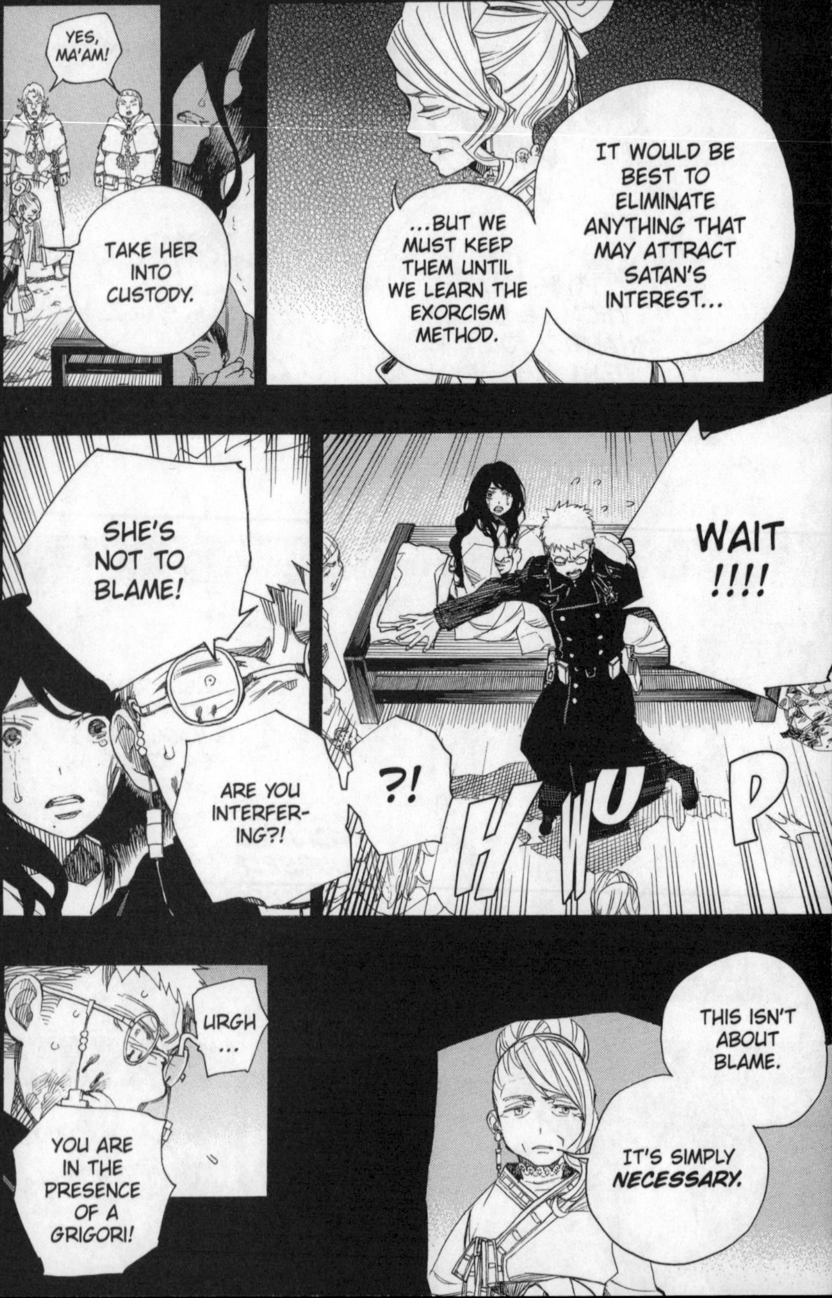
IT WOULD BE BEST TO ELIMINATE ANYTHING THAT MAY ATTRACT SATAN'S INTEREST...
...BUT WE MUST KEEP THEM UNTIL WE LEARN THE EXORCISM METHOD.
TAKE HER INTO CUSTODY.
YES, MA'AM!
WAIT !!!!
HWUMP
?!
ARE YOU INTERFER-ING?!
SHE'S NOT TO BLAME!
THIS ISN'T ABOUT BLAME.
IT'S SIMPLY *NECESSARY.*
URGH ...
YOU ARE IN THE PRESENCE OF A GRIGORI!

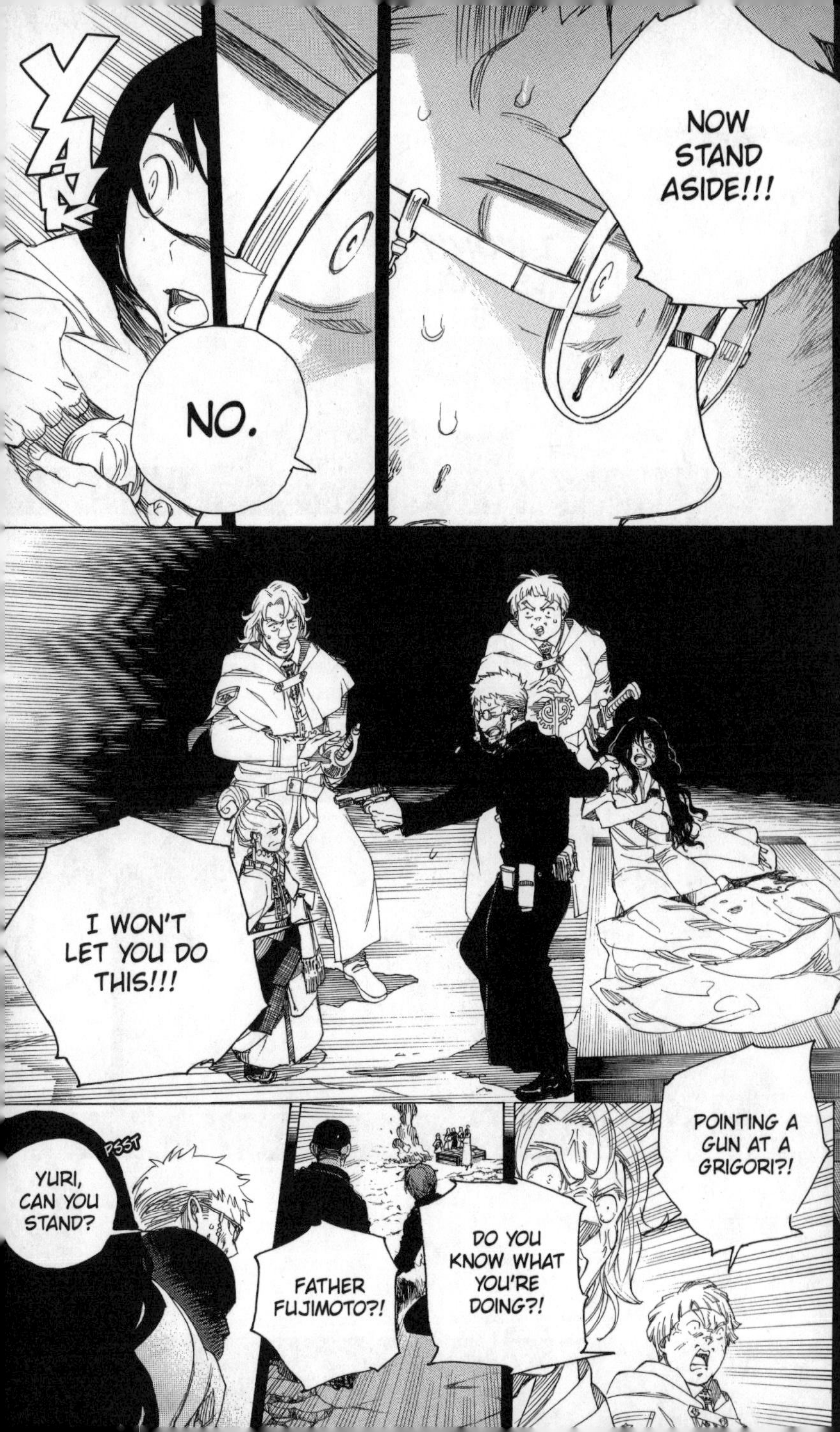
NOW STAND ASIDE!!!
YANK
NO.
I WON'T LET YOU DO THIS!!!
POINTING A GUN AT A GRIGORI?!
DO YOU KNOW WHAT YOU'RE DOING?!
FATHER FUJIMOTO?!
PSST
YURI, CAN YOU STAND?

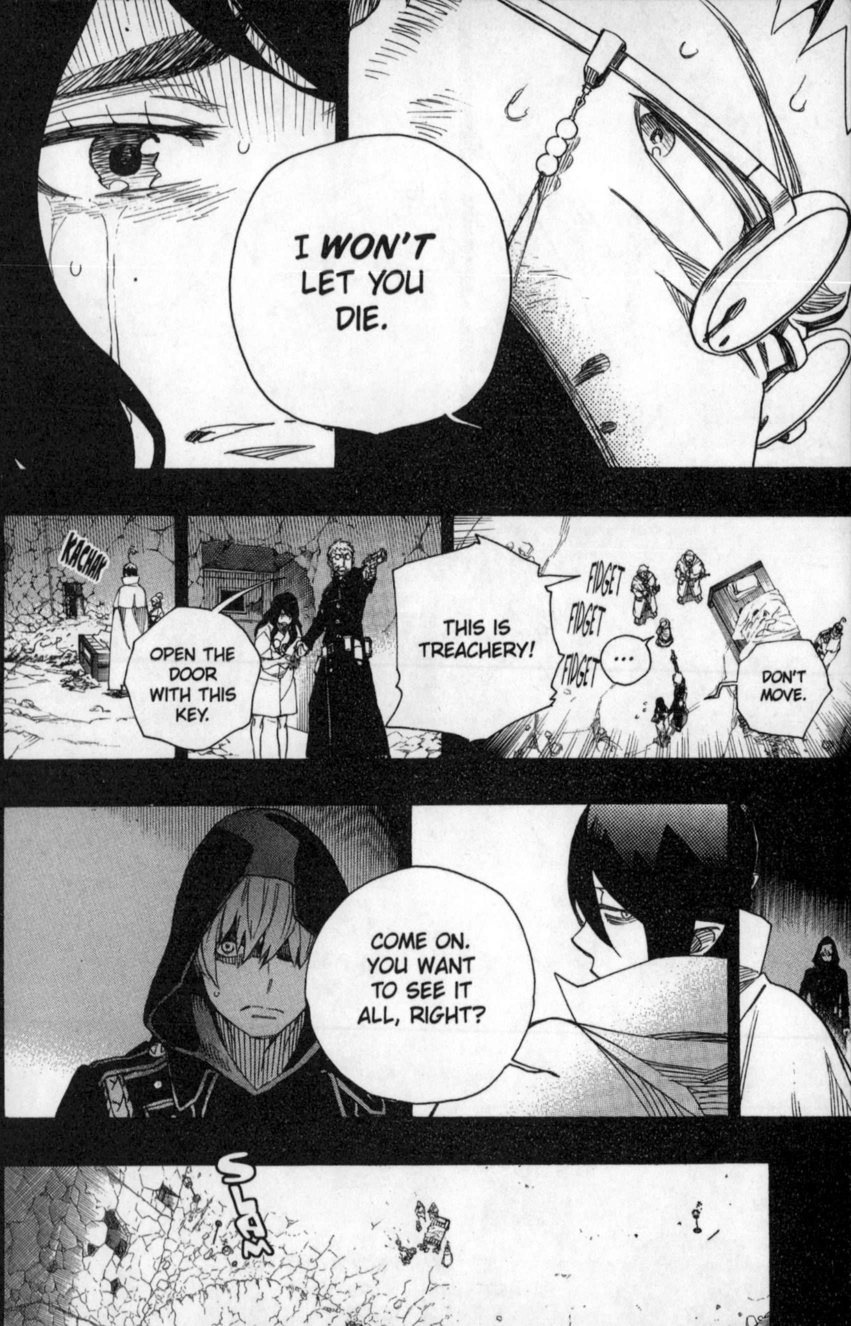
I WON'T LET YOU DIE.
DON'T MOVE.
...
FIDGET FIDGET FIDGET
THIS IS TREACHERY!
OPEN THE DOOR WITH THIS KEY.
KACHAK
COME ON. YOU WANT TO SEE IT ALL, RIGHT?
SLAM

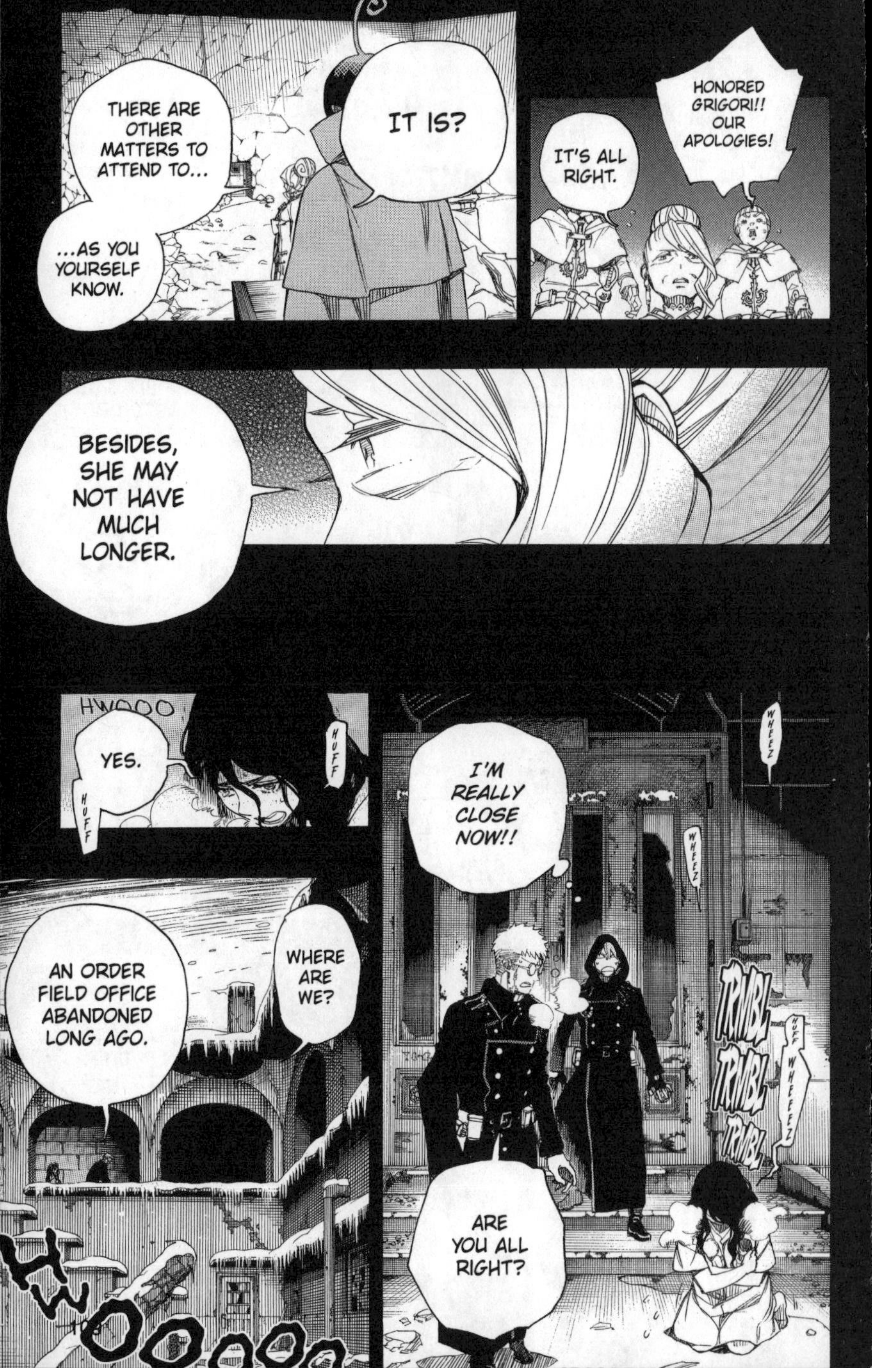
HONORED GRIGORI!! OUR APOLOGIES!
IT'S ALL RIGHT.
IT IS?
THERE ARE OTHER MATTERS TO ATTEND TO...
...AS YOU YOURSELF KNOW.
BESIDES, SHE MAY NOT HAVE MUCH LONGER.
WHEEZ
I'M REALLY CLOSE NOW!!
WHEEZ
TRMBL TRMBL TRMBL
HUFF WHEEEZ
ARE YOU ALL RIGHT?
HWOOO
HUFF
YES.
HUFF
WHERE ARE WE?
AN ORDER FIELD OFFICE ABANDONED LONG AGO.
HWOOOOO

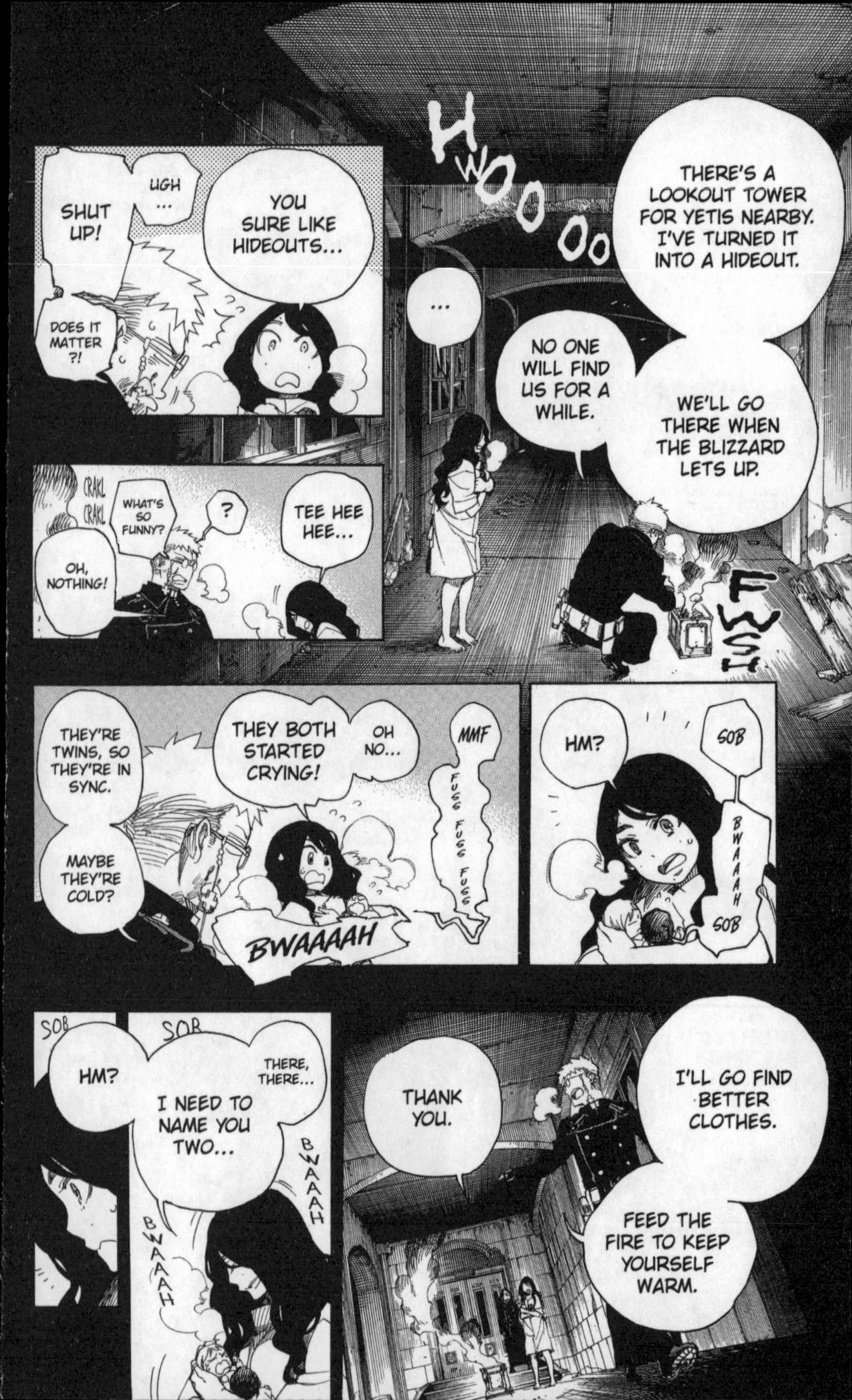
HWOOOO
THERE'S A LOOKOUT TOWER FOR YETIS NEARBY. I'VE TURNED IT INTO A HIDEOUT.
...
NO ONE WILL FIND US FOR A WHILE.
WE'LL GO THERE WHEN THE BLIZZARD LETS UP.
FWSH
YOU SURE LIKE HIDEOUTS...
UGH...
SHUT UP!
DOES IT MATTER?!
TEE HEE HEE...
?
WHAT'S SO FUNNY?
CRAKL CRAKL
OH, NOTHING!
SOB
HM?
BWAAAAH
SOB
MMF
FUSS FUSS FUSS
OH NO...
THEY BOTH STARTED CRYING!
THEY'RE TWINS, SO THEY'RE IN SYNC.
MAYBE THEY'RE COLD?
BWAAAAH
I'LL GO FIND BETTER CLOTHES.
FEED THE FIRE TO KEEP YOURSELF WARM.
THANK YOU.
SOB
THERE, THERE...
HM?
I NEED TO NAME YOU TWO...
BWAAAAH
BWAAAAH
SOB

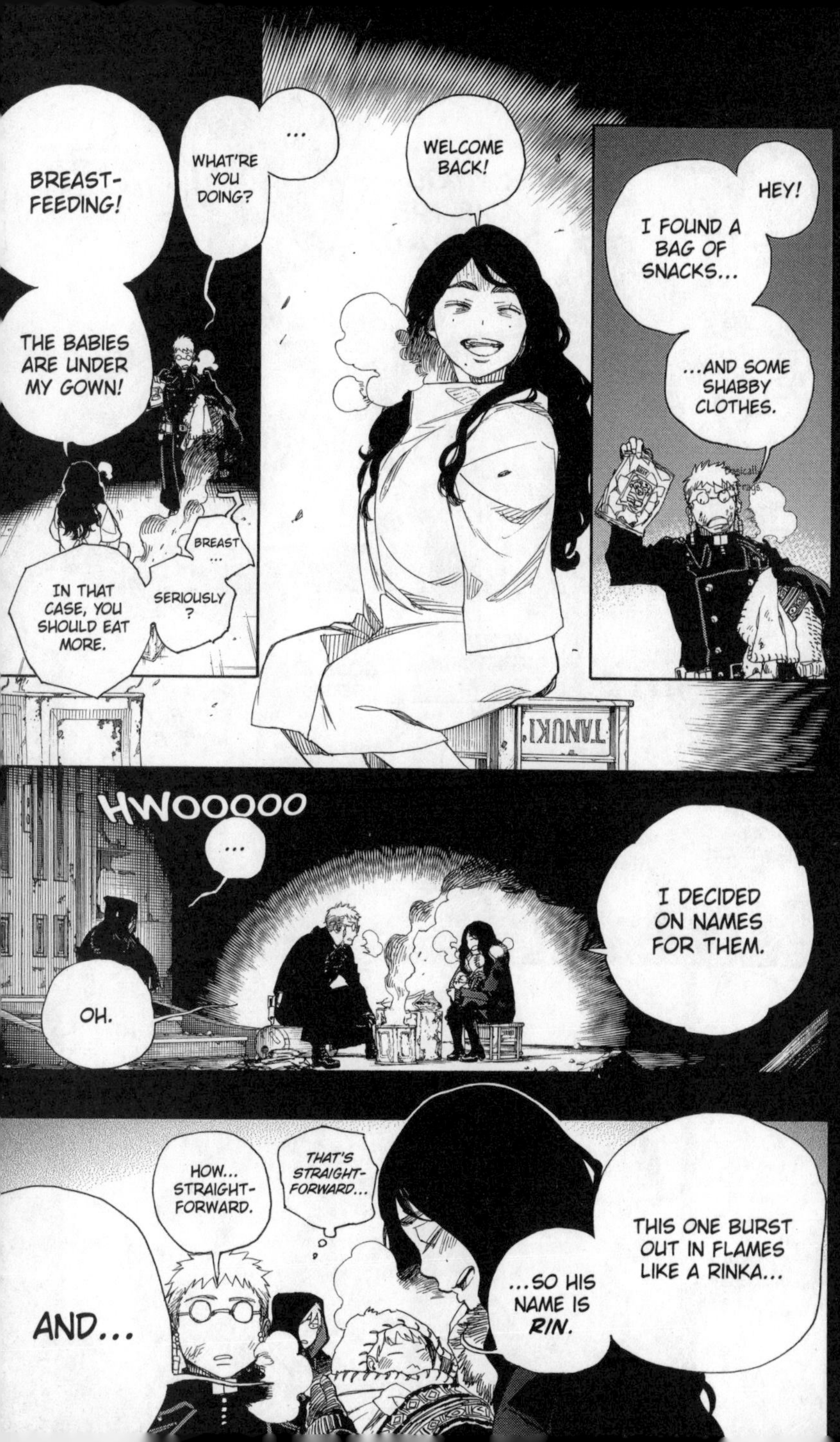
HEY!
I FOUND A BAG OF SNACKS...
...AND SOME SHABBY CLOTHES.
WELCOME BACK!
...
WHAT'RE YOU DOING?
BREAST-FEEDING!
THE BABIES ARE UNDER MY GOWN!
BREAST...
SERIOUSLY?
IN THAT CASE, YOU SHOULD EAT MORE.
TANUKI
I DECIDED ON NAMES FOR THEM.
...
HWOOOOO
OH.
THIS ONE BURST OUT IN FLAMES LIKE A RINKA...
...SO HIS NAME IS *RIN*.
THAT'S STRAIGHT-FORWARD...
HOW... STRAIGHT-FORWARD.
AND...

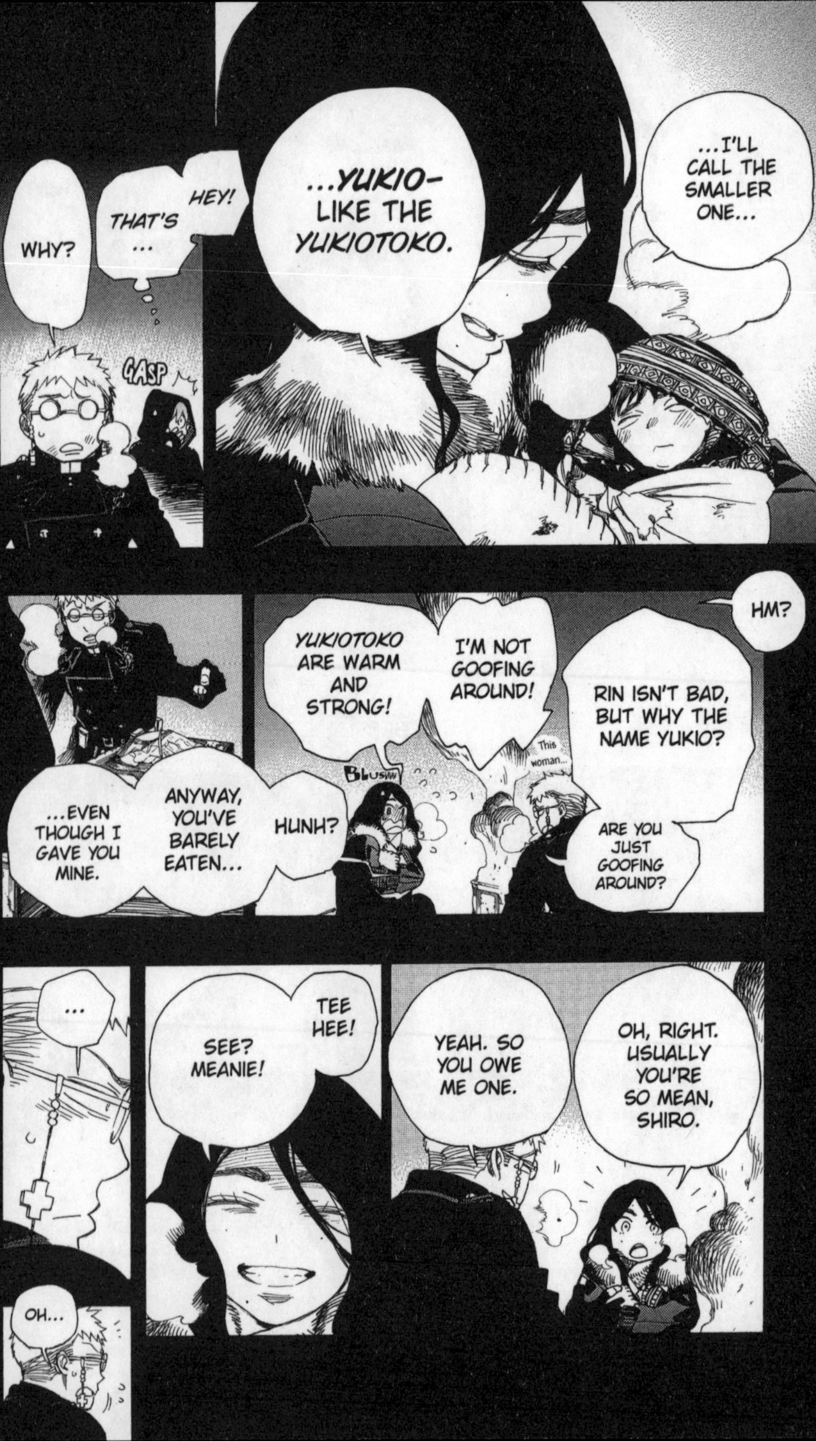
...I'LL CALL THE SMALLER ONE...
...YUKIO- LIKE THE YUKIOTOKO.
HEY!
THAT'S ...
WHY?
GASP
HM?
RIN ISN'T BAD, BUT WHY THE NAME YUKIO?
ARE YOU JUST GOOFING AROUND?
This woman...
I'M NOT GOOFING AROUND!
YUKIOTOKO ARE WARM AND STRONG!
BLUSH
HUNH?
ANYWAY, YOU'VE BARELY EATEN...
...EVEN THOUGH I GAVE YOU MINE.
OH, RIGHT. USUALLY YOU'RE SO MEAN, SHIRO.
YEAH. SO YOU OWE ME ONE.
TEE HEE!
SEE? MEANIE!
...
OH...

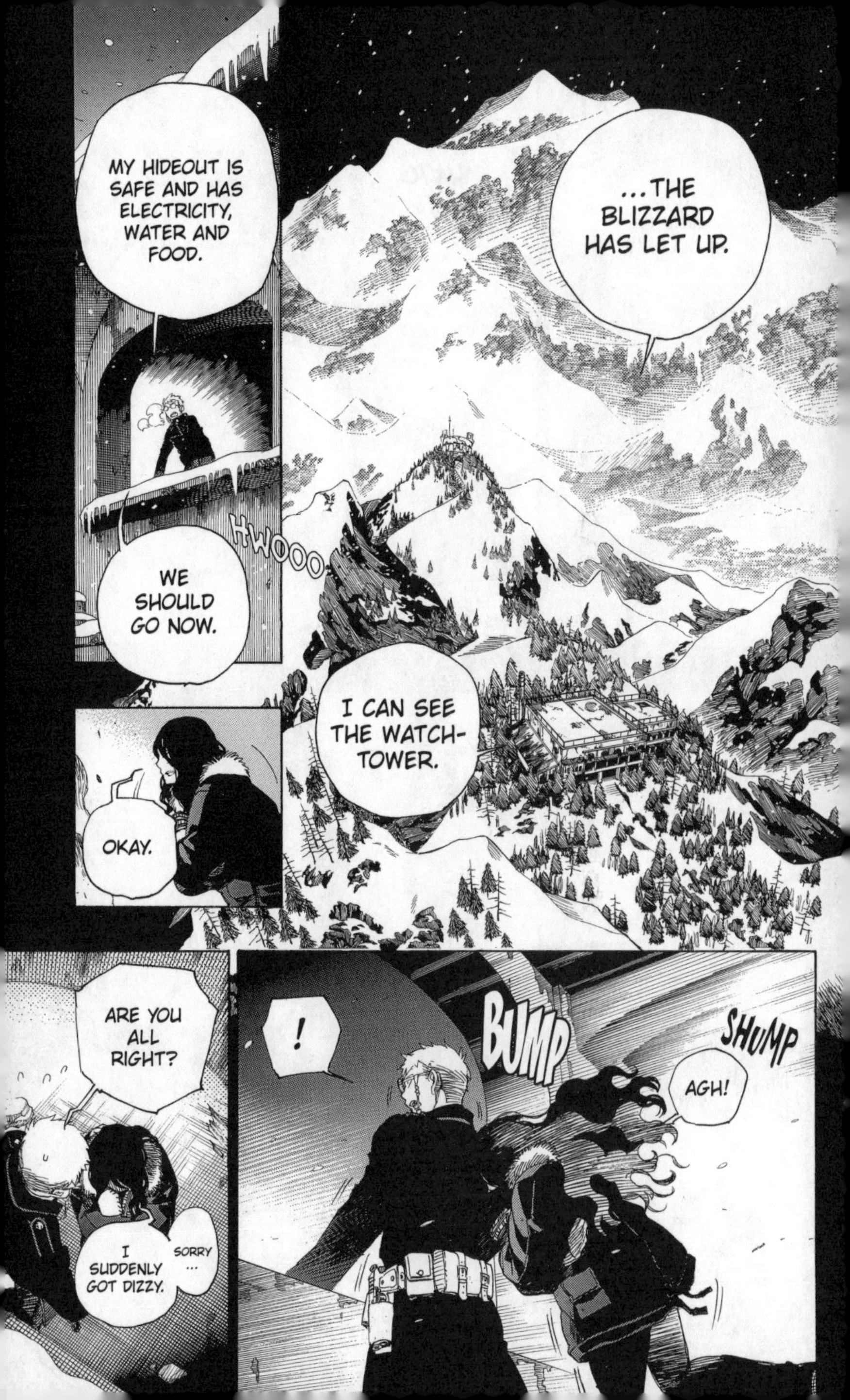
...THE BLIZZARD HAS LET UP.
I CAN SEE THE WATCH-TOWER.
MY HIDEOUT IS SAFE AND HAS ELECTRICITY, WATER AND FOOD.
HWOOO
WE SHOULD GO NOW.
OKAY.
SHUMP
AGH!
BUMP
!
ARE YOU ALL RIGHT?
SORRY...
I SUDDENLY GOT DIZZY.

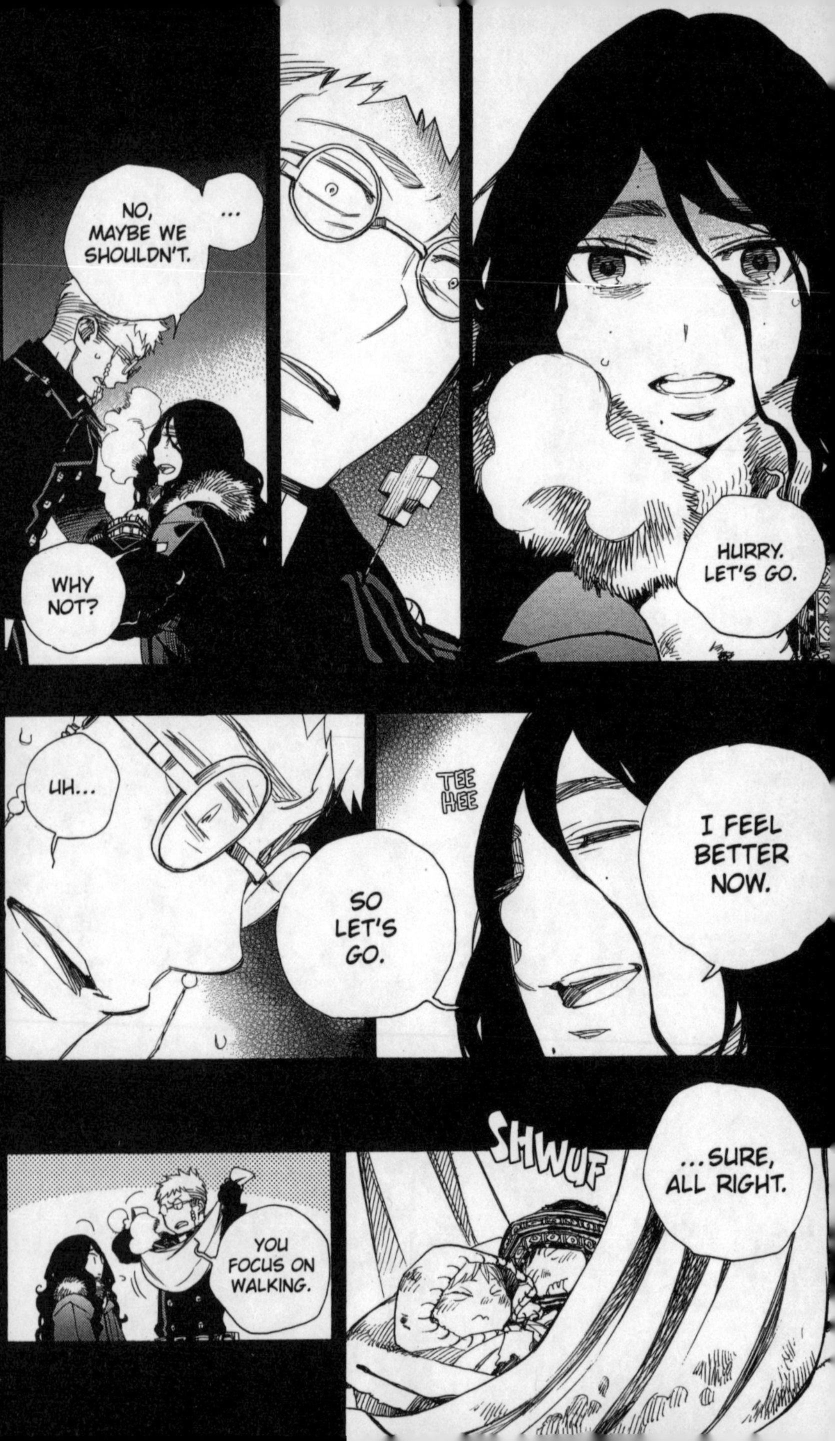
HURRY. LET'S GO.
...
NO, MAYBE WE SHOULDN'T.
WHY NOT?
TEE HEE
I FEEL BETTER NOW.
SO LET'S GO.
UH...
SHWUF
...SURE, ALL RIGHT.
YOU FOCUS ON WALKING.

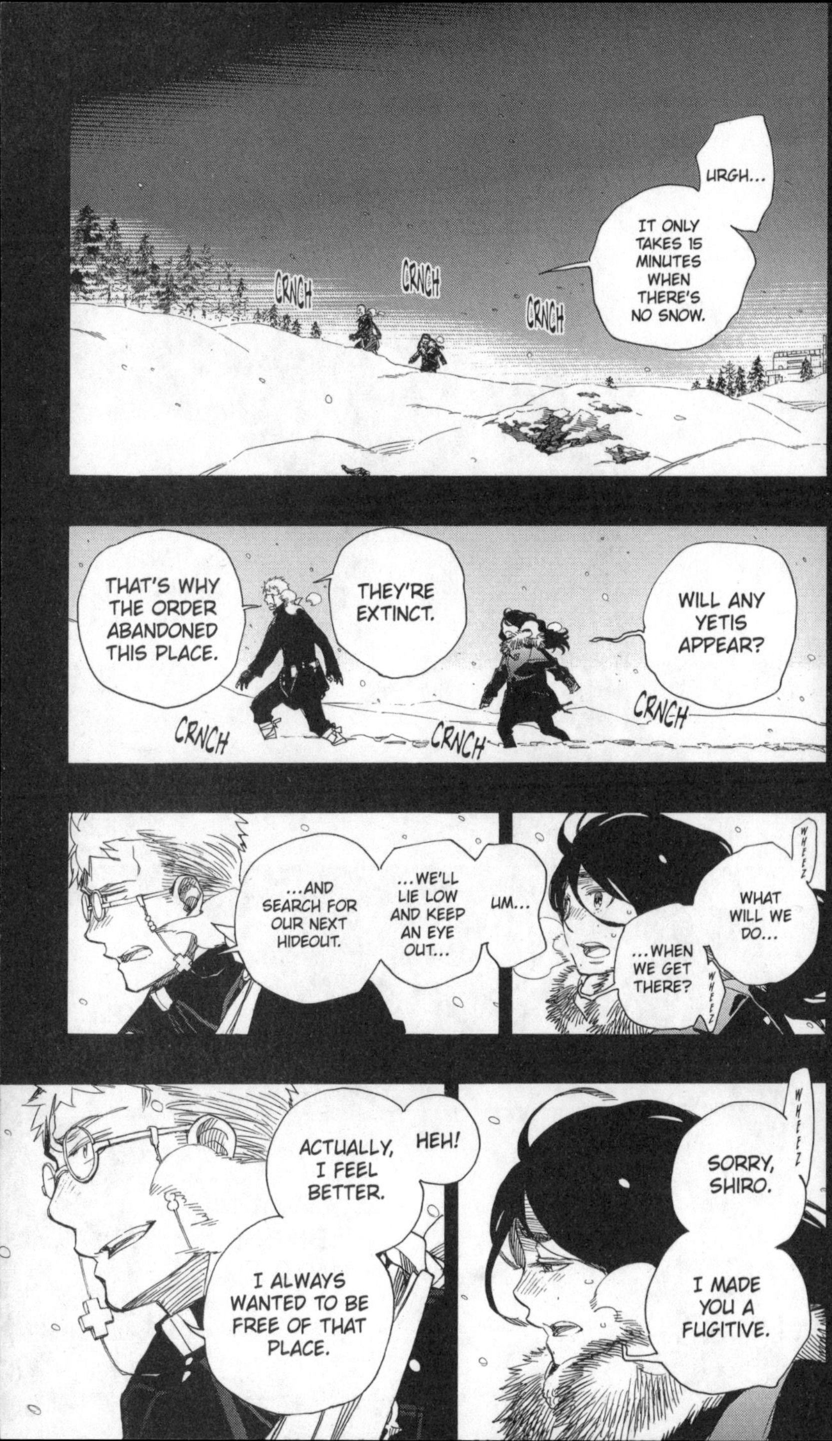
URGH...
IT ONLY TAKES 15 MINUTES WHEN THERE'S NO SNOW.
CRNCH
CRNCH
CRNCH
WILL ANY YETIS APPEAR?
CRNCH
THEY'RE EXTINCT.
CRNCH
THAT'S WHY THE ORDER ABANDONED THIS PLACE.
CRNCH
WHEEZ
WHAT WILL WE DO...
...WHEN WE GET THERE?
WHEEZ
UM...
...WE'LL LIE LOW AND KEEP AN EYE OUT...
...AND SEARCH FOR OUR NEXT HIDEOUT.
WHEEZ
SORRY, SHIRO.
I MADE YOU A FUGITIVE.
HEH!
ACTUALLY, I FEEL BETTER.
I ALWAYS WANTED TO BE FREE OF THAT PLACE.

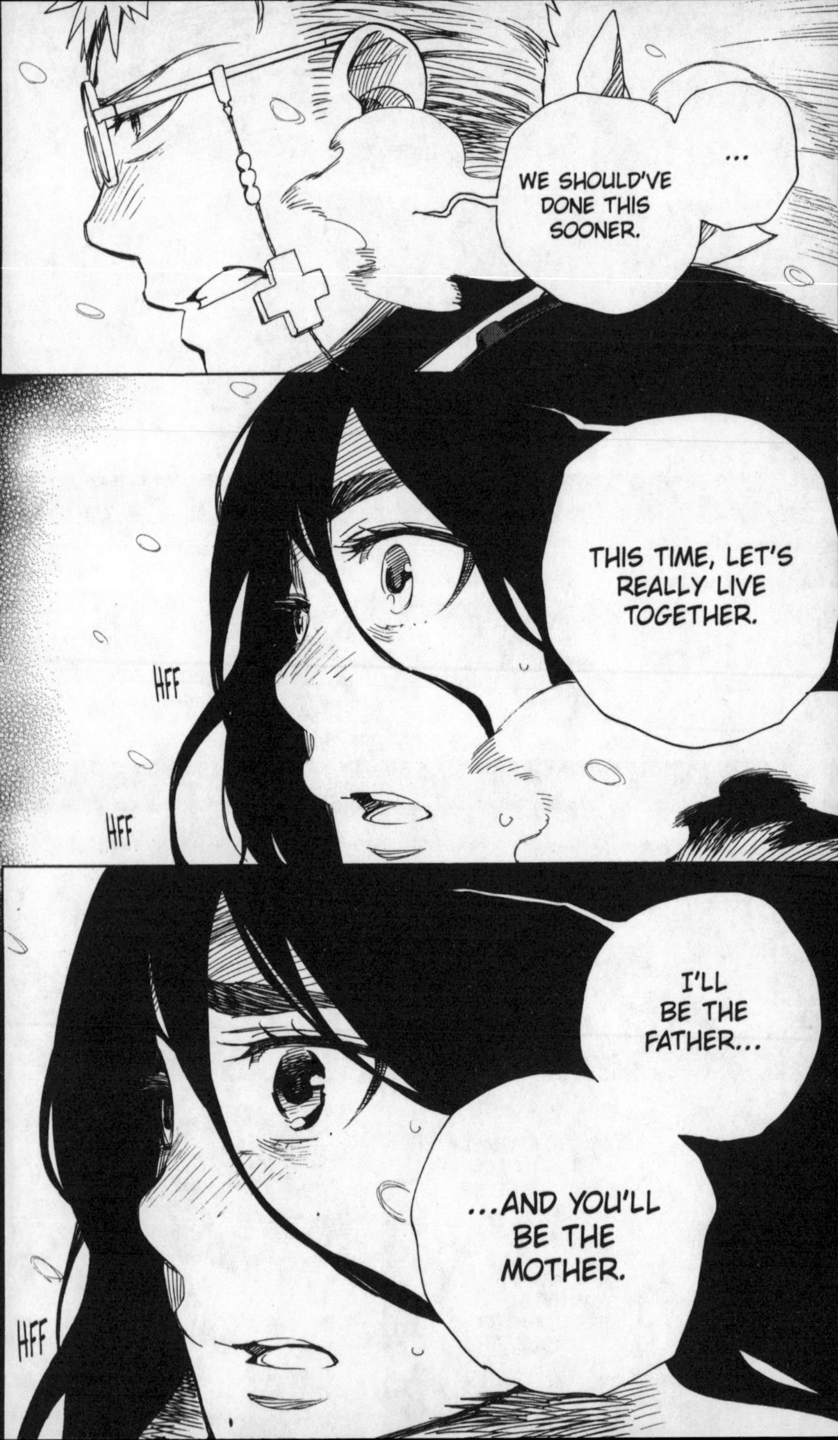
...
WE SHOULD'VE DONE THIS SOONER.
THIS TIME, LET'S REALLY LIVE TOGETHER.
HFF
HFF
I'LL BE THE FATHER...
...AND YOU'LL BE THE MOTHER.
HFF

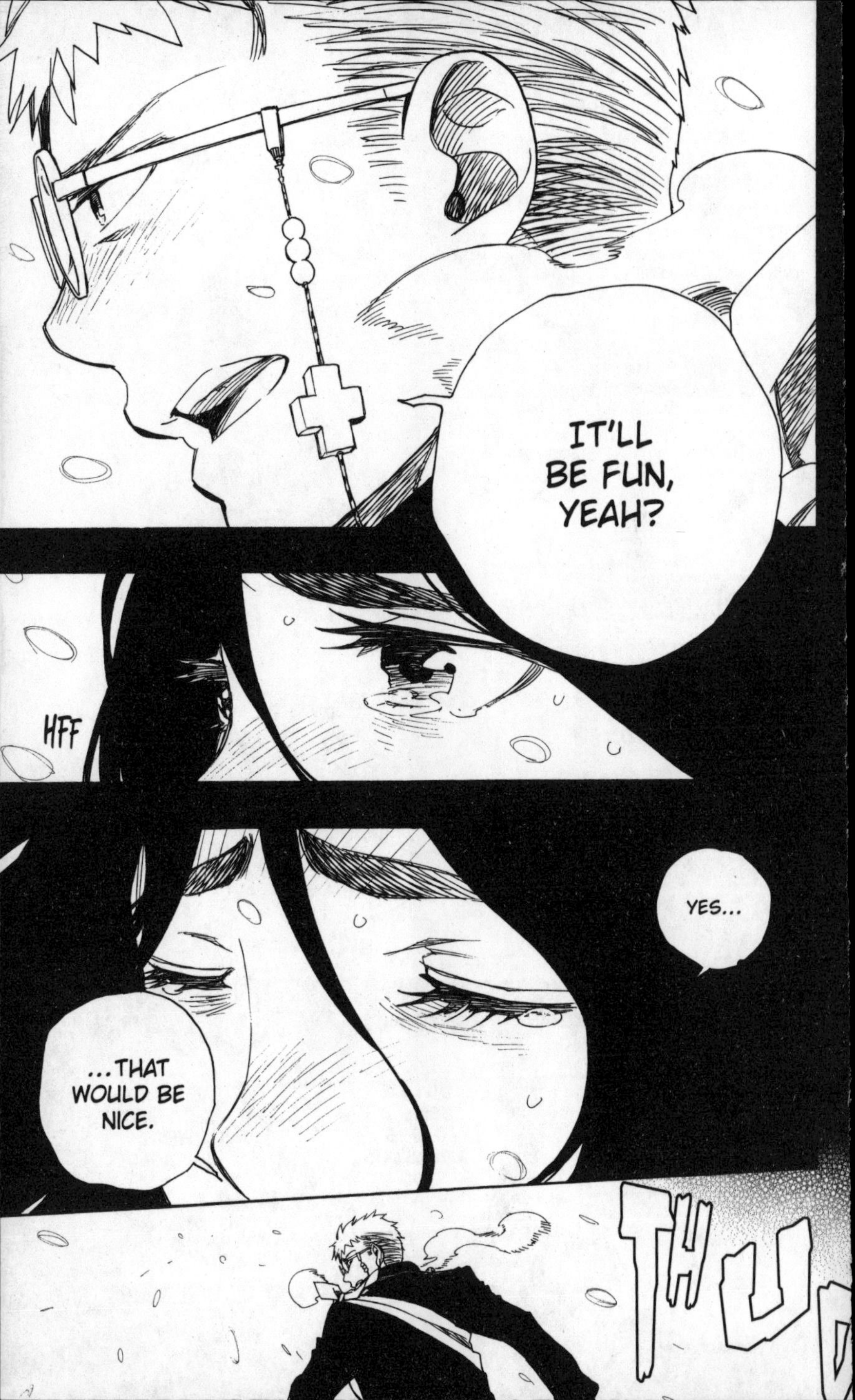
IT'LL BE FUN, YEAH?
HFF
YES...
...THAT WOULD BE NICE.
THU

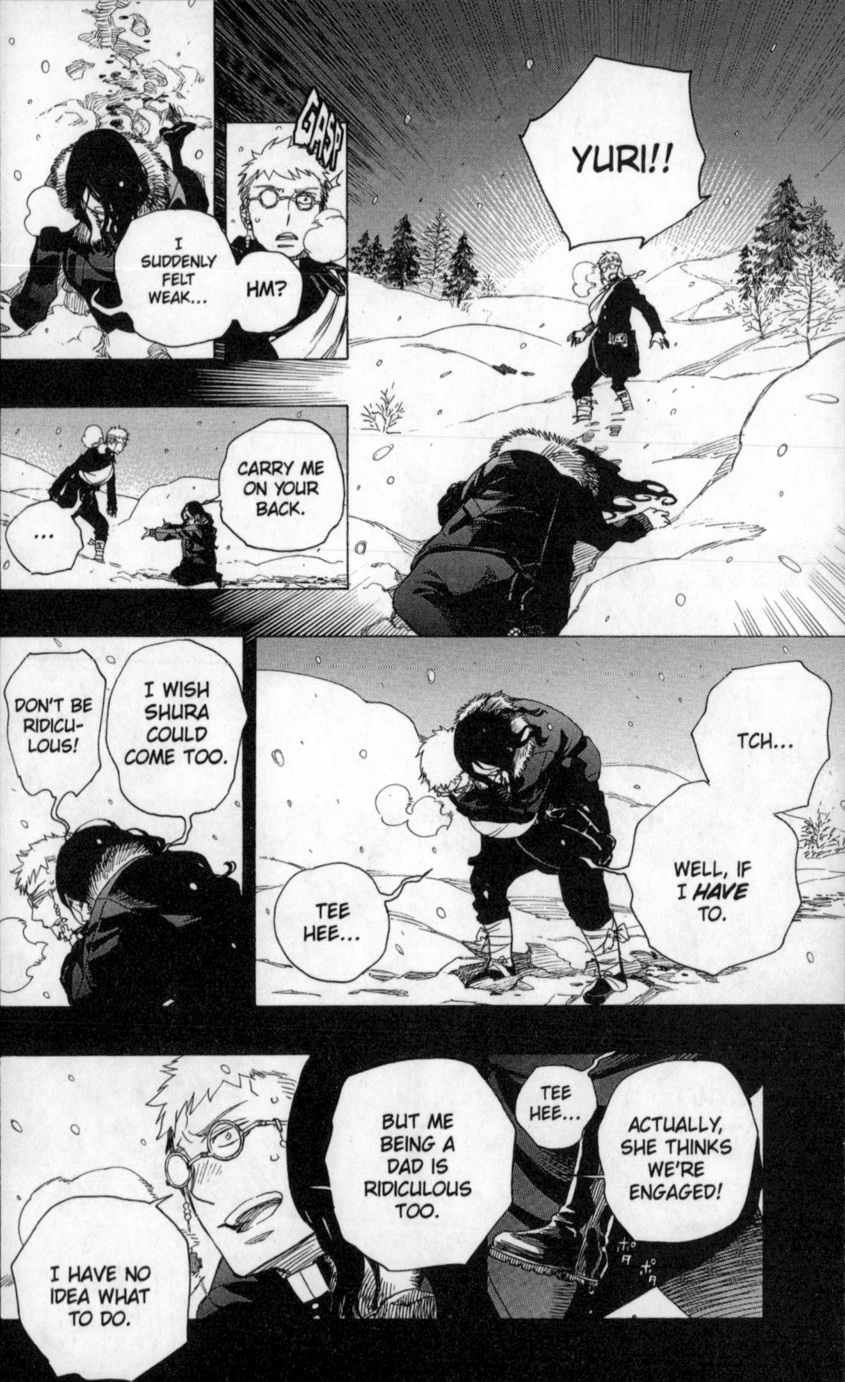
YURI!!
GASP
HM?
I SUDDENLY FELT WEAK...
CARRY ME ON YOUR BACK.
...
TCH...
WELL, IF I *HAVE* TO.
TEE HEE...
I WISH SHURA COULD COME TOO.
DON'T BE RIDICULOUS!
ACTUALLY, SHE THINKS WE'RE ENGAGED!
TEE HEE...
ポタ ポタ
BUT ME BEING A DAD IS RIDICULOUS TOO.
I HAVE NO IDEA WHAT TO DO.

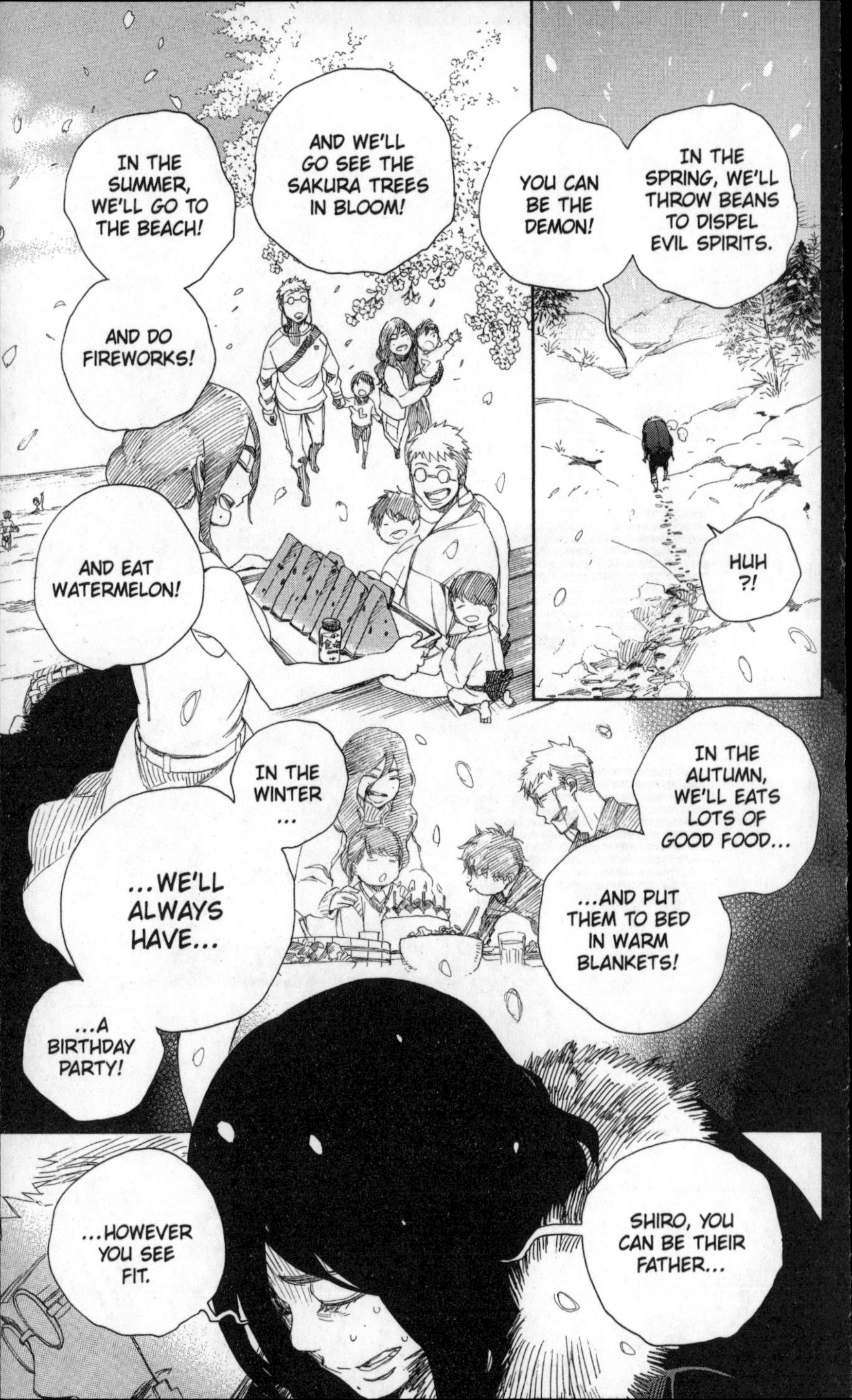
IN THE SPRING, WE'LL THROW BEANS TO DISPEL EVIL SPIRITS.
YOU CAN BE THE DEMON!
HUH ?!
AND WE'LL GO SEE THE SAKURA TREES IN BLOOM!
IN THE SUMMER, WE'LL GO TO THE BEACH!
AND DO FIREWORKS!
AND EAT WATERMELON!
IN THE AUTUMN, WE'LL EATS LOTS OF GOOD FOOD...
...AND PUT THEM TO BED IN WARM BLANKETS!
IN THE WINTER ...
...WE'LL ALWAYS HAVE...
...A BIRTHDAY PARTY!
SHIRO, YOU CAN BE THEIR FATHER...
...HOWEVER YOU SEE FIT.

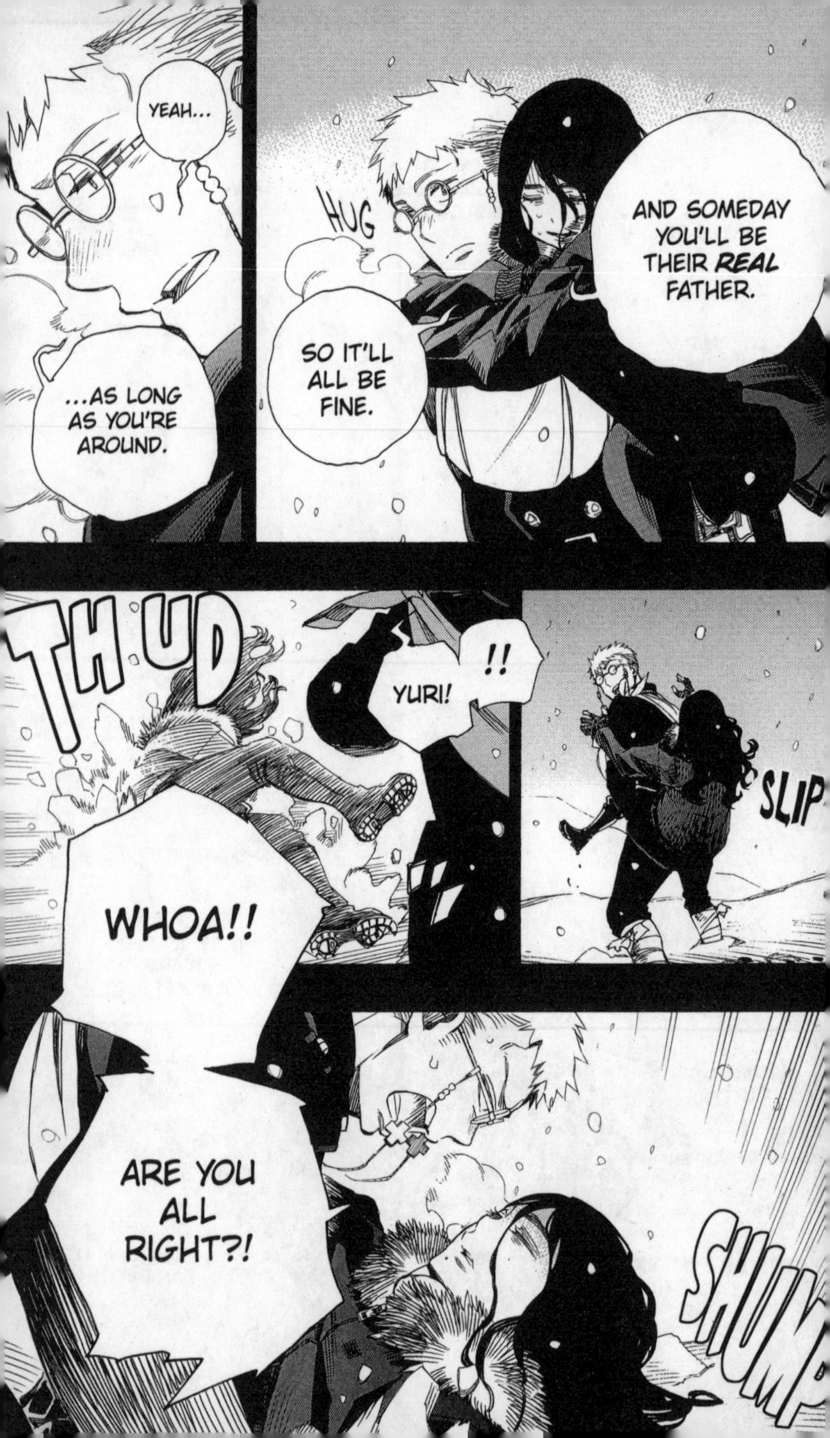
AND SOMEDAY YOU'LL BE THEIR REAL FATHER.
HUG
SO IT'LL ALL BE FINE.
YEAH...
...AS LONG AS YOU'RE AROUND.
SLIP
!!
YURI!
THUD
WHOA!!
SHUMP
ARE YOU ALL RIGHT?!

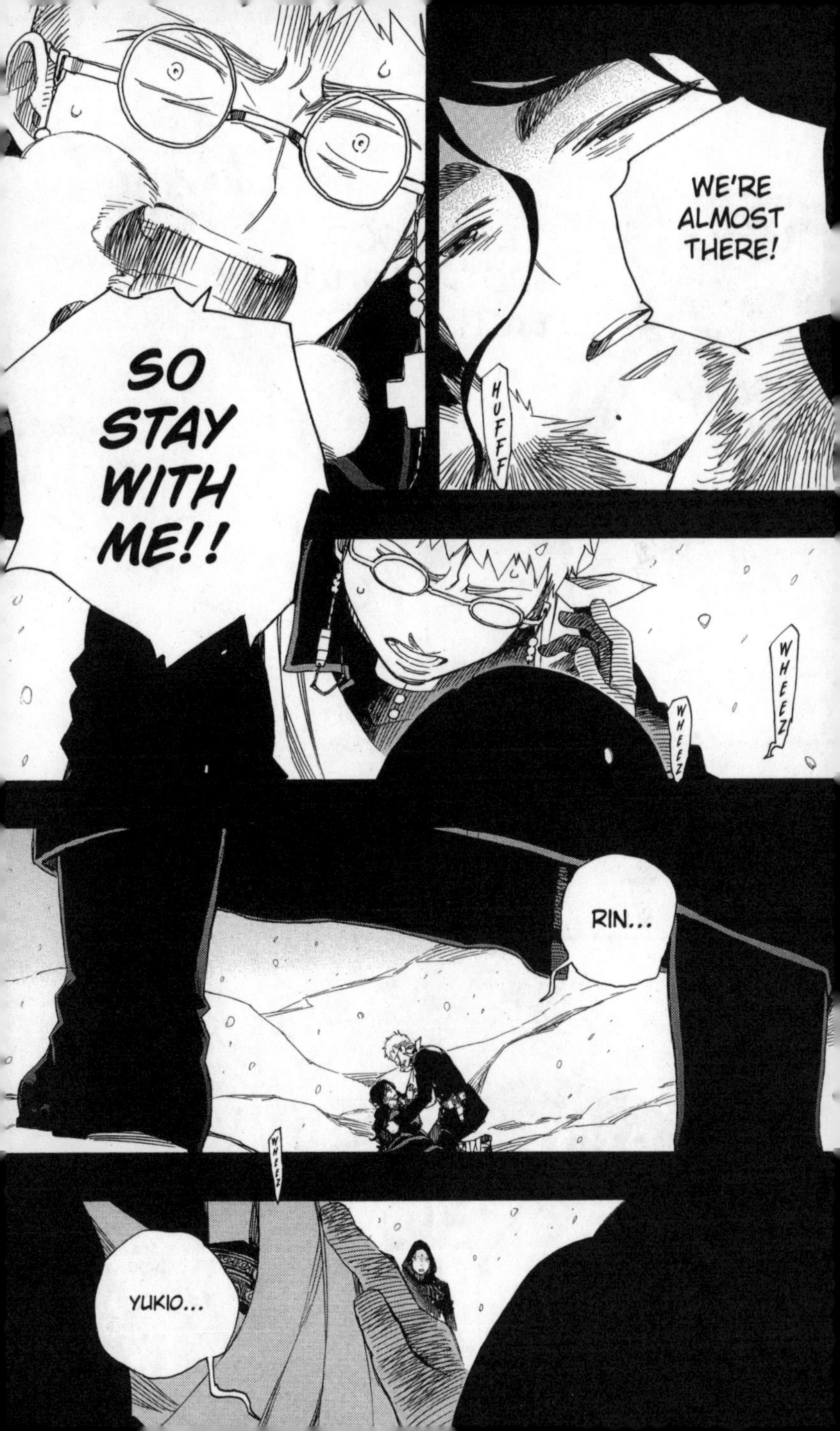
WE'RE ALMOST THERE!
HUFFF
SO STAY WITH ME!!
WHEEZ
WHEEZ
RIN...
WHEEZ
YUKIO...

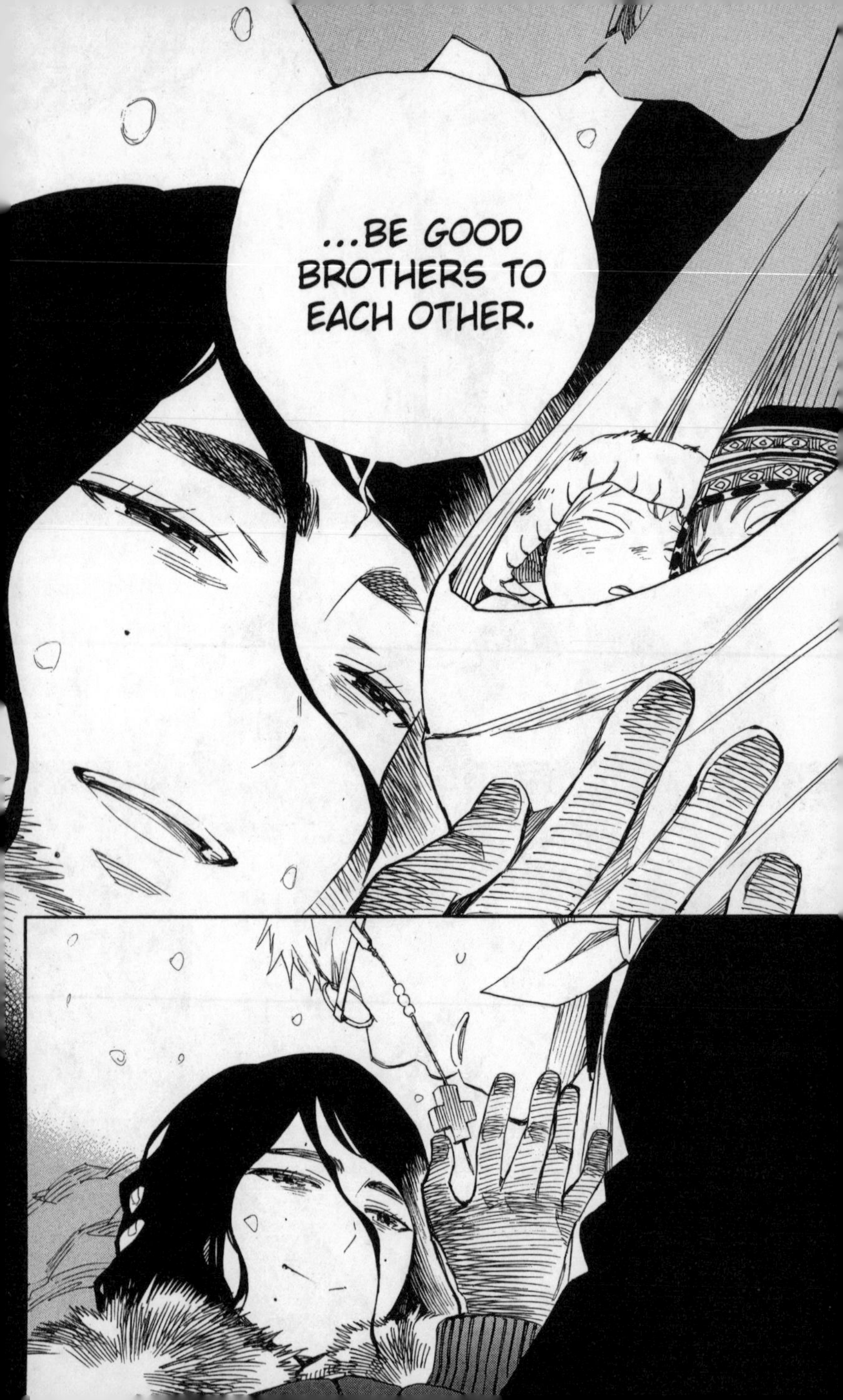
...BE GOOD BROTHERS TO EACH OTHER.

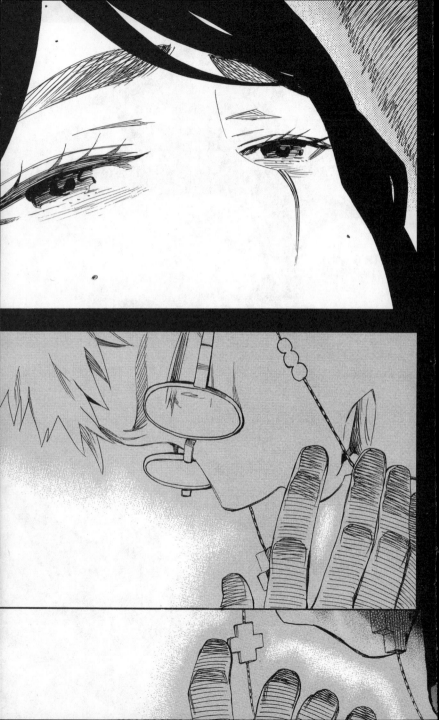

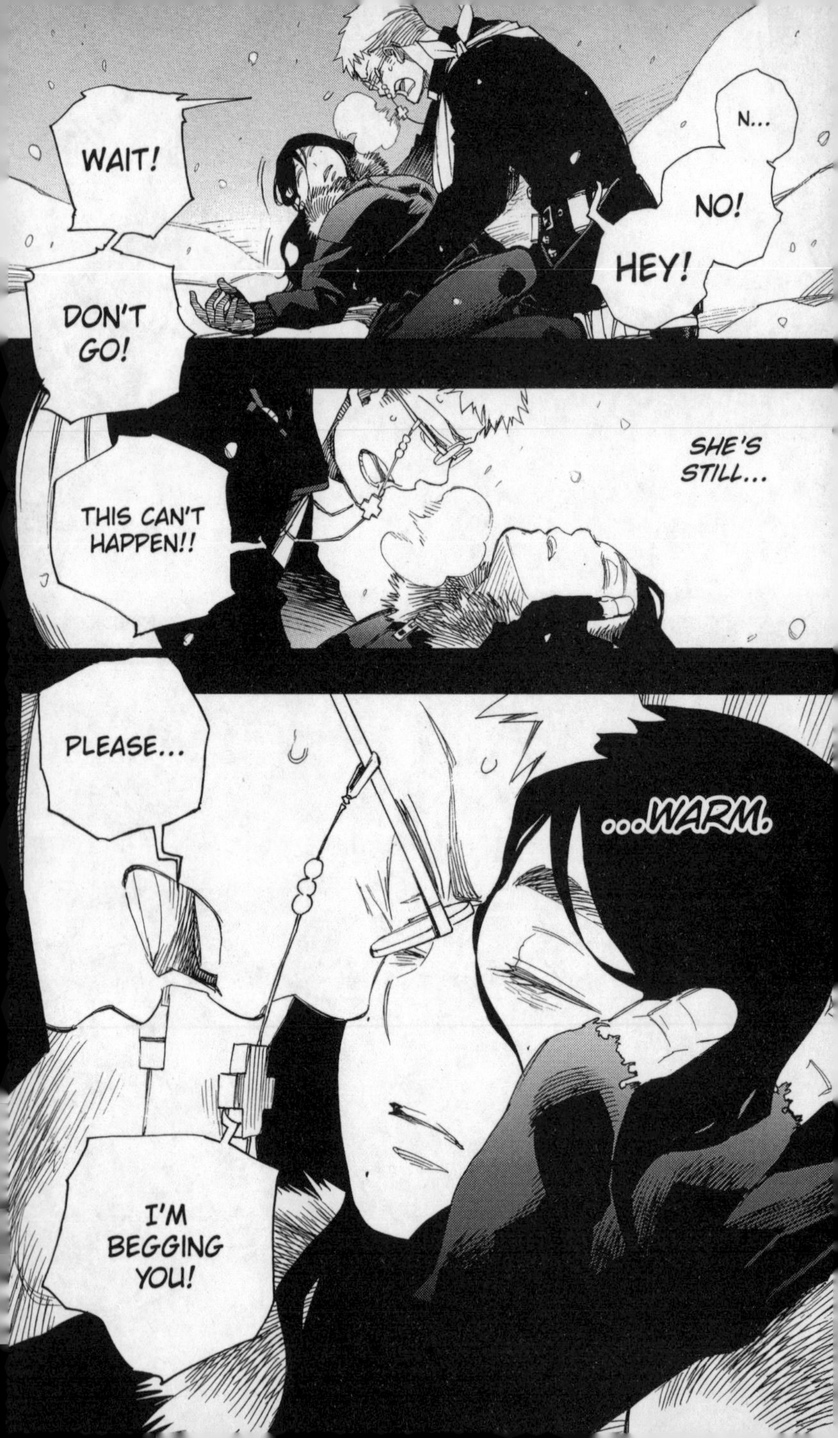
N...
NO!
HEY!
WAIT!
DON'T GO!
SHE'S STILL...
THIS CAN'T HAPPEN!!
...WARM.
PLEASE...
I'M BEGGING YOU!

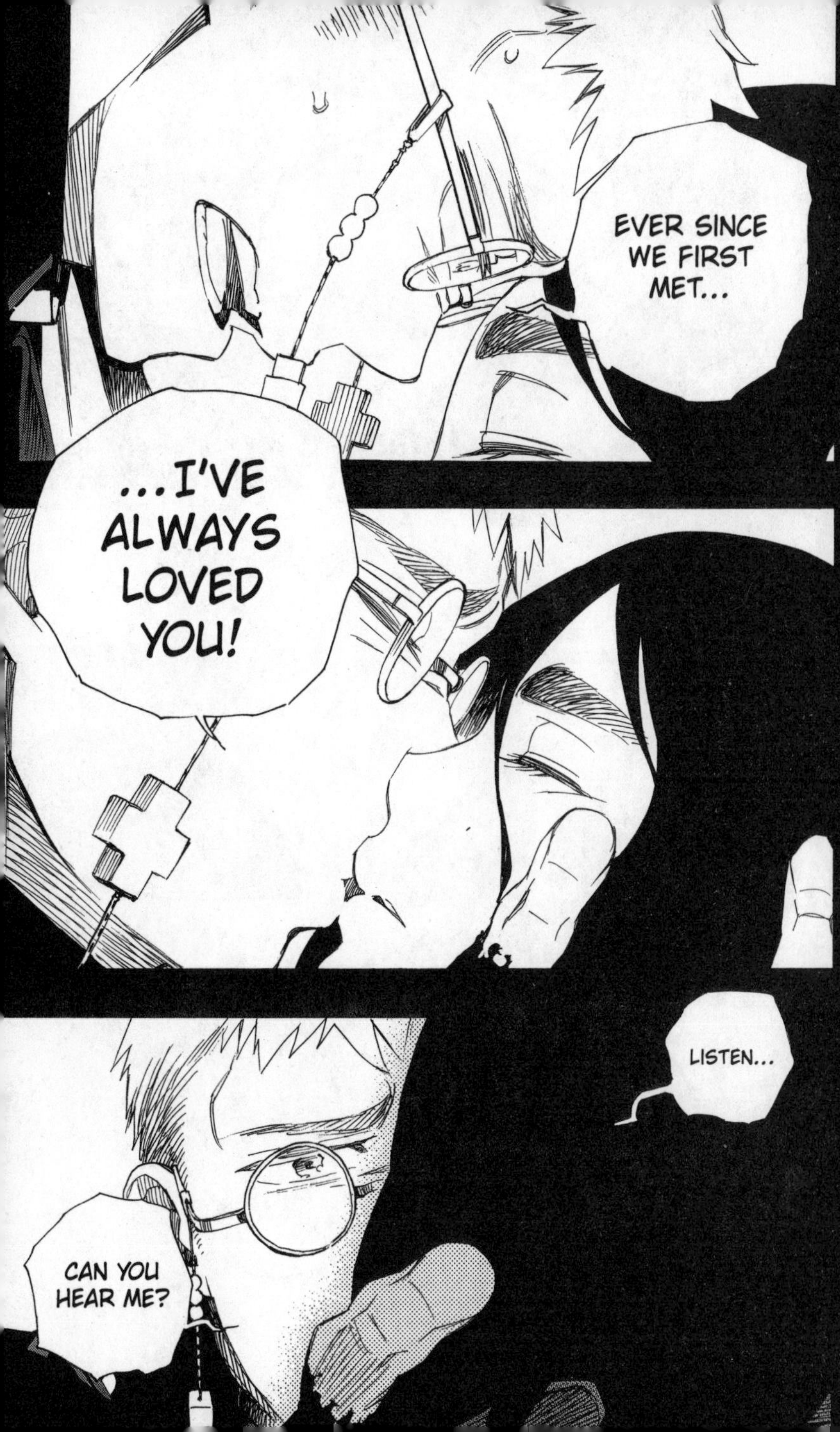
EVER SINCE WE FIRST MET...
...I'VE ALWAYS LOVED YOU!
LISTEN...
CAN YOU HEAR ME?

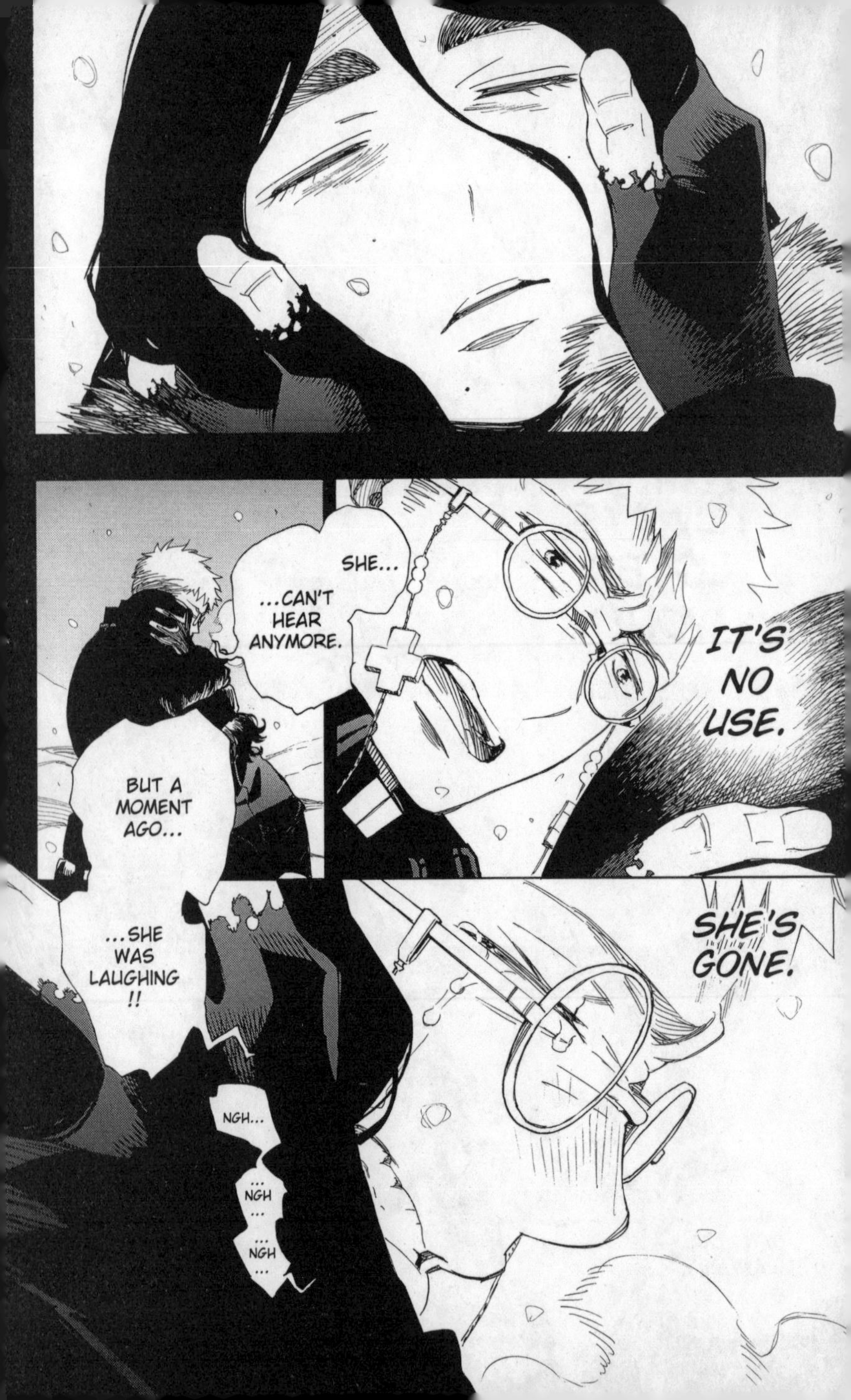
IT'S NO USE.
SHE... ...CAN'T HEAR ANYMORE.
BUT A MOMENT AGO...
...SHE WAS LAUGHING!!
SHE'S GONE.
NGH...
...NGH...
...NGH...

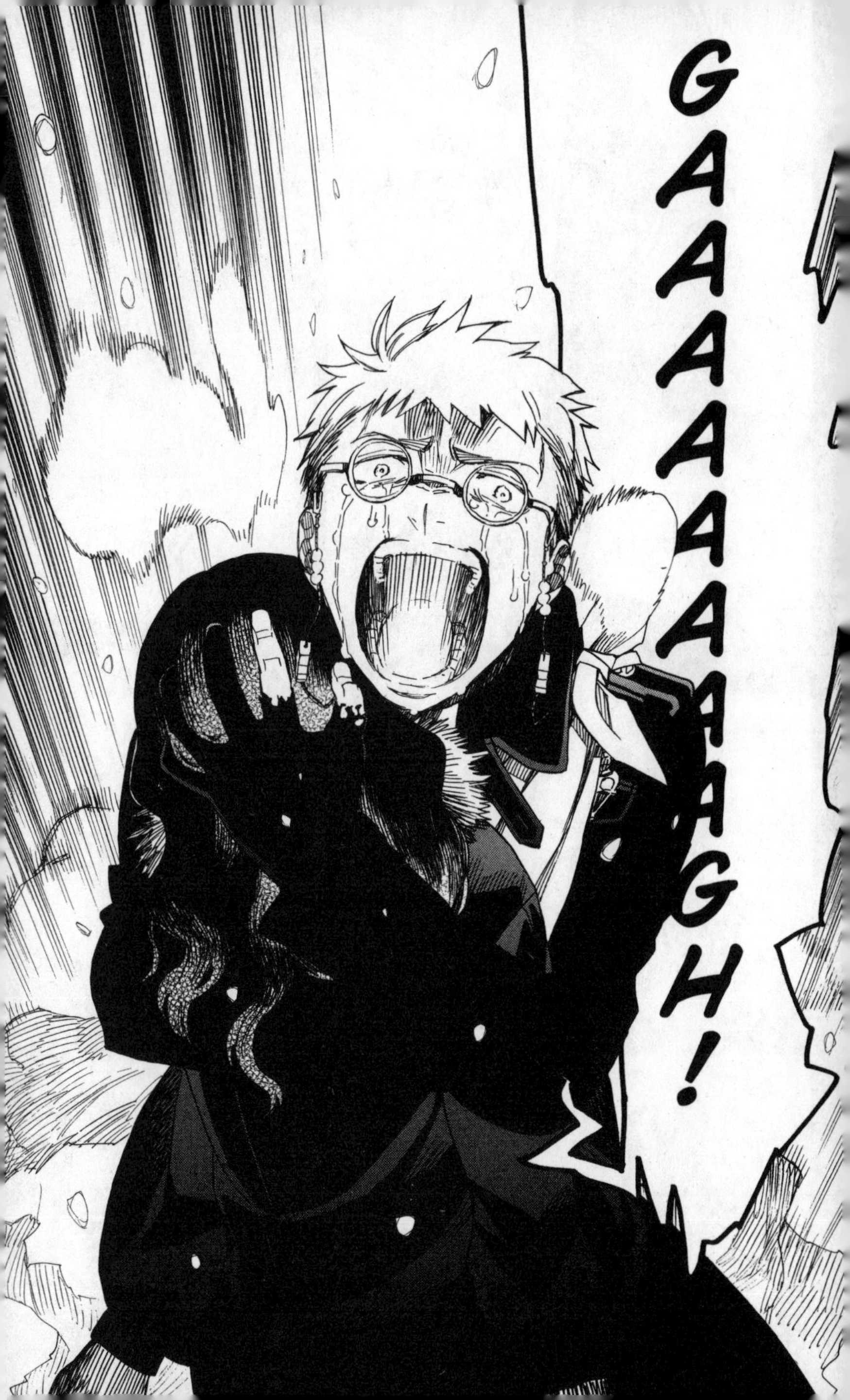
GAAAAAAAAGH!

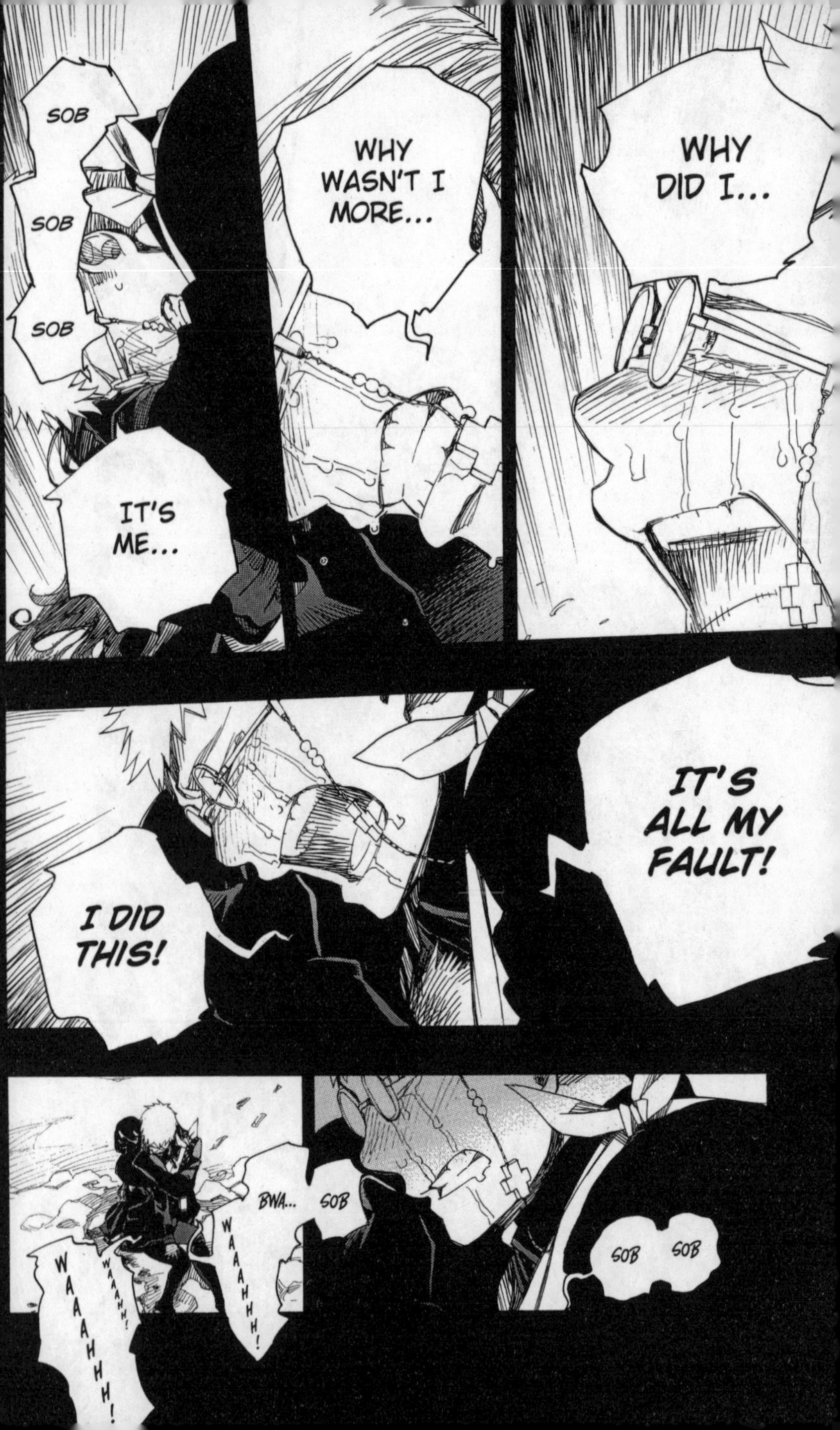
WHY DID I...
WHY WASN'T I MORE...
SOB
SOB
SOB
IT'S ME...
IT'S ALL MY FAULT!
I DID THIS!
SOB SOB
SOB
BWA...
WAAAAHHH!
WAAAAHH!
WAAAAHHH!

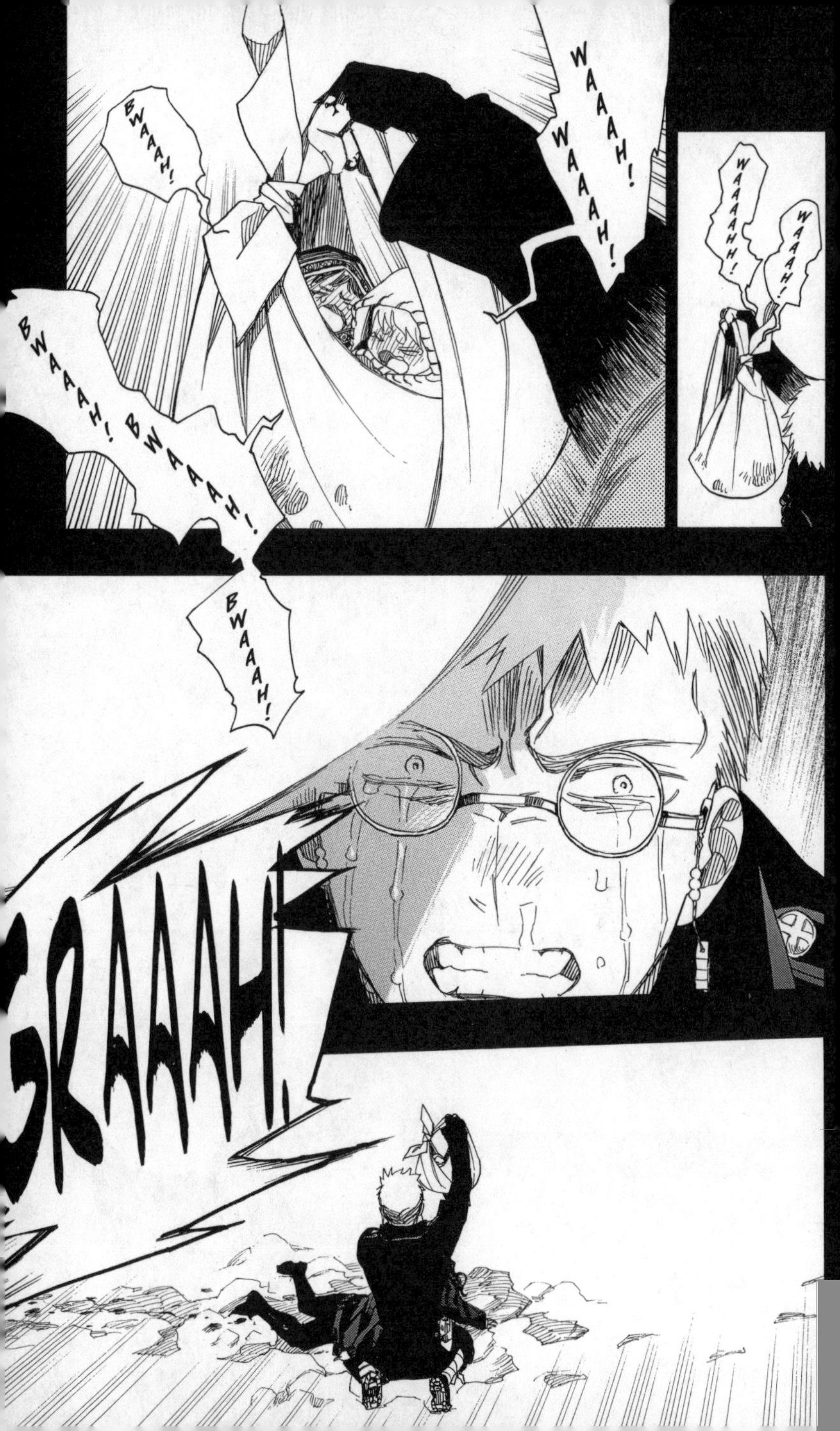
WAAAAHH!
WAAAH!
WAAAAH! WAAAAH!
BWAAAH!
BWAAAAH! BWAAAAH!
BWAAAAH!
GRAAAH!

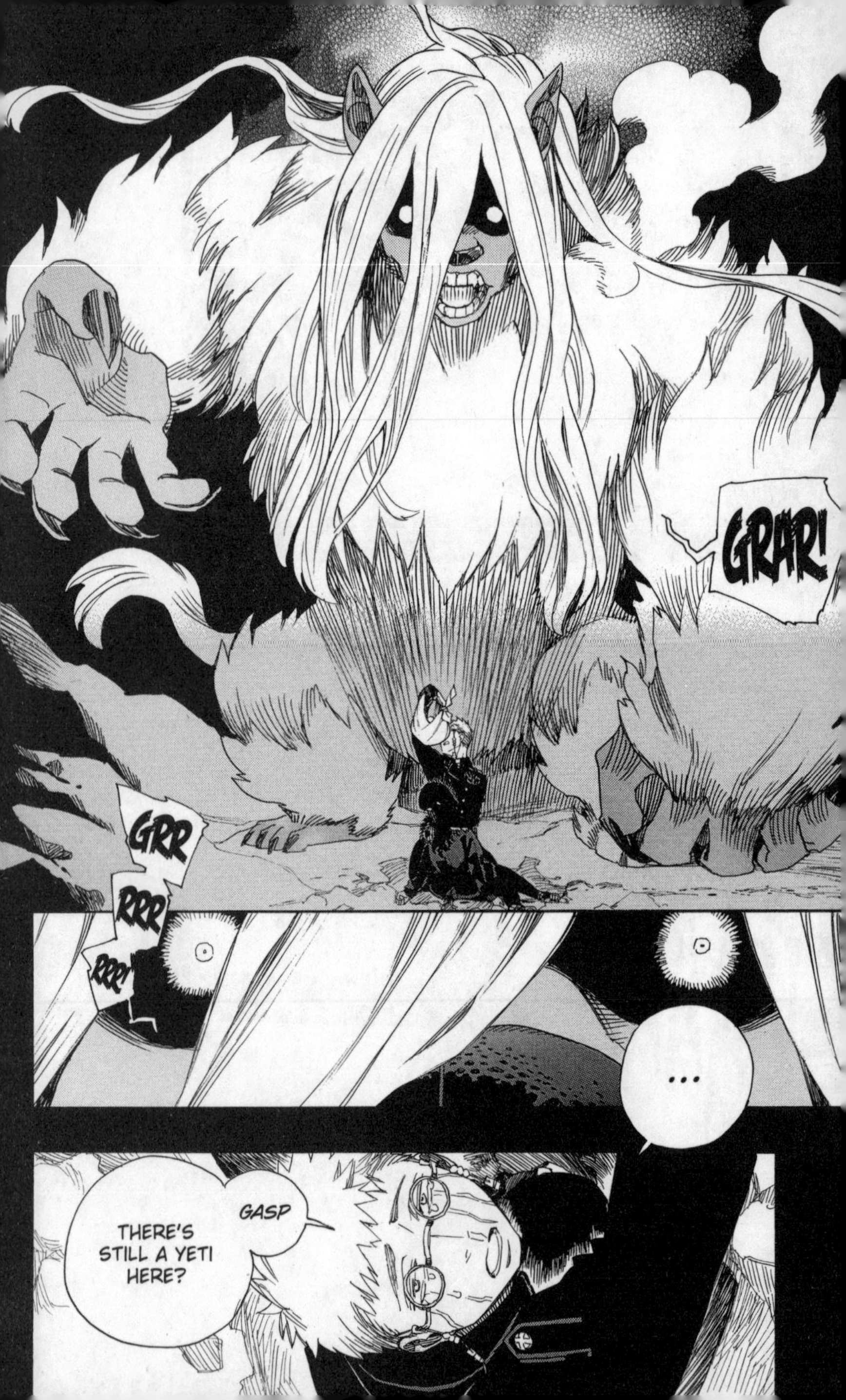
GRAR!
GRR
RRR
RRR!
...
GASP
THERE'S STILL A YETI HERE?

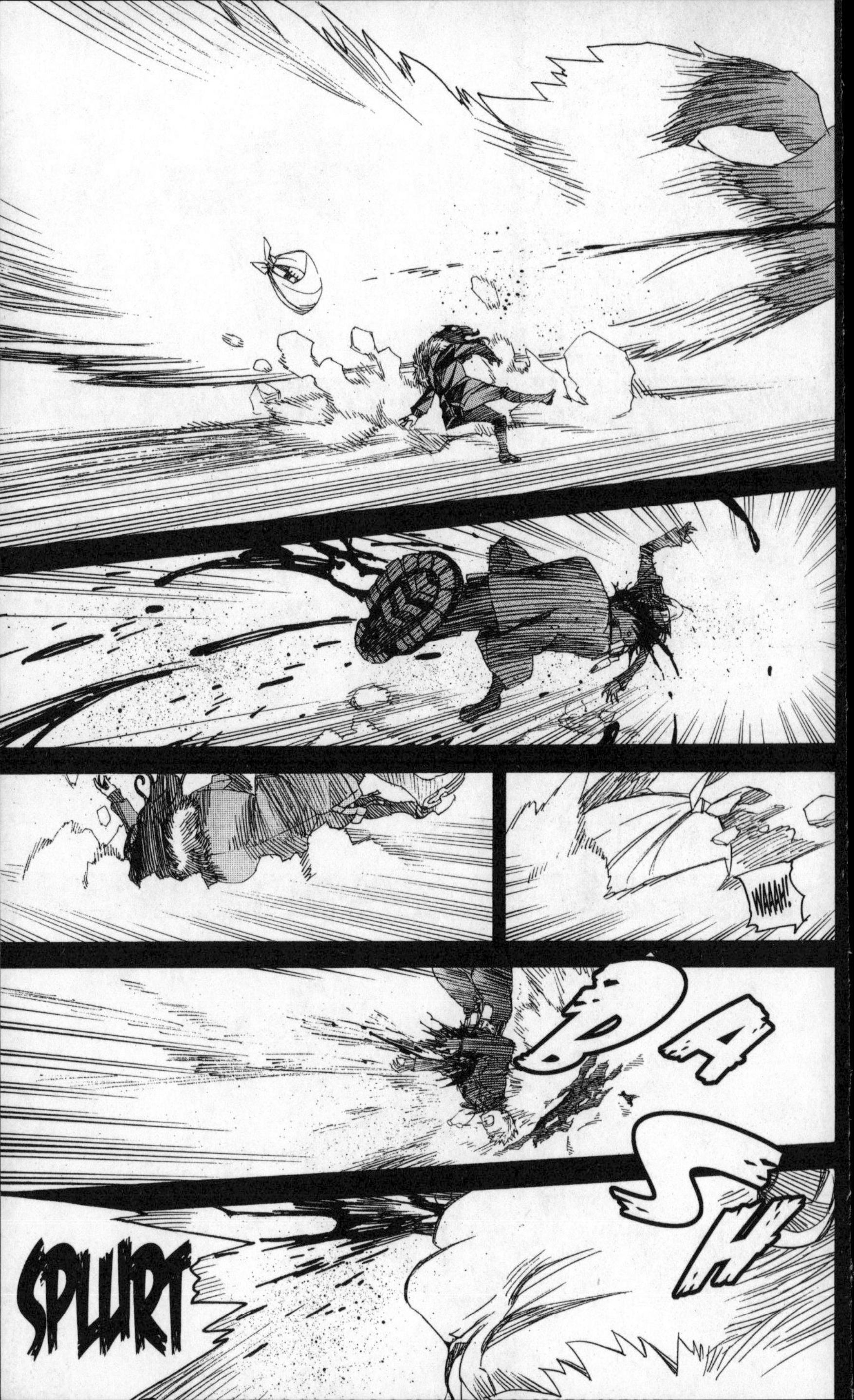
WAAAH!
BASH
SPLURT

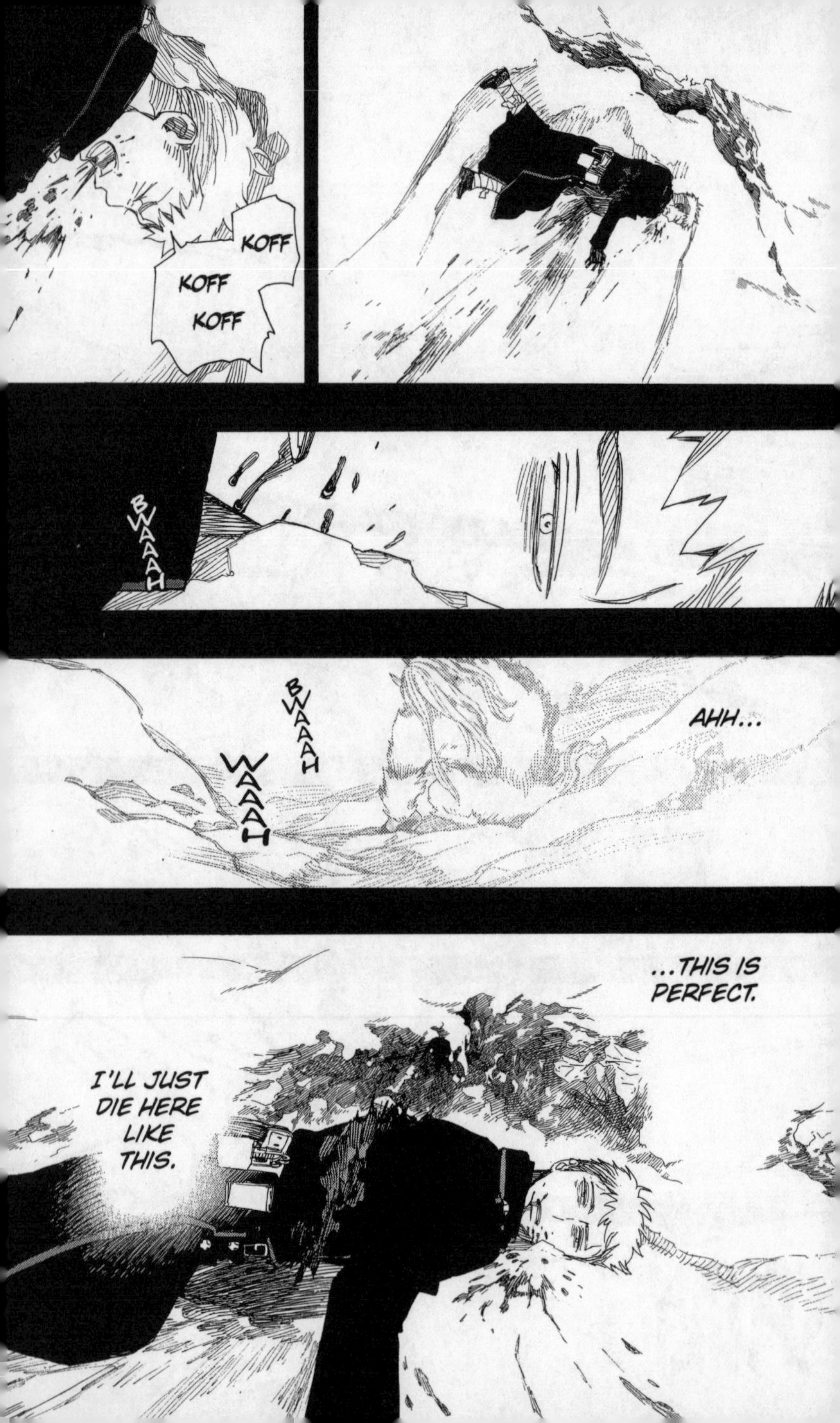
KOFF
KOFF
KOFF
BWAAAH
AHH...
BWAAAH
WAAAH
...THIS IS PERFECT.
I'LL JUST DIE HERE LIKE THIS.

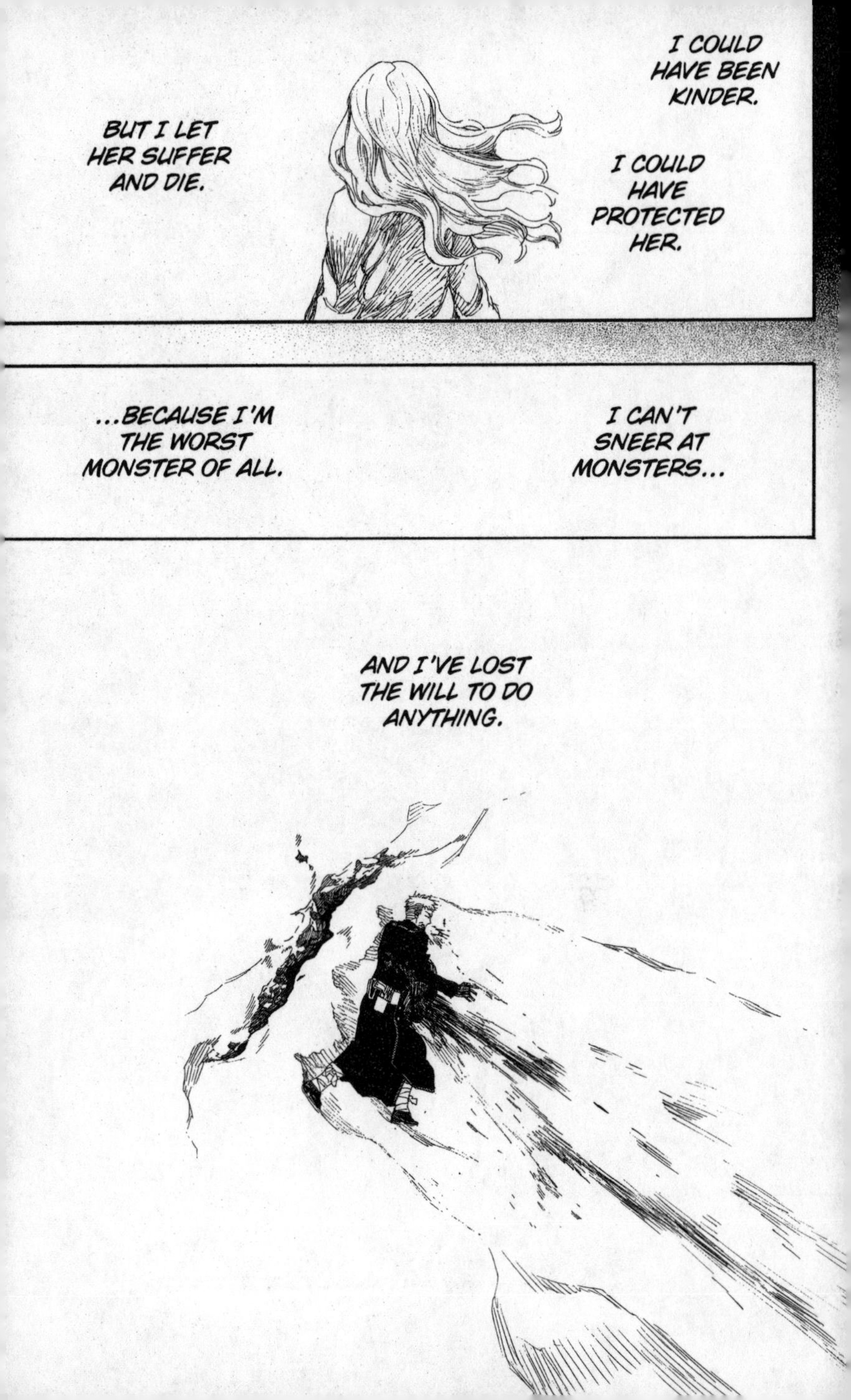
I COULD HAVE BEEN KINDER.
I COULD HAVE PROTECTED HER.
BUT I LET HER SUFFER AND DIE.
I CAN'T SNEER AT MONSTERS...
...BECAUSE I'M THE WORST MONSTER OF ALL.
AND I'VE LOST THE WILL TO DO ANYTHING.

Blue Exorcist Chapter 117: SSC23: 17Hz

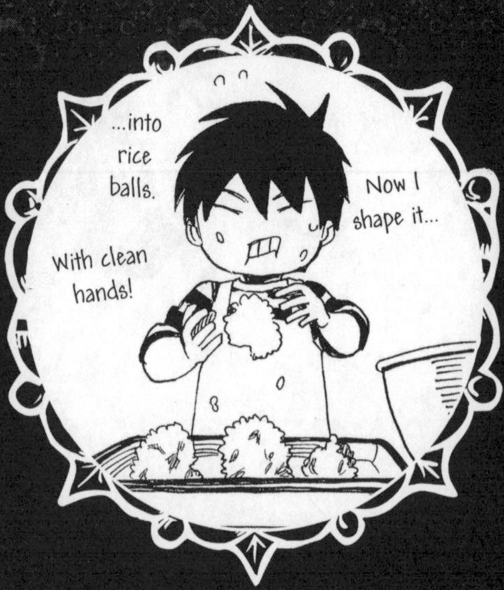
Now I shape it...
...into rice balls.
With clean hands!

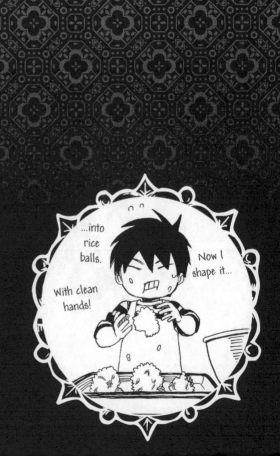

CHAPTER 118:
SsC23: 171

MY LIFE HAS
NO VALUE
ANYMORE.

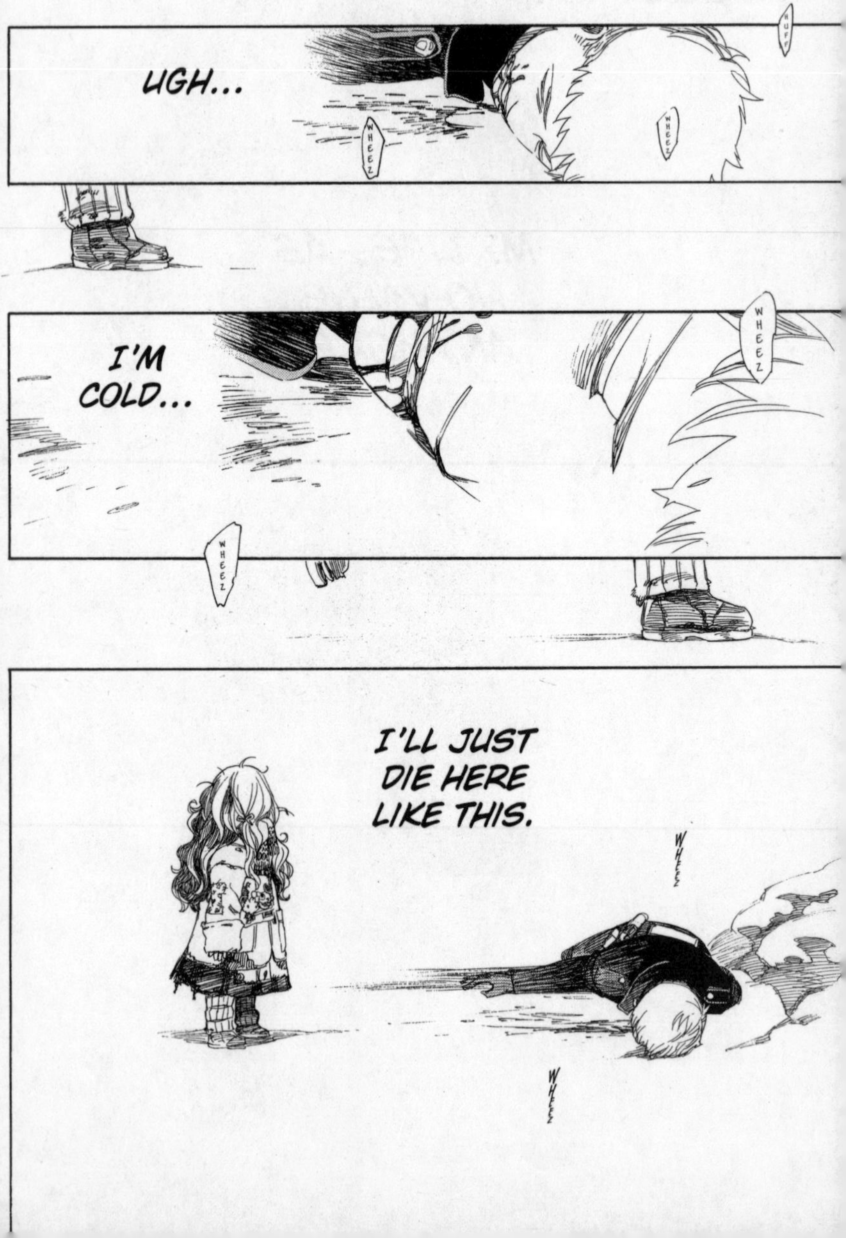
HUFF
WHEEZ
UGH...
WHEEZ
WHEEZ
I'M COLD...
WHEEZ
I'LL JUST DIE HERE LIKE THIS.
WHEEZ
WHEEZ

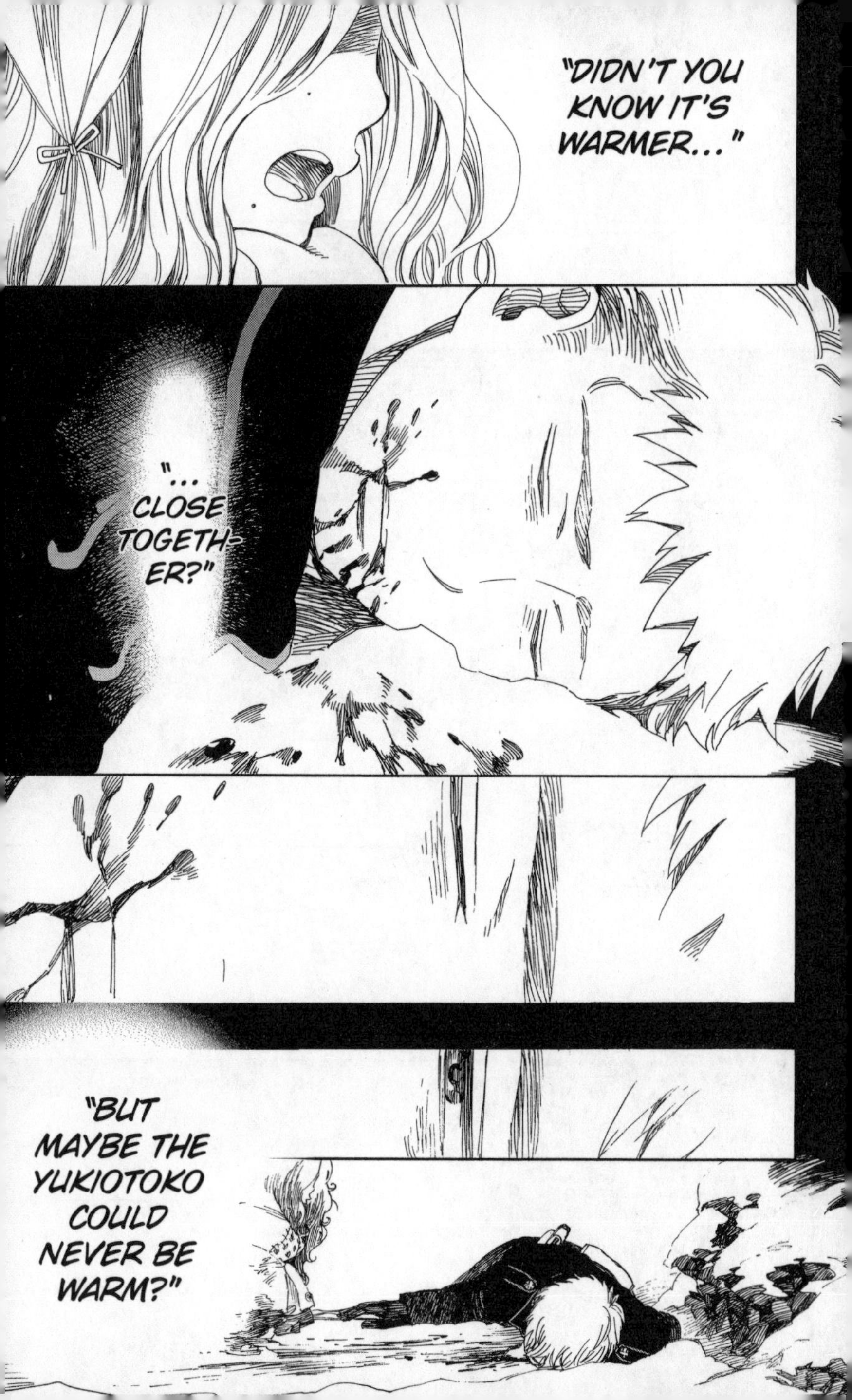
"DIDN'T YOU KNOW IT'S WARMER..."
"... CLOSE TOGETH-ER?"
"BUT MAYBE THE YUKIOTOKO COULD NEVER BE WARM?"

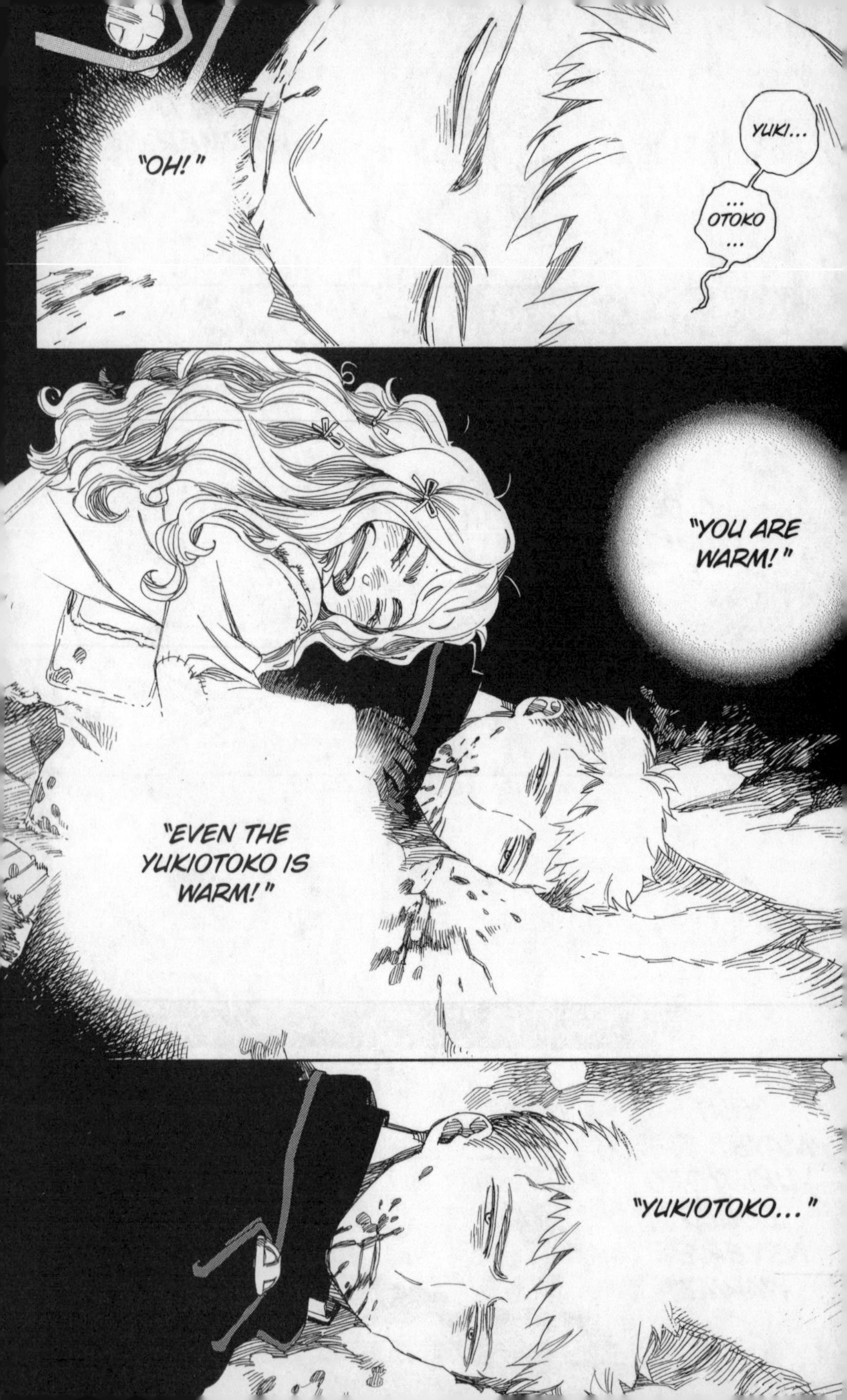
YUKI...
...OTOKO...
"OH!"
"YOU ARE WARM!"
"EVEN THE YUKIOTOKO IS WARM!"
"YUKIOTOKO..."

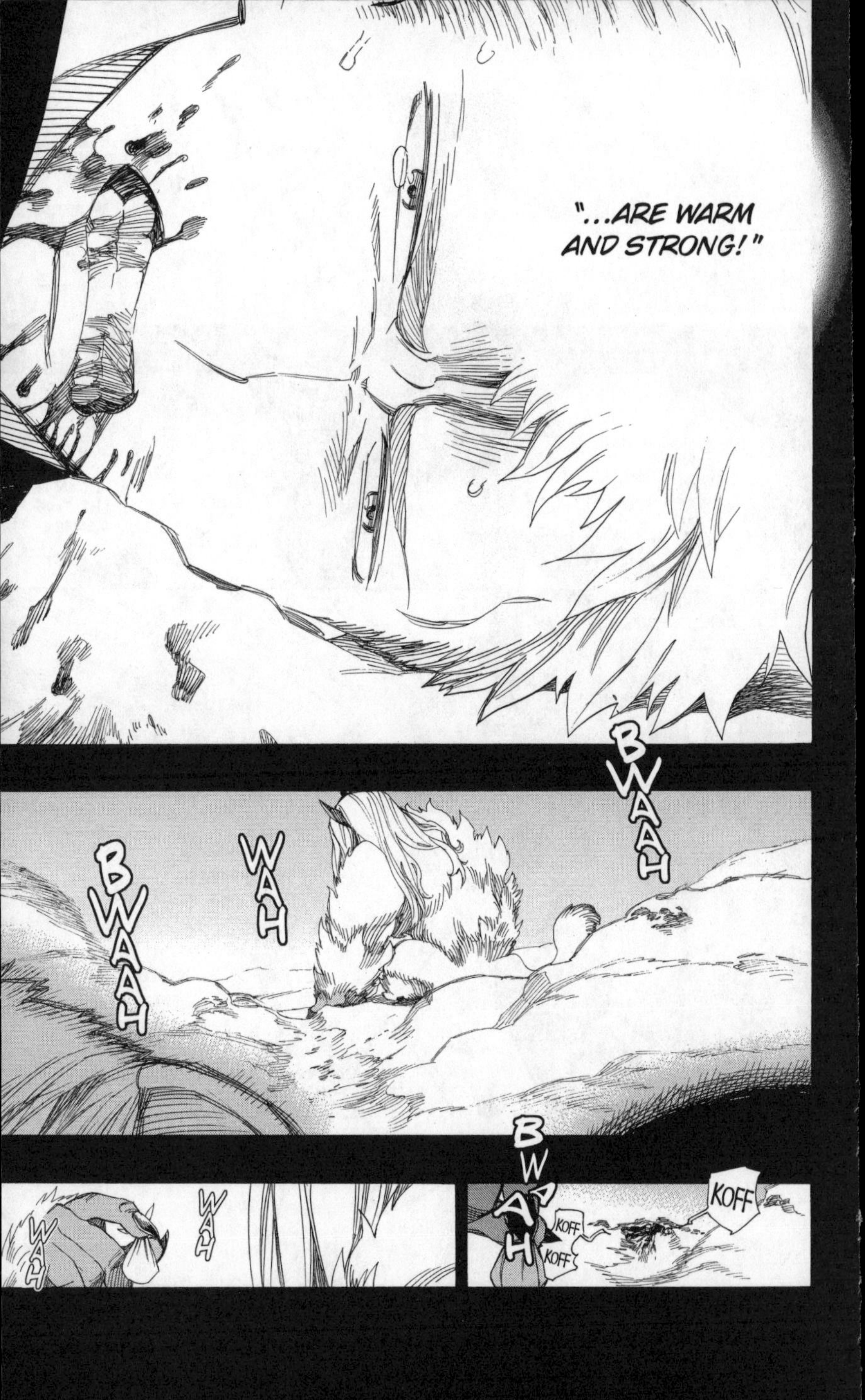
"...ARE WARM AND STRONG!"
BWAAH
WAH
BWAAH
BWAAH
KOFF
KOFF
KOFF
WAH
WAH

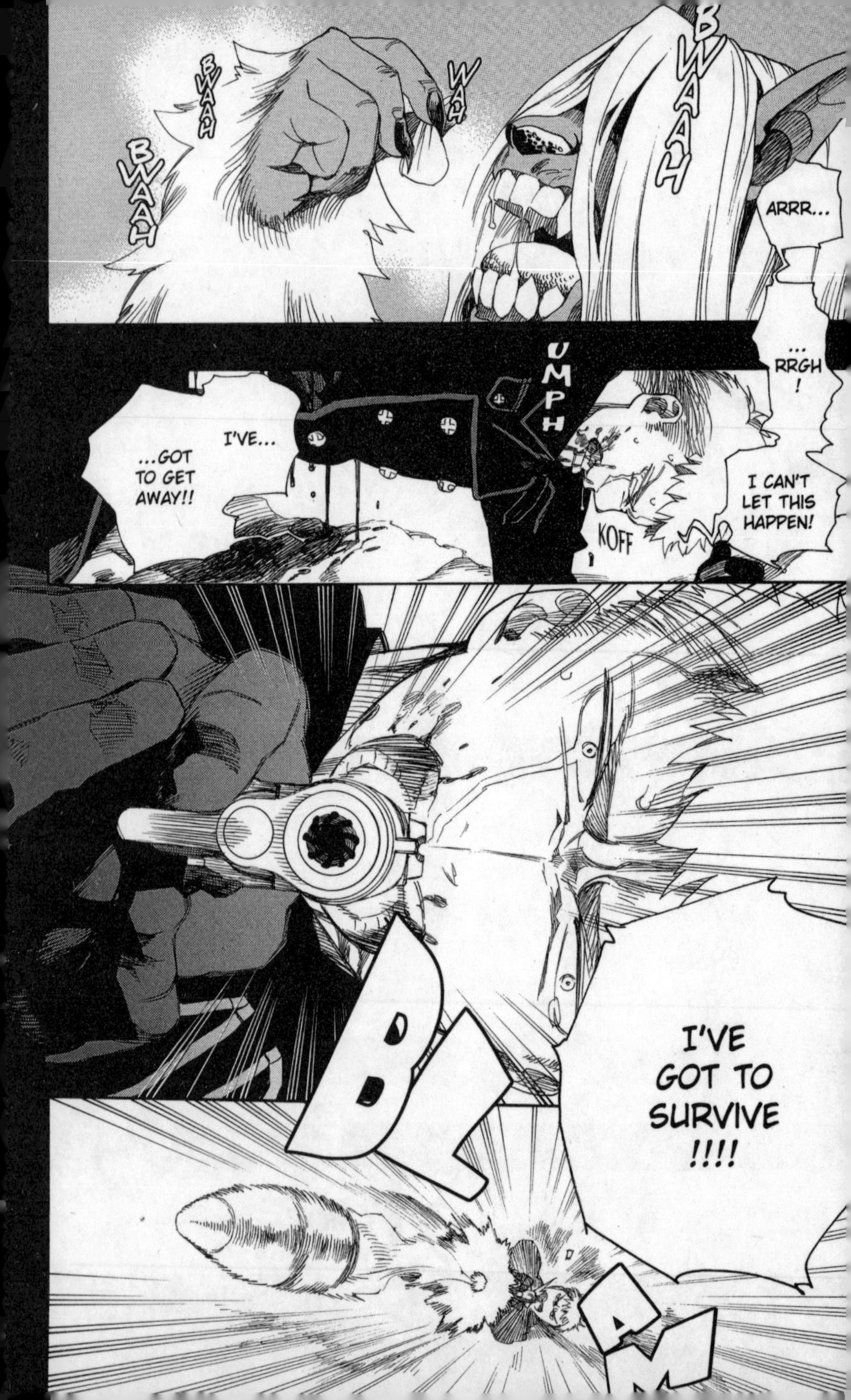
ARRR...
BWAAAH
WAH
BWAAH
BWAAH
...RRGH!
I CAN'T LET THIS HAPPEN!
KOFF
UMPH
I'VE...
...GOT TO GET AWAY!!
I'VE GOT TO SURVIVE!!!!
BLAM

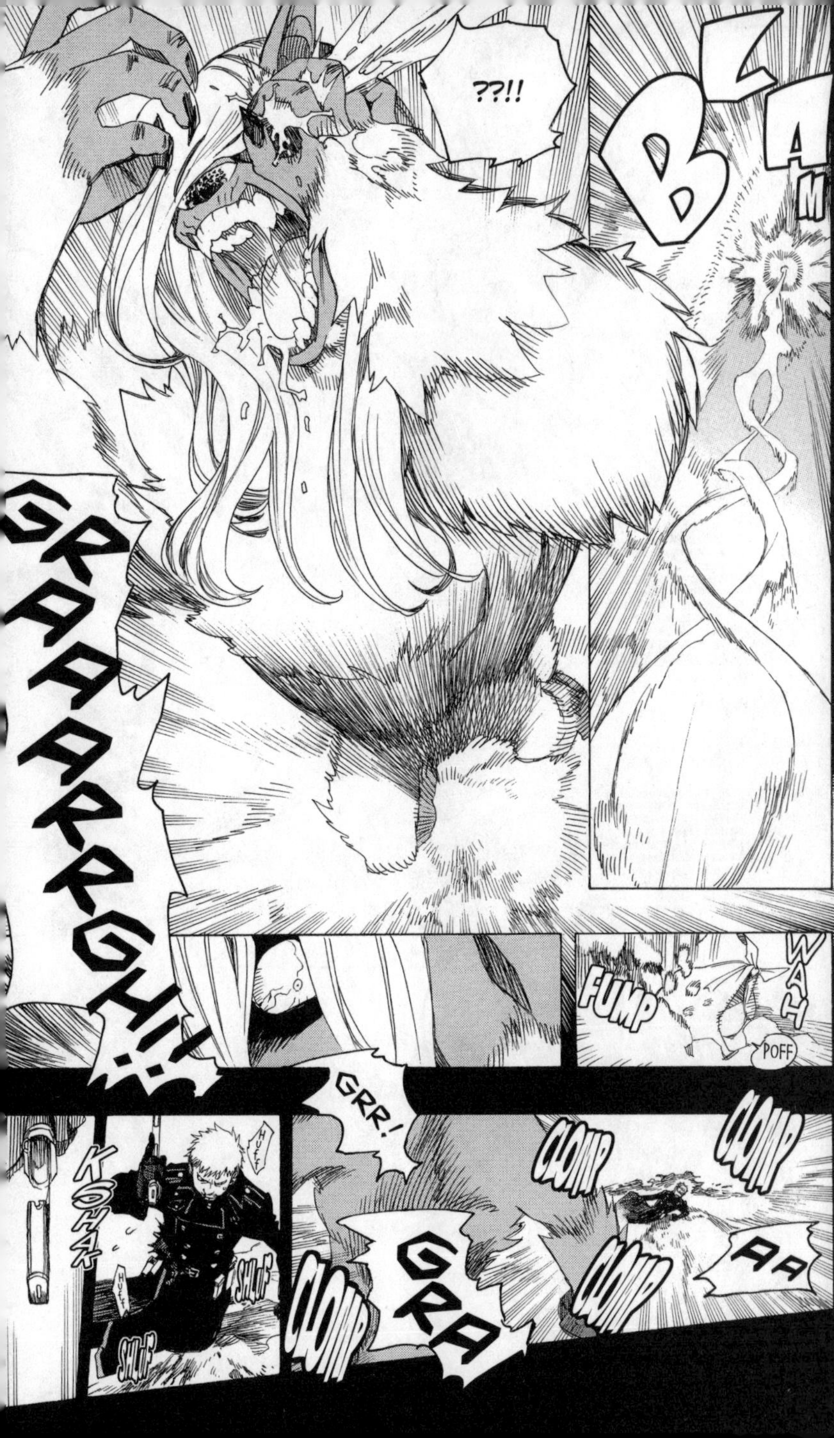
BLAM
??!!
GRAAARRGH!!
WAH
FUMP
POFF
GRR!
CLOMP
CLOMP
AA
CLOMP
GRA
CLOMP
KSHAK
HUFF
HUFF
SHUF
SHUF

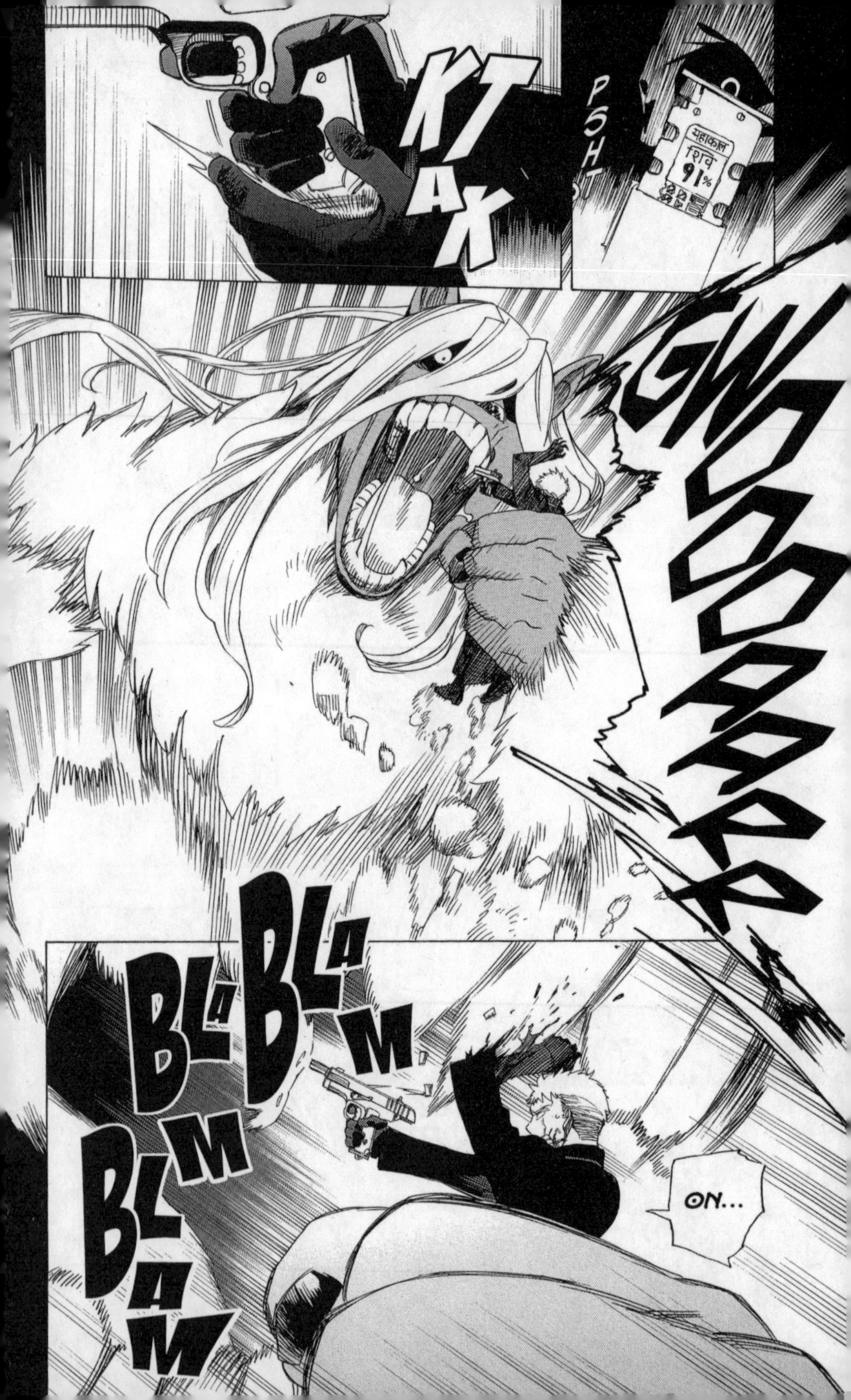
PSHT
महाकाल
शिव
91%
KTAK
GWOOOAAARR
ON...
BLAM
BLAM
BLAM

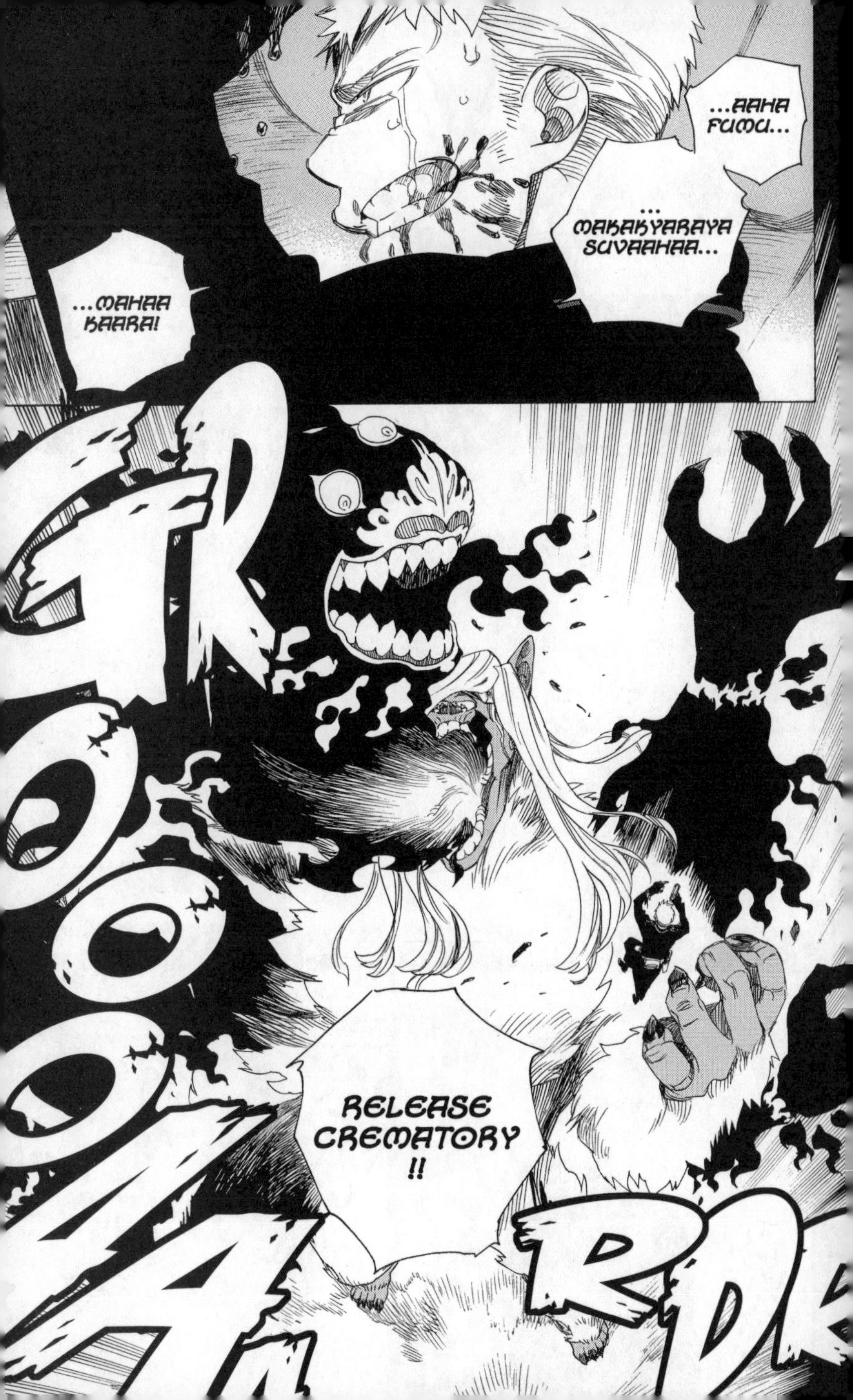
...AAHA FUMU...
...MAKAKYARAYA SUVAAHAA...
...MAHAA KAARA!
RELEASE CREMATORY !!

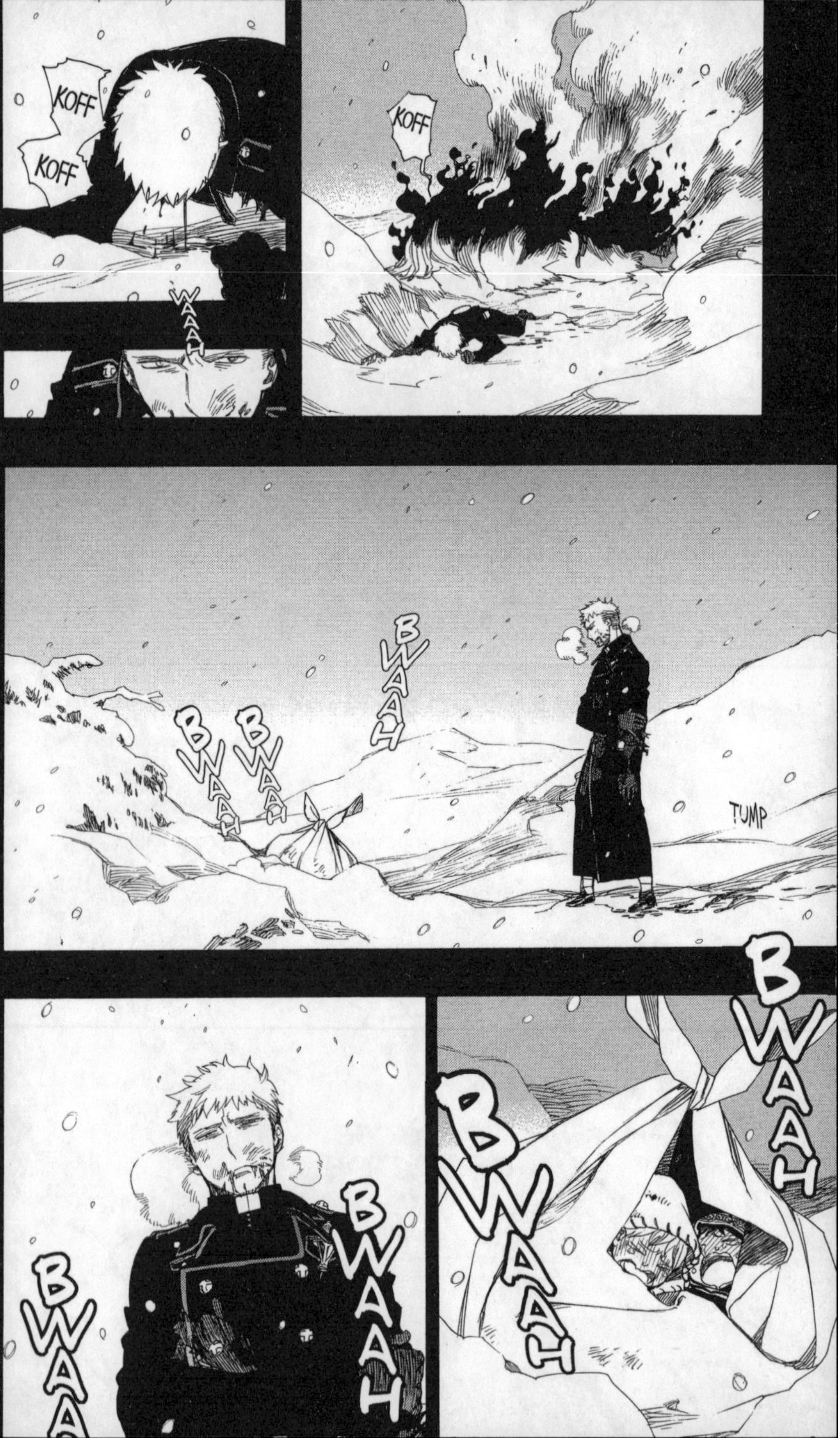
KOFF
KOFF
KOFF
WAAAH
BWAAAH
TUMP
BWAAAH
BWAAAH
BWAAAH
BWAAAH
BWAAAH
BWAA

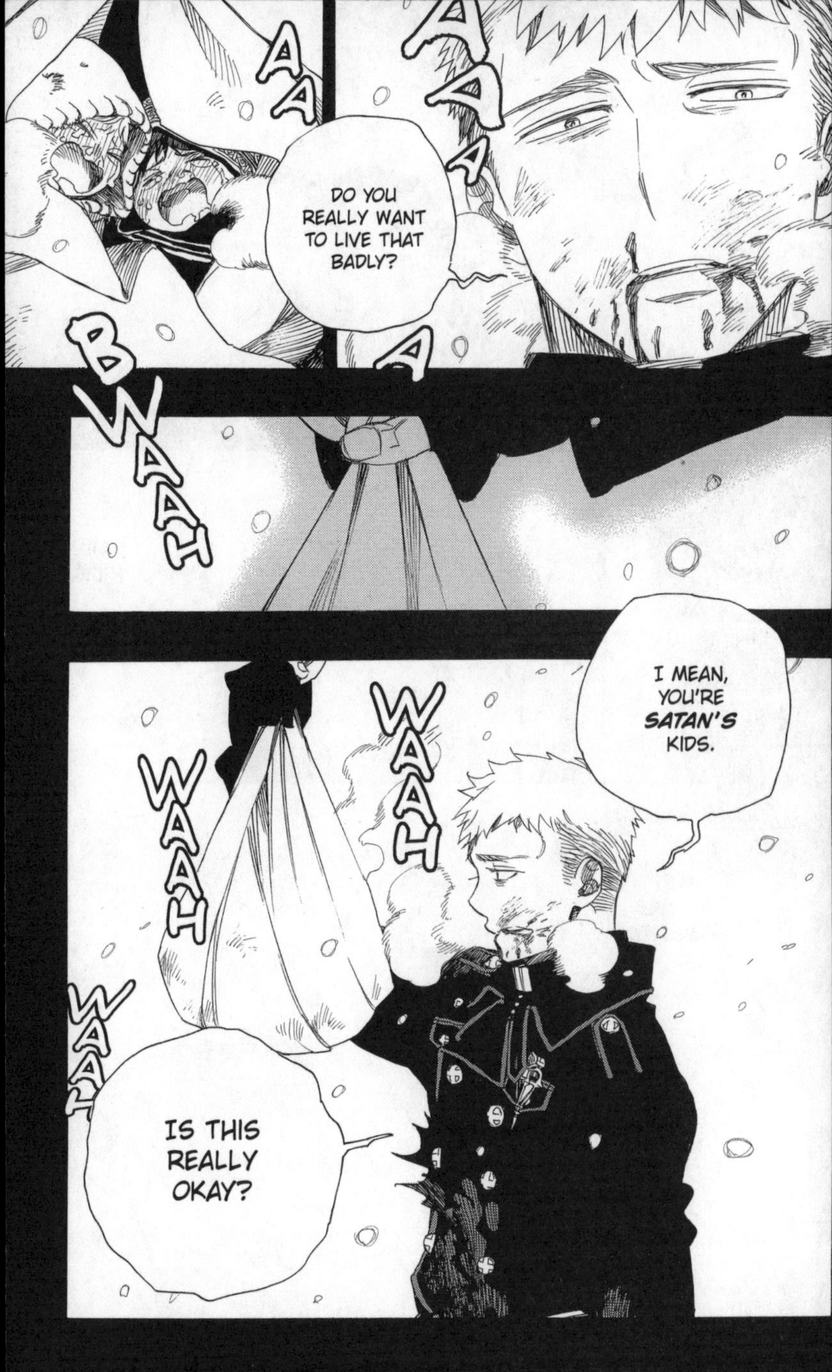
AAAAA
DO YOU REALLY WANT TO LIVE THAT BADLY?
AA
BWAAAH
I MEAN, YOU'RE **SATAN'S** KIDS.
WAAAH
WAAAH
IS THIS REALLY OKAY?
WAA

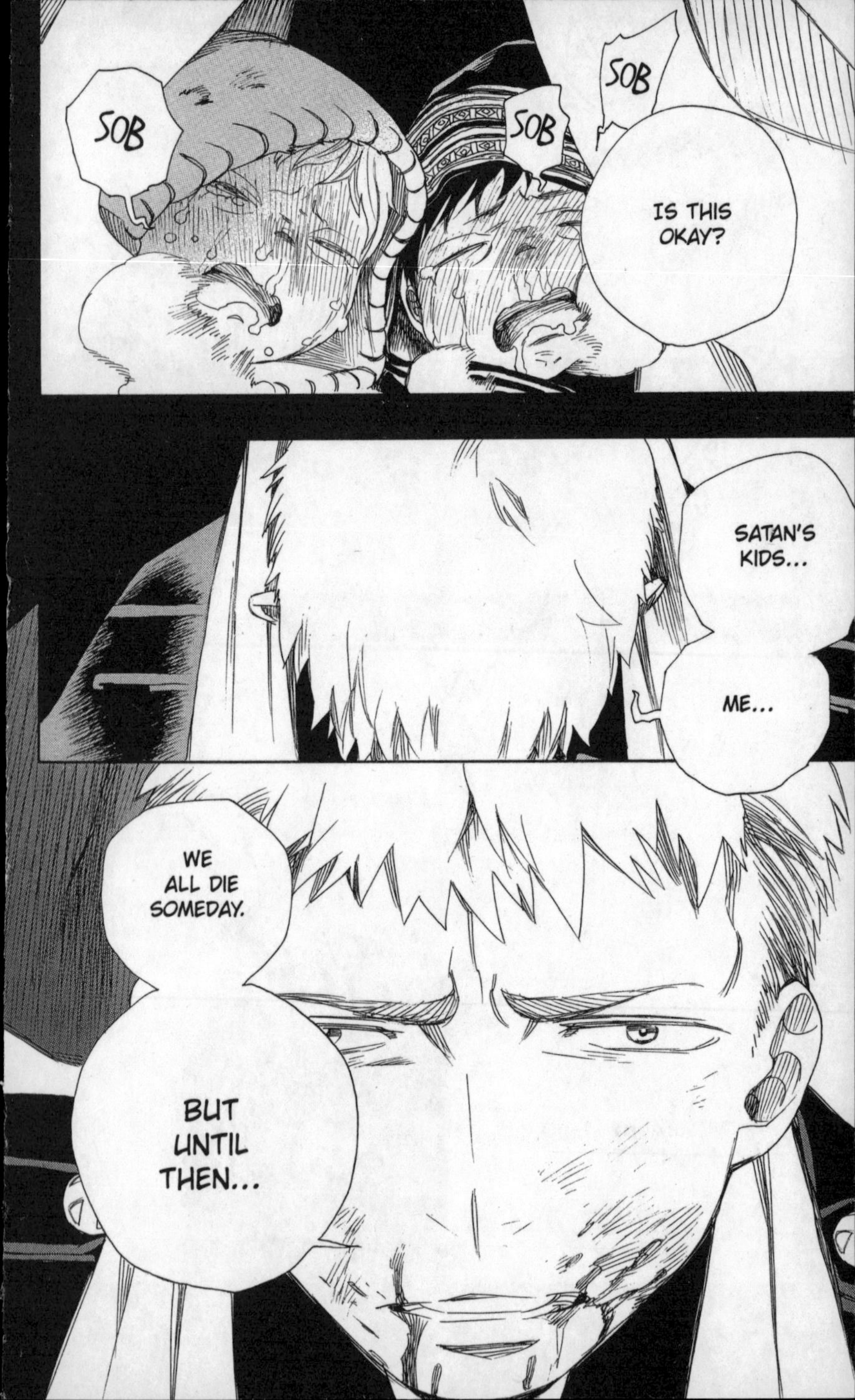
SOB
SOB
IS THIS OKAY?
SOB
SATAN'S KIDS...
ME...
WE ALL DIE SOMEDAY.
BUT UNTIL THEN...

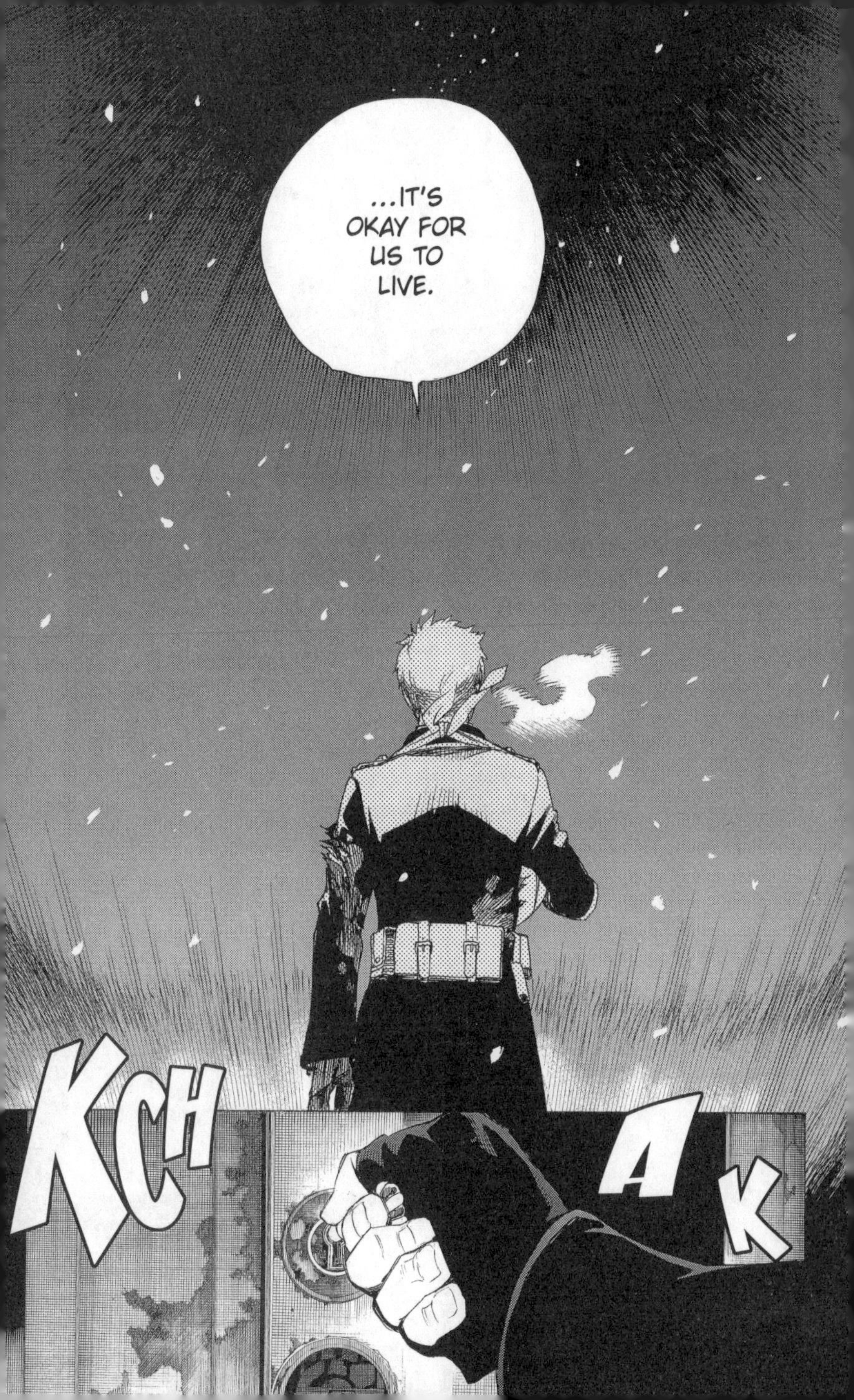
...IT'S OKAY FOR US TO LIVE.
KCHAK

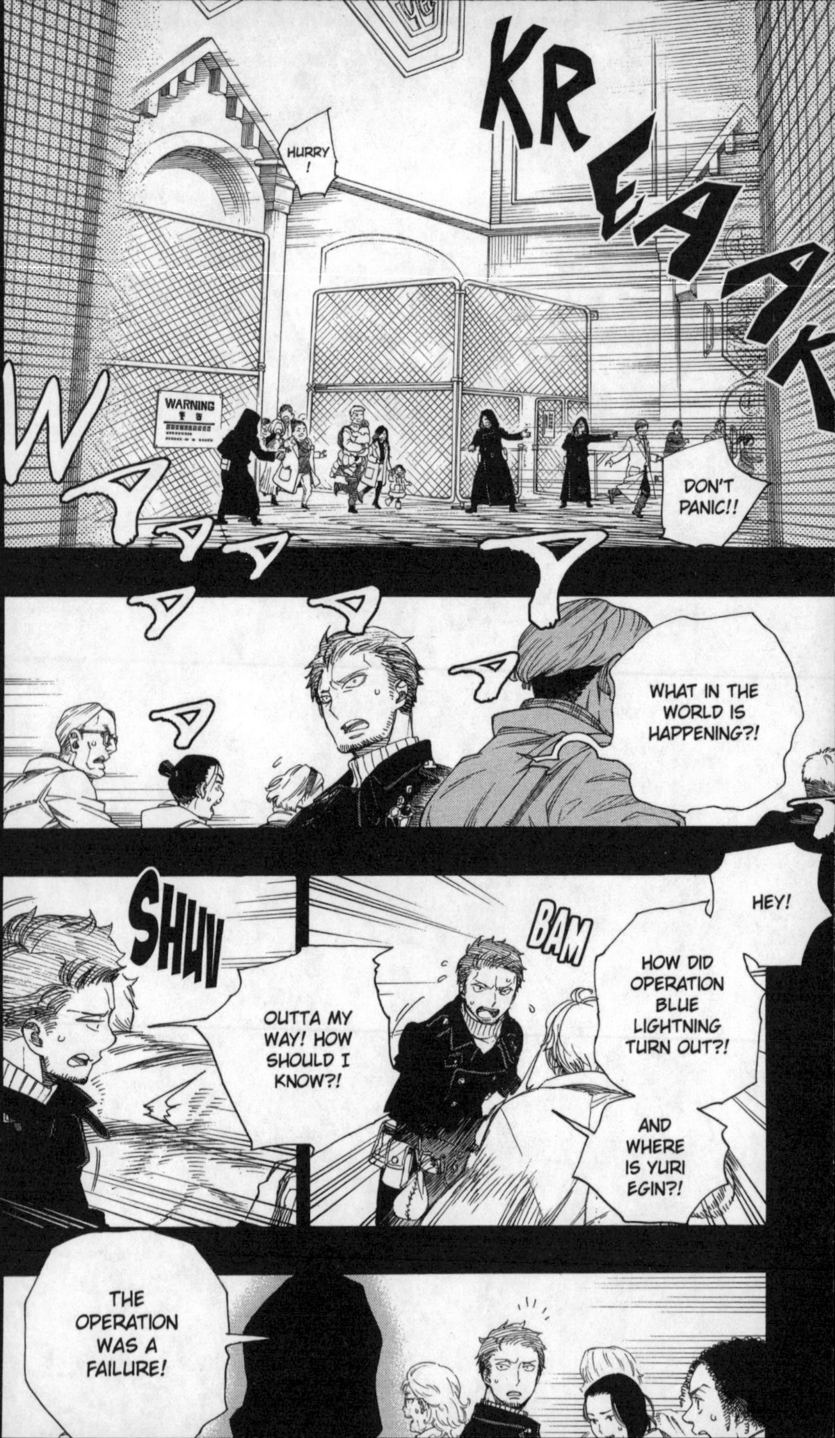
KREAAK
HURRY!
DON'T PANIC!!
WAAAAAAAAA
WHAT IN THE WORLD IS HAPPENING?!
HEY!
HOW DID OPERATION BLUE LIGHTNING TURN OUT?!
AND WHERE IS YURI EGIN?!
BAM
OUTTA MY WAY! HOW SHOULD I KNOW?!
SHUV
THE OPERATION WAS A FAILURE!

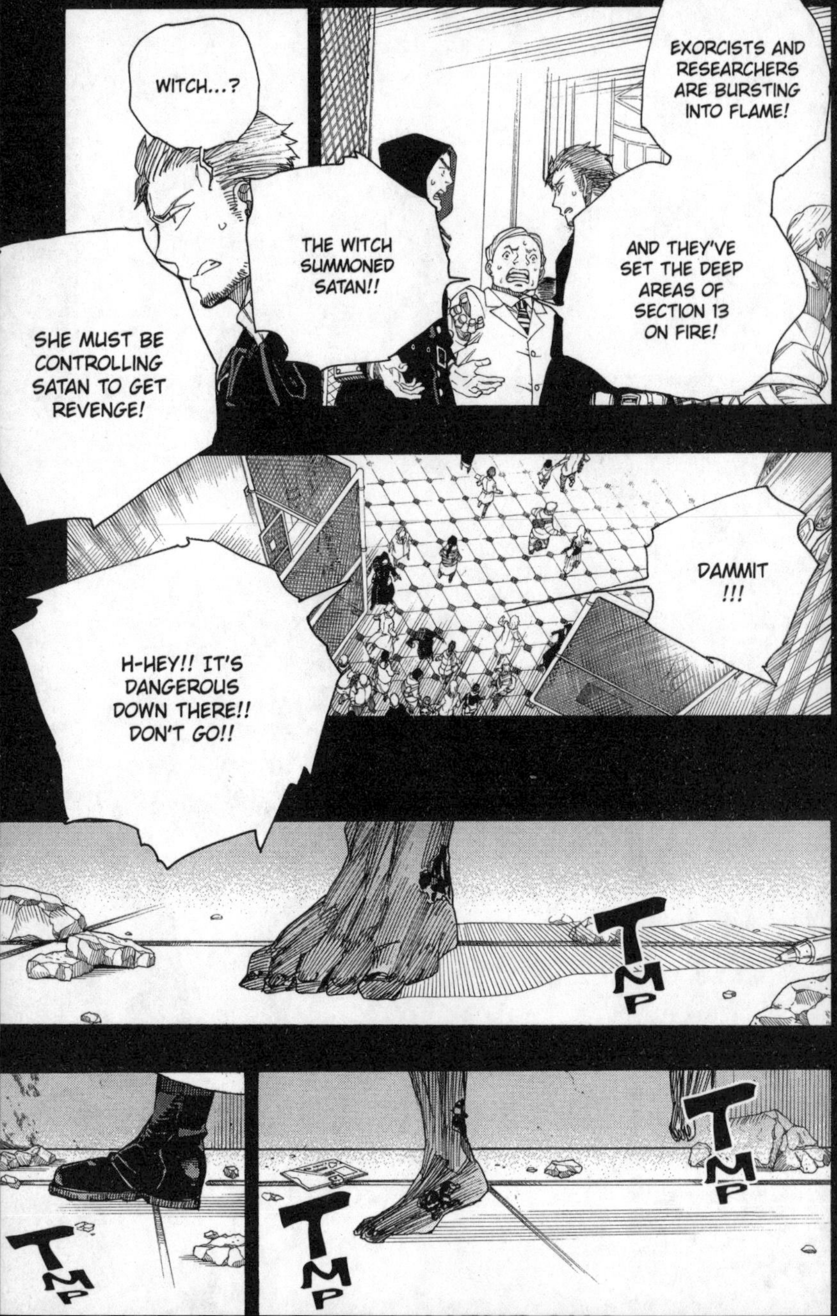
EXORCISTS AND RESEARCHERS ARE BURSTING INTO FLAME!
AND THEY'VE SET THE DEEP AREAS OF SECTION 13 ON FIRE!
THE WITCH SUMMONED SATAN!!
WITCH...?
SHE MUST BE CONTROLLING SATAN TO GET REVENGE!
DAMMIT !!!
H-HEY!! IT'S DANGEROUS DOWN THERE!! DON'T GO!!
TMP
TMP
TMP
TMP

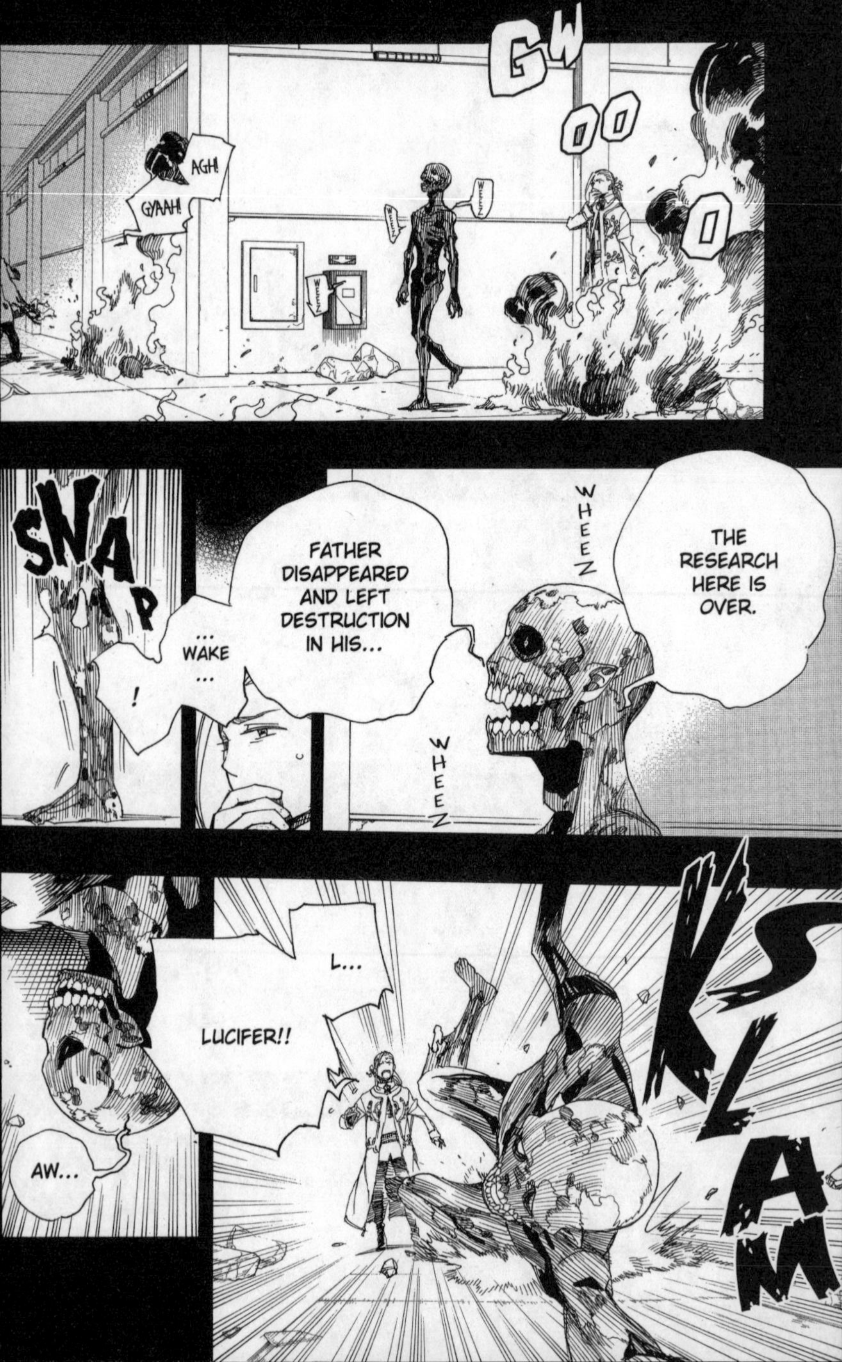
GWOOO
WHEEZ
WHEEZ
AGH!
GYAAH!
WHEEZ
WHEEZ
THE RESEARCH HERE IS OVER.
WHEEZ
FATHER DISAPPEARED AND LEFT DESTRUCTION IN HIS...
... WAKE ...
SNAP
!
KLAM
L...
LUCIFER!!
AW...

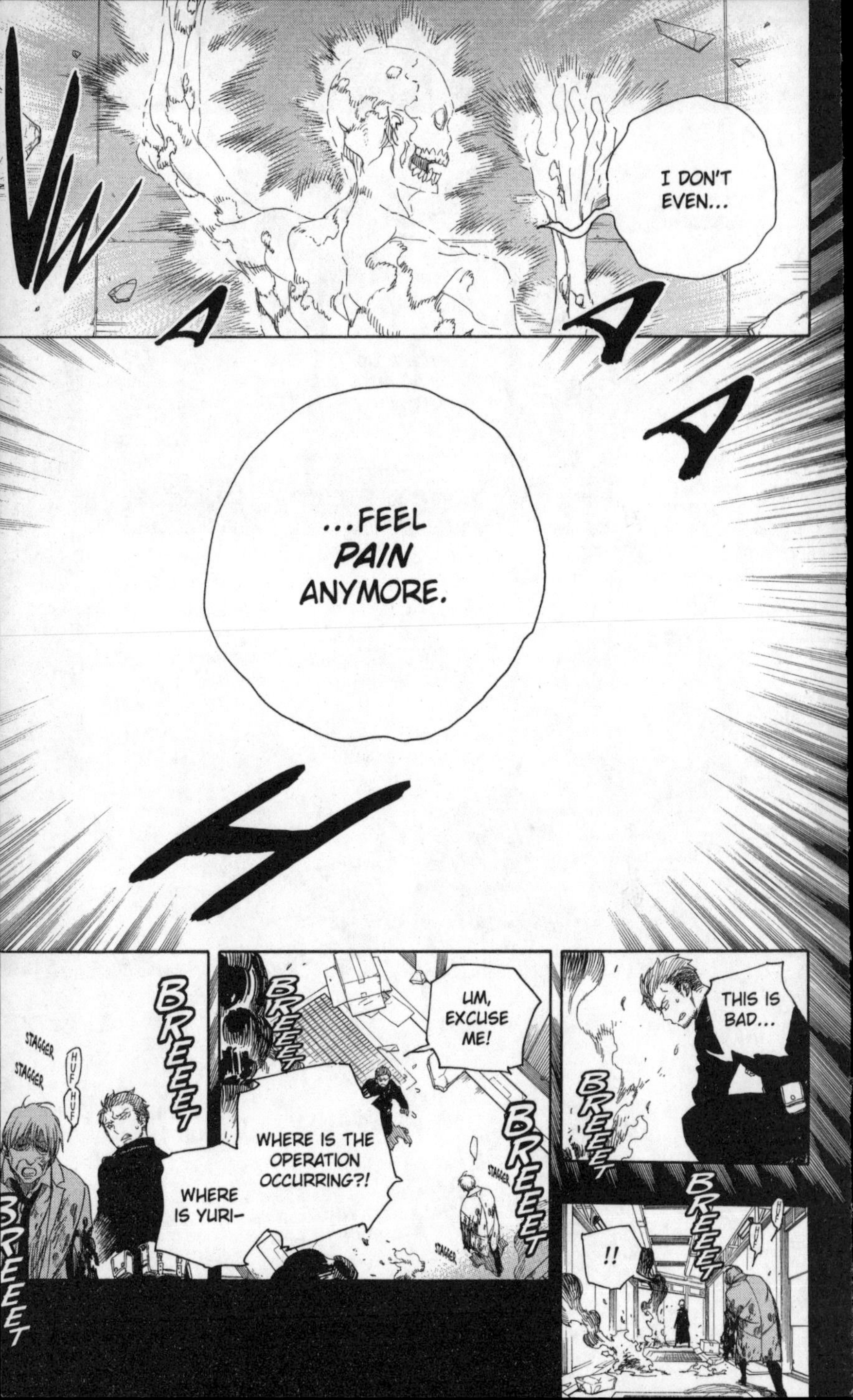

WAAAH
I DON'T EVEN...
...FEEL PAIN ANYMORE.
THIS IS BAD...
BREEET
BREEET
!!
UM, EXCUSE ME!
BREEET
BREEET
STAGGER
STAGGER
WHERE IS THE OPERATION OCCURRING?!
WHERE IS YURI-
BREEET
STAGGER
STAGGER
HUF HUF
BREEET

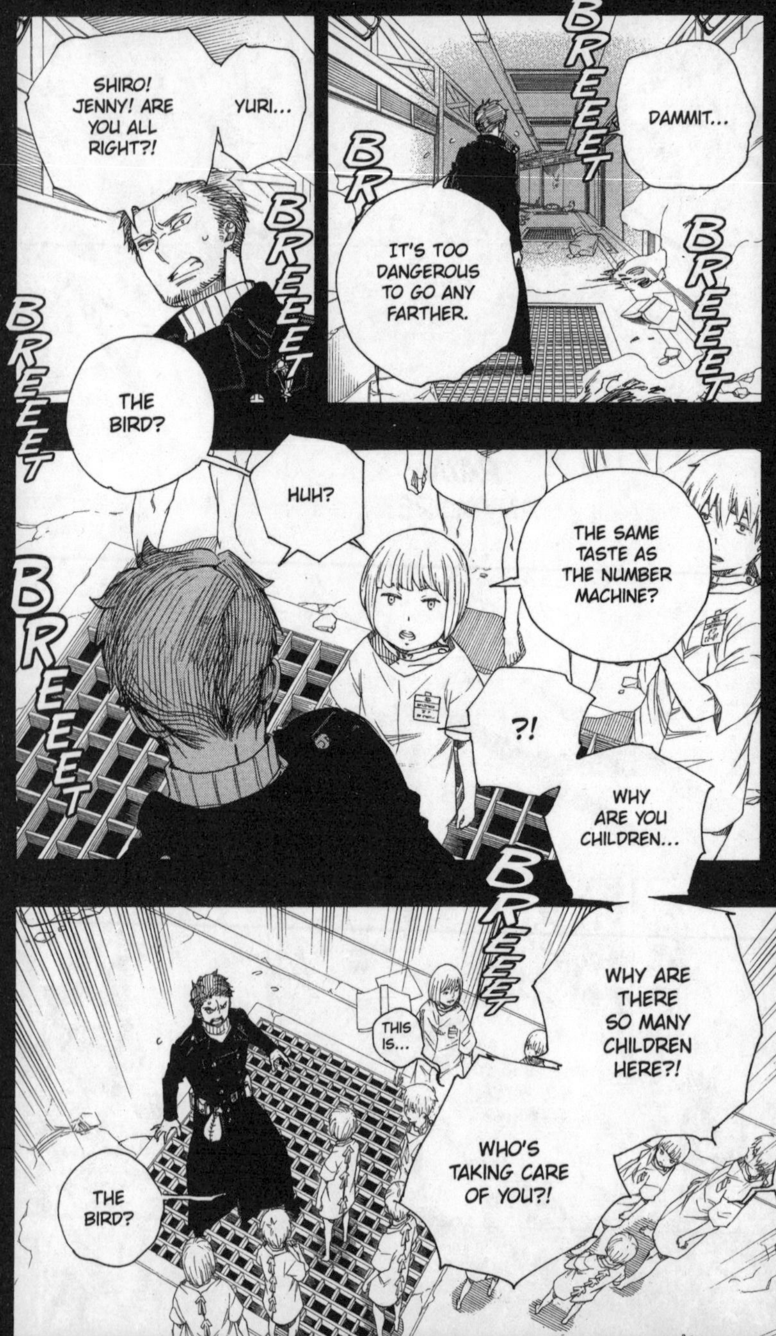
BREEET
DAMMIT...
BREEET
BR
IT'S TOO DANGEROUS TO GO ANY FARTHER.
YURI...
SHIRO! JENNY! ARE YOU ALL RIGHT?!
BREEET
BREEET
THE BIRD?
THE SAME TASTE AS THE NUMBER MACHINE?
HUH?
BREEET
?!
WHY ARE YOU CHILDREN...
BREEET
WHY ARE THERE SO MANY CHILDREN HERE?!
THIS IS...
AH HA HA!!
WHO'S TAKING CARE OF YOU?!
THE BIRD?

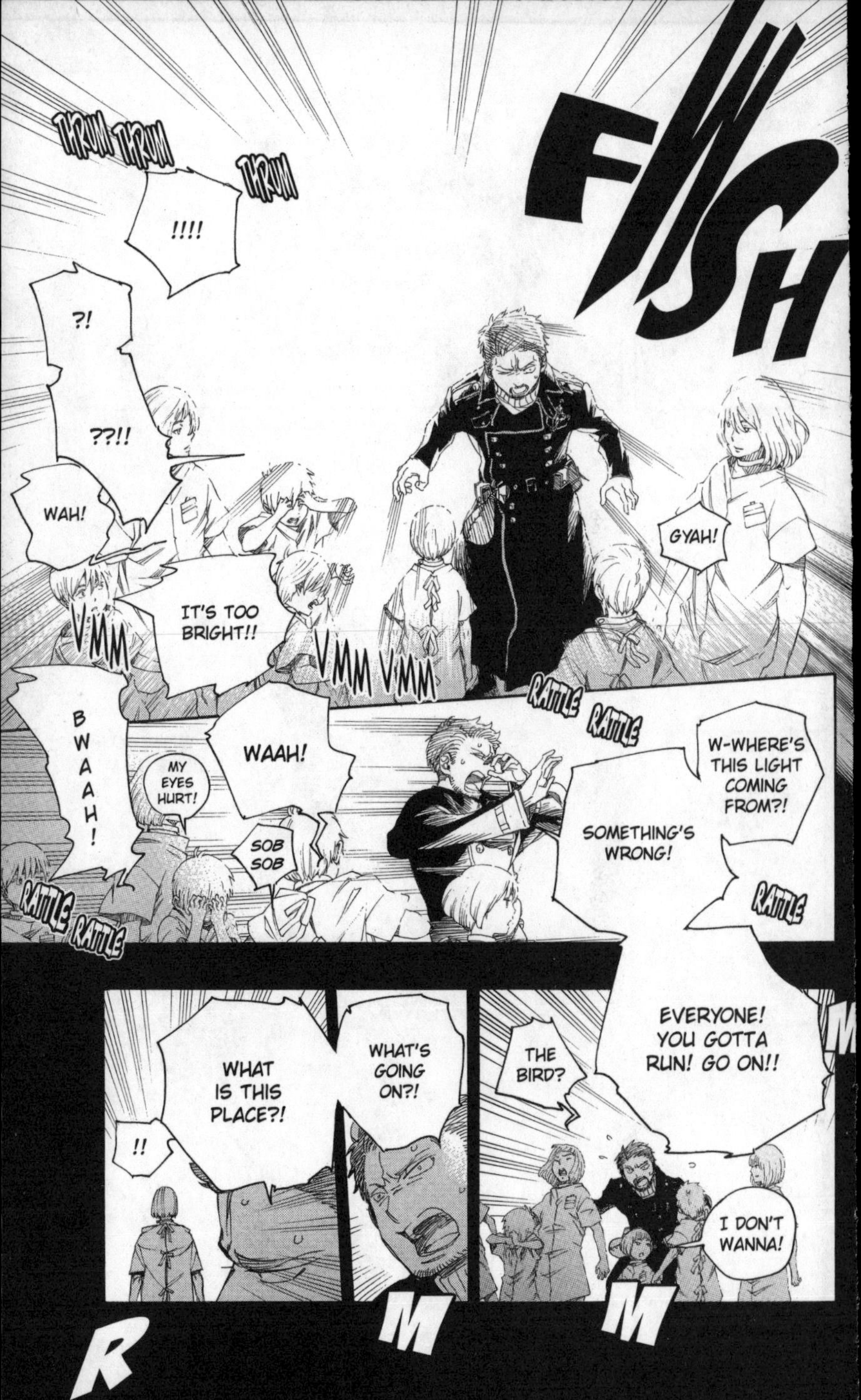
FWISH
THRUM
THRUM THRUM
!!!!
?!
??!!
GYAH!
WAH!
IT'S TOO BRIGHT!!
VMM VMM
VMM
RATTLE RATTLE
W-WHERE'S THIS LIGHT COMING FROM?!
SOMETHING'S WRONG!
RATTLE
WAAH!
MY EYES HURT!
BWAAH!
SOB SOB
RATTLE RATTLE
EVERYONE! YOU GOTTA RUN! GO ON!!
THE BIRD?
I DON'T WANNA!
WHAT'S GOING ON?!
WHAT IS THIS PLACE?!
!!
RMMM

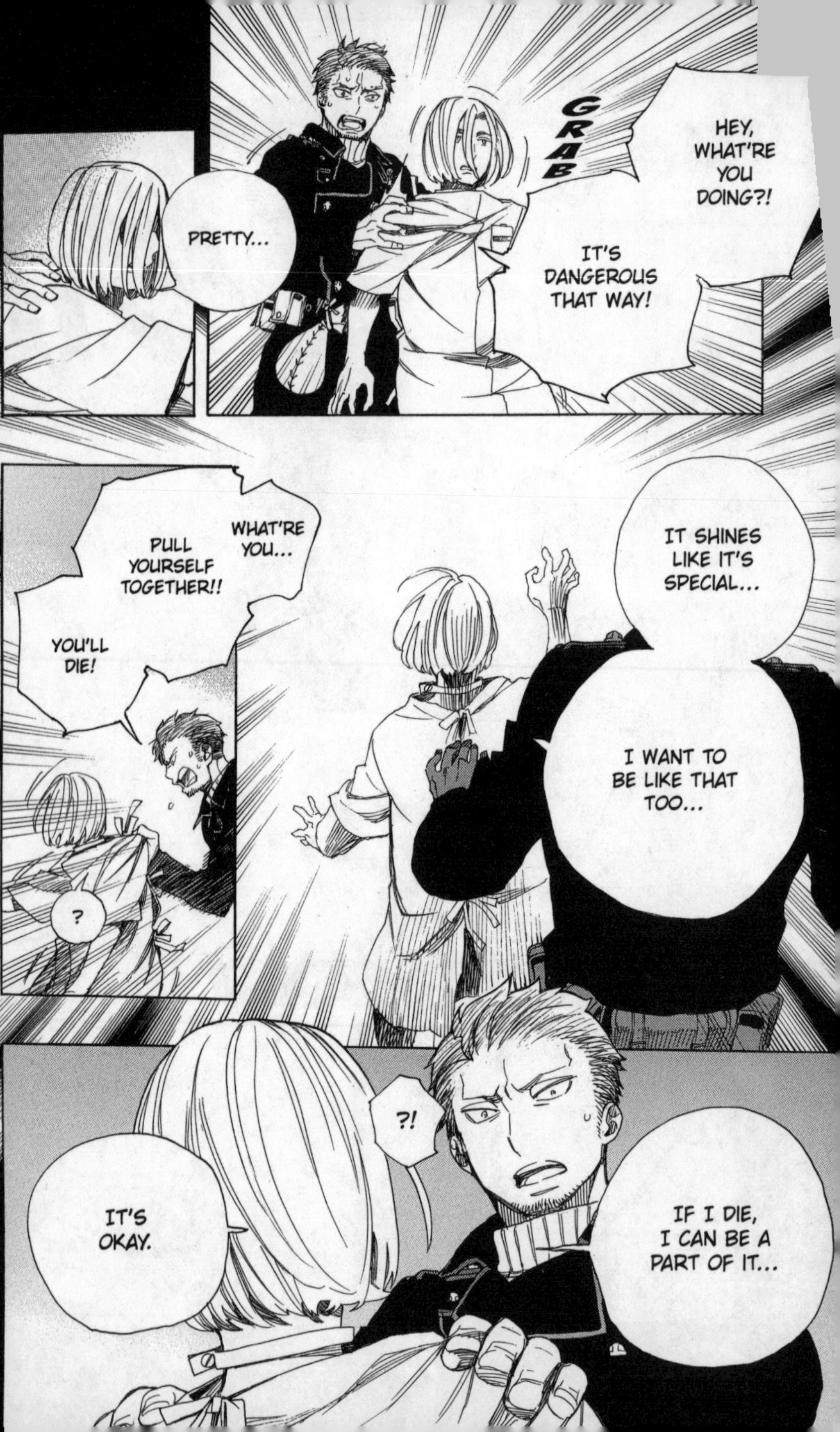
GRAB
HEY, WHAT'RE YOU DOING?!
IT'S DANGEROUS THAT WAY!
PRETTY...
IT SHINES LIKE IT'S SPECIAL...
I WANT TO BE LIKE THAT TOO...
WHAT'RE YOU...
PULL YOURSELF TOGETHER!!
YOU'LL DIE!
?
?!
IF I DIE, I CAN BE A PART OF IT...
IT'S OKAY.

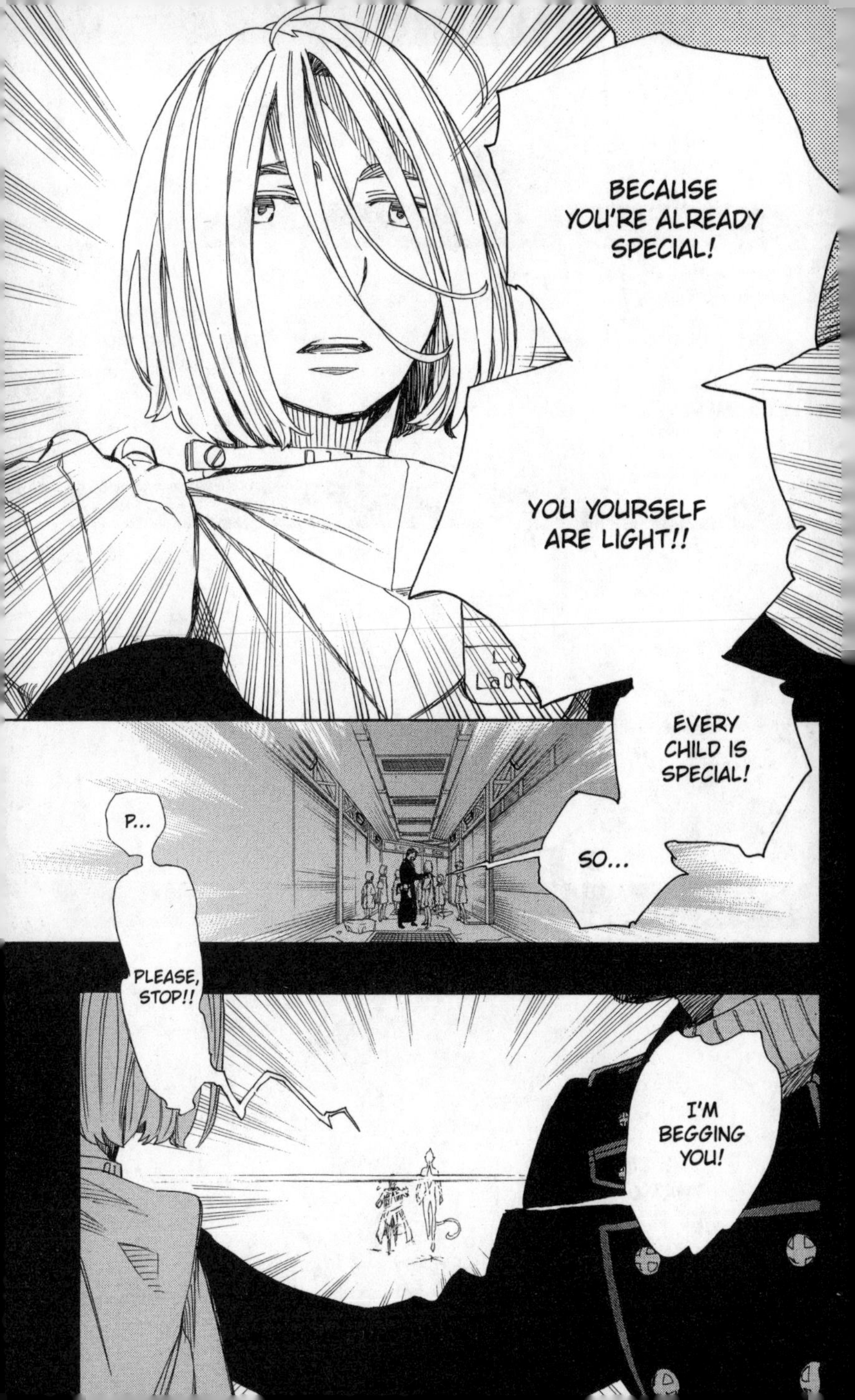
BECAUSE YOU'RE ALREADY SPECIAL!
YOU YOURSELF ARE LIGHT!!
EVERY CHILD IS SPECIAL!
SO...
P...
PLEASE, STOP!!
I'M BEGGING YOU!

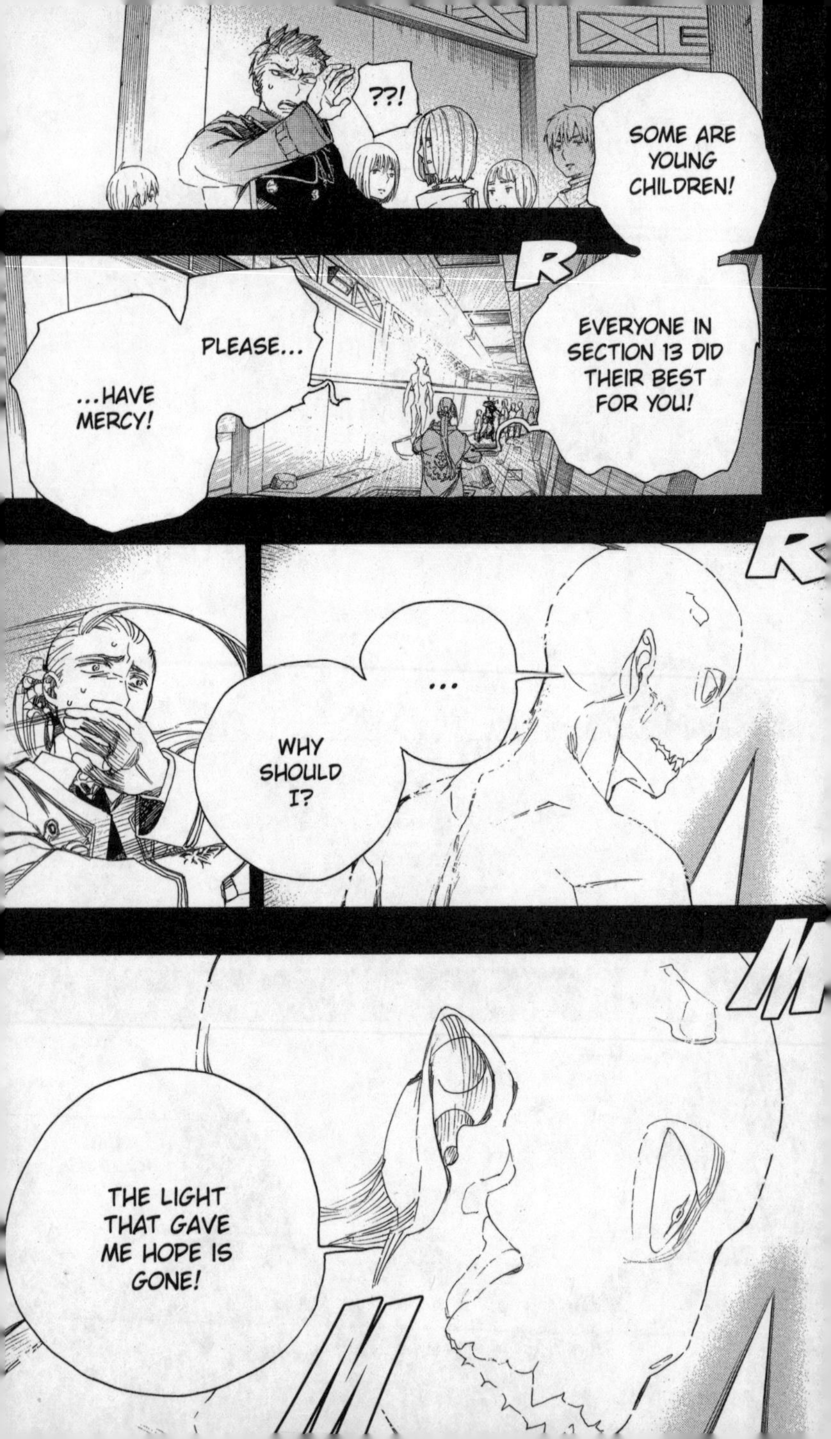
SOME ARE YOUNG CHILDREN!
??!
EVERYONE IN SECTION 13 DID THEIR BEST FOR YOU!
R
PLEASE...
...HAVE MERCY!
R
...
WHY SHOULD I?
M
THE LIGHT THAT GAVE ME HOPE IS GONE!
M

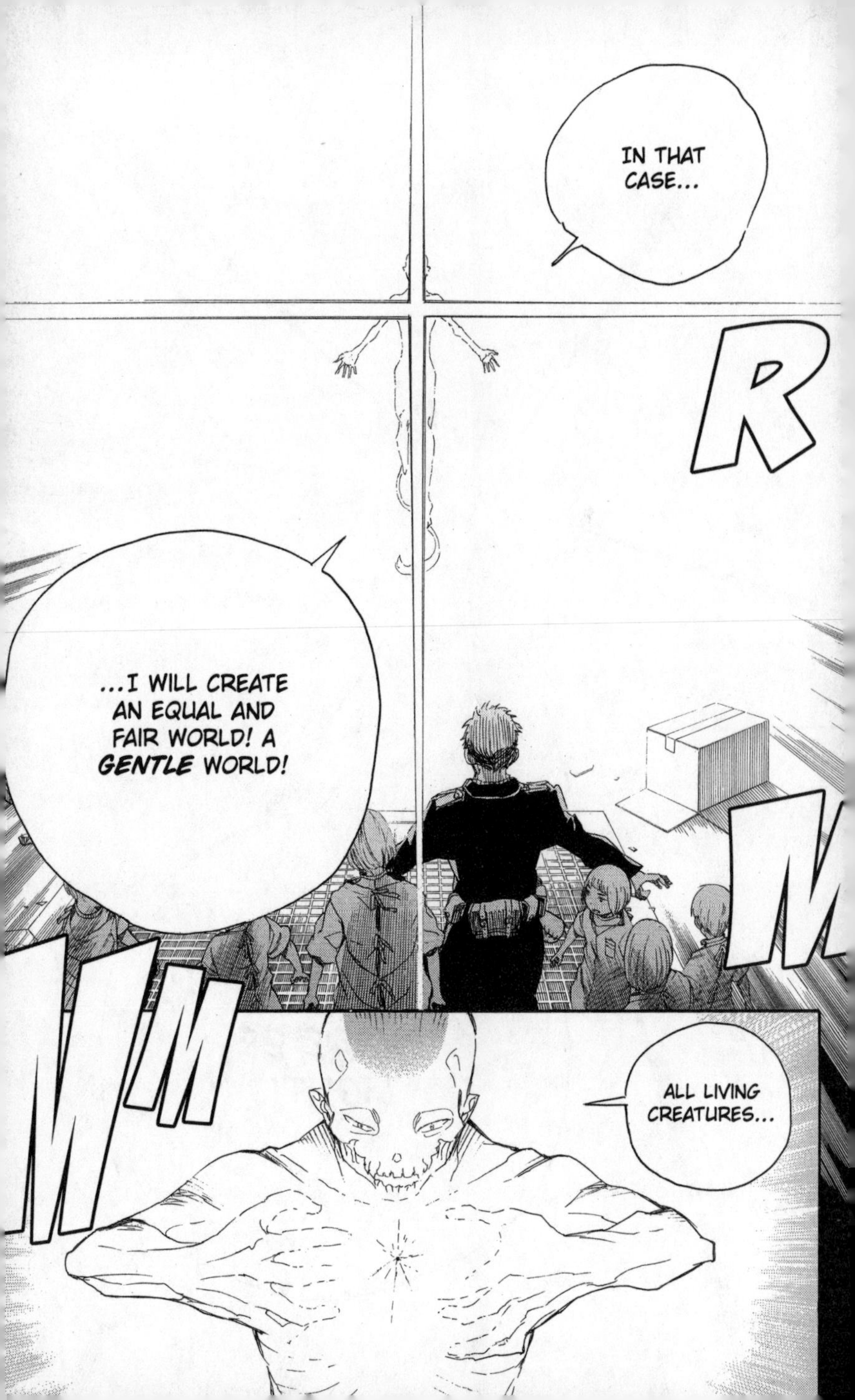
IN THAT CASE...
RMMM
...I WILL CREATE AN EQUAL AND FAIR WORLD! A *GENTLE* WORLD!
ALL LIVING CREATURES...

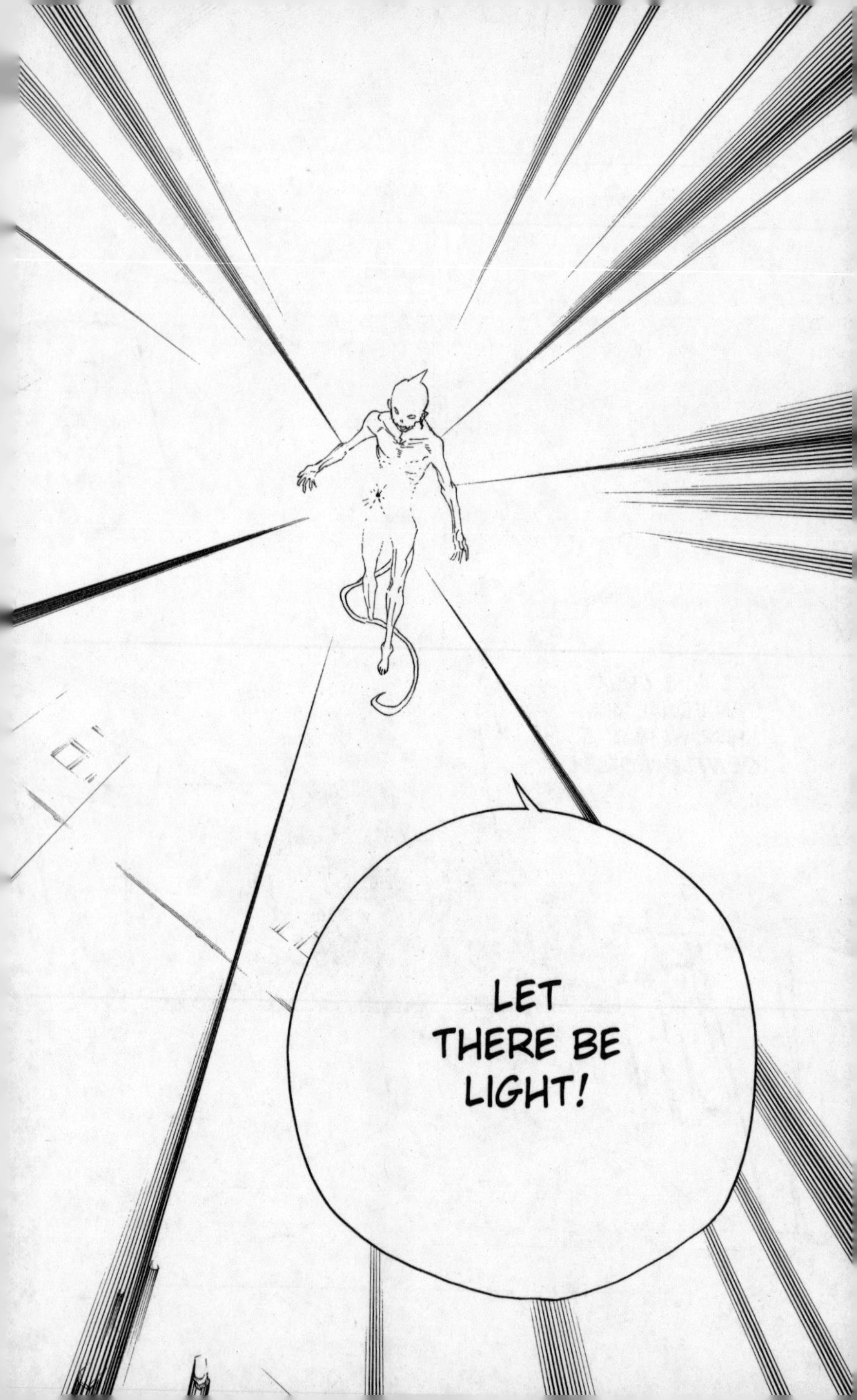
LET THERE BE LIGHT!

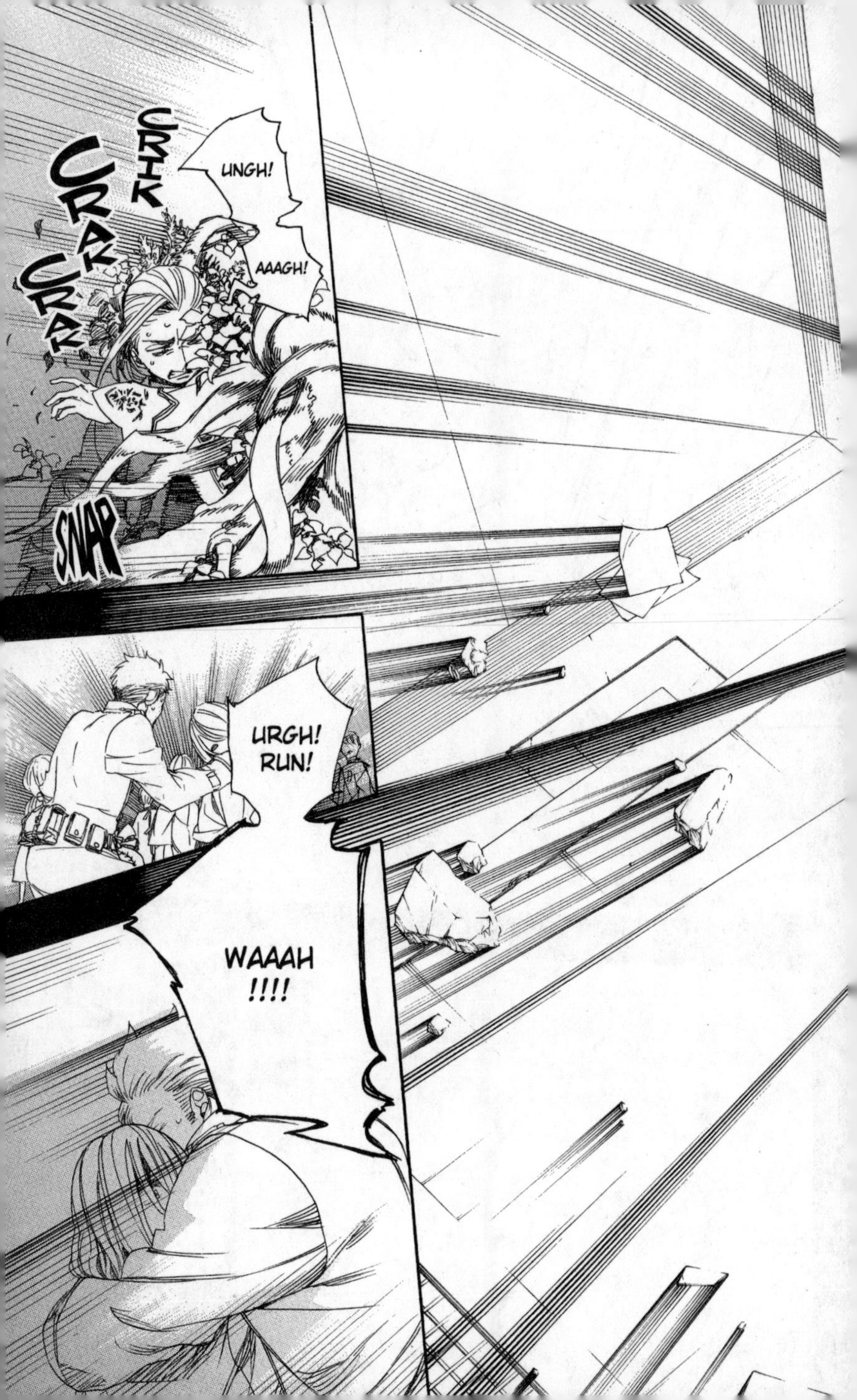
UNGH!
AAAGH!
CRIK
CRAK
CRAK
SNAP
URGH! RUN!
WAAAH !!!!

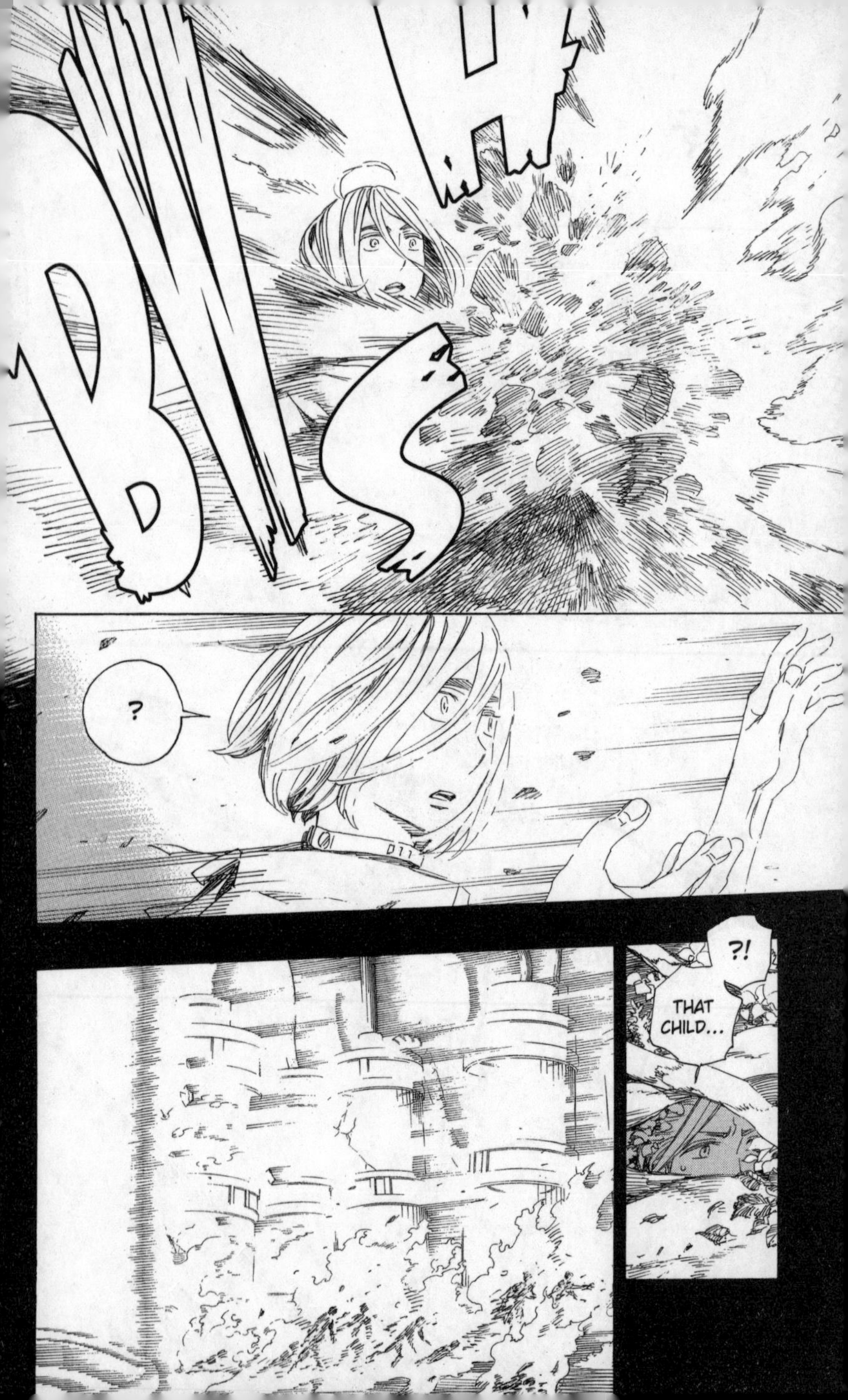
BDSH
?
?!
THAT CHILD...

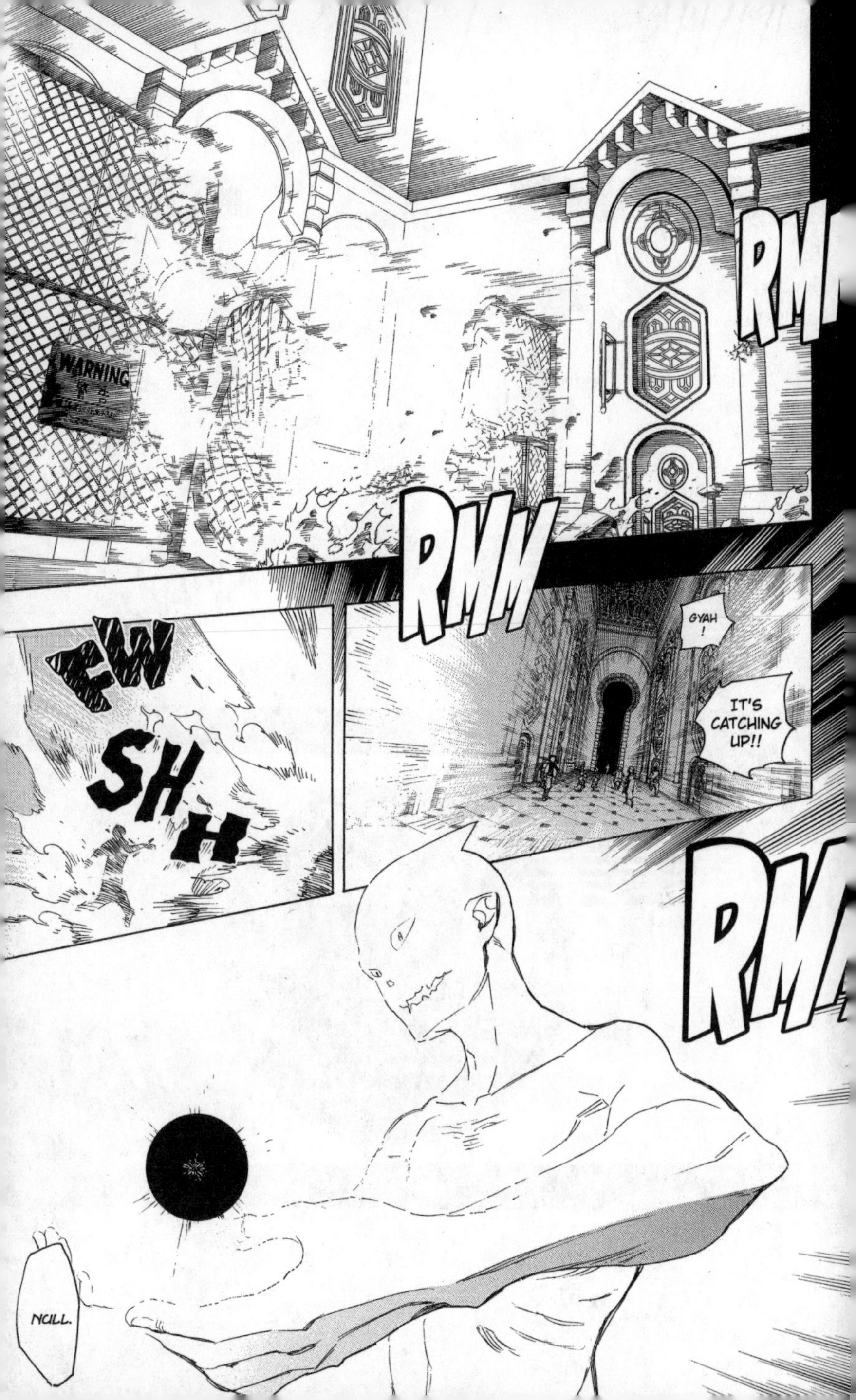
WARNING
RMM
GYAH!
IT'S CATCHING UP!!
FWSHH
NULL.

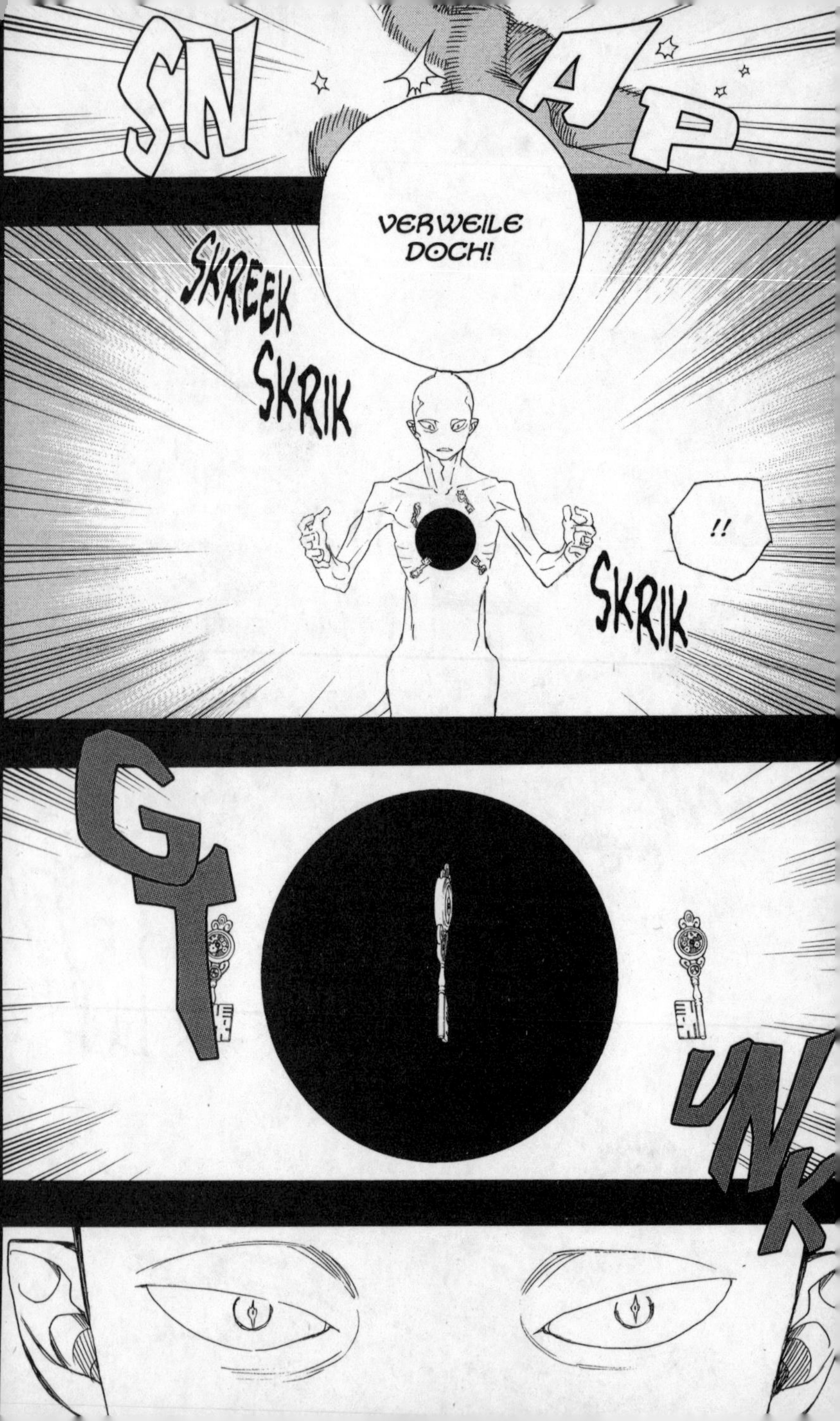
SNAP
VERWEILE DOCH!
!!
SKRIK
SKREEK
SKRIK
GUNK

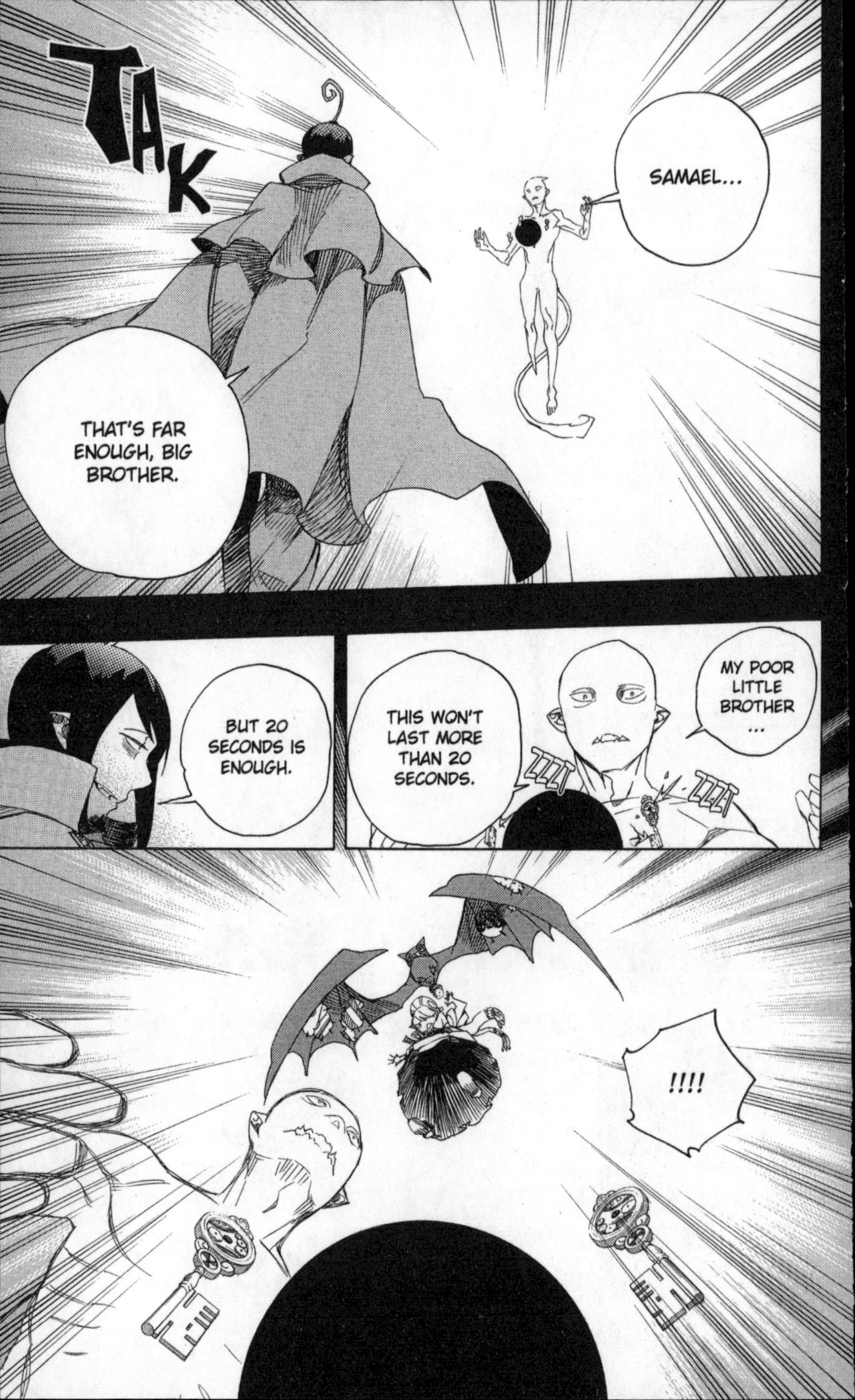
SAMAEL...
TAK
THAT'S FAR ENOUGH, BIG BROTHER.
MY POOR LITTLE BROTHER ...
ZZZT
ZZZT
THIS WON'T LAST MORE THAN 20 SECONDS.
BUT 20 SECONDS IS ENOUGH.
!!!!

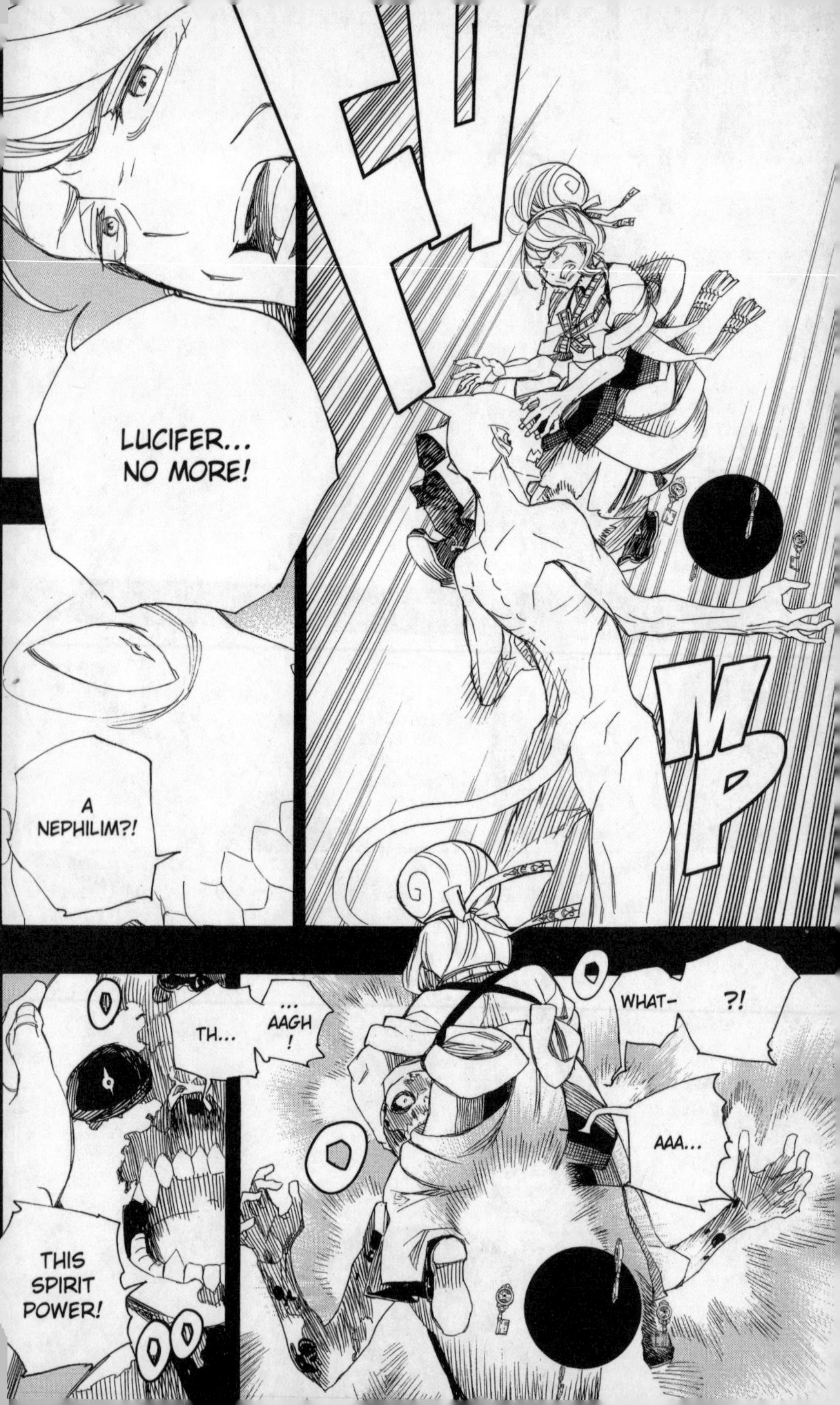
LUCIFER... NO MORE!
A NEPHILIM?!
WHAT- ?!
AAA...
...AAGH!
TH...
THIS SPIRIT POWER!

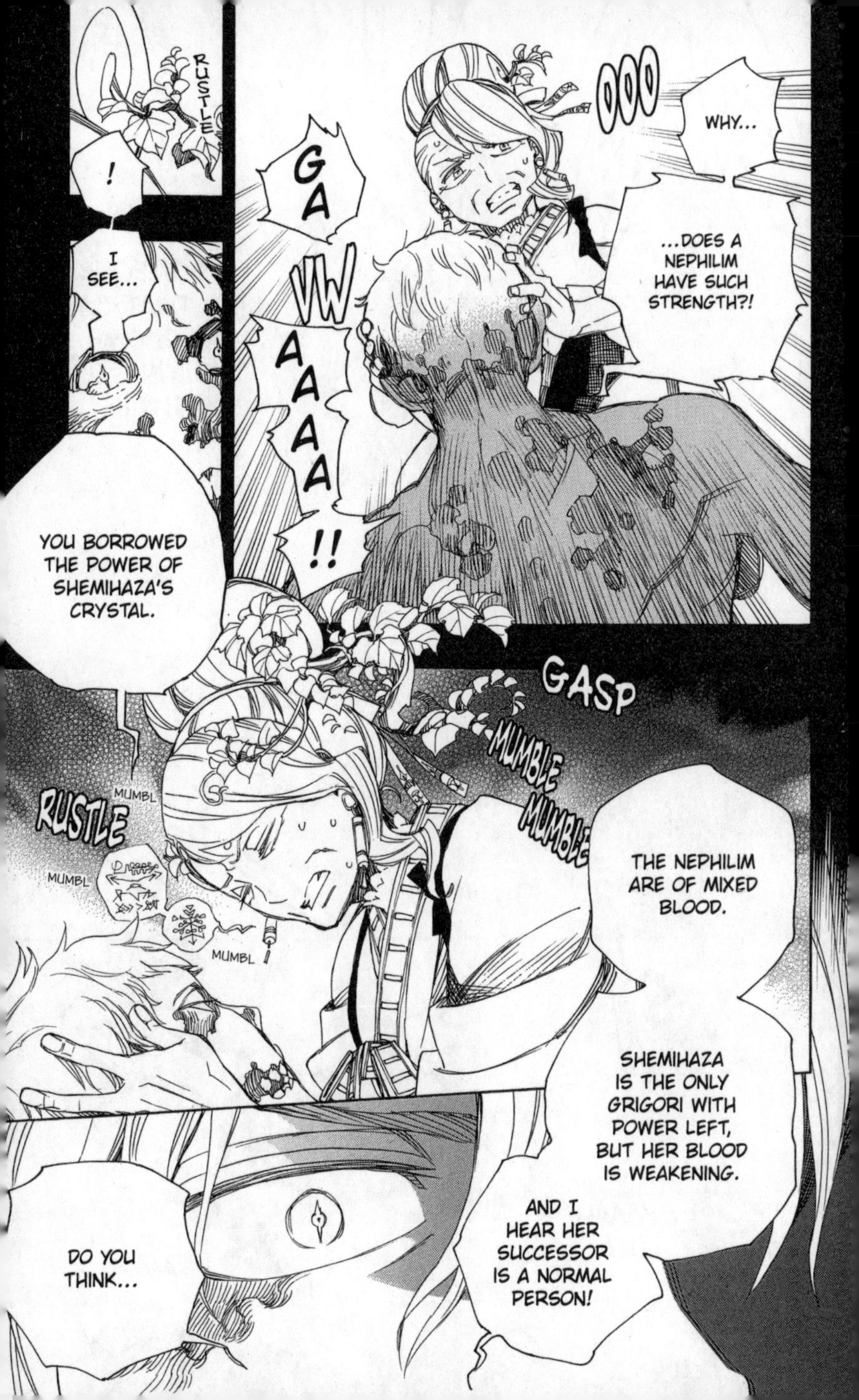
OOO
WHY...
GA
VWAAAAA!!
...DOES A NEPHILIM HAVE SUCH STRENGTH?!
RUSTLE
!
I SEE...
YOU BORROWED THE POWER OF SHEMIHAZA'S CRYSTAL.
GASP
MUMBLE
MUMBLE
THE NEPHILIM ARE OF MIXED BLOOD.
MUMBL
RUSTLE
MUMBL
MUMBL
SHEMIHAZA IS THE ONLY GRIGORI WITH POWER LEFT, BUT HER BLOOD IS WEAKENING.
AND I HEAR HER SUCCESSOR IS A NORMAL PERSON!
DO YOU THINK...

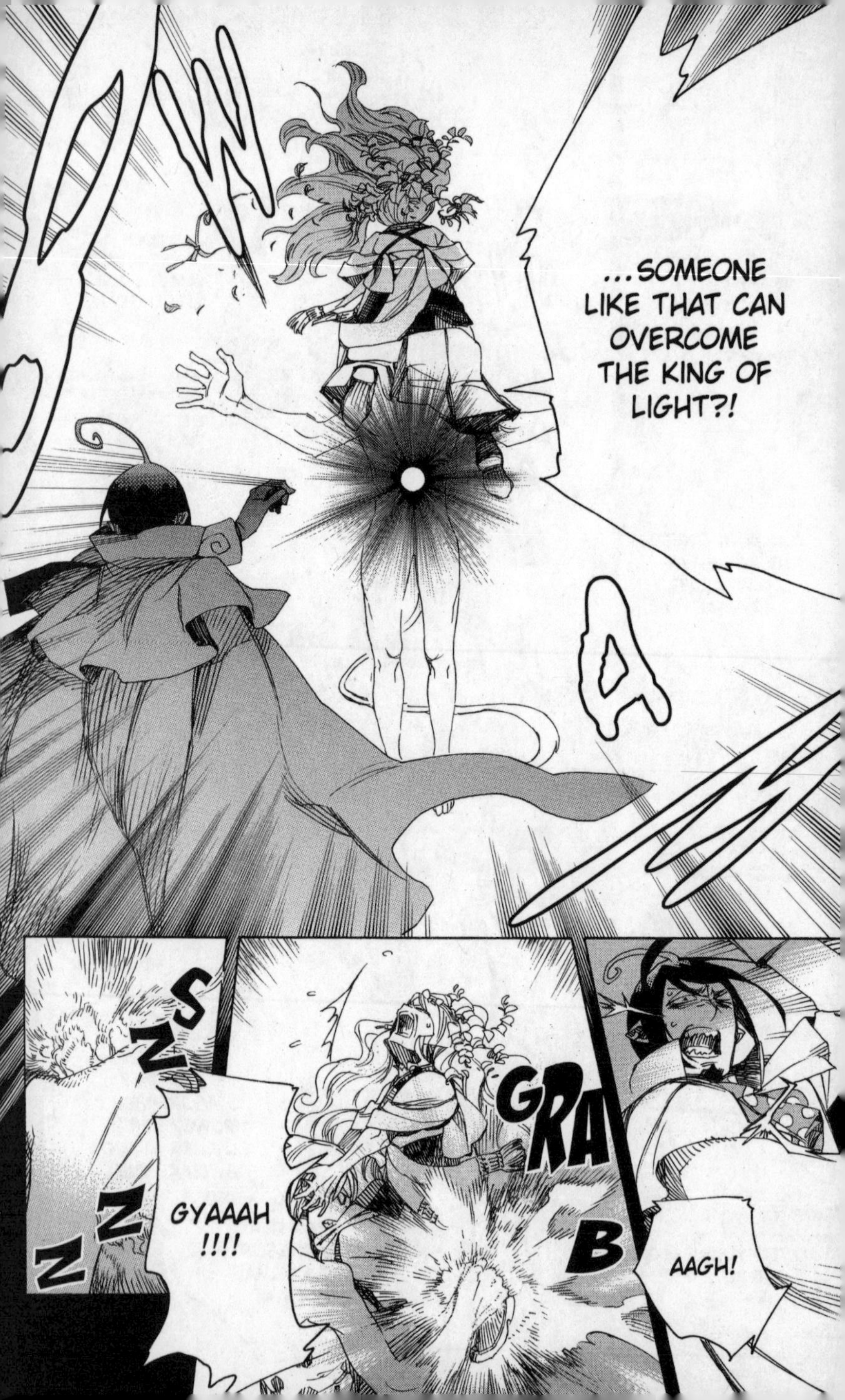
...SOMEONE LIKE THAT CAN OVERCOME THE KING OF LIGHT?!
AAGH!
GRAB
GYAAAH !!!!

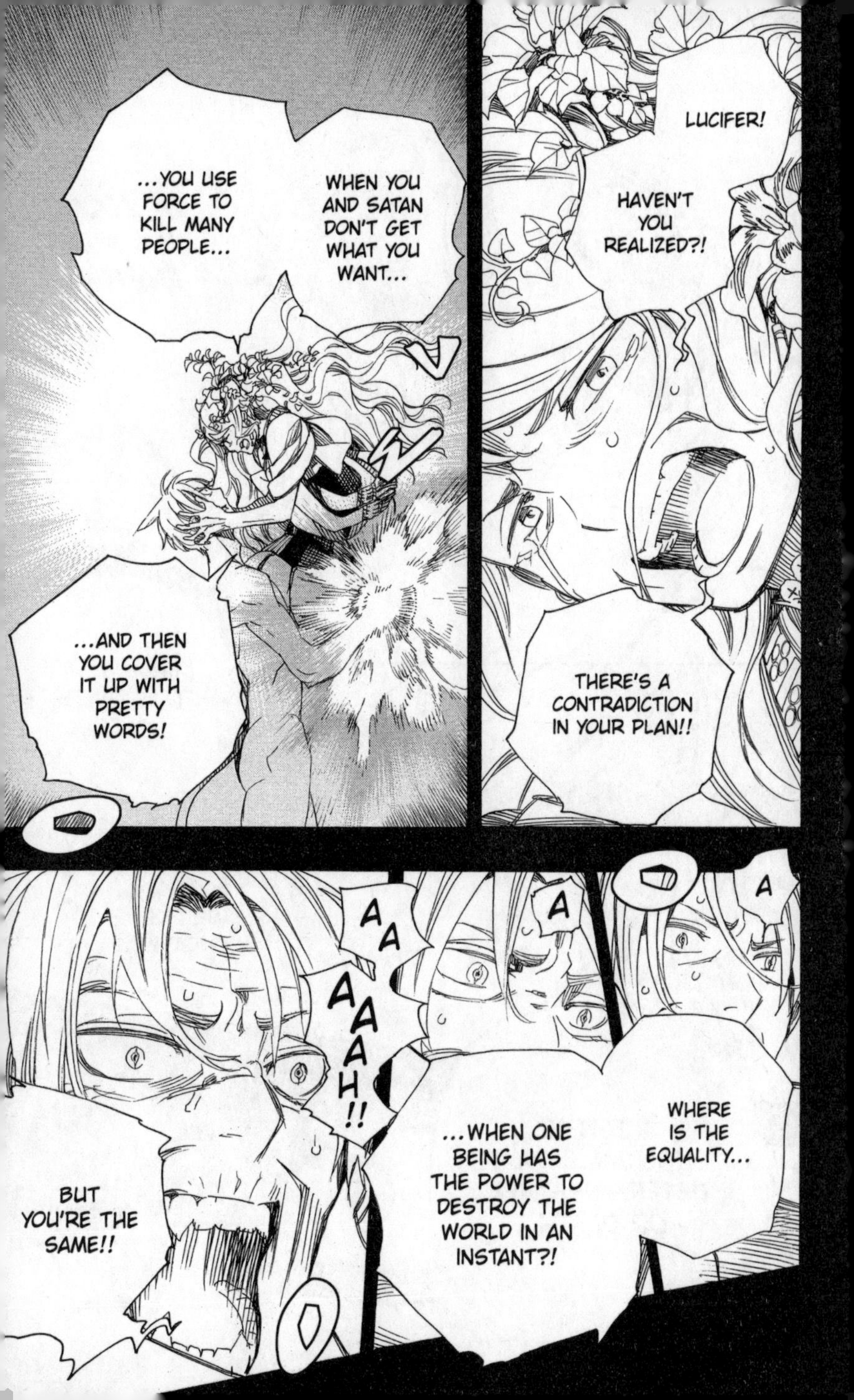
LUCIFER!
HAVEN'T YOU REALIZED?!
THERE'S A CONTRADICTION IN YOUR PLAN!!
WHEN YOU AND SATAN DON'T GET WHAT YOU WANT...
...YOU USE FORCE TO KILL MANY PEOPLE...
V
W
...AND THEN YOU COVER IT UP WITH PRETTY WORDS!
O
O
A
WHERE IS THE EQUALITY...
...WHEN ONE BEING HAS THE POWER TO DESTROY THE WORLD IN AN INSTANT?!
A
AAAAAH!!
BUT YOU'RE THE SAME!!
O

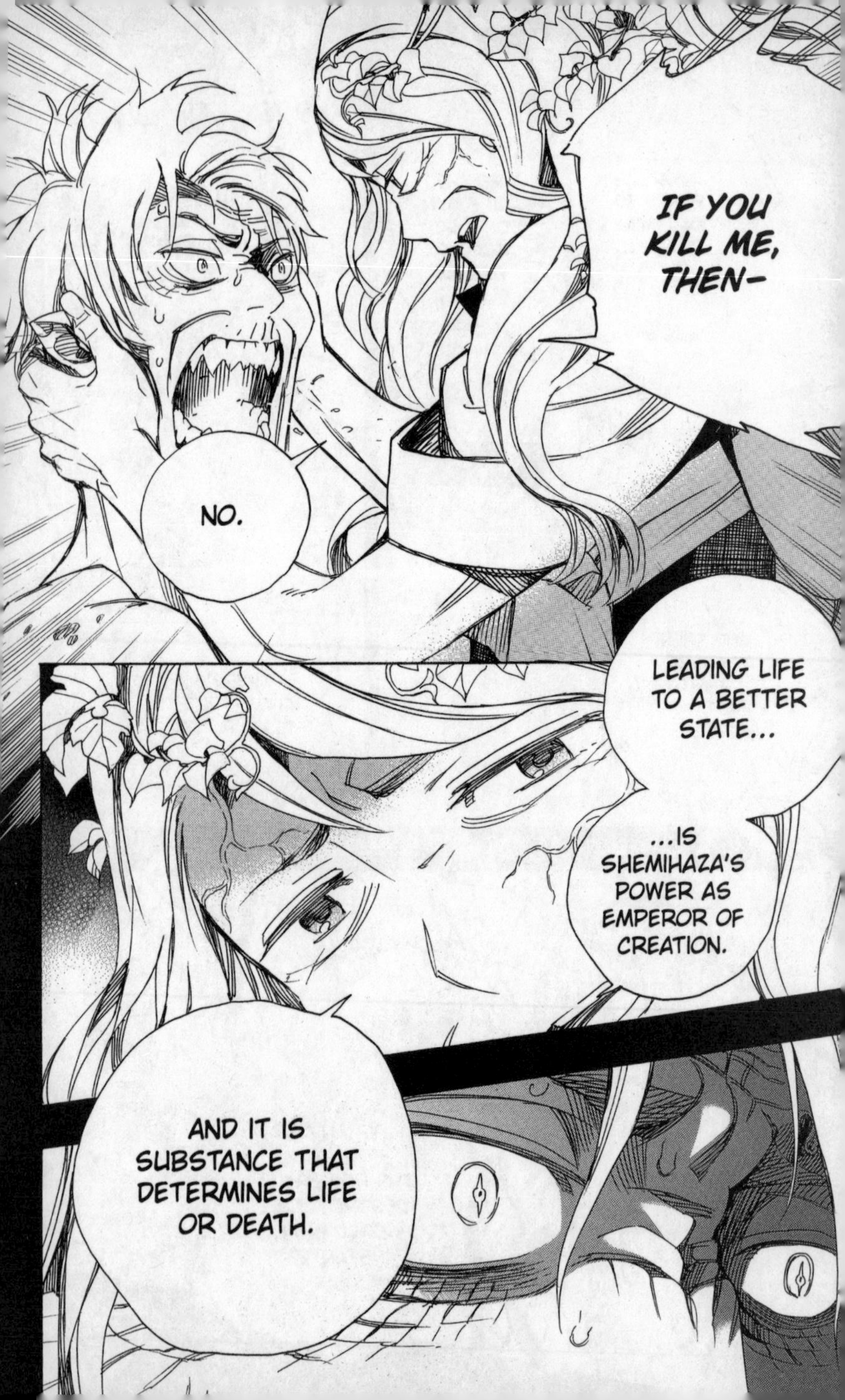
IF YOU KILL ME, THEN-
NO.
LEADING LIFE TO A BETTER STATE...
...IS SHEMIHAZA'S POWER AS EMPEROR OF CREATION.
AND IT IS SUBSTANCE THAT DETERMINES LIFE OR DEATH.

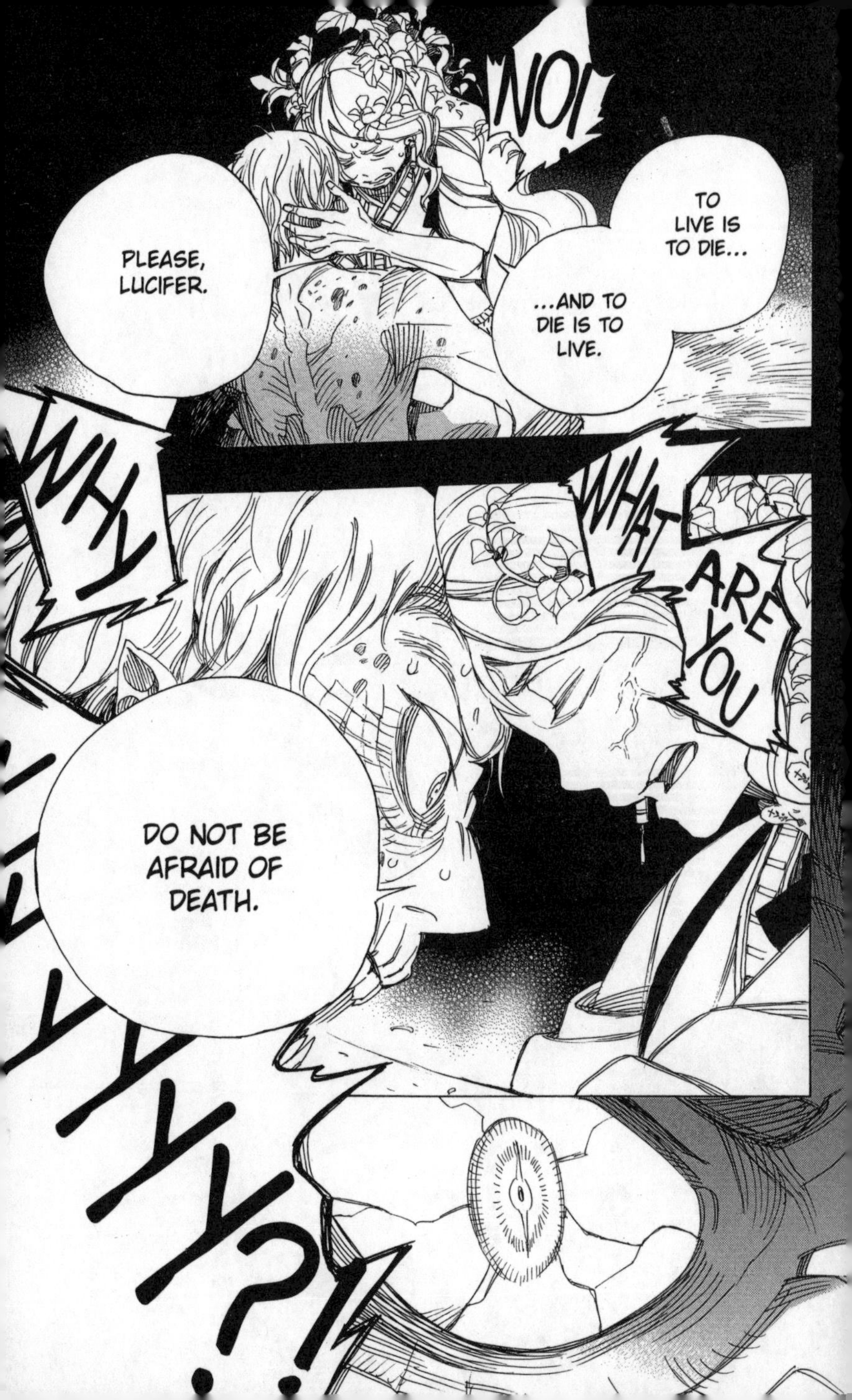
NO!
TO LIVE IS TO DIE...
...AND TO DIE IS TO LIVE.
PLEASE, LUCIFER.
WHAT ARE YOU
DO NOT BE AFRAID OF DEATH.
WHYYYY?!

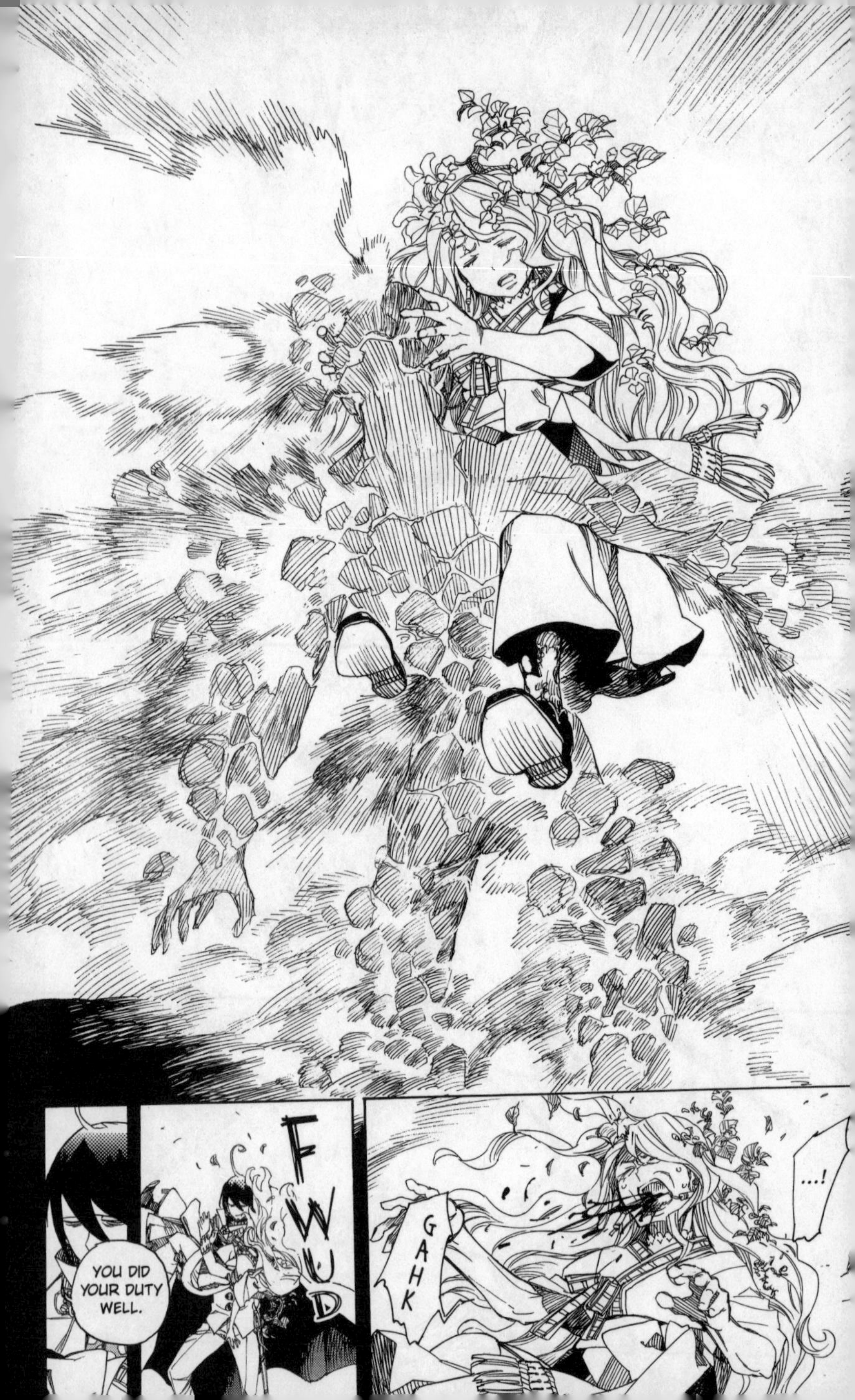
...!
GAHK
FWUD
YOU DID YOUR DUTY WELL.

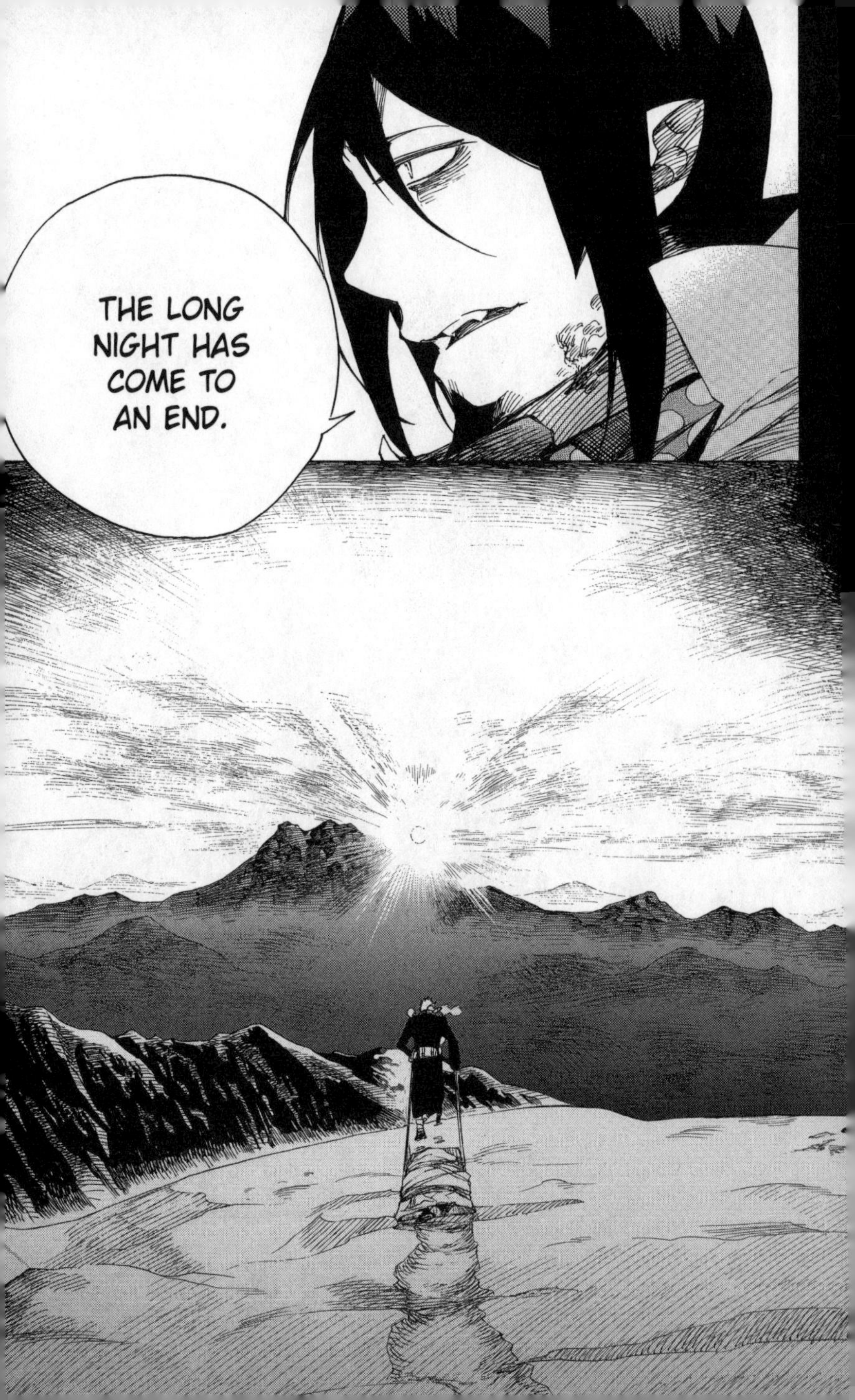
THE LONG NIGHT HAS COME TO AN END.

CHAPTER 118: SsC23:17I

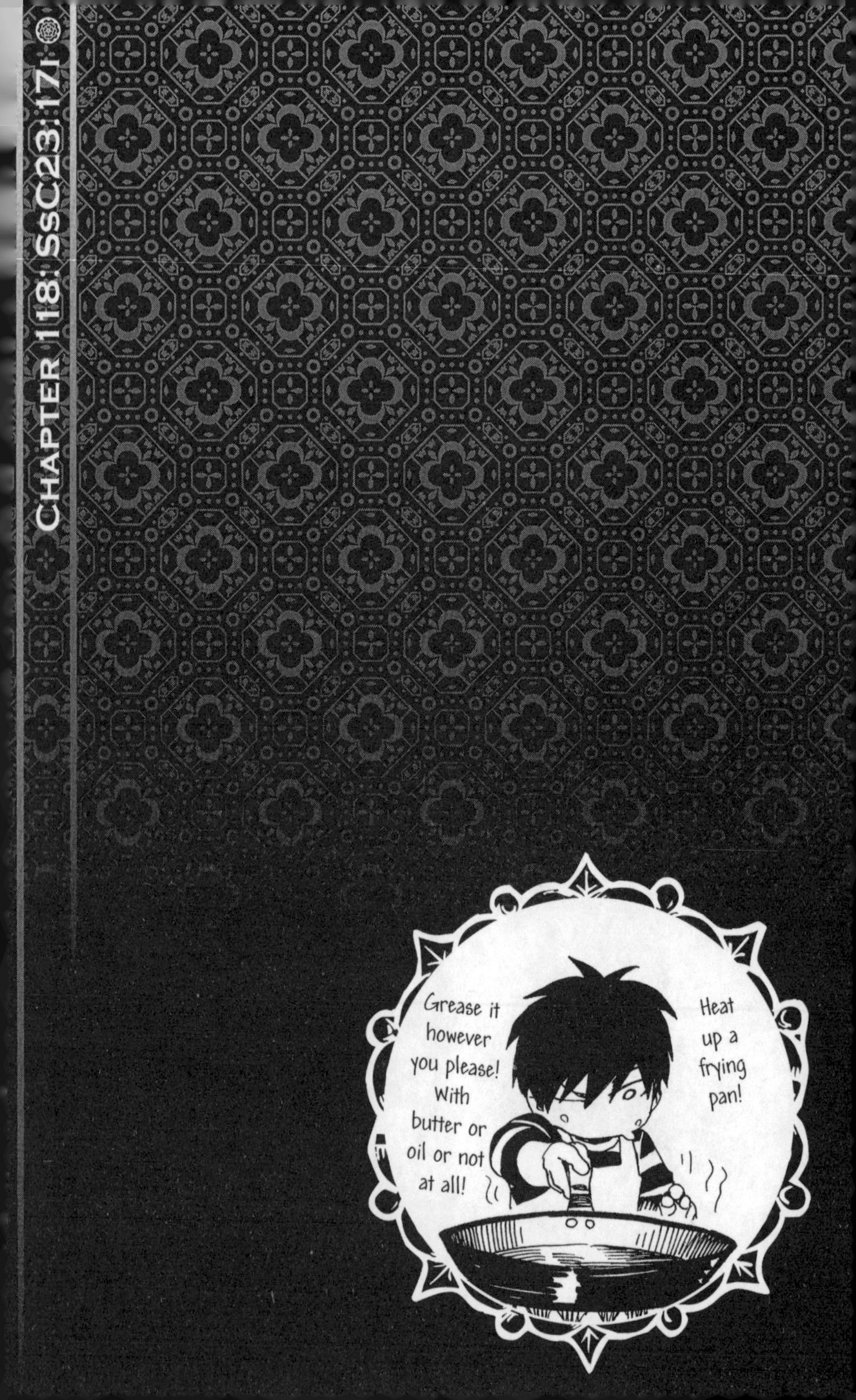
Heat up a frying pan!
Grease it however you please! With butter or oil or not at all!

Chapter 119: SsC24:16

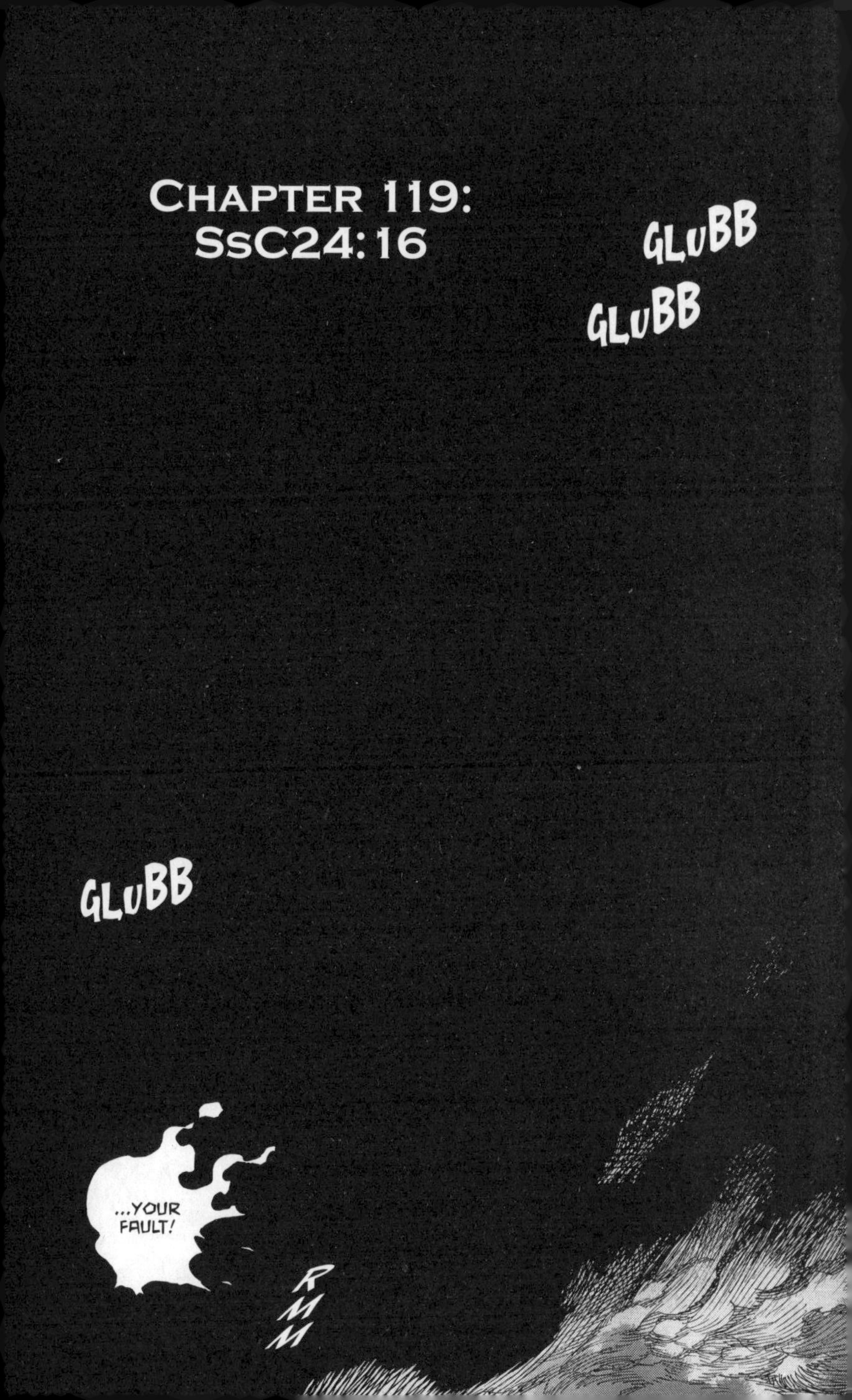
GLUBB
GLUBB
GLUBB
...YOUR FAULT!
RMMM

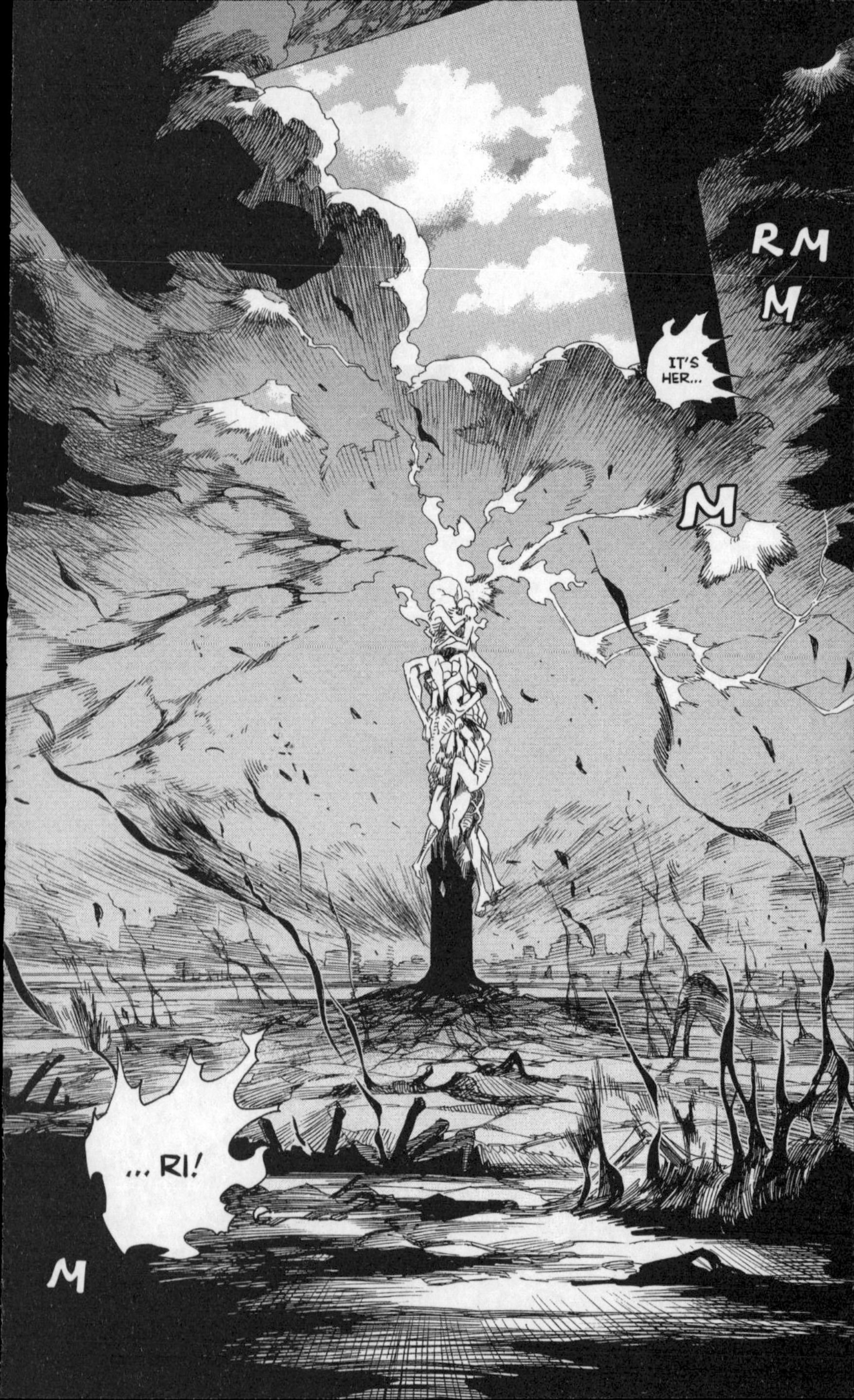
RM
M
IT'S HER...
M
...RI!
M

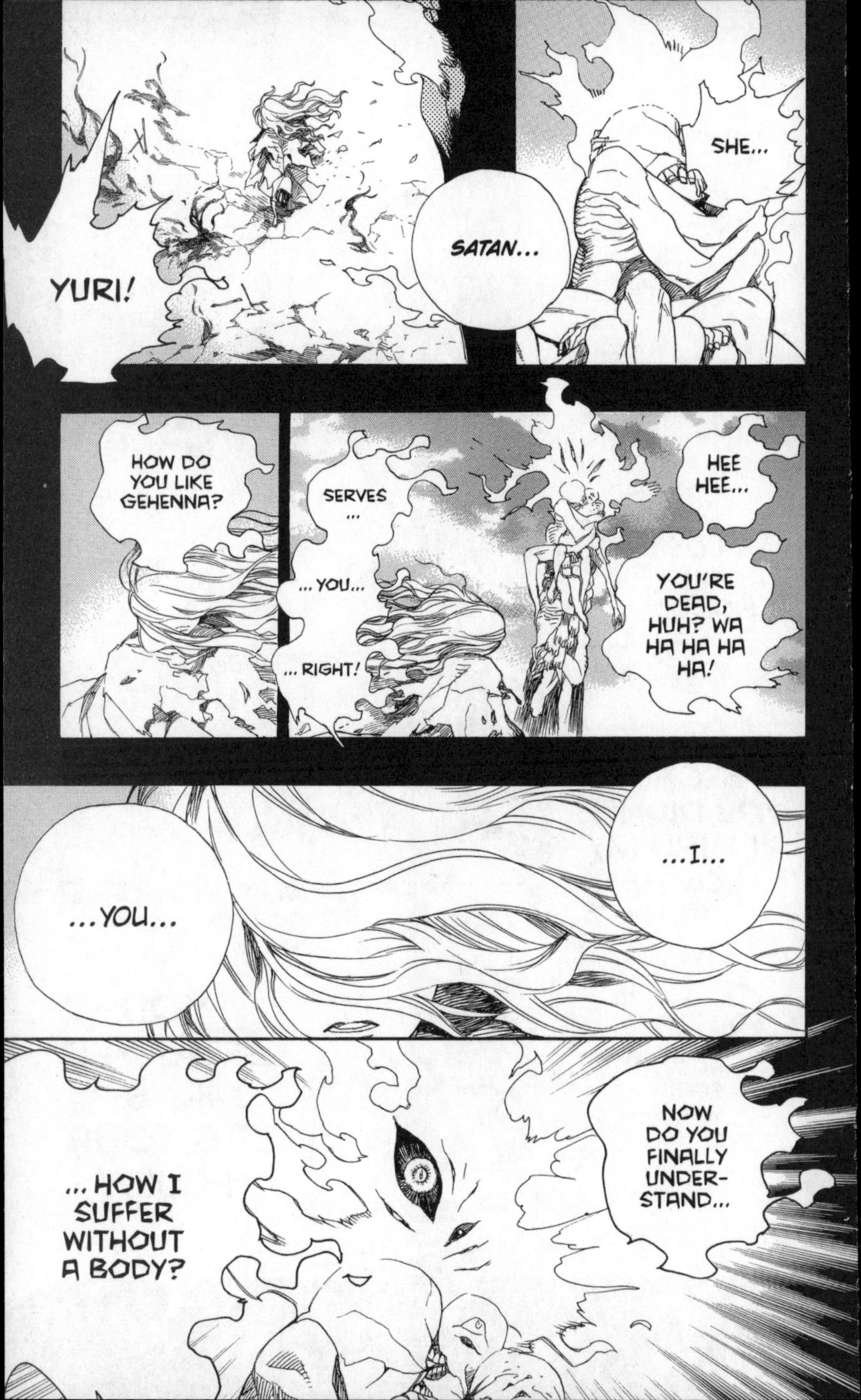
SHE...
SATAN...
YURI!
HEE HEE...
YOU'RE DEAD, HUH? WA HA HA HA HA!
SERVES ...
... YOU...
... RIGHT!
HOW DO YOU LIKE GEHENNA?
...I...
...YOU...
NOW DO YOU FINALLY UNDER-STAND...
... HOW I SUFFER WITHOUT A BODY?

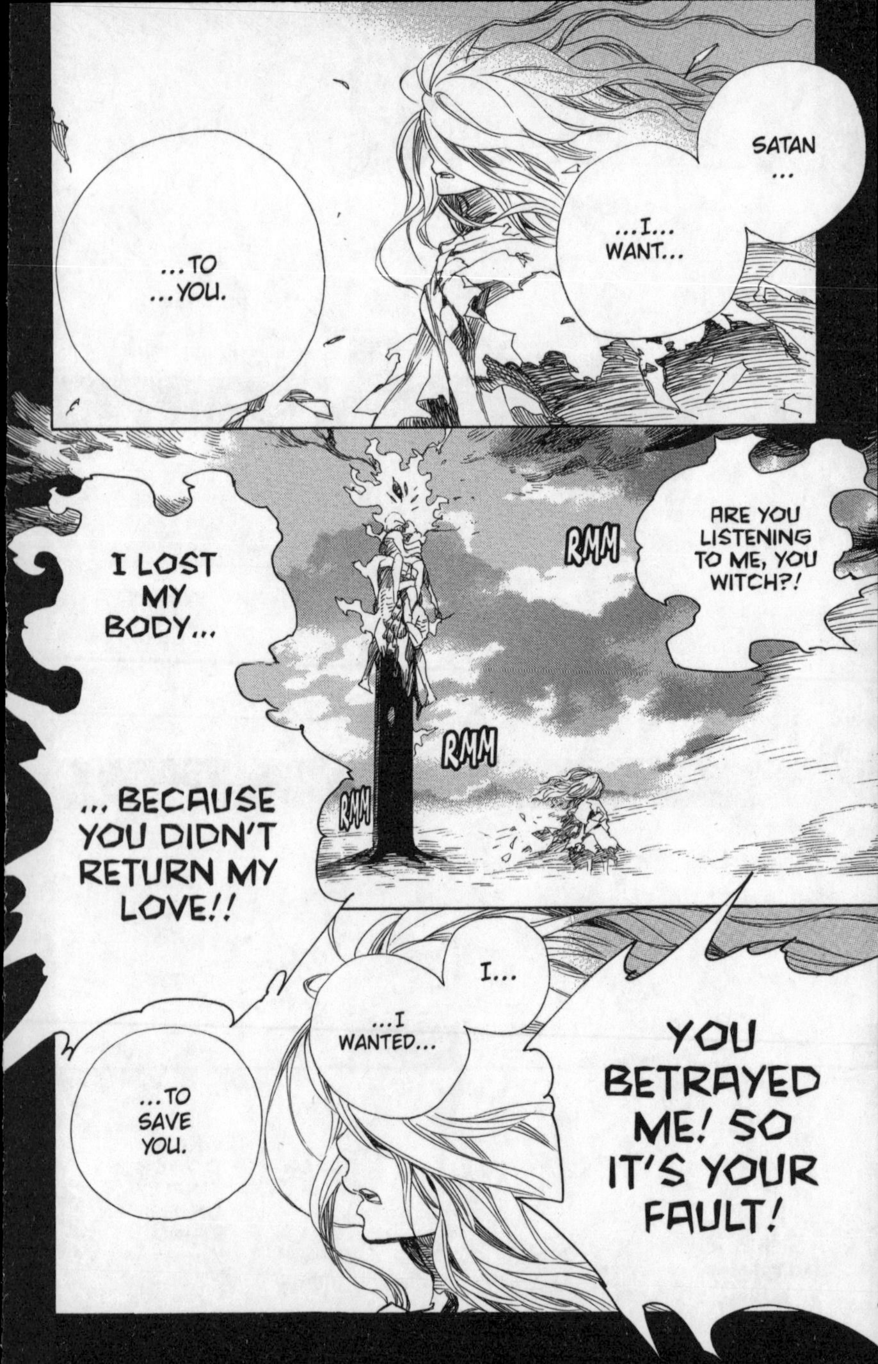
SATAN ...
...I... WANT...
...TO ...YOU.
ARE YOU LISTENING TO ME, YOU WITCH?!
RMM
RMM
RMM
I LOST MY BODY...
... BECAUSE YOU DIDN'T RETURN MY LOVE!!
YOU BETRAYED ME! SO IT'S YOUR FAULT!
I...
...I WANTED...
...TO SAVE YOU.

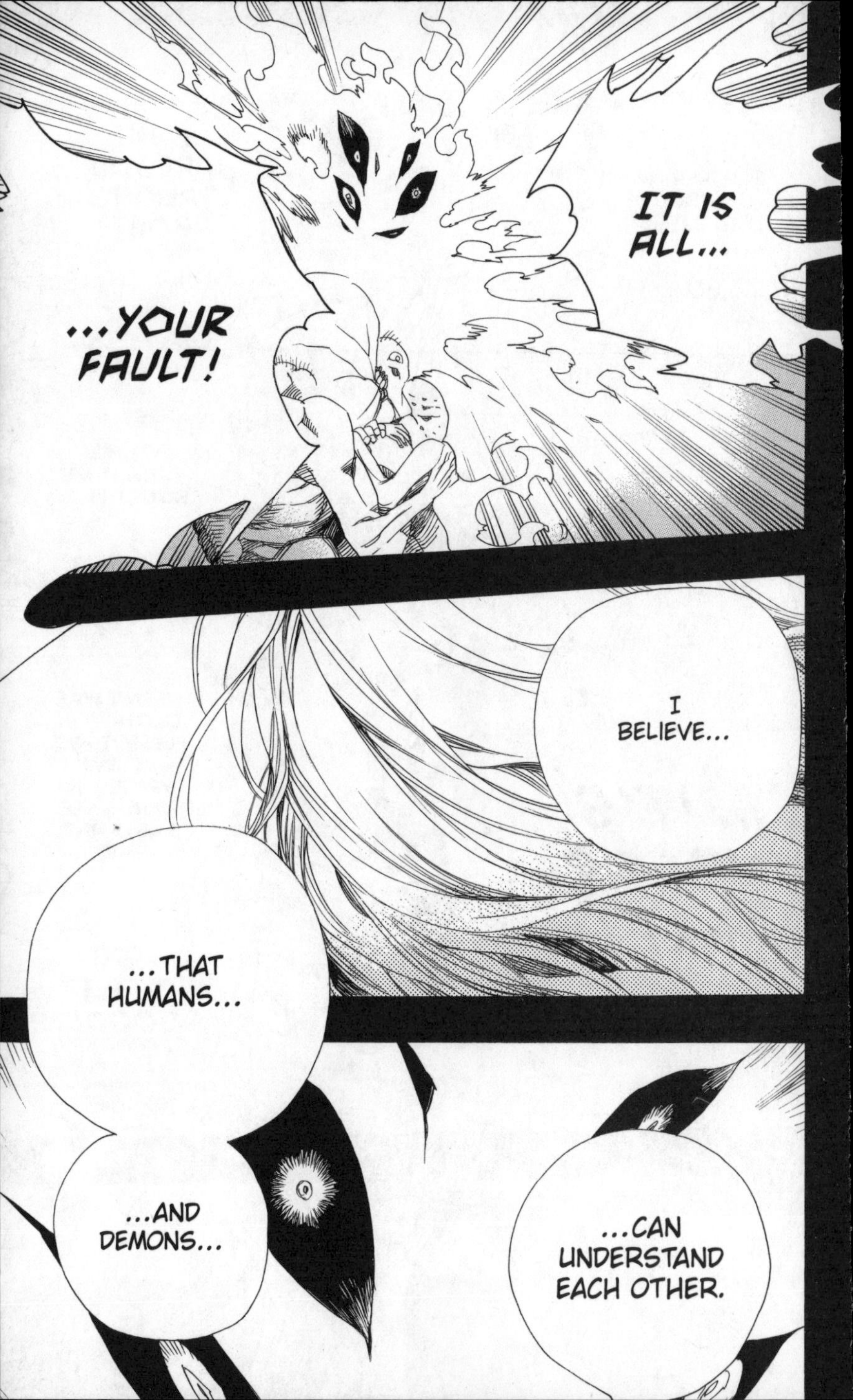
IT IS ALL...
...YOUR FAULT!
I BELIEVE...
...THAT HUMANS...
...AND DEMONS...
...CAN UNDERSTAND EACH OTHER.

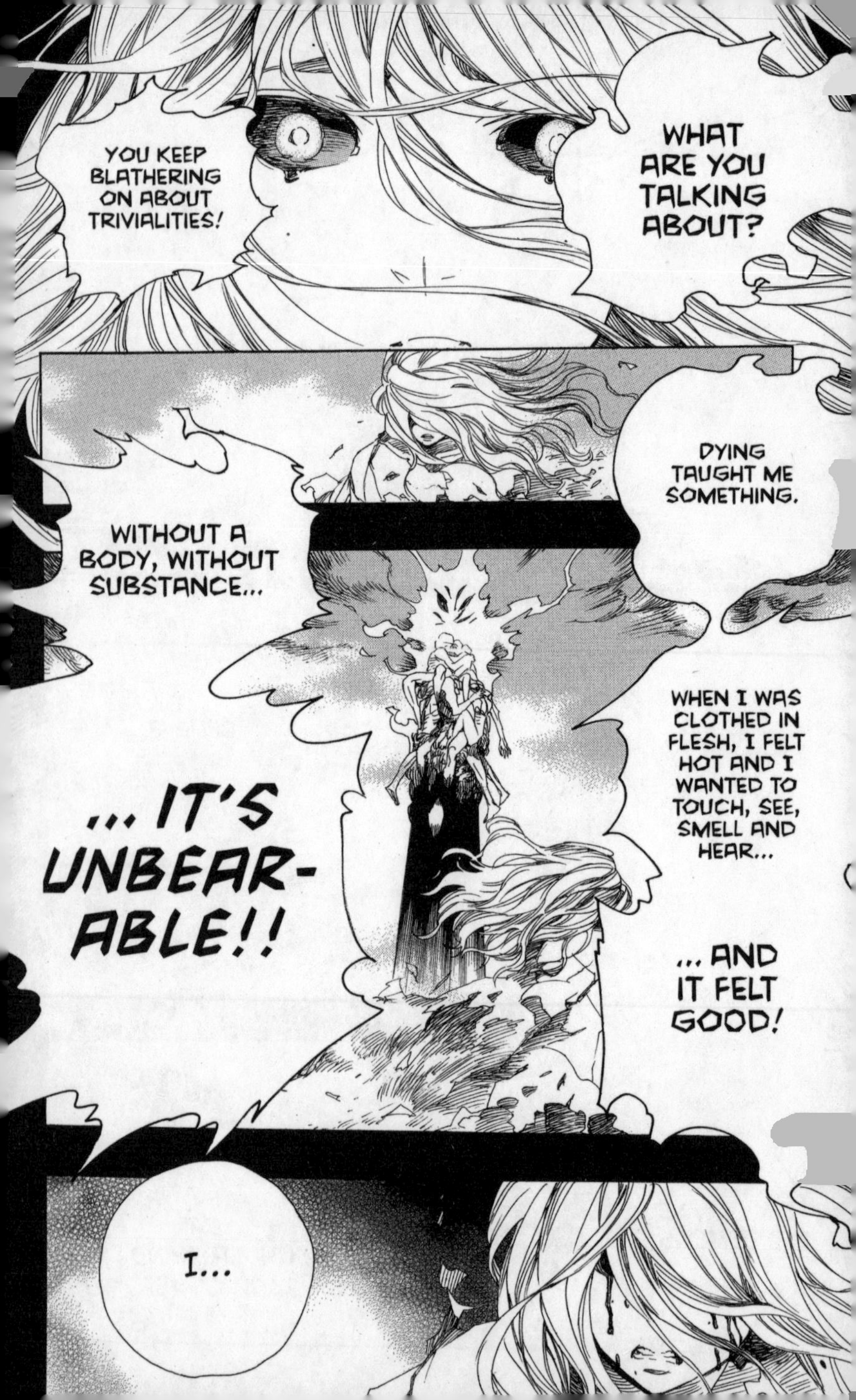
WHAT ARE YOU TALKING ABOUT?
YOU KEEP BLATHERING ON ABOUT TRIVIALITIES!
DYING TAUGHT ME SOMETHING.
WHEN I WAS CLOTHED IN FLESH, I FELT HOT AND I WANTED TO TOUCH, SEE, SMELL AND HEAR...
...AND IT FELT GOOD!
WITHOUT A BODY, WITHOUT SUBSTANCE...
...IT'S UNBEAR-ABLE!!
I...

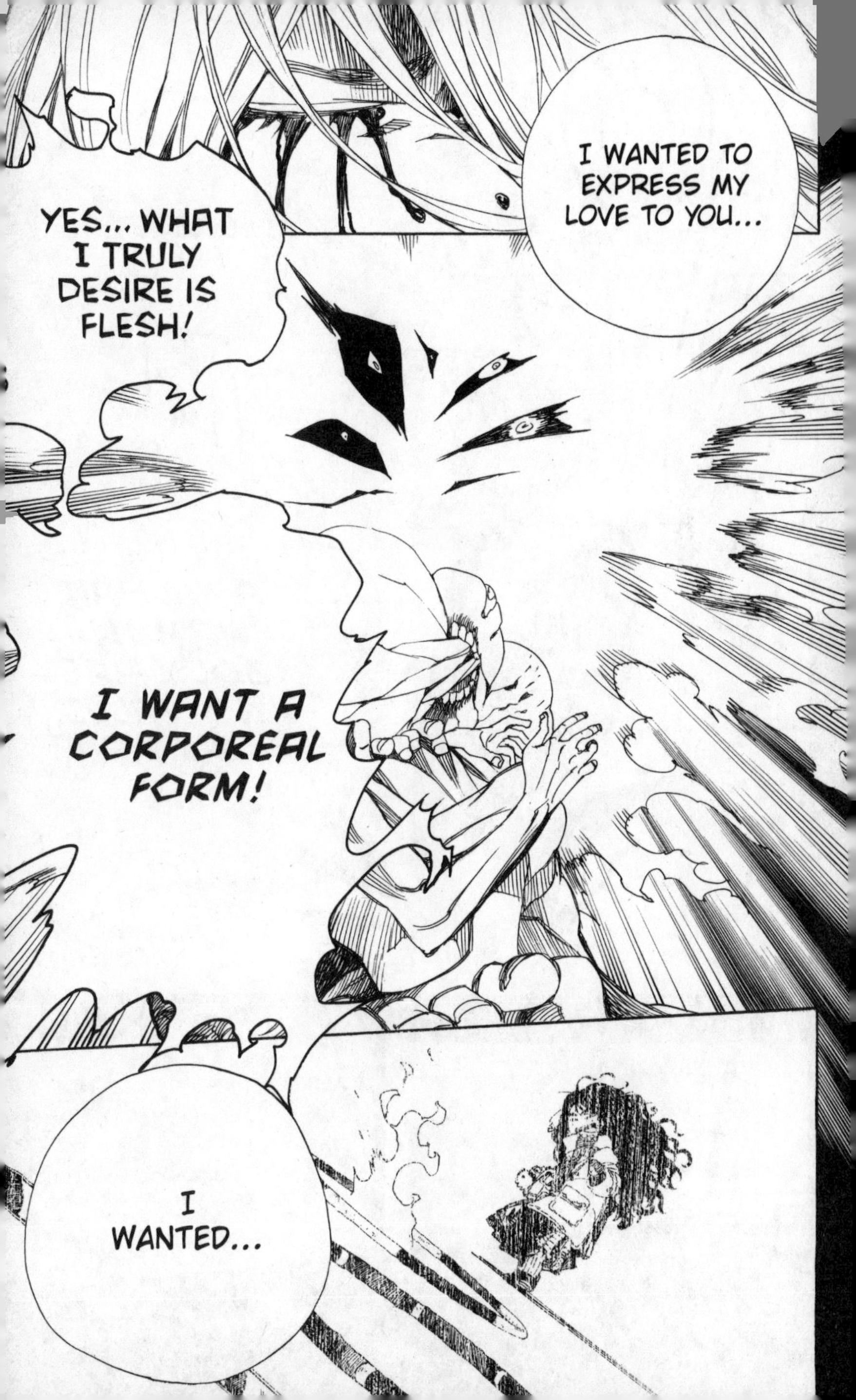
I WANTED TO EXPRESS MY LOVE TO YOU...
YES... WHAT I TRULY DESIRE IS FLESH!
I WANT A CORPOREAL FORM!
I WANTED...

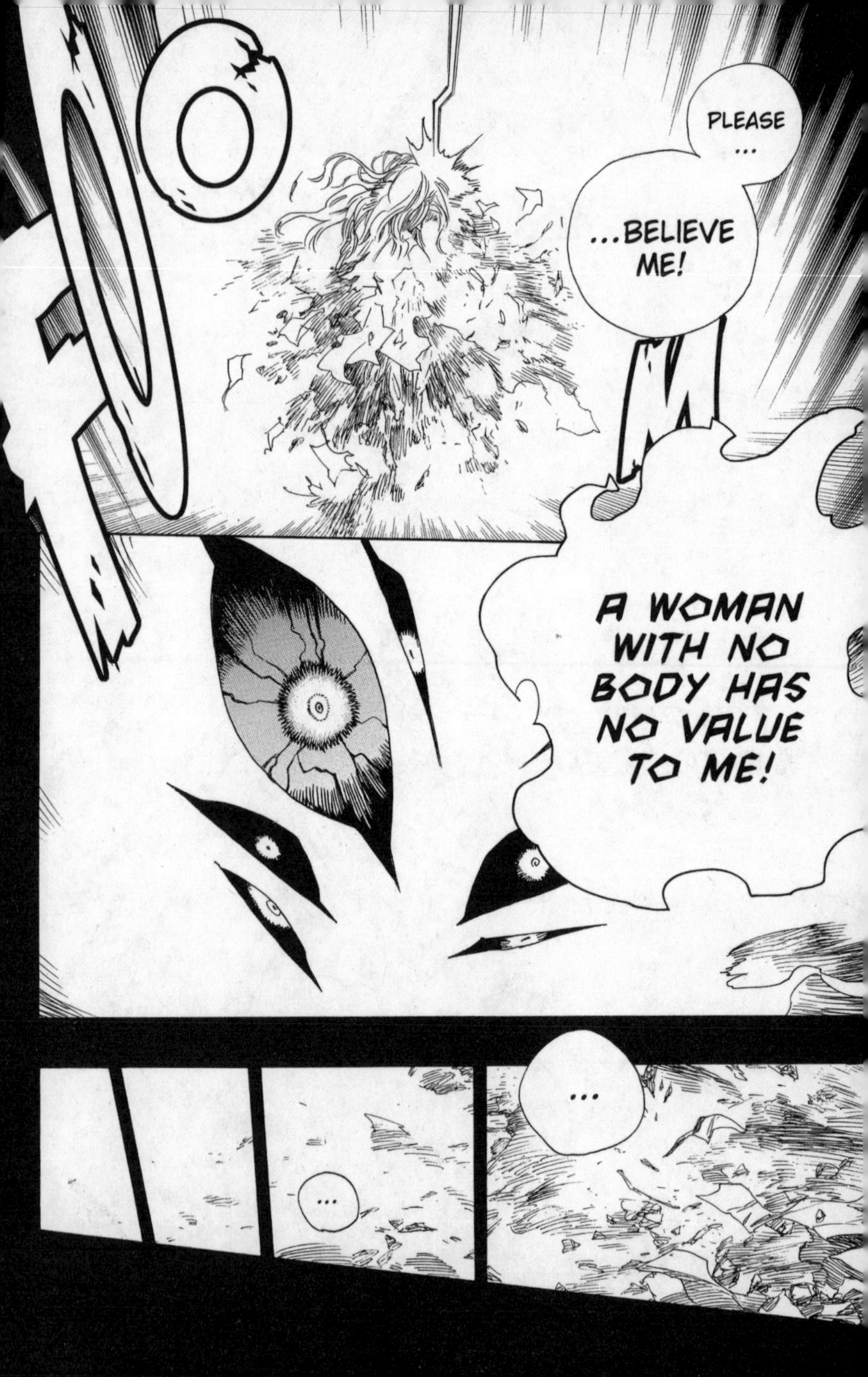
PLEASE ...
...BELIEVE ME!
A WOMAN WITH NO BODY HAS NO VALUE TO ME!
...
...

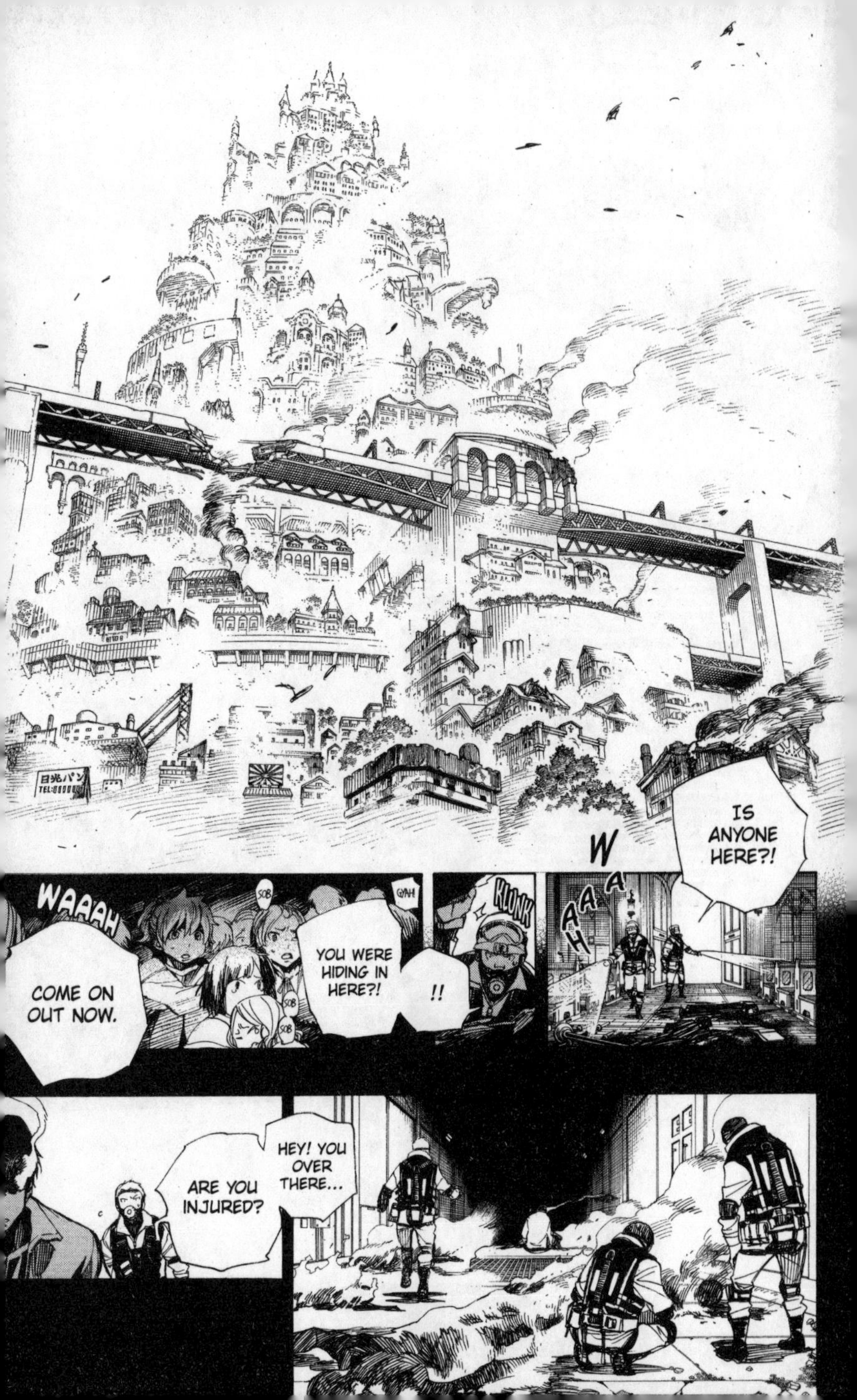
IS ANYONE HERE?!
WAAAAH
KLUNK
!!
GYAH
YOU WERE HIDING IN HERE?!
SOB
SOB
SOB
WAAAH
COME ON OUT NOW.
HEY! YOU OVER THERE...
ARE YOU INJURED?

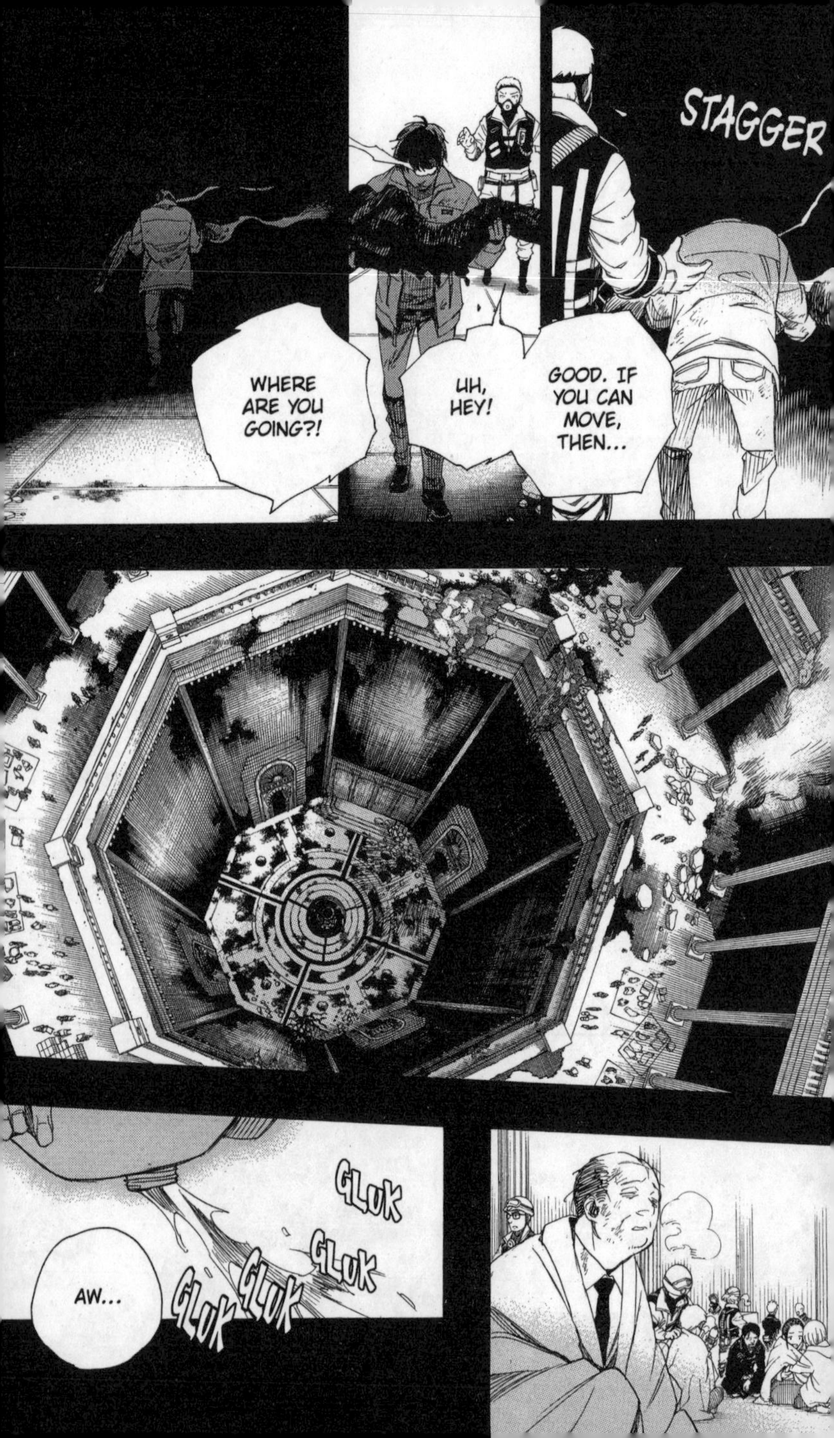
STAGGER
GOOD. IF YOU CAN MOVE, THEN...
UH, HEY!
WHERE ARE YOU GOING?!
GLUK
GLUK
GLUK
GLUK
AW...

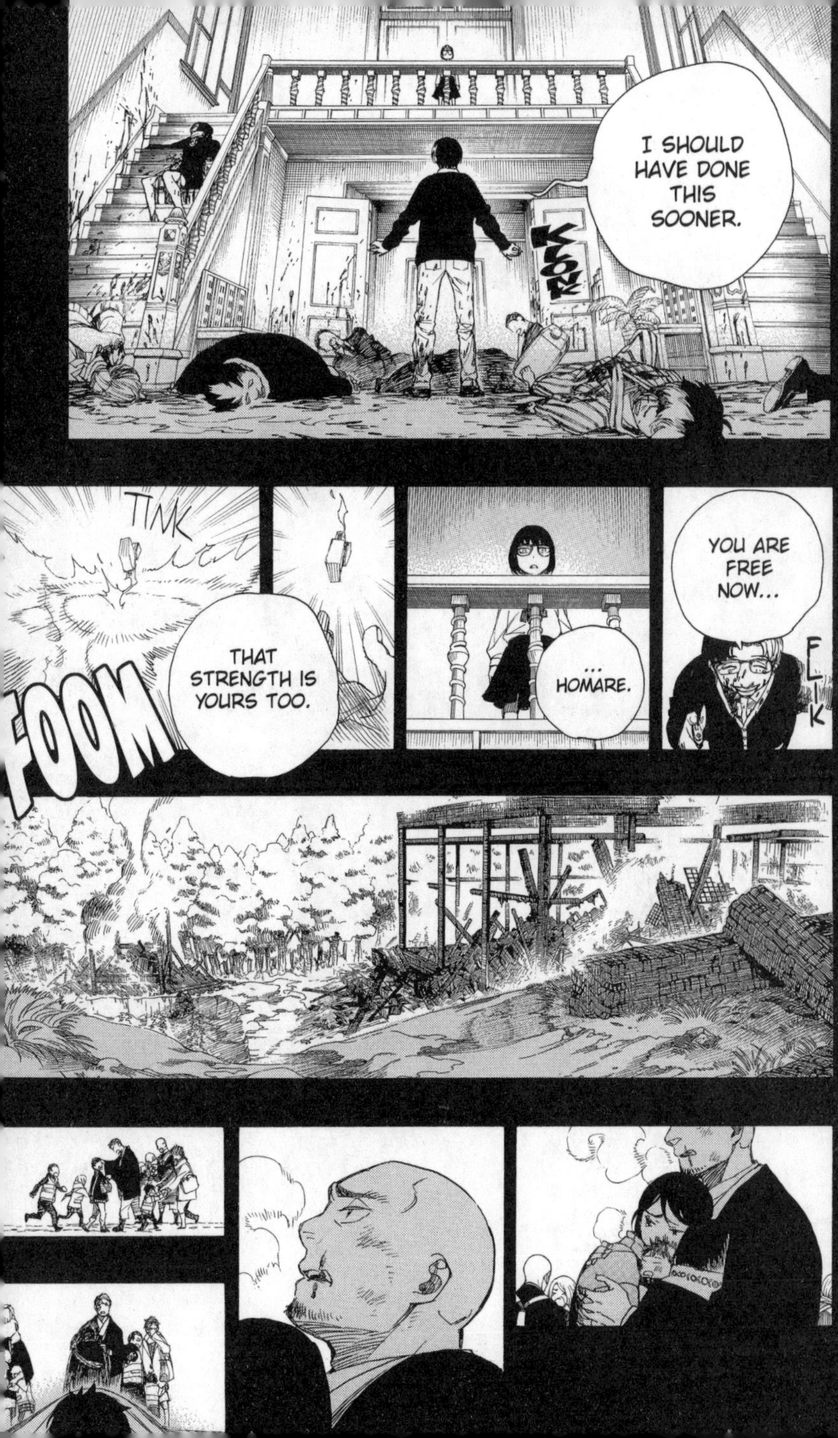
I SHOULD HAVE DONE THIS SOONER.
KLONK
YOU ARE FREE NOW...
FLIK
... HOMARE.
THAT STRENGTH IS YOURS TOO.
TINK
FOOM

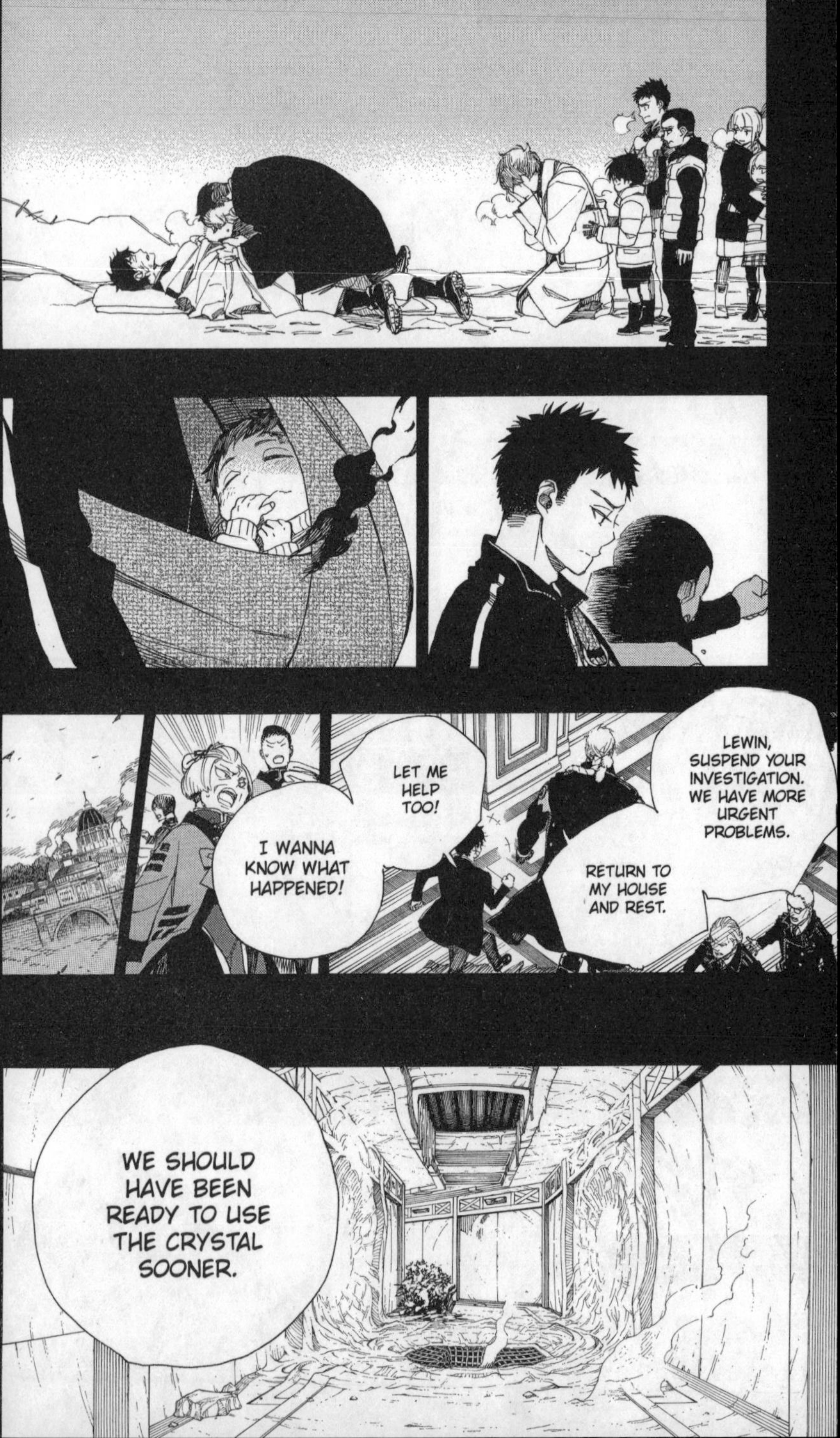
LEWIN, SUSPEND YOUR INVESTIGATION. WE HAVE MORE URGENT PROBLEMS.
RETURN TO MY HOUSE AND REST.
LET ME HELP TOO!
I WANNA KNOW WHAT HAPPENED!
WE SHOULD HAVE BEEN READY TO USE THE CRYSTAL SOONER.

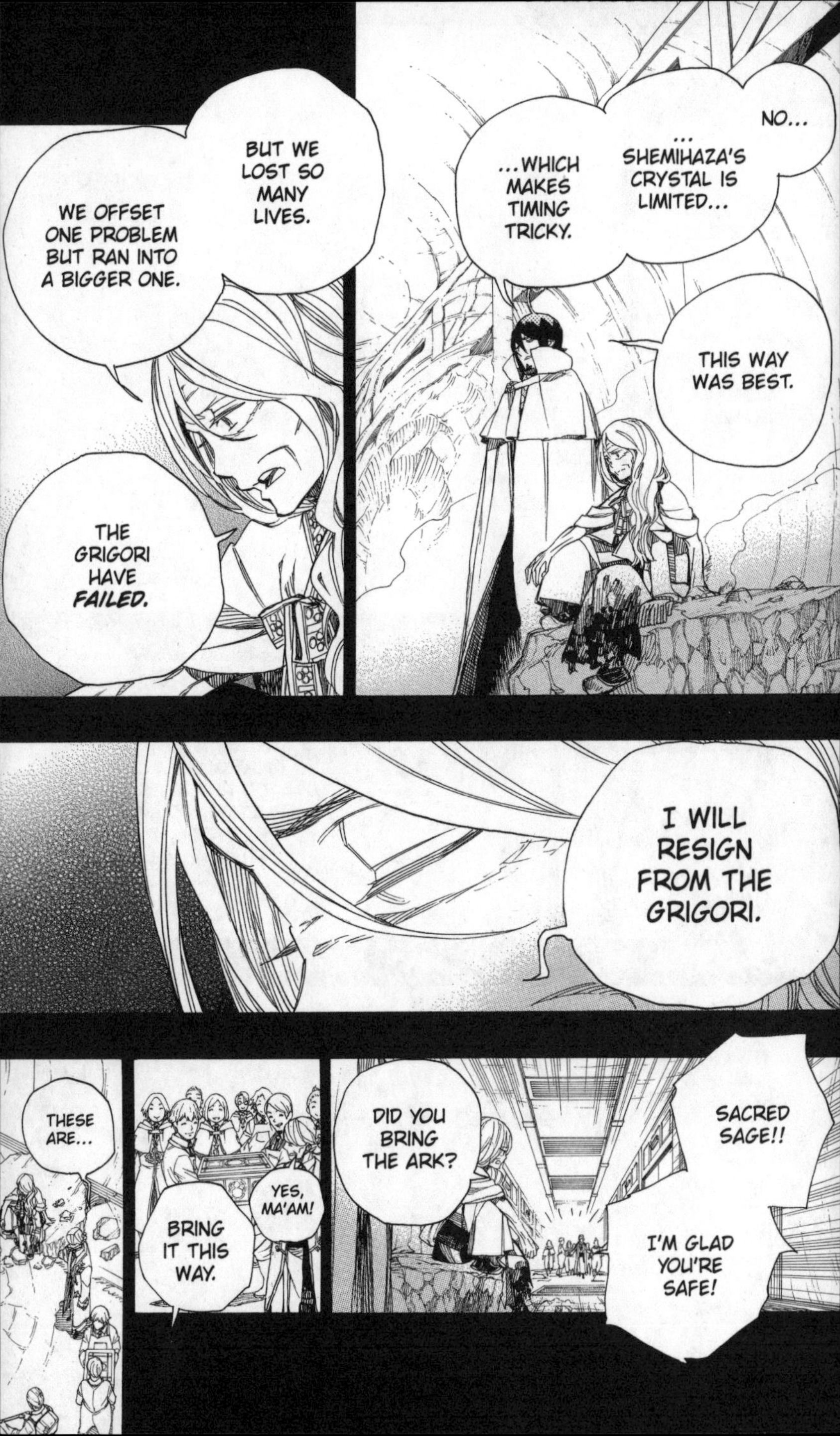
NO...
... SHEMIHAZA'S CRYSTAL IS LIMITED...
...WHICH MAKES TIMING TRICKY.
THIS WAY WAS BEST.
BUT WE LOST SO MANY LIVES.
WE OFFSET ONE PROBLEM BUT RAN INTO A BIGGER ONE.
THE GRIGORI HAVE *FAILED.*
I WILL RESIGN FROM THE GRIGORI.
SACRED SAGE!!
I'M GLAD YOU'RE SAFE!
DID YOU BRING THE ARK?
YES, MA'AM!
BRING IT THIS WAY.
THESE ARE...

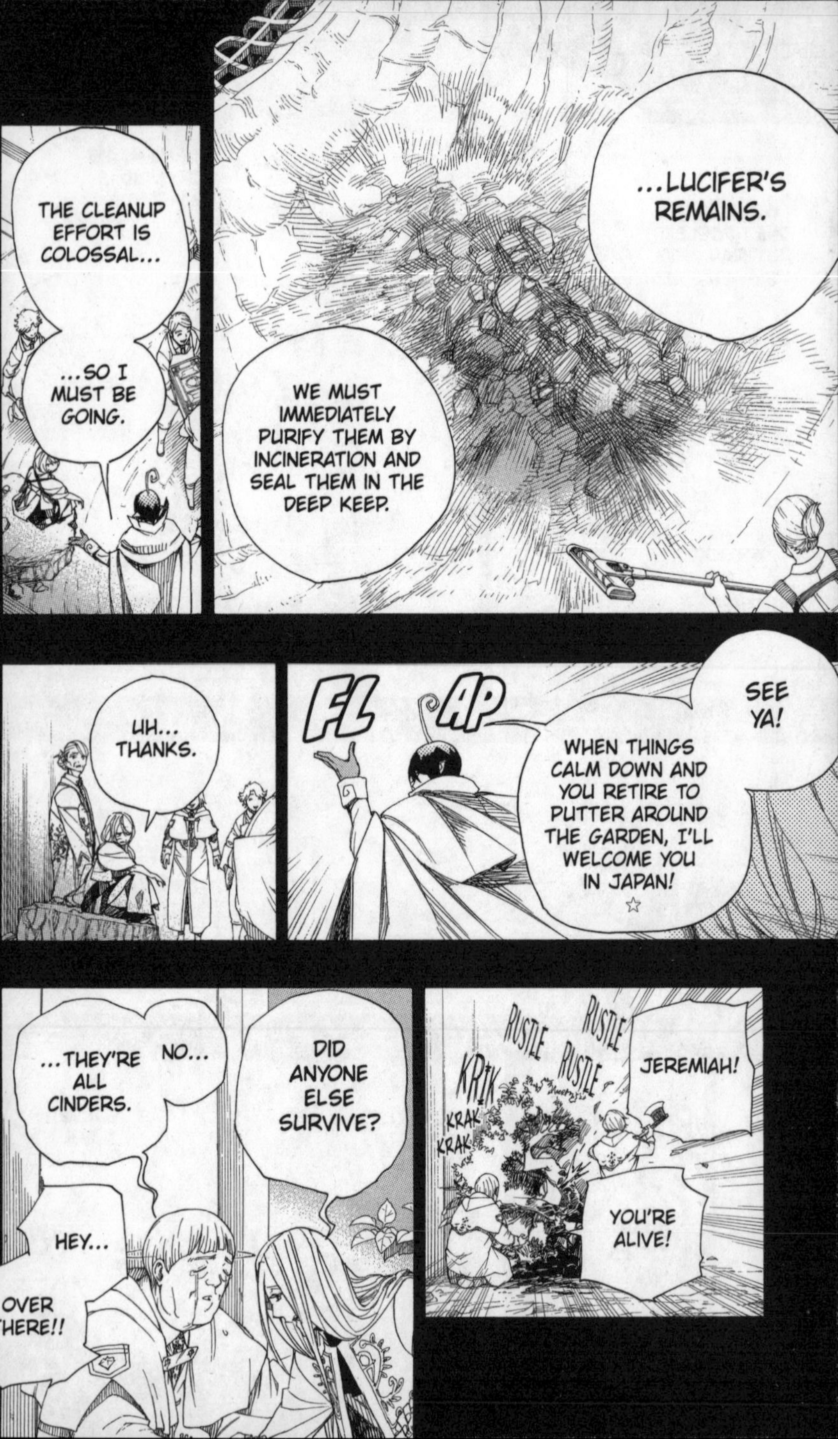

...LUCIFER'S REMAINS.
WE MUST IMMEDIATELY PURIFY THEM BY INCINERATION AND SEAL THEM IN THE DEEP KEEP.
THE CLEANUP EFFORT IS COLOSSAL...
...SO I MUST BE GOING.
SEE YA!
FLAP
WHEN THINGS CALM DOWN AND YOU RETIRE TO PUTTER AROUND THE GARDEN, I'LL WELCOME YOU IN JAPAN! ☆
UH... THANKS.
RUSTLE
RUSTLE
RUSTLE
JEREMIAH!
KRIK
KRAK
KRAK
YOU'RE ALIVE!
DID ANYONE ELSE SURVIVE?
NO...
...THEY'RE ALL CINDERS.
HEY...
OVER THERE!!

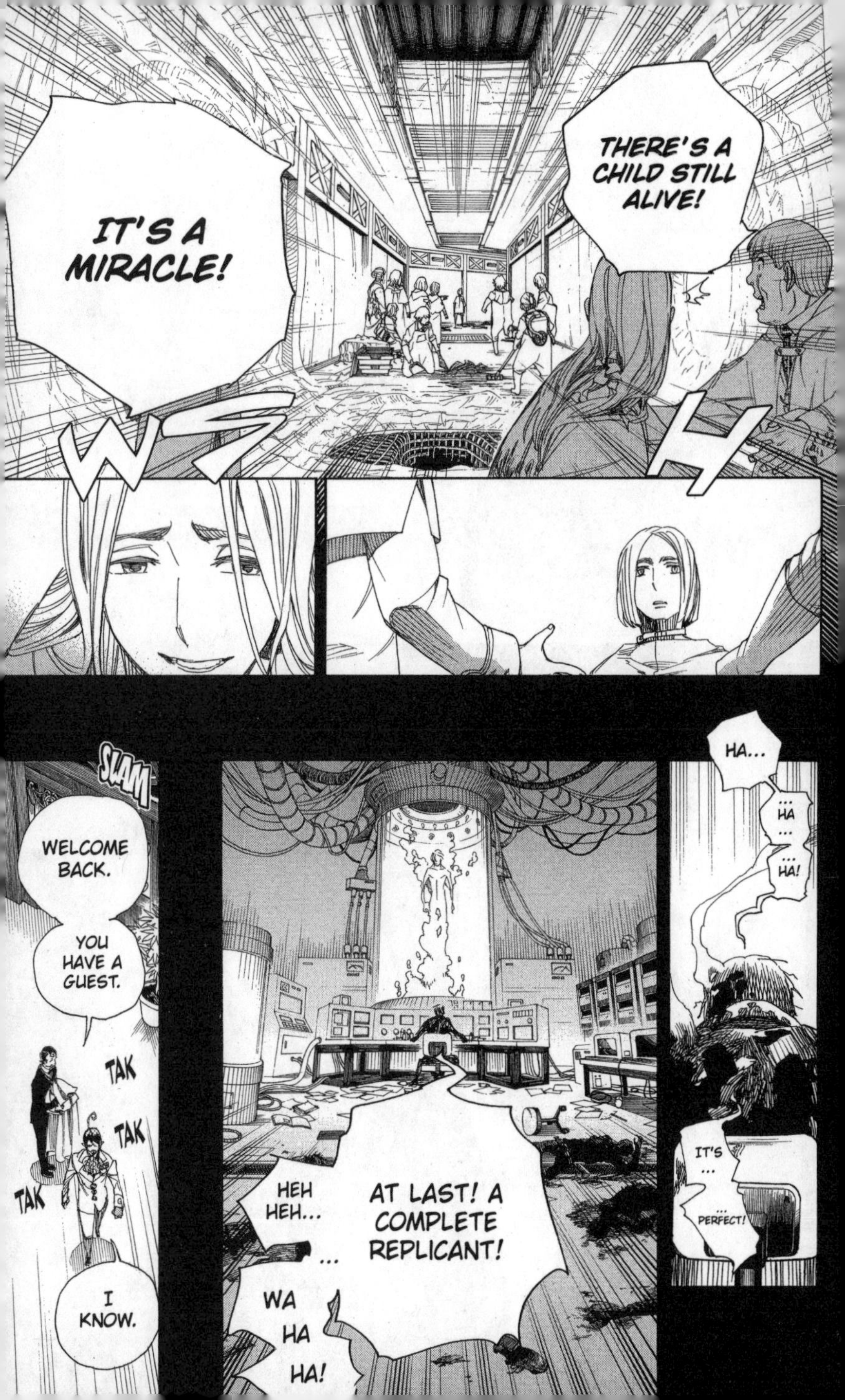
THERE'S A CHILD STILL ALIVE!
IT'S A MIRACLE!
WSH
HA...
...HA...
...HA!
IT'S...
...PERFECT!
HEH HEH...
...
WA HA HA!
AT LAST! A COMPLETE REPLICANT!
SLAM
WELCOME BACK.
YOU HAVE A GUEST.
TAK
TAK
TAK
I KNOW.

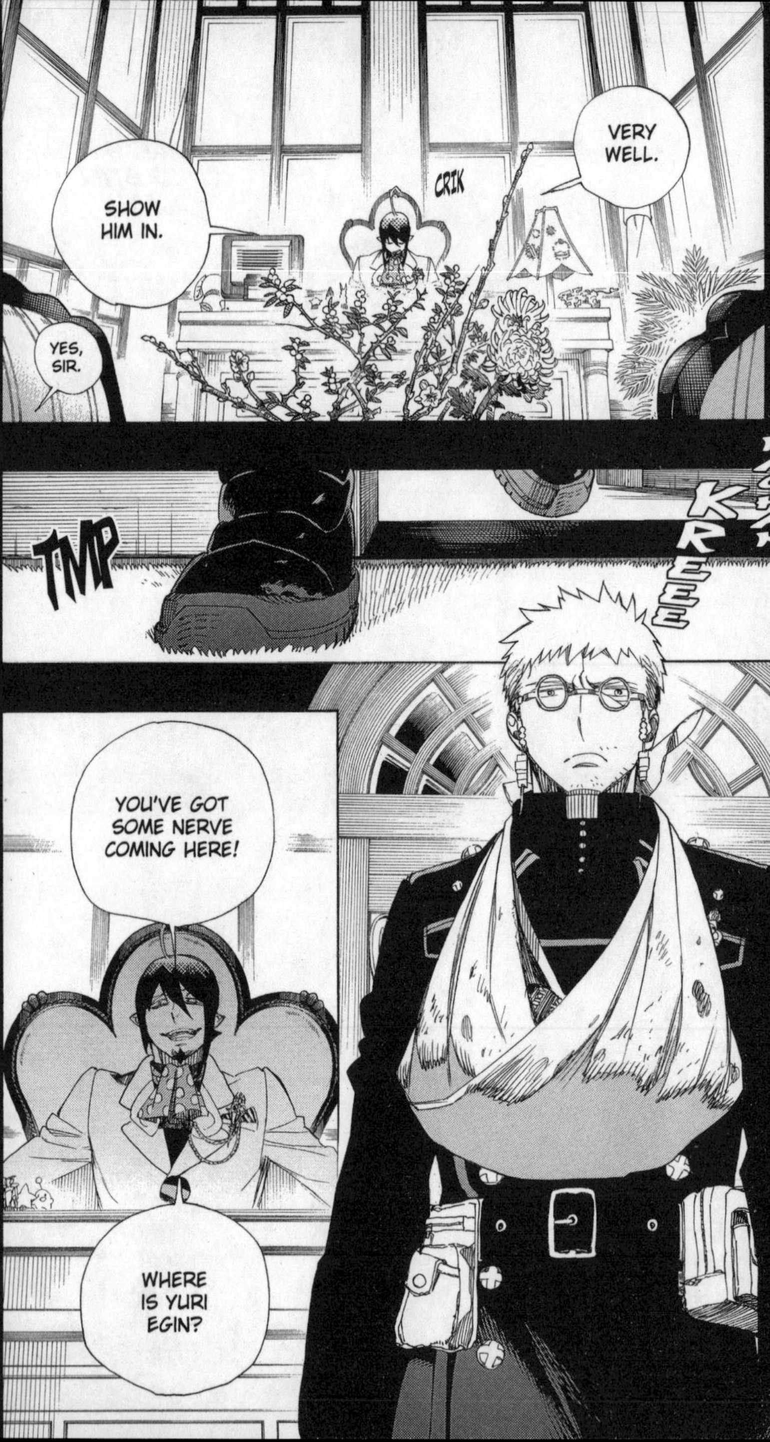
VERY WELL.
CRIK
SHOW HIM IN.
YES, SIR.
KACHAK
KREEE
TMP
YOU'VE GOT SOME NERVE COMING HERE!
WHERE IS YURI EGIN?

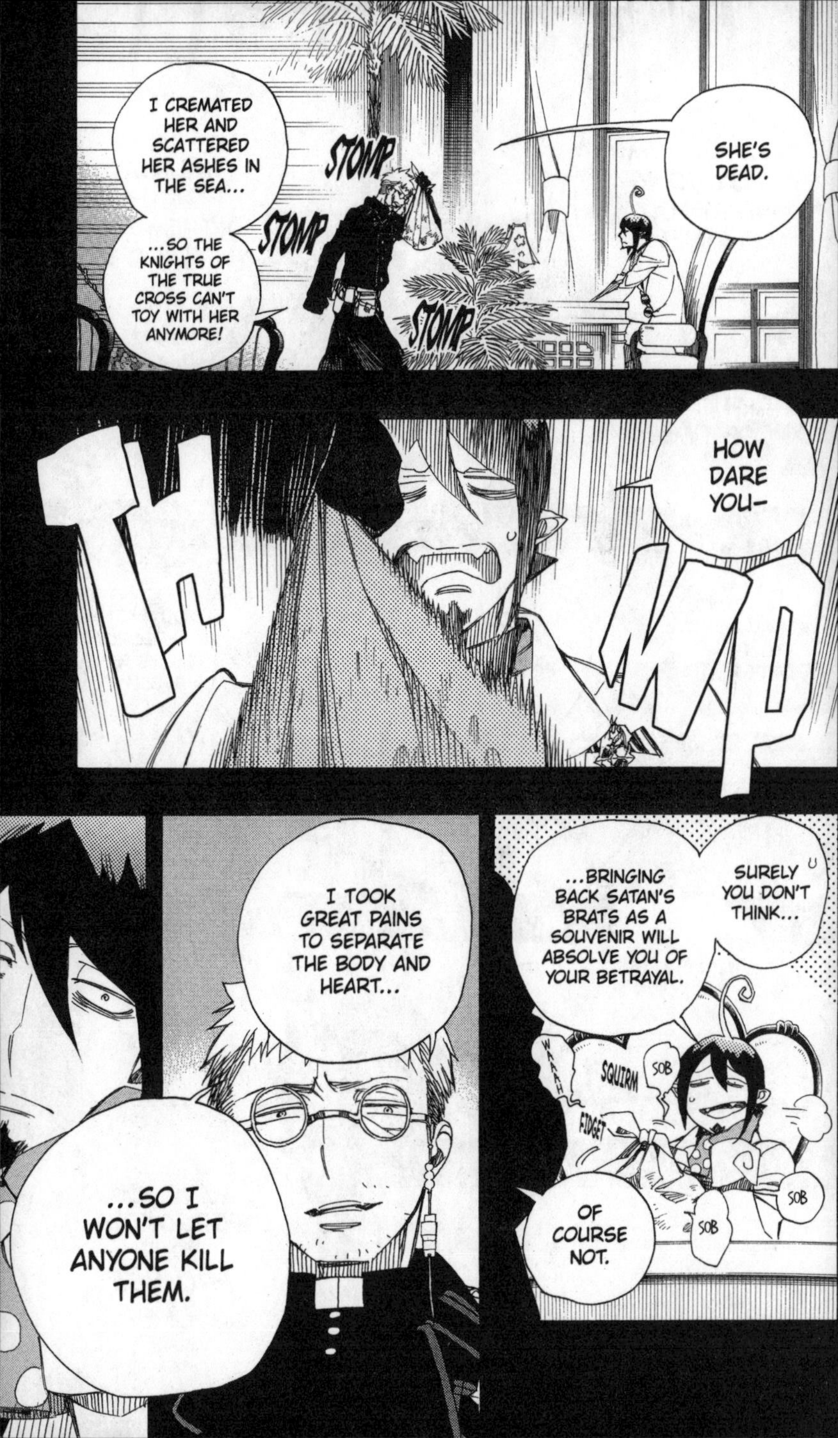

SHE'S DEAD.
I CREMATED HER AND SCATTERED HER ASHES IN THE SEA...
STOMP
STOMP
...SO THE KNIGHTS OF THE TRUE CROSS CAN'T TOY WITH HER ANYMORE!
STOMP
HOW DARE YOU-
THWMP
SURELY YOU DON'T THINK...
...BRINGING BACK SATAN'S BRATS AS A SOUVENIR WILL ABSOLVE YOU OF YOUR BETRAYAL.
SOB
SQUIRM
WAAAH
FIDGET
SOB
SOB
OF COURSE NOT.
I TOOK GREAT PAINS TO SEPARATE THE BODY AND HEART...
...SO I WON'T LET ANYONE KILL THEM.

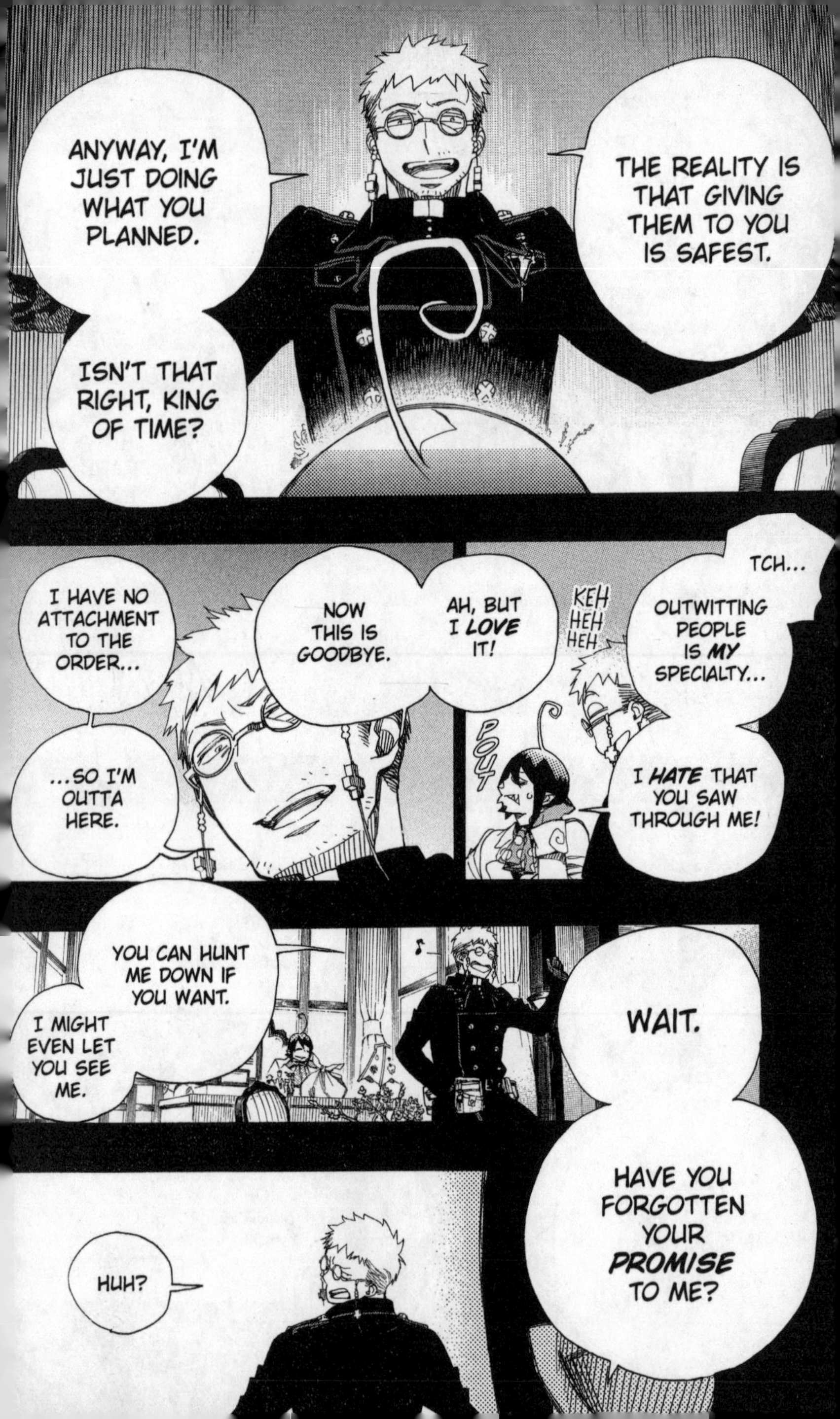
THE REALITY IS THAT GIVING THEM TO YOU IS SAFEST.
ANYWAY, I'M JUST DOING WHAT YOU PLANNED.
ISN'T THAT RIGHT, KING OF TIME?
TCH...
OUTWITTING PEOPLE IS *MY* SPECIALTY...
I *HATE* THAT YOU SAW THROUGH ME!
POUT
AH, BUT I *LOVE* IT!
KEH HEH HEH
NOW THIS IS GOODBYE.
I HAVE NO ATTACHMENT TO THE ORDER...
...SO I'M OUTTA HERE.
YOU CAN HUNT ME DOWN IF YOU WANT.
I MIGHT EVEN LET YOU SEE ME.
WAIT.
HAVE YOU FORGOTTEN YOUR *PROMISE* TO ME?
HUH?

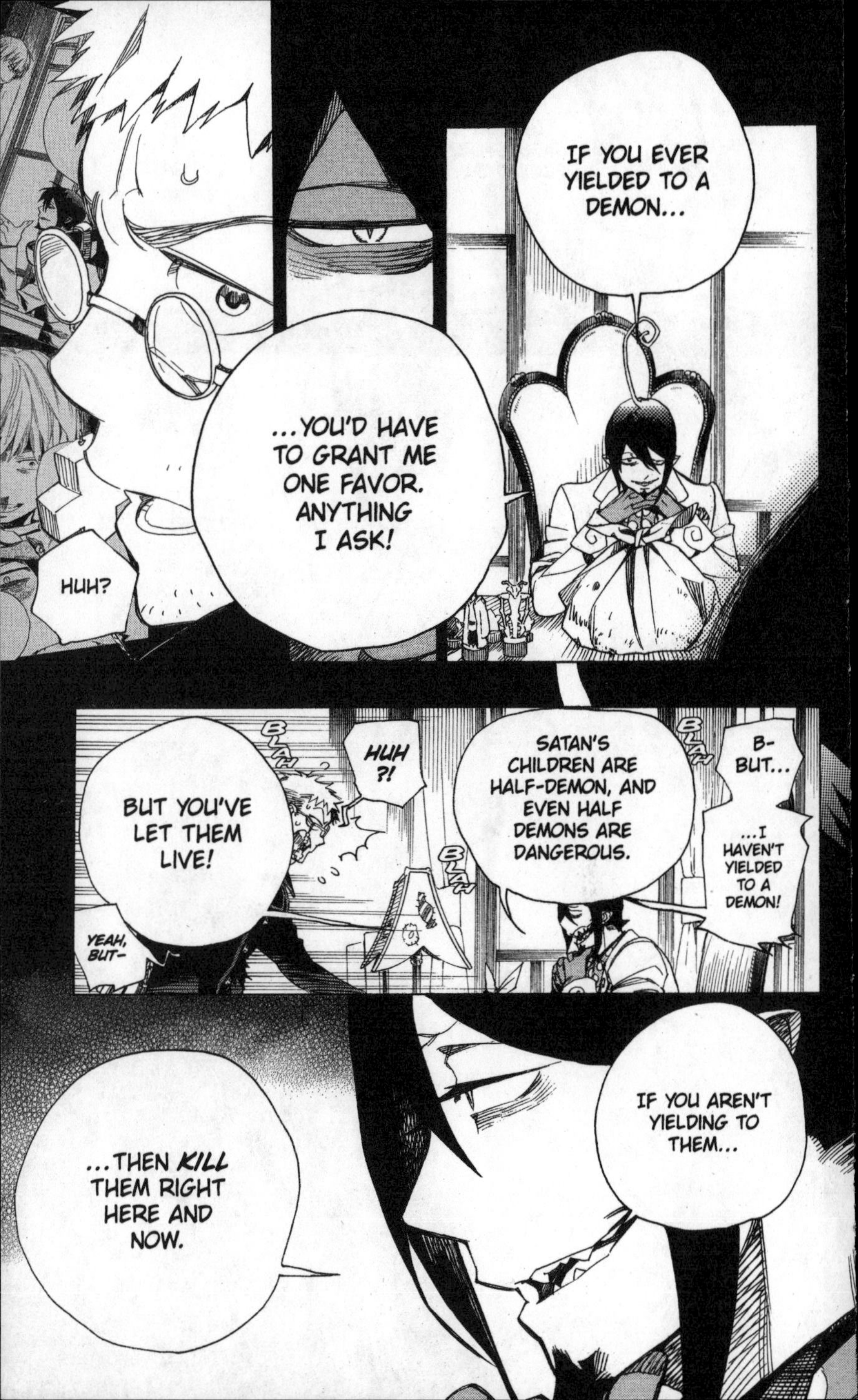
IF YOU EVER YIELDED TO A DEMON...
...YOU'D HAVE TO GRANT ME ONE FAVOR. ANYTHING I ASK!
HUH?
B-BUT...
...I HAVEN'T YIELDED TO A DEMON!
BLAH
SATAN'S CHILDREN ARE HALF-DEMON, AND EVEN HALF DEMONS ARE DANGEROUS.
BLAH
BLAH
HUH?!
BUT YOU'VE LET THEM LIVE!
YEAH, BUT-
IF YOU AREN'T YIELDING TO THEM...
...THEN *KILL* THEM RIGHT HERE AND NOW.

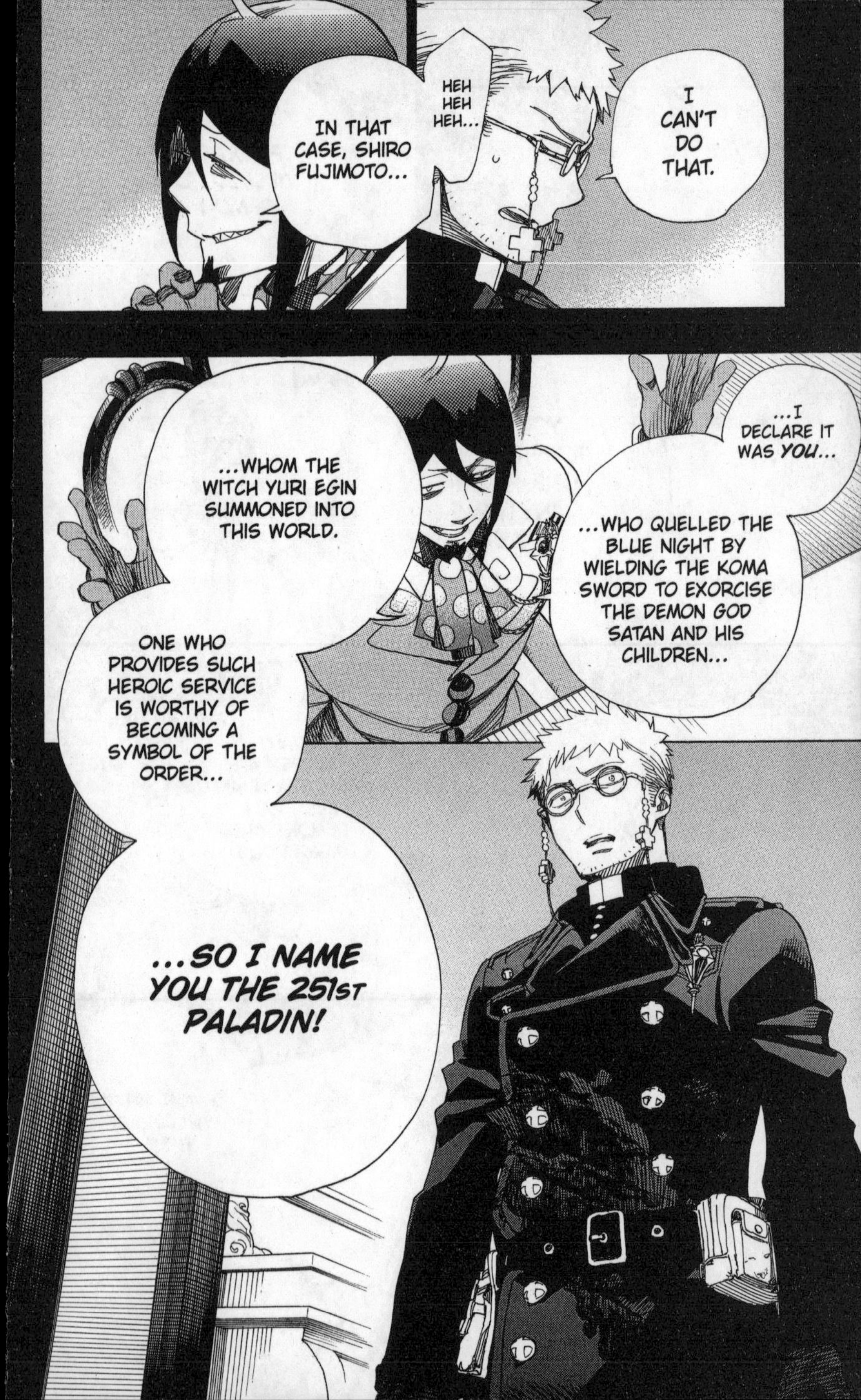
I CAN'T DO THAT.
HEH HEH HEH...
IN THAT CASE, SHIRO FUJIMOTO...
...I DECLARE IT WAS *YOU*...
...WHO QUELLED THE BLUE NIGHT BY WIELDING THE KOMA SWORD TO EXORCISE THE DEMON GOD SATAN AND HIS CHILDREN...
...WHOM THE WITCH YURI EGIN SUMMONED INTO THIS WORLD.
ONE WHO PROVIDES SUCH HEROIC SERVICE IS WORTHY OF BECOMING A SYMBOL OF THE ORDER...
...SO I NAME YOU THE 251ST PALADIN!

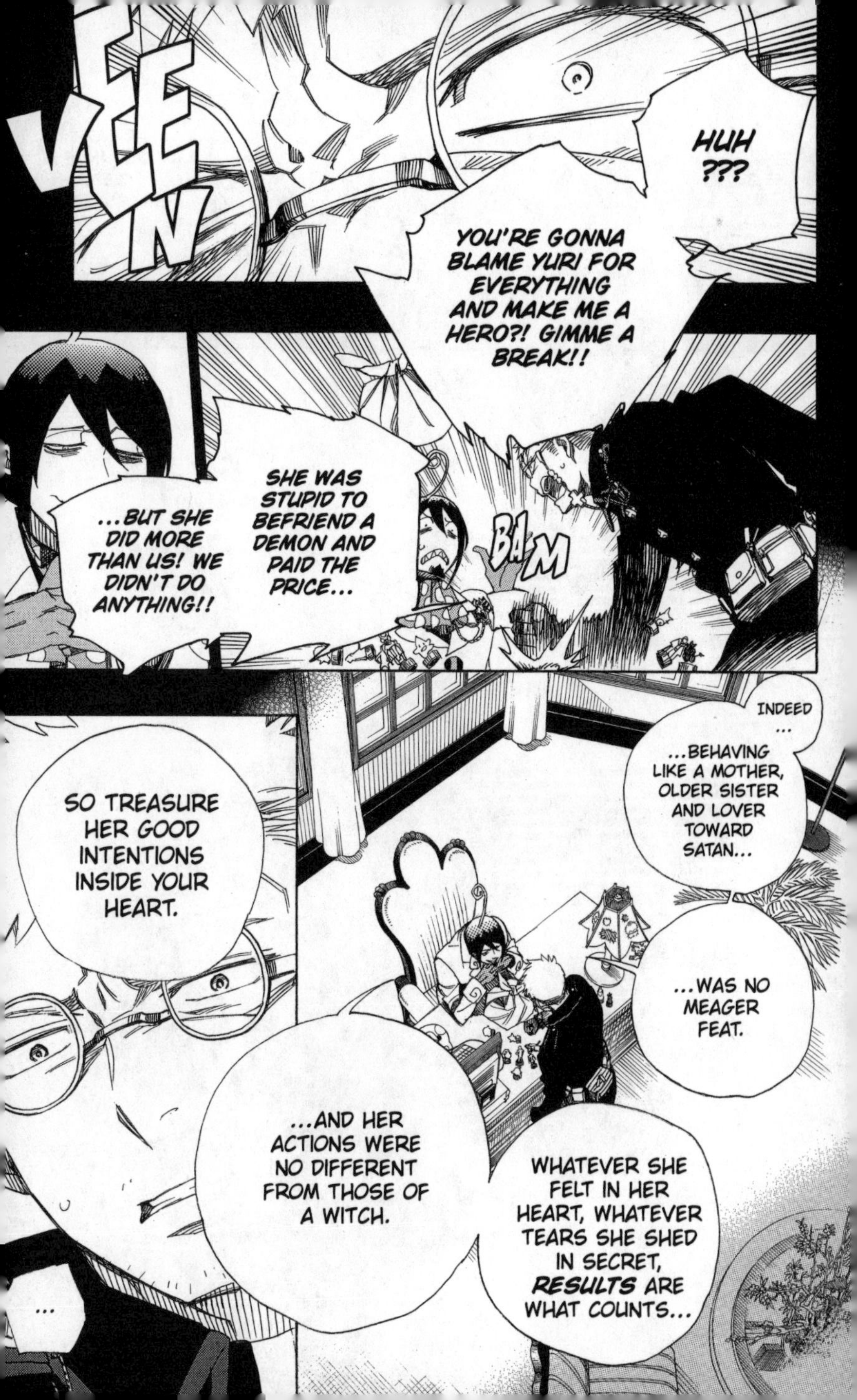
HUH ???
VEEN
YOU'RE GONNA BLAME YURI FOR EVERYTHING AND MAKE ME A HERO?! GIMME A BREAK!!
BAM
SHE WAS STUPID TO BEFRIEND A DEMON AND PAID THE PRICE...
...BUT SHE DID MORE THAN US! WE DIDN'T DO ANYTHING!!
INDEED ...
...BEHAVING LIKE A MOTHER, OLDER SISTER AND LOVER TOWARD SATAN...
...WAS NO MEAGER FEAT.
WHATEVER SHE FELT IN HER HEART, WHATEVER TEARS SHE SHED IN SECRET, RESULTS ARE WHAT COUNTS...
...AND HER ACTIONS WERE NO DIFFERENT FROM THOSE OF A WITCH.
SO TREASURE HER GOOD INTENTIONS INSIDE YOUR HEART.
...

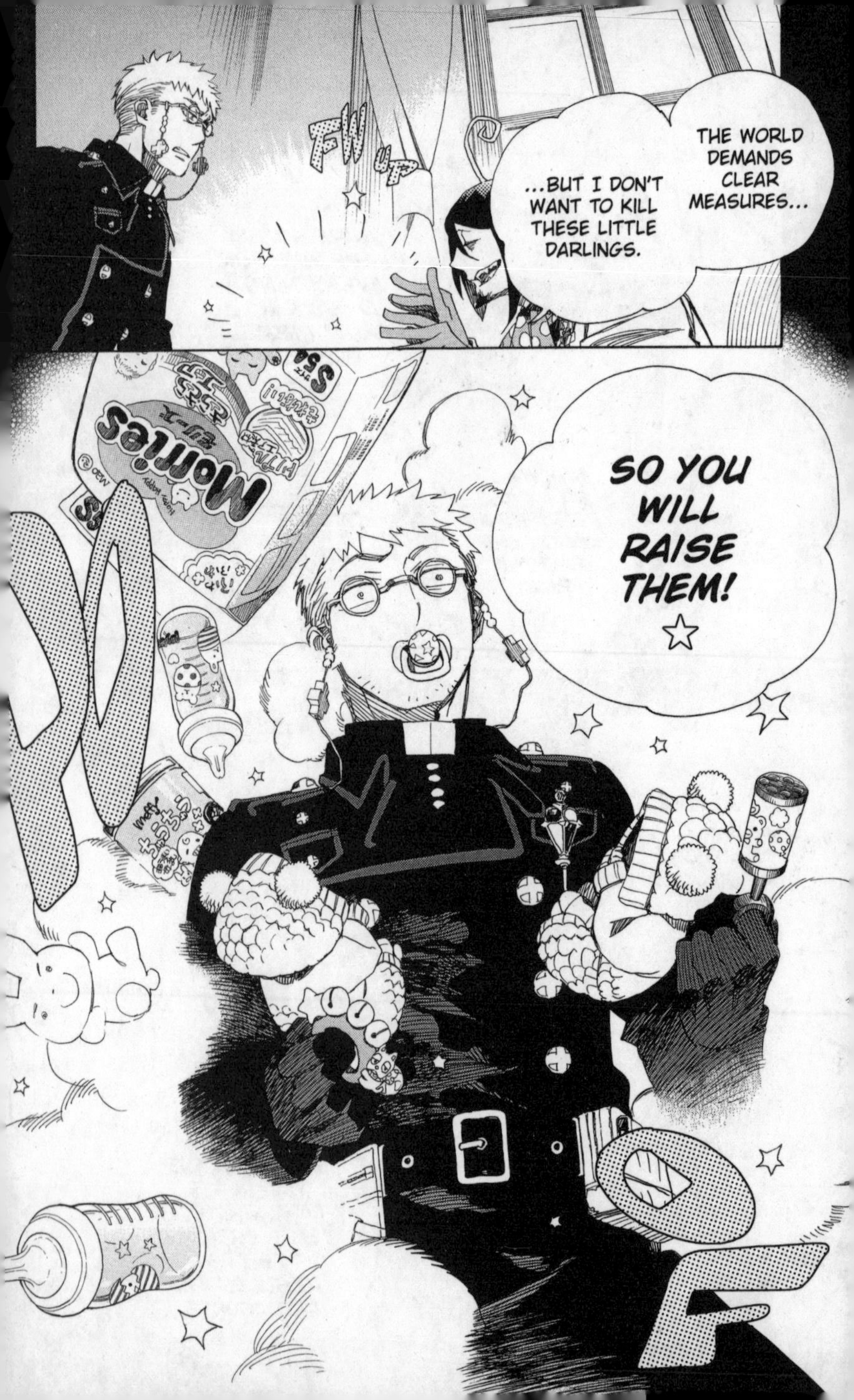
THE WORLD DEMANDS CLEAR MEASURES...
...BUT I DON'T WANT TO KILL THESE LITTLE DARLINGS.
FWUP
SO YOU WILL RAISE THEM!

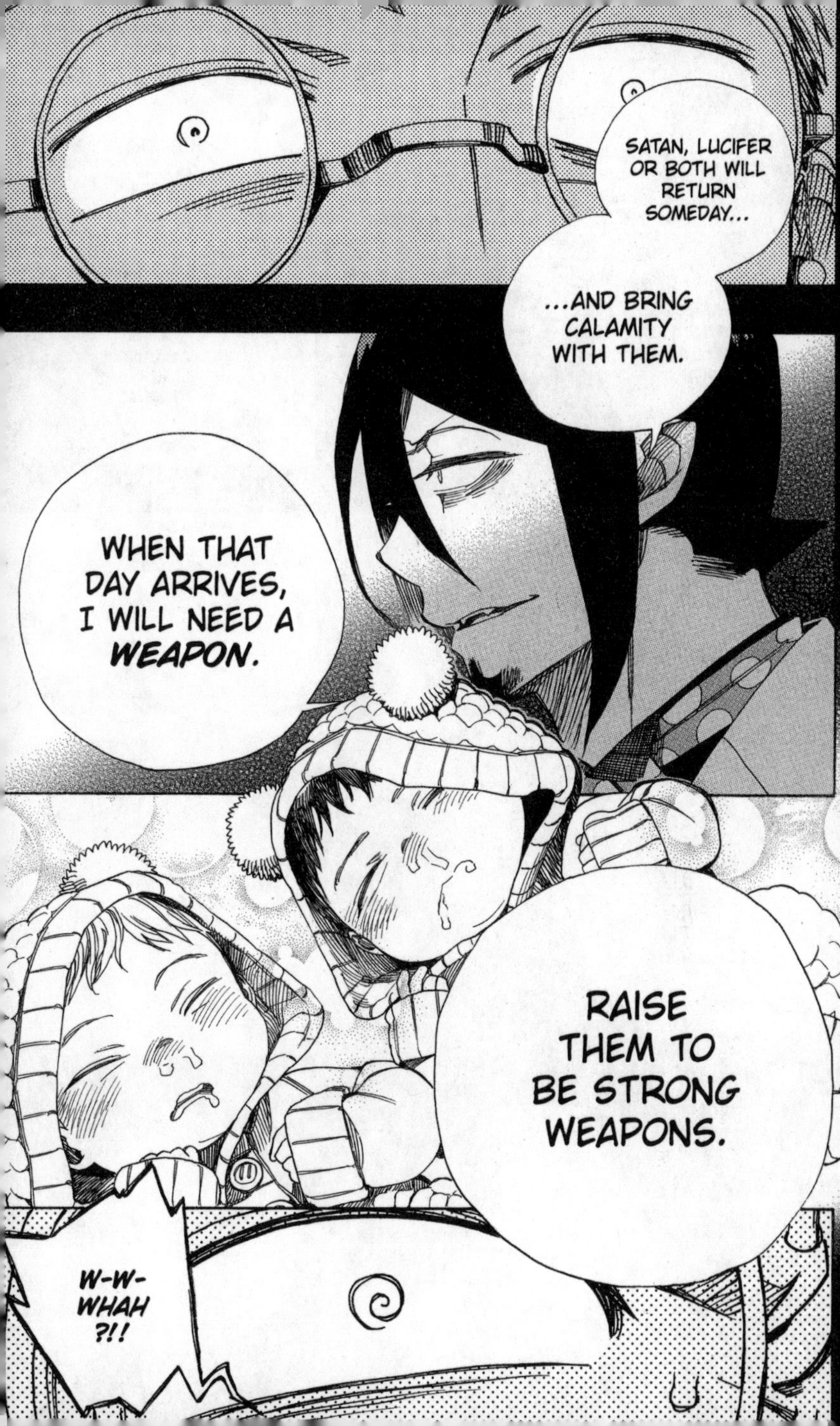
SATAN, LUCIFER OR BOTH WILL RETURN SOMEDAY...
...AND BRING CALAMITY WITH THEM.
WHEN THAT DAY ARRIVES, I WILL NEED A *WEAPON*.
RAISE THEM TO BE STRONG WEAPONS.
W-W-WHAH ?!!

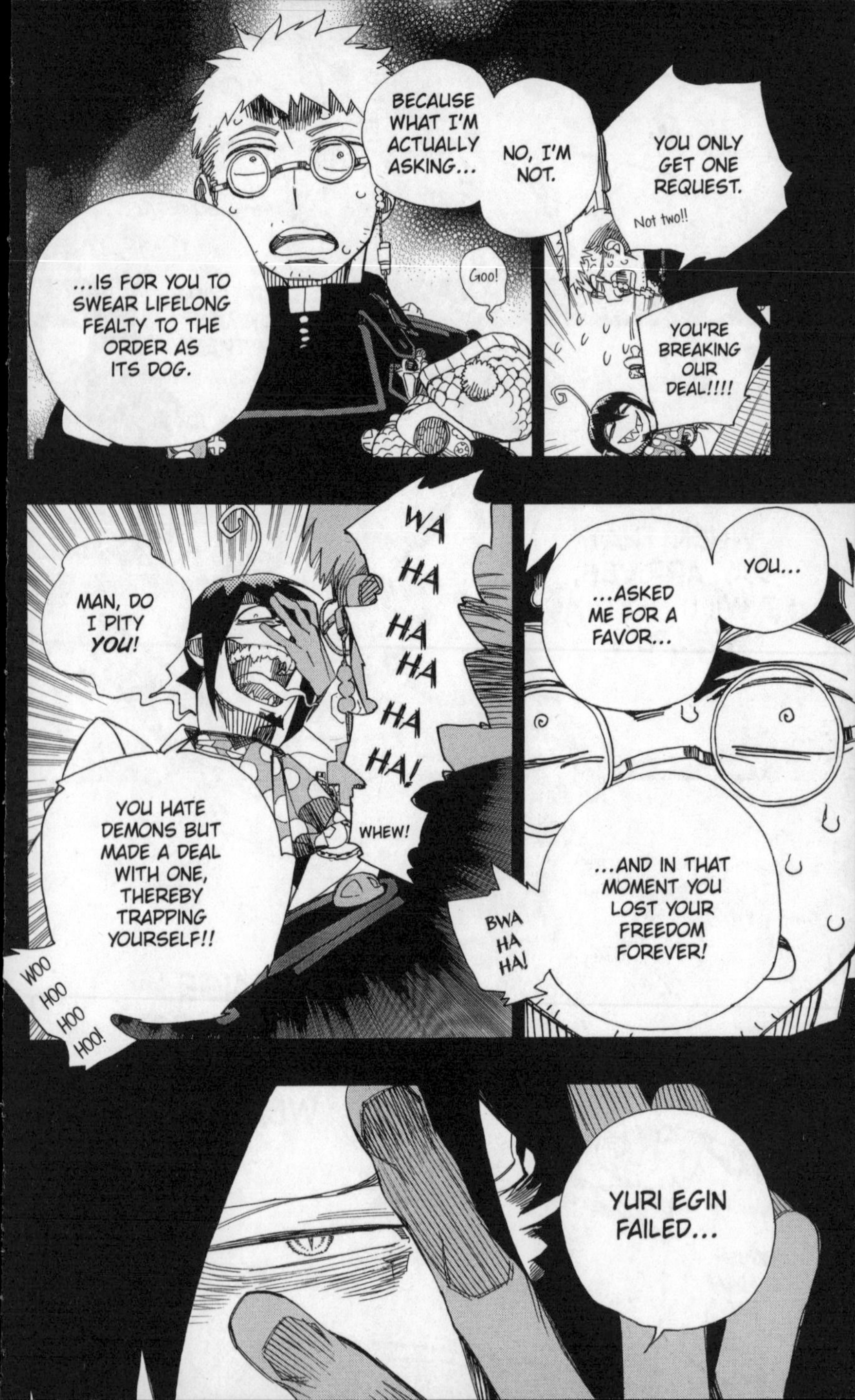
YOU ONLY GET ONE REQUEST.
Not two!!
YOU'RE BREAKING OUR DEAL!!!!
NO, I'M NOT.
BECAUSE WHAT I'M ACTUALLY ASKING...
Goo!
...IS FOR YOU TO SWEAR LIFELONG FEALTY TO THE ORDER AS ITS DOG.
YOU...
...ASKED ME FOR A FAVOR...
...AND IN THAT MOMENT YOU LOST YOUR FREEDOM FOREVER!
BWA HA HA!
WA HA HA HA HA HA HA!
MAN, DO I PITY YOU!
WHEW!
YOU HATE DEMONS BUT MADE A DEAL WITH ONE, THEREBY TRAPPING YOURSELF!!
WOO HOO HOO HOO!
YURI EGIN FAILED...

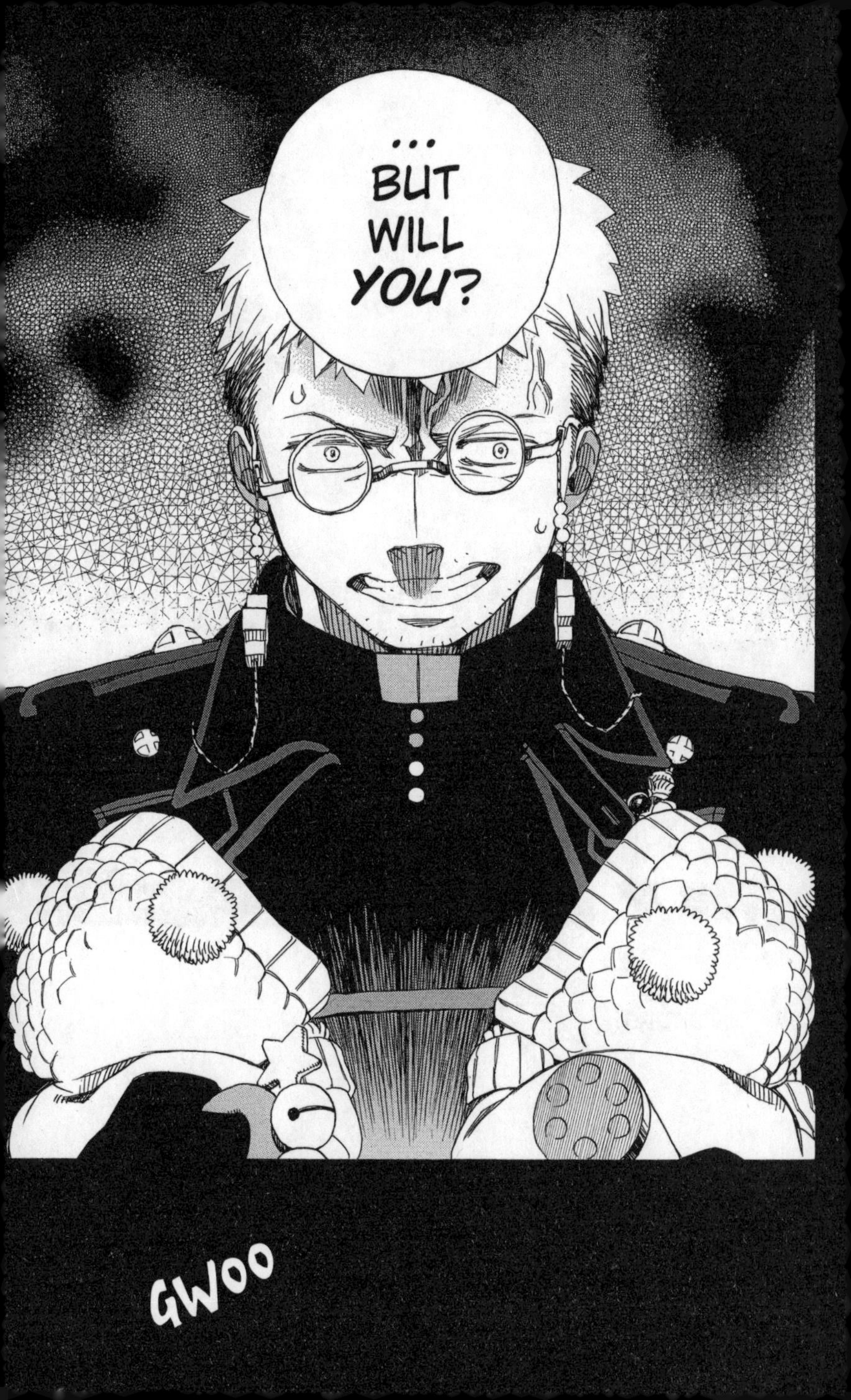
... BUT WILL YOU?
GWOO

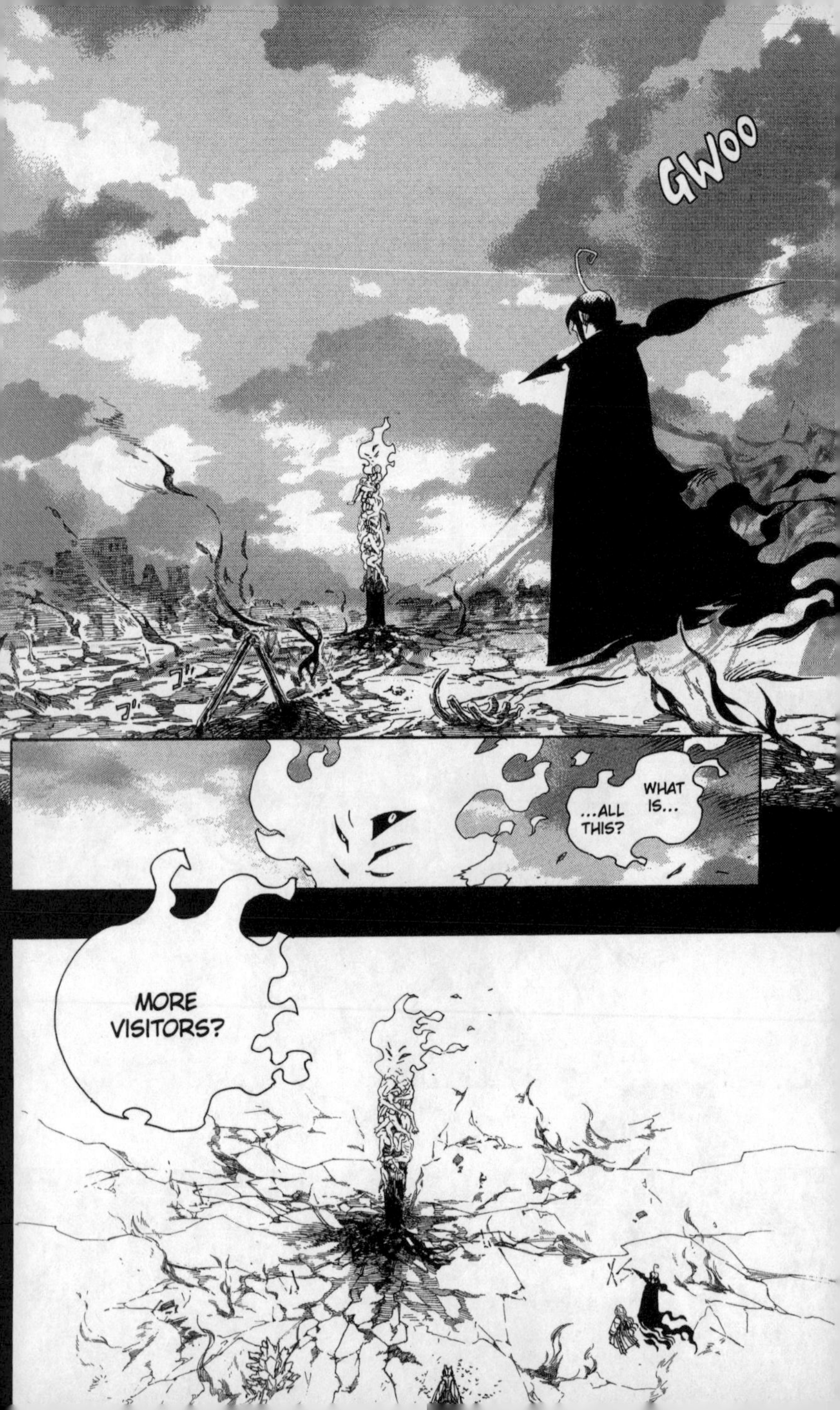
GWOO
WHAT IS... ...ALL THIS?
MORE VISITORS?

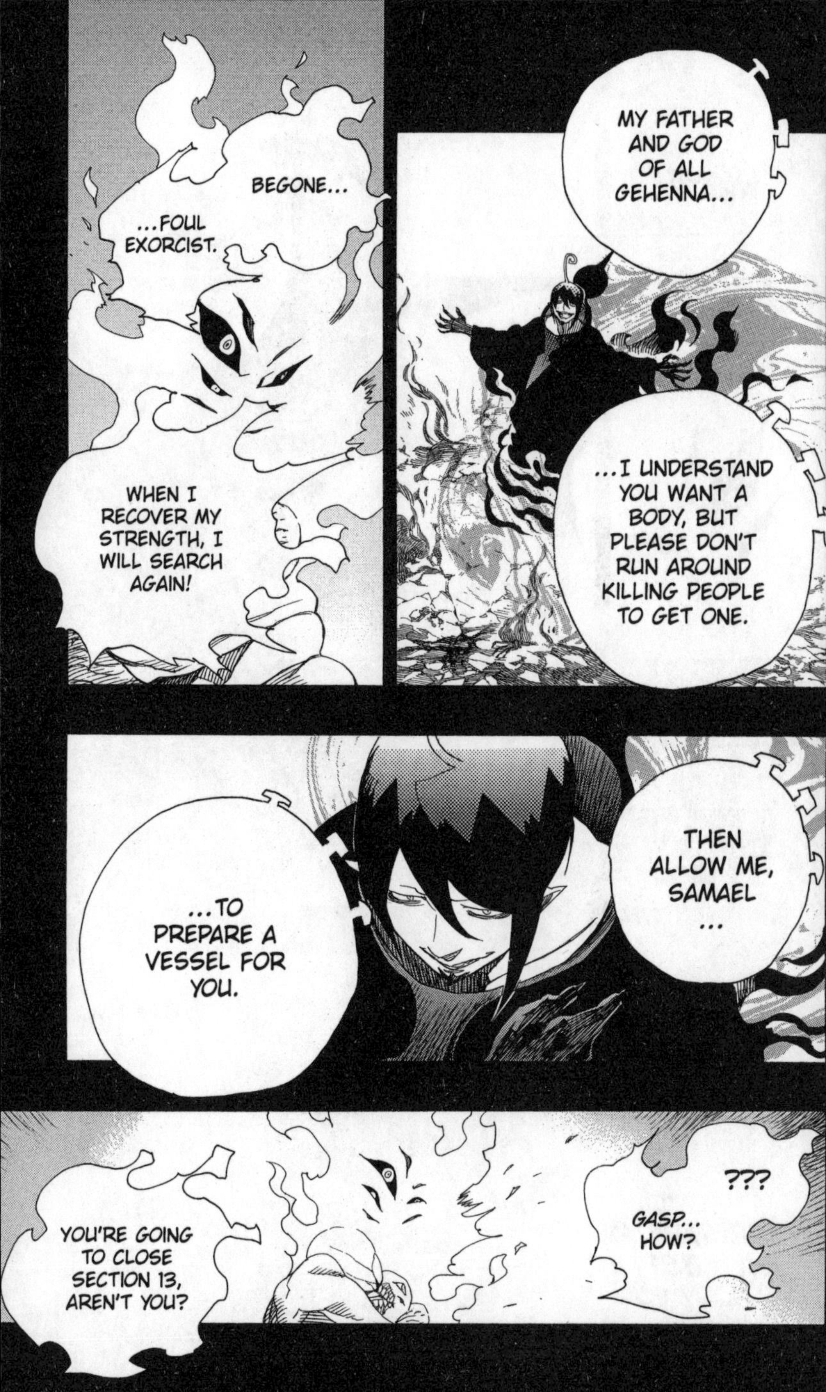
MY FATHER AND GOD OF ALL GEHENNA...
...I UNDERSTAND YOU WANT A BODY, BUT PLEASE DON'T RUN AROUND KILLING PEOPLE TO GET ONE.
BEGONE...
...FOUL EXORCIST.
WHEN I RECOVER MY STRENGTH, I WILL SEARCH AGAIN!
THEN ALLOW ME, SAMAEL ...
...TO PREPARE A VESSEL FOR YOU.
???
GASP... HOW?
YOU'RE GOING TO CLOSE SECTION 13, AREN'T YOU?

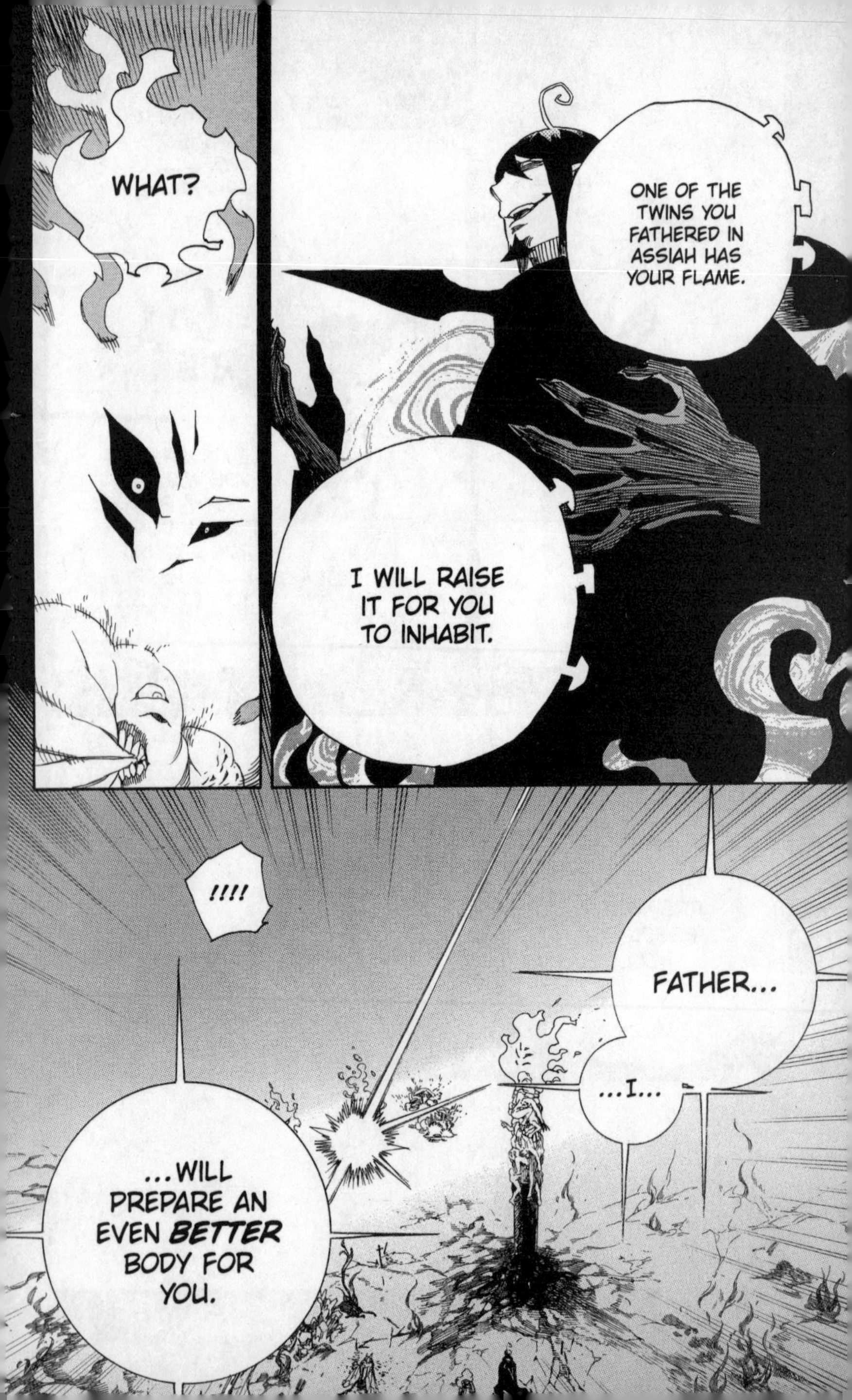
ONE OF THE TWINS YOU FATHERED IN ASSIAH HAS YOUR FLAME.
I WILL RAISE IT FOR YOU TO INHABIT.
WHAT?
FATHER...
...I...
!!!!
...WILL PREPARE AN EVEN *BETTER* BODY FOR YOU.

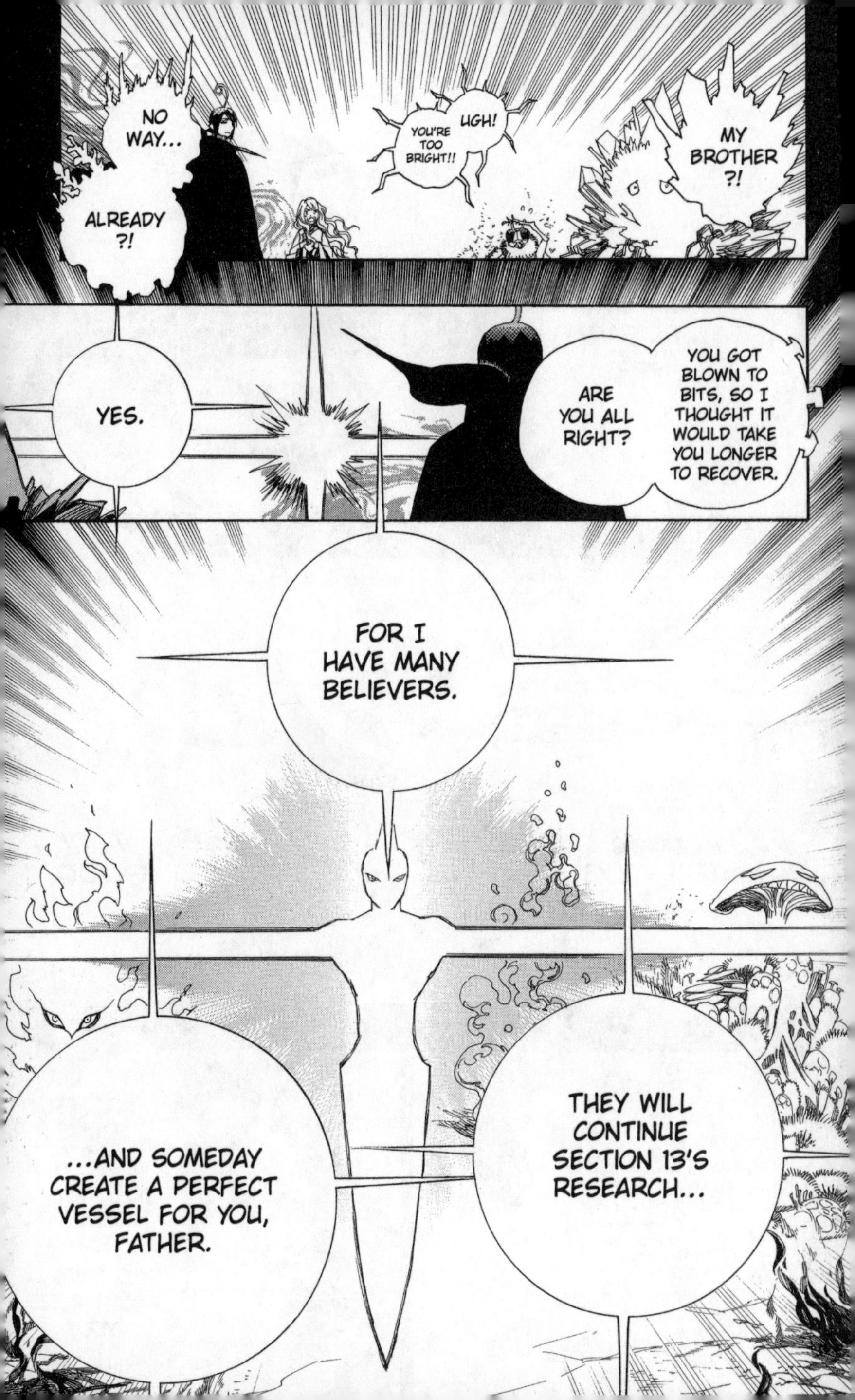
MY BROTHER ?!
UGH!
YOU'RE TOO BRIGHT!!
NO WAY...
ALREADY ?!
YOU GOT BLOWN TO BITS, SO I THOUGHT IT WOULD TAKE YOU LONGER TO RECOVER.
ARE YOU ALL RIGHT?
YES.
FOR I HAVE MANY BELIEVERS.
THEY WILL CONTINUE SECTION 13'S RESEARCH...
...AND SOMEDAY CREATE A PERFECT VESSEL FOR YOU, FATHER.

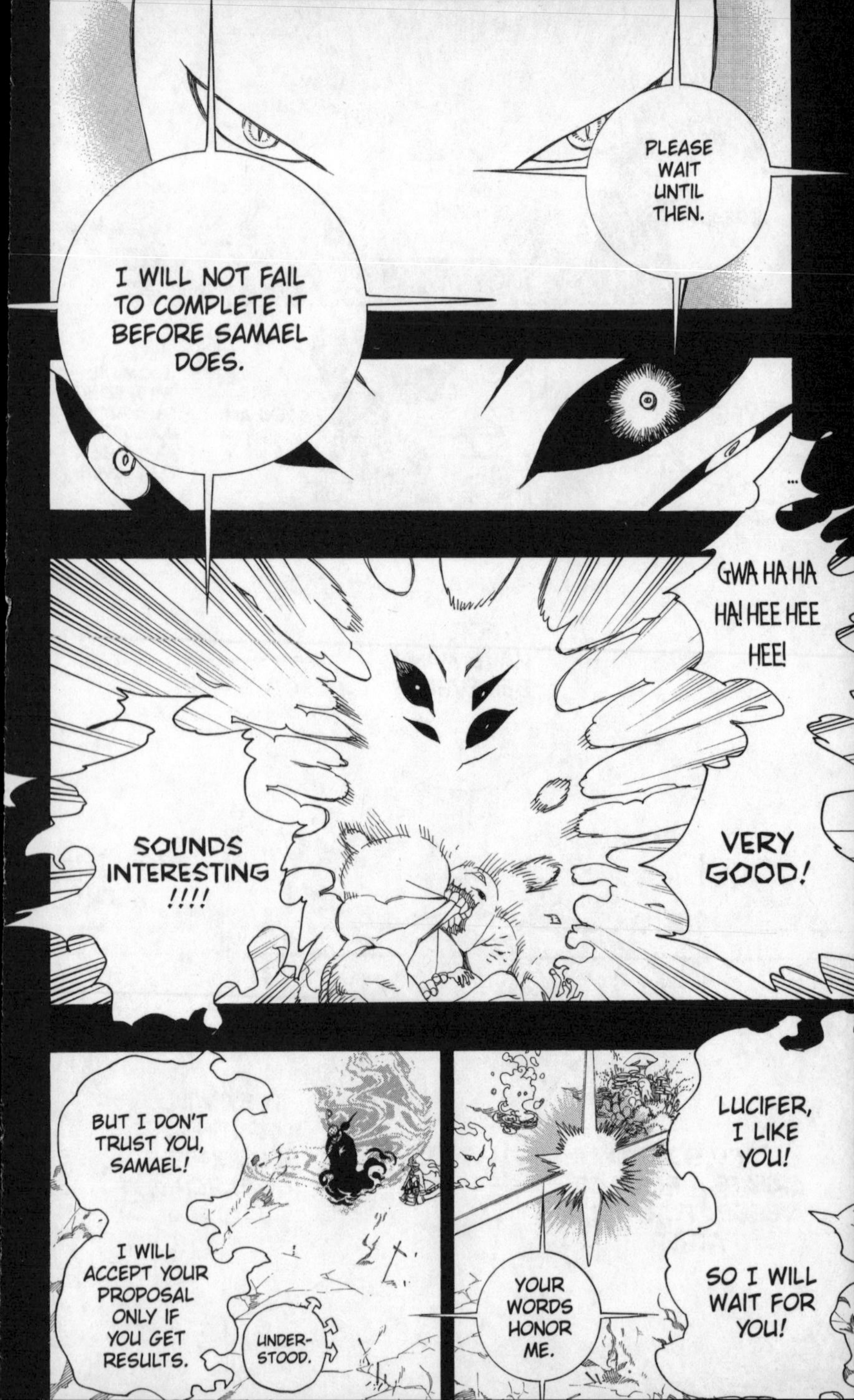
PLEASE WAIT UNTIL THEN.
I WILL NOT FAIL TO COMPLETE IT BEFORE SAMAEL DOES.
...
GWA HA HA HA! HEE HEE HEE!
VERY GOOD!
SOUNDS INTERESTING!!!!
LUCIFER, I LIKE YOU!
SO I WILL WAIT FOR YOU!
YOUR WORDS HONOR ME.
BUT I DON'T TRUST YOU, SAMAEL!
I WILL ACCEPT YOUR PROPOSAL ONLY IF YOU GET RESULTS.
UNDER-STOOD.

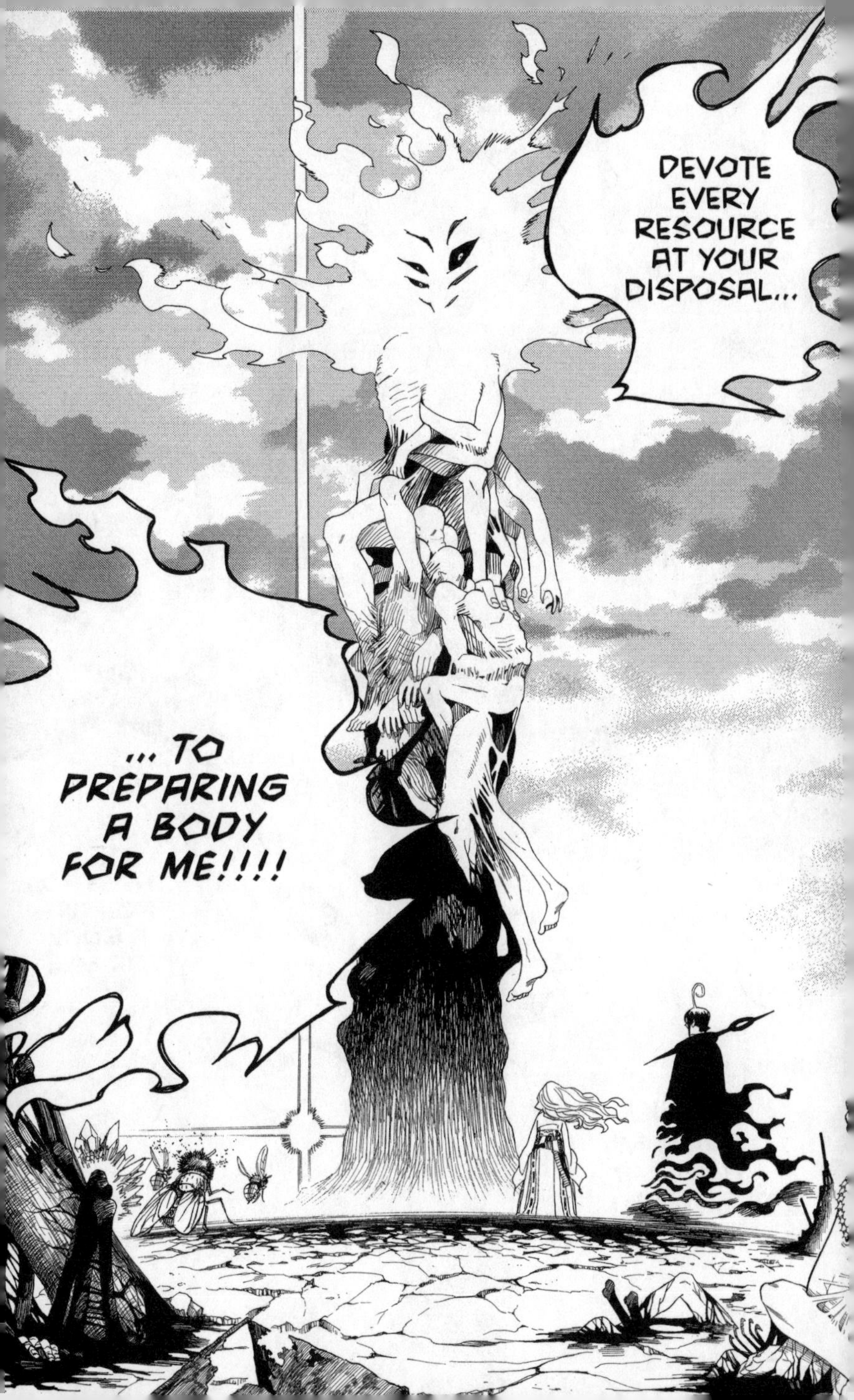
DEVOTE EVERY RESOURCE AT YOUR DISPOSAL...
... TO PREPARING A BODY FOR ME!!!!

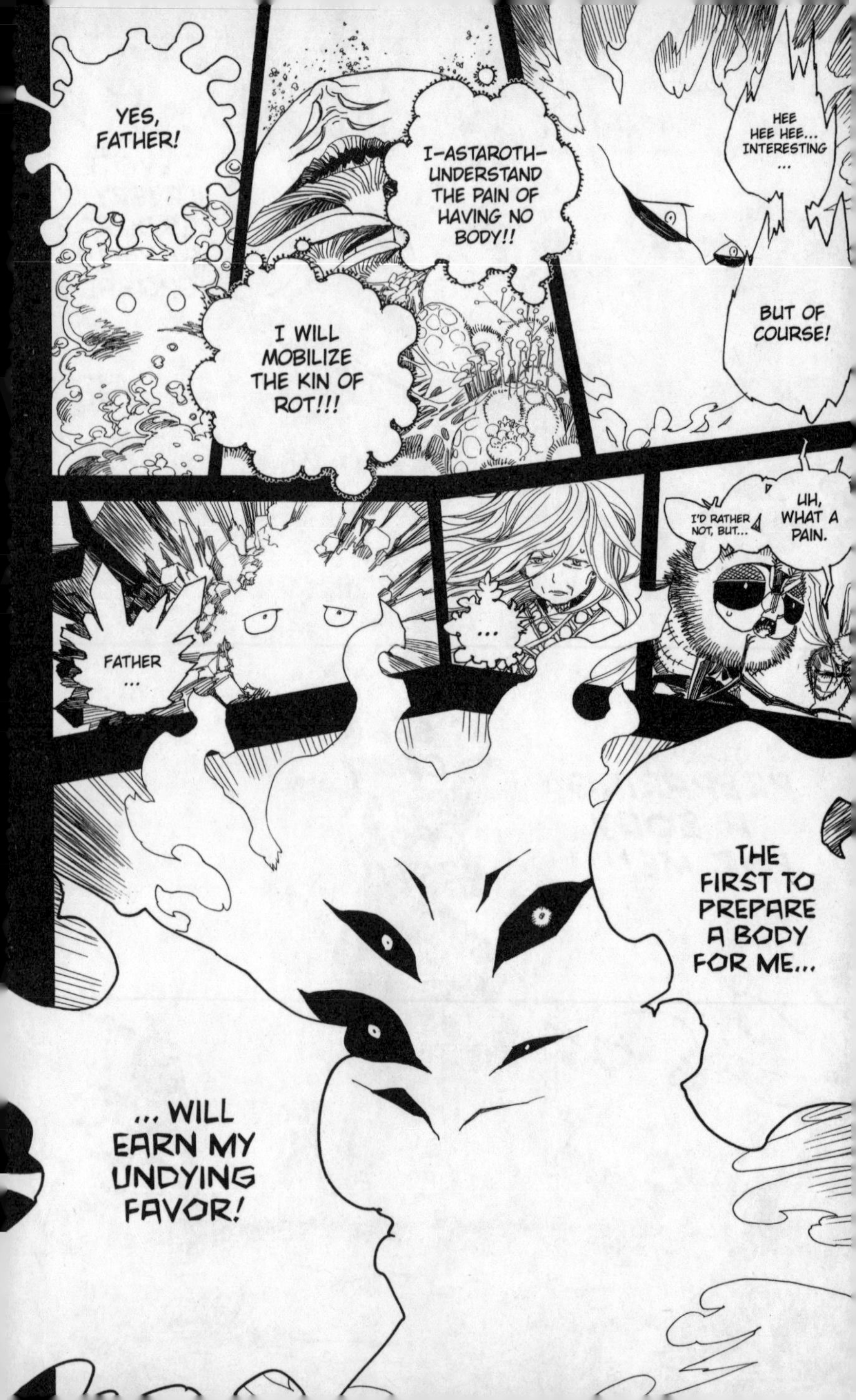
HEE HEE HEE... INTERESTING ...
BUT OF COURSE!
I-ASTAROTH-UNDERSTAND THE PAIN OF HAVING NO BODY!!
I WILL MOBILIZE THE KIN OF ROT!!!
YES, FATHER!
UH, WHAT A PAIN.
I'D RATHER NOT, BUT...
...
FATHER ...
THE FIRST TO PREPARE A BODY FOR ME...
... WILL EARN MY UNDYING FAVOR!

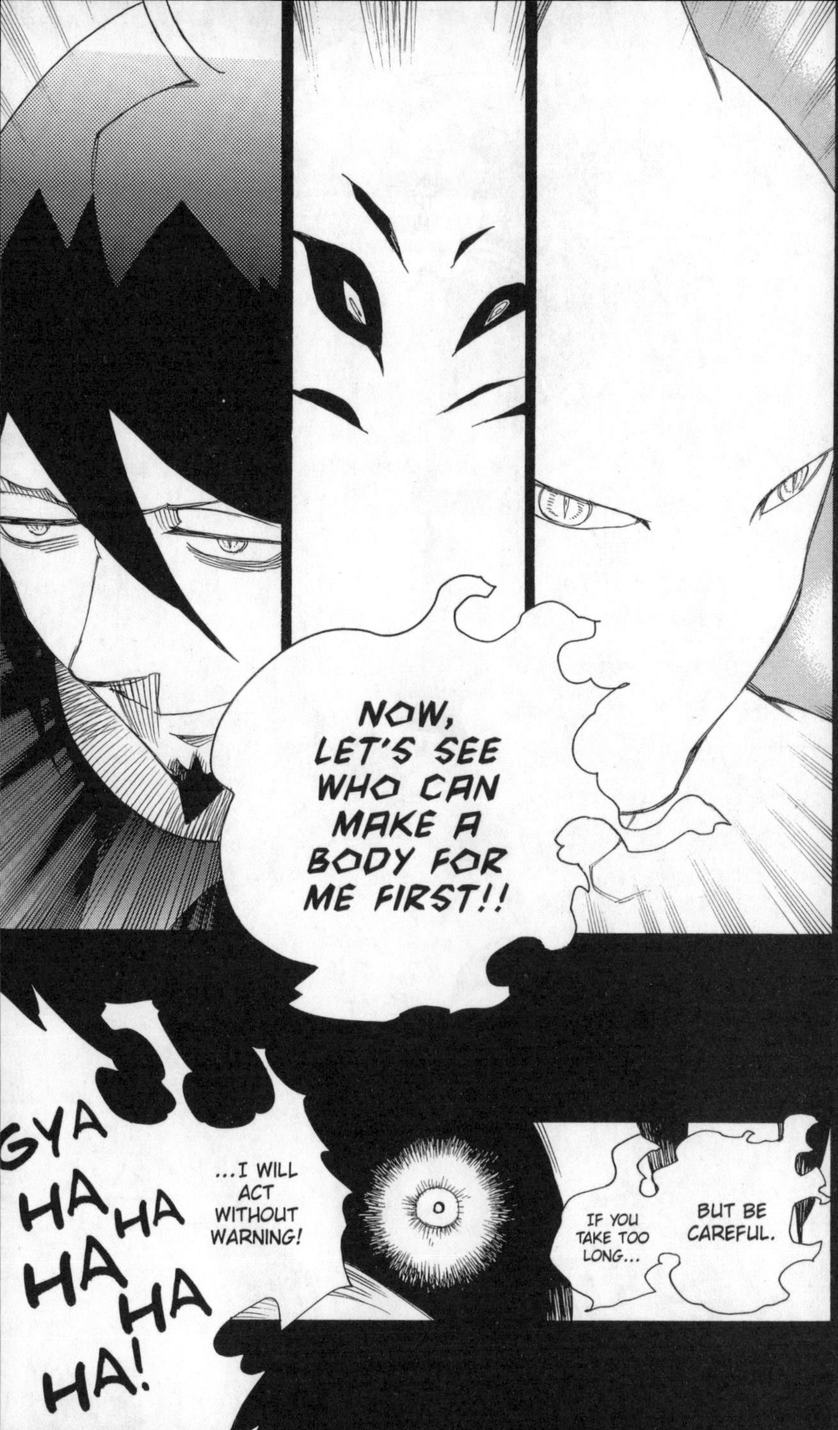
NOW, LET'S SEE WHO CAN MAKE A BODY FOR ME FIRST!!
BUT BE CAREFUL.
IF YOU TAKE TOO LONG...
...I WILL ACT WITHOUT WARNING!
GYA HA HA HA HA HA!

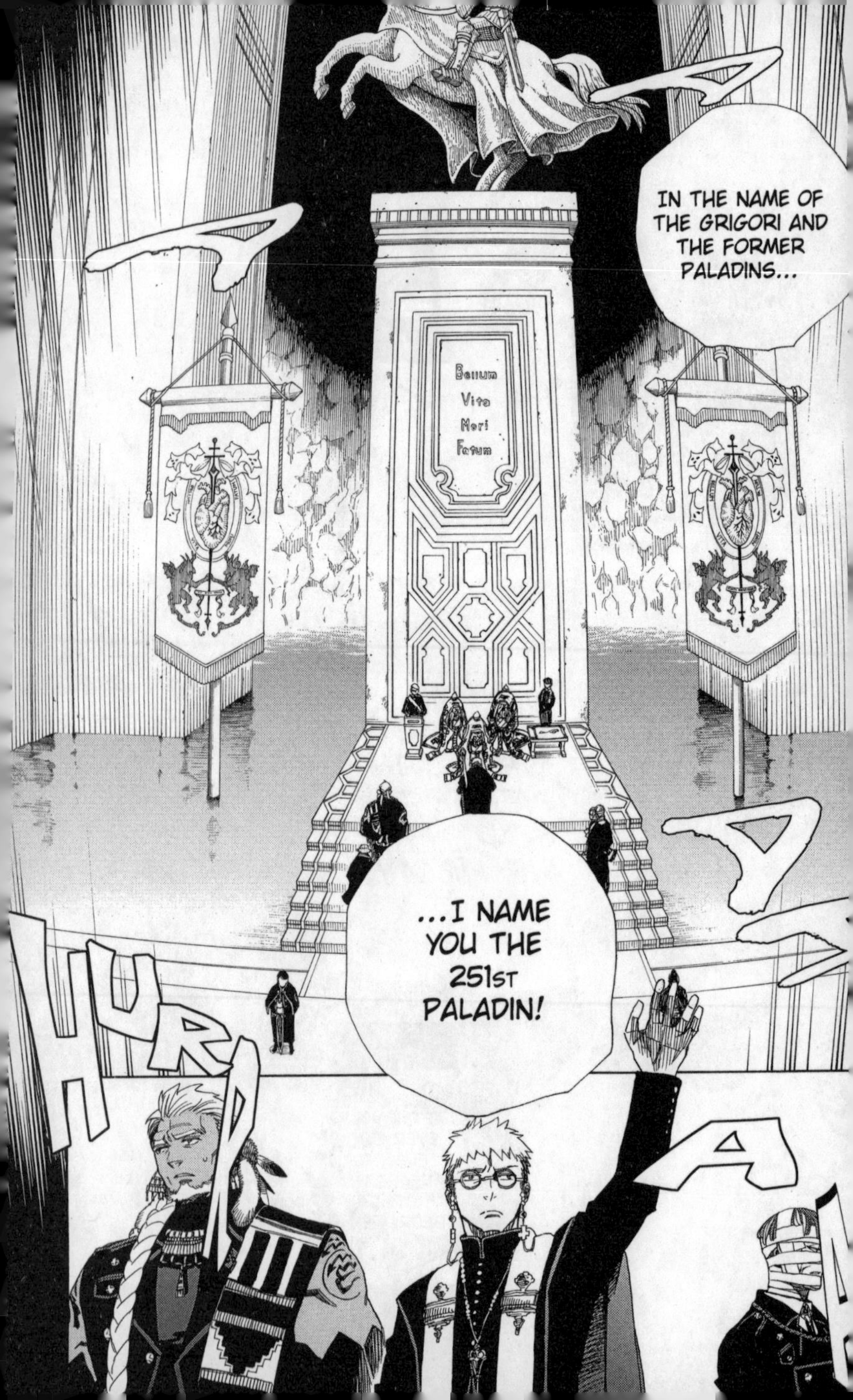
IN THE NAME OF THE GRIGORI AND THE FORMER PALADINS...
Bellum Vita Mori Fatum
...I NAME YOU THE 251ST PALADIN!

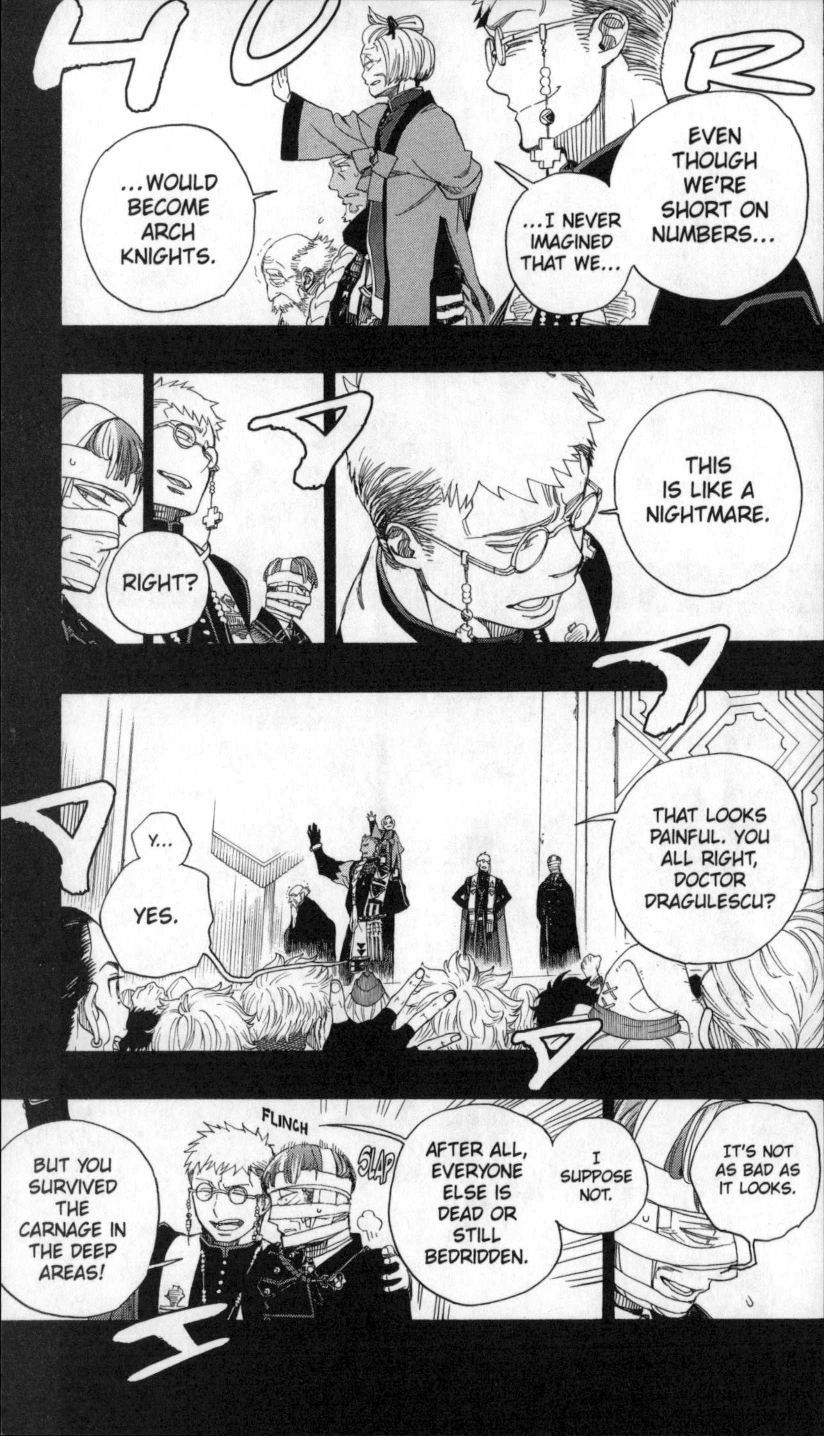
EVEN THOUGH WE'RE SHORT ON NUMBERS...
...I NEVER IMAGINED THAT WE...
...WOULD BECOME ARCH KNIGHTS.
THIS IS LIKE A NIGHTMARE.
RIGHT?
THAT LOOKS PAINFUL. YOU ALL RIGHT, DOCTOR DRAGULESCU?
Y... YES.
IT'S NOT AS BAD AS IT LOOKS.
I SUPPOSE NOT.
AFTER ALL, EVERYONE ELSE IS DEAD OR STILL BEDRIDDEN.
SLAP
FLINCH
BUT YOU SURVIVED THE CARNAGE IN THE DEEP AREAS!

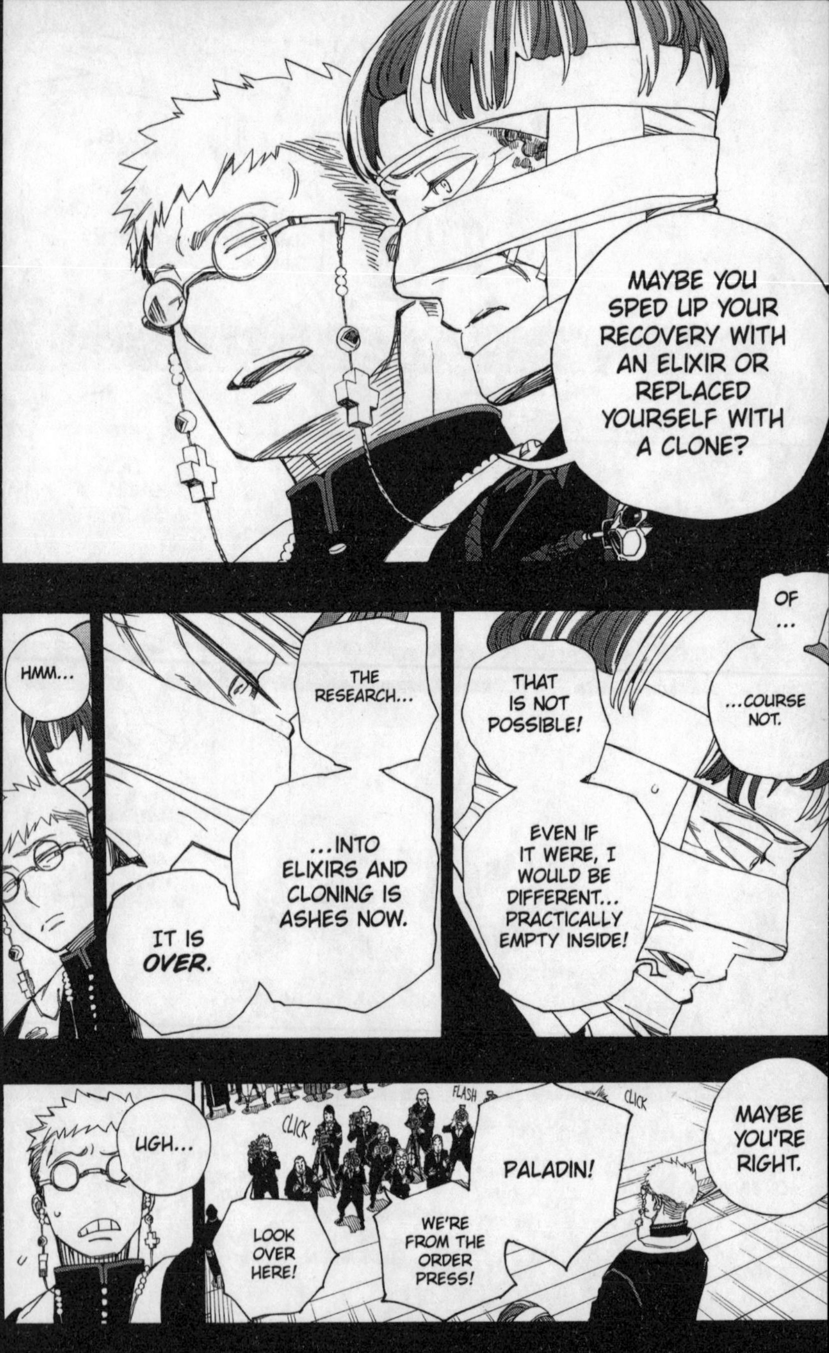
MAYBE YOU SPED UP YOUR RECOVERY WITH AN ELIXIR OR REPLACED YOURSELF WITH A CLONE?
OF...
...COURSE NOT.
THAT IS NOT POSSIBLE!
EVEN IF IT WERE, I WOULD BE DIFFERENT... PRACTICALLY EMPTY INSIDE!
THE RESEARCH...
...INTO ELIXIRS AND CLONING IS ASHES NOW.
IT IS *OVER.*
HMM...
MAYBE YOU'RE RIGHT.
CLICK
PALADIN!
FLASH
WE'RE FROM THE ORDER PRESS!
LOOK OVER HERE!
CLICK
UGH...

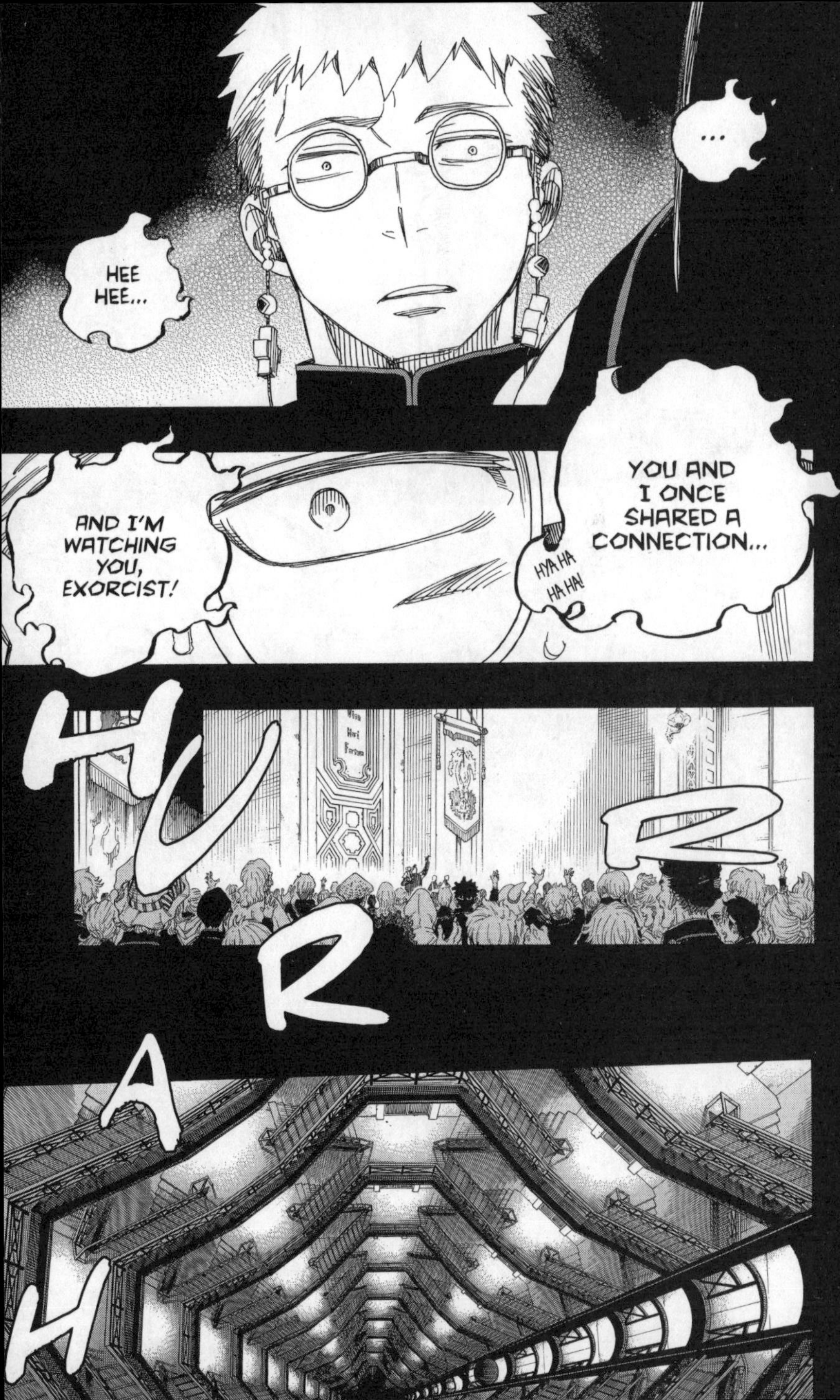
...
HEE HEE...
YOU AND I ONCE SHARED A CONNECTION...
HYA HA HA HA!
AND I'M WATCHING YOU, EXORCIST!
HURRAH

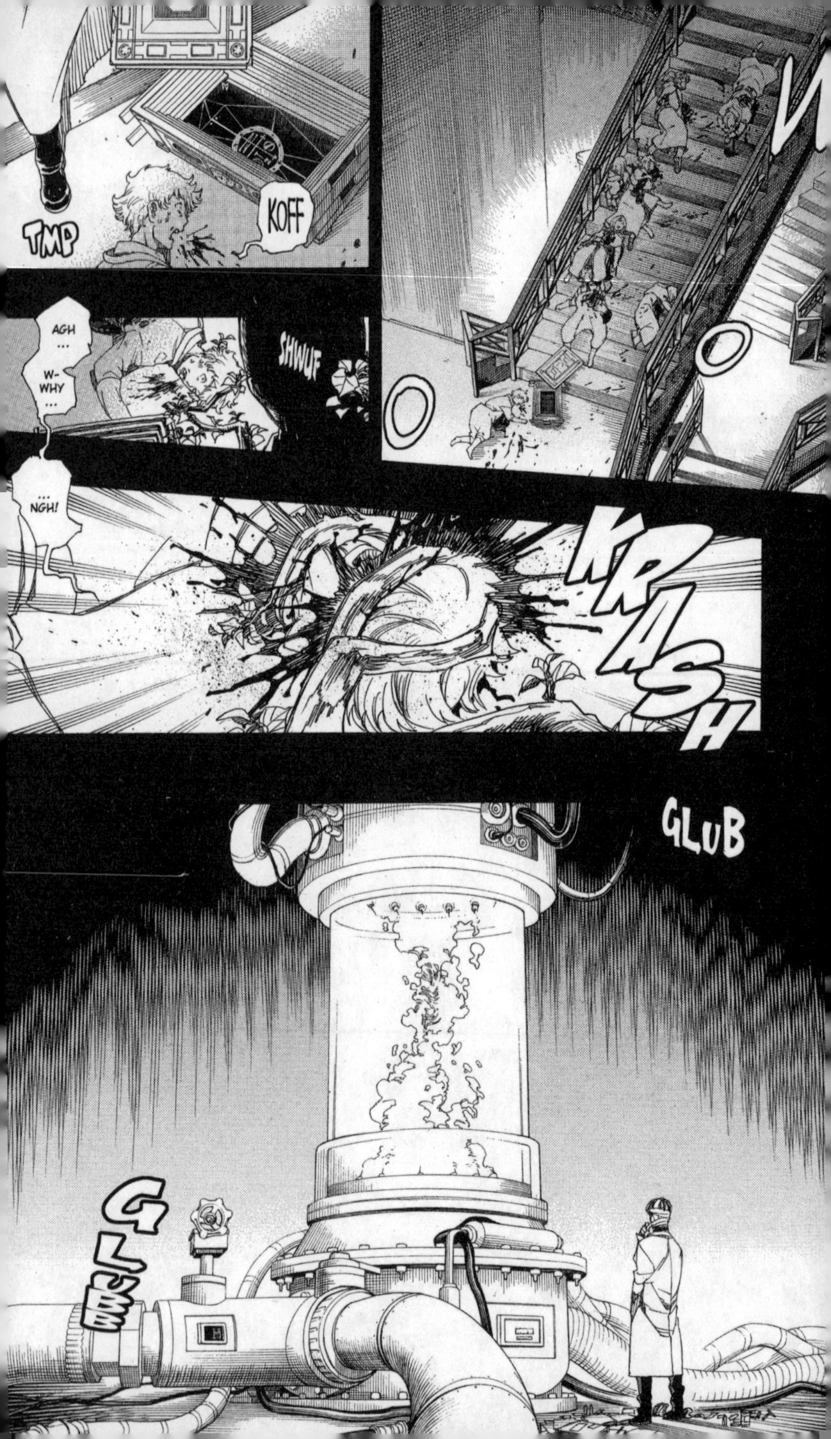
TMP
KOFF
SHWUF
AGH ... W-WHY ...
... NGH!
KRASH
GLUB
GLUBB

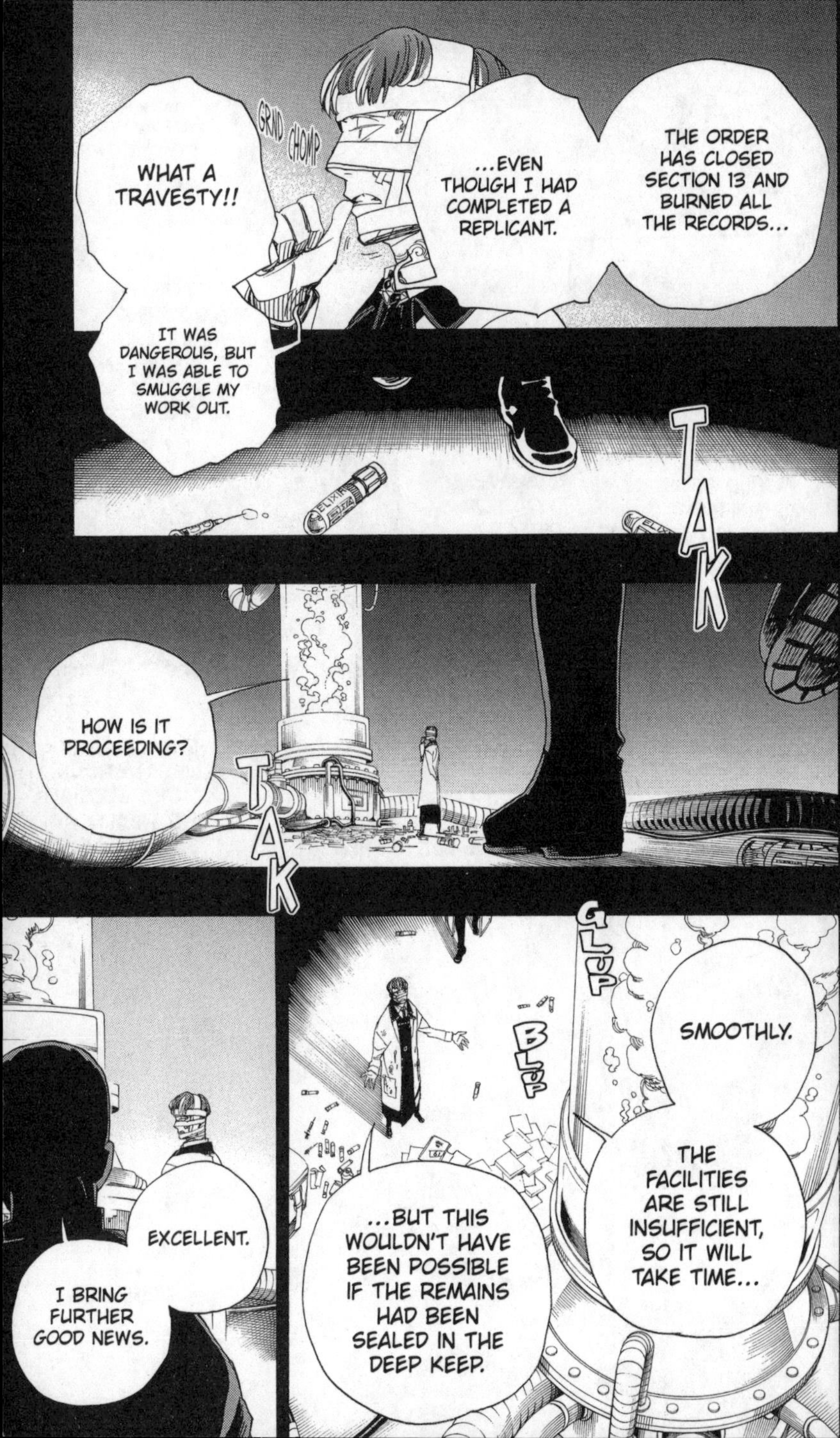
THE ORDER HAS CLOSED SECTION 13 AND BURNED ALL THE RECORDS...
...EVEN THOUGH I HAD COMPLETED A REPLICANT.
GRND
CHOMP
WHAT A TRAVESTY!!
IT WAS DANGEROUS, BUT I WAS ABLE TO SMUGGLE MY WORK OUT.
TAK
HOW IS IT PROCEEDING?
TAK
GLUP
BLUP
SMOOTHLY.
THE FACILITIES ARE STILL INSUFFICIENT, SO IT WILL TAKE TIME...
...BUT THIS WOULDN'T HAVE BEEN POSSIBLE IF THE REMAINS HAD BEEN SEALED IN THE DEEP KEEP.
EXCELLENT.
I BRING FURTHER GOOD NEWS.

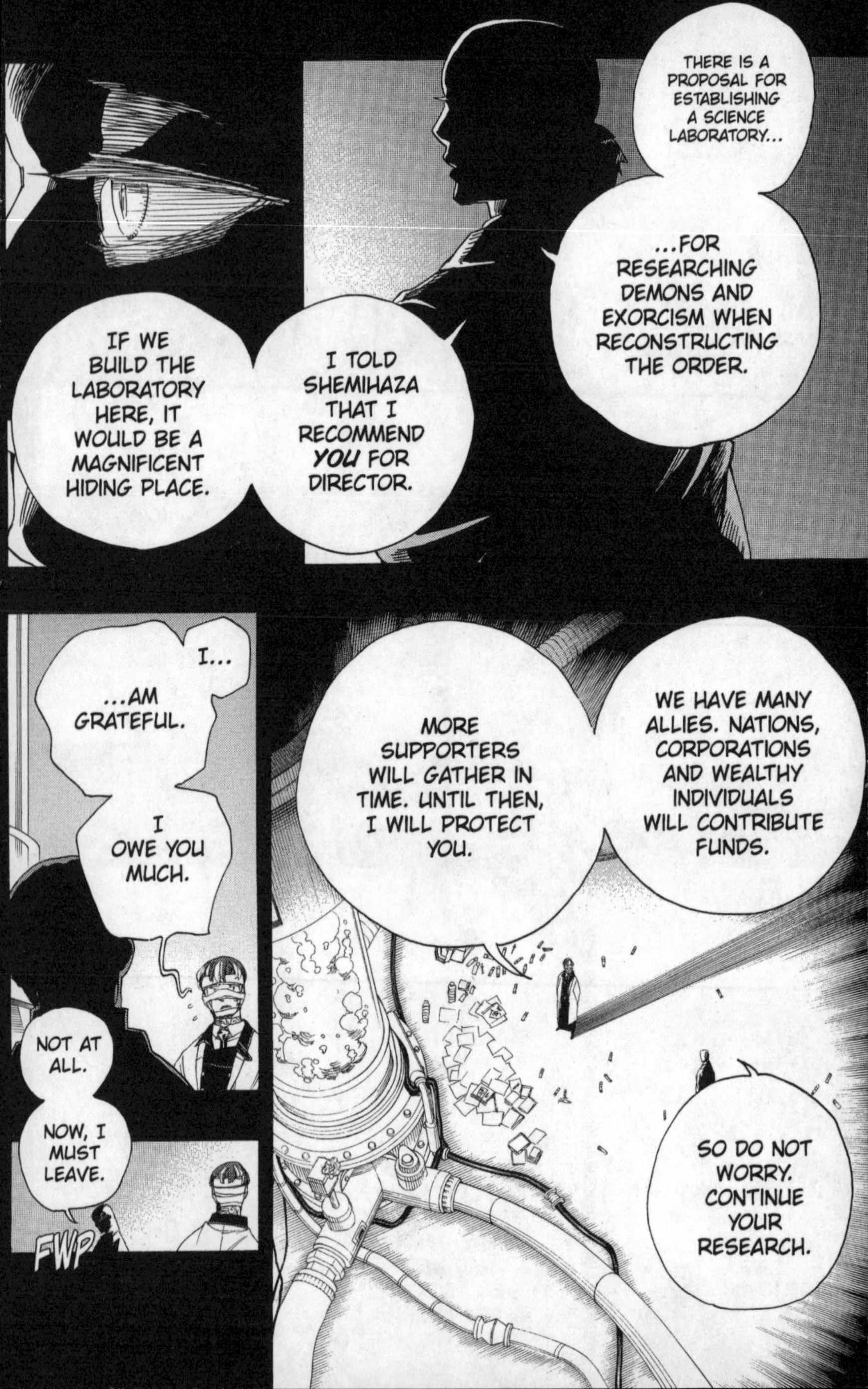
THERE IS A PROPOSAL FOR ESTABLISHING A SCIENCE LABORATORY...
...FOR RESEARCHING DEMONS AND EXORCISM WHEN RECONSTRUCTING THE ORDER.
I TOLD SHEMIHAZA THAT I RECOMMEND *YOU* FOR DIRECTOR.
IF WE BUILD THE LABORATORY HERE, IT WOULD BE A MAGNIFICENT HIDING PLACE.
WE HAVE MANY ALLIES. NATIONS, CORPORATIONS AND WEALTHY INDIVIDUALS WILL CONTRIBUTE FUNDS.
MORE SUPPORTERS WILL GATHER IN TIME. UNTIL THEN, I WILL PROTECT YOU.
SO DO NOT WORRY. CONTINUE YOUR RESEARCH.
I...
...AM GRATEFUL.
I OWE YOU MUCH.
NOT AT ALL.
NOW, I MUST LEAVE.
FWP

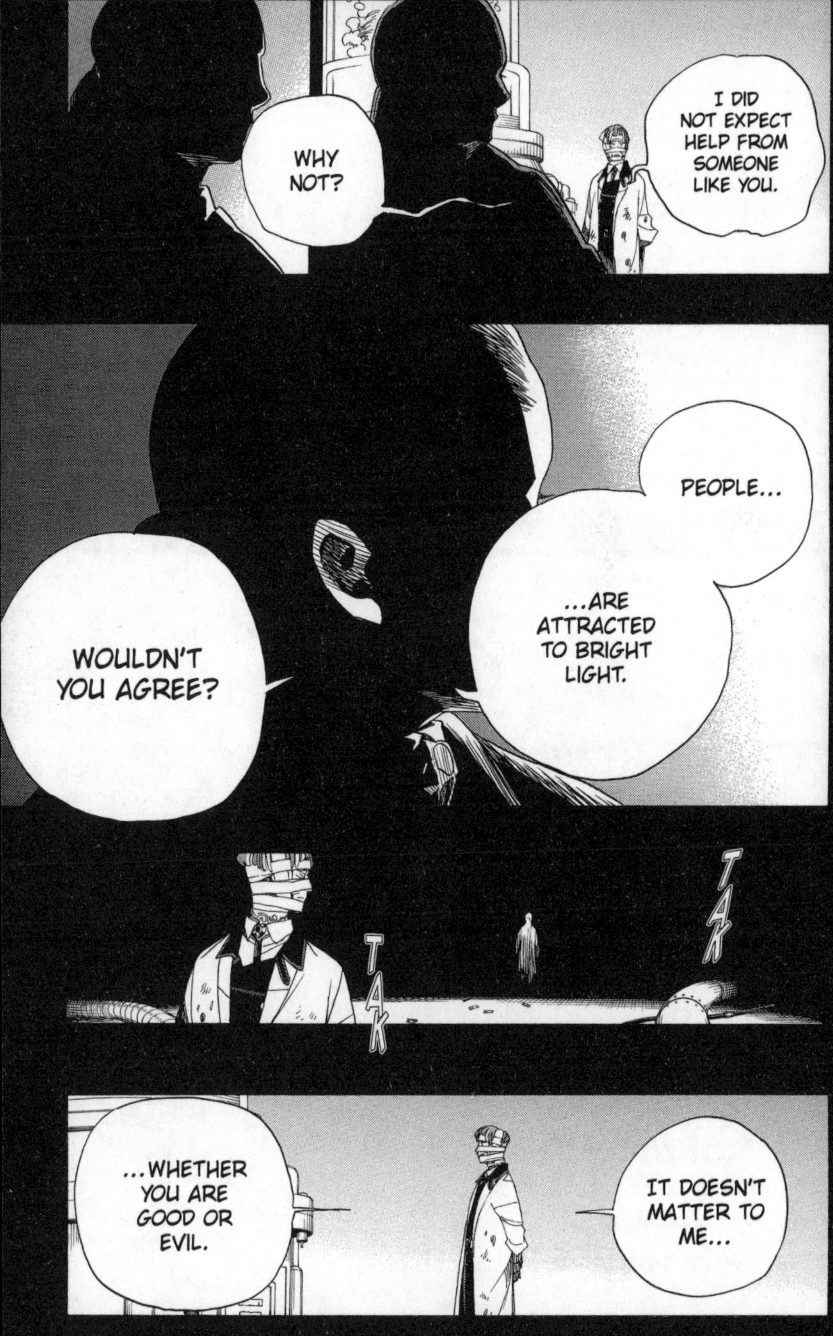
I DID NOT EXPECT HELP FROM SOMEONE LIKE YOU.
WHY NOT?
PEOPLE...
...ARE ATTRACTED TO BRIGHT LIGHT.
WOULDN'T YOU AGREE?
TAK
TAK
IT DOESN'T MATTER TO ME...
...WHETHER YOU ARE GOOD OR EVIL.

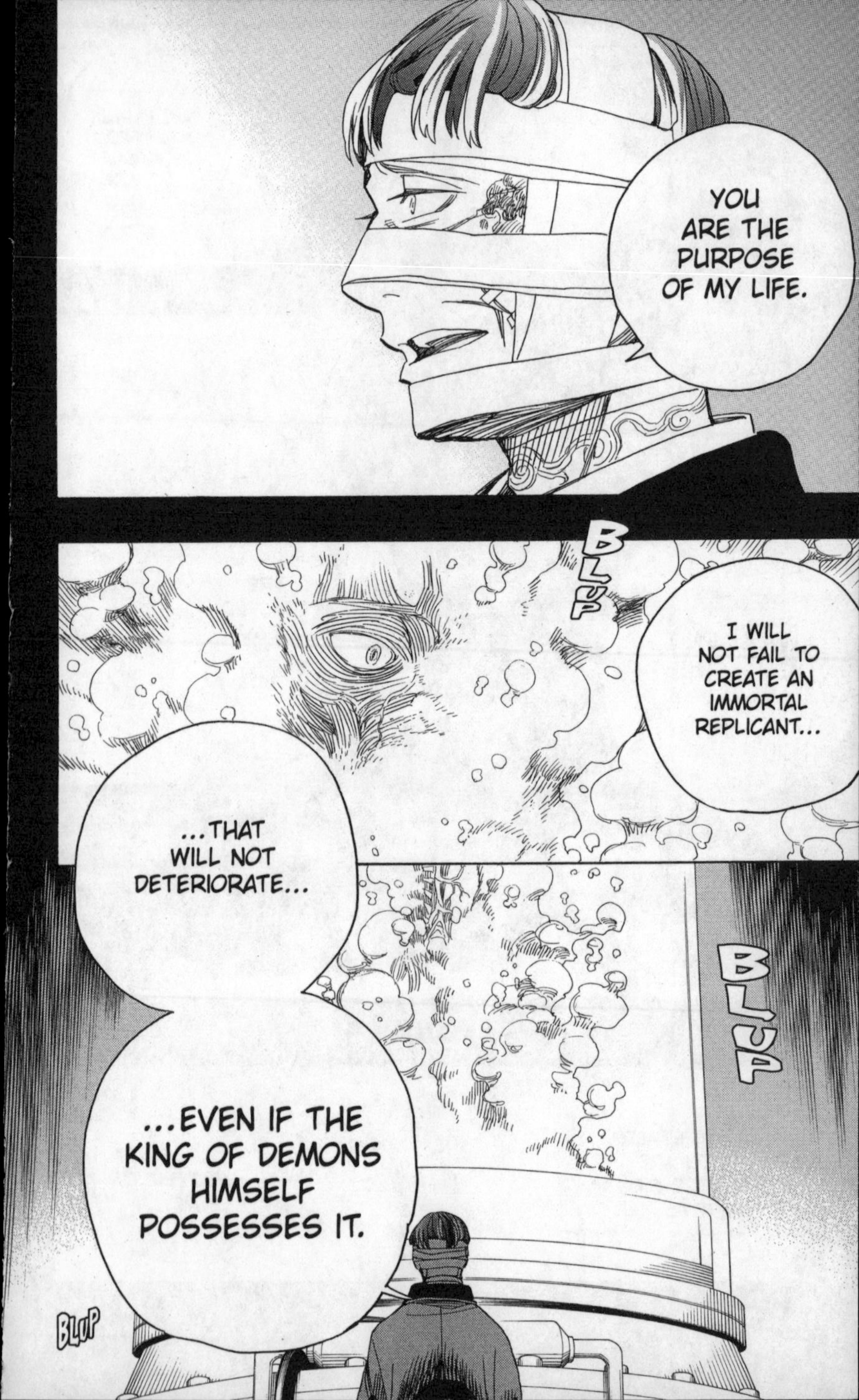
YOU ARE THE PURPOSE OF MY LIFE.
BLUP
I WILL NOT FAIL TO CREATE AN IMMORTAL REPLICANT...
...THAT WILL NOT DETERIORATE...
BLUP
...EVEN IF THE KING OF DEMONS HIMSELF POSSESSES IT.
BLUP

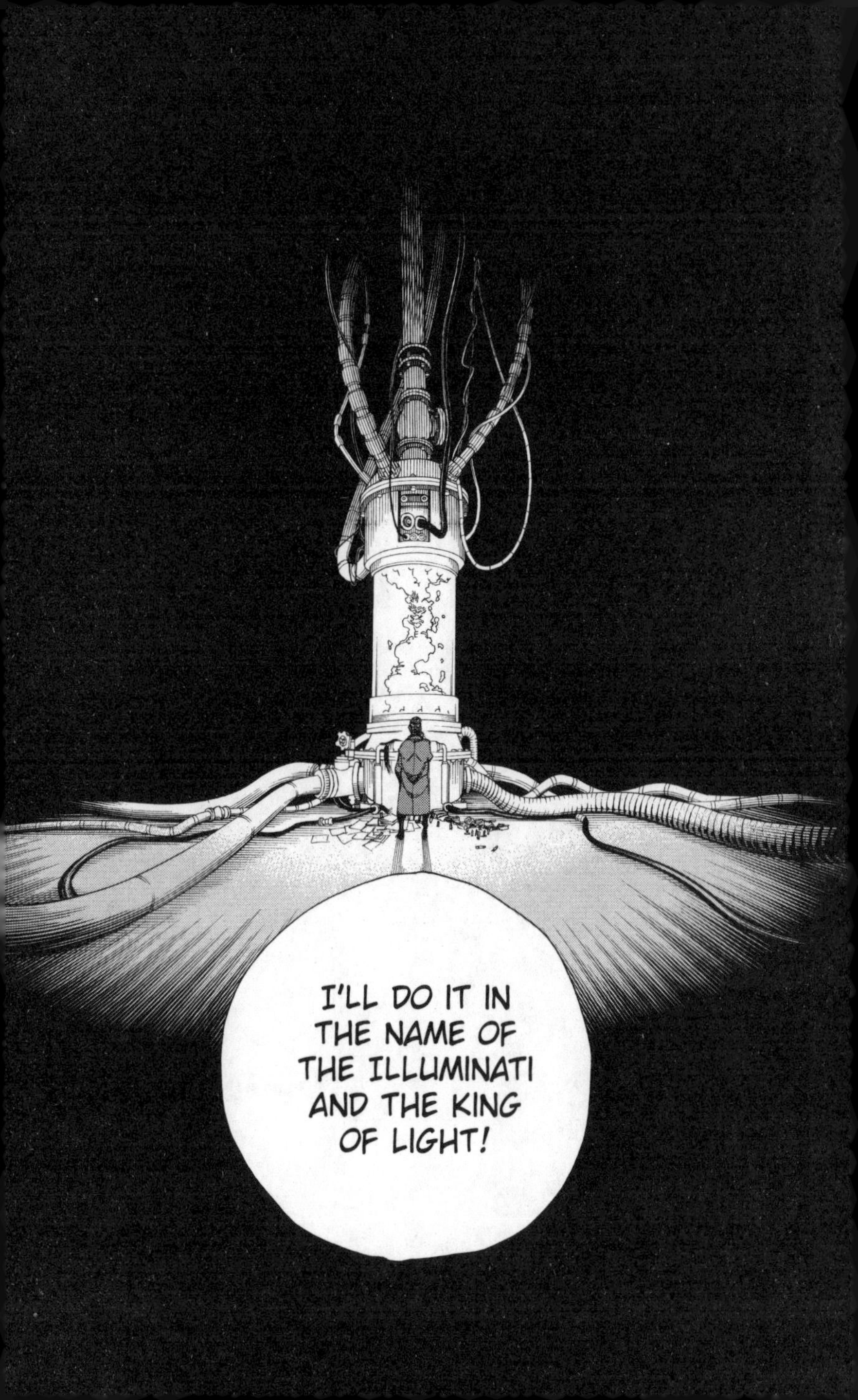
I'LL DO IT IN THE NAME OF THE ILLUMINATI AND THE KING OF LIGHT!

BLUE EXORCIST CHAPTER 119: SsC24: 16

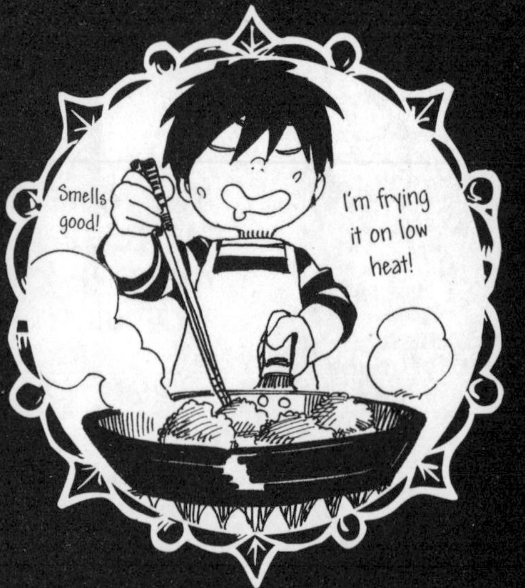
I'm frying it on low heat!
Smells good!

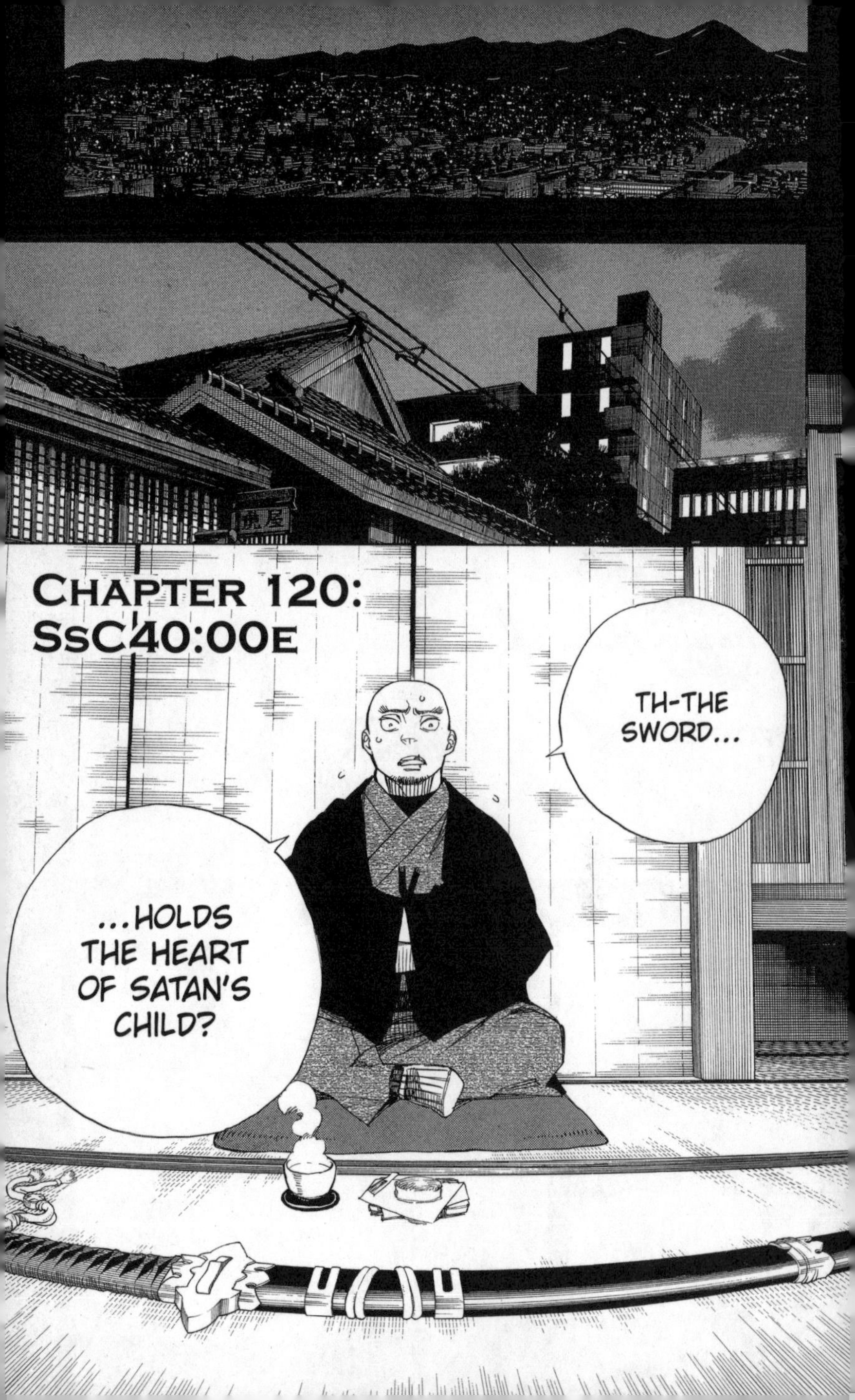
CHAPTER 120:
SsC40:00E
TH-THE SWORD...
...HOLDS THE HEART OF SATAN'S CHILD?

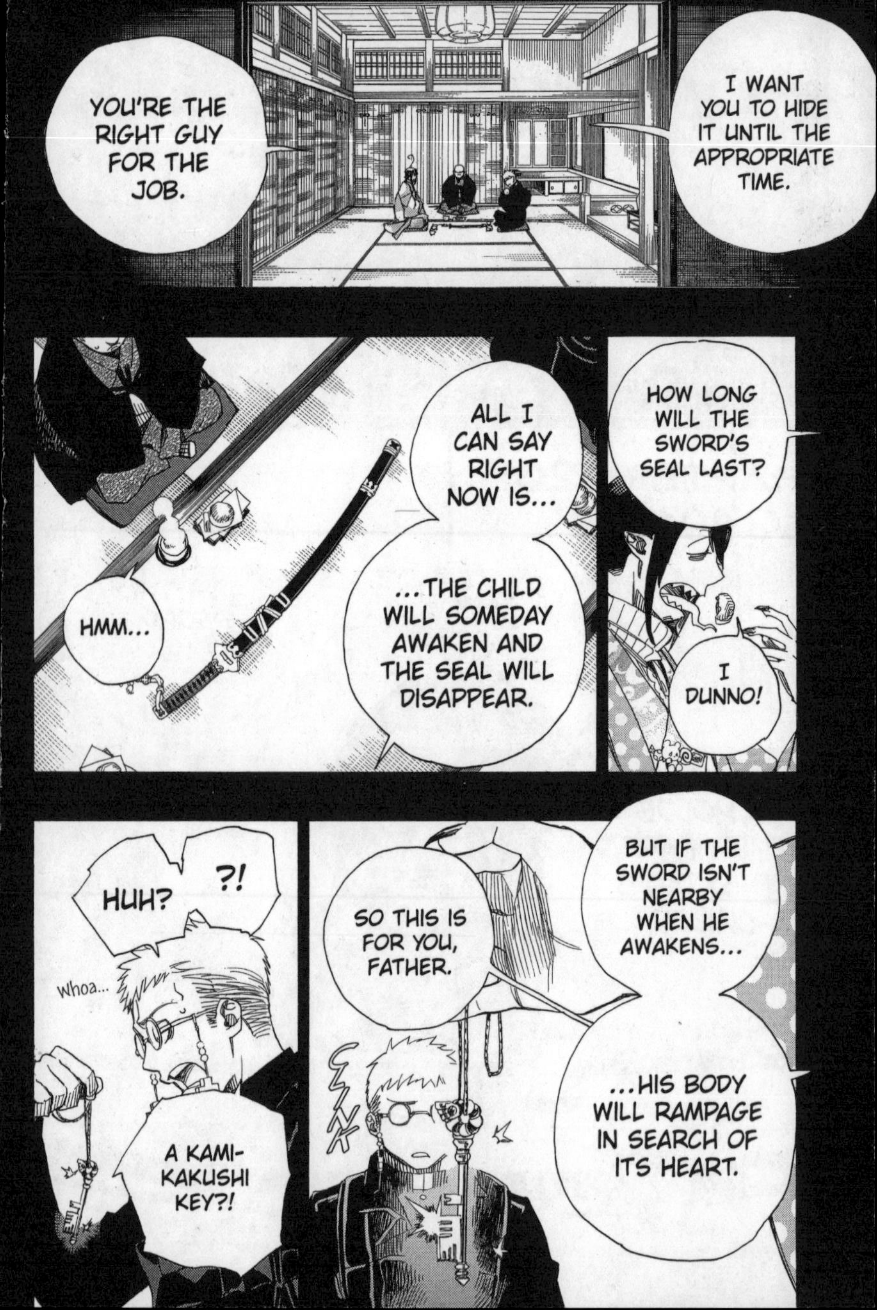
I WANT YOU TO HIDE IT UNTIL THE APPROPRIATE TIME.
YOU'RE THE RIGHT GUY FOR THE JOB.
HOW LONG WILL THE SWORD'S SEAL LAST?
I DUNNO!
ALL I CAN SAY RIGHT NOW IS...
...THE CHILD WILL SOMEDAY AWAKEN AND THE SEAL WILL DISAPPEAR.
HMM...
BUT IF THE SWORD ISN'T NEARBY WHEN HE AWAKENS...
...HIS BODY WILL RAMPAGE IN SEARCH OF ITS HEART.
SO THIS IS FOR YOU, FATHER.
HUH?
?!
whoa...
A KAMI-KAKUSHI KEY?!

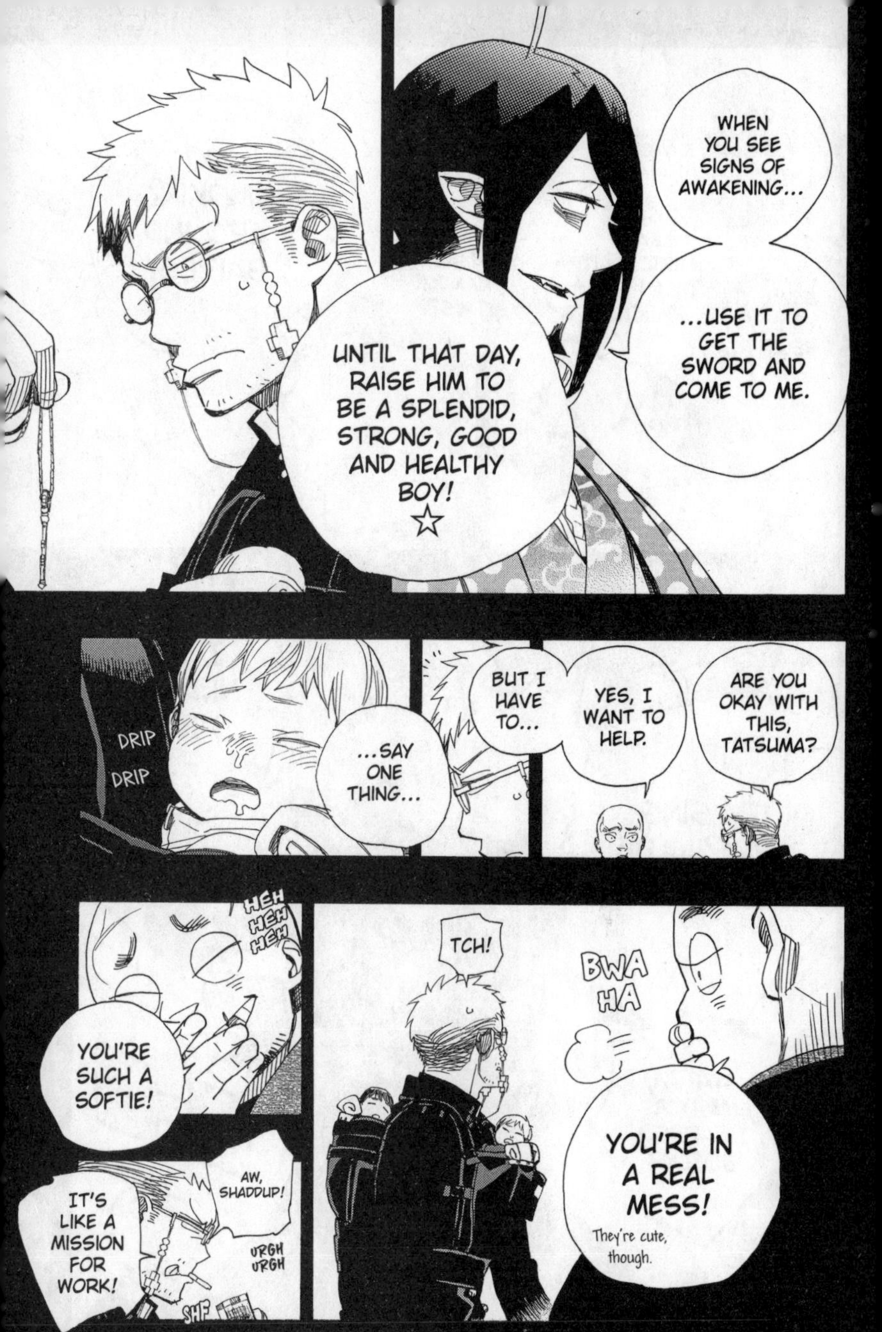
WHEN YOU SEE SIGNS OF AWAKENING...
...USE IT TO GET THE SWORD AND COME TO ME.
UNTIL THAT DAY, RAISE HIM TO BE A SPLENDID, STRONG, GOOD AND HEALTHY BOY! ☆
ARE YOU OKAY WITH THIS, TATSUMA?
YES, I WANT TO HELP.
BUT I HAVE TO...
...SAY ONE THING...
DRIP
DRIP
BWA HA
TCH!
YOU'RE IN A REAL MESS!
They're cute, though.
HEH HEH HEH
YOU'RE SUCH A SOFTIE!
AW, SHADDUP!
IT'S LIKE A MISSION FOR WORK!
URGH URGH
SHF

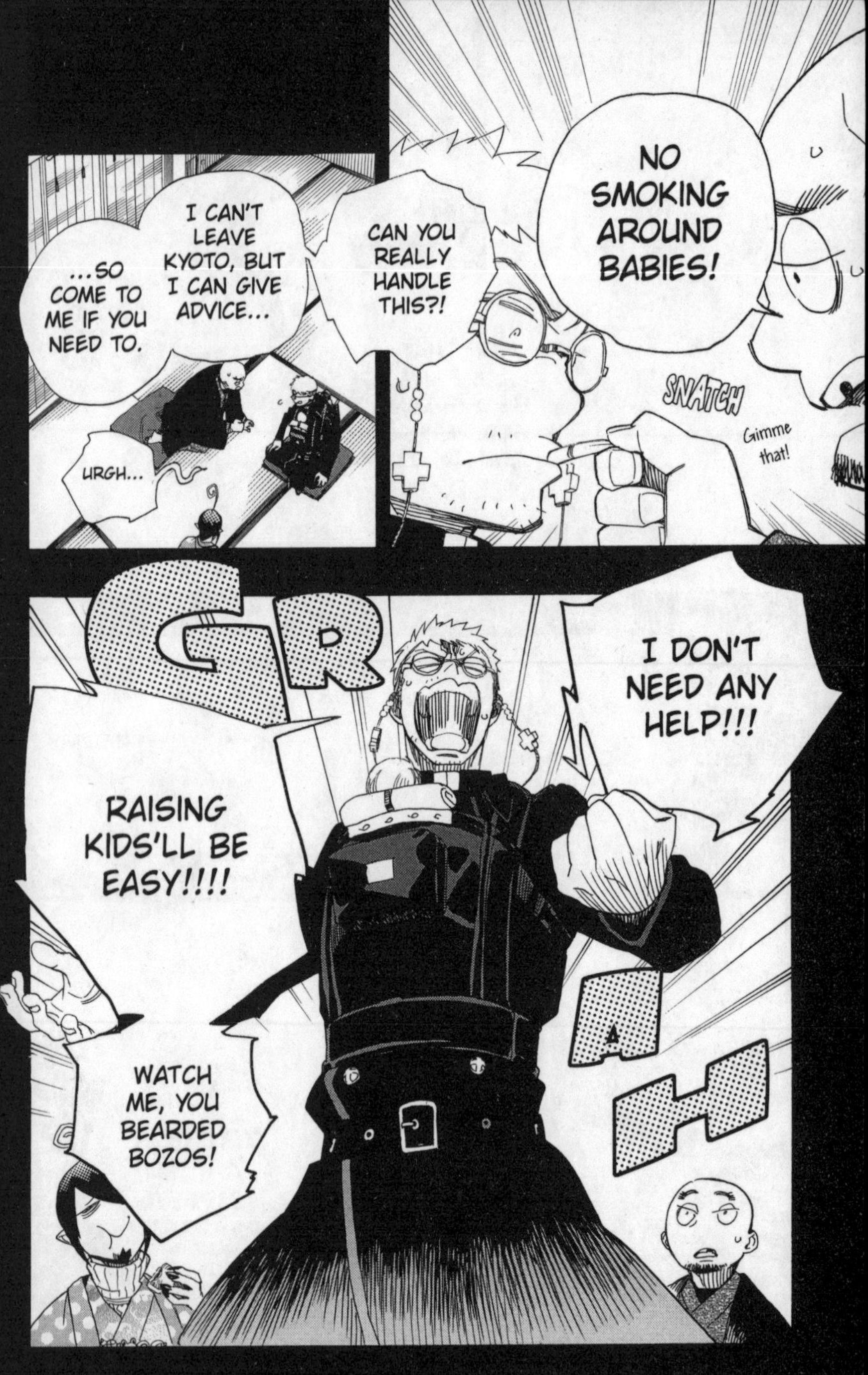
NO SMOKING AROUND BABIES!
SNATCH
Gimme that!
CAN YOU REALLY HANDLE THIS?!
I CAN'T LEAVE KYOTO, BUT I CAN GIVE ADVICE...
...SO COME TO ME IF YOU NEED TO.
URGH...
I DON'T NEED ANY HELP!!!
GRAAH
RAISING KIDS'LL BE EASY!!!!
WATCH ME, YOU BEARDED BOZOS!

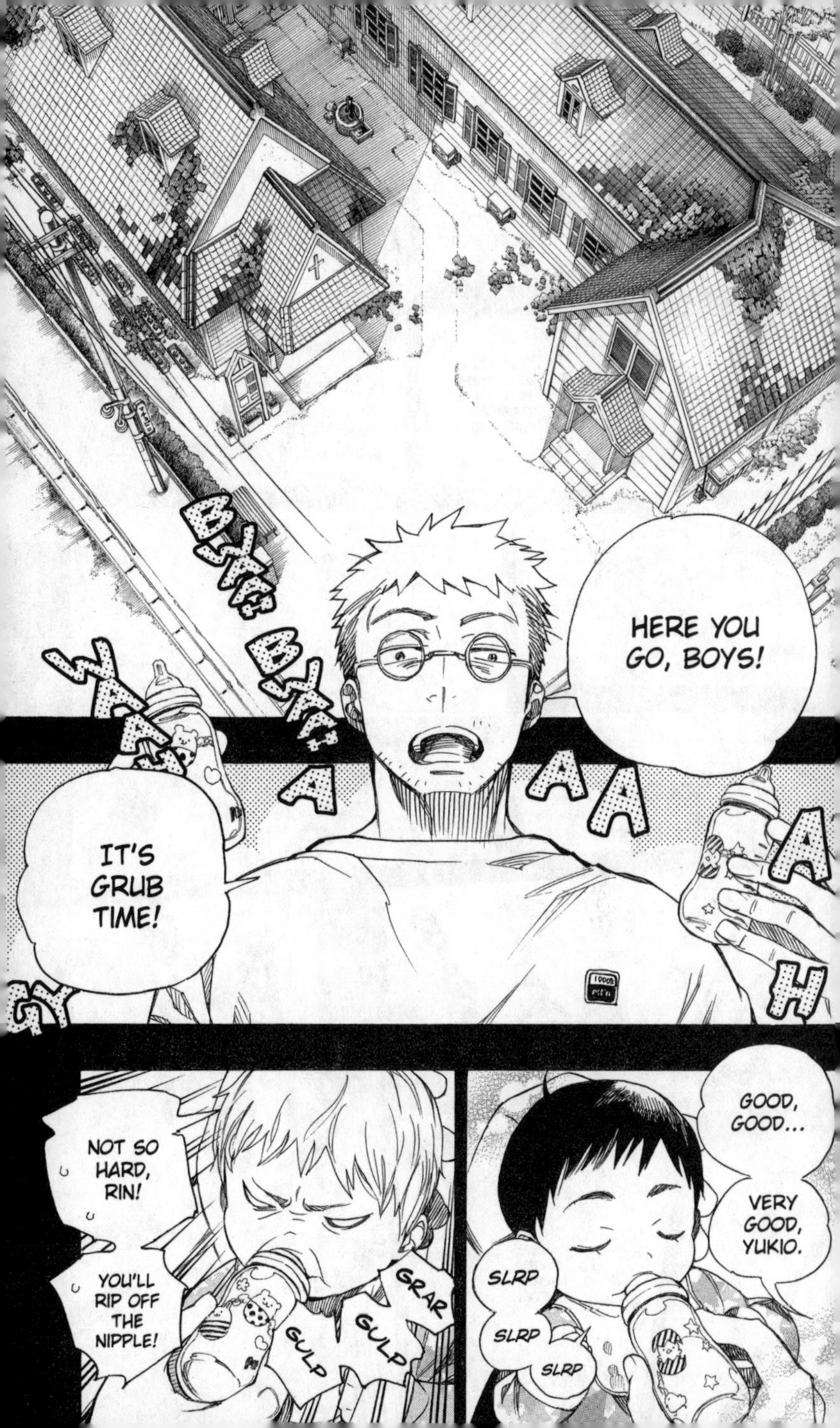
HERE YOU GO, BOYS!
IT'S GRUB TIME!
GOOD, GOOD...
VERY GOOD, YUKIO.
SLRP
SLRP
SLRP
NOT SO HARD, RIN!
YOU'LL RIP OFF THE NIPPLE!
GRAR
GULP
GULP

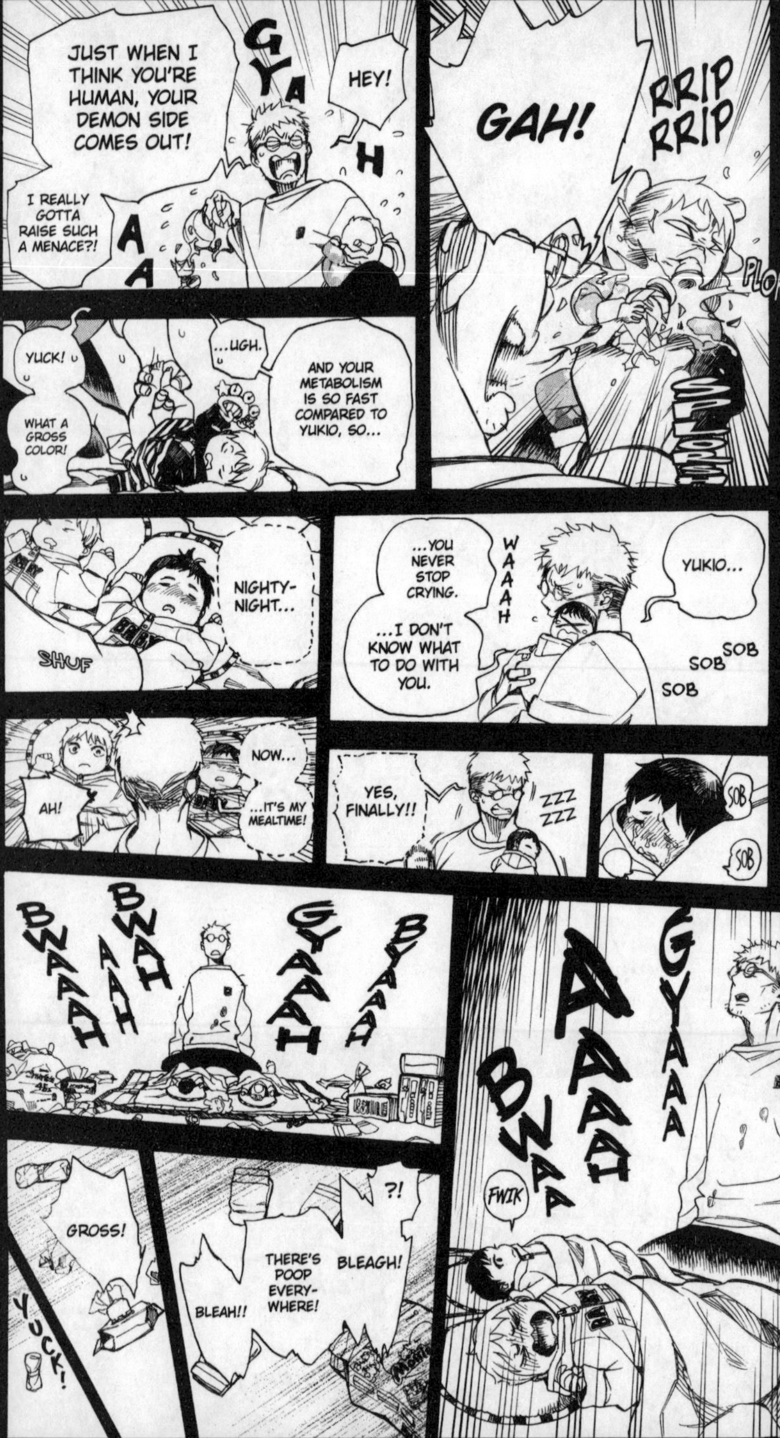
GAH!
RRIP RRIP
PLOK
SPLORSH
HEY!
JUST WHEN I THINK YOU'RE HUMAN, YOUR DEMON SIDE COMES OUT!
GYAH
I REALLY GOTTA RAISE SUCH A MENACE?!
AND YOUR METABOLISM IS SO FAST COMPARED TO YUKIO, SO...
...UGH.
YUCK!
WHAT A GROSS COLOR!
YUKIO...
SOB SOB SOB
WAAAAH
...YOU NEVER STOP CRYING.
...I DON'T KNOW WHAT TO DO WITH YOU.
NIGHTY-NIGHT...
SHUF
SOB
SOB
ZZZ ZZZ
YES, FINALLY!!
NOW...
...IT'S MY MEALTIME!
AH!
GYAAAA
AAAAH
BWAA
FWIK
BWAAAH
BWAAAH
GYAAAH
BYAAAH
?!
BLEAGH!
THERE'S POOP EVERYWHERE!
BLEAH!!
GROSS!
YUCK!

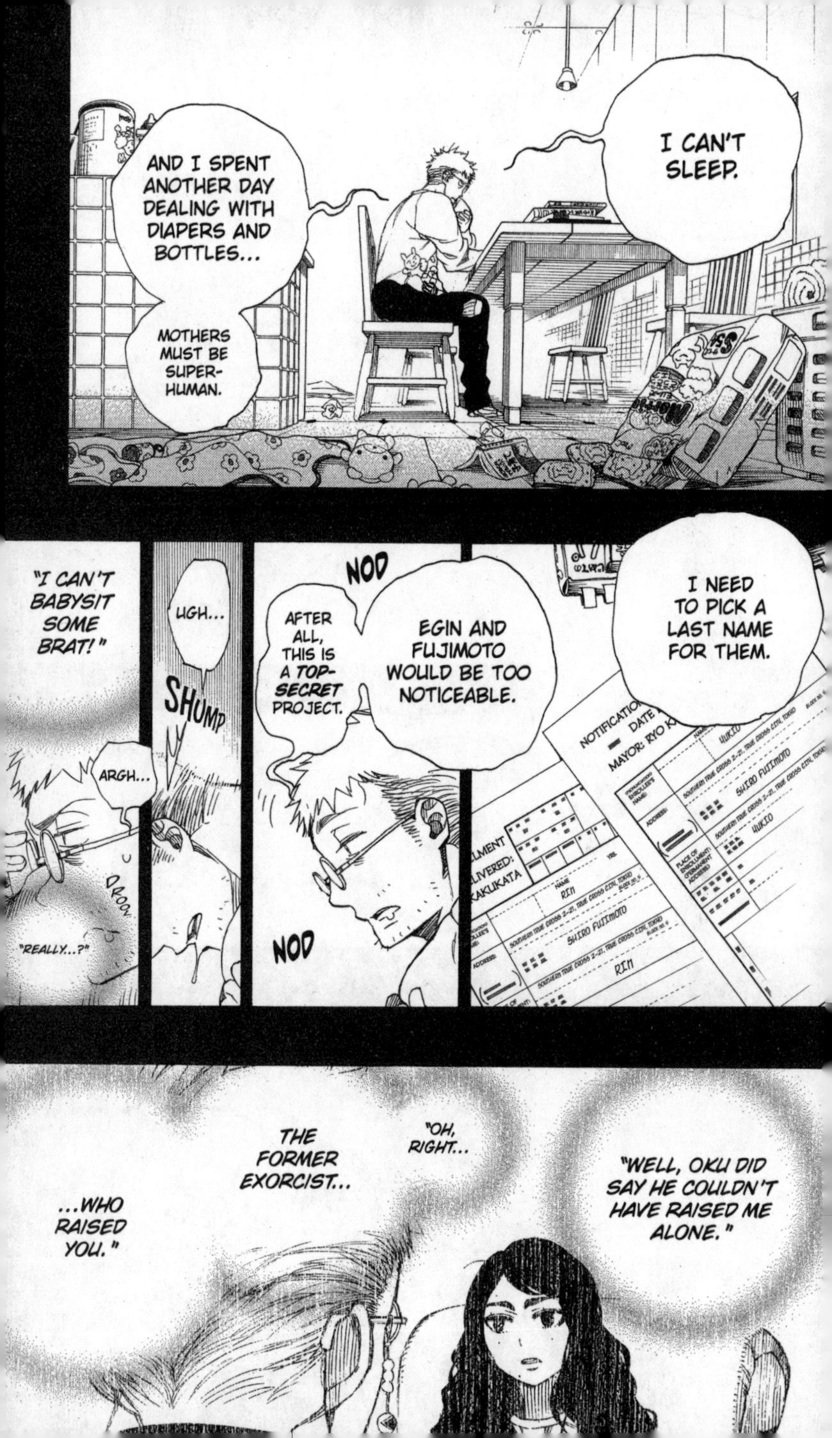
I CAN'T SLEEP.
AND I SPENT ANOTHER DAY DEALING WITH DIAPERS AND BOTTLES...
MOTHERS MUST BE SUPER-HUMAN.
I NEED TO PICK A LAST NAME FOR THEM.
NOD
EGIN AND FUJIMOTO WOULD BE TOO NOTICEABLE.
AFTER ALL, THIS IS A TOP-SECRET PROJECT.
NOD
UGH...
SHUMP
"I CAN'T BABYSIT SOME BRAT!"
ARGH...
DROOL
"REALLY...?"
"WELL, OKU DID SAY HE COULDN'T HAVE RAISED ME ALONE."
"OH, RIGHT...
THE FORMER EXORCIST...
...WHO RAISED YOU."

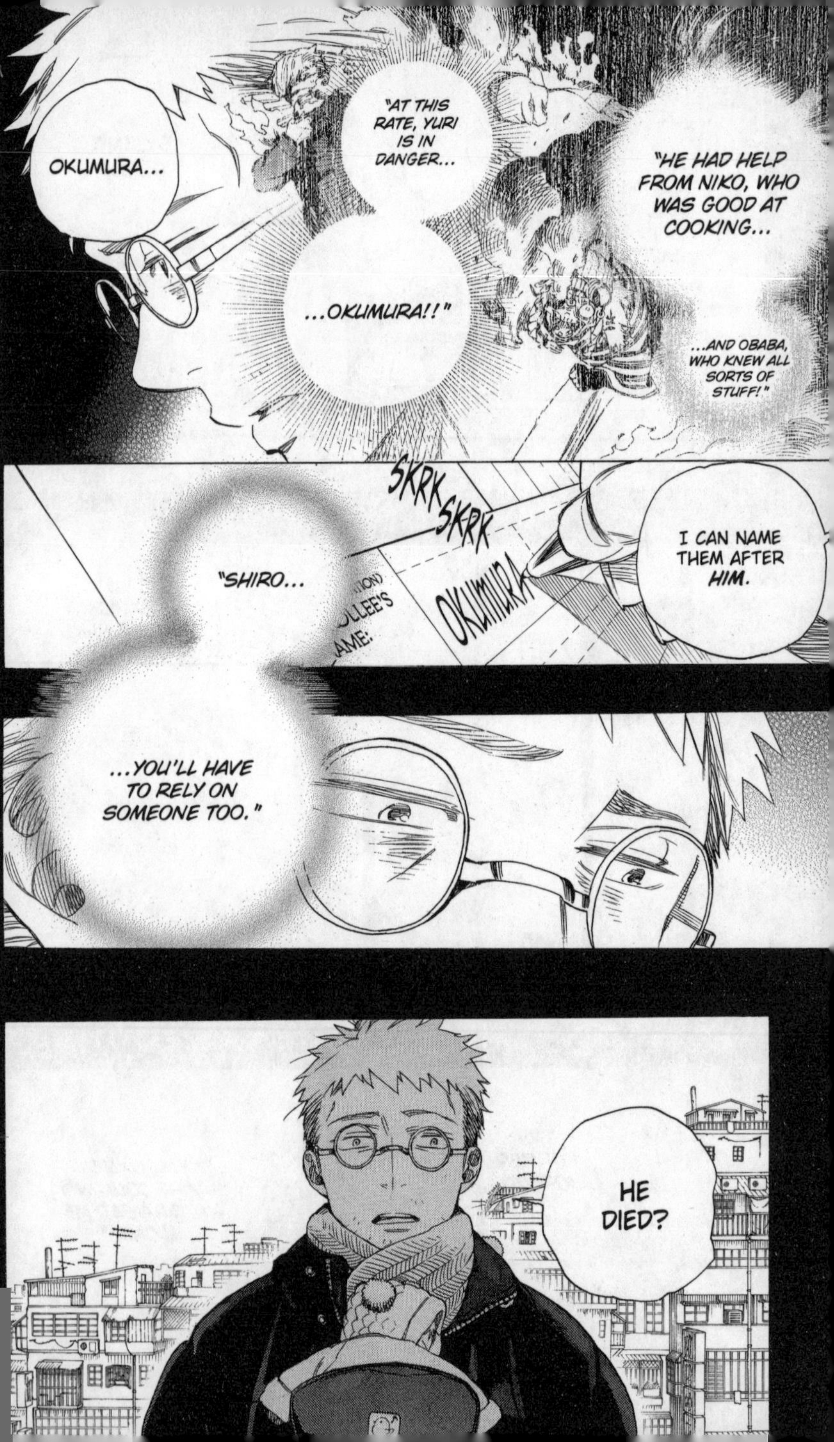
"HE HAD HELP FROM NIKO, WHO WAS GOOD AT COOKING...
...AND OBABA, WHO KNEW ALL SORTS OF STUFF!"
"AT THIS RATE, YURI IS IN DANGER...
...OKUMURA!!"
OKUMURA...
I CAN NAME THEM AFTER HIM.
SKRK SKRK
OKUMURA
"SHIRO...
...YOU'LL HAVE TO RELY ON SOMEONE TOO."
HE DIED?

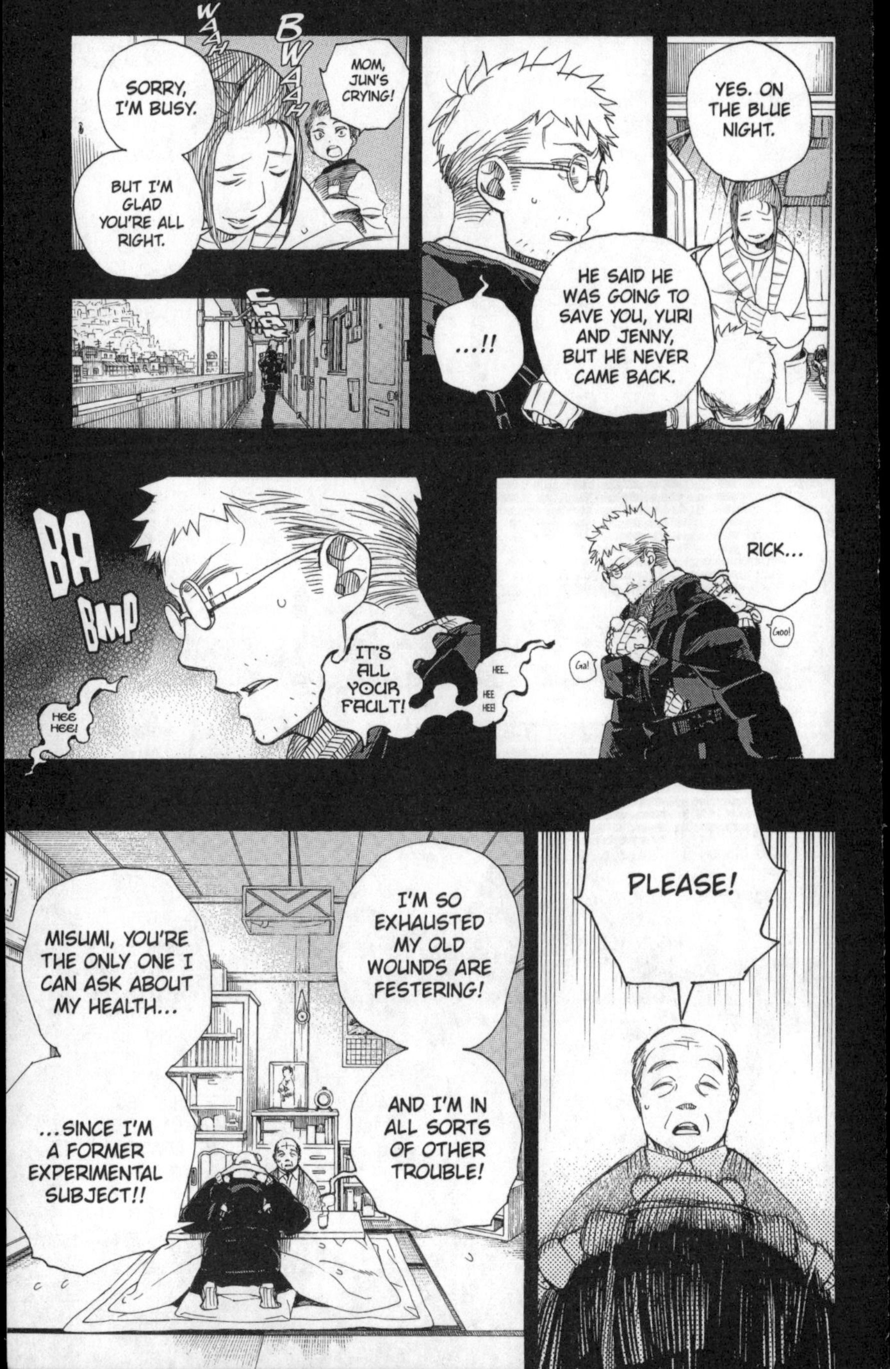
YES. ON THE BLUE NIGHT.
HE SAID HE WAS GOING TO SAVE YOU, YURI AND JENNY, BUT HE NEVER CAME BACK.
...!!
WAAH
BWAAH
MOM, JUN'S CRYING!
SORRY, I'M BUSY.
BUT I'M GLAD YOU'RE ALL RIGHT.
RICK...
Goo!
Ga!
HEE... HEE HEE!
IT'S ALL YOUR FAULT!
BA BMP
HEE HEE!
PLEASE!
I'M SO EXHAUSTED MY OLD WOUNDS ARE FESTERING!
AND I'M IN ALL SORTS OF OTHER TROUBLE!
MISUMI, YOU'RE THE ONLY ONE I CAN ASK ABOUT MY HEALTH...
...SINCE I'M A FORMER EXPERIMENTAL SUBJECT!!

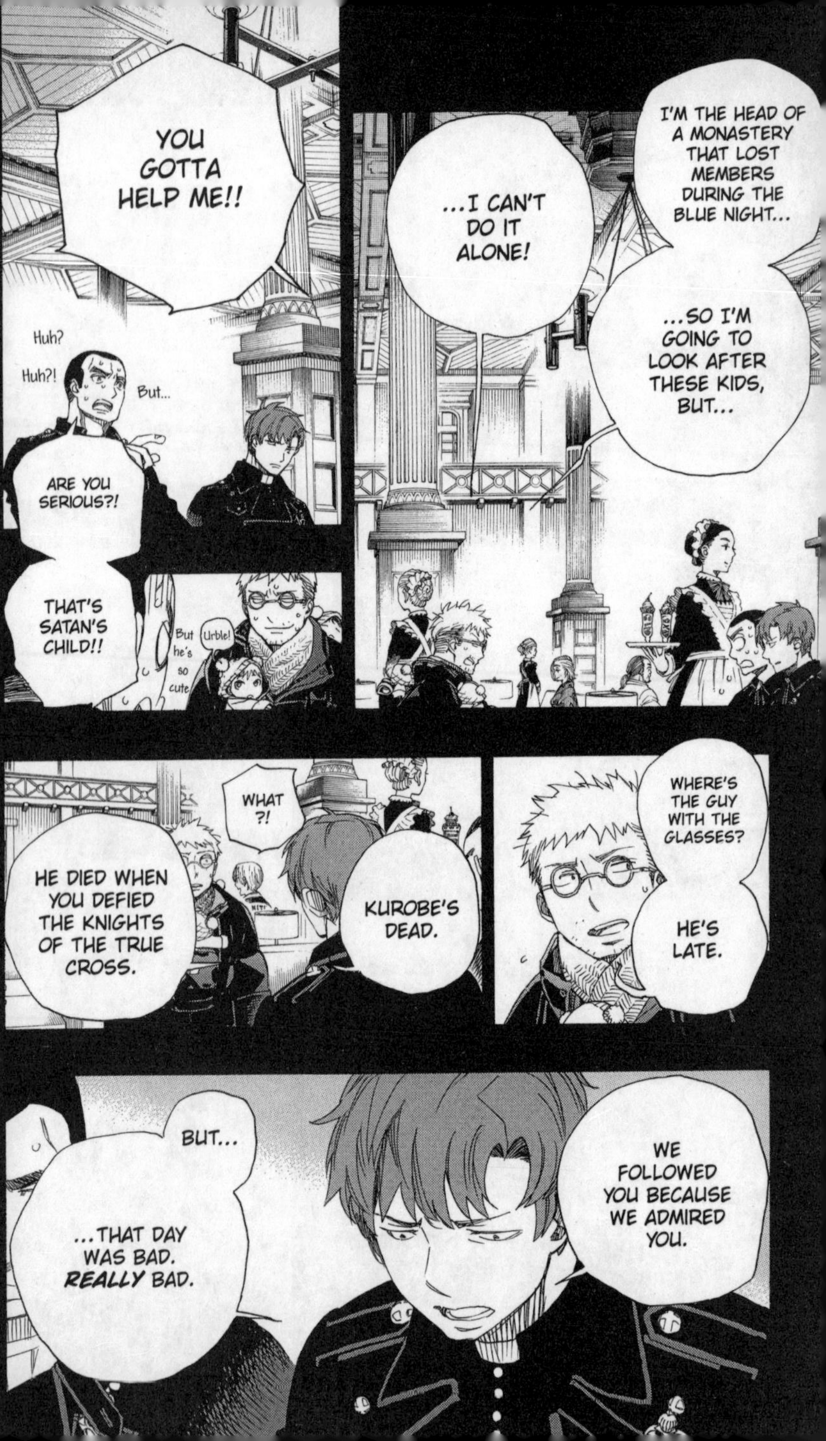
I'M THE HEAD OF A MONASTERY THAT LOST MEMBERS DURING THE BLUE NIGHT...
...SO I'M GOING TO LOOK AFTER THESE KIDS, BUT...
...I CAN'T DO IT ALONE!
YOU GOTTA HELP ME!!
Huh?
Huh?!
But...
ARE YOU SERIOUS?!
THAT'S SATAN'S CHILD!!
But he's so cute
Urble!
WHERE'S THE GUY WITH THE GLASSES?
HE'S LATE.
WHAT?!
KUROBE'S DEAD.
HE DIED WHEN YOU DEFIED THE KNIGHTS OF THE TRUE CROSS.
WE FOLLOWED YOU BECAUSE WE ADMIRED YOU.
BUT...
...THAT DAY WAS BAD. *REALLY* BAD.

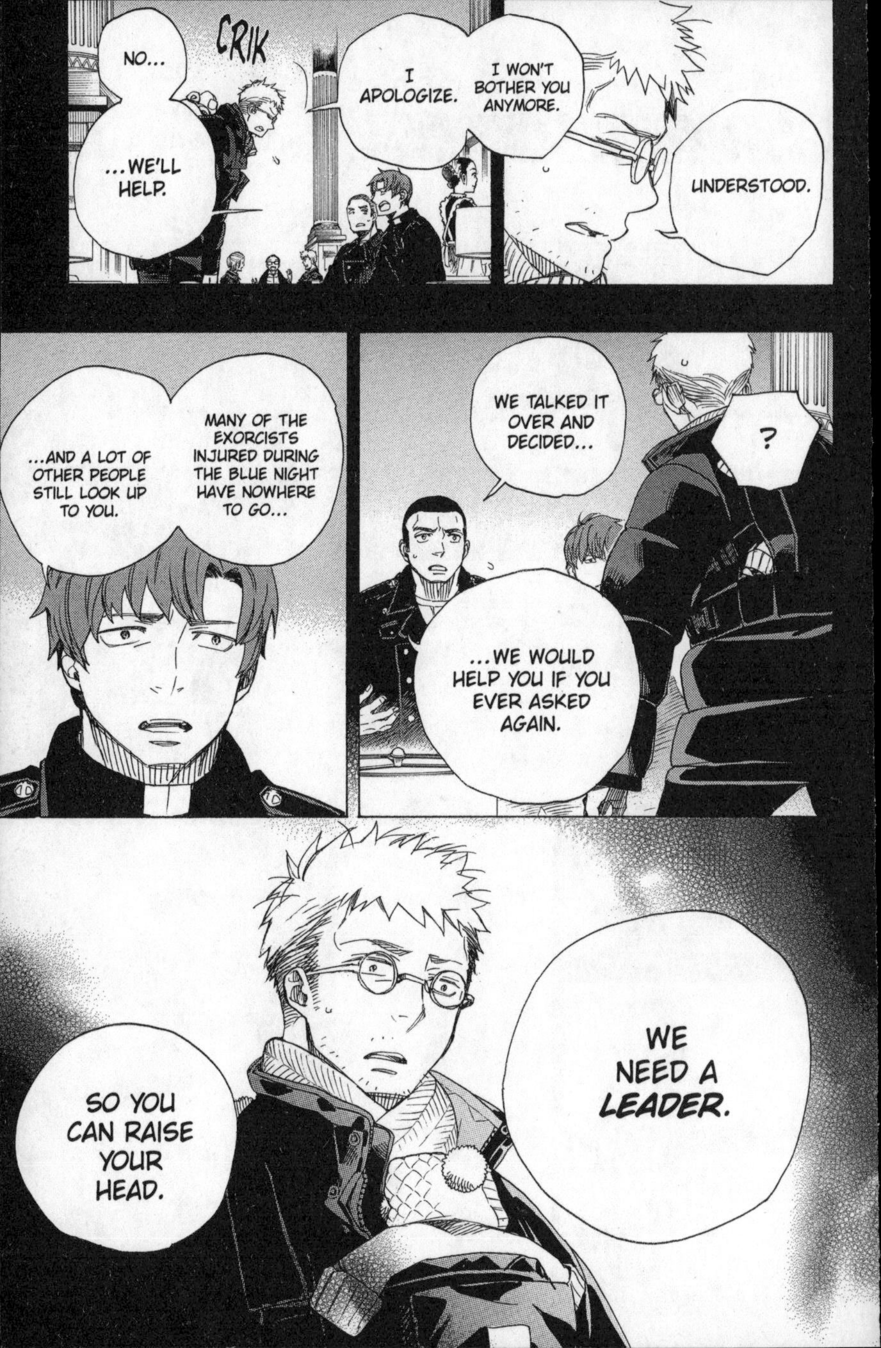
UNDERSTOOD.
I WON'T BOTHER YOU ANYMORE.
I APOLOGIZE.
CRIK
NO...
...WE'LL HELP.
WE TALKED IT OVER AND DECIDED...
?
...WE WOULD HELP YOU IF YOU EVER ASKED AGAIN.
MANY OF THE EXORCISTS INJURED DURING THE BLUE NIGHT HAVE NOWHERE TO GO...
...AND A LOT OF OTHER PEOPLE STILL LOOK UP TO YOU.
WE NEED A *LEADER.*
SO YOU CAN RAISE YOUR HEAD.

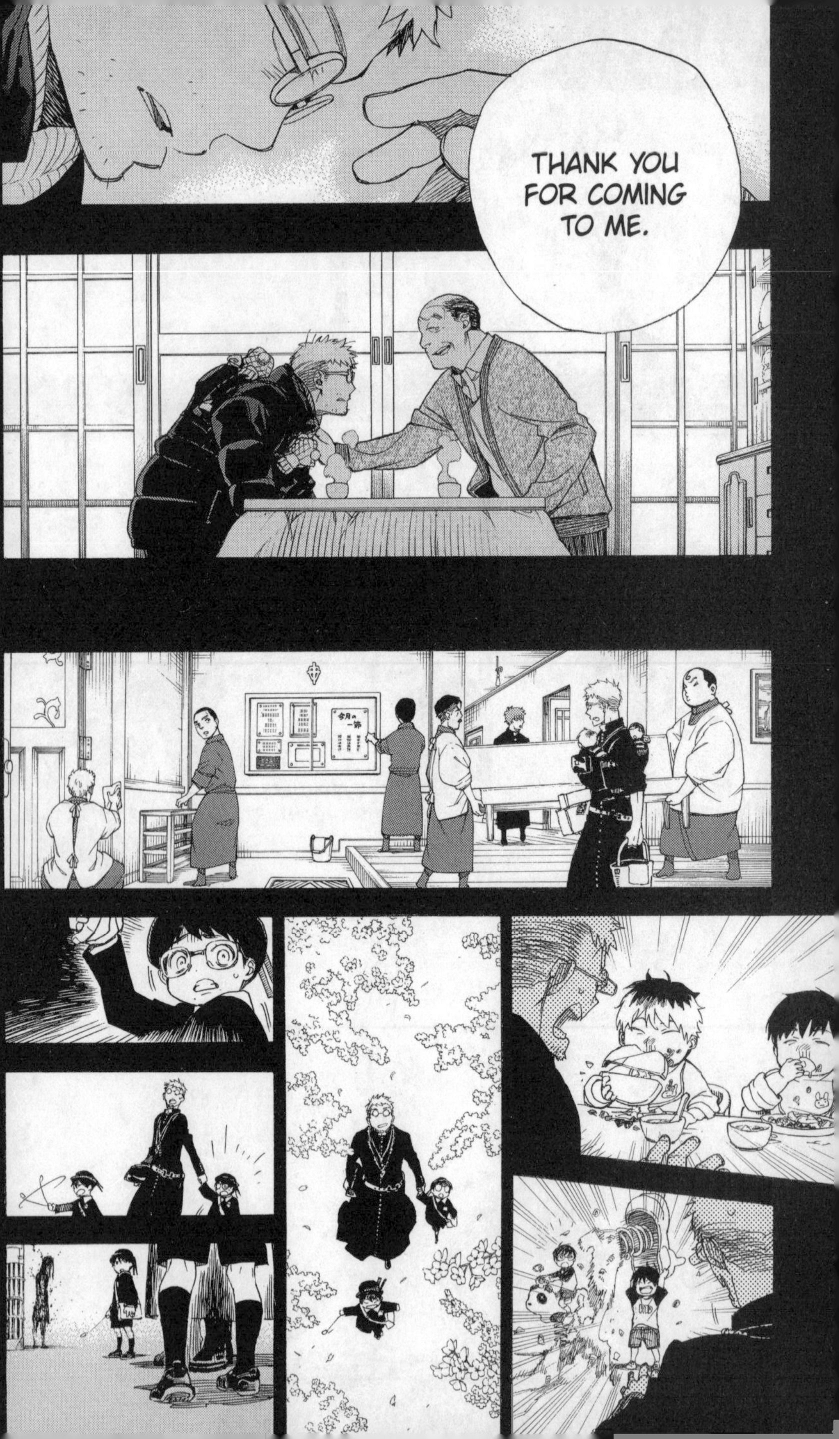
THANK YOU FOR COMING TO ME.

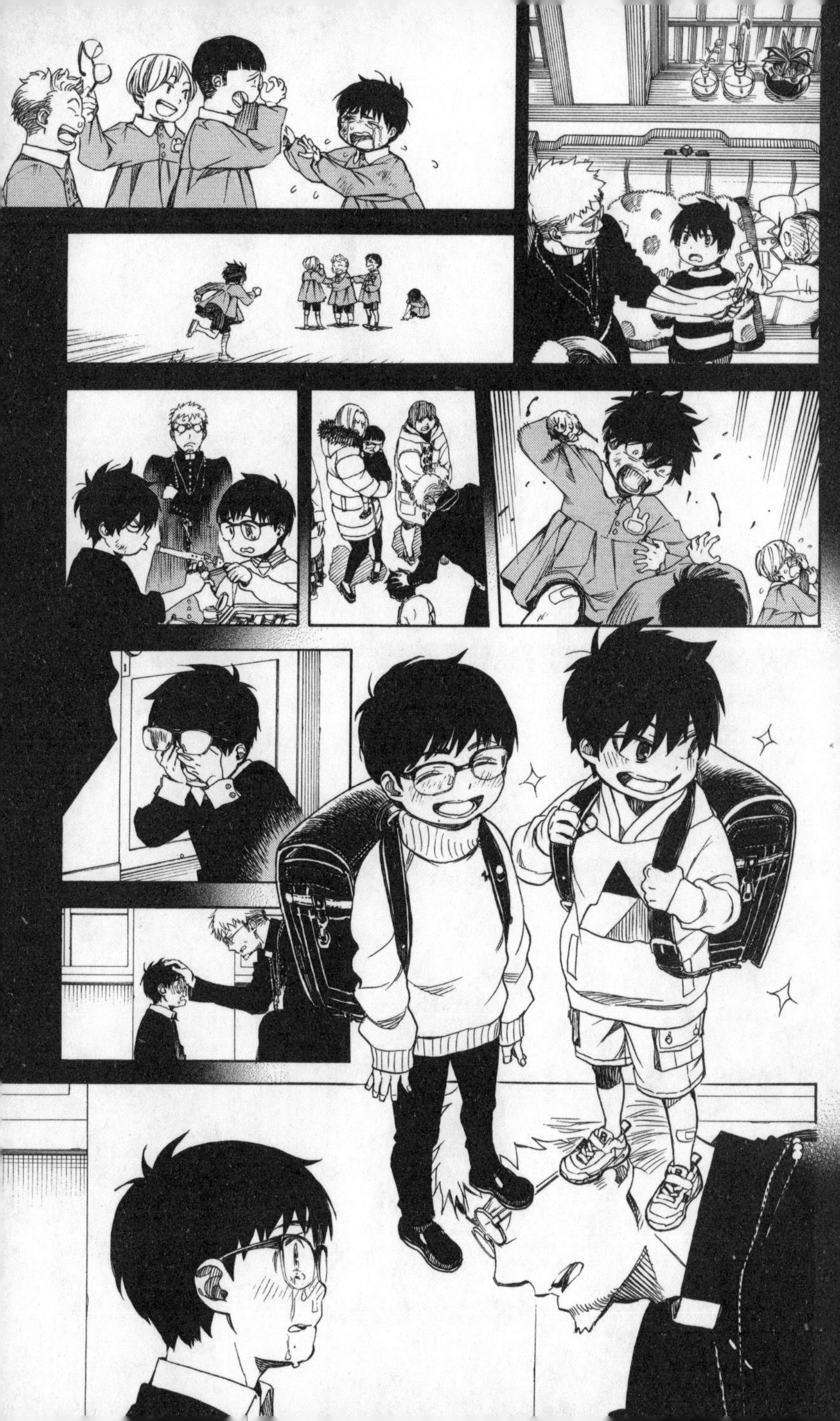

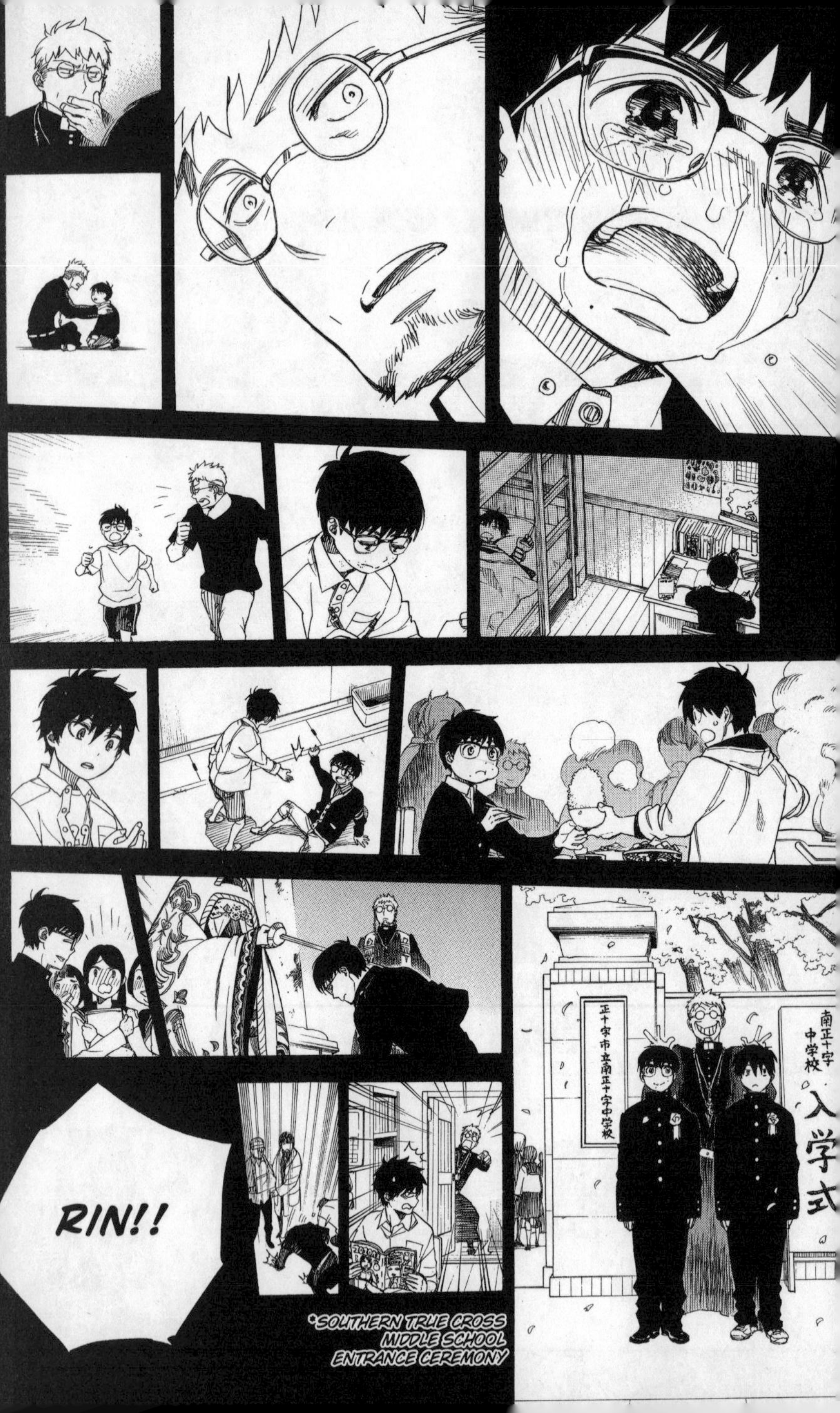
南正十字中学校入学式
正十字市立南正十字中学校
*SOUTHERN TRUE CROSS MIDDLE SCHOOL ENTRANCE CEREMONY
RIN!!

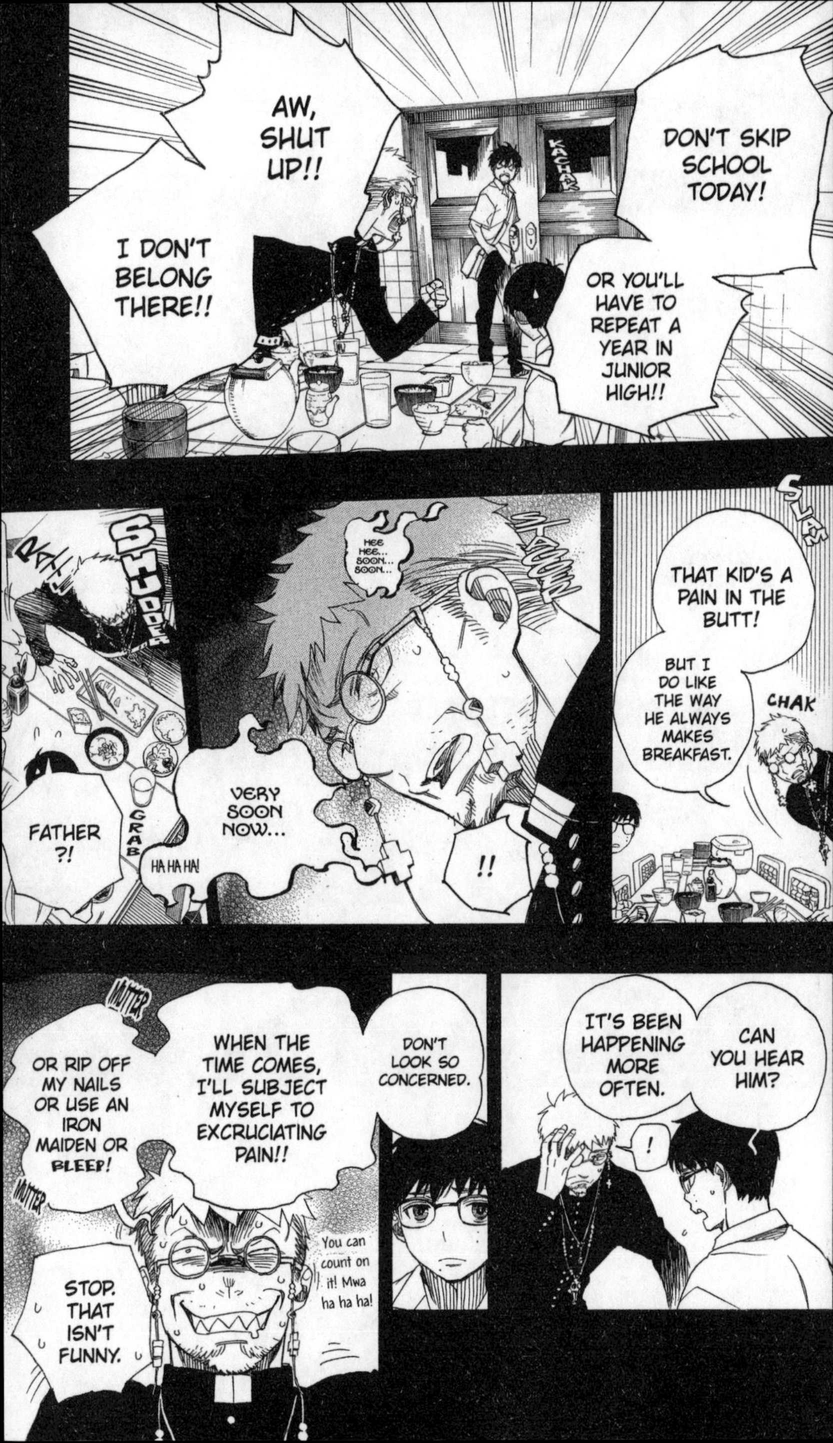
DON'T SKIP SCHOOL TODAY!
KACHAK
AW, SHUT UP!!
OR YOU'LL HAVE TO REPEAT A YEAR IN JUNIOR HIGH!!
I DON'T BELONG THERE!!
SLAM
THAT KID'S A PAIN IN THE BUTT!
BUT I DO LIKE THE WAY HE ALWAYS MAKES BREAKFAST.
CHAK
HEE HEE... SOON... SOON...
VERY SOON NOW...
!!
SHUDDER
FATHER ?!
GRAB
HA HA HA!
CAN YOU HEAR HIM?
IT'S BEEN HAPPENING MORE OFTEN.
!
DON'T LOOK SO CONCERNED.
MUTTER
WHEN THE TIME COMES, I'LL SUBJECT MYSELF TO EXCRUCIATING PAIN!!
OR RIP OFF MY NAILS OR USE AN IRON MAIDEN OR BLEEP!
MUTTER
You can count on it! Mwa ha ha ha!
STOP. THAT ISN'T FUNNY.

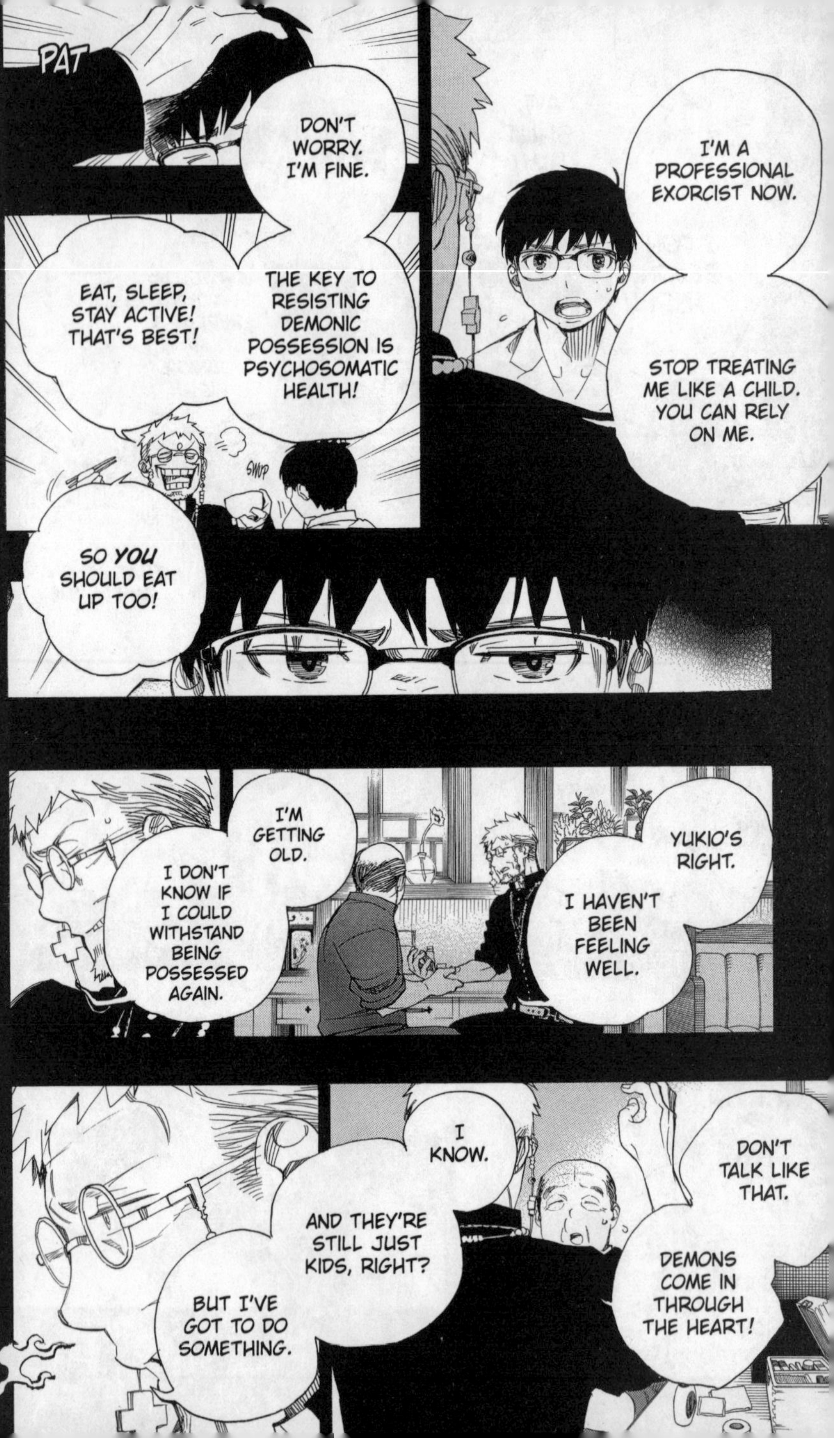
I'M A PROFESSIONAL EXORCIST NOW.
STOP TREATING ME LIKE A CHILD. YOU CAN RELY ON ME.
PAT
DON'T WORRY. I'M FINE.
THE KEY TO RESISTING DEMONIC POSSESSION IS PSYCHOSOMATIC HEALTH!
EAT, SLEEP, STAY ACTIVE! THAT'S BEST!
SWUP
SO *YOU* SHOULD EAT UP TOO!
YUKIO'S RIGHT.
I HAVEN'T BEEN FEELING WELL.
I'M GETTING OLD.
I DON'T KNOW IF I COULD WITHSTAND BEING POSSESSED AGAIN.
DON'T TALK LIKE THAT.
DEMONS COME IN THROUGH THE HEART!
I KNOW.
AND THEY'RE STILL JUST KIDS, RIGHT?
BUT I'VE GOT TO DO SOMETHING.

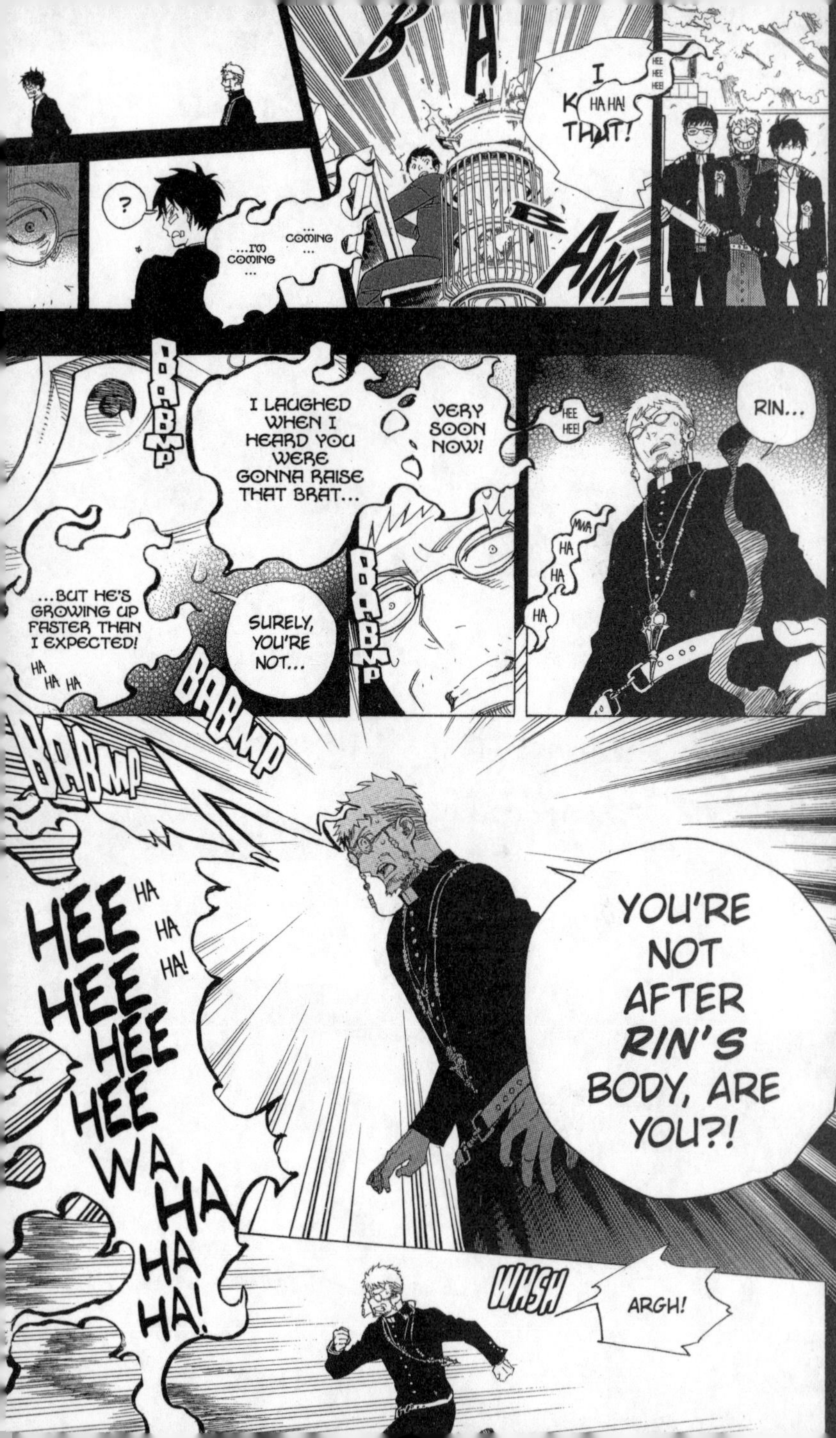
I K THAT!
HEE HEE HEE!
HA HA!
BA
BAM
?
...I'M COMING...
...COMING...
RIN...
HEE HEE!
MWA HA HA HA
VERY SOON NOW!
BABMP
I LAUGHED WHEN I HEARD YOU WERE GONNA RAISE THAT BRAT...
...BUT HE'S GROWING UP FASTER THAN I EXPECTED!
HA HA HA
SURELY, YOU'RE NOT...
BABMP
BABMP
YOU'RE NOT AFTER *RIN'S* BODY, ARE YOU?!
BABMP
HEE HEE HEE HEE WA HA HA HA!
HA HA HA!
WHSH
ARGH!

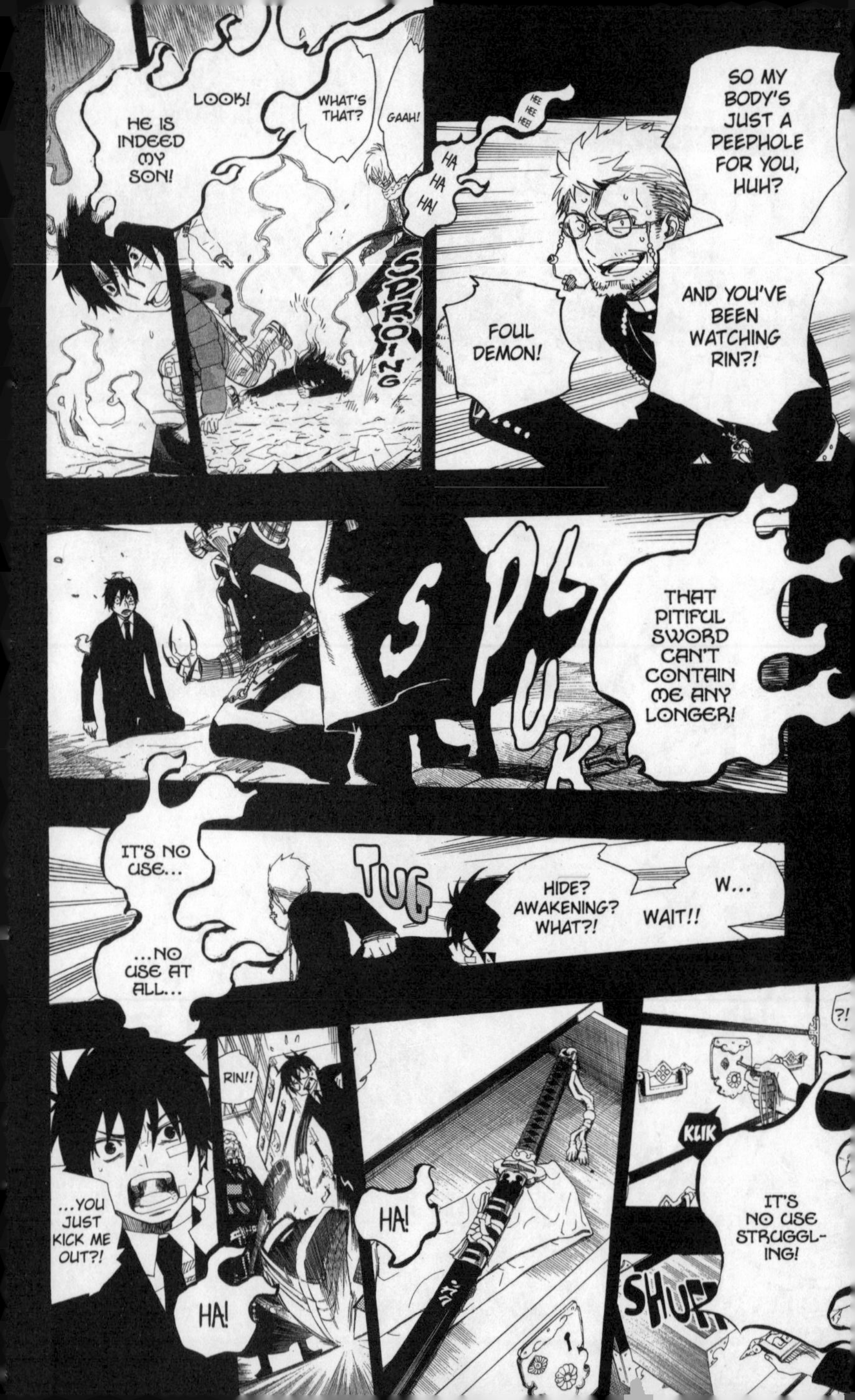
SO MY BODY'S JUST A PEEPHOLE FOR YOU, HUH?
AND YOU'VE BEEN WATCHING RIN?!
FOUL DEMON!
HEE HEE HEE!
HA HA HA!
GAAH!
WHAT'S THAT?
LOOK!
HE IS INDEED MY SON!
SPROING
THAT PITIFUL SWORD CAN'T CONTAIN ME ANY LONGER!
SPLUK
W...
WAIT!!
HIDE? AWAKENING? WHAT?!
TUG
IT'S NO USE...
...NO USE AT ALL...
?!
KLIK
IT'S NO USE STRUGGLING!
SHUP
HA!
RIN!!
...YOU JUST KICK ME OUT?!
HA!

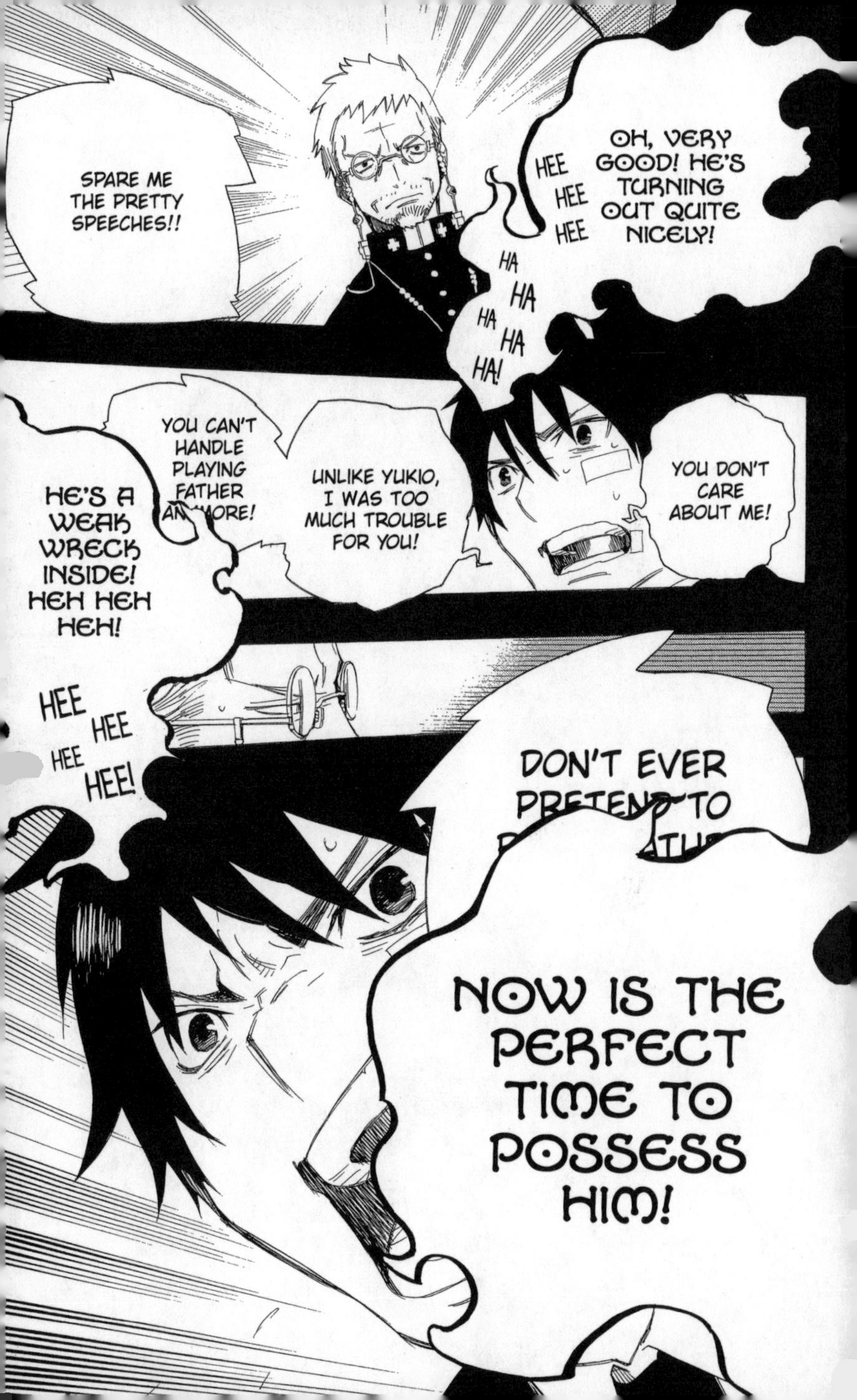
HEE HEE HEE
OH, VERY GOOD! HE'S TURNING OUT QUITE NICELY!
HA HA HA HA HA!
SPARE ME THE PRETTY SPEECHES!!
YOU DON'T CARE ABOUT ME!
UNLIKE YUKIO, I WAS TOO MUCH TROUBLE FOR YOU!
YOU CAN'T HANDLE PLAYING FATHER AN ORE!
HE'S A WEAK WRECK INSIDE! HEH HEH HEH!
DON'T EVER PRETEND TO
HEE HEE HEE HEE!
NOW IS THE PERFECT TIME TO POSSESS HIM!

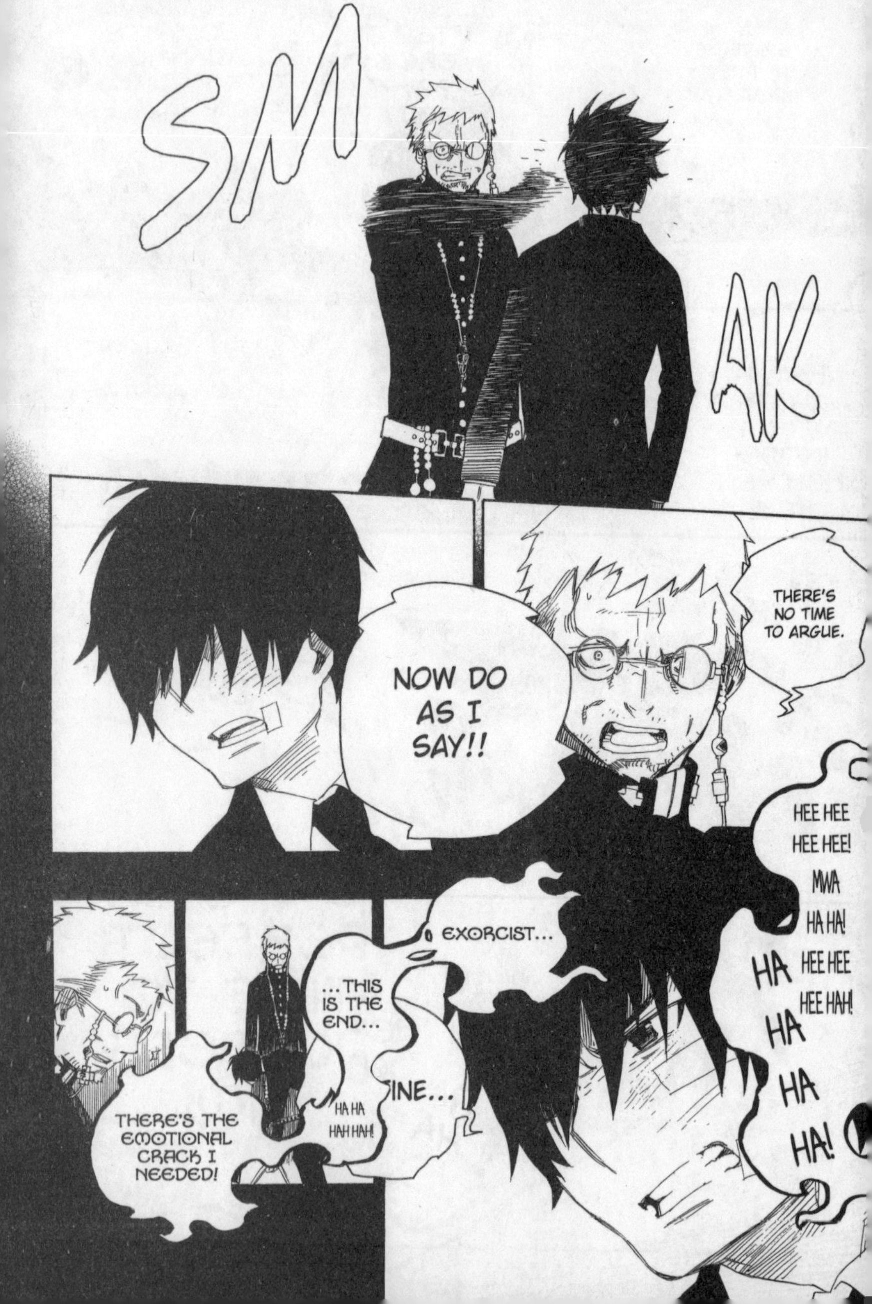
SM
AK
THERE'S NO TIME TO ARGUE.
NOW DO AS I SAY!!
HEE HEE HEE HEE! MWA HA HA! HEE HEE HEE HAH!
HA HA HA HA!
EXORCIST...
...THIS IS THE END...
INE...
HA HA HAH HAH!
THERE'S THE EMOTIONAL CRACK I NEEDED!

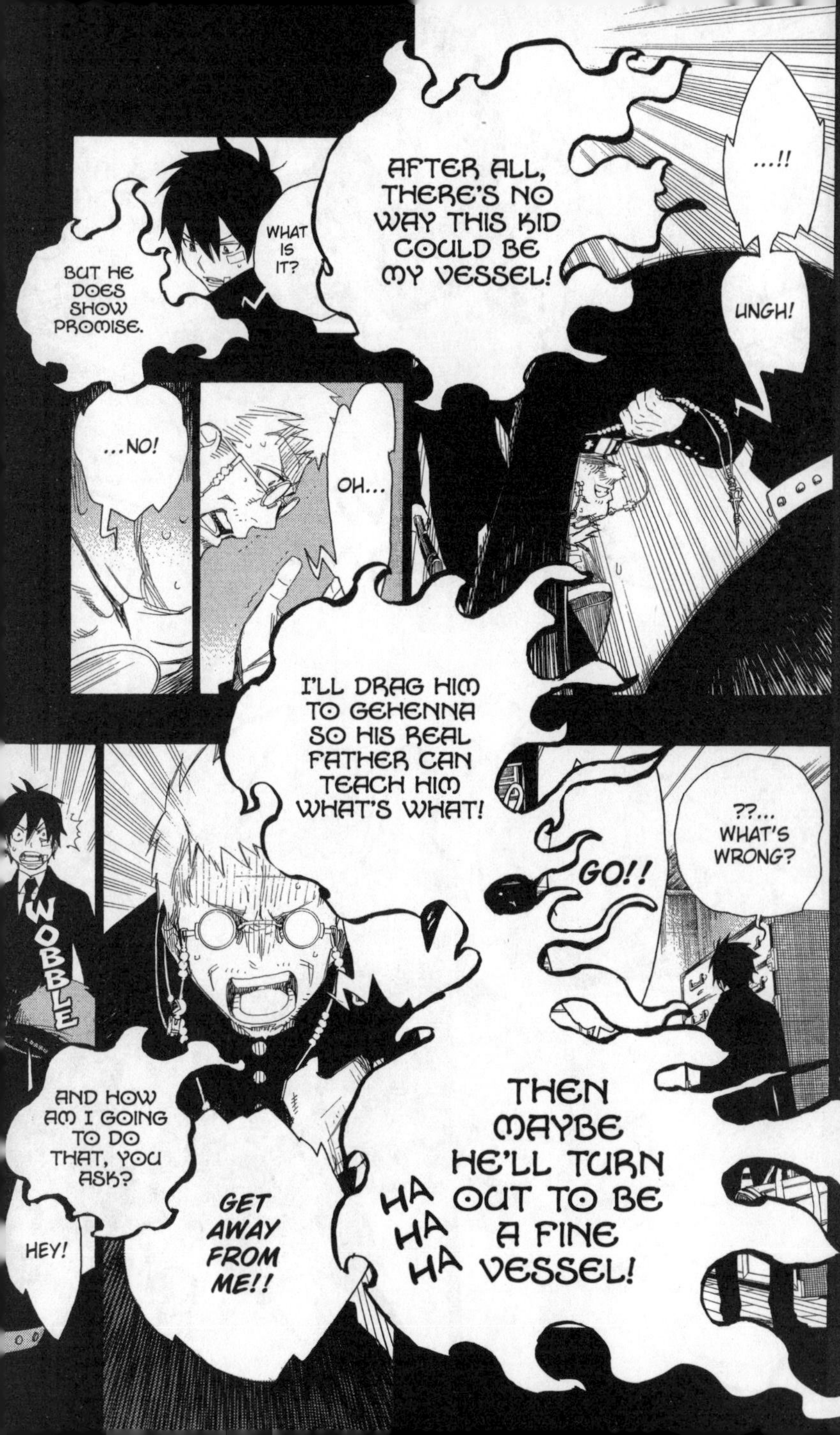
...!!
UNGH!
AFTER ALL, THERE'S NO WAY THIS KID COULD BE MY VESSEL!
WHAT IS IT?
BUT HE DOES SHOW PROMISE.
OH...
...NO!
I'LL DRAG HIM TO GEHENNA SO HIS REAL FATHER CAN TEACH HIM WHAT'S WHAT!
??... WHAT'S WRONG?
GO!!
THEN MAYBE HE'LL TURN OUT TO BE A FINE VESSEL!
HA HA HA
AND HOW AM I GOING TO DO THAT, YOU ASK?
GET AWAY FROM ME!!
WOBBLE
HEY!

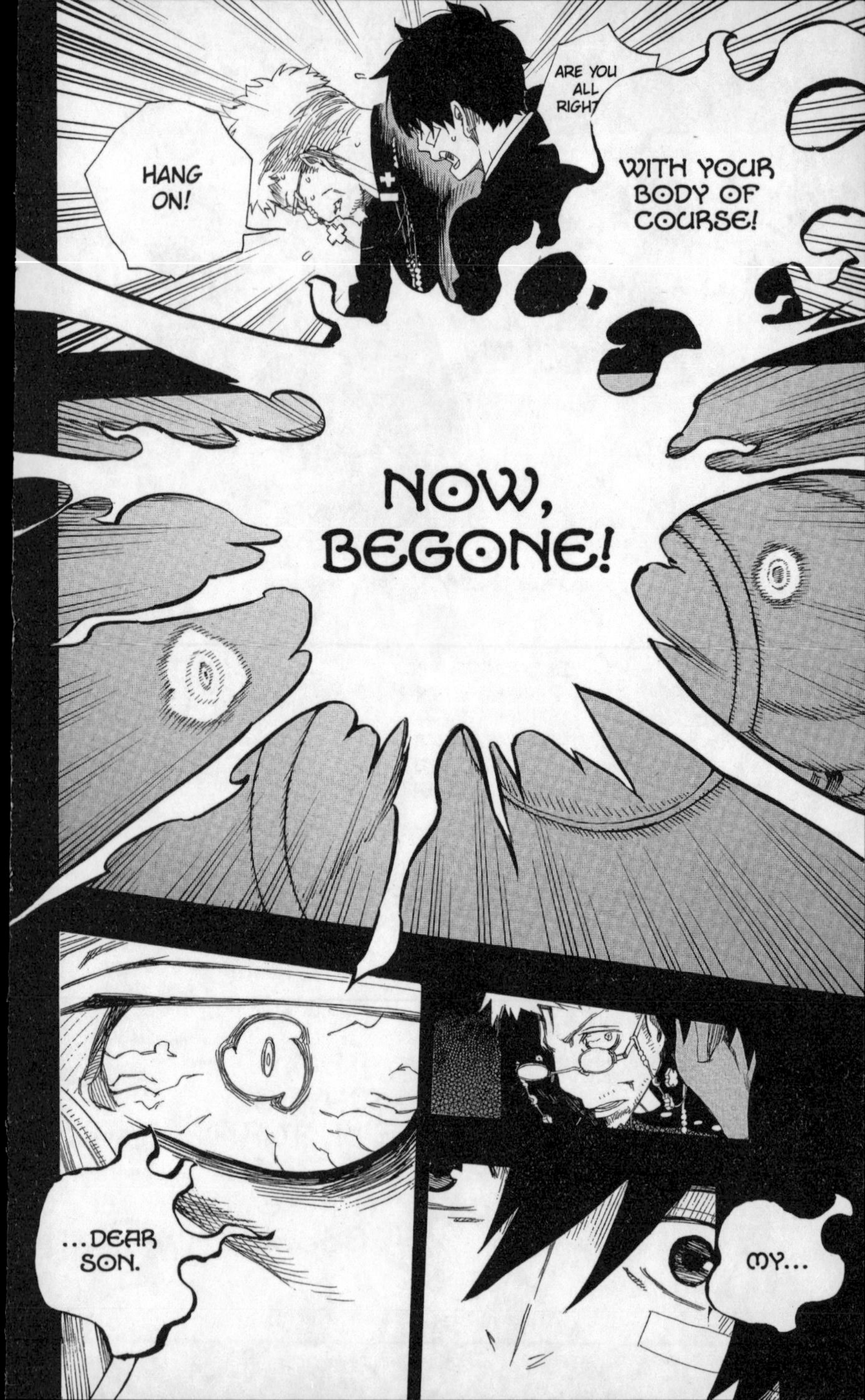
ARE YOU ALL RIGHT
WITH YOUR BODY OF COURSE!
HANG ON!
NOW, BEGONE!
MY...
...DEAR SON.

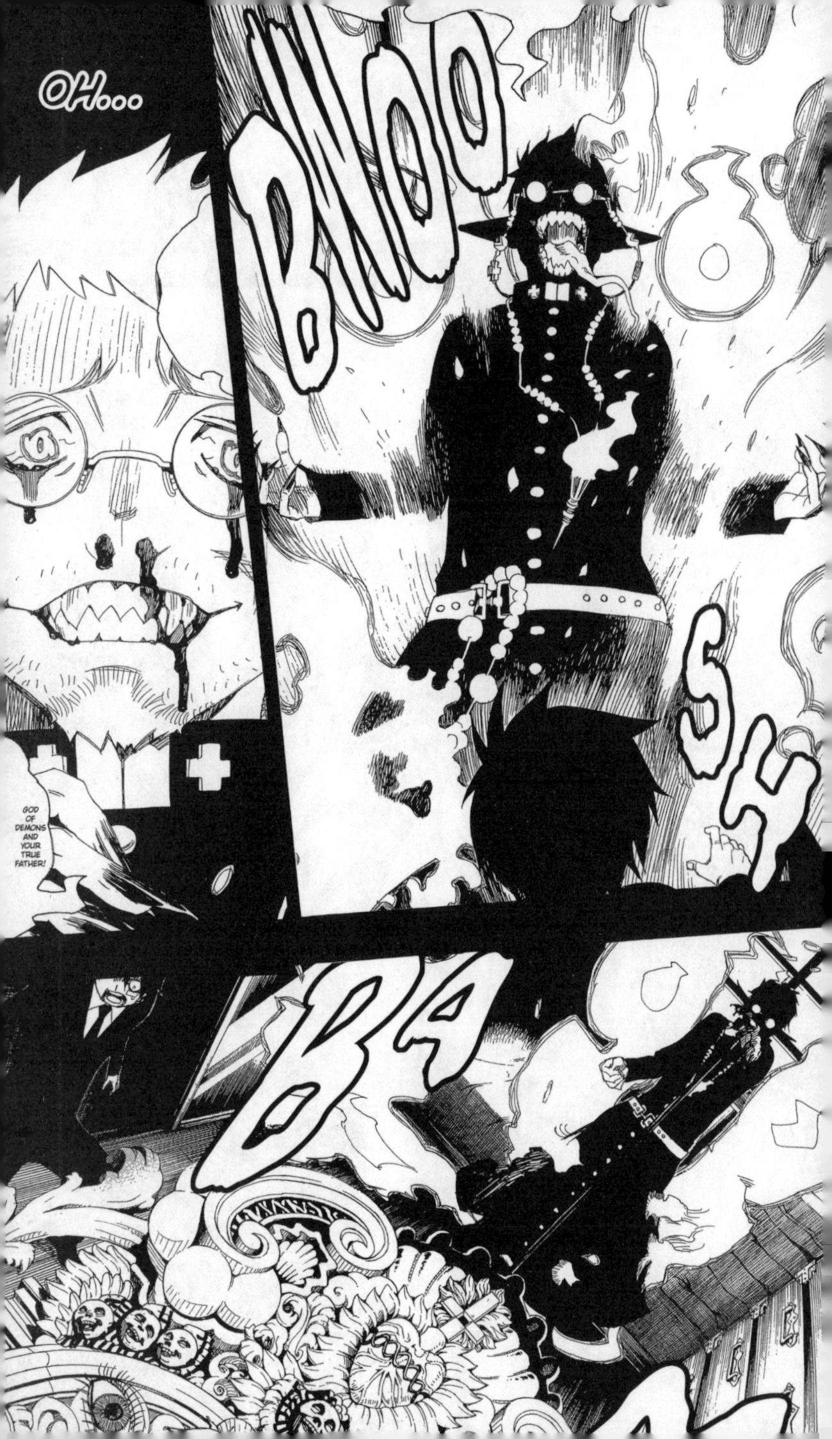
BWOOO
SH
OH...
GOD OF DEMONS AND YOUR TRUE FATHER!
BA

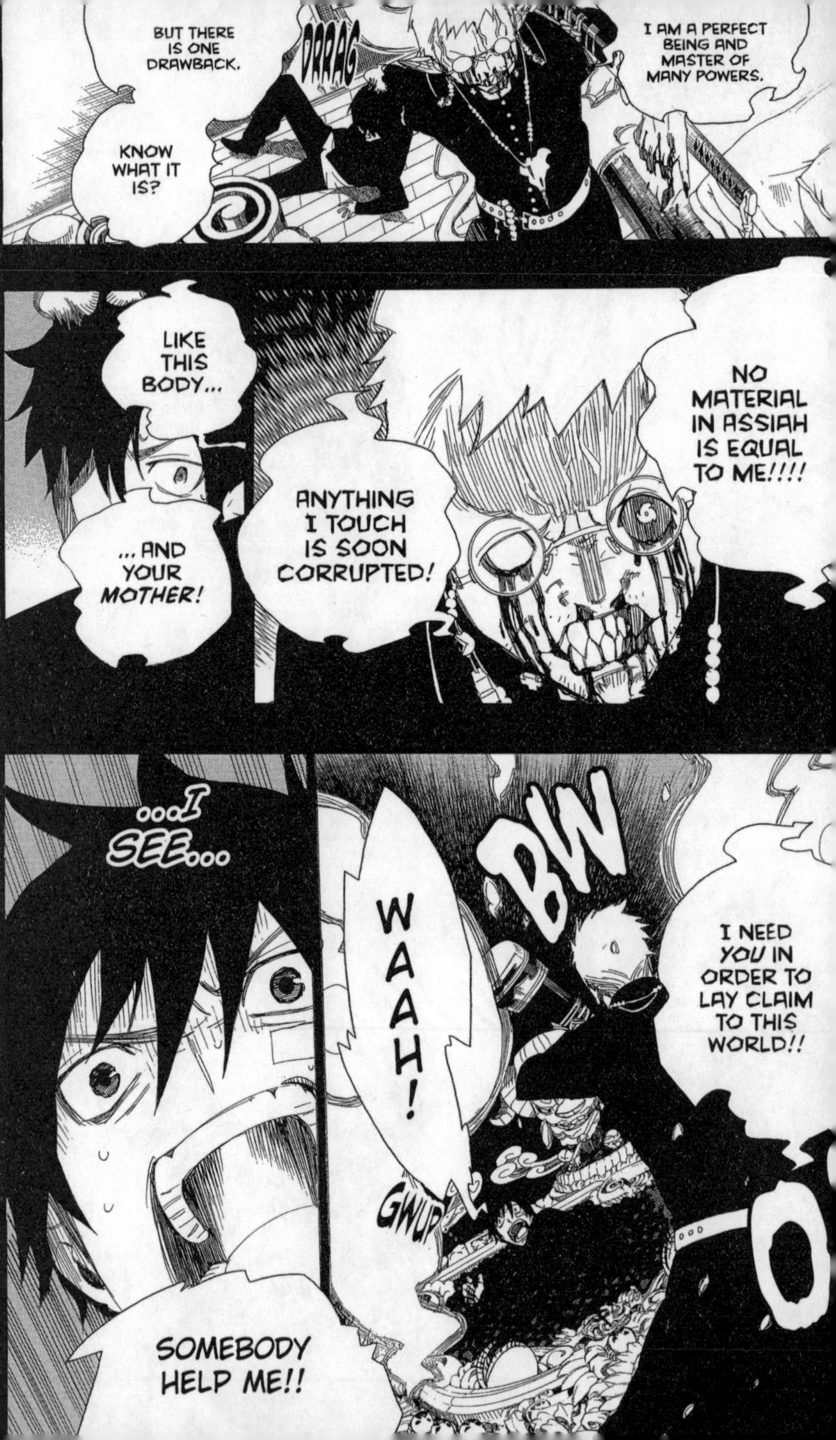

I AM A PERFECT BEING AND MASTER OF MANY POWERS.
DRRAG
BUT THERE IS ONE DRAWBACK.
KNOW WHAT IT IS?
NO MATERIAL IN ASSIAH IS EQUAL TO ME!!!!
ANYTHING I TOUCH IS SOON CORRUPTED!
LIKE THIS BODY...
...AND YOUR *MOTHER!*
I NEED *YOU* IN ORDER TO LAY CLAIM TO THIS WORLD!!
BW
WAAH!
GWUP
...I SEE...
SOMEBODY HELP ME!!

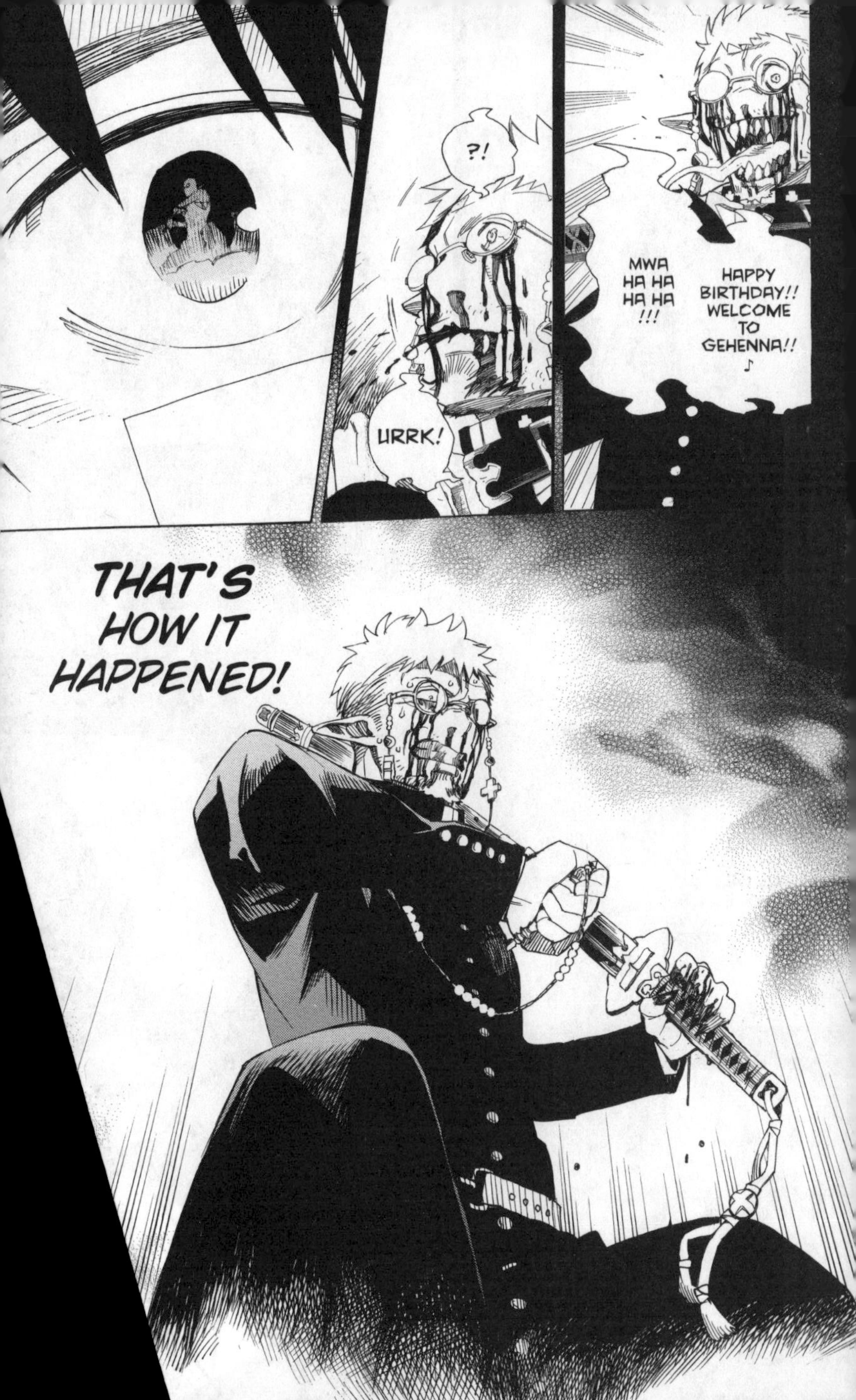
HAPPY BIRTHDAY!! WELCOME TO GEHENNA!! ♪
MWA HA HA HA HA !!!
?!
URRK!
THAT'S HOW IT HAPPENED!

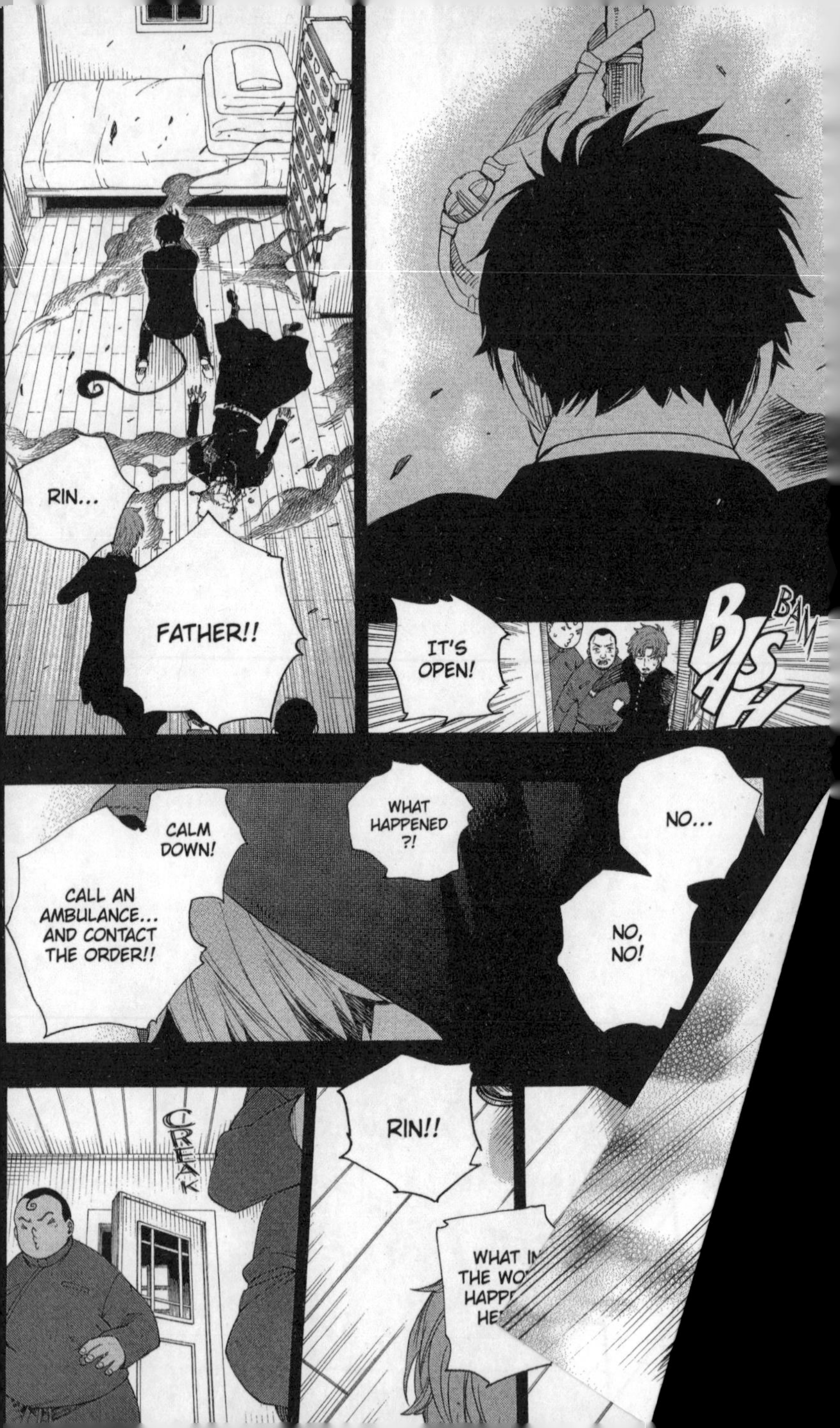
BAM
BISHAH
IT'S OPEN!
RIN...
FATHER!!
NO...
NO, NO!
WHAT HAPPENED ?!
CALM DOWN!
CALL AN AMBULANCE... AND CONTACT THE ORDER!!
RIN!!
WHAT IN THE WO HAPP HE
CREAK

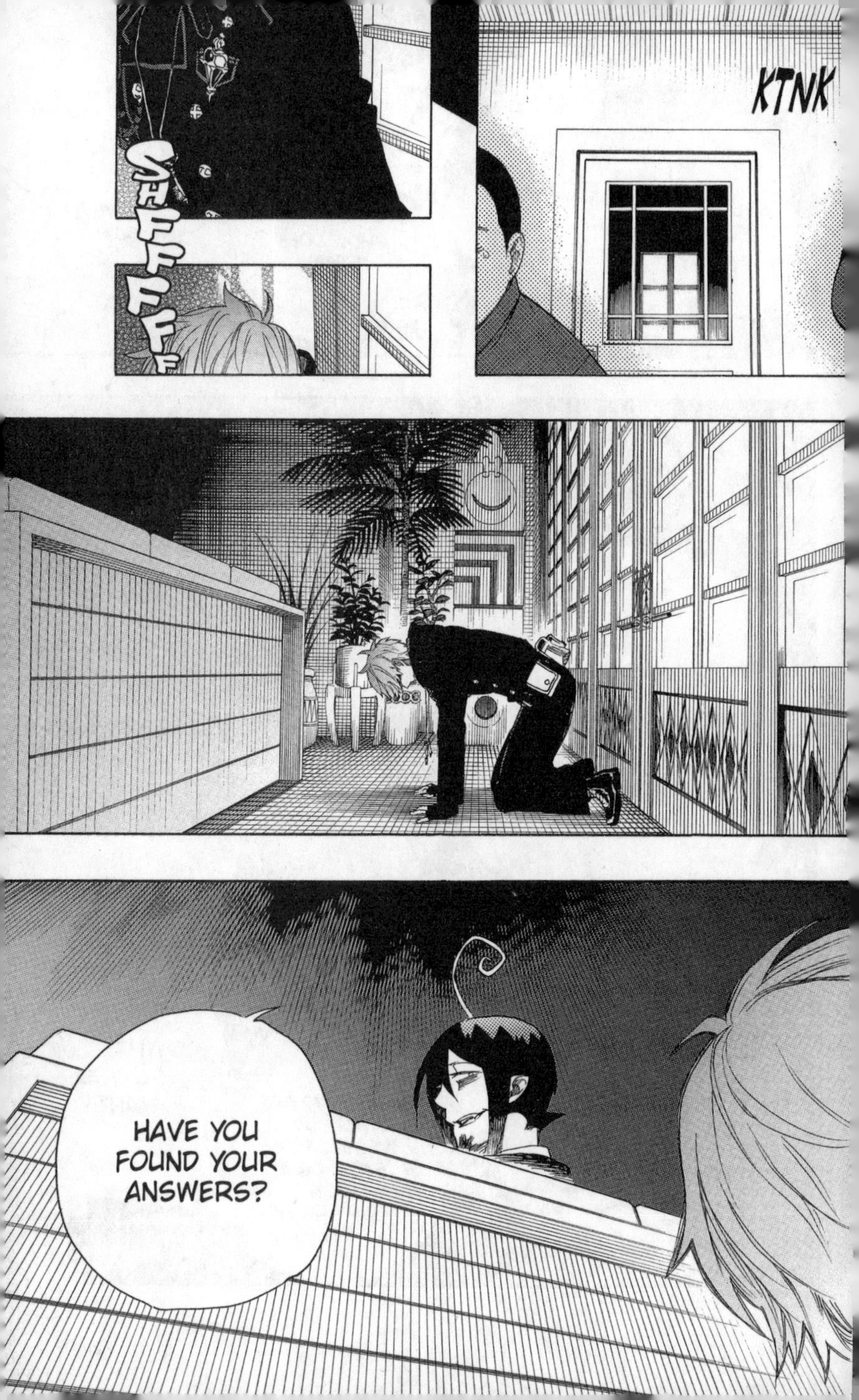
KTNK
SHFFFFF
HAVE YOU FOUND YOUR ANSWERS?

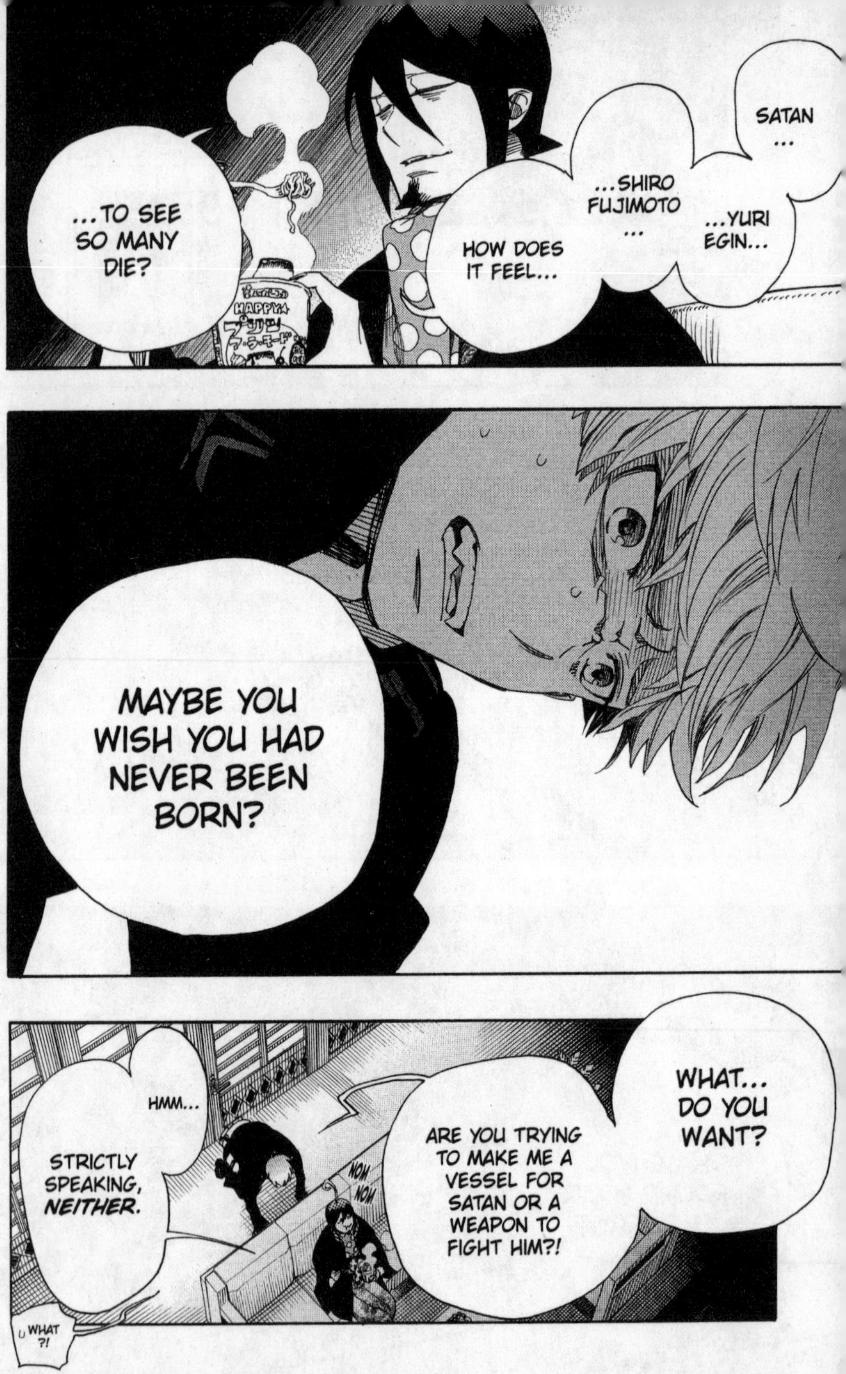
SATAN ...
...YURI EGIN...
...SHIRO FUJIMOTO ...
HOW DOES IT FEEL...
...TO SEE SO MANY DIE?
HAPPY
MAYBE YOU WISH YOU HAD NEVER BEEN BORN?
WHAT... DO YOU WANT?
ARE YOU TRYING TO MAKE ME A VESSEL FOR SATAN OR A WEAPON TO FIGHT HIM?!
NOM NOM
HMM...
STRICTLY SPEAKING, *NEITHER*.
WHAT ?!

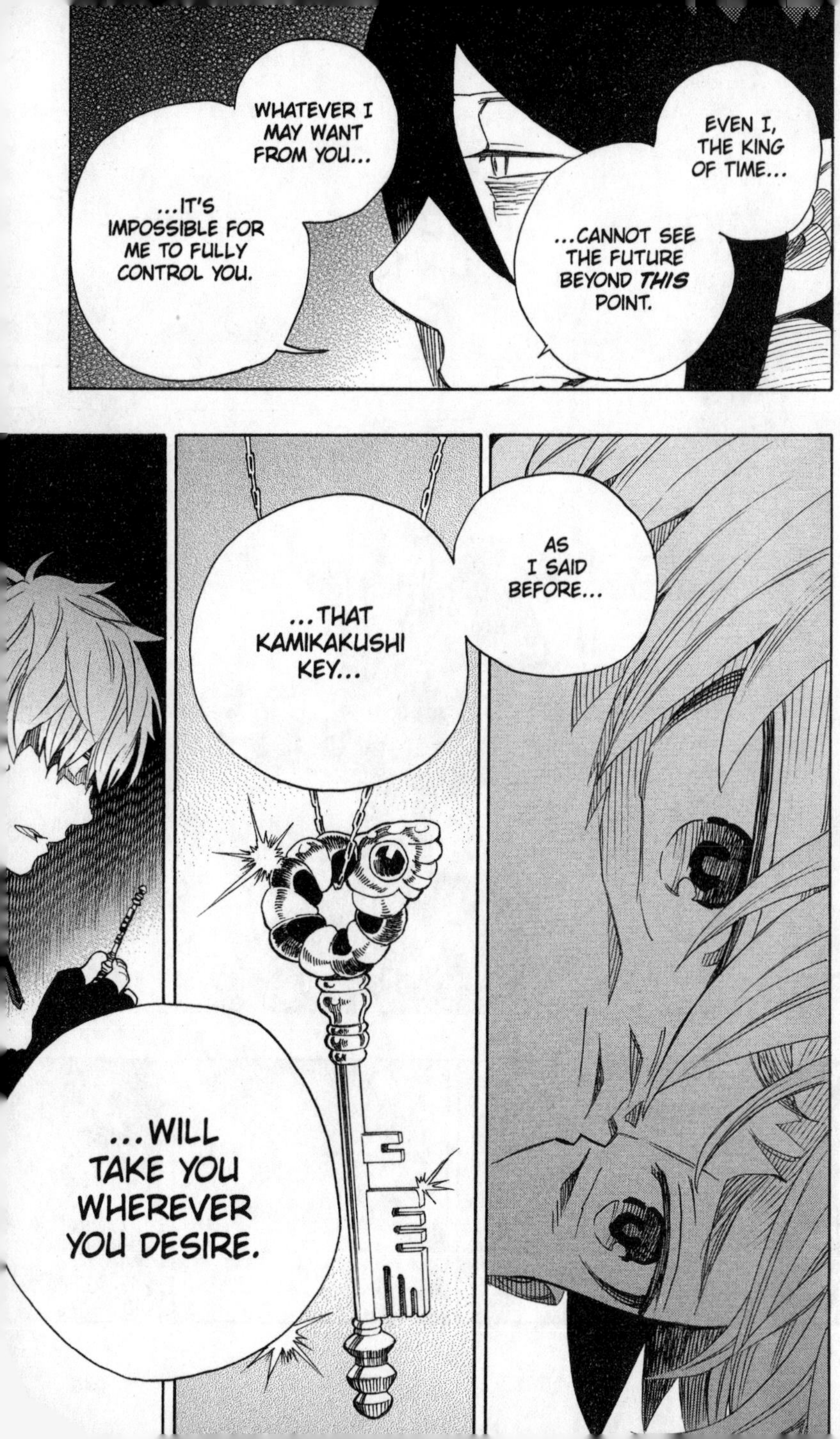
EVEN I, THE KING OF TIME...
...CANNOT SEE THE FUTURE BEYOND *THIS* POINT.
WHATEVER I MAY WANT FROM YOU...
...IT'S IMPOSSIBLE FOR ME TO FULLY CONTROL YOU.
AS I SAID BEFORE...
...THAT KAMIKAKUSHI KEY...
...WILL TAKE YOU WHEREVER YOU DESIRE.

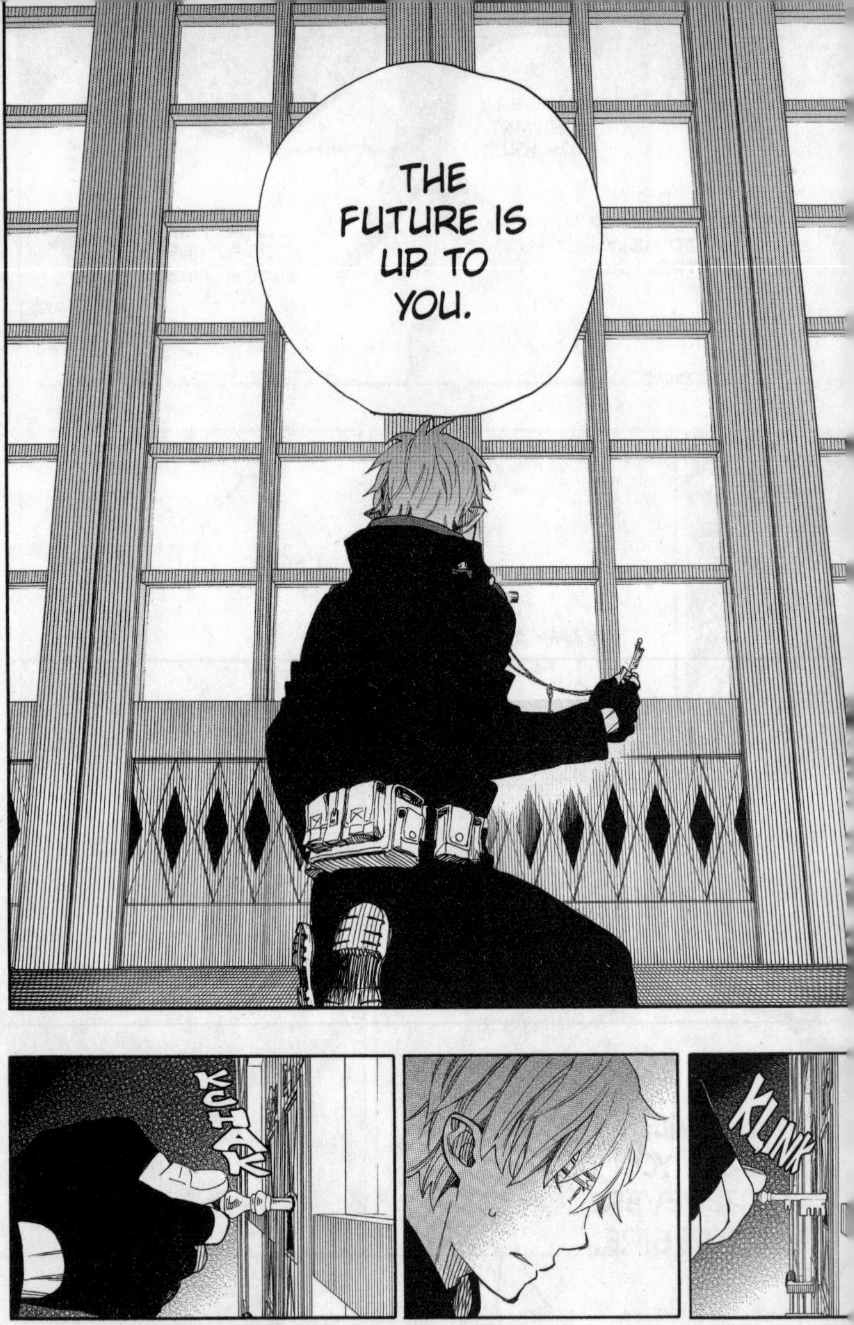
THE FUTURE IS UP TO YOU.
KLINK
KCHAK

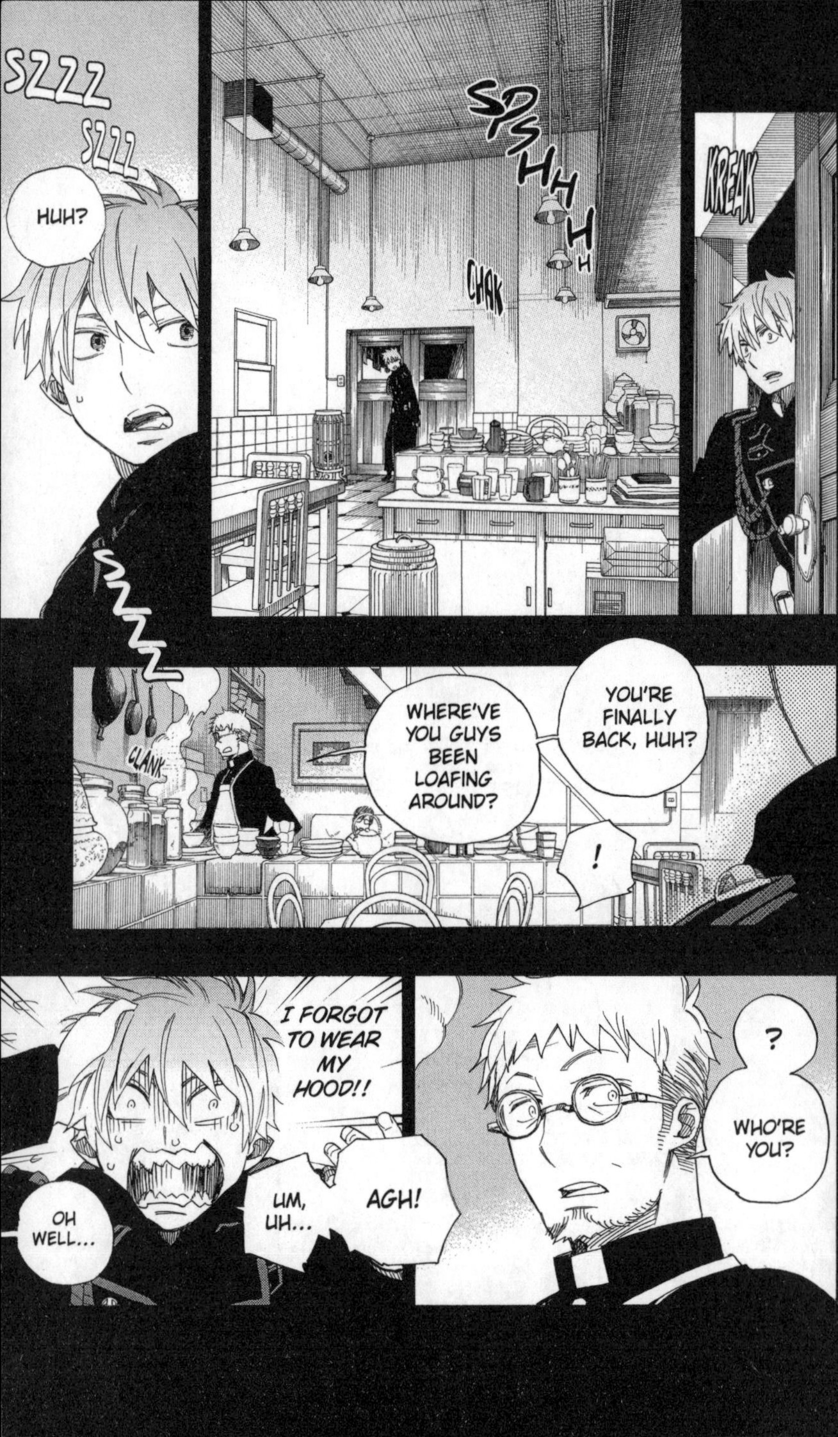
KREAK
SPSHHHHH
CHAK
SZZZ
SZZZ
HUH?
SZZZZ
YOU'RE FINALLY BACK, HUH?
WHERE'VE YOU GUYS BEEN LOAFING AROUND?
CLANK
!
?
WHO'RE YOU?
I FORGOT TO WEAR MY HOOD!!
AGH!
UM, UH...
OH WELL...

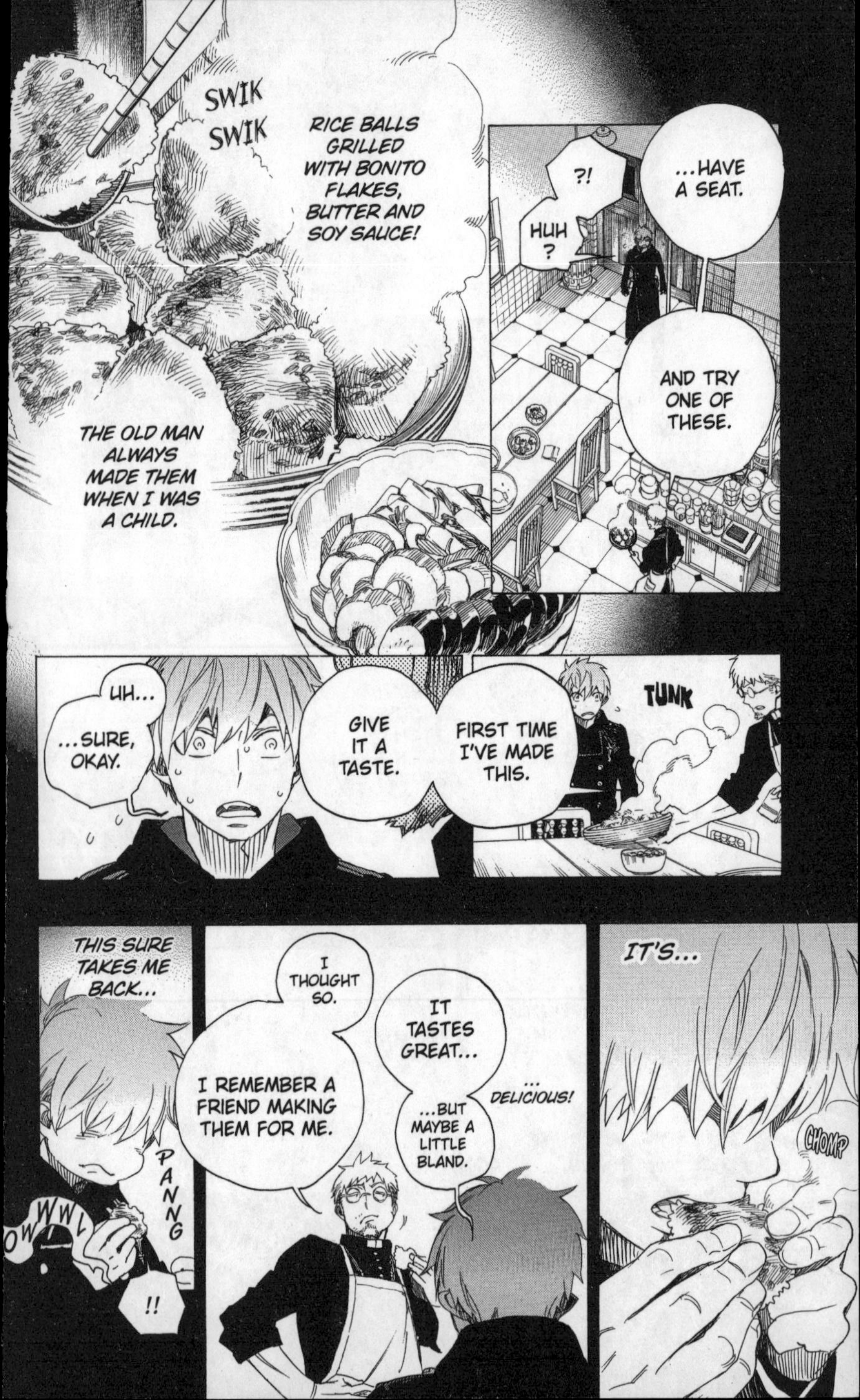
...HAVE A SEAT.
?!
HUH ?
AND TRY ONE OF THESE.
SWIK
SWIK
RICE BALLS GRILLED WITH BONITO FLAKES, BUTTER AND SOY SAUCE!
THE OLD MAN ALWAYS MADE THEM WHEN I WAS A CHILD.
TUNK
FIRST TIME I'VE MADE THIS.
GIVE IT A TASTE.
UH...
...SURE, OKAY.
IT'S...
CHOMP
... DELICIOUS!
IT TASTES GREAT...
...BUT MAYBE A LITTLE BLAND.
I THOUGHT SO.
I REMEMBER A FRIEND MAKING THEM FOR ME.
THIS SURE TAKES ME BACK...
PANNG
OWWWL
!!

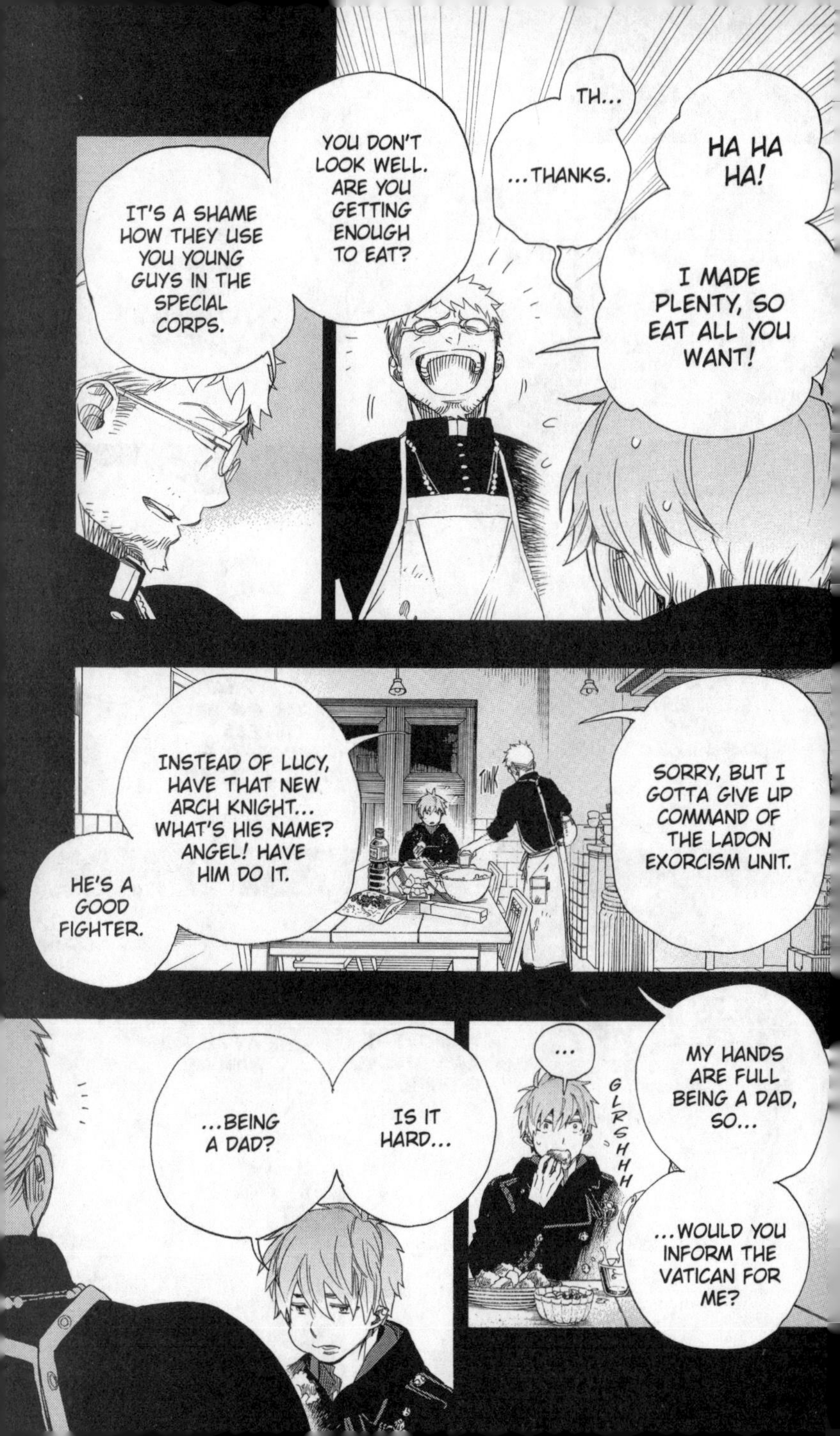
IT'S A SHAME HOW THEY USE YOU YOUNG GUYS IN THE SPECIAL CORPS.
YOU DON'T LOOK WELL. ARE YOU GETTING ENOUGH TO EAT?
TH...
...THANKS.
HA HA HA!
I MADE PLENTY, SO EAT ALL YOU WANT!
SORRY, BUT I GOTTA GIVE UP COMMAND OF THE LADON EXORCISM UNIT.
TUNK
INSTEAD OF LUCY, HAVE THAT NEW ARCH KNIGHT... WHAT'S HIS NAME? ANGEL! HAVE HIM DO IT.
HE'S A GOOD FIGHTER.
MY HANDS ARE FULL BEING A DAD, SO...
...
GLRSHHH
...WOULD YOU INFORM THE VATICAN FOR ME?
IS IT HARD...
...BEING A DAD?

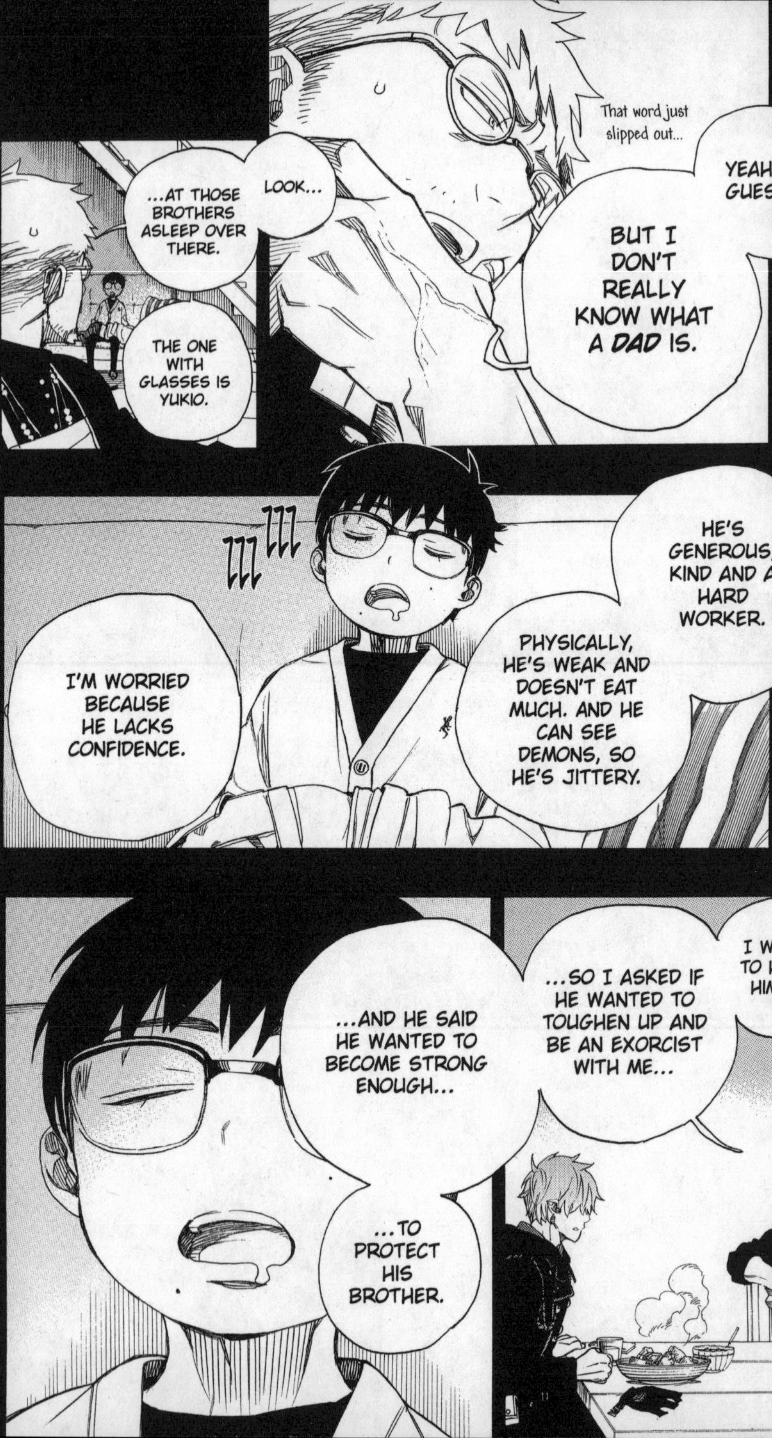
That word just slipped out...
YEAH, I GUESS.
BUT I DON'T REALLY KNOW WHAT A *DAD* IS.
LOOK...
...AT THOSE BROTHERS ASLEEP OVER THERE.
THE ONE WITH GLASSES IS YUKIO.
HE'S GENEROUS, KIND AND A HARD WORKER.
PHYSICALLY, HE'S WEAK AND DOESN'T EAT MUCH. AND HE CAN SEE DEMONS, SO HE'S JITTERY.
ZZZ ZZZ
I'M WORRIED BECAUSE HE LACKS CONFIDENCE.
I WANT TO HELP HIM...
...SO I ASKED IF HE WANTED TO TOUGHEN UP AND BE AN EXORCIST WITH ME...
...AND HE SAID HE WANTED TO BECOME STRONG ENOUGH...
...TO PROTECT HIS BROTHER.

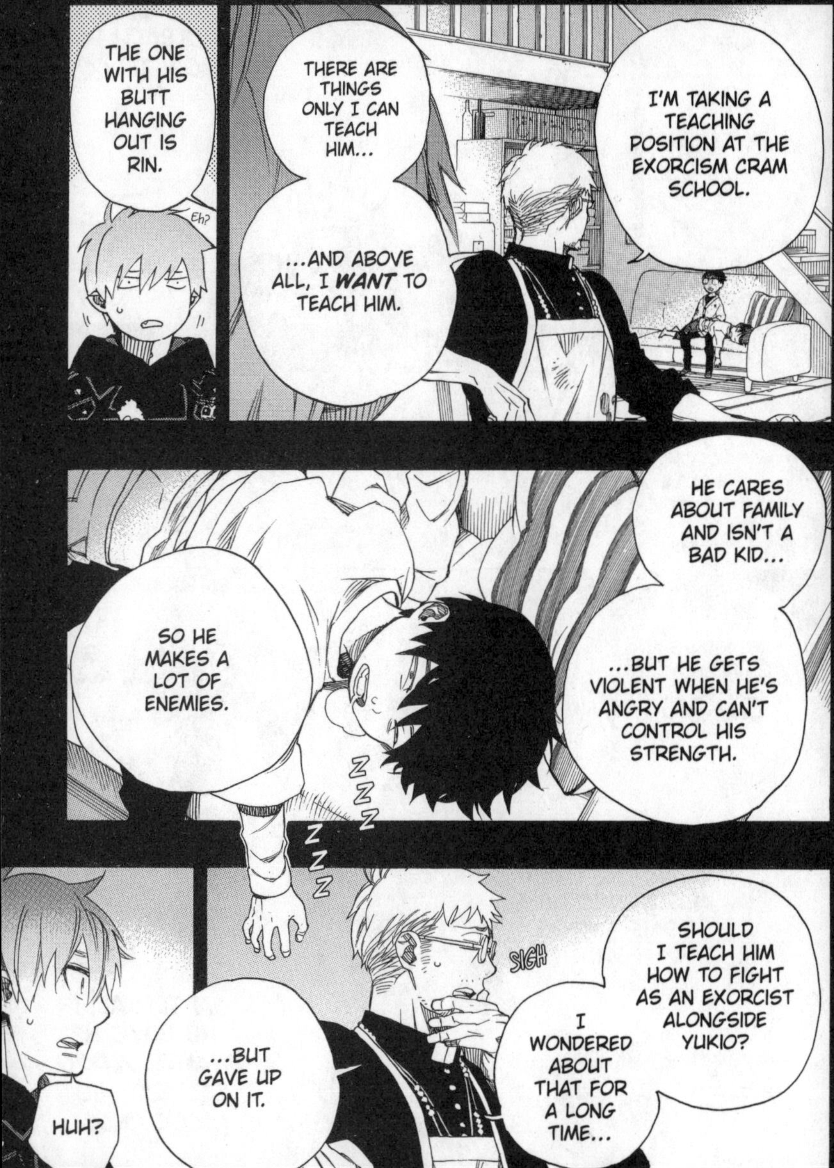
I'M TAKING A TEACHING POSITION AT THE EXORCISM CRAM SCHOOL.
THERE ARE THINGS ONLY I CAN TEACH HIM...
...AND ABOVE ALL, I *WANT* TO TEACH HIM.
THE ONE WITH HIS BUTT HANGING OUT IS RIN.
Eh?
HE CARES ABOUT FAMILY AND ISN'T A BAD KID...
...BUT HE GETS VIOLENT WHEN HE'S ANGRY AND CAN'T CONTROL HIS STRENGTH.
SO HE MAKES A LOT OF ENEMIES.
ZZZ
ZZZ
SIGH
SHOULD I TEACH HIM HOW TO FIGHT AS AN EXORCIST ALONGSIDE YUKIO?
I WONDERED ABOUT THAT FOR A LONG TIME...
...BUT GAVE UP ON IT.
HUH?

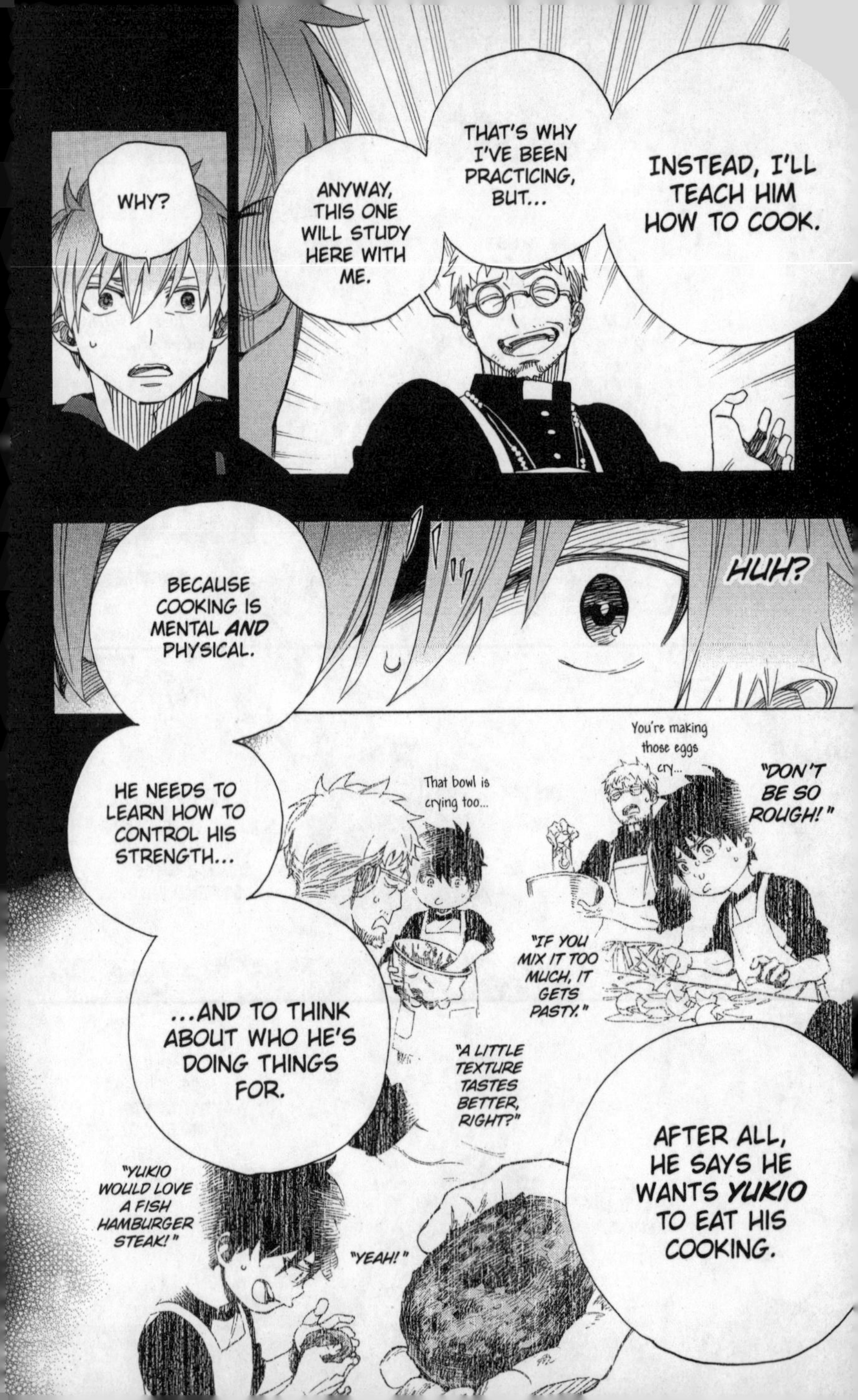
INSTEAD, I'LL TEACH HIM HOW TO COOK.
THAT'S WHY I'VE BEEN PRACTICING, BUT...
ANYWAY, THIS ONE WILL STUDY HERE WITH ME.
WHY?
HUH?
BECAUSE COOKING IS MENTAL AND PHYSICAL.
"DON'T BE SO ROUGH!"
You're making those eggs cry...
"IF YOU MIX IT TOO MUCH, IT GETS PASTY."
That bowl is crying too...
HE NEEDS TO LEARN HOW TO CONTROL HIS STRENGTH...
"A LITTLE TEXTURE TASTES BETTER, RIGHT?"
...AND TO THINK ABOUT WHO HE'S DOING THINGS FOR.
AFTER ALL, HE SAYS HE WANTS YUKIO TO EAT HIS COOKING.
"YEAH!"
"YUKIO WOULD LOVE A FISH HAMBURGER STEAK!"

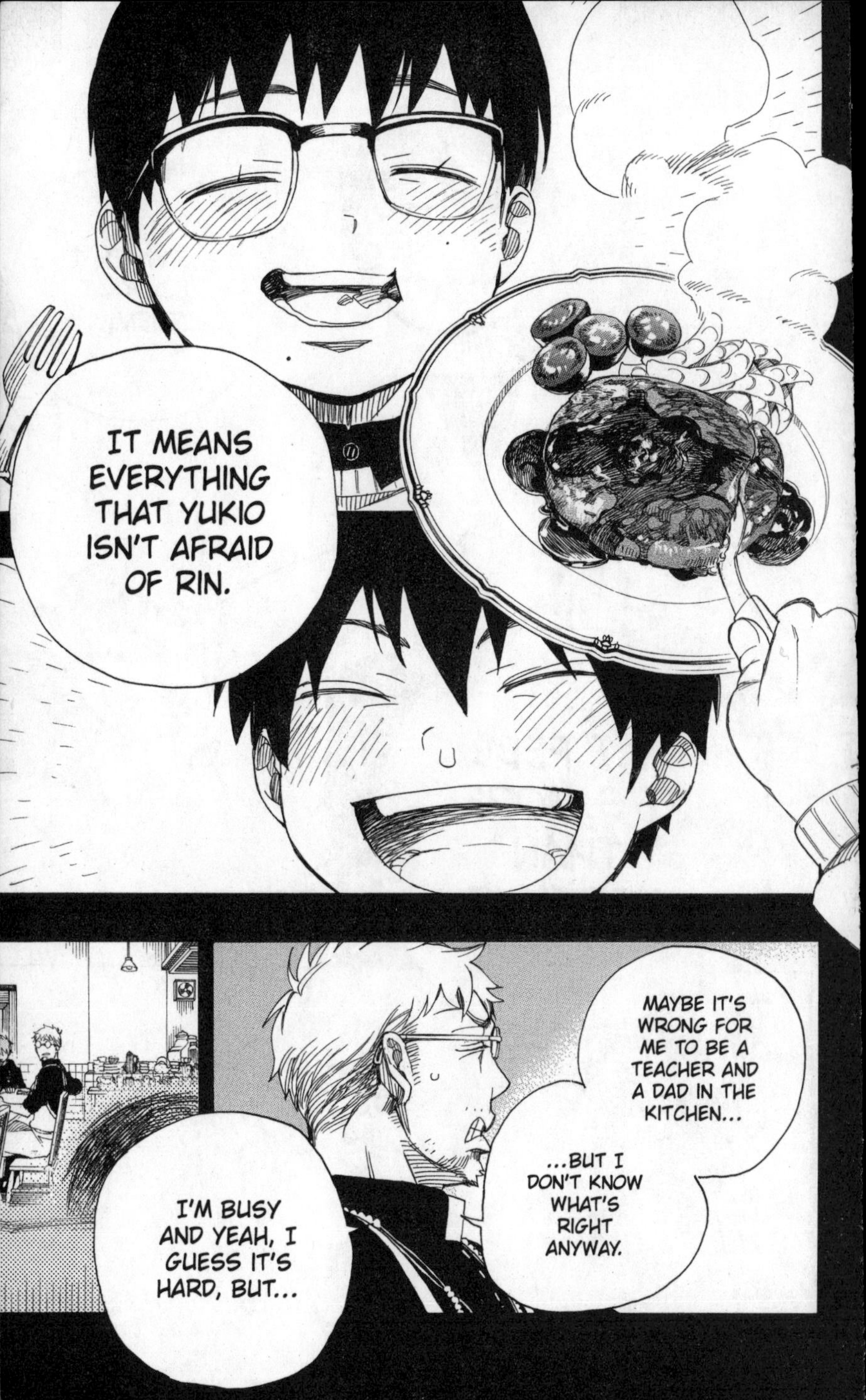
IT MEANS EVERYTHING THAT YUKIO ISN'T AFRAID OF RIN.
MAYBE IT'S WRONG FOR ME TO BE A TEACHER AND A DAD IN THE KITCHEN...
...BUT I DON'T KNOW WHAT'S RIGHT ANYWAY.
I'M BUSY AND YEAH, I GUESS IT'S HARD, BUT...

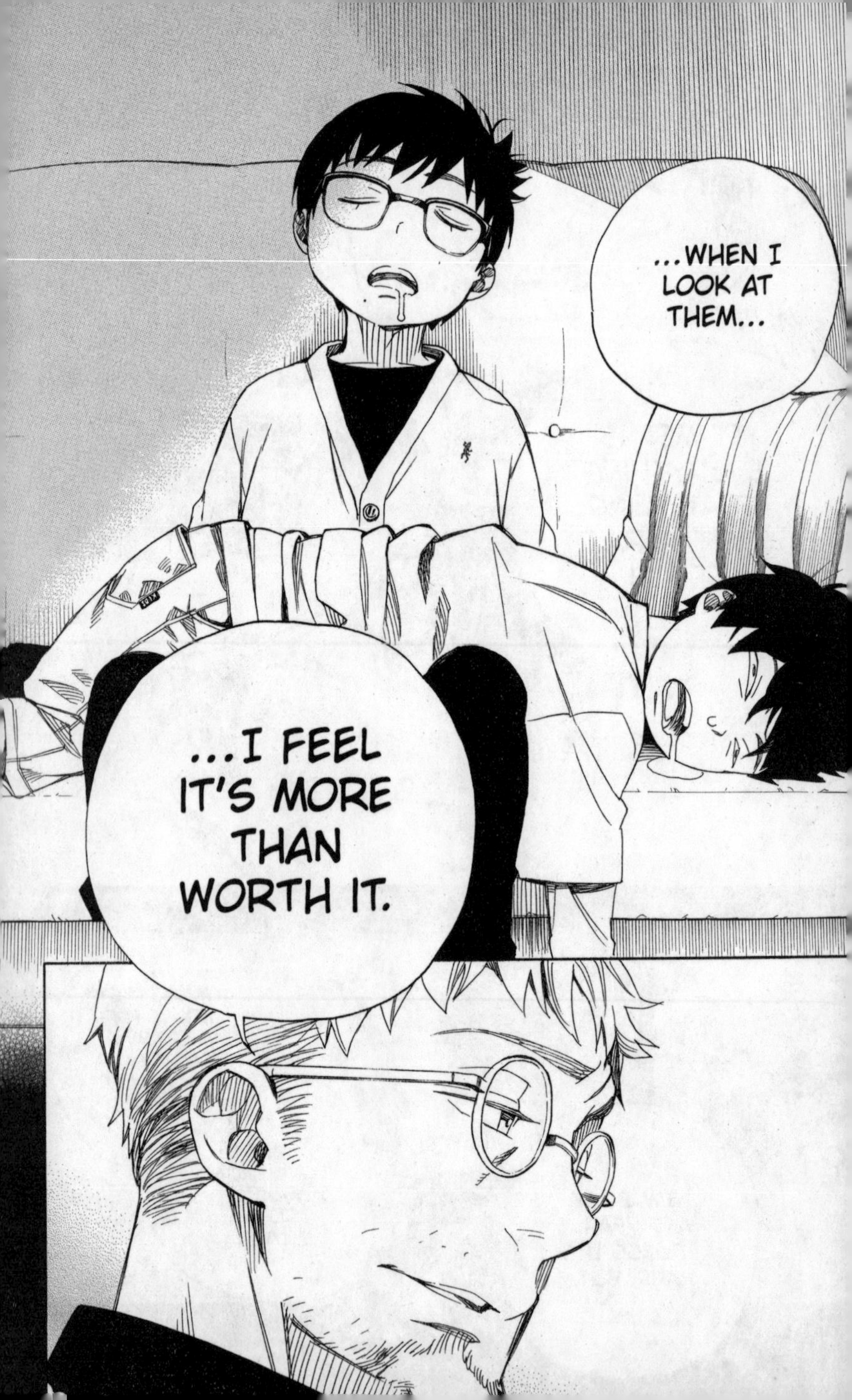
...WHEN I LOOK AT THEM...
...I FEEL IT'S MORE THAN WORTH IT.

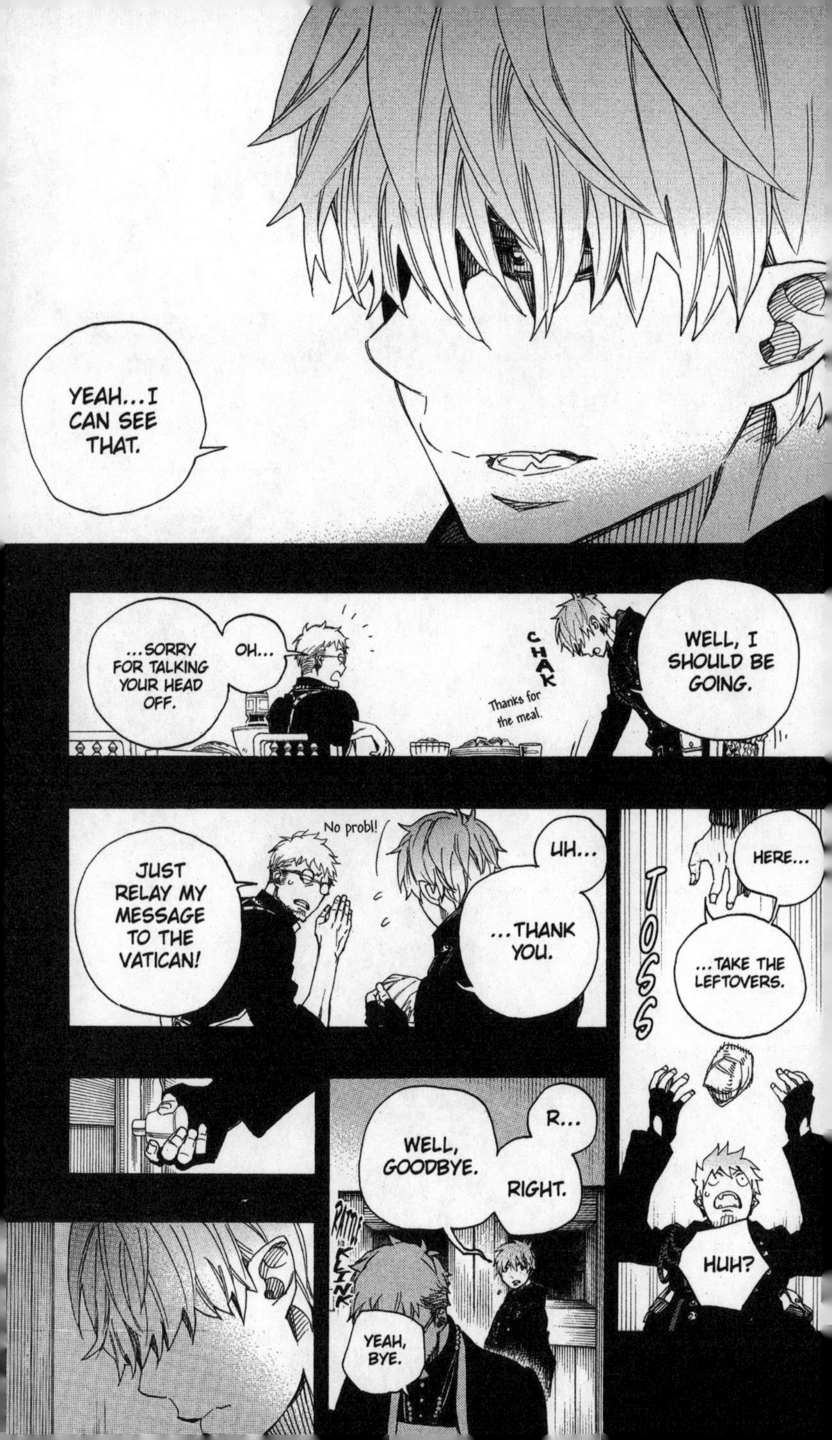
YEAH... I CAN SEE THAT.
WELL, I SHOULD BE GOING.
CHAK
Thanks for the meal.
OH...
...SORRY FOR TALKING YOUR HEAD OFF.
HERE...
...TAKE THE LEFTOVERS.
TOSS
HUH?
UH...
No probl!
...THANK YOU.
JUST RELAY MY MESSAGE TO THE VATICAN!
R...
WELL, GOODBYE.
RIGHT.
RATTL
KLINK
YEAH, BYE.

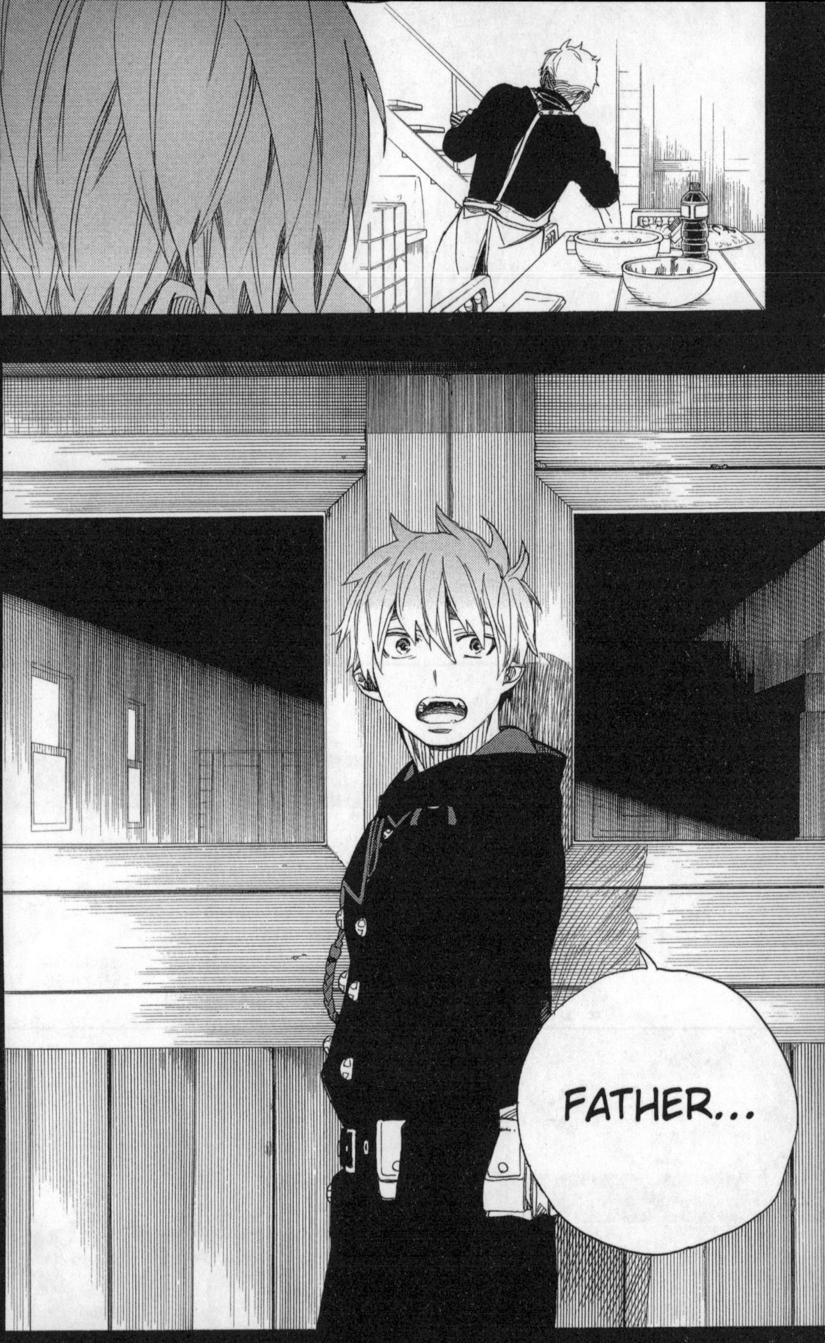
FATHER...

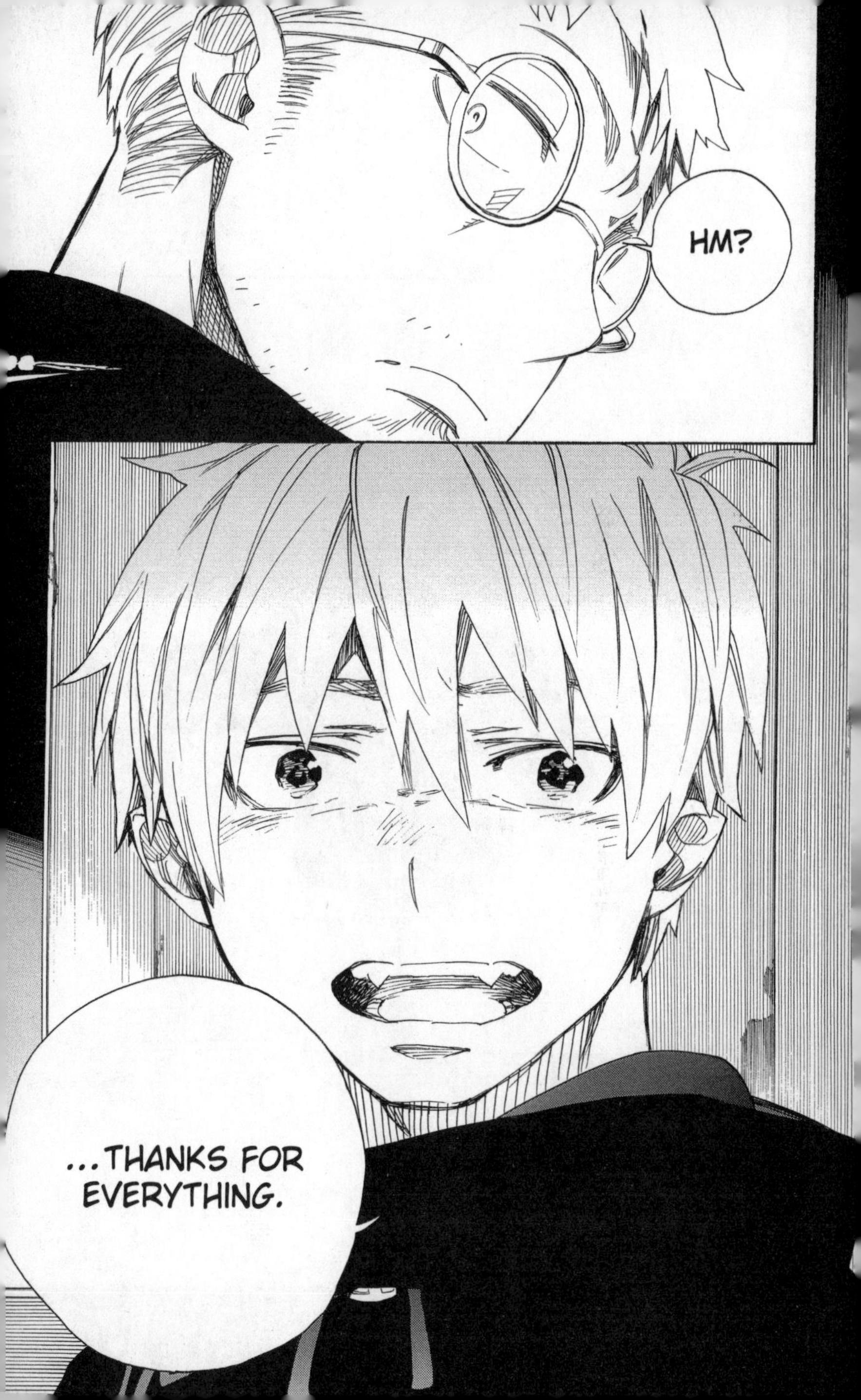
HM?
...THANKS FOR EVERYTHING.

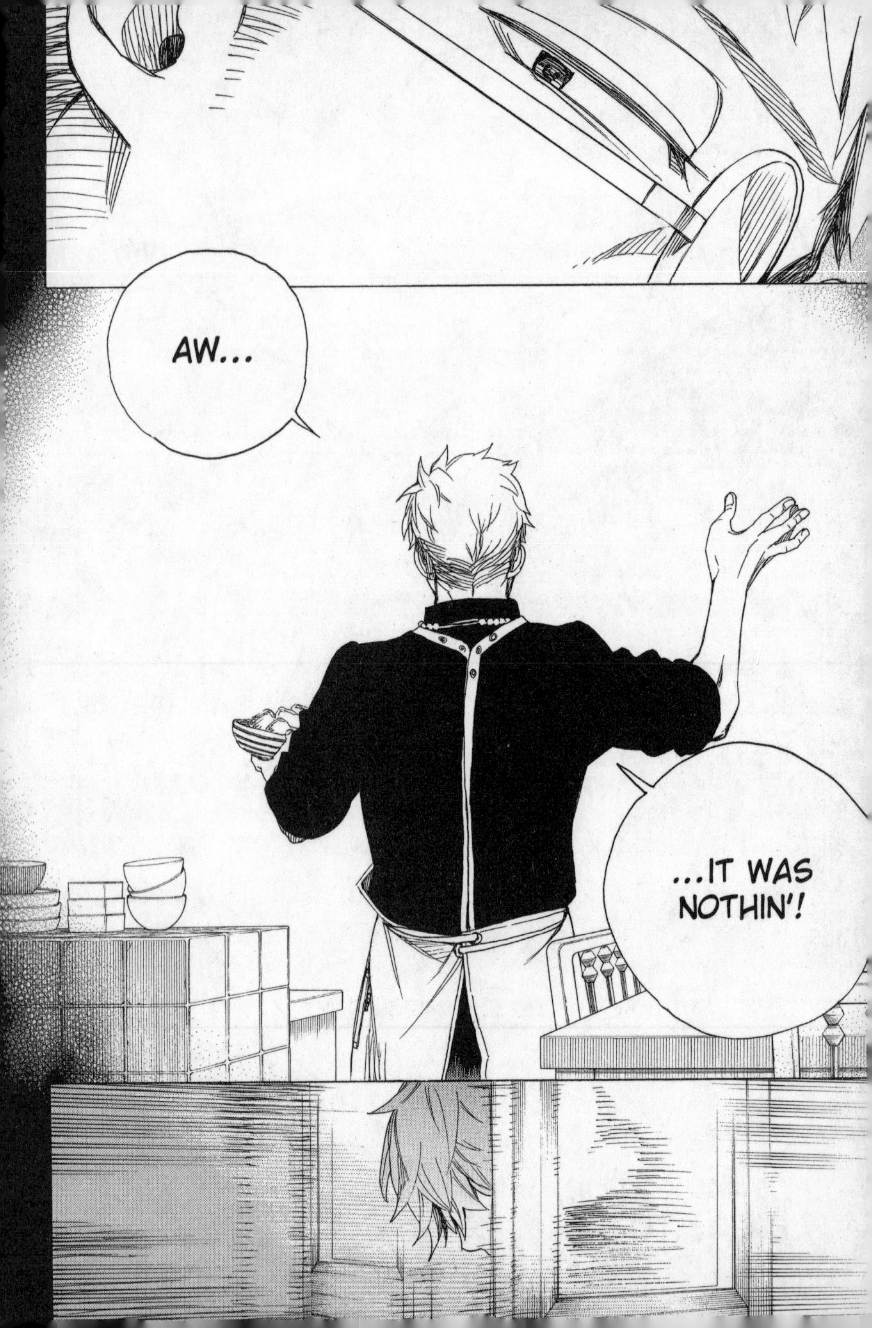
AW...
...IT WAS NOTHIN'!

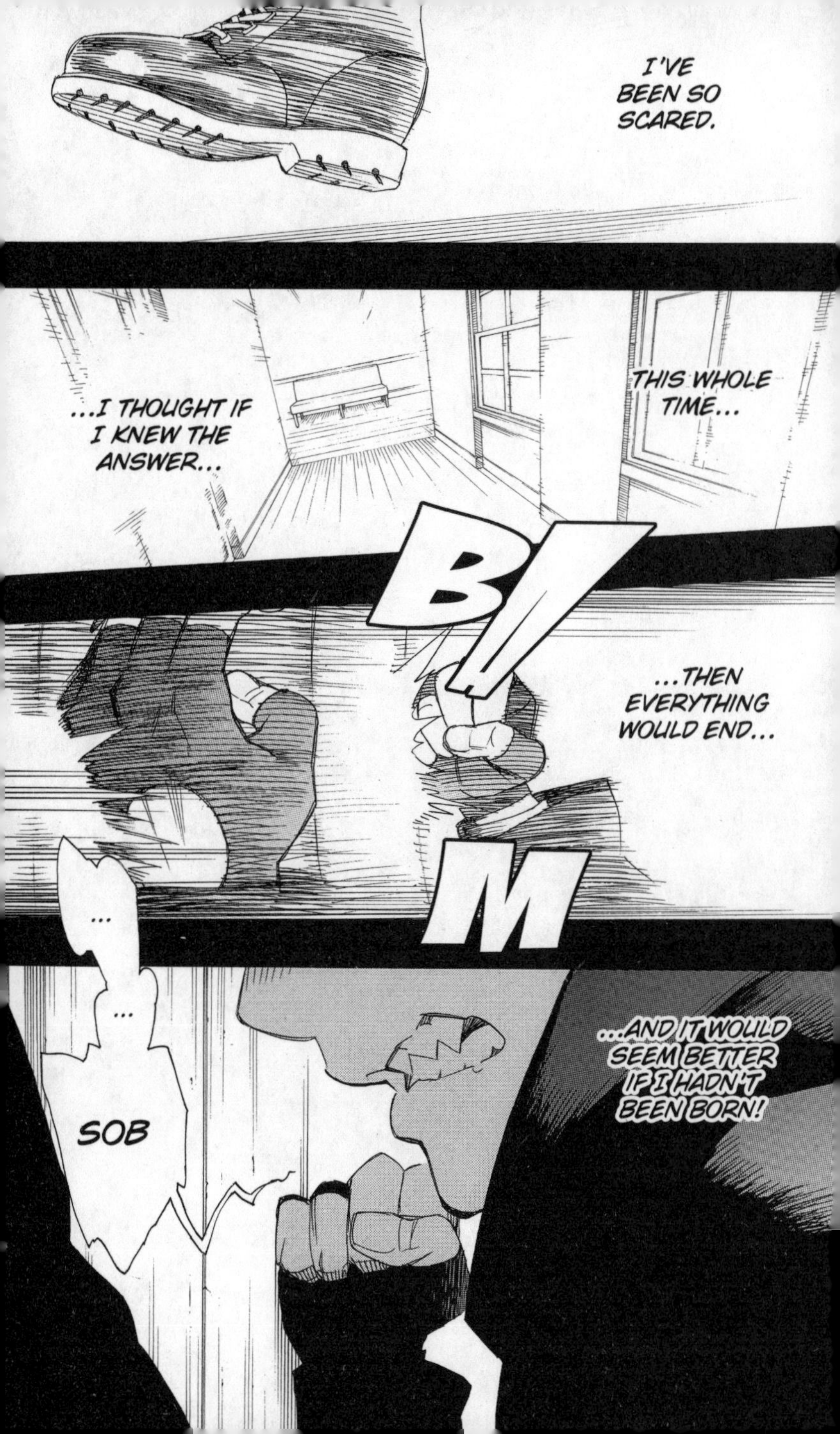
I'VE BEEN SO SCARED.
THIS WHOLE TIME...
...I THOUGHT IF I KNEW THE ANSWER...
B
M
...THEN EVERYTHING WOULD END...
...AND IT WOULD SEEM BETTER IF I HADN'T BEEN BORN!
...
...
SOB

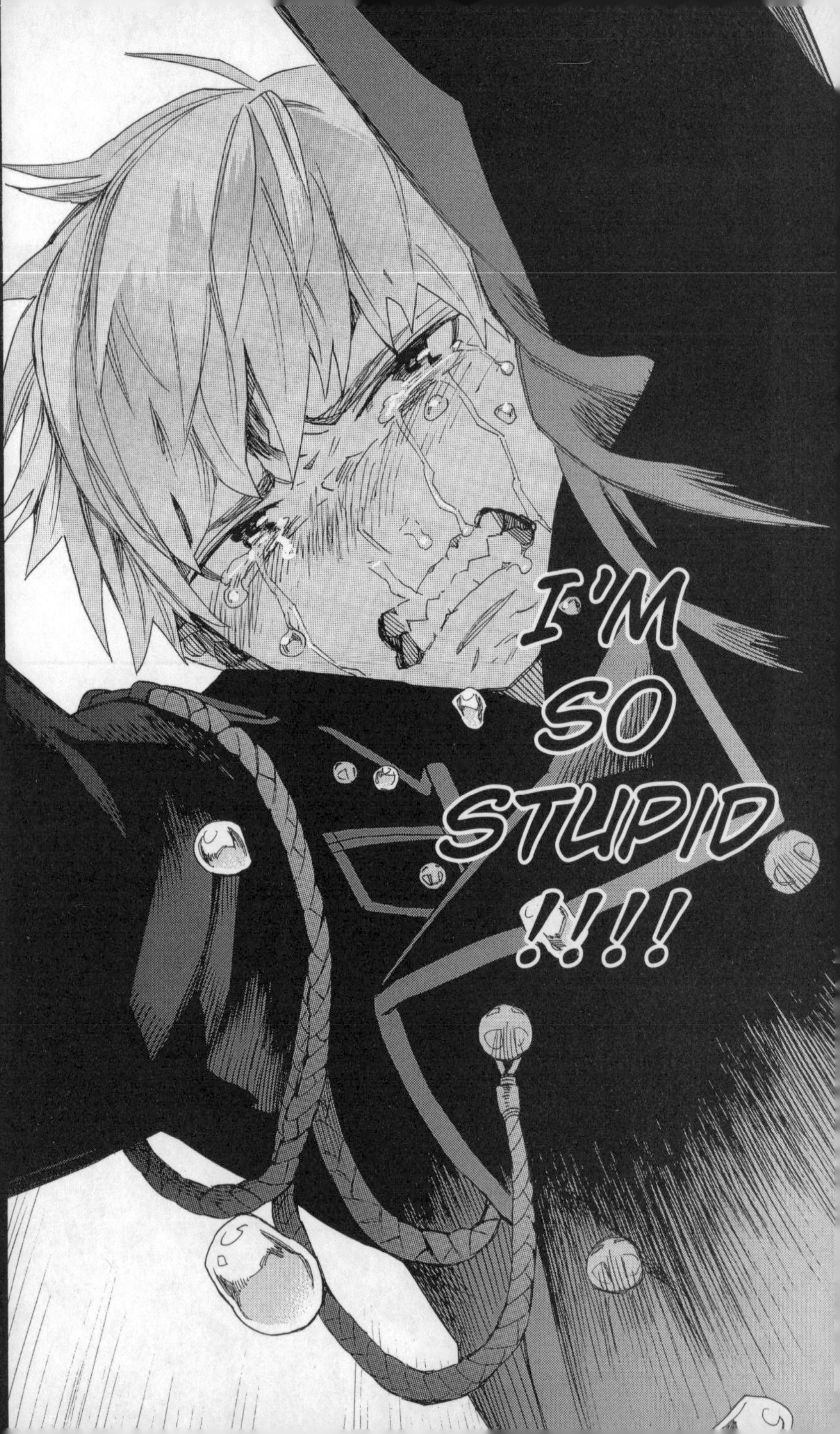
I'M SO STUPID !!!!

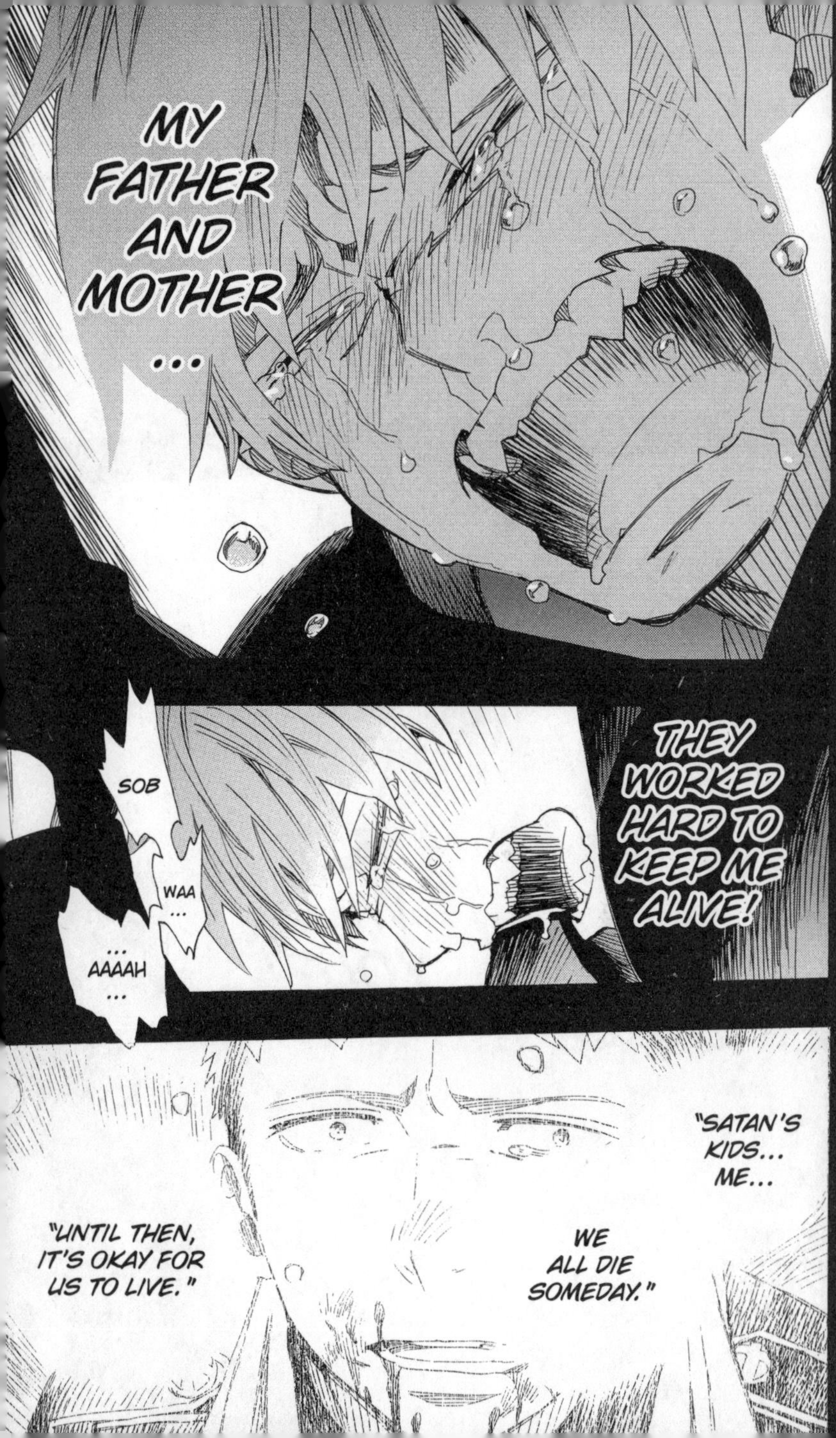
MY FATHER AND MOTHER ...
THEY WORKED HARD TO KEEP ME ALIVE!
SOB
WAA ...
... AAAAH ...
"SATAN'S KIDS... ME...
WE ALL DIE SOMEDAY."
"UNTIL THEN, IT'S OKAY FOR US TO LIVE."

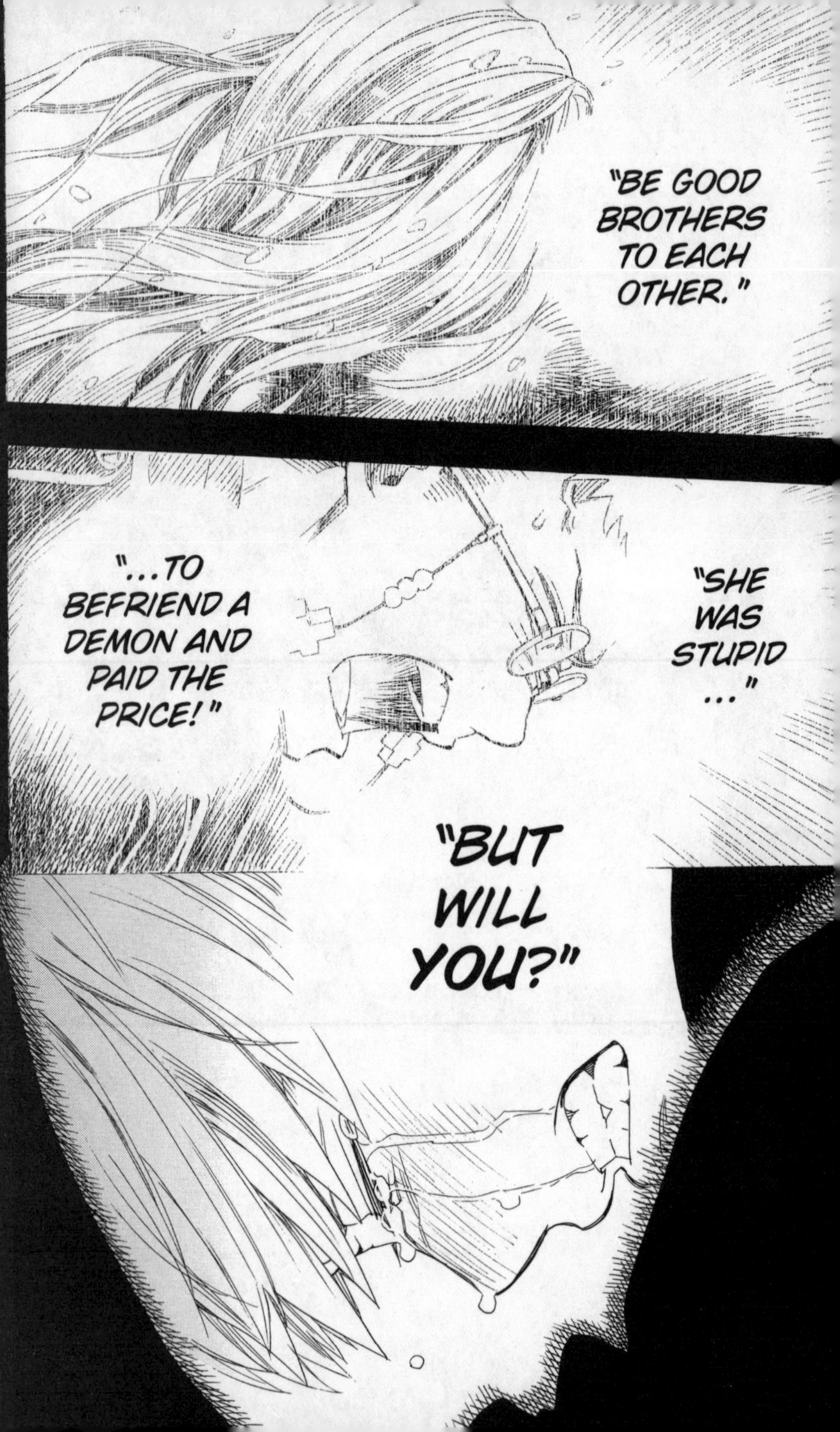
"BE GOOD BROTHERS TO EACH OTHER."
"SHE WAS STUPID ..."
"...TO BEFRIEND A DEMON AND PAID THE PRICE!"
"BUT WILL YOU?"

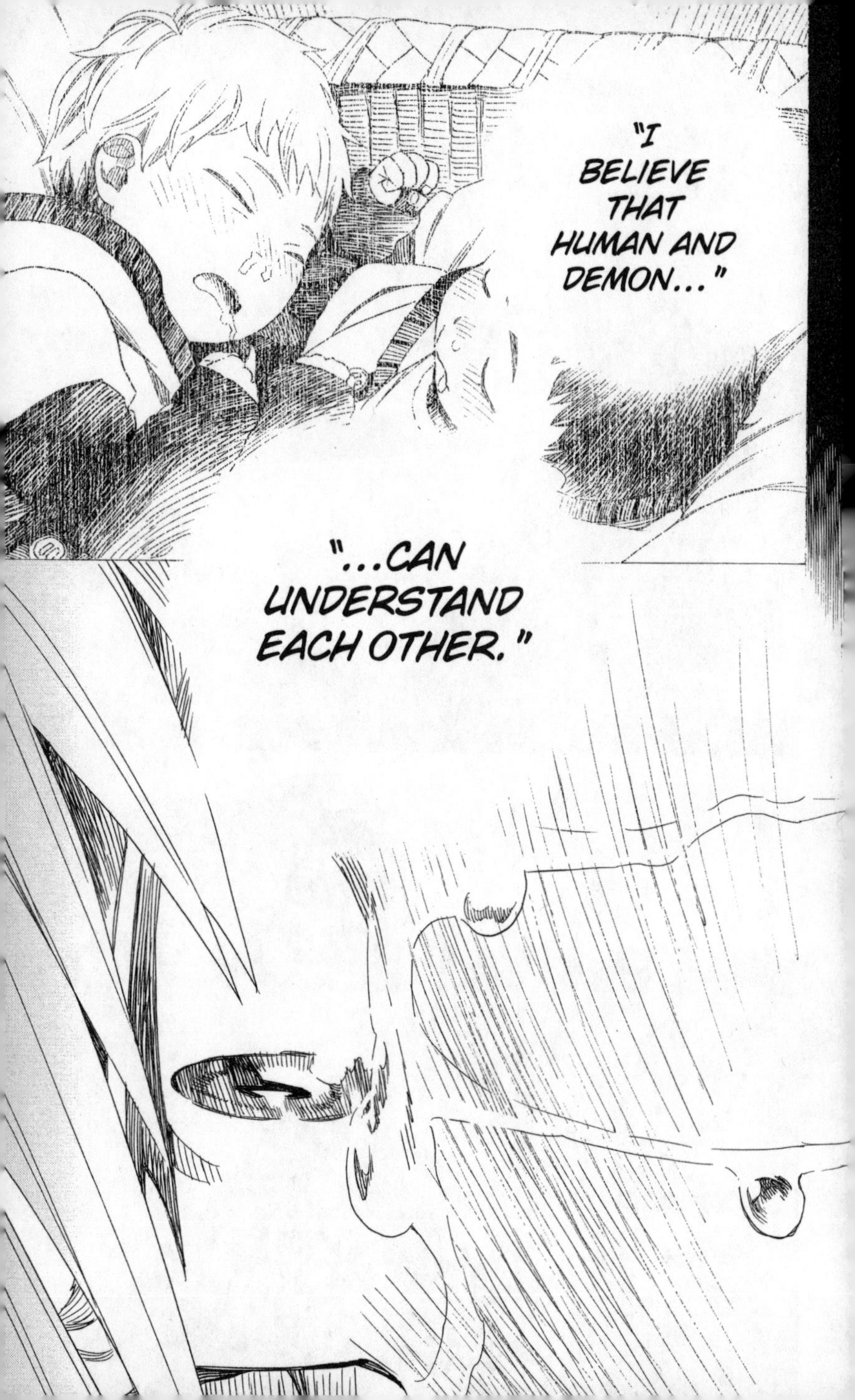
"I BELIEVE THAT HUMAN AND DEMON..."
"...CAN UNDERSTAND EACH OTHER."

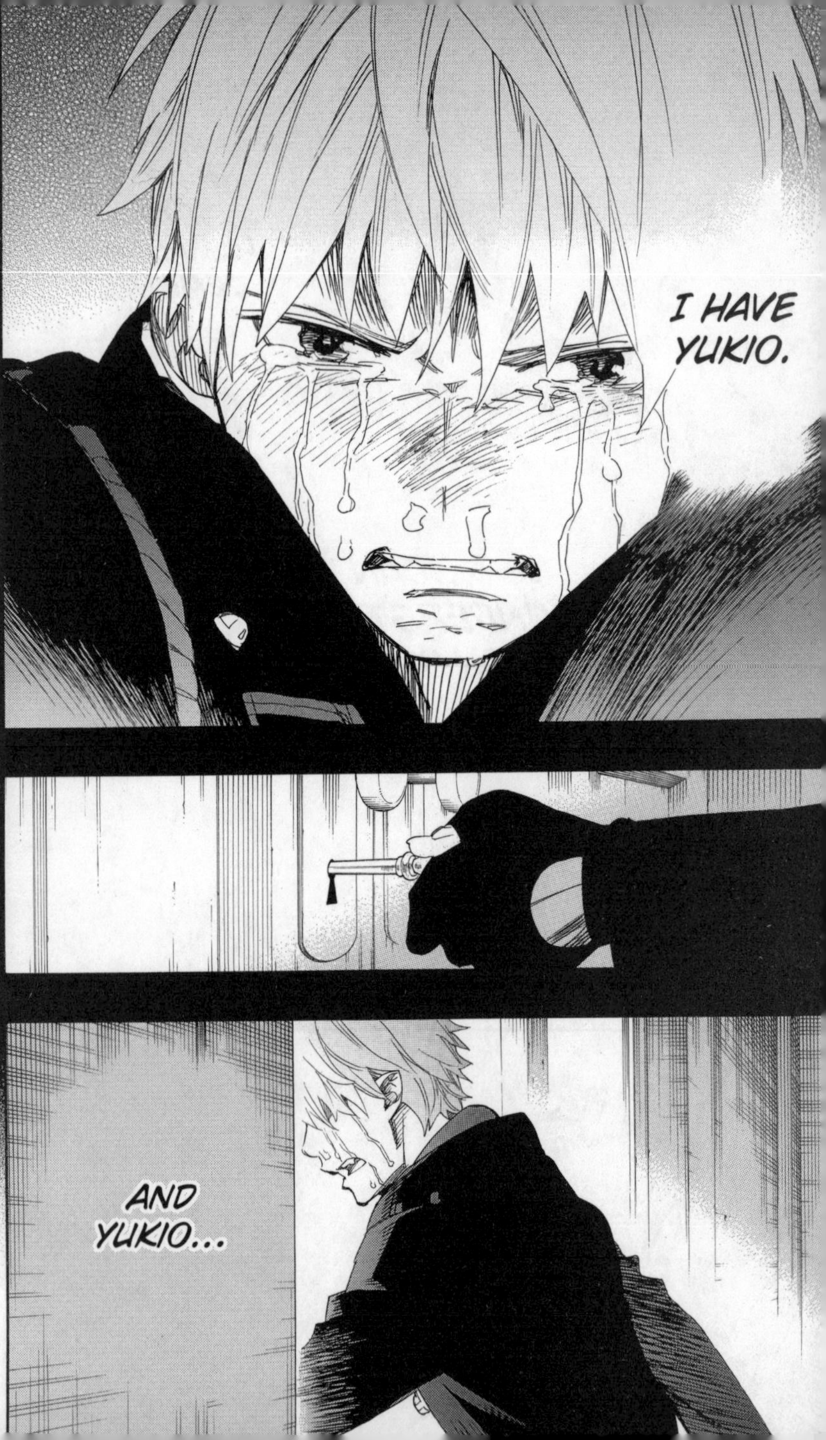
I HAVE YUKIO.
AND YUKIO...

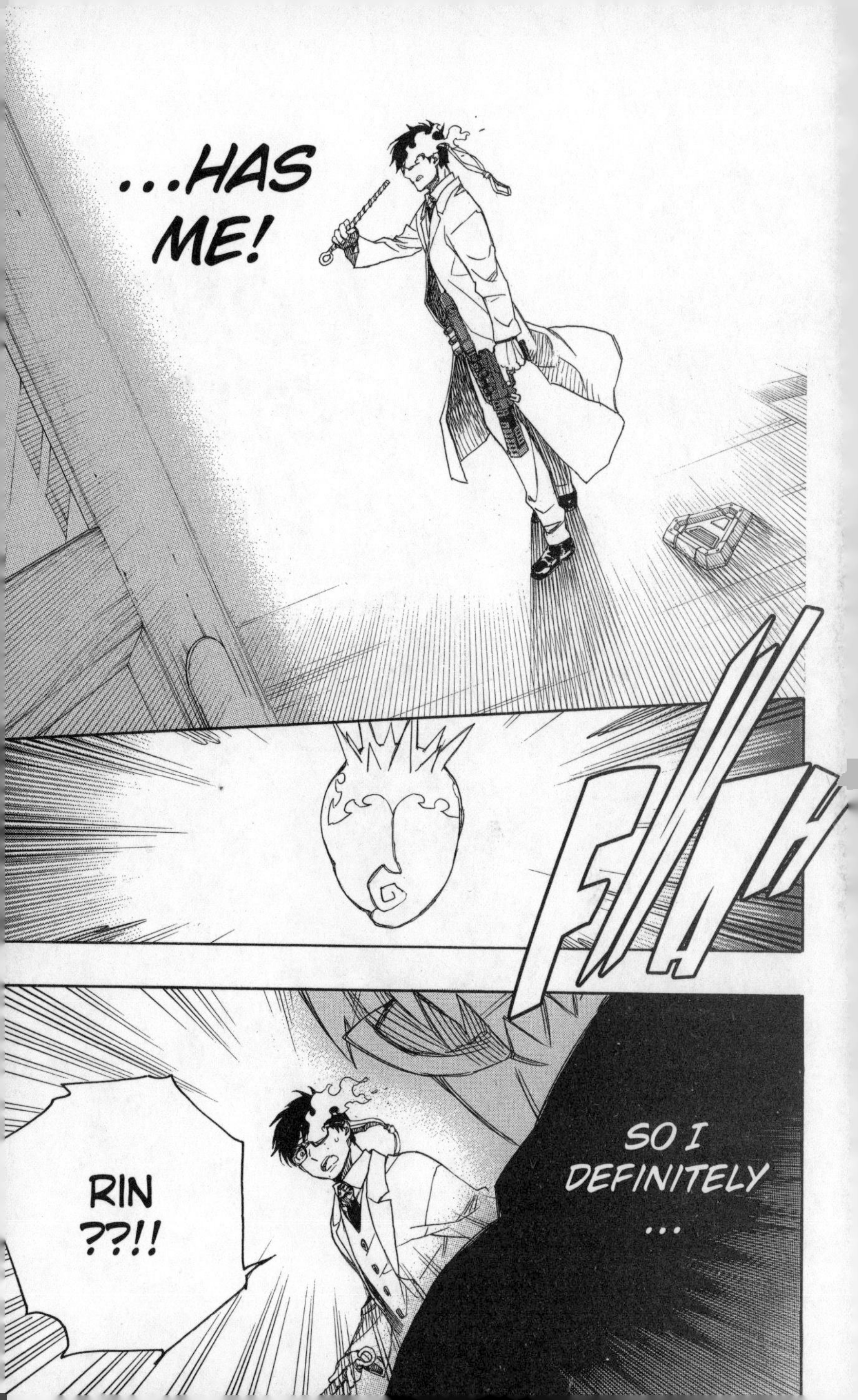
...HAS ME!
SO I DEFINITELY ...
RIN ??!!

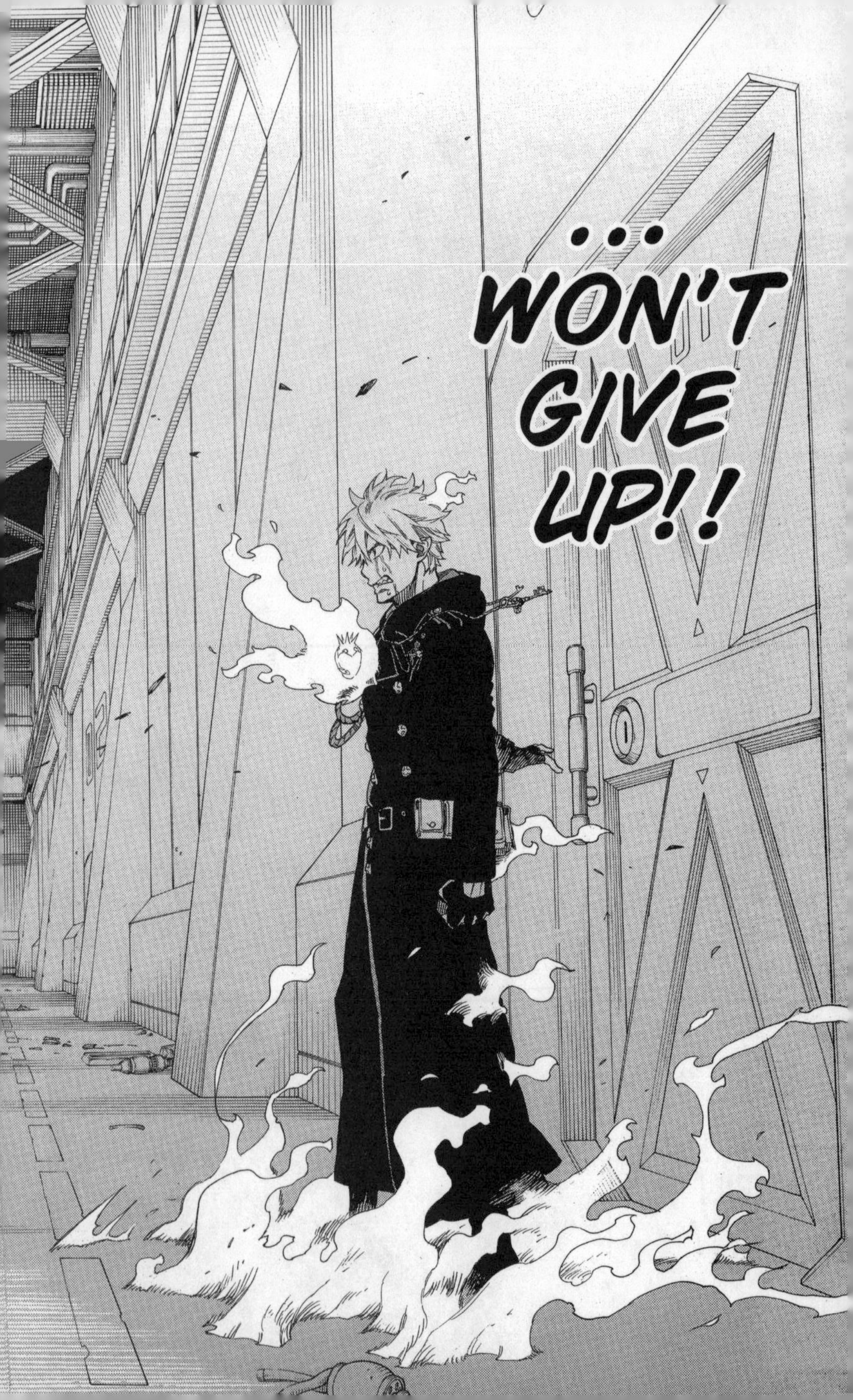
...WON'T GIVE UP!!

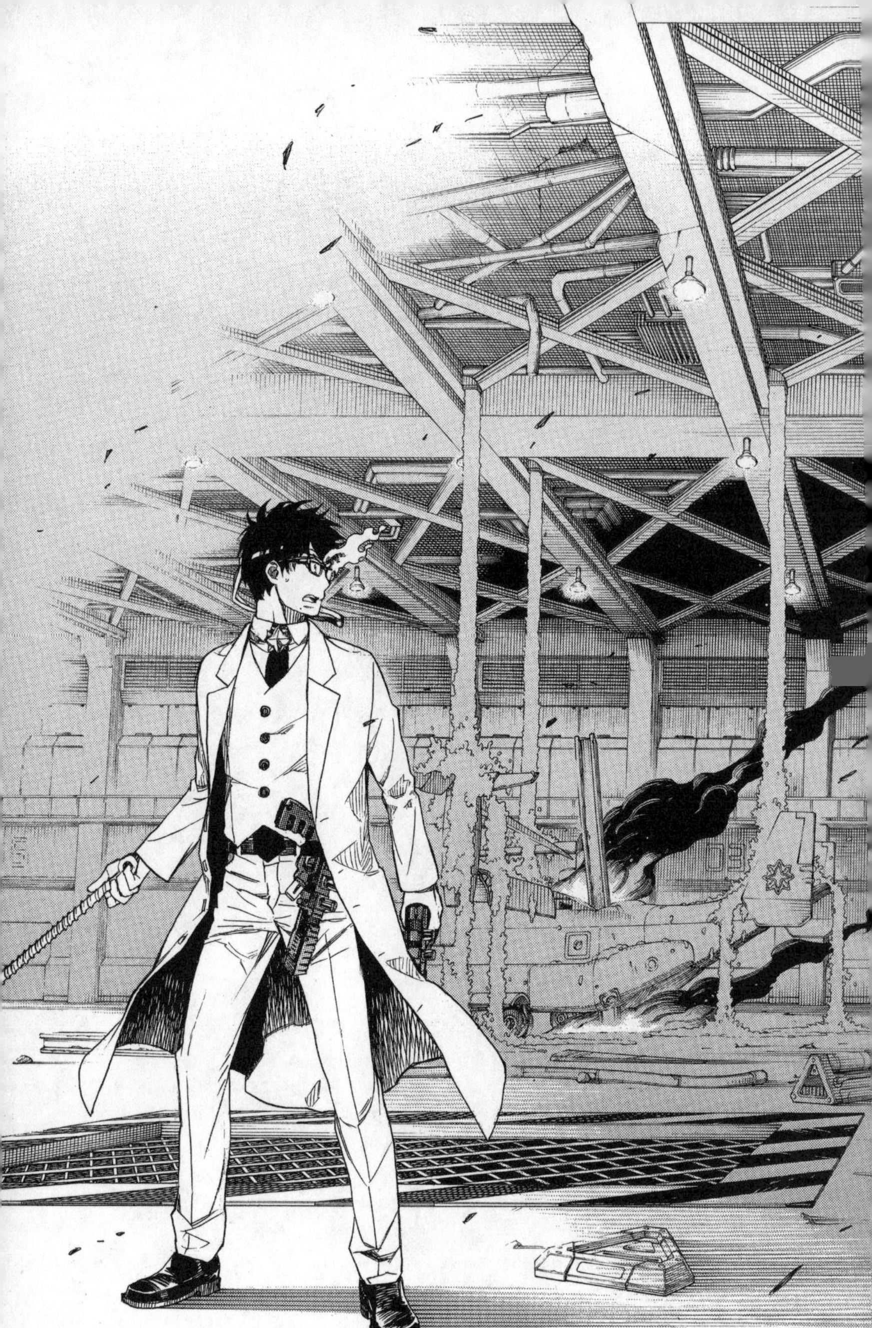

BLUE EXORCIST 25 - END -

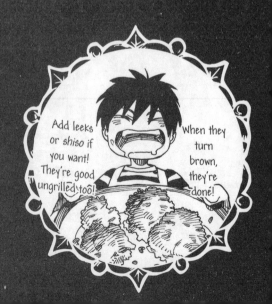

Blue Exorcist Chapter 120: SsC40:00E

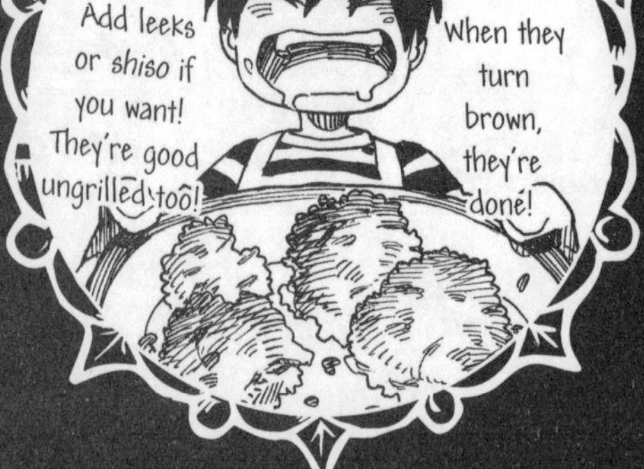
When they turn brown, they're done!
Add leeks or shiso if you want! They're good ungrilled, too!

BLUE EXORCIST BONUS

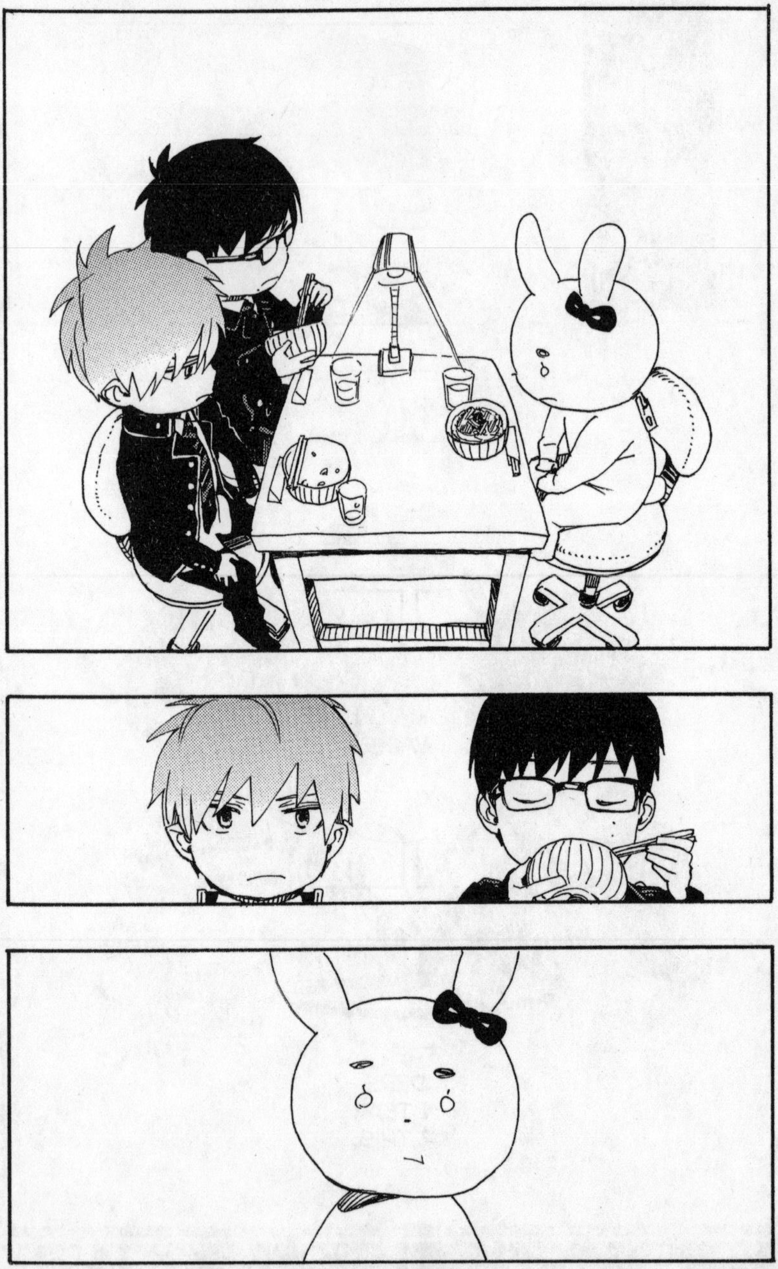

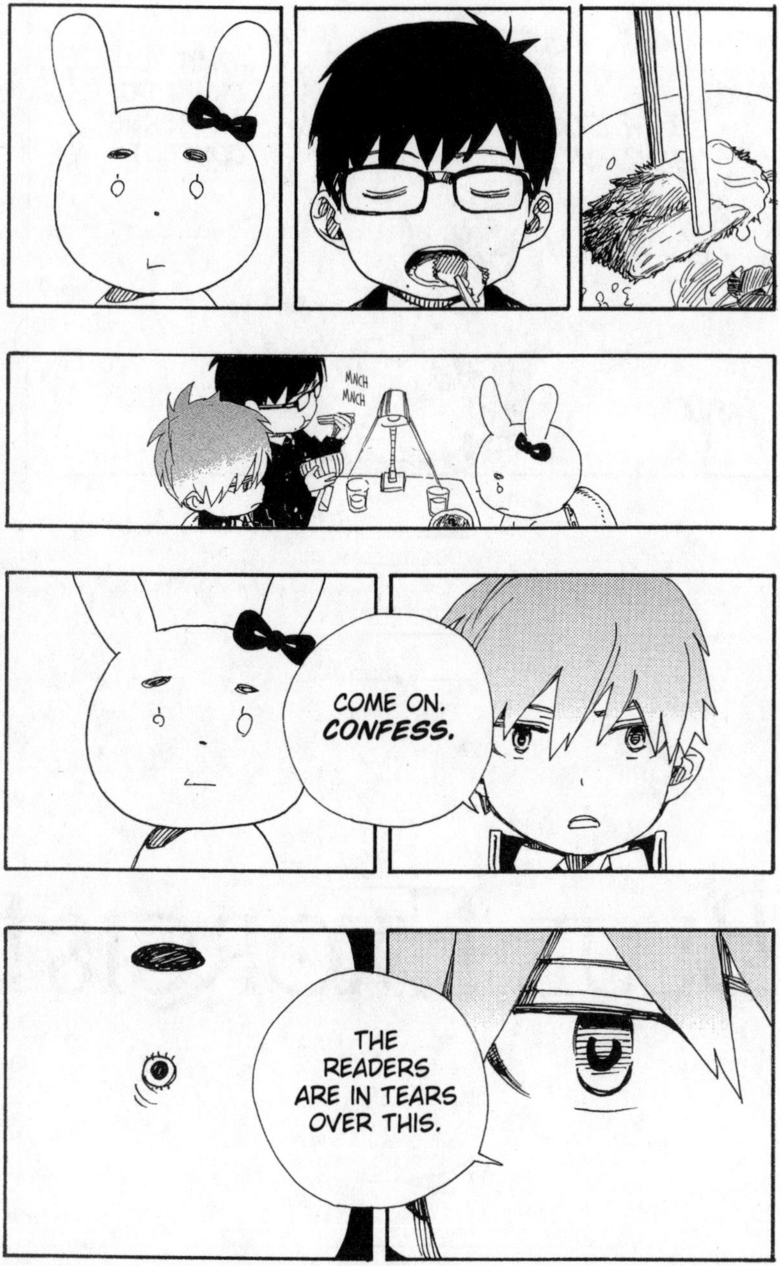
MNCH
MNCH
COME ON. **CONFESS.**
THE READERS ARE IN TEARS OVER THIS.

ADMIT YOU DIDN'T DO ANY BONUS CONTENT!
I...
I'M SO SORRY!!
END

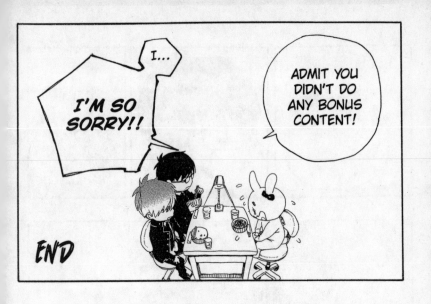

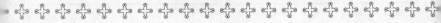

BLUE EXORCIST

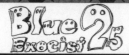

Blue Exorcist 25

Art Staff

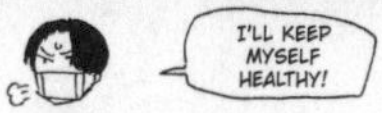
I'LL KEEP MYSELF HEALTHY!
Erika Uemura

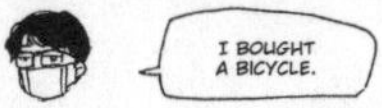
I BOUGHT A BICYCLE.
Ryoji Hayashi

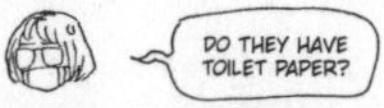
DO THEY HAVE TOILET PAPER?
Mari Oda

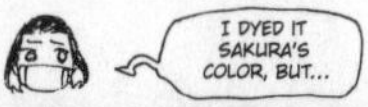
I DYED IT SAKURA'S COLOR, BUT...
Aki Shiina

Art Assistants

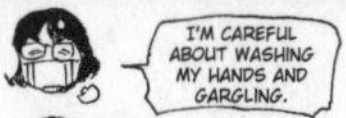
I'M CAREFUL ABOUT WASHING MY HANDS AND GARGLING.
Yamanaka-san

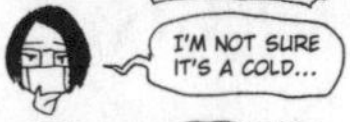
I'M NOT SURE IT'S A COLD...
Obata-san

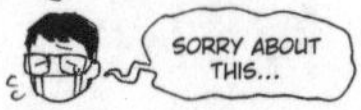
SORRY ABOUT THIS...
Ito-kun

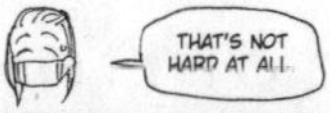
THAT'S NOT HARD AT ALL.
Seo-san

Composition Assistant

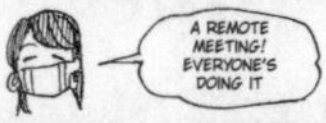
A REMOTE MEETING! EVERYONE'S DOING IT
Minoru Sasaki

Editors

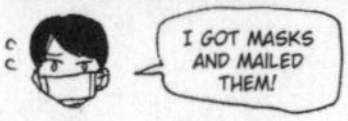
I GOT MASKS AND MAILED THEM!
Ippei Sawada

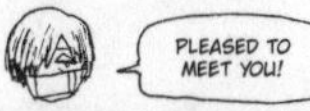
PLEASED TO MEET YOU!
Yujiro Hattori

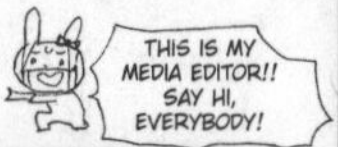
THIS IS MY MEDIA EDITOR!! SAY HI, EVERYBODY!

Graphic Novel Editor

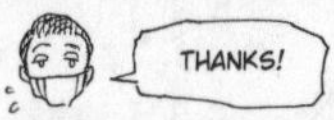
THANKS!
Ryusuke Kuroki

Graphic Novel Design

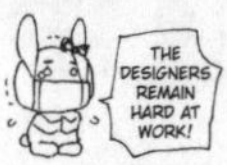
THE DESIGNERS REMAIN HARD AT WORK!

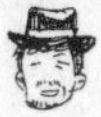
Shimada Hideaki

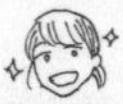
Rie Akutsu (L.S.D.)

Manga

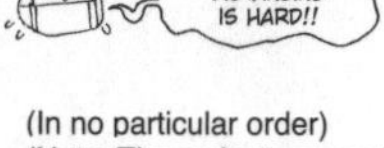
SOCIAL DISTANCING IS HARD!!
Kazue Kato

(In no particular order)
(Note: The caricatures and statements are from memory!)

These are hard times, but see you in volume 26!!!

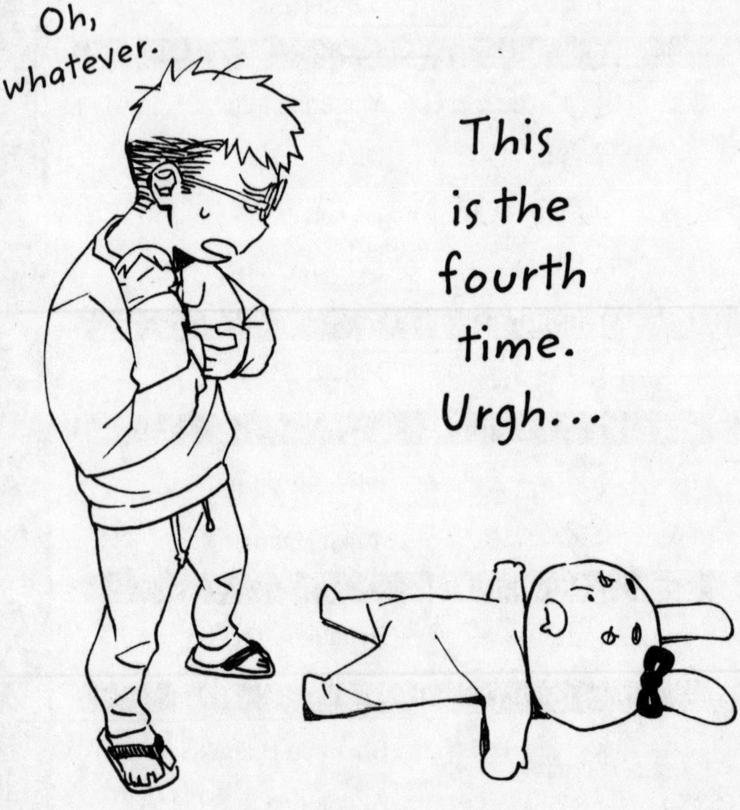

This is the fourth time. Urgh...
Oh, whatever.

It Got Really Easy

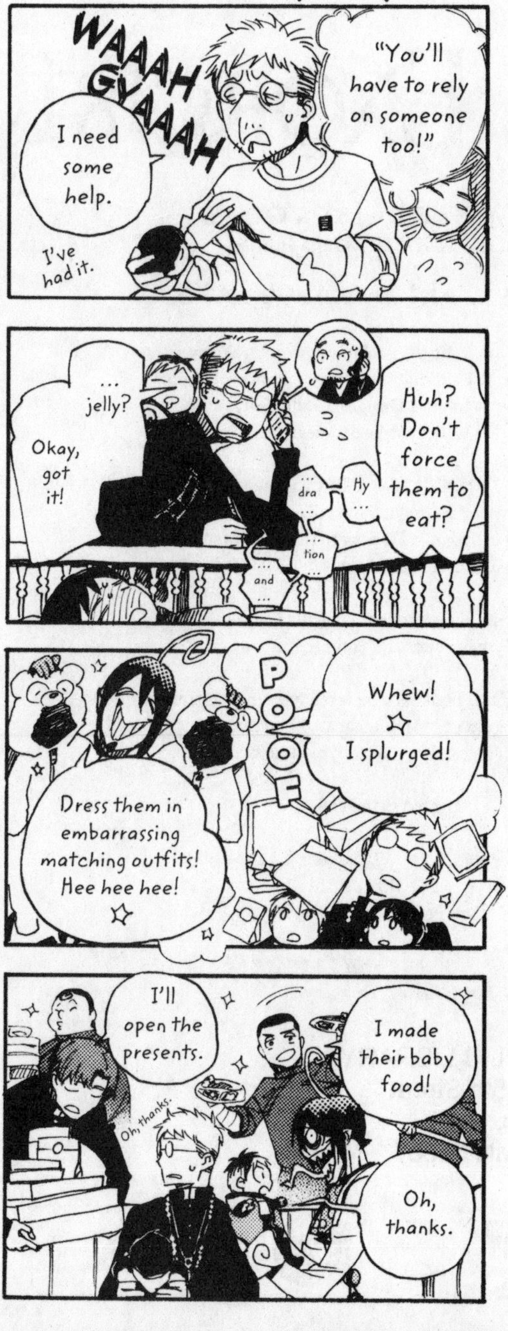
"You'll have to rely on someone too!"
WAAAAH GYAAAAH
I need some help.
I've had it.
Huh? Don't force them to eat?
Hy...
...dra...
...tion...
...and...
...jelly?
Okay, got it!
Whew! ☆ I splurged!
POOF
Dress them in embarrassing matching outfits! Hee hee hee! ☆
I made their baby food!
I'll open the presents.
Oh, thanks.
Oh, thanks.

BLUE EXORCIST

BLUE EXORCIST VOL. 25
SHONEN JUMP Manga Edition

STORY & ART BY KAZUE KATO

Translation & English Adaptation/John Werry
Touch-up Art & Lettering/John Hunt, Primary Graphix
Cover & Interior Design/Mindy Walters
Editor/Mike Montesa

AO NO EXORCIST © 2009 by Kazue Kato
All rights reserved.
First published in Japan in 2009 by SHUEISHA Inc., Tokyo.
English translation rights arranged by SHUEISHA Inc.

Printed in the U.S.A.

Published by VIZ Media, LLC
P.O. Box 77010
San Francisco, CA 94107

10 9 8 7 6 5 4 3 2 1
First printing, February 2021

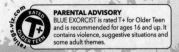

Thanks to everyone, I built a very very good office.

KAZUE KATO

I DID MORE NEW PAGES THAN EVER FOR THIS VOLUME, SO IT TURNED OUT TO BE HUGE. SORRY ABOUT THAT. BUT I'M GLAD I COULD REACH A GOOD STOPPING POINT!

PLEASE ENJOY READING VOLUME 25.

Blue Exorcist 25

Kazue Kato

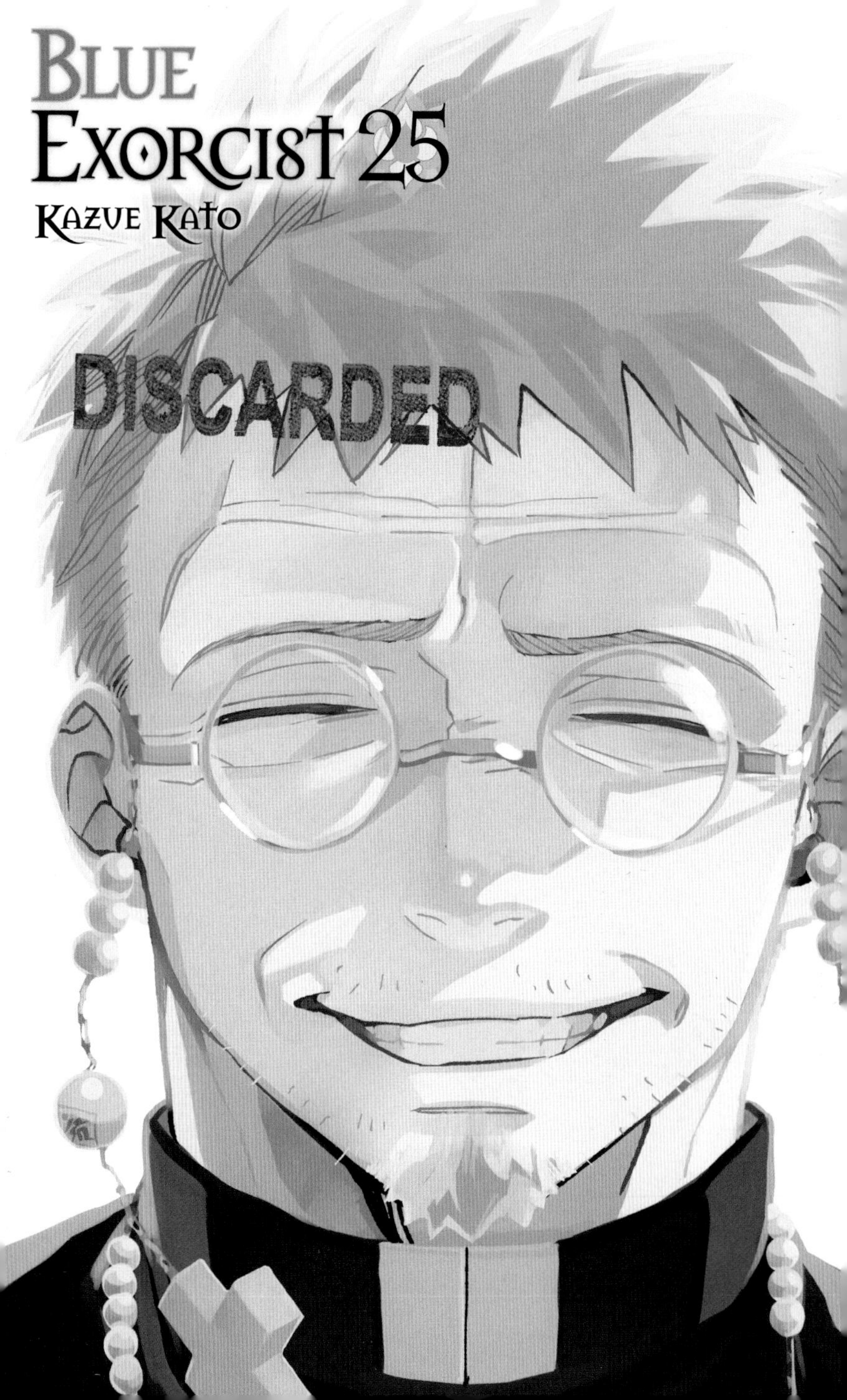

Blue Exorcist

Contents 25

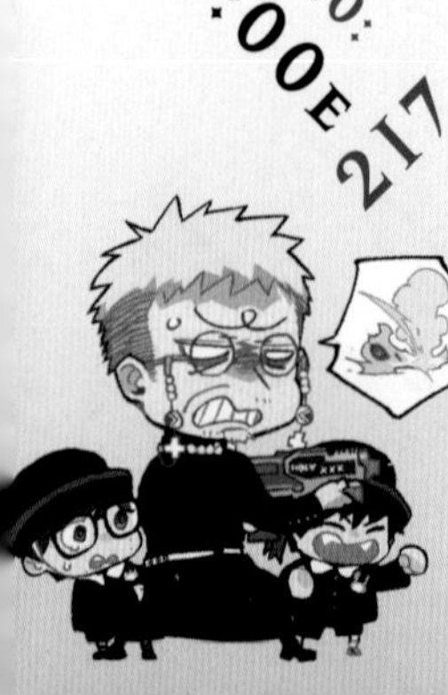

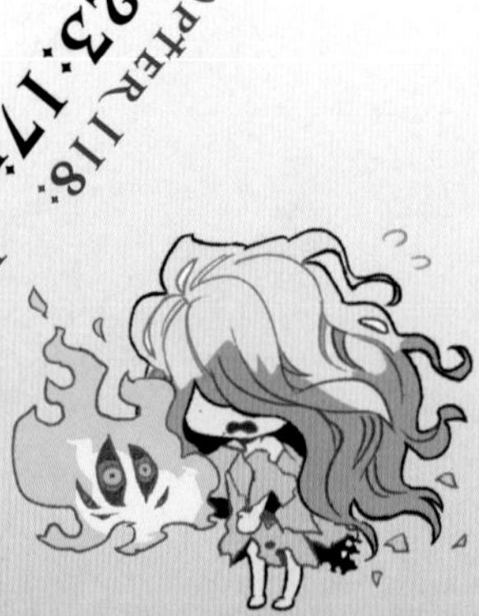